Information
Quality Applied

Information Quality Applied

Best Practices for Improving Business Information, Processes, and Systems

Larry P. English

Wiley Publishing, Inc.

Information Quality Applied

Published by
Wiley Publishing, Inc.
10475 Crosspoint Boulevard
Indianapolis, IN 46256
www.wiley.com

I dedicate this book to all of you readers who care about your Information Consumers who require Quality, Just-In-Time Information to accomplish the aim of your enterprise and serve your end-Customers for their best interests. I dedicate this book to the:

- *CEOs who want to understand how their companies can apply the TIQM Quality System as a core business management tool*

- *Knowledge Workers who require Quality Information in order to perform their work effectively and help accomplish the Enterprise Mission and delight their Customers*

- *Information Producers who perform processes to capture Quality Information required by their downstream Knowledge Workers*

- *Business and Information Systems Mangers who are accountable for the Information and Systems Quality to meet their downstream Managers' Information Requirements*

- *Information Quality professionals to help them define, standardize and integrate TIQM processes into the Culture of the Enterprise*

About the Author

Larry P. English, president and principal of INFORMATION IMPACT International, Inc., is one of the most well known authorities in information management and Information Quality Improvement.

He has provided consulting and education in over 40 countries on six continents. Mr. English was featured as one of the "21 Voices for the 21st Century" in the American Society for Quality's journal *Quality Progress* in its January 2000 issue. DAMA awarded him the "Individual Achievement Award" for his contributions to the field of information resource management in 1998. He was awarded the Heartbeat of America's "Keeping America Strong" Award in December 2008, honoring his work helping organizations to implement effective Information Quality processes that enable them to eliminate the high costs of business process failure caused by missing, inaccurate, duplicated, or untimely information. The award was broadcast by a national news magazine TV show hosted by William Shatner, Admiral Delaney, and Doug Llewelyn. English was honored by MIT for a *Decade of Outstanding Contributions to the Data and Information Quality field in July, 2009.*

Mr. English's TIQM® Quality System for Total Information Quality Management has been implemented in many organizations worldwide. Mr. English's widely acclaimed first book *Improving Data Warehouse and Business Information Quality* (Ohmsha, Ltd. 2000) has been translated into Japanese by the first Information Services organization to win the Deming Prize for Quality. It is called "the Information Quality Bible for the Information Age," by Masaaki Imai, creator of the Kaizen Quality Management System.

Mr. English has been called:

- "The most influential thought leader in the Information Quality space," Neil Foshay, Faculty, St. Francis Xavier University, Canada
- "The thought leader in the Information Quality/Data Quality field," Dr. Martin Eppler, Professor at the University of Lugano and author of *Managing Information Quality*
- "The Dr. Deming of Information Quality," by two of Deming's students
- "The leading authority in applying Dr. Deming's principles to Information Quality," Dr. Joyce Orsini, President of the Deming Institute and Director of the Deming MBA Scholars Program at Fordham University

Credits

Executive Editor
Robert Elliott

Project Editor
Adaobi Obi Tulton

Technical Editors
Andres Perez
Jeff Pettit
Lori Silverman
C. Lwanga Yonke

Production Editor
Eric Charbonneau

Copy Editors
Kim Cofer
Foxxe Editorial Services

Editorial Director
Robyn B. Siesky

Editorial Manager
Mary Beth Wakefield

Production Manager
Tim Tate

**Vice President and
Executive Group Publisher**
Richard Swadley

**Vice President and
Executive Publisher**
Barry Pruett

Associate Publisher
Jim Minatel

Project Coordinator, Cover
Lynsey Stanford

Compositor
James D. Kramer,
Happenstance Type-o-Rama

Proofreader
Nancy Carrasco

Indexer
Johnna VanHoose Dinse

Cover Image
Polka Dot Images / Jupiter Images

Acknowledgments

To write a book is not a solitary task, especially a book that addresses solving multiple, critical problems facing business, government, and society around the world.

Acknowledgements to the Quality Pioneers Who Molded My TIQM Quality System.

I must acknowledge the mentors who taught me the fundamental principles and processes of Quality Management that I have sought to *faithfully* translate into the principles of Information Quality in the TIQM Quality System for Total Information Quality Management. They include my first discovery of Quality Management, Dr. W. Edwards Deming, whom I met first, through Mary Walton's book, *The Deming Management Method*, followed by Deming's *Out of the Crisis* and *The New Economics*, followed by taking Dr. Deming's four-day video seminar, *A Four Day Seminar on the Leadership Philosophy of Dr. W. Edwards Deming*. I thank Dr. Joyce Orsini, President of the Deming Institute and founder and Director of the Deming MBA Scholars Program at Fordham University for her informative keynote presentations and tutorials at my Information Quality Conferences, and for allowing me to share with the Deming Scholars how Deming's System of Profound Knowledge applies to Information Quality. I also derived much of my learning from Masaaki Imai, who gave us the concept of Kaizen, Continuous Process Improvement involving everyone in the organization. I was privileged to attend Kaizen training from the Kaizen Institute and to participate in Kaizen events (Process Improvement Initiatives) on the manufacturing shop floor. I met Dr. Joseph Juran and studied his Quality Planning and the importance of embedding quality in the culture and behavior of the enterprise. I was privileged to hear Philip Crosby's last presentation at the American Society for Quality before his untimely death from cancer. I have applied Crosby's Quality Management Maturity Grid to TIQM to help organizations understand capability and maturity in applying Quality Principles to Information Quality within their organization as a Business Management Tool. I had the privilege to meet Genichi Taguchi and have studied his famous Quality Loss Function, for which he won the Deming Prize. This is a key concept in understanding the Business Value Proposition for proactive Continuous Process Improvement to hit the center line consistently, without variation, and that loss due to poor quality is a loss to society, affecting Customers, Investors and Taxpayers. I am further indebted to Walter Shewhart for his pioneering in statistical process control and the Plan-Do-Study-Act cycle for Process Improvement. I thank Kauru Ishikawa, for his Cause-and-Effect Diagram as a tool for finding Root Causes of quality problems. Without identifying the real Root Causes of problems, we can never fully optimize the Process Improvements. From Mizuno Akao, I learned about Quality Function Deployment and the "Voice of the Customer" as a critical tool for discovering Customers' Requirements and how to design quality into the products and processes to meet Customer expectations. I thank Dr. Harry Hertz for his leadership in the Baldrige Quality Program that acknowledges Information as a key Criterion for Performance Excellence.

Acknowledgements to My Early Clients for Implementing and Testing My Early IQ Methods That Have Matured into My Current TIQM Quality System

I must also express my gratefulness to my early clients, who pioneered the use of my methods and techniques in their IQ processes. These include: Danette McGilvray at HP and Agilent Technologies, Lwanga Yonke and David Walker at Aera Energy, Jeff Pettit at Intel Corporation, and Kathy Hunter at One-to-One in the UK. They proved that sound Quality Principles applied to Information work.

Acknowledgements to My Contributors on Special Topics

I thank three key contributors to the book writing — Don Carlson, the first person to apply Six Sigma Quality principles to information at Motorola, where Six Sigma was conceived; Graham Rhind, GRC Database Information, the expert on global Customer Information Quality; and John Smart of Smart Communications for their contributions to chapters on IQ Applied to Financial and Risk Management, IQ Applied to Customer Information Quality, and IQ applied to Document and Knowledge Management, respectively.

Acknowledgements to My Technical Editors

I thank my technical editors, Andres Perez, Jeff Pettit, Lori Silverman and C. Lwanga Yonke, for their helpful reviews and suggestions for improving the book's content.

Acknowledgements for Best Practice and IQ Anecdotes

I thank those who submitted Best Practices for those that I was able to publish, as well as those whose submissions I was not able to include because of space limitations. They include: Zahir Balaporia, Michael Gibson, Jaylene McCandlish, Jeff Pettit, Lwanga Yonke, Sunil Gupta, Almar Hijlkema, Milan Kucera, Karen Lopez, Shari Turner McKee, Liz Miller, Joyce Norris-Montanari, Eric Nielsen, Serge Pisano, Dr. Jan Philipp Rohweder, Lusani Raidani, Filip van Hallewijn, Bill Vilardell, and Lou Walters.

Acknowledgements to My Support Network

Most importantly, I must thank Diane, my wife and business partner; and Lori, our Assistant VP, for keeping me going and for providing helpful reviews well beyond the call of duty.

Contents

Foreword

In late 1997 I interviewed with the CEO of Aera Energy LLC for the position of Chief Information Officer. The interview lasted 10 minutes and turned on one question from the CEO: "I know that I need a good information system to run an oil company – can you help?" I said, "Yes, but you will need to focus on the quality of the information as well as the systems and technology in order to be successful." I got the job.

Our company had a compelling case for action. We produce oil and gas from high density oilfields, which we often compare to complex manufacturing plants. However, these fields are not only much larger than a traditional manufacturing plant but, more significantly, the barrels of oil we produce and the most essential equipment we use to produce them are deep below ground. With our product and production equipment out of sight, we require high quality information in order to intuit what's going on "down there." Without that information, we cannot run an effective or efficient operation. We knew we needed to gather quality data in order to provide quality information, but we also had to sustain that quality over time. For knowledge workers to trust the information we provided it had to be right all the time.

Our original Information Management & Technology (IM&T) purpose statement said, "Deliver the *right* information to enable business success." Obviously, we needed a clear definition of *"right."* It was about this time that I met Larry English, who helped us embark on a 10-year journey that would lead us to embrace the concept of Information Quality.

After helping us understand how to manage Information Quality, Larry facilitated the development of a framework for our Information Quality organization, including roles and responsibilities for everyone involved. Over our 10-year journey of continuous improvement, we have institutionalized Information

Quality management. We also made one change to our IM&T purpose statement. It now reads, "Provide quality information to enable business success."

Larry's book will help you:

- Reach a common understanding of the importance of Information Quality at all levels in your organization

- Establish the partnership between the business and the CIO organization, which is absolutely essential for a successful Information Quality Management process

- Acknowledge that data is as essential as systems and infrastructure in your CIO organization

- Establish information as an asset in your company with appropriate controls and standards

- Institutionalize Information Quality Management as a way of life in your company

One phrase that I have used repeatedly to explain the importance of Information Quality comes from Larry. It says in essence that "the only value coming from a CIO organization is information; all the rest is a cost."

One of the main values we have realized from improved information quality is increased productivity of our engineers. The head of one of our business units estimates that the productivity of his engineers has doubled through increased time spent analyzing information and less time spent managing it.

Using the concept of establishing value from information and with the guidance provided in this book, you will be on the right track to implement an effective Information Quality program in your company.

David C. Walker
Senior Vice President and CIO
Aera Energy LLC
July 2009

Introduction: Business Excellence through Information Excellence

This is a book about Business Excellence. My experience, time and again, across all industries, government and not-for-profits, and across all continents, is that Business Excellence cannot be achieved if the Information the enterprise depends on is *defective* (inaccurate, missing, duplicate, untimely, or biased or misleading in its presentation). Making decisions or taking actions on the basis of Poor Quality Information *causes process failure* and, if not controlled, *can ultimately lead to* enterprise failure.

Quality Information is not the result of doing work. Information Quality comes as the result of designing Quality (Error-Proofing) into processes that create, maintain, and present information to Knowledge Workers who perform the value work of the enterprise.

Information Quality does NOT come by inspecting and correcting data — these are two of the many costs of poor IQ. Rather Information Quality comes by designing quality into the processes, by following the proven quality technique of Plan-Do-Check/Study-Act cycle or the DMAIC (Define-Measure-Analyze-Improve-Control).

Author's Warranty

This author believes that organizations that make products or deliver services should stand by the quality of their work and warrant it. As a reader of this book, you are my Customer. I warrant that it will meet your satisfaction or you will get your money back. I also warrant my consulting and my training and education services.

If you are not able to apply ideas contained in this book to achieve value to your organization worth *multiple* times the cost of the book, I will personally refund you the purchase price you paid for it. Simply contact me at `Larry .English@infoimpact.com` for your refund instructions (check or credit card transaction refund). All I ask is for you to give me a copy of your sales receipt, a statement of what you tried that did not work, and your assessment of why it failed to result in value. No further questions will be asked.

Who Should Read and Apply This Book

This book is not for everyone. It is not for people who think Information Quality is just about the data. It is not for people who want to set up an organizational unit and go out and "do" Information Quality. It is not for people who are only interested in their own personal information so that they can use it to advance their own cause and goal.

This Book Is NOT For:

- People who believe that data quality is data profiling and data cleansing. These activities represent an outmoded "inspect and correct" mindset. This book contradicts this theory of quality.

- People who want to "dink" with data. These are generally technology specialists who like the technical aspects of IQ tools. They like to conduct data profiling to find the "problems" and conduct data cleansing [sic. Should be "Data Correction," "Data Corrective Maintenance," or "Information Scrap and Rework"]. This mindset only attacks the "symptoms" of IQ issues and not the "Root Causes."

- People who want to build an Information Quality empire for their own advancement. Quality Management is everyone's responsibility. The Information Quality Team is chartered to define repeatable processes for measuring and improving information processes to prevent the need for ongoing data correction by error-proofing the information processes. The TIQM Quality System provides a step-by-step guide that is easily adaptable to any given enterprise by the IQ Team, as the process owners of the discrete Information Quality Processes.

Rather, This Book IS For:

Those who care about the Customers of their organization and who want to serve and delight them. This book is for those who care that they have accurate and complete information about their Customers with the purpose of delighting them with their products and services. This includes the following:

- CEOs who want to understand how their companies can apply the TIQM Quality System as a core business management tool, especially Chapter 1, "Process and Business Failure: The High Costs of Low Quality Information" and Chapter 3, "Implementing and Sustaining an Effective Information Quality Environment."

- Knowledge Workers who require high-Quality Information in order to perform their work effectively and help accomplish the enterprise's Mission and delight their Customers.

- Information Producers who perform processes to capture quality information required by their downstream Knowledge Workers.

- Business and Information Systems Managers who are accountable for Information Quality to meet their downstream managers' Information Requirements.

- Information Quality professionals to help them define, standardize and integrate TIQM processes into the culture of the enterprise.

This book is for people who care about creating a better world, by eliminating the waste in their organizations that squander our people, financial, and natural resources.

This book is for Executives, specifically Chapter 1, a description of the high costs of poor quality information and Chapter 3, "Implementing and Sustaining an Information Quality Environment," so that they know how to implement the Information Quality Culture into the organization as a core business management tool.

It is a book for managers and staff who want to improve their processes to delight their internal Information Consumers so that they can turn around and delight their own internal or external Information Consumers.

This book is for all levels of personnel in the organization from the Customer-facing Knowledge Workers who must delight their purchasing and end-Consumers *down* to the Executive Leaders of the enterprise. An Executive Leader must operate as a symphony conductor who leads the orchestra as a single ensemble as opposed to operating in a vertical chain of command. Leaders must ensure that every level of Management and every Business Area work together as *interdependent* — not independent — sections in the orchestra as a single entity to accomplish the Aim of the Enterprise and delight its Customers.

In this book I introduce the concept of "Value Circles" in which the activities of the big Business Processes are centered around the Customers and Stakeholders of the process. These Value Circles are defined generically for several core processes in the Part III, "IQ Applied" chapters.

Representations of processes with work flow diagrams, or swim lanes, or levels of hierarchies do not adequately represent the *interdependence* of all parts of the Enterprise as a single system or ensemble that must work together, holistically. Even the term "value chain" no longer is adequate, for it still conveys separateness in the links of the chain.

I am often asked how many people there should be in the Information Quality Management Team. The answer is the same number as the number of employees, full- or part-time, including consultants, contract personnel, as well as those in outsourced or offshored entities that perform work required for your Enterprise to accomplish its Mission.

Everyone in the Enterprise has one or more specific accountabilities for Information Quality based on their role and relationship to Information. Everyone in the organization is tasked with identifying and improving broken information processes, as outlined in Chapter 3, "Establishing and Sustaining the Information Quality Environment."

Organization of This Book

This book is divided into three parts, beginning with a description of the proven principles of Quality Management, and then delving into the Six Processes of the TIQM Quality System for Total Information Quality Management. Finally, you learn to apply TIQM to seven core processes required for business effectiveness.

Part I: The High Costs of Poor Quality Information and the Principles of Quality Management Required to Solve the IQ Crisis

Part I describes the horrific problems that are crippling organizations in the Information Age. It then defines the principles, processes, and techniques in the proven Quality Systems that have successfully addressed the problems of quality in the Industrial Age. These same Quality Principles must also be applied to Information Processes if we are to solve them successfully.

> **Chapter 1: "Process and Business Failure: The High Costs of Low Quality Information."** This chapter establishes the business problem we must solve by applying Quality Principles to Information Processes.

> **Chapter 2: "The ABCs of the TIQM Quality System for Total Information Quality Management."** This chapter describes the fundamental Principles as practiced by the proven Quality Systems, such as Deming, Juran, Shewhart, Ishikawa, Crosby, Imai (Kaizen), Taguchi (Quality Engineering), Akao (Quality Function Deployment), The Baldrige Criteria, and Six Sigma.

Part II: The Six Processes of the TIQM Quality System for Total Information Quality Management

Part II describes the Six Processes of the TIQM Quality System for Total Information Quality Management, based on the Quality Principles described in Chapter 2 "The ABCs of the TIQM Quality System for Total Information Quality Management." Part II chapters include:

> **Chapter 3: "Implementing and Sustaining an Effective Information Quality Environment."** This chapter describes how to implement an effective and sustainable IQ Management System as part of your business management toolset. This is required reading for Executives and the IQ Leader.
>
> **Chapter 4: The Step-by-Step Guide to Assessing Information Product Specifications and Information Architecture Quality.** This chapter describes how to measure the Quality of Information Product Specification (data definition), Information Models, and Database designs, which are critical to the Information Production capability of the Enterprise.
>
> **Chapter 5: The Step-by-Step Guide to *Assessing Information Quality*.** This chapter describes how to measure the Quality of Information and its Presentation. It assesses the effectiveness of the processes that produce, maintain, and deliver Information to the Knowledge Workers.
>
> **Chapter 6: The Step-by-Step Guide to Measuring the Costs and Risks of Poor Quality Information.** This describes how to measure the Costs of Poor Quality Information and how to measure the Return on Investment of Information Process Improvements. This represents the business case for IQ Management.
>
> **Chapter 7: The Step-by-Step Guide to *Improving Information Process Quality*.** This describes how to apply the Shewhart cycle of Plan-Do-Check/Study-Act to Information Process Improvements. Designing Quality in to the Information Processes is the core competency and habit of a High IQ Culture.
>
> **Chapter 8: The Step-by-Step Guide to *Data Correction and Controlling Data Redundancy*.** This describes the most cost-effective way to conduct data correction. This should be performed only *after* Improving the Process.

Part III: Information Quality Applied to Core Business Value Circles

Part III consists of the application of TIQM to seven core processes required for business effectiveness in the realized Information Age. Part III introduces the concept of Information "Value Circles." An Information Value Circle is an end-to-end set of processes that begin with a request from a "Customer." In each of these seven chapters, you will see how to apply TIQM measurement and process improvement to the unique problems of the core Value Circles:

Chapter 9: IQ Applied to Customer Care. This chapter addresses the Quality of Information required to sustain a relationship of loyalty in your end Customers.

Chapter 10: IQ Applied to Product Development. This chapter addresses the Quality of Information required to innovate new products and services and to understanding Customer Requirements.

Chapter 11: IQ Applied to Supply Chain Management. This chapter addresses the Quality of Information required to ensure that the total Supply Chain is managed effectively and efficiently

Chapter 12: IQ Applied to Financial and Risk Management. This chapter addresses the Quality of Information required to manage Financial Resources, including internal Financial Management, internal Auditing, external Financial Reporting, and Risk Management.

Chapter 13: IQ Applied to e-Business Management. This chapter addresses the Quality of Information in Web documents, Web design , e-Commerce, and e-Business transactions.

Chapter 14: IQ Applied to Document and Knowledge Management. This chapter addresses Quality of Information in Documents, Technical and Procedure writing, and in Lessons Learned from Knowledge Workers' experiences.

Chapter 15: IQ Applied to Information Management and Information Systems Engineering. This chapter addresses the quality of the "Information Production Capability" required to develop Enterprise Information Models of required information, translating Information Models into enterprise-strength databases. This further describes principles for enhancing and improving Information Systems' Quality, including the quality of Functional Specifications, Human-Machine Interfaces, and the Ergonomics of Screen, Report, and Workflow design.

Chapter 16: The Journey Is the Key to Success: This chapter is an epilogue that addresses the IQ Maturity Stages and final thoughts to keep you focused on the Journey.

Information Quality Applied Web Site

In addition to the book, there is a Web site for additional materials, including:

- Errata: Corrections of errors in the book, if any
- Recommended IQ Reading
- Glossary of Information Quality terms and concepts
- TIQM Process templates
- Information Quality Software with links to Suppliers' Web sites
- Additional IQ Best Practices
- Your favorite quotes from *Information Quality Applied*
- Articles by Larry English
- And more to come

You can visit the *IQ Applied* book Web site at `www.wiley.com/go/IQApplied`.

From Information Crisis to Business Excellence through Information Excellence

Chapter 1: **"Process and Business Failure: the High Costs of Low Quality Information."** This chapter describes the omnipresence of Poor Quality Information and the process and business *failure* it causes, economically to the enterprise and socially as harmful to end Customers, Investors, Citizens, and Taxpayers.

Chapter 2: **"The ABCs of the TIQM Quality System for Total Information Quality Management."** This chapter describes the proven principles, processes, and techniques of sound Quality Systems, such as Deming, Juran, Shewhart, Ishikawa, Crosby, Imai (Kaizen), Taguchi (Quality Engineering), Akao (Quality Function Deployment), The Baldrige Criteria, Six Sigma, and others, which must be applied to Information Process to address our Information Quality (IQ) problems and the Process and Business failures they cause. We describe these IQ Principles and Processes in Part I.

Process and Business Failure: The High Costs of Low Quality Information

"In the U.S.A., about a third of what we do consists of redoing work previously 'done'." [1]

Joseph M. Juran

At about the time I started writing this book, I received an email from an Information Professional, G.P. Here are the edited words of G.P.:

"My career in Information Management has now taken me from [Company 1], to [Company 2], to [Company 3], to [Company 4]. **The thing that they all have in common is a desire to cut corners and deal with quality later.** It takes a lot of energy to be the Information Quality cheerleader, and I find it discouraging and overwhelming at times. Keep writing your articles and books to encourage all the people like me who are dealing with these issues every day."

G.P., this book is written especially for people like you who care about your end-Customers and your internal Information Consumers, who require Quality Information to perform their work effectively to accomplish the enterprise mission and to stay in business.

The principle of management by quantity or speed over quality is a failed management philosophy.

What is our experience of the costs of poor quality information?

In this chapter I provide specific real-world anecdotes of the high costs of low quality Information and Information Systems.

High Costs and Losses of Poor Quality Information

Here are sample anecdotes collected over the past twenty years that illustrate the costs and consequences of poor quality information and Information Systems.

Table 1-1 highlights the high costs of poor quality in Information Systems.

DISCLAIMER

The following anecdotes in Tables 1-1 and 1-2 have been cited from reputable sources. While I have not audited these findings, I have no reason to doubt their accuracy to within a 90 to 95 percent confidence level. I have sought to calculate the exchange rates at the prevailing time period of the failures.

Some of the examples listed are associated with biased and misleading information or fraud. Fraud, of course, is the worst scenario, and some may challenge them as not applicable. However, deliberate distortion of information also has costs to society, hurting individuals, organizations, and society as well. These truly appear as costs, financially, psychologically, and sociologically.

In virtually every disaster, Information Systems and Information Quality failures alike, there will be losses of Customers due to loss of confidence in the companies. British Gas, for one example, lost over 1 million Customers in 2006 alone. The lost revenue from this will exceed the direct cost losses from the failure.

Table 1-1 lists anecdotes of poor quality Information System Software and the costs of poor quality. The source and dates of the anecdotes are found at the end of each Outcome column cell entry. See the legend at the end of the Table.

Table 1-1: The High Costs of Poor Quality Information Systems Software and Databases

COMPANY / INDUSTRY	OUTCOME (COSTS (M = MILLION; B = BILLION; T = TRILLION) (REF/DATE))	US$ LOSS AMT
Allstate Insurance Co.	Office Automation System abandoned after deployment, costing $130 M. (WSF, 1993).	$130,000,000
Arianespace [France]	Software specification and design errors cause $350 M Ariane 5 rocket to explode. (WSF, 1996).	$350,000,000
AT&T Wireless	Customer Relationship Management (CRM) upgrade problems lead to revenue loss of $100 M. (WSF, 2003–4).	$100,000,000
Avis Europe PLC [UK]	Enterprise Resource Planning (ERP) System canceled after $54.5 M spent. (WSF, 2004).	$54,500,000

COMPANY / INDUSTRY	OUTCOME (COSTS (M = MILLION; B = BILLION; T = TRILLION) (REF/DATE))	US$ LOSS AMT
British Gas (Centrica)	£300 M overhaul of billing System over-bills Customers. BG wrote off £200 M due to complaints (11, 2006–2008) and filed suit against its contractor for £182M. (£482M * $2/£).	$964,000,000
BSkyB	After a failed Customer Relationship Management system, BSkyB sued EDS for £709 M ($1.349 B($1.9)), for misrepresented EDS' abilities. (11, 2008/05/13).	$1,349,000,000
Budget Rent-A-Car, Hilton Hotels, Marriott Int'l, and AMR	American Airlines Travel Reservation System canceled after $165 M spent. (WSF, 1992).	$165,000,000
Chemical Bank	Software error causes $15 million to be deducted from 100,000 Customer accounts. (WSF, 1994).	$15,000,000
CIGNA Corp.	Problems with CRM System contribute to $445 M loss. (WSF, 2002).	$445,000,000
Federal Bureau of Investigation	$170 M for Networked System to replace paper system. Scrapped one year after delivery. (Washington Post, 2006/08/18).	$170,000,000
Ford Motor Company	Purchasing System abandoned after deployment costing $400 M. (WSF, 2004).	$400,000,000
FoxMeyer Drug Company	$40 M ERP System abandoned after deployment, bankrupting company. (WSF, 1996).	$40,000,000
Greyhound Lines Inc.	Bus Reservation System crashes repeatedly upon introduction, causing revenue loss of $61 M. (WSF, 1993).	$61,000,000
Hershey Foods Corp.	Problems with ERP System contributes to $151 M loss. (WSF, 1999).	$151,000,000
Hewlett-Packard Company	Problems with ERP System contribute to $160 M loss. (WSF, 2004).	$160,000,000
Hudson Bay Co. [Canada]	Problems with Inventory System contribute to $33.3 M loss. (WSF, 2005).	$33,300,000
J Sainsbury PLC [UK]	Supply-Chain System abandoned after deployment costing $527 M. (WSF, 2004).	$527,000,000

(continued)

Table 1-1 *(continued)*

COMPANY / INDUSTRY	OUTCOME (COSTS (M = MILLION; B = BILLION; T = TRILLION) (REF/DATE))	US$ LOSS AMT
Kmart Corporation	Supply-Chain System canceled after $130 M spent. (WSF, 2001).	$130,000,000
London Ambulance Service [UK]	Dispatch System canceled in 1990 at $11.25 million; second attempt abandoned, costing $15 M. (WSF, 1993).	$26,250,000
London Stock Exchange [UK]	Taurus Stock Settlement System canceled after $600 M spent. (WSF, 1993).	$600,000,000
McDonald's Corporation	The Innovate Information-Purchasing System canceled costing $170 M. (WSF, 2002).	$170,000,000
Nike Inc.	Problems with Supply-Chain System causes $100 M loss. (WSF, 2001).	$100,000,000
Oxford Health Plans Inc.	Billing and Claims System problems contribute to quarterly loss; stock plummets, leading to $3.4 B loss in corporate value. (WSF, 1997).	$3,400,000,000
Snap-on-Tools	Problems with Order-Entry System causes $50 M revenue loss. (WSF, 1998).	$50,000,000
State of California	DMV System canceled after $44 M spent. (WSF, 1994).	$4,000,000
State of Mississippi	Tax System canceled after $11.2 M is spent; state receives $185 M in damages. (WSF, 1999).	$196,200,000
State of Washington	Department of Motor Vehicle (DMV) System canceled after $40 M spent. (WSF, 1997).	$40,000,000
Sydney Water Corp. [Australia]	Billing System canceled after $33.2 M spent. (WSF, 2002)	$33,200,000
Toronto Stock Exchange [CAN]	Electronic Trading System canceled after $25.5 M is spent. (WSF, 1995).	$25,500,000
UK Inland Revenue	S/W errors contribute to $3.45 B tax-credit overpayment. (WSF, 2004–5).	$3,450,000,000
U.S. Federal Aviation Admin.	Advanced Automation system canceled after $2.6 B spent. (WSF, 1994).	$2,600,000,000
U.S. Internal Revenue Service	Tax Modernization effort canceled after $4 B is spent. (WSF, 1997).	$4,000,000,000

COMPANY / INDUSTRY	OUTCOME (COSTS (M = MILLION; B = BILLION; T = TRILLION) (REF/DATE))	US$ LOSS AMT
United Way	Administrative Processing System canceled $12 M spent. (WSF, 1999).	$12,000,000
Washington, D.C.	City Payroll System abandoned after deployment $25 M spent. (WSF, 2000).	$25,000,000
U.S. Bureau of Indian Affairs	Spent $12.5 M on Maintenance Repair System for schools that failed to capture quality information. (5: 2003/08).	$12,500,000
U.S. Business spend on unwanted systems	BPN Forum survey = 10% to more than 20% of IT budget wasted on unwanted systems; Calc: $13.84 T (U.S. GDP) × 10% (IT budget) = $138.40 B X 20% (waste rate/yr) = $24.6 B wasted per year. (BPN Forum,).	$24,600,000,000
	Total Costs of Poor Quality Software in these examples in US$	**$44,589,450,000**

Sources: WSF: "Why Software Fails"; BW = *Business Week*; CEO = *CEO Magazine*; CW = *Computerworld*; IW = *InfoWeek*; FCW = *Federal Computer Week*; For = *Fortune*; NYT = *The New York Times*; Tim = *Time*; WSJ = *The Wall Street Journal*; III = Information Impact International; USA = *USA Today*; FT = *Financial Times*; LTim = *London Times*; LTel = *London Telegraph*;TN = *The Tennessean*; N&O = *News and Observer*; Aus = *The Australian*; AFR = *Australian Financial Review*; LAT = *LA Times*; NAO = UK Nat'l Audit Office; Wired.com = http://www.wired.com/science/discoveries/news/2004/02/62242.

Table 1-1 illustrates the incredibly high Costs of Poor Quality in Information Systems software. These are Information Systems with such poor quality that they had to be scrapped. For every scrapped Information System, there are hundreds more that have significant defects that Knowledge Workers have to live with. Information Producers and Knowledge Workers are struggling to perform their work when the defects are not so catastrophic as to scrap the systems. This wastes the time of our most important resource: people.

As organizations become more and more dependent on Information Technology, they must ensure they design quality into the Information Management and Information Systems Engineering processes, so they error-proof Information Systems to the extent possible.

When systems fail, business processes stop or must be handled manually, always with a risk of omission and error in capturing data.

Table 1-2 documents anecdotes of actual losses and Costs of Poor Quality Information that cause business processes to fail, requiring costs of recovery from the failure and the Information Scrap and Rework required to find and correct the information so other processes do not fail. Sources and dates of anecdotes are found at the end of each Outcome cell in Table 1-2.

Table 1-2: The High Costs of Poor Quality Business Information

COMPANY / INDUSTRY	OUTCOME (COSTS (REF DATE))	LOSS AMOUNT
AIG	Agrees to pay $1.6 B to settle allegations that it used deceptive accounting practices to mislead investors and regulatory agencies. (TN, 2006/02/10).	$1,600,000,000
AIG	Bailout money of $223 B from taxpayers. (TN, 2009/03/03).	$223,000,000,000
Arthur Andersen	Auditing failure at Enron led to $1.3 B loss in pension. (FT, 2002/01).	$1,300,000,000
AT&T	AT&T agrees to pay $177,000 in fines in Tennessee for billing Customers for services they hadn't authorized. (TN, 2004/03/06).	$177,000
Australia Dept. of Defence	Defence to lose compensation billions in reforms due to overcompensation due to error in inflation: A$ 4.3 B = US$ 2.99 B. (AFR, 2009/03/30).	$2,990,000,000
Bristol-Myers-Squibb	Fined $150 M for inflating its revenue. (USA, 2004/04/05).	$150,000,000
Bristol-Myers-Squibb	Paid $300 M to settle lawsuit (accounting re: Imclone). (USA, 2004/04/04).	$300,000,000
Cell Phone Companies	Agree to pay 32 states $5 M and required to give Customers a grace period for cancellations and better information. (TN, 2004/07/22).	$5,000,000
City Government	Free garbage pick-up due to oversight for 90 homes outside of Nashville's urban services district for almost 10 years may have cost the city as much as $55,000. (TN, 2005/03/10).	$55,000
Citigroup	Citigroup paid $2 B to settle a lawsuit over its role in helping Enron manipulate its accounting that led it to Enron's collapse. (TN, 2005/06/11).	$2,000,000,000
Citigroup	Citigroup paid $2.7 B to investors to settle a class-action lawsuit over losses in WorldCom accounting fraud. It set aside another $6.7 B for other lawsuits. (USA, 2004/05/11).	$9,400,000,000

COMPANY / INDUSTRY	OUTCOME (COSTS (REF DATE))	LOSS AMOUNT
Citigroup	Paid $18 M refunds and settlement for taking $14 M from Customers' credit card accts. (USA, 2008/08/27).	$18,000.000
Community Health Systems	CHS to pay $31 M in settlement due to billing errors. (TN, 2000/03).	$31,000,000
DirecTV	Paid $5 M for misleading program packaging. (TN, 2005/12/03).	$5,000,000
DuPont	DuPont's failure to report widespread exposures to a toxic chemical costs it $16.5 M in fines & payouts. (TN, 2005/12/13).	$16,500,000
Enron	Ex-CEO Skilling enters prison for 24-year sentence. He and Ken Lay were convicted on many counts of fraud, conspiracy, and insider trading — loss of $60 B in stock & $2 B in pension plans. (TN, 2006/12/14).	$62,000,000,000
Enron	Settled lawsuit for $168 M for misleading Stakeholders. (TN 2005/01/09).	$168,000,000
Fannie Mae	Required to restate 2004 earnings down by $11 B due to serious accounting problems and earnings manipulation. (TN 2006/05/10).	$11,000,000,000
Fannie Mae	Spent $1 B to correct years of false financial reports. (TN 2008/08/24) .	$1,000,000,000
Federal Agency	Overpaid one set of beneficiaries by $1.7 B and underpaid another set of beneficiaries by $600 M. (Private Client, 2005).	$2,300,000,000
FEMA	The GAO 95% confident that improper FEMA payments were between $600M & $1.4B re Katrina & Rita = $1 B. (USA, 2007/06/15).	$1,000,000,000
Financial A	Acquired subprime mortgage company without due diligence on data. Write-down $2.6 B & $1 B in debt & 100 M loss. (III, BW, 2000).	$3,700,000,000
Franklin Advisors	Settled lawsuit for $50 M for illegal, rapid trading transactions. (USA, 2004/08/03).	$50,000,000

(continued)

Table 1-2 *(continued)*

COMPANY / INDUSTRY	OUTCOME (COSTS (REF DATE))	LOSS AMOUNT
General Motors	Takes a $39 B charge to stay in compliance with accounting law. (USA, 2007/11/07) .	$39,000,000,000
Goodyear	Billing errors in accounting led to $100 M loss. (TN, 2003/10/23).	$100,000,000
Google	Shortchanged thousands of their advertisers and settled a lawsuit for $60M. (2006/05/08).	$60,000,000
Government	Billions in 9/11 recovery loans were misused by those who were not affected or did not need them. Estimated at $2.5 B. (TN, 2005/09/09).	$2,500,000,000
Government Contractors	U.S. Military suspends $160 M in charges due to inaccurate and incomplete files and bills. (USA, 2004/05/18).	$160,000,000
Halliburton	Report questions over $1.4B of Halliburton Bills. (USA, 2005/06/28).	$1,400,000,000
Halliburton KBR	Poor accounting costs KBR $1.2 B for contracting. (WSJ-EU, 2004/04).	$1,200,000,000
Healthways	Calls off $307.5 M merger with LifeMasters Supported Self Care over "data & reporting errors" that minimized its value. (TN, 2006/08/03).	$307,500,000
Hubble Telescope	Error in mirror specification causes a $700 M repair. (wired.com, 2004/02/11).	$700,000,000
Institute of Medicine	Report found 1.5 million people harmed by medication errors per year. Extra costs to treat medication-related injuries in hospitals alone amount to at least 3.5 B per year. (USA, 2006/07/21).	$3,500,000,000
Insurance company A	Lost $5 B one year and $3 B the next due to poor risk analysis. (III Private, 2002).	$8,000,000,000
Insurance company B	One third of staff time is Information Scrap and Rework = $23.4 M/year. (III Private, 2004).	$23,430,000

COMPANY / INDUSTRY	OUTCOME (COSTS (REF DATE))	LOSS AMOUNT
Janus Capital	Client pulls $5 B out of Janus over improper trading. Losses est. at $250 M/yr. (TN, 2004/07/30).	$250,000,000
Janus Capital Group	Fined $226 M for improper trading actions. (WSJ, 2004/04/20).	$226,000,000
KPMG	Sued $1 B (£692 M) for accounting irregularities in collapse of New Century Financial. (FT, 2009/04/02)	$1,000,000,000
L.A. County	Due to poor calculation of pension funds incurred $1.2 B liability. (LAT, 1998/04/08).	$1,200,000,000
Lucent	Fined $25 M for overstating revenue and earnings. (USA, 2004/05/18).	$25,000,000
Mazda	Fined $5.25 M for failure to disclose required information on leases. (TN, 1999/10/02).	$5,250,000
Medical Care	98,000 people a year in U.S. die from medical error @ $147 M legal costs. (USA, 2002/07/24).	$147,000,000
Medicare	35M Handbooks with wrong info. 13,000,000 Booklets @ $.55/book to replace. (TN, 2005/10/6).	$19,250,000
Medicare	Paid out $339 M in improper claims. (TN, 1998/10/01).	$339,000,000
Merck	Merck paid IRS $2.04 B due to disallowed deductions. (WSJ, 2004/05/10).	$2,040,000,000
Merck	Merck & Co. settled its U.S. personal injury claims over Vioxx for $5.2 B in 11/2007 (deceptive advertising). (Aus, 2009/03/30).	$5,200,000,000
Merck	Merck & Co. seeks to settle its personal injury claims over Vioxx in Australia. Estimated legal costs @ US $ 400 M. (Aus, 2009/03/30).	$400,000,000
Mizuho Securities	Typing error leads to 225M loss on Tokyo stock exchange. Trader tried to sell 610,000 shares at 1 yen of com co. He intended to sell 1 share at 610,000 yen. (TN, 2005/12/11).	$225,000,000

(continued)

Table 1-2 *(continued)*

COMPANY / INDUSTRY	OUTCOME (COSTS (REF DATE))	LOSS AMOUNT
Morgan Stanley	Paid $15M fine to settle charges that it hid a large trove of archived information from the U.S. Securities and Exchange Commission. (USA, 2006/05/11).	$15,000,000
Morgan Stanley	Books a quarterly loss of at least $1.2 B to $1.7 B due to wrong accounting treatment of bonds. (WSJ.com, 2009/04/09).	$1,450,000,000
Morgan Stanley	Fined $2.2 M for late communication to investors. (WSJ, 2004/07/30).	$2,200,000
Mutual Fund Companies	Fleeing investors hurt scandal-tainted fund companies worse than fines. Losses estimated at $500 M. (TN, 2004/09/03).	$500,000,000
NASA-Mars Climate Orbiter	Miscalculation of English units of measure to metric causes total loss of $125 M and lost scientific measurement. (CNN.com, 1999/09/30).	$125,000,000
Nashville Metro Govt.	Overlooked collection of fines and has lost $57 M. (TN, 2009/01/16).	$57,000,000
Natwest Bank	Derivatives pricing error led to £91 M = $152 M loss; selling off Equities division led to $1.192 B write-off (Tot = $1.344 B). (USA, 1997/12/03).	$1,344,000,000
Not-for-Profit org.	Direct Costs due to poor IQ = $42,192,000 per year. (III Private, 2008).	$42,192,000
Package Delivery co.	Failed to invoice for 4.2% of packages delivered = $340 M/year. (III Private, 2006/02).	$340,000,000
Pentagon	Pentagon's books defy auditors; fixing it costs at least $13 B. (N&O, 2006/02/12).	$13,000,000,000
Pharmaceuticals fined	Abbott fined $600 M for improper marketing of some products. (USA, 2003/07/24): AstraZeneca fined $354 M for giving drugs to MDs to bill medicare; Ross Products paid $200 M and $400 M for criminal/civil penalties; Tap Pharmaceuticals paid $875 M fine.	$2,429,000,000

COMPANY / INDUSTRY	OUTCOME (COSTS (REF DATE))	LOSS AMOUNT
Putnam Investments	Customers withdrew $4.4B from Putnam funds over accounting errors. (WSJ, 2003/11/7).	$4,400,000,000
RiteAid	Errors in accounting led to $1.81 B write-down over three years. (TN, 2002/6/22).	$1,810,000,000
Shell	Fined $151.5 M for overstating oil reserves. (WSJ, 2004/07/30).	$151,500,000
Sprint	Sprint records $29.5 B loss in Nextel write-down. Poor service and dropped calls lost Sprint 683,000 subscribers. (Blm, 2008/02/29).	$29,500,000,000
State of Tennessee	Had to compensate wrongly convicted man $833,000. (TN, 2004/10/05).	$833,000
Telco A	Costs of poor quality eliminated over 10 years $800 M. (III Private, 2004).	$800,000,000
Telco B	Losses of $50 M in un-invoiced services (III Private, 2002).	$50,000,000
Ten Wall Street firms	Fined a total of $1.4 B by SEC (misleading investors) (TN, 2004/08/27).	$1,400,000,000
UBS	Lost $664 M (911 M Swiss francs) due to poor risk management data. (NYT, 1998/11/18).	$664,000,000
UBS	Lost 19.7 B Swiss francs ($17 B) in 2008 as it wrote down the value of some debt assets and wealth management clients withdrew money. (NYT, 2009/5/29).	$17,000,000,000
U.K. Gov.	Pension calculation errors cause some pensioners to be overpaid by up to £140 M with others underpaid by £100 M. (LTim, 2009/3/9). Tot £240 M x 1.45 (exchange) = $348 M.	$348,000,000
U.K. Inland Revenue	Inland Revenue overpaid tax credits for disabled persons of between £510 million and £710 million from errors in understated income.£82M ($123.3 M). (NAO, 2003/11/19). (exchange= $1.45:£= $884.5 M).	$884,500,000

(continued)

Table 1-2 *(continued)*

COMPANY / INDUSTRY	OUTCOME (COSTS (REF DATE))	LOSS AMOUNT
U.K. Inland Revenue	Penalties caused by failed Inland Revenue processing. 300,000 at £900 ($1.504) = $406 M. (LTel, 2003/03).	$406,080,000
U.K. Office of Nat'l Statistics	Overpaid staff £11 M ($16.5 M). (FT, 2003/03/26).	$16,544,000
U.K. Revenue & Customs	A National Audit found £6.6 B overpayment in tax credits; £1-1.3 B paid in 2004–5 to claimants not entitled; £575 M in 2006; £800m not collected and £340 M overpaid by taxpayers. £135 M (US$ 191 M) a year lost because tax due on pensions is not collected. (FT, 2007/7/13). £1 = $2.037. (exch on 2007/07).	$17,926,000,000
U.S. Bureau of Indian Affairs	After spending $12.5 M on the system software, they had to spend $13 M to correct the records. (FCW, 2003/08).	$13,000,000
U.S. Government	Costs to upgrade voting equipment: $3.8 B after the 2000 Presidential election failure. This did not solve the problem. (USA, 2002/10).	$3,800,000,000
U.S. Government	Owed more than $35 B in fines from criminal and civil cases but collects less than half of that ($20 B). (TN, 2006/03/09).	$20,000,000,000
U.S. Government	An error in an addendum that required oil and gas companies to pay federal royalties on offshore leases cost the US $7B (TN, 2006/03/02).	$7,000,000,000
U.S. Internal Revenue Service	A study conducted by Treasury Department investigators posing as taxpayers determined that IRS employees gave wrong answers to 28% of the questions. $50 M est. losses. (TN, 2003/09/04).	$50,000,000
U.S. Internal Revenue Service	The U.S. tax gap of taxes owed to taxes collected is a deficit of $290 B per year in 2001 and 2002. (TN, 4/17/2006).	$290,000,000,000

COMPANY / INDUSTRY	OUTCOME (COSTS (REF DATE))	LOSS AMOUNT
U.S. Internal Revenue Service	"Tax gap" for the IRS in failure to collect taxes is around $350 B per year in lost revenue in 2005 and 2006. (S. Hrg. 110-698, 2007/04/18). (http://finance.senate.gov/hearings/46363.pdf).	$350,000,000,000
U.S. Internal Revenue Service	Loses from $200 to $300 M in taxes because software that screened for fraudulent refunds was not working. (TN, 2006/07/15).	$250,000,000
University of California	Sued AOL for overstating ad revenues and subscribers. Loss of $450 M in value. (USA, 2003/04).	$450,000,000
WorldCom	Former WorldCom head, Bernie Ebbers jailed over the $11 B accounting manipulation. (FT, 2005/03/16).	$11,000,000,000
WorldCom	Fined $500 M by SEC for its $9 B accounting scandal. (USA, 2003/05).	$500,000,000
Xerox and Arthur Andersen	Xerox fined $10 M and Andersen fined $7 M for inaccurate financial reporting. (USA, 2002/04).	$17,000,000
Subtotal	*Poor Quality Information Costs – from Table 1-2*	**$1,167,785,029,000**
Poor Software Quality Costs	*Poor Quality Software Costs – from Table 1-1*	**$44,589,450,000**
Grand Total	*Total Costs of Poor Quality Information & Systems*	**$1,212,374,479,000**

Sources: WSF: "Why Software Fails"; BW = *Business Week*; CEO = *CEO Magazine*; CW = *Computerworld*; IW = *InfoWeek*; FCW = *Federal Computer Week*; For = *Fortune*; NYT = *The New York Times*; Tim = *Time*; WSJ = *The Wall Street Journal*; III = Information Impact International; USA = *USA Today*; FT = *Financial Times*; LTim = *London Times*; LTel = *London Telegraph*; TN = *The Tennessean*; N&O = *News and Observer*; Aus = *The Australian*; AFR = *Australian Financial Review*; LAT = *LA Times*; NAO = UK Nat'l Audit Office; S. Hrg. = Senate Hearing; Wired.com = http://www.wired.com/science/discoveries/news/2004/02/62242.

If the costs of Poor Quality Information of: $1,212,374,479,000 — nearly **One and a Quarter Trillion Dollars** — of waste in these 122 mostly reputable organizations, not counting recurring annual costs, *doesn't shock the heck out of you,* I do not know what will motivate you to address Information Quality within your own organization.

Many organizations may read about these companies and government entities and write them off. "But we are different," they may say. But if they are not in Stage 3 of Information Quality Management maturity, they will only be misleading themselves.

Remember that these are direct costs only and do not list missed or lost opportunity. Also know that your costs to create and develop a sustainable Information Quality Management capability and culture will be a fraction of the waste you are incurring every year in out-of-control information processes.

Also know that you cannot solve your problems by simply buying IQ software and inspecting and correcting your way out of your IQ problems. You must attack this as a serious threat to your enterprise, with your IQ initiative being driven by your Top Leadership Team.

Societal Costs and Losses Caused by Poor Quality Information

It is not just the direct and opportunity costs of poor quality information to the enterprise that are harmful, it is also the societal losses, causing Customers to pay higher prices for goods and services and causing Citizens to pay higher taxes. Defective information can cause death and injury due to medication error or wrong medical procedures. Students may be denied entrance to universities because of errors in scoring required entrance exams. Consumers may buy harmful foods if nutritional labels are not accurate to a minimum level. People will be convicted of crimes they did not commit or guilty offenders may be released in error, putting citizens at risk. See the following sidebars for a small, but representative, examples of such losses.

STUDY: MEDICAL ERRORS KILL AS MANY AS 98,000 U.S. PATIENTS YEARLY

Journal of the American Medical Association reports as many as 98,000 people in the U.S. die from medical errors, despite increased focus on attempts to reduce errors.[2]

U.S. NAVY SUB HITS MOUNTAIN NOT ON ITS NAVIGATION CHARTS

The nuclear attack submarine, the San Francisco, was severely damaged when it cruised at high speed, around 30 knots, into an underwater mountain that was not on its navigation charts. One sailor was killed, while 23 others were injured. Fortunately, the nuclear reactor was not damaged. If damaged, it could have caused long-term problems.[3]

FATAL AEROBATICS AS NAVIGATION MAP OMITS GONDOLA LOCATION

Maps given to Marine flight crews did not show a gondola lift on the steep mountainside at Cavalese in the Italian Alps, even though lifts have been there for decades. Also, the flight rules issued did *not* include a ban on flying below 2,000 feet above the terrain. The Marine pilot was showing off that day, flying faster than authorized and dipping below 400 feet above the terrain.

Whether he was aware of the gondola, his reckless behavior led to his slicing the gondola cable, causing the car to come crashing down, killing the 20 people on board.[4]

RAPIST REMAINED AT LARGE FOR EIGHT YEARS BECAUSE OF "TYPING ERROR"

A violent rapist in the U.K. remained at large for eight years because of a "typing error" in recording DNA evidence, police said. The rapist attacked and tried to strangle a 19-year-old woman who was walking home in Rainham, Kent, in 1996. But the rapist was not arrested for some time, despite giving a DNA sample that matched police evidence three months after the attack. He was jailed for 12 years by Maidstone Crown Court after admitting to the crime.[5]

DIALYSIS EQUIPMENT SENT TO WRONG PLACE

Four new dialysis chairs were sent to a remote hospital in north Queensland, Australia, where no patients with kidney problems lived. At the same time, no dialysis chairs were provided in locations where many dialysis candidates reside.[6]

EURO COINS ORDERED TO BE REMINTED

Nine million of the first Euro coins minted in France had to be melted down and minted again in 1998. Some of the coins were not minted to specification. The 10-cent and 50-cent coins had to be reminted because they did not conform to the previously agreed specifications that called for raised ridges along the edges.

Vending machine operators found that the 50-cent coin was too light, making it impossible for machines to tell it apart from the 20-cent coin.

This example illustrates the importance of correct product specifications.[7]

SMART BOMBS DESTROY HOUSE, KILLING INNOCENTS

In January 2005, U.S. forces mistakenly dropped a 500-pound bomb on a house, destroying it and killing from five to 14 people, injuring five others. The house was not the intended target.

There have been many unfortunate failures of so-called "smart bombs" and attacks on innocents, due to poor quality information and communication in the Afghanistan and Iraq "wars."[8]

In another incident, a U.S. pilot failed to clearly identify a target and fired on friendly forces, killing a British soldier and injuring several others.[9]

PASSENGER WEIGHT A CAUSE OF CRASH OF FLIGHT US5481

US Airways Express flight 5481 came crashing down just after take off due to two causes. One was the inaccurate average weight of passengers was too low, and the other was that poor maintenance of the cables that attached to the elevator that adjusted the plane's tail flap. As a result of these two problems, the pilots were unable to control the flight, killing all 21 people aboard.

As the American population has grown, literally, in weight, airlines must measure their passengers' weight and adjust the weight measurements to ensure safety of all. The FAA issued a temporary order to add 10 pounds to each passenger's weight and five pounds to the weight of each bag.[10]

INCORRECTLY GRADED SAT TEST SCORES LOWERED SCORES FOR 4000

Errors in software that graded the SAT exams of U.S. college applicants in October 2005 caused 4,000 exam takers' scores to be wrong, lower than their actual results. In 5% of the tests, scores were 100 points lower than they should have been. This could have caused college applicants to be denied entrance.

In another incident in Minnesota, a scoring error led to 8,000 students being told they failed a 2000 state math test.

In 2005, 4,000 students taking an ACT Chemistry exam were given wrong scores.[11]

MISLEADING FOOD LABELS LEAD TO POOR HEALTH DECISIONS

Nutritional information on some food products is "wildly inaccurate," a U.K. consumer magazine has warned. They looked at 570 nutrients in 70 products and found just 7% exactly matched the quantities on the labels. Some 17% fell outside the accepted 20% margin of error, including a kids' pizza with 47% more sugar than stated.

Currently there is no specific law about how accurate the information on food labels should be. They need only show average nutrition values in the U.K.

Worst offenders:

- Rivington's Pink Panther wafers had three times more saturated fat than stated.

- Cadbury's Light Trifles contained 23% more fat than stated.

- Tesco Kids Hot Dog Pizza contained 47% more sugar than claimed.

The consequences are that food choices are made based on misleading nutritional information, which will cause health problems.

Editor Malcolm Coles said: "Nutrition labels help people compare foods and make healthy choices, but only if they're accurate. How can you trust what you're eating when so many labels fall outside even the fairly generous margins of error allowed?"[12]

28% OF MOTOR LICENSES IN SOUTHWEST ENGLAND ARE NOT ACCURATE

A government study reveals that almost 28% of all drivers in the region do not update their licenses when they get married or move. Accurate information is required for police to track down stolen vehicles and for emergency crews at the scene of an accident. Failure to keep data accurate can lead to a £1,000 fine.[13]

FIRM SEEKS 200,000 TIRES SUBJECT TO RECALL

Poor quality information is hampering Bridgestone/Firestone from locating some 200,000 defective recalled tires that may still be on Ford Explorers. Owners may be at risk if they are driving on them, and are urged to notify Bridgestone/Firestone.[14]

LOSS OF NASA'S MARS CLIMATE ORBITER IS LOSS OF KNOWLEDGE

While the loss of the $125 million Mars Climate Orbiter wasted money, the real loss was the inability to capture knowledge about Mars to better understand our universe.[15]

The Orbiter's loss was caused by the use of English units of measure to calculate the trajectory and altitude of the Orbiter as it was supposedly sent into orbit around Mars. However, the NASA team entered the data as metric data (NASA's standard). By the time the NASA team realized that the data provided was not metric, it was too late to transmit the corrected data, and the Orbiter was sent in to an altitude below the gravitational pull, sending it crashing down on the backside of Mars.

A BROKEN SYSTEM: ERROR RATES IN U.S. CAPITAL CASES 1973–1995

- Overall rate of prejudicial error (serious, reversible error) in the American capital punishment system was 68%.[16]

- Capital trials produce so many mistakes it takes three judicial reviews to catch them.

- Of the 2,370 death sentences thrown out due to serious error, 90% were overturned by state judges; many had imposed the sentence in the first place.

Most common errors:

- Defense lawyers didn't look for, or missed evidence that the defendant was innocent.

(continued)

A BROKEN SYSTEM: ERROR RATES IN U.S. CAPITAL CASES *(continued)*

- Police/prosecutors discovered missed or important evidence, but suppressed it.

- 82% of the people whose capital judgments were overturned by state post-convictions courts due to serious error were found to deserve a sentence less than death.

- In 20 out of 23 study years, more than 50% of capital cases had serious flaws. In 10 of the study years, the error rate was 60%.

- Over 90% of death-sentencing states have error rates of 52% or higher. 85% have rates of 60% or higher. Three-fifths have error rates of 70% or higher.

BROKEN ELECTIONS PROCESSES DISENFRANCHISE MILLIONS OF VOTERS

The 2000 Presidential election saw from four to six million voters lose their votes because of over-voting (voting for two or more candidates) or under-voting (not recording a vote, failed chad penetration, or too light pencil marks). The number of disenfranchised voters was the equivalent of more than all the voters who voted in Florida that year![17]

25 PERCENT OF U.S. CONSUMER CREDIT REPORTS CONTAIN MATERIAL ERRORS

Conducted by the U.S. PIRG Education Fund studied reports from thirty states and found 25 percent contained material errors that would deny credit for the individuals affected. In addition:

54% contained personal information that was inaccurate or missing.

22 % of reports listed the same mortgage or loan twice.

8 % were missing major credit, loan, or other consumer accounts that demonstrated creditworthiness of the consumer.

30 % contained credit accounts that had been closed by the consumer but remained listed as open.

Altogether, 79 % contained serious errors or other mistakes.[18]

The sad truth in all of these examples and many others ends up costing the Consumers, Citizens, innocent bystanders, and Voters in time and money, paying for the recovery from process failure and Information Scrap and Rework because of organizations' broken information processes.

Revisiting the Costs of Poor Quality Information

The costs of poor quality in manufacturing, service, and government have been well documented over the past seven decades. Table 1-3 lists what the quality gurus peg as the costs of poor quality.

Table 1-3: The High Costs of Low Quality in Manufacturing and Service Sectors

QUALITY AUTHORITIES	INDUSTRY	PERCENT OF REVENUE		
		LOW	TO	HIGH
Philip Crosby	Manufacturing	15%	to	20%
Siegel & Shim	All Sectors	20%	to	25%
F. Steingraber	Manufacturing	25%	to	30%
	Service Sector	20%	to	30%
A.V. Feigenbaum	Manufacturing	15%	to	40%
W.E. Deming	Manufacturing	25%	to	50%
Joseph M. Juran	Manufacturing	20%	to	40%
L.P. Carr	Manufacturing	25%	to	30%
	Service Sector	30%	to	50%
Average for All		22%	to	35%

The Quality thought leaders have clearly identified the significant costs and losses in manufacturing and the service sectors when poor quality exists.

What is our experience of the Costs of Poor Quality Information? In the Costs of Poor Quality Information analyses that we have conducted, combined with the anecdotal evidence we have collected over the past twenty years, the evidence is clear. The Costs of Poor Quality Information as a percent of operating revenue or budget (for government and not-for-profit) is roughly equivalent to the costs of poor quality in the manufacturing and service sectors. In fact, manufacturing costs of poor quality often are caused by Information Quality issues such as errors in engineering and manufacturing specs or inaccurate inventory counts that cause materials shortages or materials and product overages.

In my first book *Improving Data Warehouse and Business Information Quality*, Wiley, (1999), I estimated the Costs of Poor Quality Information at from 10 to 25 percent of operating revenue. I was wrong!!! For the typical immature organization, the costs are much higher.

The costs of poor quality associated with the 122 anecdotes in Tables 1-1 and 1-2 totals US$1.2 Trillion, with several of these costs being annually recurring costs, see Figure 1-1.

> The costs of Poor Quality Information — based on updated research and measurement — are from 20 to 35 percent of an organization's operating revenue wasted in recovery from process failure and Information Scrap and Rework.

Figure 1-1: The High Costs of Poor Quality Information

Information-intensive enterprises such as banks, insurance companies, government agencies, and information brokers can have higher costs, reaching to 40% of operating revenue or budget or more.

Why Do We Have a Glut of Poor Quality Information and Information Processes?

There are many root causes, but a predominant cause is that business is managed out of the old, obsolete Industrial-Age principles of management by specialization of labor:

- Most organizations' Leadership Teams have failed to heed Peter Drucker's Information Age model of managing the Information-Based Organization[19] as an orchestra ensemble (performing together as one entity) and W. Edwards Deming's Pillar of the Enterprise as a (single) System.

- Management creates performance measures and reward systems that compromise quality for speed and cost-reduction, failing to understand "Total Cost of Ownership."

- Western management tends not to go to *Gemba* (the Japanese word for the Real Place where the Value Work takes place) to observe the information processes and find and fix the Root Causes of the broken processes. For more about *Gemba*, see the section "Solve Information Quality Problems at the Source — Not Downstream" in Chapter 2, "The ABCs of the TIQM Quality System for Total Information Quality Management."

- Management focuses on the needs of the investors over the needs of the end-Customers and Knowledge Workers who must delight the end-Customers.

Often, the truth of the matter is that Executive Management is out of the loop of feeling the pain of Poor Quality Information. Executives simply have to give the word to a staff member, "go get me this information," and it is done. But the executive does not see how much hunting and chasing goes into finding and collating the information. On the other hand, Knowledge Workers who receive defective information are the ones who feel the pain. If management does not manage by walking around in *Gemba* (the "Real Place") in which the value work goes on, they may never realize the enterprise-threatening costs they are incurring in process failure, Customer alienation, and Information Scrap and Rework to recover from the failure.

You cannot expect management to understand the real costs of poor quality information until they go measure it in their own organization. Right now, leading-edge organizations that have matured their Information Quality competencies and have transformed their culture to a habit of continuous IQ process improvement are putting pressure on their competitors.

When management does measure the Costs of Poor Quality Information, they often find them so high as to dispute them as, "this cannot be true!!!" If they write these costs off, they put their organization in jeopardy of failure.

Organizations that do not understand the Taguchi Quality Loss Function (any variation from the nominal valve causes loss and waste) are in danger. This is true in manufacturing as well as Information Quality used to manage the business and manufacturing processes. The traditional measurement of costs of poor quality are warranty costs incurred by the *manufacturer*. Taguchi defines Quality Loss as "the loss imparted by the product to the *society* from the time the product is shipped."[20]

How We Got into This Mess: The Root Causes of Business Failure in the Post-Industrial, Information Age

It should be well known that organizations cannot survive without having quality information. But simply having processes that capture information does not guarantee that information captured, maintained, and delivered to Knowledge Workers has the quality to enable business effectiveness. In fact, to have consistent quality information requires an organization to apply the same kind of Quality Management Principles and processes to information as they have applied to manufacturing in order to produce quality products and services.

The irony of this is that Western business was precisely successful in applying the Industrial-Age principles to business. But when the paradigm shifted with the dawning of the Information Age, Business and Information Systems Management did not seem to recognize, understand, or embrace the paradigm shift. Business management failed to see that success in the emerging Information Age requires a fundamental rethinking of how it manages the enterprise. It was comfortable managing down the vertical functional organization lines, creating a spirit of competition rather than a spirit of cooperation, collaboration, and ensemble.

Even when the U.S. re-discovered Dr. Deming in 1980 through an NBC documentary film describing the transformation Japan made by applying sound principles of Quality Management, organizations jumped on the "TQM" bandwagon, without really understanding the fundamental principles and processes required. Many only paid lip service to Total Quality Management, without seeking to learn and understand. As a result the emphasis on TQM started falling away in most organizations, whose philosophy was quantity and speed, without understanding Costs of Ownership.

Where was Information Systems (IS) management? IS management seemed clueless as to the significance of database management technology and its unifying potential for managing Enterprise-Strength, Shared Information. Many IS leaders failed to see their work as a business function. This is clearly seen in the fact that many CIOs, by and large are NOT Chief *Information* Officers — but Chief Information *Technology* Officers. Falling into the techno-trap of believing their job was to put in place the information technology infrastructure, their job was then to build or acquire and deploy hardware, networks, and applications, period. Few CIOs saw and understood the Information-Age paradigm. Caught up in the ever-accelerating technology "innovation" spiral, they were not able to reason through what is the purpose — or need — for this or that technology. They could not see that their true purpose is to transform how work could be done in the realized Information Age, and that application "solutions" sic. "systems" is not their product — INFORMATION and empowered Knowledge Workers are.

The Information-Age purpose of the CIO has always been to deliver Quality, Just-In-Time Information to the Knowledge Workers, and transform how they perform work.

Avoiding the Crisis

You, the reader and your management, have three choices in addressing Information Quality:

1. You can maintain the status quo of your current rate of defective information, incurring the high costs of process failure and Information Scrap and Rework, possibly leading to risk of enterprise failure. You and your management cannot just write this off as, "but we're different." If you ignore the potential waste, it will only increase your losses.

2. You can embrace a conservative, reactive approach of "Playing at Quality" by implementing an "Inspect and Correct" model of data profiling and data "cleansing" [*sic.* "Information Scrap and Rework"]. This will also lead to competitive disadvantage if your competitors scoop your organization.

3. You can embrace the proactive model of Total Information Quality Management by designing quality and error-proofing into the processes.

You can lead the transformation in your organization to the Stewardship that everyone in the organization is accountable for in their role and relationship to Information and make IQ management a habit for everyone. In this model, your organization will create competitive advantage, and you will scoop your competitors.

I hope you embrace the third choice and help bring your organization into the *realized* Information Age.

Summary

The Costs of Poor Quality Information represent an incredible *loss to society* and all Stakeholders. The costs are not just economic, but they affect safety, well-being, and equitable treatment of all in the civilized societies around the world.

The total costs of poor quality Information and Information Systems in the 122 anecdotes represent nearly one and a quarter Trillion dollars of actual waste caused by poor quality Information and Information Systems, some of which are recurring annual costs.

The cost of a proactive IQ Management function is a fraction of the monies the IQ function will recover in Information Scrap and Rework as it creates the habit of Continuous Process Improvement.

As you read the following chapters and start applying the TIQM Quality System for Total Information Quality Management, I look forward to seeing you take your profits to the bank.

Remember that 122 major organizations have lost or cost others

$1,212,374,479,000 plus or minus a few $ Billion in Information Process failure.

While these costs are for mostly major organizations, no one is exempt from broken information processes. The more *immature* an organization is in applying Quality Management Principles, Processes, and Practices to its Information Processes, the higher the costs of recovery from process failure and Information Scrap and Rework it incurs.

Consider what your organization may be losing as a result of poor quality, Out-of-Control Information Processes. Then go find them, measure them, improve them and measure the return on your investment.

Then study Chapter 6, "The Step-by-Step Guide to *Measuring the Costs and Risks of Poor Quality Information*" and go measure these costs for the sake of your Enterprise and Enterprise Stakeholders. Remember, you have a stake in the survival of your Enterprise, as well.

The ABCs of the TIQM Quality System for Total Information Quality Management

"Creative thinking involves breaking out of established patterns in order to look at things in different ways."
Edward de Bono, *Lateral Thinking*, **p. 11**

Why Total Information Quality Management

Organizations cannot perform their work or accomplish their mission effectively in the emerging *realized* Information Age without *Quality Information*. Most organizations, however, lack information of sufficient quality to enable them to have a competitive advantage. The implicit perception among most Executive Leadership is that "our information must be 'okay' — after all, we are making a profit." The message in Chapter 1 should dispel this *misconception* that abounds in organizations that do not have an Information Quality culture.

Purpose of the TIQM Quality System

Total Information Quality Management (TIQM) has two meanings. First, it is the name of the Information Quality Management System I developed, beginning in 1992. But secondly, and more importantly, it can refer to any Quality System applied to information that addresses a holistic approach to managing Information Quality and that is based on proven Quality Management Systems (QMS), such as Deming, Juran, Crosby, Imai (Kaizen), the Baldrige Criteria, and Six Sigma. It should address all aspects of Information Quality, including:

- Quality of "Information Product Specification" data (data definition, valid values, business rule specifications, information model correctness, and database design stability, flexibility, and reuse)

- Quality of Information Content (accurate and complete)
- Quality of Information Presentation (relevant, objective, intuitive)
- Quality Culture transformation to sustain Business Performance Excellence through Information Excellence as a result of Continuous Information Process Improvement

The real purpose of TIQM is to provide a means for organizations, whether in the private or public sector, whether large or small, to accomplish their missions efficiently and effectively to delight their Customers by eliminating process failure, recovery from failure, Information Scrap and Rework, and *Muda*, or waste of resources caused by poor quality information.[1]

Muda elimination — the elimination of waste — is a major component of Kaizen, the system of "Continuous Process Improvement" developed by Masaaki Imai. Information processes either add value or they add waste. A goal of TIQM is to eliminate the waste of non-value adding processes, such as reactive Information Scrap and Rework.

As Japan experienced its awakening to the Value Proposition of quality management, beginning in 1948, the successive results demonstrated that improved quality improves productivity. Dr. W. Edwards Deming would always write on the blackboard of meetings with top management the chain reaction of quality on business performance, illustrated in Figure 2-1.[2]

Figure 2-1: The Impact of Quality Improvement on Business Performance

TIQM is a complete, yet practical system of quality principles, processes, and techniques that can be easily applied to measure Information Quality and improve processes to eliminate the causes of poor quality information and its resulting process failure, losses, and costs.

Total Information Quality Management can be summarized as ABC:

A. *Assessment*: Measure Information Quality capability and information processes to identify process capability (degree of defects), and measure the costs of poor quality information that causes process failure, recovery from failure, and Information Scrap and Rework to:

- Determine how mature the Enterprise is in applying Quality Management Principles, processes, and techniques to its information processes as a business management tool.

- Determine if processes are in control and consistently producing quality information.

- Identify where processes need improvement to meet the Information Quality Requirements of *all* Knowledge Workers.

- Identify where data definition or information content and presentation processes need to be improved to prevent communication failure.

- Quantify the real Costs of Poor Quality Information and its effect on business profit (surplus) and on customer and Knowledge Workers satisfaction and productivity.

B. *Betterment*: Continually improve processes to:

- Eliminate the causes of defects at the source to prevent defective information, using a Pareto Diagram of most important to next most important Information and using an Impact Pareto to identify the magnitude of the costs or impact of defective information on the organization.

- Prevent process failure and costs to recover from failure caused by defective information.

- Eliminate the costs and waste of Information Scrap and Rework to fix the defects or scrap the unfixable defects.

- Prevent Customer alienation and loss of Customers and Customer Lifetime value.

- Increase end-Customer satisfaction and Customer Lifetime Value.

- Increase Knowledge Worker satisfaction and productivity by reducing Information Scrap and Rework, providing them more time for value work and innovation.

- Increase the satisfaction of all Stakeholders, including Shareholders, Suppliers, Business Partners, and Communities, all of whom benefit from the organization's success.

- Achieve successful accomplishment of the Enterprise Mission for the betterment of its Stakeholders, society, and the world.

C. **Culture Transformation:** Transform the culture of the Enterprise to value "Information Customers" and empower "Information Producers," providing training and other resources to manage information horizontally across the business Value Circles to meet the quality requirements of all Information Consumers, enabling them to effectively and efficiently perform their value-adding work and to innovate to meet tomorrow's Customer needs.

Dr. Deming cautions us that, "the transformation can only be accomplished by [hu]man, not by hardware (computers, gadgets, automation, new machinery). A company cannot buy its way into quality."[3]

All three ABC Components are required for a complete and sustainable Information Quality environment that optimizes the enterprise as a whole system — not just a collection of dis-integrated organization or business units. W. Edwards Deming's Management System of Profound Knowledge describes four components required for effective management. The first is "Appreciation for a system." The enterprise is a [single] system consisting of a "network of interdependent components that work together to try to accomplish the aim of the system [enterprise]."[4] Dr. Deming illustrated these interdependencies with his "Flow diagram" that he used from 1950 until the last presentation he gave before he died in 1993. See Figure 2-2.

Enterprise as a System

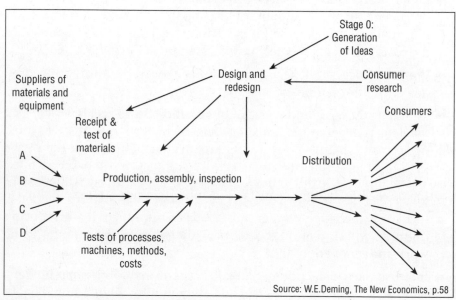

Figure 2-2: Dr. Deming's "Enterprise as a System" Flow Diagram

The Enterprise must be understood and managed as a *single system of interdependent divisions and departments that work together* to accomplish the aim of the enterprise. In this regard, an enterprise is much more like a symphony orchestra than the disjointed industrial specializations of labor that have grown into silos that not only have a little knowledge of how they fit into the enterprise mission, but often lead to competition with each other for resources. Orchestra musicians cannot perform as prima donna soloists, even if they have a solo passage. The music must all fit together as a whole.

Peter Drucker writes that executive management must operate more like a symphony conductor than a military commander, who provides orders within his chain of command. This means assuring that all groups work as an ensemble, defined as "a system of items that constitute an organic unity, or a congruous whole."[5] In an orchestra concert, if one part is missing, the entire performance is compromised. In business if one unit works toward its own goals, it can compromise the accomplishment of the aim of the Enterprise.

The Executive Leadership of an organization must clearly communicate the aim of the enterprise, like the orchestra conductor communicates the interpretation of the composer's intention of the music to be performed. Everyone must understand how their part fits into the whole and performs together.[6]

In businesses, government agencies, and not-for-profit organizations, Executives must clearly communicate the enterprise purpose and aim and lead the Enterprise to work as a single "ensemble," even if they have very diverse tasks.

Many organizations today are managed up and down the functional specialties, often with relatively autonomous or self-defined goals that may not be tightly bound to the enterprise mission.

Most large organizations' Information Systems are anything but an ensemble of work processes. Even with robust database management system technology that enables a single database to share information across the enterprise, most systems are designed as functional, stand-alone prima donna applications with interfaces that transform data from one database design to a disparately defined database based upon that unit's functional needs. This is a primary cause of muda in today's supposed state-of-the-art Information Technology functions.

ENSEMBLE OR COMPETITION?

One large software company actually encourages multiple software project teams to compete against each other for the same software product, with the "winning" team — whoever delivers first — being rewarded.

"Large organizations will have little choice but to become information-based,"[7] Drucker says. But most large organizations are choking under ever-growing *data proliferation* of data redundantly stored, excessively transformed, and moved to support ever-increasing islands of automation with functionally created data from one business area with quality that often fails to meet the needs of those dependent on it in downstream business areas.

The cultural change required to sustain effective business Leadership means transforming the management of the enterprise away from managing specialties and units *vertically* to managing the business Value Circles *horizontally* or *laterally* to optimize the interdependencies of all specialties.

The cultural change will not come easily, for Knowledge Workers do not necessarily want to give up their private, proprietary Information Stores, and managers do not want to give up their ability to work toward their own objectives. For a comprehensive treatment of the 14 Points of Transformation for Information Quality, see Chapter 11, "The 14 Points of Information Quality" in *Improving Data Warehouse and Business Information Quality*.[8]

What Is Information Quality?

Information Quality is both a concept and a function.

> **INFORMATION QUALITY CONCEPT DEFINED**
>
> Information Quality is "'Consistently meeting or exceeding *all* Knowledge Workers and end-Customer expectations' with information, so that Knowledge Workers can perform their work effectively and contribute to the enterprise mission, and so that Customers are successful in conducting business with you and are delighted with the products, services and communications [information] they receive."[9]

Information Quality is not an end in and of itself. It exists as a business tool to enable the accomplishment of the Mission of the Enterprise, whether business, government, not-for-profit, or in our own personal lives.

It is always the Customer who decides whether a product, service, or information meets their needs. Armand Feigenbaum states it pointedly, "Quality is what the *Customer* says it is….Quality is a *Customer* determination, not an engineer's determination, not a marketing determination or a general management determination. It is based upon the *Customer's* actual experience with the product or service, measured against his or her *requirements* — stated or unstated, conscious or merely sensed, technically operational or entirely subjective — and always representing a moving target in a competitive market."[10] Peter Drucker echoes this fundamental truth, " What is value for the Customer is…anything but obvious."[11]

Likewise, Information Quality is not an Information Quality analyst's determination, nor an Information Producer or producer manager's determination, nor a system professional's determination. Rather, it is the Knowledge Workers who depend on information to perform their work, who will make the real determination of Quality based on how well it supports their ability to perform their work to realize the Enterprise Mission.

INFORMATION QUALITY MANAGEMENT DEFINED

1. **Information Quality Management is "The application of sound Quality Management Principles, processes, and practices to information as a product of business, manufacturing, and service processes to meet all Information Consumers' expectations so they can accomplish the mission of the enterprise."**

2. **Another way to define IQM: "Increasing mission effectiveness by increasing information effectiveness through the application of sound Quality Management Principles and Processes to Information."**

TIQM is much more than the Quality Management of "data" content. TIQM requires quality not just of the data; TIQM requires quality of three components:

- Information Product Specification Quality (Data Definition, valid value sets, business rules, data formats, and Information Model and Database Design Quality)

- Information Content Quality

- Information Presentation Quality

Information Product Specification Data Quality

Information Product Specification (IPS) is to data what a Manufacturing Product Specification is to the manufactured product.[12] IPS includes:

- **Data Name:** Represents an attribute or characteristic about a real-world object or event the enterprise needs to know.

- **Data Definition:** A clear definition of the characteristic of the real-world object or event

- **Valid Value Set:** The complete set of discrete values for the attribute

- **Data Value Format:** The structure of the value, such as NNN-NN-NNNN for a U.S. Social Security number

- **Business Rules:** Clear and correct specification of rules that govern integrity of the valid values

- **Derived Data Calculation Formula:** The correct algorithm or formula used to calculate a fact of derived data

- **Information Model:** Represents the objects and events and the attributes — or facts — that the enterprise needs to know in order to be successful and accomplish its mission.

Information Models that represent the Information Requirements of an *enterprise* (all Knowledge Workers) become the blueprints for database designs that house the information. Information Models must express the *inherent* relationships of the real-world objects and events and all facts about them the enterprise needs to know to enable quality of database design.

Physical database designs need to have structural integrity to allow Knowledge Workers across the enterprise to share information from a single Record-of-Reference database rather than from redundant, functional, and (usually) disparately defined data stores. Quality database design produces databases that contain all required facts (data elements), are stable to allow new applications with additive change only (no modification of the data structure), and are flexible to support business process reengineering with *minimal* structural change to the databases.

Information Content Quality

Data stored in a database or data warehouse represents the raw material of information. Data Content Quality is equivalent to the Quality of Raw Materials in manufacturing. Defects in the content cause defects in the Information Presented to Knowledge Workers or in applications that use the defects in their calculations or processing, causing them to fail.

Data values must be complete, valid, accurate to the right level of precision, consistent across all data stores that house them, and of the right currency (age) for each specific use.

Information Presentation Quality

Quality, relevant information must be accessible, available, and presented in a timely, intuitive, and un-biased way, enabling Knowledge Workers to understand the significance in the Information, so they can take the *right* action or make the *right* decision.

Many practices that use the label "Data Quality" focus only on the data content. This addresses only part of the Information Quality problems. Focusing on data content only is like Manufacturing Quality focusing only on the quality of the raw materials and not the assembled, Finished Product. A sound Quality System must also address Data Definition and Design Quality and Presentation Quality of the assembled, finished Information Product. A sound Information Quality (IQ) Management System must also address the cultural transformation required to sustain an ongoing Information Quality environment.

COMMON MISCONCEPTIONS ABOUT INFORMATION QUALITY DISPELLED

■ *IQ is quality of data in databases.* No! Data in databases represents the raw material. IQ must also address the quality of the Information Product Specifications (definition, valid value set, business rule specifications, and calculation formulas) and the presentation mode and format.

■ *IQ is "data cleansing."* No! When most people unfamiliar with Quality Management Principles hear the term *Data Quality* they think of data cleansing, or fixing defective data. But a Total Quality Management approach to Information Quality confirms that IQ is *NOT* data cleansing. Data cleansing is a euphemism for Information "Scrap and Rework" or Corrective Maintenance. In auto manufacturing, no one speaks of vehicle cleansing unless it is about running the vehicle through a car wash. Data *Corrective Maintenance*, the more accurate term, represents the cost of poor quality information processes. Information Preventive Maintenance or Process Improvement by designing quality into the information process is the means to delivering quality information. Information Quality Management means: (1) training and equipping people to understand and perform their processes effectively; and (2) designing Quality into the processes that define, create, maintain, and present information to prevent errors and biased information presentation. TIQM is about quality of people. "A company able to build quality into its people is already halfway toward producing Quality [Information] Products." [13]

■ *IQ is data profiling or data measurement.* No! Any data measurement represents the cost of appraisal or inspection. We must measure to identify broken processes. But if we only conduct inspections without improving processes, we will fail to achieve the Value Proposition of eliminating the costs and waste in process failure caused by defective information. PS: providing data measurement results back to responsible management is insufficient. Management must know how to *improve* processes to prevent defects.

■ *IQ is "fitness for use" or "fitness for purpose."* No! Although these definitions are valid for manufacturing quality where parts or products have a singular or small set of uses, information is required to support *many different* purposes within an organization. Information may be fit for one purpose but cause others to fail.

INFORMATION MUST HAVE QUALITY FOR MULTIPLE PURPOSES

A call-center order taker was able to take Customers' credit orders if they did not have their Social Security number (SSN) — a required field — by inserting her own SSN. This was fit for purpose to place an order, but caused the credit authorization process to fail.

- ■ *Quality is best-of-breed.* No! Popular in software evaluations, best-of-breed looks only at a comparison of the software features and functions *without respect* to the specific requirements of an organization. Organizations must evaluate software data structures against their own Information Requirements to determine the Costs of Ownership of the interfaces they will have to design and to find what required information is missing from the software.

- ■ *Quality is zero defects in all information.* No! Zero defects in information that is marginally important to accomplishing the mission represents the waste of "overkill." The most important information that truly requires zero defects is the information that Six Sigma and TIQM call Critical-to-Quality (CTQ). Defects in this Information can cause high Costs of Failure and losses. Genichi Taguchi is right that any variation (defects) in required information causes a loss to society; the organization must prioritize IQ based on the Pareto of CTQ information first, then focus on the next most important information.

- ■ *IQ problems are created by Information Producers.* No! The truth is that Information Producers do exactly what they are paid to do and measured for. A major inhibitor to high quality information is measures that reward speed without considering the costs of process failure and Information Scrap and Rework caused to downstream processes.

- ■ *IQ improvement is what the Information Quality Team/Organization does.* No! This is a major misconception based on the notion that IQ can be delegated. The IQ Team will define the processes and help transform the organization to make Quality Improvement a normal part of everyone's job and accountability.

- ■ *IQ problems can be edited out.* No! Implementing well-defined business rules for data edit and validation is *part* of Process Improvement, but this alone will only guarantee "business rule conformance" or validity of the data. Data could conform to all business rules and still be inaccurate, presented in a biased way or not delivered in a timely manner. Quality Information must meet or exceed all Quality Requirements — not just validity.

- ■ *TQM or TIQM is only a program or a project or a methodology.* No! Total Information Quality Management is a:
    - ■ *Quality System* that values the information "Customer,"

> - *Mindset of Excellence* in all products, tangible, intangible, or information, and a
>
> - *Habit of Continuous Improvement* of all core information processes, using proven Quality Management Principles, processes, and methods to continually drive out the waste of poor quality information and increase Information Customer satisfaction.
>
> ■ *IQ is too expensive.* No!!! When planned and implemented properly, IQ is a *profit maker!* If an Enterprise treats IQ as "inspect and correct," it will condemn its IQ function to be an ineffective *cost center*, reactively and systematically performing Information Scrap and Rework. If, however, the enterprise treats Information as the product of its processes and concentrates on making quality *certain*, the IQ function will become a profit center, continually eliminating the waste of poor quality information.[14]

Total Information Quality Management

The principles that drive Total Information Quality Management are not new. They already exist in the principles that drive the proven Quality Management Systems of the Quality gurus that led to the industrial economic (quality) revolution and the *maturation* of the Industrial Age. Those gurus include Walter Shewhart (Quality Control and Plan-Do-Study-Act), W. Edwards Deming (System of Profound Knowledge), Joseph Juran (Trilogy of Quality Planning, Quality Control, Quality Improvement), Kaoru Ishikawa (Total Quality Control), Armand Feigenbaum (Total Quality Control), Masaaki Imai, (Kaizen and Gemba Kaizen), Genichi Taguchi (Quality Engineering), Philip Crosby (Quality is Free and the 14 Steps), and Yoji Akao (Quality Function Deployment [QFD]). Other non–individual-based, proven quality systems include ISO 9000-2000, the Baldrige Criteria for Performance Excellence, and the EFQM Excellence Model and Six Sigma.

The Importance of Total Quality Management Principles

Principles are fundamental truths, laws, or assumptions that represent guidelines required to achieve a successful result in an endeavor. Understanding the Principles common to effective Quality Management Systems helps us implement the fundamental components to achieve effective *Information* Quality Management Systems and environments.

True principles of Quality Management seen in the proven Quality Systems have transformed the organizations that adopted and implemented them. These same principles can and must be applied to Information Quality Management for effective and sustainable High Quality Information that increases Business Performance Effectiveness.

To understand Information Quality Management Principles, we must first understand the Quality Principles that are the foundations of the proven Quality Management Systems of the Industrial Age.

Because information is a product of our business, manufacturing, and service processes, understanding the universal Quality Principles that have been applied successfully to manufacturing enables us to create a sound and effective Information Quality Management culture.

Universal Principles of Quality Management Applied to Information Quality

Study of the sound Quality Systems that developed during the maturing of the Industrial Age reveals *common Principles* and *Critical Success Factors* that must be applied to Information, the *differentiating* resource of the Information Age. Why? Although Information is intangible and non-consumable, it is manufactured by processes just as real as the automobile coming off the production assembly line.

UNIVERSAL PRINCIPLES OF QUALITY MANAGEMENT

- **Poor quality causes high costs of process failure and Scrap and Rework, hurting Customers, the enterprise, and society.**
- **Everyone adopts a strong Customer focus.**
- **Quality exists when products and services consistently meet or exceed Customer Expectations.**
- **To solve Quality problems we must "speak with data (facts)."**
- **Process improvement that eliminates Root Causes is the means to realize quality.**
- **Solve Quality problems at the source — not downstream.**
- **Process Improvement is continuous.**
- **Use proven scientific methods for Quality Management.**
- **Executive Leadership commits to and is actively involved in driving the Information Quality System.**
- **Management assumes Accountability for Quality.**
- **Training and resources are provided to enable everyone to make quality their job.**

Next, these common Quality Principles are translated to their Information Quality Principles counterparts and described.

Poor Quality Information Causes High Costs of Process Failure and Information Scrap and Rework

The real driver for Quality Management is the fact that poor quality causes process failure, scrap or rework to recover, alienated and lost Customers and their Customer Lifetime Value, missed opportunity, and ultimately, Mission failure. This is true whether the product is a consumer goods product or an "Information" Product.

If the organization's processes are optimized, then there is no need for improvement. But the reality is that without a sound Quality Management System, an organization's information processes are not just sub-optimized — they are severely broken. Chapter 1 has illustrated the high costs caused by Poor Quality Information that have resulted in more than just a few companies going out of business. Chapter 6 describes how to measure these costs as well as how to measure the ROI on your Information Process Improvements.

HOW BROKEN ARE OUR PROCESSES?

- *Philip Crosby:* "Quality is measured by the cost of quality which is the expense of the cost of nonconformance — the cost of doing things wrong. These costs are divided into prevention, appraisal, and failure categories. But they all are a result of not doing things right the first time. You can spend 15 to 20 percent of your sales dollar on such expenses without even trying hard."[15]

- *Joseph Juran:* "Costs of poor quality, including Customer complaints, product liability lawsuits, redoing defective work, products scrapped, and so on. The total of those costs is huge. In most companies they run about 20 to 40 percent of sales. In other words, about 20 to 40 percent of the companies' efforts are spent in redoing things that went wrong because of poor quality."[16]

- *Samuel Boyle:* "We have learned the hard way that the cost of poor quality is extremely high. We have learned that in manufacturing it is 25-30 percent of sales dollars and as much as 40 percent in the worst companies. Moreover, the service industry is not immune, as poor quality can amount to an increase of 40 percent of operating costs."[17]

- *Joel Siegel and Jae Shim:* "Quality costs are costs that occur because poor quality may exist or actually does exist. These costs are significant in amount, often totaling 20 to 25 percent of sales."[18]

- *Lawrence Carr:* "The costs of rework and scrap, which can amount to 25 to 30 percent of sales revenue in manufacturing companies and as much as 30 to 50 percent for service firms."[19]

(continued)

> **HOW BROKEN ARE OUR PROCESSES?** *(continued)*
>
> ■ *Larry P. English:* "The Direct Costs of Poor Quality Information, including irrecoverable costs, rework of products and services, workarounds, and fines and Customer compensation can be as high as 20 to 35 percent of a large organization's (operating) revenue or budget."[20]
>
> ■ *English:* "As much as <u>40 to 50 %</u> or more of the typical IT budget is really 'Information Scrap and Rework' when you count the redundant databases and interfaces that move and transform data between them with cost-adding only, when quality designed databases allow data to be shared by all operational application systems."[21]
>
> ■ *English:* "Poor Quality Information often causes <u>40 to 60 %</u> of manufacturing Scrap and Rework costs."[22]
>
> ■ One formal Cost of Poor Information Quality analysis in a major financial institution, signed off by its Internal Auditors and Legal Counsel, found its direct costs alone of poor quality information were 33 percent of its operating revenue!

In Chapter 6, you learn how to measure these costs; in Chapter 7 you learn how to Improve Processes to prevent the Root Causes of Information Quality problems; and in Chapter 6 you learn how to measure the ROI (Return-on-Investment) of your Process Improvement initiatives.

Everyone Adopts a Strong Information "Customer" and Knowledge Worker Focus

Quality exists in the eye of the Customer. The organization must listen to and understand what Customers care about in the products and services it provides, so they can measure and ensure they address the Quality Characteristics they need.

The earliest manufacturing Quality Systems focused first on finding and fixing defects, then on reducing variability (defects) in manufactured products. This product-out mindset led to meeting "internally defined" quality requirements that may or may not meet "Customer expectations."

What is accomplished if one makes quality-engineered products that Customers don't want or buy? This is what happened to Motorola, even as it pioneered the Six Sigma Quality System. Focusing on engineering quality, Motorola failed to take notice of the softer Customer expectations, such as style. It belatedly regrouped to design style into its mobile phones, but only after losing the digital mobile phone market to Nokia.

So, who are the Customers of Information?

■ Purchasing Customers, with whom you communicate, invoice, and apply payments

- End-Consumers who use products or services and the Owner's Manual or instructions and Warranty data
- Internal Knowledge Workers, who require Quality Information to perform work that meets the needs of your purchasing Customers and end-Consumers
- External Regulators, who evaluate compliance
- Shareholders, who require financial data to evaluate investments
- Web site Visitors who evaluate your products or services and other information as a prospective supplier

HOW IMPORTANT ARE CUSTOMERS AND KNOWLEDGE WORKERS?

- **Deming:** "The consumer is the most important part of the production line."[23] "The obligation to the Consumer never ceases."[24]

- **Juran:** The first step of Quality Planning is "Identify who are the Customers," followed by "Determine the needs of those Customers."[25] "The word "Customer" has popular appeal. That is why we adopt it to designate those who are impacted by our processes and products, even if they are not [purchasing] clients."[26]

- **Crosby:** The Quality Policy recommended is: "Perform exactly like the requirement...or cause the requirement to be officially changed to what we and our Customers really need."[27]

- **Masaaki Imai:** TQC (Total Quality Control) activities have shifted emphasis from "maintaining Quality throughout the Production Process to building Quality into the Product by developing and designing products that meet Customer Requirements."[28]

- **Armand V. Feigenbaum:** "While today's buyers continue to purchase with strong attention to price...they place increasingly high emphasis upon Quality, expecting acceptable products at *any* price level. It is Quality as well as price that sells today, and Quality that brings Customers back for the second, third, and fifteenth time."[29]

- **Six Sigma:** "Identify the Customer(s) for your product or service; determine what they consider important; Identify your needs to provide the product/service so that it satisfies the Customer."[30]

- **Baldrige National Quality Program:** Customer and Market Focus examines how an organization "determines requirements, needs, expectations, and preferences of CUSTOMERS and markets," and how the organization "builds relationships with CUSTOMERS and determines the KEY factors that lead to CUSTOMER acquisition, satisfaction, loyalty and retention and to business expansion and SUSTAINABILITY."[31]

In the Information Age, Customers and end-Consumers as well as internal Employees or Associates are Information *Customers*. Organizations communicate with their Customers in many ways, such as marketing catalogs, emails or phone calls, Web sites, billing statements, and newsletters, among others.

Employees or Associates who require Information to perform their work are *Knowledge Workers*, according to the management gurus Peter Drucker and Stephen Covey. Drucker coined the term Knowledge Worker when he foresaw the impact of computing and Information Technology on business and society as early as 1960. In 1966 Drucker writes, "Modern society is a society of large organized institutions. In every one of them, including the armed services, the center of gravity has shifted to the Knowledge Worker, the man who puts to work what he has between his ears rather than the brawn of his muscles or the skill of his hands."[32]

INFORMATION-AGE BUSINESS PERSONNEL ARE KNOWLEDGE WORKERS AND INFORMATION CONSUMERS — NOT "USERS"

Stephen Covey rightfully notes, "The most valuable assets of a 20th-century company were its *production equipment*. The most valuable asset of a 21st-century institution, whether business or non-business, will be its *Knowledge Workers* and their *productivity*."[33]

If the Father of Modern Management, Peter Drucker, recognized the importance of employees, as *Knowledge Workers*, since the 1960s, why have the Software industry and Information Systems Professionals persisted in applying the label *user* to the very people who do the Value Work of the enterprise? Is it not an oxymoron to speak of "Knowledge Management" on the one hand, and call the source of the Knowledge "users"?

The term *user* originated to differentiate the maker of something from those who used the something. So, the term *computer user* arose. However, that connotation has been lost, as illustrated in an IQ Software provider's reference to "IT *professionals* and business *users*" made at an IQ Conference a few years ago. Here the term *user* does *not* refer to someone who uses the business, but computers. It is used as a synonym of non-IT employees. Question: If we have IT Professionals, do we not have Business *Professionals*?

Someone defended the use of the term *user* with the argument that a carpenter requires a saw to do his work; therefore the carpenter is a saw user. I wrote back asking him when was the last time he called a carpenter a "saw user." He has not yet replied.

Quality Exists When Information Products and Services Meet or Exceed Information Consumer Expectations

Products will not be rated as quality even if they last the duration of the warranty if they are not easy to use or meet other soft Expectations of the Consumer.

When manufacturers or retailers try to convince an unhappy Customer that the product is a quality product it only increases the number of "prospective Customers" they will share their complaints with.

Juran tells us we must understand not just the Customers' stated needs, but also their unstated needs. "Customers' perceptions may seem 'unreal' to us, but they are a reality to Customers and hence must be taken seriously."[34]

And Imai reminds us that, "Quality begins when everybody in the organization commits to never sending rejects or imperfect [missing, inaccurate or untimely] Information to the next process."[35]

Information as a Product

Information is the resource that drives the Information-Age enterprise, requiring the discipline of "Information Management" to exploit the Information Resource. Information is not a Resource that appears automatically. Information is a *Product* of the processes that acquire, produce, gather, or create Information about the objects and events the organization must know about. It is this aspect that drives the discipline of "Information Quality Management." This Characteristic is why the principles of Manufacturing Quality Management apply *directly* to Information Quality. Just as in manufacturing, defective processes produce defective products, whether an automobile or the loan-agreement Information to finance the automobile.

Understanding Information Consumers' Expectations

Two major differences exist between Information as a Product and manufactured, tangible products. The first is that electronic Information is not tangible. As such, it is the only *non-consumable* Resource within the Enterprise. The second difference is that manufactured products tend to have a single or small set of uses. Information, however, is very multi-purposeful. The same Customer information may be used by:

- Sales reps to maintain mutually beneficial relationships
- Marketers to develop a profiled marketing campaign, and then to evaluate its effectiveness
- Accounts Receivable to invoice the Customer
- Customer Care to resolve a Complaint
- Quality Engineers to analyze product failure
- Product Developers to design the next generation products or services
- Business analysts to understand emerging Customer trends
- Compliance Officers to ensure Regulatory Compliance
- Legal department to monitor privacy compliance
- Fraud department to identify any suspicious activity

Therefore, Information must meet the needs of all work groups that depend on it. The data definition and base data content will remain constant wherever data is used, but the Information Presentation, or its aggregation or computation will vary based on the specific use by specific sets of Knowledge Workers. Each presentation must be designed to meet the needs of its Knowledge Worker group for their specific purpose or purposes. The Quality of the Information Content must meet the needs of the most rigorous requirement of any of the various Information Consumer groups.

To Solve Information Quality Problems We Must "Speak with Data (Facts)"

Before we can solve information problems, we must know what and where they are along with the extent of the problem. This requires gathering accurate and complete data about the Information Processes. It is not an accident that the great Japanese Quality thought leader, Kaoru Ishikawa, *Guide to Quality Control*, entitles Chapter 1, "How to Collect Data."[36] In *Japanese Quality Control*, Ishikawa says that to solve problems, "we should talk with facts and data." But he warns, "When you see data, doubt them! When you see the measuring instrument, doubt it! When you see chemical analysis, doubt it!" reminding readers that there are real scenarios of "false data, mistaken data, and immeasurables."[37] He continues, "even if accurate data are available, they will be meaningless if they are not used correctly." Ishikawa was aware that much information gathered to "please the boss" can be biased.

Ishikawa reminds us that just as business processes can be defective, producing Poor Quality Information, the measurement processes that gather data can also be defective, giving us a faulty view of the Process or Information we are measuring. Solving these problems is the very purpose of this book!

But the essence of this principle is that we must analyze data to discover the nature and extent of the poor quality — if any — and analyze and understand the Root Causes *before* we can improve to eliminate the problems. We must always work on the Pareto of most significant issues first, then move to the next most significant issues based on impact to the enterprise and our Customers.

Information Process Improvement That Eliminates Root Cause of Defects Is the Means to Realize Information Quality

As we said earlier, data cleansing — really "Data Correction" or "corrective maintenance" — is *Information Scrap* and *Rework*. Information Scrap and Rework, like Manufacturing Scrap and Rework, is not only more costly than doing it right "the first time," it also creates unintended Negative Side Effects in the process failure the defects cause. Scrap and Rework is the penalty and result of broken processes that create the defects or variation.

The second of Philip Crosby's "Four Absolutes" of Quality is, "The System of Quality Is Prevention."[38] Quality is accomplished *not* by Scrap and Rework, but by Process Improvement and Defect Prevention that eliminates the Causes of the Defects and Variation. Likewise, Information Quality is accomplished *not* by "data cleansing" but by "Information Process" Improvement and Defect Prevention that eliminates the Root Causes of the Information Defects and waste.

Defect Prevention can only be realized by understanding and defining improvements that eliminate the Causes of the Information Defects. All the edits and validation in an application will not prevent defects if the Root Cause is that claims processors are paid for how many claims a day they process.

World-class organizations set high ratios of money *invested* in Process Improvement (Preventive Maintenance) versus money *squandered* in failure recovery and Scrap and Rework.

Solve Information Quality Problems at the Source — Not Downstream

Always solve problems at the source to avoid passing defects on. The Japanese word *Gemba* means the *real place*, and in Kaizen *Gemba* is the place where products are produced or services delivered.[39] Defects are created here, and they must be resolved and prevented here. Never delegate rework to the downstream Customers. Because the next process is the Customer, we must commit to *"never to pass on defective parts or inaccurate pieces of information to those in the next process."*[40]

Information *Gemba* is wherever Information is discovered, captured, exchanged, or applied in Business Processes. Examples include:

- In the call center when Customers place orders with Customer Reps
- In the hospital operating room when the surgical team confirms they have "the Right Patient, Right Procedure, and Right Site"
- At the bank teller's window when a Customer makes a deposit
- At an oil well, when a field engineer measures the oil production equipment
- In cyberspace as a Visitor browses and buys something from an Internet merchant
- In a tornado damage zone when a claims agent assesses damage to a property
- At a computer when an Information Producer creates the features of a new insurance product
- In a seismograph as it records the vibrations of an earthquake
- In a report that presents Information to knowledge Workers

Information Processes that are the point of capture or update or presentation of Information need to be error-proofed at that point. Defects *not* Prevented at the source will cause processes using it to fail. If defective data is moved downstream and corrected in a redundant database, it causes a new problem of inconsistent data and does not prevent failure of processes that use it from the source. Reports from the source and downstream — now corrected — databases will not reconcile, possibly causing Knowledge Workers to trust neither.

Information Process Improvement Is Continuous

Quality Improvement is not a one-time activity, but a habit of Continuous Improvement of critical Enterprise Processes. "Improve constantly and forever the system of production and service," is Deming's Point 5 of Management Transformation.[41]

With each Process Improvement founded on eliminating Root Causes, the next Improvements to eliminate additional elements of waste become feasible. The more we improve, the more time and money Information Producers and Knowledge Workers have to concentrate on Value-Adding work and on Innovations for tomorrow's needs.

Use Proven Scientific Methods for Information Quality Management

Over time a number of Quality Management Tools and Techniques have been developed that have been demonstrated to be effective for quality management. The tools and methods that have been effective in general quality management can also be applied, often without modification, for TIQM. Some of these tools include:

- **Plan-Do-Study/Check-Act (Cycle):** Also called the Shewhart Cycle created by Walter Shewhart, this is the fundamental Process Improvement method. It is the basis of Six Sigma's DMAIC (Define-Measure-Analyze-Improve-Control) cycle.

- **Cause and Effect Diagram:** Created by Kaoru Ishikawa, the great Japanese quality guru, this is used to analyze Root Causes of Quality Problems to enable effective process improvements. The Information Cause and Effect Diagrams are called Ishikawa-English Diagrams by some people.

- **Statistical Quality Control Chart:** Used first by Shewhart to illustrate the variation in a process, this indicates whether or not a process is "in control."

- **SIPOC (Supplier-Input-Process-Output-Customer) Chart:** These are used to document process interdependencies and identify Customer Requirements.

- **Quality Function Deployment (QFD) and the Voice of the Customer (VOC):** This tool is used to capture Customer Requirements and Expectations and involves Customers in the design of products.

A variety of other tools, too numerous to mention here, are available, but will be discussed later in respective chapters.

Executive Management Commits To and Is Actively Involved in Driving the Information Quality System

Early Quality Management experts made it clear that Executive Leadership cannot simply *delegate* the task of Quality to others. They must be personally involved to make Quality happen:

THE ROLE OF EXECUTIVE MANAGEMENT IN INFORMATION QUALITY

▪ *Crosby:* "The Executive Leadership must make it clear [to everyone] where Management stands on Quality."[42]

▪ *Juran:* But Executives must not just tout their commitment. They must demonstrate it with tangible actions. "Upper managers must become personally involved in establishing corporate and divisional Quality Policies, Goals, Plans, Controls."[43]

▪ *Imai:* "Declared Commitment at Senior Management level is not, therefore, sufficient — it must be made credible by visible support from the Management Team.... Clear communication is required to explain fully to all employees the nature and implications of the initiative...[along with] an intensive program of training."[44]

▪ *Juran:* "The Upper Managers must participate extensively in the Quality Initiative. It is not enough to create awareness, establish goals, and then leave all else to subordinates. This has been tried and has failed over and over again. I know of *no company* that became a quality leader without extensive participation by Upper Managers."[45]

▪ Deming cites an actual, but typical, report that analyzed a specific organization's failing quality initiative, "My opening point is that *no permanent impact* has ever been accomplished in Improvement of Quality unless the top management carry out their responsibilities. These responsibilities never cease: they continue forever.... Failure of your own management to accept and act on their responsibilities for Quality is, in my opinion, the prime cause of your trouble."[46]

Remember that the degree of Poor Quality Information in the status quo is the result of the current Management Systems, values (as acted out — not as published), and performance measures that the Executive Leadership Team has put in place.

Executives must actively educate themselves in Quality Management Principles and processes, serve as the ultimate Governance Body on Information Quality concerns, and establish the infrastructure and provide resources to make Information Quality happen as a Normal Part of Business.

Executives must evaluate their performance and reward systems and revise them if they cause the defects that must be corrected or scrapped. When executives create bonuses for meeting "production" Targets based on Quantity *without considering the costs incurred by defective physical and information products*, they inadvertently *drive up the costs of doing business*. This creates enormous incentives for defects that cause unintended failure and waste!

Executives must measure the Costs of Poor Quality, including understanding how much manufacturing Scrap and Rework is caused by Poor Quality Information.

IQ practitioners must engage, educate, and coach Executives into new behaviors. Masaaki Imai describes a problem in Western management with top management perceptions of what *Quality Control* (QC) or *Total Quality Control* (TQC) means. Most often he found executives' reaction to those terms conjured up "inspection of finished products," which to them meant QC = higher costs, and, believing that "they [executives] have very little to do with Quality Control, lose interest immediately."[47]

IQ practitioners must help Executives *feel the pain* of the cost of the status quo and *demonstrate through Process Improvement Initiatives* that TIQM is a profit maker — not a cost center.

Management Assumes Accountability for Information Quality

In Quality Management, Managers are responsible for establishing Quality standards, for meeting them and for elevating those Quality Standards to meet the increasing requirements from their Customers. Management must accept accountability for achieving QCD (Quality, Cost, Delivery) for all the characteristics that result in a Quality Product.[48]

Once Executives have taken on Accountability for making Quality happen, they can turn and implement Accountability in their Management Team. "Management [who oversee Information Producers or the production of products] must accept accountability for achieving QCD [Quality, Cost, Delivery]"[49] to meet all Information Stakeholders' needs.

During the maturing of the Industrial Age, Management became Accountable for the proper use and maximization of the key Industrial-Age resources, *capital* and *people*. "The *administrative* job of the manager is to *optimize* the yield from these resources."[50]

In the Information Age, the differentiating resources are *Information* and *People*. "In an Industrial Society, the strategic resource is Capital. In the new Information Society, that key resource has shifted to *Information, Knowledge, Creativity*. And there is only one place where the corporation can mine this valuable new resource — in its Employees."[51]

Because Information is a "Product" of the processes that create and update it to keep it current, and because that information is a resource and the business uses it to manage every other resource, from money to inventory to facility and equipment maintenance to staff, every Manager must be held Accountable for the Quality of Information being produced. The accountability statements for Managers in the Information Age will look something like the following:

MANAGEMENT ACCOUNTABILITY FOR INFORMATION

RESPONSIBILITIES / ACCOUNTABILITIES:[52]

1. *Responsible for management and control of fiscal resources*: **Develop budgets and manage expenses within approved guidelines.**

2. *Responsible for personnel management of the department*: **Provide employee development. Uphold policies, schedule, oversee salary administration of staff, resolve staff problems.**

3. *Responsible for management, control and use of Information*: **Ensure Quality of Information created or maintained within the process or department meets all Information Consumers' needs, internal staff, other business areas' staff, and Customers and other external Stakeholders. Ensure Information Policy is understood and followed. Provide training of personnel in Information Quality Principles and Standards and provide Resources to accomplish Information Quality goals.**

If managers have a *different* performance measure than staff, especially if it is not aligned with the Enterprise Aim, they have a potential conflict of interest: to provide resources to staff to meet the Information Quality needs of downstream Information Consumers, or to meet productivity goals on which their bonus depends.

Training and Resources Are Provided to Enable Everyone to Make Information Quality Their Job

Once Managers are held Accountable for Information Quality and once training and other resources are made available to Employees or Associates, they can likewise be empowered to improve their processes and be held Accountable for the Quality of their Information.

Process Overview of Total Information Quality Management

TIQM is a complete and comprehensive Quality Management System based upon the principles incorporated in the proven Quality Systems that developed during the maturing of the Industrial Age to address the Quality of manufactured goods.

The same processes of Assessment, Improvement, and Culture Transformation apply to Information Quality, just as to Product Quality. An overview of the six TIQM processes is illustrated in Figure 2-3.

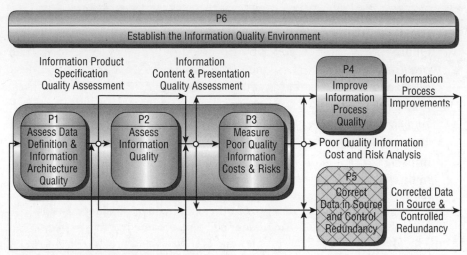

Figure 2-3: TIQM Process Overview

TIQM Processes

The six processes of TIQM are numbered (P1-P6), but this does not define the physical sequence of process execution. The six processes include three processes for Assessment (Inspection or Measurement), one for Betterment P4, through Process Improvement, one for controlled Information Corrective Maintenance, P5 and one (P6) for Culture Transformation:

TIQM Overview

Processes and objectives of TIQM. Remember the ABCs (Assessment, Betterment, and Culture Transformation).

ASSESSMENT

P6. Assess Information Quality Management Maturity: You must understand your enterprise's maturity in its ability to apply IQ Management Principles, Processes and practices as a *Business Management Tool*. From here you identify gaps that you must overcome to establish an effective IQ Culture and Habit.[53]

P1. Assess Information Product Specification Quality: This process measures the correctness, completeness, and clarity of the definition of the Business Information the Enterprise needs to know, to ensure that all Information Stakeholders, from the Knowledge Workers who apply Information and Information Producers who create, capture, or gather the Information have a common understanding and clearly communicate with one another in their work.

P2. Assess Information Quality: This process measures Critical-to-Quality Attributes required by Knowledge Workers to perform their processes optimally. These include completeness, accuracy, timeliness, relevance, and presentation intuitiveness and utility of the information provided to Knowledge Workers, among others.

P3. Measure Poor Quality Information Costs and Risks: P3 is the "Business Case" process. From a business standpoint, it is not as important to know that 57 percent of the Customer records have errors in them or that 23.3 percent of the Marital-Status codes are not correct, or that 37 percent of Customer records are duplicate records as it is for the business to know how much those defects *cost* the Enterprise, both in direct costs of failure and Information Scrap and Rework, and in lost Customer Lifetime Value and missed or lost opportunity.

P3 is critical for getting and sustaining the attention, commitment, and action of management.

BETTERMENT

P4. Improve Information Process Quality: The core competency of any sound IQ Management system. Describes how to conduct Plan-Do-Check/Study-Act process improvements to identify and eliminate Root Causes of Poor Quality Information and the High Costs of Information Scrap and Rework.

P5. Correct Data in the Source and Control Data Redundancy: Warning: This process is not a value-adding activity — it is a Cost of Poor Quality caused by broken information processes and by redundant databases and interface software and programs. It describes how to correct the defects found in the P1 and P2 assessments. Any Data Correction should be conducted as a *one-time event* for defective information in a given data store if data is still used from that source, following a P4 Process Improvement and Control Initiative that prevents future defects. If corrections are not made, current processes will continue to fail. Any Data Correction activity should be preceded with Process Improvement to prevent ongoing defects. P5 also defines how to control the transformation and movement of data when it is really required.

CULTURE TRANSFORMATION

P6. Establish and Sustain the Information Quality Environment: TIQM P6 is the framework for and the umbrella process that includes the ongoing transformation of the culture that has created the status quo. P6 describes the Transformations that must be effected over time in order to sustain a Culture and Value System of Customer Care, and Continuous Process Improvement for the good of all Stakeholders. This helps you implement the 14 Points of Information Quality as a Business Management Tool in the Enterprise. This transformation is not only counter-intuitive — it will be resisted vehemently by many who have a vested interest in preserving the status quo.

How important is P6? Consider that the costs of the status quo, whatever they may be, are the result of the culture that has produced the status quo.

Guidelines for Evaluating Information Quality Methods and Consultancies

As IQ issues have become more exposed and more attention is placed on addressing these problems, consultancies and software developers are jumping on the Data Quality (DQ) bandwagon. Unfortunately many Data Quality consulting practices and "methodologies" are *not* grounded in sound Quality Management Principles. One should evaluate IQ consulting methodologies and training offered by IQ consultancies and software providers against the principles described herein.

Evaluating IQ Methodologies

There are two approaches to creating Information Quality practices:

1. Develop your own methods using a trial-and-error approach.

2. Adopt — and adapt — existing proven IQ Quality Systems that are grounded in proven Quality Management Systems.

The message of Publilius Syrus around the first century BC is best guidance for those establishing, or enhancing your IQ practices: "From the errors of others, a wise man corrects his own."[54] In other words, should someone develop their own methodology, learning from their own mistakes as they go? The wise person will evaluate IQM methodologies based upon how well they apply the proven principles of the sound, proven Quality Management Systems. The wise person will understand and evaluate based on total cost-of-ownership:

- ☑ Ability to accelerate time-to-market — getting success early

- ☑ Avoiding the pitfalls other IQ practice start-ups invariably experience

- ☑ Increase the likelihood of success in your important Proof-of-Concept (PoC) initiative and ongoing IQ initiatives.

- ☑ Ability to increase enterprise acceptance and IQ maturity growth due to minimized mistakes and successful Process Improvement Initiatives with their elimination of the costs of failure and Information Scrap and Rework

Not all IQ methodologies are equally effective. If an IQ methodology is based on an *"inspect and correct"* principle, it will not stand the test of time. Inspect and correct approaches to Information Quality will always fail to become profit centers, because they attack the symptoms and not the Root Cause of the problems.

IQ methodologies based on IQ software systems will address how to use the software, but will generally fail to address Cost-of-Poor Quality Measurement, Process Improvement and the Culture Transformation.

IQ Methodology Evaluation Checklist

Table 2-1 provides a checklist for evaluating the methodologies provided by consultants and software providers. The methods, processes, and software you select will either help you solve the Root Causes of IQ problems — or they will *sub-optimize* your attempts to solve your IQ problems.

Table 2-1: Checklist of Essential Ingredients of a Sound "Information *Quality* Management" Methodology[55]

☑	1.	The IQ Quality System can trace its roots to one or more proven Quality Management Systems, such as Deming, Juran, Crosby, Imai (Kaizen), Shewhart, Ishikawa, Taguchi, Six Sigma, ISO 9000-2000, or Baldrige.
☑	2.	The IQ Method holistically addresses the Business Processes and not just the Application Systems and Database aspects. It implements IQ Processes as a Management Tool to increase Business Process effectiveness and to eliminate the Costs of Failure and Waste caused by poor quality.
☑	3.	The IQ Method has been implemented *successfully* in multiple organizations and references are able to be contacted in a final evaluation process.
☑	4.	The IQ Method has a *strong focus* on the "Information Customers" to understand and meet their Quality Expectations, and a *strong focus* on the Information Producer and Manager to provide them with training and resources so both can accomplish their jobs successfully across the business Value Circles.

(continued)

Table 2-1 (continued)

☑	5.	The IQ Method addresses and assures Quality of Data Definition and Information Model and Database design (as "Information Product Specification") and Information Presentation (the *finished product*) Quality as well as content.
☑	6.	The IQ Method differentiates between Validity and Accuracy and never presents a measure of Validity (conformance to business rules) as if it represents Accuracy (correct to the characteristic of the real-world object the data represents, such as "birth date"). It emphasizes Accuracy assessment for important data even if less frequently than Validity assessment and with smaller samples.
☑	7.	The IQ Method addresses the proper perspective between defined processes for IQ management coupled with IQ software products to exploit their capabilities. The IQ processes have procedures for performing IQ functions not capable of being provided by the IQ software.
☑	8.	The IQ Method measures the Costs of Poor Quality Information, so management understands the *Business* Costs of the status quo and as the basis for measuring the benefits of Process Improvements. The IQ Method measures the Costs of Information Process Improvement and calculates the ROI compared to the Cost of Ownership of the Defective Process.
☑	9.	The IQ Method has an effective *Process Improvement* Process, such as the Shewhart Cycle (Plan-Do-Check/Study-Act), that analyzes Root Cause and defines Improvements, implements and confirms improvements that eliminate recurrence of the defects, and puts the Process In Control as a repeatable process. The method emphasizes training to everyone in how to conduct Process Improvements and encourages them to do so.
☑	10.	The IQ Method emphasizes Information Quality Improvements and Control at the *Source* Processes that capture and maintain it, not on correcting data for only downstream Stakeholders.
☑	11.	The IQ Method emphasizes Training to Managers and Information Producers to provide them the tools to better perform their jobs in creating and maintaining High Quality Information.
☑	12.	The IQ Method actively encourages and facilitates a Cultural Transformation, helping Executive Management understand its role in IQ, emphasizing Management Accountability for Information Quality, and creating Customer-Supplier awareness among Management and Staff with "Customer Satisfaction" in Knowledge Workers and end-Customers as Key Performance Measures.
☑	13.	IQ Methodology training is available for Knowledge Transfer to different audiences, including IQ professionals, Executive Management, Business Management, Information Producers and Knowledge Workers, and Information Systems staff.

Do's and Don'ts in IQ Methodology Evaluation

Some guidance on evaluating IQ Methodologies:

☑ **Do** question the developer as to what Quality Management System or systems provide the basis for their methodology. Have them illustrate with references mapping their IQ principles, processes, and techniques to sound Quality System principles, processes, and techniques described herein. Are the IQ practices faithful equivalents for information compared to the quality system practices?

☑ **Do** explore whether the IQ Quality methods of IQ software providers is a true IQ Quality Management System or simply a procedure for using the software. Most IQ software providers, like software providers in general, develop methodologies to use the software — not necessarily to solve the business problems. As such, they may not address critical aspects, such as cultural changes, and performing necessary IQ functions that are not supported by their tools, such as process improvement initiatives. *Please do not take this as a criticism of IQ software providers. There is a need for effective and efficient IQ software to provide support to real IQ problems that lend themselves to automation.* For example, the various software capabilities can help you:

 ☑ Analyze data efficiently for value frequency distribution, pattern recognition, and missing values (profiling) to help you understand *certain* kinds of errors.

 ☑ Validate data efficiently for conformance to valid values or specified business rules.

 ☑ Correct *certain kinds* of data errors to valid values, but not necessarily to accurate values.

 ☑ Identify *potentially* duplicate records for consolidation.

 ☑ Prevent *certain kinds* of validity defects in applications that create or update data. Defect prevention is the highest quality capability in IQ software. You should require it in your IQ software selection.

☑ **Do not** be misled by supposed authoritative "advisory" sources that specialize in *Information Technology* areas that do *not* demonstrate an understanding of sound Quality Management Principles. Reports by "analysts" who are not grounded in sound Quality Management Principles may *not* be helpful to evaluate IQ Methods based on sound quality principles.

☑ **Do** listen to IQ software providers to see if they truly support or adopt sound IQ methods outside of their own methods. Software providers' expertise is in developing software — not developing comprehensive methods that address the human and management factors and the required culture transformation that is outside the capability of software. Their expertise will be in effectively using the capabilities of their tools.

☑ **Do** recognize that you will need *both* an effective IQ Management Methodology based on proven Quality Management Principles *and* effective IQ software if your organization has large volumes of information.

Summary

The principles, processes, and techniques of sound and proven Quality Management Systems are well-known today. Any valid Information Quality Management System will be grounded in those principles, processes, and techniques and will adapt them in ways that apply to information, as an intangible product of the enterprise.

To recap those Information Quality Management Principles:

- Poor Quality Information Causes High Costs of Process Failure and Information Scrap and Rework.

- Everyone Adopts a Strong Information "Customer" and Knowledge Worker Focus.

- Quality Exists When Information Products and Services Meet or Exceed Information Consumer Expectations.

- To Solve Information Quality Problems We Must "Speak with Facts."

- Information Process Improvement That Eliminates Root Causes Is the Means to Realize Information Quality.

- Solve Information Quality Problems at the Source — Not Downstream.

- Information Process Improvement Is Continuous.

- Use Proven Scientific Methods for Information Quality Management.

- Executive Leadership Commits To and Is Actively Involved in Driving the Information Quality System.

- Management Assumes Accountability for Information Quality.

- Training and Resources Are Provided to Make Information Quality Everyone's Job.

The Step-by-Step Guide to the TIQM Quality System for Total Information Quality Management

"Creative thinking involves breaking out of established patterns in order to look at things in different ways."

Edward de Bono, *Lateral Thinking*

Part II consists of six chapters, each of which describes a critical process of the TIQM Quality System.

Chapter 3: **"Implementing and Sustaining an Effective Information Quality Environment."** This chapter describes Critical Success Factors necessary to transform the Enterprise's culture and to create an effective IQ Management System as a Business Management System. Here, we address the Principles and Techniques required to create an effective and sustainable habit of Continuous Information and Business Process Improvement to reduce and eliminate the High Costs of Poor Quality Information.

Chapter 4: **"The Step-by-Step Guide to** *Assessing Information Product Specifications and Information Architecture Quality.***"** This chapter describes how to assess the quality of your Information Management processes and the Quality of Information Product Specifications. Information Product Specifications are to Information Quality what manufacturing Product Specifications are the Product Quality.

Chapter 5: **"The Step-by-Step Guide to** *Assessing Information Quality.***"** This chapter describes how to Assess the Quality of Information and its Presentation. The basis for IQ Assessment is understanding the Critical-to-Quality (CTQ) IQ Characteristics required by Knowledge Workers.

Chapter 6: **"The Step-by-Step Guide to Measuring the Costs and Risks of Poor Quality Information."** This chapter describes how to Measure the Costs of Poor Quality Information as well as the Return-on-Investment of Process Improvement Initiatives. This process is the Business Case Process, enabling you to see the Costs of Poor Quality Information in your status quo environment. The process further establishes the reduction in costs of process failure and Information Scrap and Rework to calculate the Return-on-Investment of Information Process Improvement Initiatives.

Chapter 7: **"The Step-by-Step Guide to** *Improving Information Process Quality.***"** This chapter describes how to Improve Information Processes and keep them in Control. This follows the fundamental Shewhart cycle of Plan-Do-Check/Study-Act to improve processes.

Chapter 8: **"The Step-by-Step Guide to** *Data Correction and Controlling Data Redundancy.***"** This chapter describes how to conduct data correction and control data redundancy. This process is fundamentally a Cost of Poor Information Quality activity. It tells when and how to correct data as a one-time event after you have improved the process to prevent further errors from the status quo processes.

Implementing and Sustaining an Effective Information Quality Environment

"The significant problems we face cannot be solved at the same level of thinking we were at when we created them."

Albert Einstein[1]

The TIQM Quality System is a comprehensive Quality Management System for Total Information Quality Management based on proven Quality Management Systems (QMS). The discrete processes of measuring IQ, measuring the Costs of Poor Quality Information, and Improving Information Processes are not sustainable without having a Culture and Habit of Continuous Information Process Improvement. This chapter describes how to transform the organization's culture to establish a sustainable Total Information Quality Management Environment that encourages everyone to take accountability for the Quality of Information they produce, update, or apply in the performance of their Value Work.

The purpose of this chapter is twofold:

1. To outline how to establish an environment that leads to a culture of effective, Continuous Business and Information Process Improvement

2. To identify why TQM and IQM implementation initiatives fail and what you can do to avoid failure

TIQM Process 6: Establish the Information Quality Environment

TIQM begins and continues with the umbrella Process of TIQM P6: "Establish the Information Quality Environment." This Process is not a discrete Process, but rather, an ongoing transformation of the Enterprise to a culture of Continuous

Process Improvement and Stewardship of the Enterprise's second most important resource — its Information.

This Process provides analysis of the current status quo of the Enterprise, evaluation of business management systems, education, training, and coaching. The goal is to dismantle the barriers to Information Quality and to empower management and staff to Continually Improve Processes to prevent the high costs of recovery and Information Scrap and Rework.

While TIQM Processes P1–P5 are discrete Processes with definable beginning and end points, P6 is a continuous Process of transformation and education to continually mature the organization's capability for delivering Quality Information for Business Effectiveness. Figure 3-1 illustrates the six Processes of TIQM with P6 as the umbrella Process of Culture Transformation.

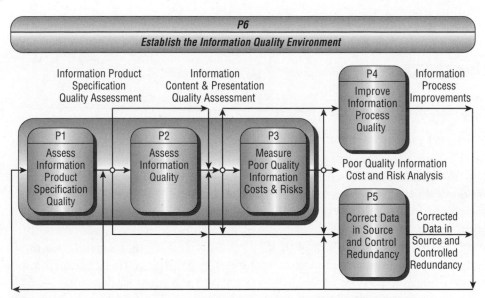

Figure 3-1: TIQM Process Diagram with P6: Establish the Information Quality Environment as the Framework for Sustainable Information Quality Management

Chapter 2 describes how the shared principles of proven Quality Management Systems will fundamentally transform an organization to Business Excellence. This happens through continuous improvement of the Information Processes that provide the Information used to manage every other resource of the Enterprise. This chapter describes how to implement these shared principles and how you can avoid failure by learning why TQM implementations of the past have failed.

The 14 Points of Information-Age Transformation

TIQM is not a program, a project, and certainly not just a methodology. TIQM is a Quality System for establishing sustainable business effectiveness through continuous improvement of all processes, including the Information Processes that are required to capture, maintain, and deliver essential Information to Knowledge Workers who depend on it for performing their Value Work.

Dr. Deming's System of Profound Knowledge and his 14 Points of Transformation are fundamental to the development, cultivation, and sustainability of an effective Quality Management System, whether for manufacturing Quality, service Quality, or Information Quality.

The 14 Points are outlined here for your reference. They are described in detail in my earlier book, *Improving Data Warehouse and Business Information Quality:Methods for Reducing Costs and Increasing Profits* (Wiley, 1999).[2]

The 14 Points Applied to Information Quality

Dr. Deming's 14 Points of Transformation provides a sound basis for establishing an effective IQ Management culture and environment. Here, I give a brief synopsis of Deming's Points and how they apply to IQ.

1. Create Constancy of Purpose toward Improvement of Product and Service, with the Aim to Become Competitive and to Stay in Business, and to Provide Jobs.

- Management has two sets of problems:
  - **Those of today:** "It is easy to stay bound up in the tangled knots of the problems of today, becoming even more efficient in them."
  - **Those of tomorrow:** "For the company that hopes to stay in business."[3]
- "The obligation to the Customer *never ceases*."[4]

IQ 1. Create Constancy of Purpose toward Improvement of Information Product and Service, with the Aim to Become a Competitive, Intelligent, Learning Organization, and to Stay in Business, and to Provide Jobs.

Management must not stay bound up in the tangled knots of poor Quality Information, simply perpetuating never-ending data cleansing, [*sic.* "Corrective Maintenance" or "Information Scrap and Rework."] It must plan for tomorrow's

Information needs as to what the Customers need and what Knowledge Workers need. The Enterprise Strategy must drive the Enterprise to capture, maintain, and deliver quality, Just-in-Time Information to meet Knowledge Workers' requirements. This is required so they have the Information they need to perform their Value Work and contribute to the accomplishment of the Enterprise Mission and to delight all of their Information "Customers."

To create Constancy of Purpose for Information Quality, you must:

- Understand the Mission of the Enterprise. Always start here.
- Define the IQ Vision, and Strategies driven by the Enterprise Mission. The culture of Quality must enable the Enterprise to effectively accomplish it's Mission. This is accomplished by improving the Quality of Information required to perform work effectively and efficiently and to enable optimized decisions.
- Develop IQ plans with both long-term strategies and short-term deliverables that enable accomplishment of *Strategic* Business Objectives.
- Implement and define IQ Processes and Techniques with a *Customer* focus that leads to Quality and Continuous Process Improvement.
- "The *obligation* to the *Knowledge Worker* never ceases, so they can perform their work effectively."[5]

2. Adopt the New Philosophy. We Are in a New Economic Age. Western Management Must Awaken to the Challenge, Must Learn Their Responsibilities, and Take on Leadership for Change.

The economic realities of today require new standards:

- "Reliable Service Reduces Costs."[6]
- "Point two really means … a Transformation of Management"[7] This transformation is a transformation away from Quality by "inspect and correct" to Management through Continuous Process Improvement.

IQ 2. Adopt the New Paradigm in the New Economic Era of the Information Age: Reliable Information Reduces Costs.

- We cannot compete without Information Quality in the Age of Information.
- Implement a philosophy that recognizes that:
  - "Reliable, *managed* Information reduces costs and increases value."
  - "Reliable, *quality*, Shared Information reduces costs and increases value."

- This means a Transformation of Business and Information Systems Management.
  - Business Management must become *Accountable* for Information created or updated by their Information Producers or retrieved and applied by their Knowledge Workers.
  - Systems Management must be *Accountable* for design and engineering of Value-Adding applications and for design of Enterprise-Strength Information Models and Database Designs.[8]

3. Cease Dependence on Mass Inspection to Achieve Quality. Eliminate the Need for Inspection on a Mass Basis by Building Quality into the Product in the First Place.

- Quality assurance (inspection) has a goal to discover faulty products and fix them (Rework) or throw them out (Scrap) before they get to the Customer.
- "Quality comes *not* from inspection but from Improvement of the Production process."[9]

IQ 3. Cease Dependence on Mass Data Profiling and Information Assessment to Achieve Information Quality by Designing Quality into Information Processes.

- Eliminate the need for inspection by Designing Quality into the Information Production and Delivery (Presentation) Processes.
- "Quality comes not from Data Profiling and IQ Assessment, but from Improvement of the Information Processes that create, update, and deliver Information to Knowledge Workers."

4. End the Practice of Awarding Business on the Basis of Price Tag. Instead, Minimize Total Cost. Move toward a Single Supplier for Any One Item, and a Long-Term Relationship of Loyalty and Trust.

- The practice of choosing the lowest price has had the impact of actually *Increasing Costs* while Increasing Defects.
  - Instead, minimize *"Total Costs"* of Ownership.
  - "Price has no meaning without a measure of the *quality* purchased."

- "Purchasing should be a team effort and … include … representatives … of [all] departments involved with the product."

- "A buyer will serve his company best by developing a long-term relationship of loyalty and trust with a single vendor."

IQ 4. End the Practice of Awarding or Rewarding Information Systems and Database Design on the Basis of Price Tag or "On-Time, Within-Budget" Alone or Capturing Information at the Lowest Price.

Instead, minimize Total Cost of *Ownership* of Information Systems, Database Design, and Information Production.

- The practice of choosing the lowest price for Information Systems Consulting or for Information Systems Development as to "On-Time, Within-Budget" alone has had the impact of actually *Increasing Costs* and *Increasing Defects* at the same time.

  - Instead, minimize *"Total Costs of Ownership"* by Designing Quality Into the Information Models, Databases, Information Systems, and Information Creation Processes.

  - Price has no meaning without a measure of the *Quality* of the Information Purchased, whether from internal Information Producers or external Information Brokers.

  - Development of Resource (Subject) Information Models should be a team effort involving representatives of *all* departments involved with the "Information Products" to be developed, created, maintained, and applied.

  - Develop a long-term relationship of loyalty and trust with the business area where Information Producers are the *natural* source of Knowledge.

  - Insist on a Warranty for any Information Purchased from Information Brokers. Warranties must contain Remedies for Non-Compliance with agreed-upon IQ requirements.

5. Improve Constantly and Forever the System of Production and Service, to Improve Quality and Productivity, and Thus Constantly Decrease Costs.

- Improvement is not a one-time effort. Management is obligated to Continual Process Improvement.

  - Quality "must be Built In at the Design Stage."[10]

- "Everyone and Every Department in the company must subscribe to Constant Improvement."[11]
- Fixing a problem is not the same as Process Improvement. Fixing the problem only attacks the symptom. Process Improvement seeks to eliminate the Root Cause.

IQ 5. Improve Constantly and Forever the Processes of Information and Systems Engineering and Information Production

- Data Cleansing (sic., Information Scrap and Rework) is not the same as Information Process Improvement.
- Identify and involve the Customers of Information Products and Services — understand their Information Requirements and Design Quality Into the Information Model, Database Design, and the Processes to Create, Update, and Retrieve and Present the Information.
- Design Quality into Information Development Processes, including Information Systems and Database Designs by involving Information Producers and Knowledge Workers in the Design, using such tools as Quality Function Deployment (QFD) and SIPOC Charts for capturing Information and Information Quality requirements.

  QFD is described in Chapter 10, "Information Quality Applied to Product Development." The SIPOC is described in Chapter 15, "Information Quality Applied to Information Management and Information Systems Engineering."
- Everyone and Every Business Area must participate in Continual Information Process Improvement.

6. Institute Training on the Job

- Proper training is essential for workers to perform their jobs effectively.
- Training must be formal with standardized processes.

IQ 6. Institute Information Quality Training on the Job.

- Information Quality Training must be provided for Information Producers.
- Business Management requires a customized set of IQ training based on their Accountability for IQ. They must understand their downstream Information Consumers and their IQ requirements. They must provide resources and empower their Information Producers to perform their work to meet their Information Customer Requirements.

- Executives require yet another focus on IQ. This focus is on the *Strategic Imperative and Absolute Requirement* to apply Quality Principles to Information Processes *that will enable* the Transformation of the Enterprise into an effective Information-Age Enterprise.

7. Institute Leadership. The Aim of Supervision Should Be to Help People and Machines and Gadgets to Do a Better Job. Supervision of Management Is in Need of Overhaul, as Well as Supervision of ... Workers.

- Management is *Leadership* — not "supervision."
  - Leaders Empower Workers to Improve their Processes.
  - Most supervisors are just the opposite, because they implement *inappropriate* measures and rewards.

IQ 7. Institute Leadership for Information Quality.

- Take the lead in IQ improvement by being proactive, and develop relationships of trust with your circle of influence.
- IQ Leaders must Educate and Coach Executives through their circle of influence. Bring in IQ Management authorities for your coaching and for coaching the CEO.
- Implement Management Accountability for Information Quality.
- Measure and Reward the *right* things: Teamwork, Customer Satisfaction, Information Scrap and Rework Reduction, and Total Cost of Ownership.

8. Drive Out Fear, So Everyone May Work Effectively For the Company

- Improvement in Quality requires people to feel *secure*.
  - "Most people ... do not understand what their job is, or what is right or wrong."
  - "So seldom is anything done to *correct problems* that there is *no incentive* to expose them."

IQ 8. Drive Out Fear So Information Producers and Knowledge Workers Can Work Effectively.

- Establish a Non-Blame, Non-Judgmental Environnent for IQ.

- Provide Training to Producers in IQ Improvement-Techniques and IQ Expectations; Empower them to Improve Processes.

- Implement Accountability and encourage *eliminating* the causes of information problems and taking action.

- Create an anonymous Information Quality hotline.

- Allow staff to try new behaviors without fear of punishment should they "fail."

9. Break Down Barriers between Departments. People in Research, Design, Sales, and Production Must Work as a Team, to Foresee Problems of Production and In Use That May Be Encountered with the Product or Service.

- Enterprise failure occurs when organizational units *operate autonomously toward their own goals*.

IQ 9. Break Down Barriers between Business Areas So Information Producers Can Provide Quality Information to Meet Their Information Consumers' Needs.

Critical Business Area relationships include:

- **Business Area to Business Area:** Manage Value Circles across all Business Areas with Information interdependencies. We can no longer manage functions within the isolation of a Business Area without knowing the impacts on interdependent downstream Business Areas. Use the SIPOC Chart to identify Knowledge Workers and their IQ Requirements.

- **Information Systems to Business Areas:** Chapter 15, "Information Quality Applied to Information Management and Information Systems Engineering" treats this relationship in depth. Information Systems is a Supplier to the Business for transforming how work is done. It must not simply automate work activities, but must rethink and reengineer work processes. Most importantly for Information Systems is to reengineer its "Requirements Specification" and "Information Systems Design" processes to deliver Value to all Information Stakeholders. Business Subject Matter Experts (SMEs) must be actively involved in Requirements Definition and Information System Design with the Systems Engineering Team.

- **Information Systems Engineering to Information Resource Management:** These two areas must work together toward the creation of Enterprise-Strength Information Models and Database Designs and Value-Centric

Information Systems. See Chapter 15 for more details about effective relationships and processes.

- Executive Leadership must *drive* the Transformation from functional to a cooperative "ensemble" relationship for working together toward a single goal — accomplishing the Mission of the Enterprise!

- Develop Supplier-Customer "Contracts" between Business Area Managers for Information Quality with Warranties to all interdependent Knowledge Workers.

- Provide Training and Resources to staff to enable the delivery of Quality, Just-in-Time Information.

10. Eliminate Slogans, Exhortations, and Targets for the Work Force Asking for Zero Defects and New Levels of Productivity. Such Exhortations Only Create Adversarial Relationships, as the Bulk of the Causes of Low Quality and Low Productivity Belong to the System and Thus Lie beyond the Power of the Work Force.

- Slogans and Quotas do not motivate. Rather, they tend to demoralize workers, especially if the targets are unrealistic. Instead eliminate superficial "motivators," and train, and empower your most important resource — your Knowledge Workers.

IQ 10. Eliminate Slogans, Exhortations, and Targets for Information Work.

Most causes of poor quality information are *not* attributable to the Information Producer or the Process, but to *Management Systems* that encourage *counterproductive* employee behavior.

- Develop *effective* Information Management and IQ Improvement Processes based on sound Quality Management Systems.

- Develop IQ Improvement Processes *that prevent information defects by eliminating the causes*.

- Then, when you discover data defects, don't just fix or ignore them — *identify and eliminate* the Causes.

- Provide Information Producers with the Training and Tools to develop the capability to Improve their Processes and provide *high-quality* Information for the downstream Knowledge Workers.

IMPROVEMENT BY SLOGANS — NOT!!!

I was called into an insurance company to help them create a shared data environment. They had brought in object-oriented technology to increase data sharing and reuse and reduce the costs of redundancy. Their Information Systems Department cubicle walls were littered with posters of cute slogans, such as "The Bug Stops Here." I reviewed their Information Standards for the *object classes* and found their naming convention started with a two-character "application system" code! Their proof-of-concept project failed spectacularly, and many of the most capable systems personnel left the company.

11a. Eliminate Work Standards (Quotas) on the Factory Floor. Substitute Leadership.

11b. Eliminate Management by Objective. Eliminate Management by Numbers, Numerical Goals. Substitute Leadership.

- Quotas and other work standards hurt quality probably more than any other single working condition.
- Quotas cause above-average Workers to slow their output and cause below-average Workers frustration.

IQ 11. Eliminate Work Standards (Quotas) for Quantity of Information Work. Substitute Leadership.

- Replace information "productivity" quotas with focus on Quality, *real* Business Performance, and Cost of Ownership:
  - Management Ownership (Total) Costs of doing business
  - Reduced costs of Information Scrap and Rework
  - Internal Knowledge Worker satisfaction surveys of Information Products, both immediate and downstream, and both after implementation and on a continued basis
  - External end-Customer satisfaction, including satisfaction with Communication and Information

12a. Remove Barriers That Rob the Hourly Worker of His Right to Pride of Workmanship. The Responsibility of Supervisors Must Be Changed from Sheer Numbers to Quality.

12b. Remove Barriers That Rob People in Management and in Engineering of Their Right to Pride of Workmanship. This Means, Inter Alia, Abolishment of the Annual or Merit Rating and of Management by Objective.

- Workers, apart from management, know the problems of their jobs and, given an opportunity, will fix them.

- *Management must listen* to their Employees, *involve them actively* — not with "quick fix" programs to *defuse employee frustration* — but to solve the real problems.

IQ 12. Remove Barriers That Rob Information Producers and Their Managers of Their Right to Pride of Workmanship.

The responsibility of Supervisors must be changed from Information *quantity* to Information Quality.

13. Institute a Vigorous Program of Education and Self-Improvement.

- It is not good enough to know today's skills. We must constantly learn *tomorrow's skills* of the Information Age and learn how to apply information technology for business transformation.

- The Enterprise must be able to compete in a new economic era of Information and Knowledge, which are the *new capital* of the Information Age.

IQ 13. Institute a Vigorous Program of Education and Self-Improvement in Information Process Quality Improvement and Innovation.

- Provide comprehensive training in Information Process Improvement.

- Empower all Employees to perform Information Process Improvements as a habit.

- Empower all Employees to share their knowledge from Lessons Learned (Critical Success Factors (CSFs) and Root Causes of poor Quality) in Improvement and Innovation.

14. Put Everyone to Work to Accomplish the Transformation.

- The Transformation is everybody's job. Management will explain by seminars and other means why change is necessary, and that the change will involve *everybody*.

IQ 14. Put Everyone to Work to Accomplish the IQ Transformation.

Everybody participates in the Transformation. Management must provide the rationale and the training necessary to make the Transformation happen for sustainable IQ Management.

- The Executive Leadership Team (ELT) will put IQ on its regular meeting agendas to:
  - Focus on the *progress* of the Transformation of Culture to TIQM.
  - Monitor the progress of the habit of Continuous Information Process Improvement.
  - Monitor the *reduction in costs* of recovery of process failure and Information Scrap and Rework.
  - Monitor Information Producer and Knowledge Worker Satisfaction.
  - Monitor end-Customer Satisfaction with the information services.
  - Communicate progress and status of the TIQM transformation to management and staff.
- Empower all Employees to perform Information Process Improvements as a habit as they become trained.

The Information Quality Management Maturity Grid

Before you can address changes to the Culture of the Enterprise, you must know where you stand in terms of maturity in applying Quality Management Principles, Processes, and Practices to the Information and Information Processes in your organization. The IQMM Grid is such a tool to help organizations discover their strengths and weaknesses.

The IQMM Grid shown in Figure 3-2 represents a continuum of maturation to increase business effectiveness through TIQM as a business management tool. It is a framework for developing your Strategic Plan for IQ Management introduction, development, and maturation.

Measurement Categories	Stage 1: Uncertainty (Ad hoc)	Stage 2: Awakening (Repeatable)	Stage 3: Enlightenment (Defined)	Stage 4: Wisdom (Managed)	Stage 5: Certainty (Optimizing)
1. Management Understanding and Attitude	No comprehension of Information Quality as a management tool. Tend to blame Data Management or I/S org. for "Information Quality problems" or vice versa.	Recognizing that Information Quality Management may be of value but not willing to provide money or time to make it all happen.	While going through Information Quality Improvement Program learn more about quality management; becoming supportive and helpful.	Participating. Understand absolutes of Information Quality Management. Recognize their personal role in continuing emphasis.	Consider Information Quality Management an essential part of company system.
2. Information Quality Organization Status	"Data" Quality is hidden in application development departments. Data audits probably not part of organization. Emphasis on correcting bad data.	A stronger Information Quality role is "appointed" but main emphasis is still on correcting bad data.	Information Quality organization exists, all assessment is incorporated and manager has role in development of applications.	Information Quality Manager reports to CIO; effective status reporting and preventive action. Involved with business areas.	Information Quality Manager is part of management team. Prevention is main focus. Information Quality is a thought leader.
3. Information Quality Problem Handling	Problems are fought as they occur; no resolution; inadequate definition; lots of yelling and accusations.	Teams are set up to attack major problems. Long-range solutions are not solicited.	Corrective action communication established. Problems are faced openly and resolved in orderly way.	Problems are identified early in their development. All functions are open to suggestion & improvement.	Except in the most unusual cases, Information Quality problems are prevented.
4. Cost of Information Quality as % of Revenue	Reported: unknown Actual: 20%	Reported: 5% Actual: 18%	Reported: 10% Actual: 15%	Reported: 8% Actual: 10%	Reported: 5% Actual: 5%
5. Information Quality Improvement Actions	No organized activities. No understanding of such activities.	Trying obvious "motivational" short-range efforts.	Implementation of the 14 Point program with thorough understanding and establishment of each step.	Continuing the 14 Point program and starting to optimize.	Information Quality Improvement is a normal and continued activity.
Summation of Enterprise Information Quality Posture	"We don't know why we have problems with Information Quality."	"Is it absolutely necessary to always have problems with Information Quality?"	"Through management commitment and Information Quality Improvement we are identifying and resolving our problems."	"Information Quality problem prevention is a routine part of our operation."	"We know why we do not have problems with Information Quality."

Adapted from P. B. Crosby Quality Management Maturity Model

IQMM is a registered trademark of Information Impact Int'l. L. English, Improving Data Warehouse and Business Information Quality, p. 428

Figure 3-2: The IQMM Information Quality Management Maturity Grid

The IQMM Grid is a framework for developing your Strategic Plan for implementing an effective and sustainable IQ Management Culture and maturing it to World-Class capability. The IQMM characteristics are described by maturity stage:

Stage 1: IQ Uncertainty

This is the least mature organization.

Management Understanding and Attitude:

- No awareness that IQ can solve their *Business problems*.

- Management unaware of the costs of IQ because they are being shielded from real costs, or they believe they are being "handled" by the Information Systems group.

- Business Management blames Information Systems for problems that are brought to their attention.

- Information Systems Management blames business for problems actually created by IS.

Information Quality Organization Status:

- No formal IQ organization or it will be invisible to the business.

- If there are measures in place, they will *not* be ones that are *important* to the business.

- If IQ measures are in place, they will be used for Data Correction only.

Information Quality Problem Handling:

- The organization attacks problems as they occur — if they cannot cover them up.

- Problems tend to be "solved" by finding someone to blame.

- Work relationships tend to be combative, with a lot of back-biting and criticism made about others, but not to them face-to-face,

- Teamwork comes only out of necessity, often with resentment.

Cost of Information Quality as a Percentage of Revenue:

- No measures of cost of poor IQ (*Information* is simply "documentation").

- Attempts to guess will be all over the board, but only the business persons suffering from Poor Quality Information will have close estimates.

- The typical organization in Uncertainty has from 20% to more than 30% of its operating revenue wasted in Information Scrap and Rework.

- 40–50% or more of an Information System's budget is spent in Information Processing Scrap and Rework. This includes costs of *redundant* data handling in *multiple* databases and systems, and in the interfaces that do not add value but simply add cost of moving data from one proprietary database to another proprietary database.

Information Quality Improvement Actions:

- The organization takes *no formal actions for IQ Improvement*, nor does it understand what kinds of actions should be taken.

- The *organization just reacts to each problem*, accepting this and the Information Scrap and Rework activities as *normal* costs of doing business.

Stage 1 is characterized by the phrase: "We do not know why we have a problem with IQ," or "Do we have a problem with IQ?"

Stage 2: IQ Awakening

There is increasing awareness that there may be problems with IQ. Often this emerges because of some catastrophic event or public embarrassment, such as divulging confidential information or poor quality information causing regulatory non-compliance. It is characterized by the phrase: "Is it absolutely necessary always to have problems with Information Quality?"

Management Understanding and Attitude:

- Management has realized that an IQ Improvement program may have some value, but they are not willing to put resources into it.

- Management may know some of the Costs of Poor Quality Information, but need to work some problems out before they can pay attention to it.

Information Quality Organization Status:

- An Information Quality Leader will be appointed, often part-time, or an organization may be formed, sometimes with dual roles.

- The emphasis and goals will be mostly reactive inspection and Data Correction, rather than Preventive Actions.

Information Quality Problem Handling:

- Organization recognizes problems and sets up teams to solve them.

- The predominant approach is reactive data inspection and correction.

- Software tools are seen as the "solution."

Cost of Information Quality as a Percentage of Revenue:

- Typically, the cost of data inspection and correction initiatives, without knowing how to measure costs of Information Scrap and Rework.

- Minimal quantification of total Costs of Poor Quality Information.
- Management does not know clearly the extent of IQ problems, nor the true costs of Information Scrap and Rework and recovery from process failure.

Information Quality Improvement Actions:

- "We want to get the low hanging fruit" (the quick wins). Beware that this is often used by management to get a feather in their cap without caring about the IQ Management processes for all Information Stakeholders.
- Motivational efforts are implemented to get people to improve and do the right thing, but nobody changes the incentives for people to "improve processes' and do jobs right the first time."
- Large danger here to give up and fall back into old habits and continue the defective processes.
- IQ Leaders must *quantify* the Costs of Poor Quality Information and communicate this to the ELT Management to help them understand their personal involvement and responsibility and the actions they must take.

Characterized by the phrase: "Is it absolutely necessary to always have problems with IQ."

Stage 3: IQ Enlightenment

This is the *minimum* Maturity for sustainable IQ. Sound IQ Management Principles and Processes are repeatable and implemented in phases based on IQ priorities and organizational readiness. Attitudes are noticeably different.

Management Understanding and Attitude:

- Management has begun to see the correlation between IQ Management and Business Effectiveness.
- Management has begun to take Accountability for driving the IQ Culture Transformation.
- The Chief Executive Officer begins receiving Coaching as to his or her understanding of TIQM and the actions and communications that she or he needs to take to *continue maturing* the Enterprise in TIQM.
- This represents the true beginning of the Enterprise's Transformation.
- Everyone in the Enterprise is *beginning* to have Accountability for their role in IQ as they receive training and develop capability for IQ Process Improvement.
- Management is sponsoring the IQ Process Improvement Initiatives to implement IQ Processes and make systemic changes.
- IQ is a *regular* agenda item at the ELT meetings.

Information Quality Organization Status:

- The IQ organization is elevated to a higher level of importance as a Leader in the Cultural Transformation with the goal of implementing the Processes for Information Process Improvement and in making Continuous Information Process Improvement a *habit for all*.

- The IQ organization may be part of a Business Area or part of Information Systems with *authority* to effect the Transformation of the Culture across the Enterprise.

- A Business Information Stewardship Team consisting of business SMEs has begun to attack problems in Data Definition across disparate organizational units and Information Systems.

Information Quality Problem Handling:

- Teams analyze IQ problem *causes* and attack them to prevent recurrence.

- IQ problems across organizational boundaries are addressed openly by cross-functional IQ Teams.

- Long-term solutions are sought and implemented.

Cost of Information Quality as a Percentage of Revenue:

- The organization is gaining more significant cost reductions through Information Process Improvement and Defect Prevention.

- There are more architected Databases and *a higher degree* of data sharing, *reducing the costs* of application development and increasing the speed of application delivery. After Process Improvements are made, data corrections are made to source data in sharable Enterprise-Strength Databases.

- There is *reduction* of private databases as business people begin to trust the "production" data sources.

Information Quality Improvement Actions:

- Formally implementing the 14 Points of Total Information Quality Management

- Process Improvement Initiatives are conducted on a regular basis, always solving the Root Cause problems.

Characterized by the phrase: "Through Management *commitment* and IQ *improvement*, we are identifying and resolving our problems."

Stage 4: IQ Wisdom

Reaching Stage 4 puts the organization in World-Class status.

Management Understanding and Attitude:

- Management *recognizes and accepts* its own Accountability in IQ.

- Management *participates in and sponsors* systemic changes in the Performance Measures of the Enterprise to include IQ Measures and Customer and Employee Satisfaction measures.

Information Quality Organization Status:

- IQ Organization reports directly to the Chief Information Officer (CIO) or to a high-level Enterprise Business Area.

- Applications are not viewed as *end-deliverables* of Information Systems. They are seen as the *intermediate* products from Business Information Producers, and *deliver Information Products* to Knowledge Workers.

- There is strong involvement with the Information Stewardship Team, the business community in general, and the application and data development organizations.

Information Quality Problem Handling:

- Improved its Information and Information Systems Engineering Processes and its core business processes *to design in quality* and to identify potential problems early in the cycle.

- Defect Prevention is the norm.

- All organizations are open to suggestions for Improvement even when they come from outside organizational groups.

Cost of Information Quality as a Percentage of Revenue:

- *Reaping significant cost reductions* through widespread Information-Process Quality Improvement Initiatives.

- Production Databases are highly reliable.

Information Quality Improvement Actions:

- Continues the implementation of the 14 Points of IQ and improves them.

- These points are becoming *ingrained* in the Culture of the Enterprise.

Characterized by the phrase: "Continuous Information Process Improvement is *a routine part* of our operations."

Stage 5: IQ Certainty

This is the highest degree of maturity. It is the required maturity stage for industries where IQ has life or death implications or where true Zero-Defect-Level Quality is required, such as nuclear power plants, NASA's space program, health care, and capital justice. It is characterized by the phrase: "We know why we do not have problems with Information Quality."

Management Understanding and Attitude:

- Management would not consider managing the business *without having an IQ Management system* in place.
- TIQM Leader is the CIQO (Chief Information Quality Officer).

Information Quality Organization Status:

- The IQ Organization is an essential part of the Management Team.
- Information Quality is part of any Business Reengineering or Business Transformation Initiatives.
- The IQ Team ensures that new processes and systems are designed to eliminate or reduce to nearly zero the possibility for error.

Information Quality Problem Handling:

- IQ problems *have been all but eliminated*.
- New processes routinely have IQ designed in from the outset.

Cost of Information Quality as a Percentage of Revenue:

Costs of Quality consists, almost exclusively, of costs of regular assessment of critical data to ensure control, and costs of Information Process Improvements of business processes and Information Systems Process Improvements.

Every two dollars spent in IQ results in one dollar of ***profit!***

Information Quality Improvement Actions:

- The 14 Points are a routine part of Business Processes and Systems.
- Information Process Improvement is a normal and *regular habit*.
- Customers are happy.
- Knowledge Workers are happy.
- Information Producers are happy.
- Market share is increasing.
- Information is used to create new business opportunities.

Characterized by the phrase: "We know why we do not have problems with Information Quality."

Establishing a Sustainable IQ Environment

New methods can be implemented in a matter of 18 to 24 months. However, fundamentally shifting existing paradigms requires *cultural and organizational changes* that can take three to five years or more.

Establishing a sustainable IQ environment requires two types of plans, shown in Figure 3-3.

1. Strategic IQMM+ Implementation Plan
   ➤ Process P6:* Establish the IQ Environment
      through the 14 Points of IQ Transformation.

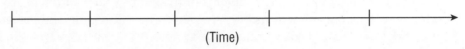

(Time)

2. Immediate "Improvement Initiative" Plan(s)
   ➤ Processes P1-P5:* (1 or more)

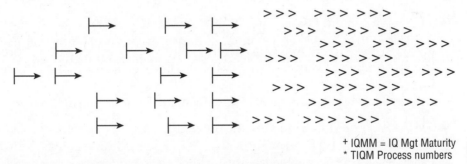

+ IQMM = IQ Mgt Maturity
* TIQM Process numbers

Figure 3-3: Two Sets of Plans for Establishing the IQ Environment, the First to Establish the Culture Transformation and the Second, Delivers Value through Planned and Continuous Information Process Improvement Initiatives

An immediate plan for implementing an IQ Process Improvement Initiative is required to establish the business case and develop commitment and support for the next IQ Process Improvement Initiatives to continue the gains and elimination of information waste. Your Strategic Plan must guide the Culture Transformation, and should identify several critical Information Process Improvement (IPI) initiatives in a Pareto approach by impact to the Enterprise. These IPIs eliminate Root Causes of Information Defects and the process failure, recovery, and Information Scrap and Rework the defects cause, and prove the Value Proposition of IQ Management.

A long-term, Strategic Plan is required to ensure that the Enterprise develops an awakening to the imperative of IQ Management and a commitment to the *education* of all personnel based on their particular IQ Management capability needs. This is required to drive the ongoing maturing of the Enterprise in terms of Principles, Values, and Habits that will establish a Culture of High IQ and increase the Business Performance Excellence throughout the Enterprise.

Essentially, this Strategic Plan drives the Enterprise through the IQMM Maturity stages *to mature at a healthy pace*. The first goal is to reach and sustain Stage 3, "Enlightenment," in three years and then achieve Stage 4 within four to five years.

There are three phases required to transform the culture of an Enterprise, whether large or small. They include:

- **TIQM Start up Phase:** Raise Awareness, and create Dissatisfaction and a sense of Urgency as to the problems of the status quo. Gain Executive Management commitment through Just-in-Time Education, and deliver a Proof-of-Concept (PoC) Initiative that delivers Business Value from the Executives' perspective, so TIQM demonstrates it pays for itself and produces a profit.

The goal is moving through Stage 2, "Awakening," within one year and beginning to mature in Stage 3, "Enlightenment."

- **TIQM Alignment Phase:** This phase begins the *formal Transformation* of the Enterprise to a Culture of "Continuous Information Process Improvement," leveraging the PoC Information Process Improvement Initiative into other Business Areas.

Aim to reach and sustain Stage 3, "Enlightenment," within two to three years.

- **TIQM Integration Phase:** This phase integrates TIQM into the Core Values and Culture of the Enterprise; drives new organizational Beliefs, Values, Practices, Systems, and Measures for the *intelligent learning organization*. TIQM is now a habit that transcends personnel changes.

The goal is to sustain Stage 3, "Enlightenment," and mature into, and sustain, Stage 4, "Wisdom" within four to five years. Zero-Defect Information Enterprises, such as nuclear power facilities, NASA's space programs, the capital justice system, and health care should strive to reach Stage 5 within six to eight years.

We will address why organization's Quality Management initiatives fail during the three phases, and how you can avoid them.

TIQM Startup Phase

Startup requires the establishment of the Value Proposition for IQ in a way that the Executive Leadership will recognize this is a concept worth pursuing. This requires *providing proper education and coaching to key Executives*, raising the level of dissatisfaction with the status quo and demonstrating the value of the PoC IQ Improvement Initiatives. Proper education is also required for the

IQ Leadership and personnel who will be implementing the components of IQ Management into the fabric of the enterprise.

Why Organizations Fail during Startup

Brown, Hitchcock, and Willard identify four major causes of failure of implementing TQM in the startup phase.[12] They include:

- **Lack of Executive Leadership Commitment:** Inability to engage Executive Management and establish the Value Proposition, or *the inability* of Executives *to see information as a real business resource* required to manage every other resource of the enterprise

- **Poor Timing and Pacing:** Attempt implementation before understanding the Principles, Processes and Practices, and not connecting them with a *compelling* Business Problem and Value Proposition.

- **Wasted Education and Training:** Training at the *wrong time, with the wrong purpose, with the wrong personnel*, or with trainees *not applying their new skills*. This can cause Management to perceive IQ is cost-adding.

- **Lack of Short-Term, Bottom-Line Results:** IQ Management must solve the *real business problems* and produce *real business results* that increase the ability to attain the Enterprise Mission effectively and efficiently. The PoC Information Process Improvement Initiative is key to demonstrating Business Value.

Failure Cause: Lack of Executive Leadership Commitment to IQ

Executives may see IQ as a *technical* IT activity and, therefore, believe it should be managed as such. IQ is a business problem, however. High-Quality Information is required to perform operational processes and to support tactical and strategic decisions, ensuring that the Enterprise can accomplish its Mission for the benefit of all Stakeholders. But quality does not happen by accident. "Best efforts" will not cause IQ to increase in a sustainable way.

Lack of Executive Leadership understanding and commitment is among the top three reasons that Information Quality Initiatives fail.[13]

Ensuring Executive Leadership Understanding, Commitment, and Behavior Transformation

In order to gain an audience with Executive Leadership, you must understand their issues, objectives, drivers, and KPIs. What keeps Executives awake at night, worrying about the Enterprise?

To do this, you must "think like a CEO." Covey's Fifth Habit is "Seek first to understand, then to be understood." So, you must seek to find out the real concerns of the Executives, which IQ Management can help mitigate. D. A. Benton describes 22 traits of effective CEOs, as shown in Table 3-1.[14]

Table 3-1: Benton's 22 CEO Traits

TWENTY-TWO TRAITS OF EFFECTIVE CEOS			
1.	Secure in yourself	12.	Theatrical
2.	In control of your attitude	13.	Detail oriented
3.	Tenacious	14.	Willing to lead
4.	Continuously improving	15.	Fight for your people
5.	Honest	16.	Admit to mistakes
6.	Think before you talk	17.	Straightforward
7.	Original	18.	Nice
8.	Publicly modest	19.	Inquisitive
9.	Aware of your style	20.	Competitive
10.	Gutsy	21.	Flexible
11.	Humorous	22.	Story teller

Benton describes the relative percent of time spent in key CEO responsibilities in Table 3-2.

Table 3-2: Key CEO Responsibilities and Percentage of Time Expended[15]

	KEY CEO RESPONSIBILITIES	% OF TIME
1	Provide Strategic Direction, Planning, and Customer Focus.	10–20%
2	Monitor and evaluate operations.	5–20%
3	Organize, utilize, and develop the Management Team.	10–15%
4	Create appropriate environment and Value Systems that stimulate the morale and productivity of the workforce and Leadership.	5–15%
5	Provide external representation and stay abreast of influential events and trends.	5–20%
6	Maintain positive relationships with the Board of Directors and Shareholders.	5–10%
7	Attend to personal development and care.	5%

W. Edwards Deming confirms that Executive Leadership and Management must Transform itself in his second point of Management Transformation, "Adopt the New Paradigm: Reliable Product Reduces Cost." Manufacturers with sound Quality Systems know this. He says that adopting this point means a Transformation of Management. But, Executives today may not yet recognize that "Reliable *Information* Reduces Costs." In IQ, this means a Transformation of Business Management at all levels and a Transformation of Information Systems Management at all levels.

Once you understand the issues and concerns of the Executives, you can develop your Value Proposition as to how proactive IQ Management helps the Enterprise overcome the problems and create value by eliminating the costs of process failure and Information Scrap and Rework. To do so, measure the Costs of Poor Quality Information for the processes that are failing because of defective information. See Chapter 6, *"The Step-by-Step Guide to Measuring the Costs and Risks of Poor Quality Information."*

If you, the reader, are an Executive tasked with leading in the IQ Management Transformation, study the fundamental Quality Management Principles, Processes, and Techniques described in Chapter 2, *"The ABCs of the TIQM Quality System for Total Information Quality Management."* They are founded on the proven Quality Systems that can be applied to IQ Management.

TIP Be sure to tie your results to the specific objectives, business drivers, and Key Performance Indicators (KPIs) Executives watch. Also, be sure to understand the meaning, and use the language the Executives use in talking about the drivers or KPIs.

NOTE Not all KPIs are true indicators of Enterprise Health. Often you will have to challenge the KPIs by comparing them to Enterprise health. An example is the percent of employees attending quality training. Compare this with how much costs of Information Scrap and Rework are eliminated.

If you are tasked with communicating to the Executives:

- **Educate yourself thoroughly in the principles, processes, and Value Proposition of TIQM:** You must become an expert in the Principles, Processes, and Value Proposition, so that you can communicate the message effectively and convincingly.

- **Customize Executive briefings to the Executives' needs and preferred presentation style:** This is one audience, and they require training that is appropriate to their preference for learning at a strategic level for effective Leadership. Understand their issues and be able to address them with authority.

- **Develop Coaching for the Chief Executive Officer:** The paradigm shift from the Industrial Age to the Information Age is a 180-degree reversal of how the Enterprise *must be managed*. This requires a combination of external consulting and coaching at first. As the IQ Leader increases his or her knowledge, there will be a shift to internal and continued external coaching until new habits are developed and the IQ culture is sustainable.

> **TIP** Paradigm shift messages need to be heard about seven times in order for individuals to fully understand the ramifications of Information Quality Management. Coaching is required for Executives to understand not just the Principles but also their own new behaviors and accountabilities.

External coaching is required for the IQ Leader tasked with implementing the IQ Management environment, both for the Leader's sake and for the ability to conduct ongoing coaching of the CEO.

The role of an external consultant in coaching is to ensure that the IQ Leader is thoroughly versed and knowledgeable in IQ Management Principles, Processes, and the Culture Transformation process required. The external coach also conducts one-on-one coaching with the CEO, to provide the Knowledge Transfer, to provide message development to the Stakeholders, and to enable the CEO to understand and embrace the IQ Business Value Proposition and to enhance the CEO's ability to lead the Transformation.

> **NOTE** External coaching and internal coaching must be consistent or confusion may arise, threatening the ability to make the transformation.

Executive Behavior that Demonstrates Commitment[16]

- **They Invest Time with Purchasing Customers and end-Consumers.**
  This requires a significant amount of time with Customers — not just to market to them but to *listen* to their *complaints, concerns, or ideas* about the quality of product, service, and information. Observing how they use the products, services, and information also yields tremendous insights that Customers often do not verbalize. Keeping in touch with Customers and suppliers is vital to understanding their real "expectations."

- **They Consider Suppliers as Partners — Not "vendors" or Competitors.**
  Quality of products and service depends on quality of information as well as raw materials and component parts.

- **They Spend Time Going to Gemba to Observe How Value Work is Performed.**
  Gemba is the Japanese word meaning "the real place." In manufacturing, Gemba is the factory where products are made.
  In IQ, Gemba is wherever Information is Learned, Captured, Exchanged, or Presented to Knowledge Workers so they can perform their work. IQ requires us to solve problems at Gemba.

- **They Spend Time Attending Quality-Related Educational Activities and in Quality-Related Team Meetings.**

  To commit to TIQM, Executives must understand the fundamental Principles and Processes. Once Executives understand and experience the Value Proposition, they will embrace it and provide time to lead it.

- **They Spend Time Analyzing Internal and External Information Customer satisfaction and Information Quality Results as Well as Operational Results.**

  Remember that the most important people here are the Customers of the products and services and the Knowledge Workers who *require* Quality Information *to serve and satisfy* their Customers, along with the Information Producers *who create* the Information.

- **They Commit Money and Other Resources to TIQM.**

  A key factor in the success of any Quality System, once you have commitment, is to *have the resources provided to make TIQM happen*, and to sustain it through the Integration Phase. Strong discipline is required, especially when resistance arises.

  Remember, even in this phase, Executives *generally provide money and resources with a tentative commitment*, based on their expectations of the Value Proposition. Staying true to the principles of TIQM will keep you delivering real business value. Managing the Value Proposition for success is critical to sustaining ongoing commitment.

- **Review IQ Assessment and Customer and Knowledge Worker Satisfaction in Relation to Their Information Needs:** These are two of the most critical KPIs for IQ Management. Customers are the ones who pay the bills, and the Knowledge Workers are the ones who perform the Value Work to delight Customers. If they *do not have* the Right Information with the Right Quality at the Right Time, they will struggle to satisfy Customers.

- **Establish reasonable IQ goals:** Ensure that your PoC IQ initiative can be managed and delivered with success. If this will be your first initiative to be presented to management, it is best for you to engage outside support from someone who has expertise to help you be successful.

NOTE Do not expect that a single Improvement will be the final Improvement. For processes with the highest quality requirements, you may have to make multiple improvements over time to achieve a Six-Sigma level of quality. Every World-Class Enterprise follows this approach of Continuous Process Improvement over time.

NOTE If you attempt to Improve *more than the process can support* in a single initiative, you run the risk of failing. It may not be possible to see the best improvement for the process from the status quo of broken processes.

> **TIP** Always estimate the value you expect to deliver as accurately as you can. Costs of Poor IQ are generally much higher than expected. The Executive Leadership Team *must feel the pain of the status quo*. Be sure to measure the costs of poor quality before and after any Process Improvement. Expect half a $, €, ¥, or £ for every $, €, ¥, or £ wasted in recovery from process failure and resulting Information Scrap and Rework.

Set stretch goals that require Process Owners to make Improvements to accomplish the defect-reduction goal within a timetable acceptable to the downstream Management whose staff depends on the Information.

> **TIP** Your ability to deliver value will be constrained by the number of trained IQ Process Improvement Facilitators you have. Do *not* move faster than you have the ability to manage for success.

> **TIP** Be sure to include training in Process Improvement facilitation to Business and Information Systems Process Owners and Managers.

> **NOTE** Each successful Process Improvement Initiative will give you permission — and funding — for the next initiatives.

- **Have Executives Implement Their Own IQ Process Improvement Initiatives.** As they experience the Value, *they will increase their support and ownership* of the Information Quality Culture Transformation.

- **Have Executives Go to Gemba to Observe and Talk About IQ with Front-line Knowledge Workers.** Executives must hear the issues of the Knowledge Workers and assure them that they are fully supportive and are "walking the talk" by applying quality to their own processes and information.

- **Executives Must Allocate the Appropriate Resources to Make Continuous IQ Process Improvement a Habit.** They must do this area-by-area until the Enterprise has adopted TIQM as a habit.

- **Measure the right things to ensure Continuous Improvement.** Measures include:
    - ☑ **Financial Measures:** Reduction in costs of process failure and Information Scrap and Rework
    - ☑ **Operational Measures:** Decreased time to market
    - ☑ **Employee Satisfaction Measures:** Increased work effectiveness and results
    - ☑ **Customer Satisfaction Measures:** Increased satisfaction and increased Customer Lifetime Value

NOTE Accurate measurement of all important aspects of Enterprise Performance is an *absolute requirement* for Continuous Improvement.

Failure Cause: Poor Timing and Pacing

If one attempts IQ *without connecting it to a compelling business problem, management will lose interest and will not see IQ Management as a value-adding activity.* Some organizations require a crisis before they see the need. One major bank brought me in to help them after they received a $200+ million fine for non-compliance with Customer Care considerations. On the other hand, two mortgage lenders brought me in to help them solve IQ problems that prevented them from understanding the value of the loan packages they sold to investors prior to the 2007 mortgage crisis.

Ensuring Proper Timing and Justification for IQ in Startup

Proper timing and justification is not just "picking the low-hanging fruit," which is often a euphemism for "I want a quick win for a feather in my cap — but am not interested in the transformation to a culture of IQ."

However, there are critical ramifications for your initial PoC projects, which are the prototype for all IQ Process Improvements.

- **Conduct a Formal Proof-of-Concept (PoC) Initiative to Establish the Justification for Investment in IQ Management.** Processes include:

- **TIQM P4.1:** Establish a project for a critical business capability where IQ is causing significant failure and Information Scrap and Rework. See Chapter 7, "The Step-by-Step Guide to *Improving Information Process Quality*."

- **TIQM P1:** Measure the Quality of Information Product Specifications (IPS) and Architecture Quality. See Chapter 4.

- **TIQM P2:** Measure the Quality of Information Content and Presentation. See Chapter 5, "The Step-by-Step Guide to *Assessing Information Quality*."

- **TIQM P3.3–6:** Measure Poor Quality Information Costs and Risks, including Direct and Opportunity Costs. See Chapter 6.

- **TIQM P4.2–5:** Improve Information Process Quality (Plan-Do-Check/Study-Act). See Chapter 7.

- **TIQM P3.7:** Measure the ROI of Information Process Improvements. See Chapter 6.

Failure Cause: Wasted IQ Education and Training

IQ Management requires extensive training of a number of different Stakeholders. However, if the *timing* of training is off, or if training addresses the wrong audience, or the *wrong* skills, management may become convinced that IQ Management is too expensive and will not support your IQ initiatives.

Training fails when:

- It addresses the *wrong skills* for the audience, such as data profiling or Data Correction rather than Process Improvement (Plan-Do-Study-Act).

- It addresses the *wrong skill level* for the audience, such as IQ concepts rather than skill in conducting Root Cause Analysis and IQ error-proofing techniques.

- It is taught at the *wrong time,* when the audience is not ready to perform the skills, such as when the training is introduced several weeks before executing the skills.

- It teaches the *wrong audience*, those who will not be performing the skills taught, such as teaching Information Producers how to conduct data profiling, which is a technical skill for the Information Systems staff.

- It addresses the *wrong objective*; for example, when it focuses on the "why" (selling/convincing), when the audience is ready for the "what" (ready to go do something specific and tangible).

Ensuring Just-in-Time IQ Education and Training

Training and education for Information Quality Management are not simple skills training. Training must drive a fundamental paradigm shift that requires one to completely rethink the paradigms of the status quo.

The Information Quality revolution brings about a shift from managing the Enterprise vertically, down the business areas, to doing so horizontally, across the Value Circles.

- **Conduct IQ Management education for the Executives to establish the Value Proposition:** Topics include the Industrial-Age paradigm of vertical, Command-and-Control Management versus the Information-Age paradigm of horizontal, collaborative management. Also taught are the concepts of Value Circles and Information Producer–to–Information Consumer inter-dependencies and Supplier-Input-Process-Output-Customer (SIPOC) as a tool for understanding Information Requirements.

Executives must learn their new Accountabilities for Information Quality for all stakeholders, from Customers, Investors, Employees, Suppliers, and Business Partners, and Regulatory Authorities.

Executives must take action to organize *themselves* to make Information Quality happen, communicating to all staff Why this change is necessary and Why everyone will be involved in the Information Quality activities.

- **Enable Just-in-Time Education and Training to Key Audiences:**
  - The Executive Leadership Team
  - The Information Quality Team
  - Business Management and Process Owners who will facilitate Information Process Improvements with their Information Producers in the proof-of-concept IQ initiatives. The PoC's will identify Root Causes and define improvements to prevent recurrence.
  - Information Systems staff developing support for the Proof-of-Concept IQ initiatives to identify Root Causes in Information Systems that support the process

- **Ensure that Training Equips the Right Audience with the Right Skills:** Follow the systematic approach of ADDIE[17] for developing skills-based training for Line Management, Knowledge Workers, and the Information Quality Team:
  - Analyze the job and tasks.
  - Develop requirements for the training based on the analysis.
  - Design training to meet the requirements.
  - Implement the training.
  - Evaluate the training and job performance.

- **Use SEDUCE: Effective Approach to Experiential Learning for Executives.** Developed by Lori L. Silverman of Partners for Progress and Linda Ernst of Training Resource, it has been proven effective as an approach for Executive education.[18] This approach includes:
  - **Startup:** Introduce the learning experience. Review objectives.
  - **Experience:** An activity, a case study, a participative lecture, a small-group discussion, for example
  - **Debrief:** Discuss the learning experience. What did you do? What did you learn?
  - **Unveil Concepts:** Take a broader view. What are the concepts and principles that were learned?
  - **Execute:** Discuss the application of the concepts and principles to everyday work and to the real world.

Table 3-3 addresses education and training in Information Management and TIQM.

Table 3-3: IQ Training by Audience, Subject, and Duration[19]

AUDIENCE	EDUCATION / TRAINING SUBJECTS	TIME
All New Employees	General orientation on Information Policies, Information Management, and in IQ Principles, and Accountabilities	2 hr
Information Producers and Knowledge Workers	IQ standards, guidelines, resources	½ -1 day as req
	Information policy regarding use; responsibilities for updating data	
	Data definition, values, business rules	
	Information Value Circle and processes producing and requiring the information, and SIPOC Chart (Supplier-Input-Process-Output-Customer)	
	Knowledge Worker expectations of Information Quality	
Business Management and Process Owners	Creating the Information-Age Organization	1 day+ upd
	Information Policies, Principles, Accountabilities	2 hr "awareness"
	IQ techniques and resources to provide staff	
	Downstream Knowledge Worker expectations	
	Information Value Circle management (See SIPOC above)	
Executive Leadership	IQ Management principles and processes, information policies, information as a strategic resource	1-2 day + 1-2 hr;
	IQ Principles and Executive Accountabilities	1 day + reg upd
	Information Stewardship roles and Accountabilities	1 day
	Creating the Information-Age organization (strategic view of information management)	1 day
	Model for Organizational Change	1-2 day
Business Information Stewards	Information Stewardship: roles/responsibilities, data definition guidelines	1 day+
	IQ Management Principles	½ day
	Information Management Principles	2 hr
	Information Value Circles and Information Stakeholders	2 hr

AUDIENCE	EDUCATION / TRAINING SUBJECTS	TIME
Information Resource Management Staff	Information Resource Management	3 day
	Information Modeling and Advanced Information Modeling	3 day + 2 day
	Information Stewardship and Accountability	2 day
	IQ Management	3 day
Application Development Staff	Information Management Principles, Roles, Responsibilities	1 day
	Information Modeling and Value-Centric Information and Systems Engineering Principles	3 day
	IQ Processes Applied to Applications and Information Presentation Guidelines	½ day
Strategic Information Mgt Staff (DW&BI)	Information Management Principles	1 day
	Information Modeling and Advanced Information Modeling	2 day
	IQ Management Principles in Data Warehouse and Business Intelligence	1 day
	IQ Assessment and Data Transformation and Movement Control Principles	1 day
Information Quality Staff	Information Management Principles	1 day
	Information Stewardship	2 day
	IQ Improvement	3 day
Information Systems Management	Creating the Information Age Organization	1 day
	Value-Centric Information and Systems Engineering	2 day
	Information Stewardship and Accountability	1 day
	IQ Management Principles	1 day

NOTE Personnel undergoing training must have an opportunity to apply their new skills as soon as they have completed their training, in order to reinforce their knowledge and skills and provide continuing value.

Failure Cause: Lack of Immediate, Bottom-Line Results

Many organizations fail to conduct and/or control a Proof-of-Concept initiative to measure the extent of poor Information Quality, measure the Costs of Poor Information Quality, and then to Improve the Process effectively to eliminate or significantly reduce the defects and produce a positive Return-on- Investment over the lifetime of the process being improved.

Ensuring Bottom-Line Results in IQ Process Improvement Initiatives

If you do not select a problem that demonstrates immediate, tangible results that the Executives expect, their commitment will vanish. Remember, you never get a second chance to make a first impression.

- ▪ **Select a Proof-of-Concept IQ Project Where:**
  - ▪ IQ issues are a threat to the health of the Enterprise and are on the Executives' radar as critical Information and Processes.
  - ▪ The potential payoff is high if Process Improvement is successful.
  - ▪ A process owner is willing to sponsor and implement Process Improvements.
  - ▪ The initiative is small and simple enough to manage for success.
  - ▪ The Process Improvement Team and participants (Information Producers and other key subject experts) are trained and capable.
  - ▪ No unmanageable obstacles or roadblocks prevent success.
  - ▪ You can manage and control the initiative for a successful result.

NOTE Again, remember that you do not get a second chance to make a first impression.

IQ Alignment Phase

During the Alignment Phase, you take the success of the PoC IQ initiative and begin replicating the results in other critical Information Processes. As this increases in scale, it creates numerous new problems and obstacles.

Why Organizations Fail during Alignment

As you begin implementing IQ Best Practices in the Enterprise, you will find status quo processes, systems, and practices that conflict with TIQM. You find *inappropriate measurement systems* that measure what is easy rather than what is right.

During the Alignment Phase, organizations usually fail for four reasons:[20]

- ▪ **Divergent or Conflicting Strategies:** Many employees believe Quality is *not* part of their job — they see it as the responsibility of the IQ Team.

- **Organizing IQ as an IT Function:** This relegates IQ Management to being only a technical function. As such, it will minimize focus on the Business Processes and the Information Consumers' needs to accomplish the Enterprise Mission.

- **Inappropriate Measures:** Most organizations measure things that are easy to count, not necessarily the things that correlate to effectiveness.

- **Outdated Performance Appraisal Methods and Inappropriate Rewards:** Most appraisal methods reinforce wrong behaviors, creating competition rather than collaboration and teamwork. Most compensation systems, again, reward individual performance rather than collaboration, skill development, and downstream Knowledge Worker success.

Failure Cause: Divergent or Conflicting Strategies

You will fail if you create an IQ Team that *does* the quality work, such as creating job positions to perform IQ assessments or to facilitate Information Process Improvements. All managers and all staff must eventually see Process Improvement as part of their job description.

Creating Synergistic Strategies

Every job role in the organization has natural accountability with respect to their role with information. Managers who oversee information creation processes *are accountable* for the Quality of Information produced by their staff. Once managers and Information Producers are trained and have resources to make IQ happen, they can be *held accountable* for the Quality of the Information they produce. Knowledge Workers who require information in the performance of their work *are accountable* for their work results and for the protection of confidential information once they have proper training and resources.

To create a synergistic organization:

- **Create a Name for the TIQM Initiative that is Tied to the Enterprise Mission or Core Strategies.** Such as, "Information Excellence for Business Performance Excellence," or "20/20 Vision through 20/20 Information Insight."

- **Focus on Implementing the Fundamental Core Competencies for IQ.** The IQ Leader is the Process Owner for defining the six TIQM processes for the enterprise. All managers are expected to execute them, or bring in IQ Specialists to assist them in conducting assessments, provide Cost of Poor Quality Measurement, and facilitate Information Process Improvements.

- **The TIQM Team Should Not Exist as a Stand-Alone Entity. Rather, the Team should be the Process Owners for the TIQM Processes.** Remember that every person in the Enterprise is accountable for IQ at some level. IQ is part of every person's job to ensure they are satisfying their internal and external Information Consumers.

- **Do Not Create a New IQ "Steering or Governance" Committee.** Use your existing governance teams, with the ELT being the top IQ Governance Team. Put IQ updates on the agenda of the regular ELT meetings.

As you execute your IQ Improvement Initiatives, provide feedback on the Information Scrap and Rework and all other Costs or Revenue Increases recovered. As you return *more profits*, you will gain *more and more credibility and support*.

This will in turn generate more interest by those who may have been skeptical at first and do not want to be left out.

Failure Cause: Organizing IQ as an IT Function

IQ Management is no more an IT function than Manufacturing Quality Management was a production machinery function. If IQ becomes an IT function, business management may lose interest, especially if IT implements only technology capabilities, such as validity assessments and Data Correction (inspect and correct) without understanding the business processes, the Root Causes, or eliminating the Root Causes through controlled Process Improvements.

Creating and Sustaining IQ as a Business Function

- Integrate TIQM with an effective Quality Management function already in place. Learn from the Quality Management function.
- Create a Chief IQ Officer or an IQ Leader at the highest level possible.

NOTE The Chief IQ Officer must be placed high in the Enterprise to get the credibility needed to effect the IQ Culture Transformation. If this position is not in the ELT, it must be close enough for the individual to be promoted to the ELT as the TIQM Transformation grows.

- Provide ongoing coaching to the CEO to keep his or her learning curve growing to maturity.
- Ensure that the CEO *drives the key messages* to the management teams and staff as to why IQ is essential to the success of the Enterprise.

Failure Cause: Inappropriate Measures

If we measure the *wrong things* we get the *wrong behavior* from our teams. If the organization measures how many calls a Call Representative takes, it will find a lot of "hang-ups" and recalls that do NOT add value but are a way of meeting quotas to get favorable performance ratings.

These behaviors follow Maslow's Hierarchy of Needs: If my well-being is threatened, I will work for my own survival, rather than the benefit of my internal and external Customers.

Creating and Sustaining Appropriate Measures

The key is to measure the right things in staff and management:

- Measure Customer Satisfaction, including Information Needs.
- Measure end-Consumer Satisfaction, including Information Needs.
- Measure Product Quality Failure caused by IQ issues, such as wrong product specs, inaccurate inventory counts, and wrong materials.
- Measure Knowledge Worker (internal Information Consumer) Satisfaction.
- Measure Investor Satisfaction, based on long-term stock price performance.
- Measure Costs of Process Failure and Information Scrap and Rework caused by Poor Quality Information. See Chapter 6.
- Measure annualized reduction in Costs of Process Failure and Information Scrap and Rework caused by Poor Quality Information based on Information Process Improvements. See Chapters 7 and 6.
- Measure the relationship of increased IQ and the accomplishment of critical KPIs, such as financial results, time to market, and market share.

Failure Cause: Outdated Performance Appraisal Methods and Inappropriate Rewards

Most employee performance appraisal methods encourage negative behaviors. They often *create competition* that is harmful to the Enterprise, Customers, fellow workers, and employees' families.

Creating and Sustaining Appropriate Appraisal Methods and Appropriate Rewards

"We must throw overboard the idea that competition is a necessary way of life. In place of competition, we need cooperation, collaboration, and synergy toward the accomplishment of the Enterprise Mission."[21]

- **Eliminate Individual Ratings:** Rating is berating, with most people falling into a category considered average, making them more angry rather than aspiring to improve.

- **Eliminate Management by Objectives:** MBOs end up being low-hanging targets easily met but not contributing to the Value Proposition and accomplishment of the Enterprise Mission.

- **Measure How Well Employees Share Knowledge and Increase Peer Performance:** This cooperative teamwork increases team value and performance.

- **Measure Downstream Information Consumer Satisfaction in Information Producer Managers' Performance:** This measures how well teams enable their Customers to perform their work effectively. Again, this is effective collaboration.

- **Ensure that All Employees Participate in the Financial Success of the Enterprise:** The days of the grossly exorbitant Executive pay schemes has got to come to an end. Ensure that workers receive bonuses commensurate with their pay grades in relative proportion to Executive bonuses.

Information Quality Integration Phase

The Integration Phase of TIQM embeds the principles, processes, and techniques as habits and behaviors in all employees, rolled out in increments throughout each Value Circle, Business Area, or Business Unit at a time. This generally starts from the core Value Circles of the Enterprise (Executive Leadership) and moves through the Value Circles on a Pareto basis. This will eventually Effect all Information Producers and Knowledge Workers who do their Value Work.

> **FEDEX NEARLY MISSED QUALIFYING FOR BALDRIGE AWARD**
>
> **Because FedEx had so embedded their quality practices in their processes, they were almost invisible to the examiners, which would have cost them qualification as a finalist.**[22]

Why Organizations Fail during Integration

During integration, the Concepts, Principles, and Processes and Techniques become embedded in the *behavior of management and staff*. The Golden Rule is, "I will create the quality of information for my Customers that I would have them create for me." Information Producers seek out their Knowledge Workers to find out their Requirements for the Information the Information Producers create for the Knowledge Workers. Employees seek to provide Excellence in all work, whether producing tangible goods or capturing Information. As the

Enterprise moves up the IQMM Maturity ladder, an increasing percentage of employees seek to improve constantly and forever their processes to enable their enterprise to become and stay World-Class.

During the Integration Phase, organizations usually fail for the following reasons:

- **Failure toTransfer True Power to Employees:** If IQ Improvement Teams in the Alignment Phase have only recommendation power, they may be *marginalized* during the Integration Phase. They must have more real authority and power during integration.

- **Maintaining Outmoded Management Practices:** Employees will notice inconsistencies in management behavior during integration. Many managers will resist change, especially when they feel threatened by Employee Empowerment. The temptation of management is to talk the talk but not walk the walk. I have seen numerous instances of deliberate sabotage of IQ implementations.

- **Poor Organization and Job Design:** The *vertical* organization design and *management structure* are the real Root Cause of many IQ issues in the Information Age. This must be dismantled and replaced with a collaborative, ensemble management approach.

- **Outdated Business Systems:** Business systems that are not transformed in the Alignment Phase must be *transformed and stabilized* during integration to prevent a relapse back to old behaviors.

- **Failing to Manage Learning and Innovation Diffusion:** Innovative solutions to IQ problems tend to happen in pockets around the Enterprise, *but* the Lessons Learned are *rarely shared*, let alone assimilated into the rest of the Enterprise.

Failure Cause: Failure to Transfer True Power to Employees

The staff in IQ Improvement Teams must have more real authority and power during the Integration Phase. Without that authority, the IQ Process Improvement Team may have their Improvements overridden by *unknowledgeable* managers who are still operating out of the status quo.

How to Empower Employees

Customer-facing Employees are the most important people in the organization, as they interact with Customers. In each and every Customer/Employee interaction, the first 15 seconds creates a "Moment of Truth."[23] This Moment of Truth is an event in which a Customer or prospective Customer has an experience with the organization. In this event, the Customer will have a positive or negative experience. The aggregate of all Customer experiences will signal the success or failure of the Enterprise.

The question is, who should make decisions that affect the well-being of the Customer? Management or the Employee in the interaction? Of course, the Employee who is at the point of contact with the Customer!

But how does it work in your Enterprise? Jan Carlzon, the CEO of Scandinavian Airlines (SAS), literally turned the traditional pyramid organization chart upside down. His message? The Executives are not the "bosses" and "decision makers" of SAS. They create the context for the business. Of course, Executives must provide a Mission, Vision, and Strategic Direction, but when it comes to Customer contact, Employees must be empowered to provide a positive Moment of Truth in every interaction if the Enterprise is to thrive.

RITZ-CARLTON EMPOWERS EMPLOYEES TO RESOLVE COMPLAINTS

Ritz-Carlton, a two-time recipient of the Baldrige Award, and keenly aware of Customer Lifetime Value, empowers its Customer-facing employees to resolve Customer complaints with a value of up to $2000 without management approval.[24]

There are five levels of empowerment, according to AXIS Performance Advisors on an escalating degree of staff empowerment. They include:[25]

1. **Traditional Industrial-Age Management:**
    This is the classic, *vertical management authority up and down the Business Area, Unit, or Division*. No real decision-making authority exists in staff Employees. The aggregation of people in their specialized functions causes fiefdoms to arise, with *competition* — rather than cooperation and collaboration — across business areas.

    Dismantle this style of management and replace it with the *Orchestra Model* of Management. Here, all Business Areas work collaboratively as a *single ensemble* performing a single composition (Mission) as a single entity.

2. **Quality of Work Life:**
    Quality of Work Life (QWL) came about in the 1970s and became popular among employees. QWL work teams came together periodically to focus on improving their work life. While they generally improved work life, there was minimal improvement of overall Enterprise Performance.

3. **Quality Circles:**
    Quality Circles (QC) also became popular in the 1970s, especially in Japan. QC teams were more productive than QWL teams because all QC team members received extensive training in Quality Improvement and Problem-Solving Methods.

While this increased quality, one study showed that QCs could have negative financial impact, *mostly because of overly bureaucratic governance structures.*[26]

4. **Participative Management:**

   Participative Management means that managers share their power and influence by seeking Employees' input with a *minimum* veto power. While this led to a significant increase in empowerment, the Command-and-Control Structure remained dominantly in place, with management making the decisions after evaluating the employee input.

5. **Self-Directed Teams:**

   Self-directed teams represent a *real transformation* in the power structure, for here management gives up its veto in clearly defined areas of responsibility. Teams plan, conduct, improve, and evaluate their own work. Team members are often cross-trained, and may work directly with Customers and Suppliers.

   More than 45 years of data confirm the conclusion that Reengineering the workplace around high-performance self-directed teams produces significant performance gains.[27]

Failure Cause: Maintaining Outmoded Management Practices

Outmoded management practices, such as *employee ranking* and even the *traditional performance appraisal* by one's supervisor, are inaccurate at best and harmful at worst.

Obstacles to self-directed teams include:

- Conflict in manager's and staff *objectives* and *motives*. Managers may be measured according to a different agenda than Information Producers, who need training and support in order to provide Quality Information to their Stakeholders.

- Lack of clear management expectations and understanding of downstream Knowledge Workers' Expectations as to their IQ Requirements

- Resistance to change

- Lack of participative skills

- Lack of Executive Leadership Commitment and Support

Everyone in the Enterprise should be focused on the same *single* Mission of the Enterprise. When managers set local goals and work expectations that are counter to the Mission, they will create competition that harms their downstream Stakeholders.

This, in turn, fosters *competition* among Business Areas that is detrimental to the health of the Enterprise.

How to Transform Management Practices

When setting strategies, goals, or work expectations:

- Always begin with the Enterprise Mission and Values as *the* single goal. Teach others how Quality Information helps enable the accomplishment of the Strategic Objectives and Mission of the Enterprise and keeps them performing their Value Work rather than having to perform "Information Scrap and Rework."

- Have Information Producers change roles or visit with their downstream Knowledge Workers. This gives them an idea of the problems their Information Consumers have with any IQ problems in the data they provide. Knowledge Workers will also get a sense of the problems in the capture of the Information from their Information Suppliers.

- Provide *true* 360-degree performance feedback. Do not get just manager and team member feedback. Solicit your downstream Information Customers' feedback. The SIPOC Chart is an excellent tool for getting this feedback and understanding your Information Consumers' requirements

- Hold frequent team meetings to share stories and anecdotes about new ideas and successes, as well as failures, to keep people generating new ways to transform work quality.

- Listen to staff who fear loss of status or control in the new collaborative environment as their old roles and practices become obsolete or minimized. Help staff who perform Information Scrap and Rework, to see and move to new roles of proactive Information Process Improvement that increase their value by eliminating the need for Information Scrap and Rework.

- Executive Commitment will come automatically when Information Process Improvements eliminate the *causes* — and *costs* — of Defective Information Processes. Ensure that in your early Process Improvements you have the Critical Success Factors in place to realize significant gains from the Improved Processes.

NOTE Remember that Process Improvement is *Continuous*. Do not stop with one or two successful improvements. Keep identifying improvement opportunities using the Pareto approach of moving from the most important (to the Enterprise) to the next most important.

Failure Cause: Poor Organization and Job Design

Most organizations still operate out of the old, now-outdated Command-and-Control Structure. This management model is even considered obsolete by the U.S. Department of Defense, as control has been turned over to the commanders in the field in its current conflicts.

How to Create Effective Organization and Job Design

As mentioned earlier, Jan Carlzon created the new organization model by flipping the traditional Pyramid upside down. This Model empowers those closest to the Customers to make the decisions that delight the Customers.

Peter Drucker in 1980s challenged the Command-and-Control Model with the Orchestra Model of ensemble. Covey describes this as Synergy. Deming used the Orchestra Model in his Executive presentations.

How does the Orchestra Model work? Well, the orchestra performs one musical composition at a time. Many specialists in their Sections (violins, violas, cellos, bass viols, trumpets, flutes, clarinets, and many others) have their own "parts" to play. If any sections are out of tune, or "come in" too early or too late, the performance is ruined. But when the Conductor reaches the podium and gives the down beat to start the music, the orchestra will rally to perform as a single ensemble. W. Edwards Deming agrees with this model and likens it to the different functional units in the Enterprise. They must operate like a single organism — not a dysfunctional set of *uncooperative business units*.

This is the basis for my describing work in what I call Value Circles, where Information is captured in one Business Area that is required by one or more downstream business areas to be successful. The Management of the Information Production must understand their downstream Knowledge Workers' Requirements for the Information they produce. Each of these Value Circles should operate as an interdependent section of the larger ensemble that is the Enterprise.

Darcy Hitchcock describes the principles for Flexible Organization Design as the Eight Ss.[28] They include: Strategy, Skills, Structure, Systems, Symbols, Staff, Style, and Shared Values.

Strategy

Strategy is the Vision and plan of action that defines what an organization intends to achieve and how it intends to achieve it.

- Develop clear and elevating goals with a *Customer Focus* with a long-term horizon that is communicated to and instilled in the workforce.

- Develop a strategy to implement Enterprise-Wide Information Management and Information Quality Management as *core competencies* in the realized Information Age to drive business strategies.

Skills

Skills refer to the competence level of an organization's workforce.

- Develop resources to provide Continuous Learning. For Information Quality, develop and deliver skills-based training in Information Quality Improvement to error-proof Information Creation, Updating, and Presentation processes.

- Deliver training only in a *Just-in-Time approach* at a point where trainees will actually be able to perform their new skills.

- Observe training to determine its effectiveness in teaching and knowledge interchange.

- Observe newly trained staff at work to see how well the learning was "taken" and applied effectively.

Structure

Structure illustrates how an Enterprise is organized for work and how accountabilities are applied. Most organizations are managed up and down the functional business areas with interfaces to other business areas. Figure 3-4 illustrates the typical, hierarchical organization structure with compartmentalized specialties.

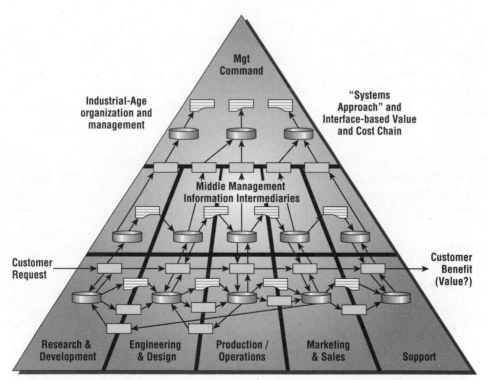

Figure 3-4: The Obsolete Hierarchical, Interfaced, Systems Approach to Management Structure

The Hierarchical Management Model is *obsolete*, creating pockets of *competition* in the various specializations of labor.

The new model is an Information-Age collaborative approach in which information is shared across the Enterprise on a Just-in-Time basis from shared, Enterprise-Strength Databases. See Figure 3-5 for the orchestral ensemble, sharing from single Enterprise-Strength Databases and collaborating through shared Knowledge Management and Lessons Learned.

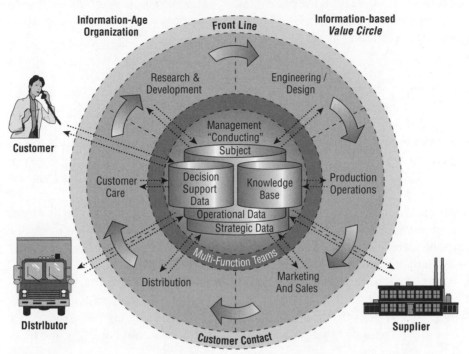

Figure 3-5: The Information-Age Value-Centric Model for Managing Collaboration through the Value Circles

Create a flexible organizational structure that empowers workers, creates a Stewardship mindset of producing High-Quality Information for one's Information Consumers, with open communication and collaboration and with few management layers. Organize Value Circles around products and processes — not functions.

Systems

Systems are the mechanisms, policies and procedures, and work methods to support operations, including Human Resource Management, Financial Management, Planning, and Information Systems and Information Resource Management.

- Develop Systems that *support* Quality and Teamwork, especially in Information Systems that support all Information Stakeholders — not just departmental or functional activities.

- Challenge and change *competitive, counterproductive* performance appraisal systems by providing rewards for collaboration, Knowledge sharing, Team Improvement, and satisfying one's downstream Information Consumers.

Symbols

Symbols represent the organization's Values and Mission.

Align your Symbols with the organization's stated Values. Symbols must promote cooperation and Enterprise Values, and support Continuous Information Process Improvement.

Staff

Staff are people who carry out the Value Work of the Enterprise.

Tap an IQ Leader who understands the Principles of Quality Management applied to Information to lead the internal transformation and implementation of IQ Management. This individual must be able to converse with all levels of management and staff and establish the business case while defining the processes for IQ Management. Coaching the CEO, along with coaching from an external CEO coach is *critical to success* in the Integration Phase.

Leverage diversity among the workforce and develop and promote those who are Stewards for the good of the Enterprise — not just their own interests. Design jobs around value-adding activities and eliminate jobs that conduct cost-adding activities.

A major bank had a department of 400 employees who did nothing more than reenter bank transactions that failed to get entered correctly at the bank branches. At $56 per hour, their work cost the bank more than $46 million per year in people costs of Information Scrap and Rework, not counting facilities and equipment costs.

Style

Style represents the way *managers behave* in interactions with their staffs and their peers, especially in the Customer-Supplier relationship of the Information.

Hire or develop managers who are open, honest, good communicators; are respectful of the needs of their Stakeholders, *valuing collaboration, sharing power*; and are able to manage conflict effectively.

Shared Values

Shared values are the *common culture* or commonly exhibited Enterprise values.

Develop high standards of excellence in all products and services, and conduct Continuous Information Process Improvement, as well as Product and Service Process Improvement. *Encourage* diversity and Knowledge sharing.

Failure Cause: Outdated Business Systems

- Most organizations' Business Systems have *poor* Requirements Specifications, *poor* designs, and produce *mediocre* results at best.

- Strategic Planning Systems, for example, often do not support *real* Strategic Planning nor translate plans to tactical and operational actions to accomplish *strategic goals*. Often strategic planning occurs *without input from* Customers, Suppliers and other critical Stakeholders or those close to them. As a result, strategic plans can be "hit or miss" in the absence of real Stakeholder Feedback.

- Financial Planning Systems are generally flawed in assuming that next year's budget will look much the same as this year's. The financial closing of the books is often cumbersome with many financial adjustments made with many trial closings taking place. Closings are not timely and mistakes are common.

- Incredibly expensive ERP (Enterprise Resource Planning) systems are so huge and complex that no one consultant or consultancy can understand all of the parts nor how they work together. The worst part of ERP systems are that the *databases* for their standard processes do not capture *all* of the required Knowledge that most organizations really need to know. As a result, ERP Customers have to create *additional* databases to capture the additional data. This is like buying a brand-new automobile and then having to build the braking system yourself because the manufacturer left it out.

How to Transform Outdated Business Systems

1. Involve Employees in the evaluation of current Business Systems.

2. Involve the Line Managers and their Staffs in evaluating business plans that affect their work.

3. Empower Line Management and staff to negotiate and collaborate based on interdependencies with other business areas' work plans.

4. Ensure that you enable people to design quality into the processes they must perform as part of their jobs.

5. Ensure you have the *right* people involved in the Business Systems, that is, that they have the competency and they have the *empowerment* to make the decisions or take actions for which they are accountable.

6. Redesign Business Management Systems and Information Systems as required.

NOTE These problems in Information Systems are treated in Chapter 15, "Information Quality Applied to Information Management and Information Systems Engineering."

Failure Cause: Failing to Manage Learning and Innovation Diffusion

Most organizations hoard knowledge as a source of power among the *elite* management or staff. The problem with this is that it creates divisions and competition, resulting in *resentment* among the "have-nots." This decreases motivation for working *for the best interests* of the Enterprise. Competition leads to self-preservation behavior, putting personal needs above the needs of the Enterprise, the Customers, and other Stakeholders.

How to Effect Learning and Innovation Diffusion

1. Open up the Databases and Knowledge Bases to all Employees, unless there is a real reason for restricting read access. The only reasons for restriction are legal requirements, such as those relating to privacy, or which require training to ensure that someone does not breach privacy or confidentiality requirements. The other reason is that Knowledge Worker training may be required to understand the meaning of complex information and how to apply it properly.

2. Bring Work Teams together to share ideas and Knowledge. What are Critical Success Factors that lead to effective results? What are factors that can cause failure? How do you rise above the failure factors and maximize the Critical Success Factors?

3. Document Successes *and* Failures in open Knowledge Bases that are accessible to others.

Guidelines for Transforming the Enterprise for the Information Quality Culture

John Kotter, a foremost expert on *leading culture change* describes the eight mistakes in leading transformative change in the Enterprise, and the Eight-Stage Change Process.

The Eight Mistakes That Cause Transformation to Fail

The eight mistakes include the following:

Error 1: Allowing Too Much Complacency

"By far the biggest mistake people make when trying to change organizations is to plunge ahead *without establishing a high enough sense of urgency* in fellow Managers and Employees. This error is fatal because transformations always fail to achieve their objectives when complacency levels are high."[29] Management must create a *sense of urgency* and *raise dissatisfaction* about the status quo and *communicate their dissatisfaction with the status quo* that is harming Enterprise Effectiveness.

Error 2: Failing to Create a Sufficiently Powerful Guiding Coalition

"Major change is often said to be impossible unless the head of the organization is an active supporter. What I am talking about here goes far beyond that. In *successful* Tansformations, the President, Division General Manager, or Department Head *plus another* five, fifteen, or fifty people with a *commitment to improved performance* pull together as a team."[30] You must develop *a coalition of committed people at many levels* to create success.

It is rare to have most of the Executive Leaders on board at first, because some will not buy in — at first. Individuals alone *cannot* create the Transformation. And weak governance or appointed committees are even less effective.

Failure here is usually caused by *underestimating the difficulties* one faces in creating change.

Error 3: Underestimating the Power of Vision

A sensible and powerful *Vision* is a critical element in successful Transformative Change, for it is a *unifier* that can rally people and help to direct, align, and inspire actions by them.

Without a singular, shared Vision, a major Transformation can evaporate into a bunch of incompatible and time-consuming projects that fail or go in a wrong direction. *Without a shared Vision* for decision making, people can fall back into their comfort zone and inhibit meaningful debate.

If you cannot describe the Vision driving a change initiative in five minutes or less and get a reaction that indicates both understanding and interest, you will have trouble succeeding.

Error 4: Undercommunicating the Vision by a Factor of 10 (or 100 or Even 1000)

Major Change will not happen unless *most* Employees are willing to help, even to make short-term sacrifices. They will not make sacrifices, even if they are unhappy with the status quo, unless they believe that the change holds benefits for them and that a Transformation is possible. This requires a lot of Credible Communication to capture the hearts and minds of the Employees.

Communication takes the form of both words and deeds, with the latter being the most powerful and critical to capture the participation of the employees.

Error 5: Permitting Obstacles to Block the New Vision

Major Change *requires action from a large mass* of people. Even when employees embrace the Vision, new initiatives fail if the Employees feel disempowered by huge obstacles in front of them. Obstacles include organizational structure, narrow job categories, and performance-appraisal systems that cause people to choose self-interest over the new Vision.

A manager at a large financial services organization paid lip service to his firm's major change efforts. However, he failed to change his own behavior or encourage others to change theirs. He would have been disruptive to the Transformation in any Management job — but he was not just any manager — he was the number *Three* Executive. Needless to say, the change initiative failed!

I have seen more than one Information Quality Management initiative fail as a result of Executive sabotage.

Error 6: Failing to Create Short-Term Wins

While Major Transformation takes time, you must create regular short-term gains and wins to prove and sustain the Transformation.

The journey to a mature Total Information Quality Culture will take three to five years, but you should be able to produce powerful results in IQ initiatives that demonstrate the Costs of Poor Quality Information in a four-to-eight week timeframe. Subsequent Information Process Improvements should be made within another four to six weeks, including measuring the Return-on-Investment of the Improvement. Each Improvement initiative will yield more ROI that can be invested in the next Improvement.

Error 7: Declaring Victory Too Soon

As you move from Stage 2, Maturity of "Awakening," you increase the scope of the effort and involve more people. Often, some quick wins early in the process may tempt you to believe you have arrived. Avoid the early celebration.

The behavior changes are deep and must become a natural part of employees' and management's behavior.

If you bring in consultants to help you create the change, remember that they may lead you through the initial PoC Initiative, but you must develop competency in your own staff and Leadership Team to continue the Improvement Initiatives until they become habits in all Employees.

Error 8: Neglecting to Anchor Changes Firmly in the Corporate Culture

'Corporate Culture' is the way people in the organization behave," according to David Walker, the CIO of a California oil production company. They successfully implemented an IQ Culture creating a Habit of Improvement sustainable from the third year of their Transformation. In the oil production business, the key success indicator is the "operating cost of barrel of oil equivalent." David's company has the lowest operating cost among their competitors in the industry.

Consequences of Errors

Consequences of errors include:

- New strategies are not implemented well.
- Acquisitions do not achieve expected synergies.
- Reengineering takes too long and costs too much.
- Downsizing does not get costs under control.
- *Quality programs* do not deliver hoped-for results.

The David Gleicher Model for Change

Lori Silverman introduced me to David Gleicher's formula for Culture Transformation, which transcends the older Kurt Lewin Model of Culture Change.[31] Gleicher sees the formula for successful Culture Transformation as:

$$C = f(D \times V \times F > R),$$

where:

C = Culture Change

f = "is a function of"

D = Dissatisfaction with the status quo

$\times$ = "multiplied by"

V = Vision of positive possibility, more than absence of pain of status quo

F = First steps (first concrete actions toward accomplishing the *Vision*)

$>$ = "is greater than"

R = Resistance to Change

If any of the components is missing, the following will occur:

- Have D but no V or F = *Frustration*.
- Have D and F but no V = *Fad of the month*.
- Have V and F but no D = *Wishful thinking*.[32]

The Eight-Stage Change Process

The eight stages include the following:[33]

1. Establish a Sense of Urgency

Timing is everything in establishing the *urgency*. If you are outside of the Guiding Coalition, you must raise the sense of urgency and create *Dissatisfaction* among those who have the authority to create Transforming Change. You must be prepared with the *Vision* of what is *Possible* and the *First Steps* with which to direct tangible actions that will bring about meaningful change. If you are in the Guiding Coalition, you should take a hard look at the strengths and weaknesses of your Enterprise in comparison to your competitors.

- Examine the market and competitive realities.

- Identify and discuss crises that have affected the Enterprise, potential crises that pose risks, or major opportunities that the Enterprise could lose without taking action to change.

- Examine Customer Complaints to identify IQ issues affecting your Customers.

- Measure the Costs of Poor Quality Information. See Chapter 6, "The Step-by-Step Guide to *Measuring the Costs and Risks of Poor Quality Information.*"

Translate these realities into messages that convey *urgency*.

Ways to Raise the Urgency Level

- If a crisis occurs, creating a financial loss, use this event to create dissatisfaction in the status quo, exposing Managers to Major Weaknesses Compared to Competitors, or allowing Information Issues to blow up instead of being corrected at the last minute.

- Eliminate obvious examples of excess, such as corporate jets and other perks that are perceived as greed to staff Employees and Customers.

- Stop measuring business area performance based only on narrow functional goals. Insist that more people be held Accountable for broader measures of Business Performance. Document the negative consequences of these "performance" measures that cause downstream processes to fail.

- Provide more Information about Customer Satisfaction, Financial Performance, or Poor Quality Information and its costs to more Employees, especially Information that demonstrates *Weaknesses* compared to the Competition.

- Insist that people talk regularly to *unhappy* Customers or internal Knowledge Workers.

- Use *qualified* consultants and other means to present *relevant* Information and conduct honest discussions of serious problems in management meetings.

- *Publish honest discussions* of the firm's *problems* in company newsletters and Executive speeches. Do *not* "sugar coat" the situation. *Masking* or *avoiding* the problems simply exacerbates them.

- Promote the *Vision* vigorously to people with Information on *future opportunities*, and *the rewards for capitalizing* on those opportunities, and raise dissatisfaction with the organization's current inability to pursue those opportunities.

2. Create the Guiding Coalition

- Put together a group with *enough power to lead* the change.
- Get the group to work together as a team.

Creating the Guiding Coalition requires four key characteristics:

1. **Positional power:** Are enough key players on board, especially the mainline managers, so that those left out cannot easily block progress?

2. **Expertise:** Are the various points of view — in terms of discipline, work experience, and nationality, for example, relative to the task at hand adequately represented so that informed, intelligent decisions will occur?

3. **Credibility:** Does the group have enough people with good reputations in the organization so that its pronouncements will be taken seriously by other employees?

4. **Leadership:** Does the group include enough proven Leaders to be able to drive the change process?

The Leadership concern is significant. You need people with both *Management* and *Leadership* skills, working in tandem and in teamwork. Avoid or carefully manage the high-ego individual who can substitute their immediate interests, which negatively affects the greater good, and those who could create enough mistrust to sabotage the transformation.[34]

- Find the right people with strong positional power, broad expertise, and high credibility, along with those with Leadership and Management skills, especially the former.

- Create trust through carefully planned off-site events and with lots of dialog and joint planning and work activities.

- Develop a common goal, sensible to the head and appealing to the heart.

3. Develop a Vision and Strategy

These are components of the Strategic Plan we introduced earlier in this chapter.

- Create a *Vision* of what a High IQ Culture that will eliminate the problems of the status quo would be like. This helps direct the change effort and garner staff participation in the Vision.

- Develop Strategies for achieving that Vision.

The Vision Must Have the Following Characteristics:

- **Imaginable:** It conveys a *picture* of what the future will look like. Is the Vision graphic enough to evoke positive emotions? Will it rally the troops?

- **Desirable:** It appeals to the *long-term interests* of Employees, Customers, Stockholders, Business Partners, and Communities. Will Employees have easier work conditions? Will Customers receive higher-quality products at lower costs? Will Stockholders receive higher dividends or share value increases?

- **Feasible:** It has *realistic, attainable goals*. Can we accomplish them within a reasonable budget and timeframe?

- **Focused:** It is *clear enough to provide guidance in decision making*. Will it keep people on a track to accomplish the Vision?

- **Flexible:** It is *general enough to allow individual initiative and alternative responses* if conditions change. Does it require minimal infrastructure change to accomplish the Vision?

- **Communicable:** It is *easy to communicate and can be explained successfully within five minutes*. Is it understandable to every level of staff and management?

The Guiding Coalition creates the Vision for the new Information Quality Culture with broad input from staff and management.

Leadership creates the Strategies that represent the logic for how to achieve the Vision.

Management develops the plans and timetables to implement the strategies.

Management converts the plans into goals with financial projections.

4. Communicate the Change Vision

- Use every vehicle possible to *communicate frequently* the Vision and Strategies.

- Ensure that the Guiding Coalition *become "role models"* of the behavior expected of employees.

The Guiding Coalition must keep talking about the Vision and how they will drive it into reality and how they will involve the staff and management in accomplishing the Vision.

The Guiding Coalition (GC) must keep *their ears open for concerns of management and staff* and address their concerns on a timely basis. Here is a potential concern from Information Producers (IP):

> IP: "I understand I will be held accountable for the Quality of Information I create, but I do not have time to verify it. We have quotas of how many calls we must take."

> GC: "We will analyze every job that Creates Information to ensure there is enough training, time, and resources to enable you to capture the information with quality."

5. Empower Broad-Based Action

The more empowerment people have to think outside the box, the more they will become engaged and feel more important to the organization.

- Get rid of obstacles. Review *unrealistic performance measures* that cause Information Producers to take short cuts or have to create their own hidden Information Factories, so they have the information (in a proprietary spreadsheet or database) that they need to perform their jobs.
- Change systems or structures that undermine the change Vision.
- Encourage risk-taking and nontraditional ideas, activities, and actions.
- Train and empower people to improve their own Information Processes.

6. Generate Meaningful Short-Term Wins Regularly

- Plan for *visible improvements in performance* (wins).
- Provide training in TIQM and *empower people* to start improving their processes.
- Create those wins through training, coaching, and ensuring effective improvements based on the Plan-Do-Check/Study-Act cycle that is the foundation for effective Process Improvement.
- Visibly recognize and reward people who made the wins possible.
- Establish IQ Process Improvement Teams to identify broken Information Processes and conduct Cost of Poor Quality Information measurement, Improving the Process to error-proof it, following the Plan-Do-Check/Study-Act cycle and then measure the ROI of the Improvement.
- Document, report, and communicate on all IQ Process Improvement Initiatives and the benefits and experiences achieved.

7. Consolidate Gains and Produce More Change

- Use increased credibility to change *all systems, structures, and policies that do not fit together and do not fit the* Transformation Vision.
- Hire, promote, and develop people who can implement the change Vision.
- Reinvigorate the process with new projects, themes, and change agents.
- Provide Just-in-Time TIQM training and keep improving defective Information Processes based on a Pareto approach of addressing the most important element, then the next-most important, and so on.

8. Anchor New Approaches in the Culture

This step seeks to establish the new behavior as a habit in all Employees. This step seeks to create the habit of Continuous Information Process Improvement that will transcend personality or organizational changes.

- Create better performance through Customer- and productivity-oriented behavior, more and better Leadership, and more effective management.
- Articulate the connections between new behaviors and organizational success.
- Develop means to ensure Leadership development and succession planning.
- Establish an Information Quality day, in which all employees seek out broken processes and seek to error-proof them.
- Provide recognition for all who participate.

Organizing the IQ Function and Environment

Work in the organization is carried out through people in specific role assignments that allow work to be performed in a standardized way, based on the nature of work and the skills required. Each role has one or more unique relationships with information. Based on these relationships, there are natural accountabilities for Information Quality required of these roles. Remember that every Employee, Manager, and Leader in the Enterprise has specific, defined accountabilities for making Information Quality happen.

This is true for the IQ Management function as well.

IQ Management as an *Enterprise* Function and Accountability

The mature IQ Management organization should have a number of IQ roles, depending on both the size of the Enterprise and its Maturity in the use of IQ Management capabilities as a business management tool. There are role descriptions found in Appendix B on this book's Web site at `www.wiley.com/go/IQApplied`.

Enterprise Roles in the IQ Culture Transformation

There are four sets of roles of important teams with unique accountabilities in making the IQ culture Transformation. They include:

- Executive Leadership Team
- Middle Management Team
- First-line Supervision Team
- Employees

I strongly believe that the Orchestra Model of Leadership in the Enterprise is the right approach. The military "Command-and-Control" Model has created, inadvertently, silos of autonomous control and has resulted in internal competition because of the nature of the performance incentive programs. Departmental managers often silently or openly compete with their peers for up-line management positions, where the pay and benefits are significantly greater.

Here are the roles of the four important Teams bulleted above, and how they help make the transformation to a High IQ Culture.

Executive Leadership

The Executive Leadership Team establishes the Vision of the Enterprise in the same way that an orchestra conductor establishes the interpretation of the music the orchestra is to perform and leads them in the performance. The Executive Leadership Team has the same responsibility and accountability for the performance of the Enterprise.

NOTE Sarbanes-Oxley is exactly correct that the Chief Executive Officer and the Chief Financial Officer are accountable for the quality of the Financial Information that the Enterprise provides to Investors and Market Analysts.

The Executive Leadership Team (ELT) is not just accountable for the Quality of Critical Information. They also require accurate, complete, and timely Information to provide the strategic Leadership required for their organization to survive in the emerging "Realized" Information Age, where managed, Quality, Just-in-Time Information is becoming the new currency of the Information Age.

Why?

Executives have absolute accountability for the success of the Enterprise, whether it is a private sector, not-for-profit, or government entity, and its fidelity to its Stakeholders, from Customers to Shareholders to Business Partners to Employees and their families to Communities affected by the Enterprise.

What?

Executives must clearly establish and present the Vision for the culture transformation. If the Executive Leadership is not the initiator of the IQ Culture Transformation, they must have a strong relationship with the Change Agents who act to bring in the change.

How?

- Understand the Costs and Business Consequences of Poor Quality Information. Direct the IQ Team to Measure the Costs of Poor Quality Information, both direct costs and opportunity costs.

- Learn about IQ Management as a Business Management tool. What is its purpose? What are the fundamental principles, processes, and methods required to make IQ happen?

- What is the ELT's role in making this Transformation happen?

- How do we make the Transformation part of the Habit and Behavior of the Enterprise?

- Identify the barriers in the status quo that will cripple the IQ Culture Transformation. How do performance incentives inhibit Information Quality?

- Identify the mechanisms to break down the barriers to change.

Middle Management

Middle Management is accountable for chunks of the Enterprise, often in major functions, such as Accounting, or Marketing and Sales, or as Divisional Heads of Operations in various locations.

Often viewed as the "lynchpin" between the ELT and First-Line Supervisors, this intermediation role must be transformed. The role of Middle Management must be to break down barriers at their level of control to ensure that the Customer-facing workers have the resources and training to delight their end-Customers.

Why?

Middle Management exists to provide proper "span of control" to ensure that work is performed properly. Each unit works together as an ensemble across the interdependent work groups. The new model for Middle Management is collaborative, like the various sections in the Orchestra, which come together as a single ensemble when they perform a Symphony.

What?

Middle Managers must communicate and share the Vision with their peers and their direct reports to ensure that everyone in their scope of control is on the same page. They must communicate to their staff and listen to their concerns, addressing them as necessary.

How?

- Middle Managers must also understand the Costs of Poor Quality Information. Direct the IQ Team to measure the Costs of Poor Quality Information, both Direct Costs and Opportunity Costs.

- Learn about IQ Management. What is the purpose? What are the fundamental principles, processes, and methods necessary to make IQ happen? How do we make this part of the habit of the Enterprise?

- Identify barriers in their area that are inhibiting Information Quality. Are we being good providers of information for our downstream Stakeholders?

First-Line Supervisors

First-line supervisors are like the section Leaders in the Orchestra, who provide standards for the music, for example, when the concert master defines the bowing for the first violins.

They must ensure that their staff have the right skills, training and resources to carry out their jobs effectively, providing High-Quality Information to their downstream Knowledge Workers.

Why?

If Information Producers in one part of the business do not provide High-Quality Information, the downstream processes of the Knowledge Workers will fail, causing High Costs of Failure and Information Scrap and Rework.

What?

Line Supervisors must provide the resources and training to their staff who perform the Value Work. The goal is for their staff to create the Quality of Information required for the downstream Stakeholders to perform their work properly.

How?

- Line supervisors must also understand the Costs of Poor Quality Information. Direct the IQ Team to measure the Costs of Poor Quality Information, both direct costs and opportunity costs.

- Learn about IQ Management. What is the purpose? What are the fundamental principles, processes, and methods necessary to make IQ happen? How do we make this part of the habit of the Enterprise?

- Provide Training and Resources so that Information Producers can provide the proper Quality of Information required downstream.

Employees

Employees are the ones who perform the Value Work of the Enterprise. It is they who delight the Customers and create Information required by downstream Knowledge Workers so that they can perform their work efficiently and effectively to delight *their* Customers, internal or external.

Why?

If Information Producers in one part of the business do not provide Quality Information, the downstream processes of the Knowledge Workers will fail, causing high costs of failure and Information Scrap and Rework.

What?

Because Employees are at the heart of the Enterprise, creating the Information they learn so that others can benefit from their Knowledge. In return, their Information Providers are capturing and providing Quality Information they need to perform their own work.

How?

- Call attention to broken processes and barriers to effective IQ work.

- Use the SIPOC (Supplier-Input-Process-Output-Customer) chart to identify your Information Customers and their Information Requirements.

- Learn IQ techniques like the Plan-Do-Check/Study-Act cycle for Process improvement and apply it to Improve your own Processes.

- Improve your processes to meet the IQ needs of your Information Customers.

Nemawashi as a Change Management Tool

"One of the major stumbling blocks of successful implementation of great ideas (ranging from appropriate technologies, sustainable agriculture, or social justice) is meticulous, step-by-step preparation of the social ecology.[35] *Nemawashi* is a key tool for creating and implementing plans where all the Stakeholders have a chance to voice concerns and needs, providing opportunity for consensus without getting bogged down in the process.

The word *nemawashi* literally means "to dig around the roots" in order to prepare a plant for transplantation. Without proper *nemawashi*, a bonsai tree transplanted to new soil may die. Hence a groundwork is important.[36]

Nemawashi is the process of discussing problems and potential solutions with all of those affected, to collect their ideas and get agreement on a path forward. This consensus process, although time-consuming to obtain, helps broaden the search for solutions, and once a decision is made, the stage is set for rapid implementation.

Nemawashi is one of the most important tools in Japanese management.[37] It is not just a tool for acquiring consensus. It is a tool that allows the major Stakeholders in a decision to evaluate multiple alternative ideas, with possible strengths and weaknesses in the ideas; evaluate carefully alternatives, risks, and rewards; and come to a consensus decision. This takes time in the decision-making process, but in the long run, the bad ideas and alternatives are weeded out, and the optimum decision is made. Once the decision is made, implementation goes quickly. Hence, the Japanese saying, "go slow, so you can go fast."

This system was developed to avoid discrepancies, and gain agreement from everyone in advance, when making a decision in a formal meeting. It is also to keep relationships harmonious.

Nemawashi is best used to let people of differing opinions have time to adjust their opinions. When the principles of *nemawashi* are put into effect first, people have the time to adjust opinions beforehand without wasting time.

The result in decision making eliminates resistance, as all have come to consensus and considered all alternatives before the decision is made. The process minimizes poor decisions through the process of evaluating alternatives.

IQ Roles and Organization in the IQ Culture

Figure 3-6 reflects the major roles and organization of the Information Quality function. The various IQ Job Positions and Business and System Information Stewardship accountabilities are found in the book's Web site: `www.wiley.com/go/IQApplied`.

On the one hand, it does not matter much where the IQ Team is positioned, as long as it has the ability to define the processes for an effective IQ capability. On the other hand, it needs to have access to provide ongoing coaching and direction to the Executive Leadership Team, so that there is proper Leadership of IQ Processes throughout the Enterprise as part of everyone's job. The Information Quality Team is made up of all Employees and Managers throughout the Enterprise. The official IQ Team merely defines the Information Quality Processes and provides training to make IQ happen, across the Enterprise.

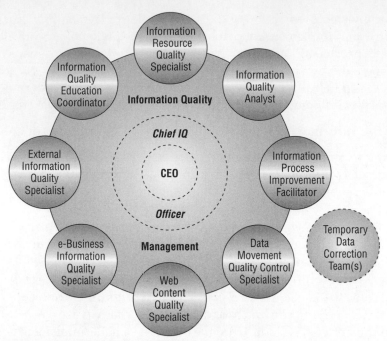

Figure 3-6: The Mature Information Quality Management Organization Roles

Every Employee, every Manager, and every Executive have specific activities and *accountabilities* for Information Quality that is inherent to the job position. The following are specific IQ Management job positions:

Standard IQ Management Job Positions

- Chief Information Quality Officer (CIQO)
- Information Quality Champion or Sponsor
- Information Quality Management Leader
- Information Resource Quality Specialist
- Information Quality Analyst
- Information Process Improvement Facilitator
- Data Movement Quality Control Specialist
- Information Quality Education Coordinator

Specialized Information Quality Roles or Positions

- Web Content Quality Specialist
- e-Business Information Quality Specialist

- External Information Quality Coordinator
- Information Presentation Quality Specialist
- Data Correction Team (ad hoc)

Business Information Quality Roles and Stewardship

Remember that the Information Quality Management Team does not *do* Information Quality work. They provide the capability, and implement principles, processes, methods, and techniques to enable the Enterprise to execute Information Quality work. The TIQM Team becomes the Process Owners of the six TIQM processes. They define those processes in a way that embeds them as part of the Enterprise's Culture without compromising the Quality Management Principles that undergird a sound Quality Management System applied to Information.

Peter Block has the seminal definition of "Stewardship" as an alternative to supervisory management. He describes Stewardship as, "the willingness to be accountable for the well-being of the larger organization by operating in service of, rather than in control of those around us."[38] People are good Stewards when they perform their work in a way that benefits their Internal and External Customers (the larger organization), not just themselves or their department. Valuable workers understand how others depend on their work products, and work *to provide Customer Service.*[39]

Information Stewardship, then must be, "the willingness to be accountable for a set of Information for the well-being of the larger organization by operating in service, rather than in control of those around us."[40]

Business Information Stewardship Roles

- Knowledge Worker as "Knowledge Steward"
- Information Producer as "Operational Information Steward"
- Data Entry Clerk as "Information Transcription Steward"
- Information Translator as "Information Translation Steward"
- Information Agent as "Information Preparation Steward"
- Business (Production) Manager as "Managerial Information Steward"
- Process (Definition) Owner as "Process Steward"
- Business Subject Matter Expert as "Business Information Steward"
- Executive Business Leader as "Strategic Information Steward"

SAMPLE MANAGEMENT ACCOUNTABILITY STATEMENT

Responsible for management, control, and use of information. Ensure that the quality of information created or maintained within the process or department meets all Information Consumers' needs, internally, to other business areas and to Customers and external Stakeholders. Ensure that Information Policy is understood and followed. Provide training to personnel in Information Quality Principles and Standards and provide resources to accomplish Information Quality goals.[41]

Information Systems' Roles and Information Quality Stewardship

There are 19 major Information Systems roles that impact the capability of an Enterprise to manage its information effectively. Their Information Quality Stewardship accountabilities are found on the book's website at www.wiley.com/go/IQApplied.

Information Systems roles include:

- Applications Development/Engineering Manager
- Application Project Manager
- Systems Analyst/Engineer
- Application Systems Designer/Engineer
- Computer Programmer
- Information Resource Management Leader
- Information Architect/Modeler
- Information Resource Analyst
- Database Administration Manager
- Database Designer
- Data Movement Control Specialist
- Knowledge Management Leader
- Business Intelligence/Strategic Information (Data Warehouse) Manager
- Virtual Information (Web) Manager
- Information Resource Data/Repository/Dictionary Manager
- Information and Systems Security Officer
- Computer Operations Manager
- Chief Information Officer (CIO) as "Strategic Information Resource Steward"
- Chief Business Information Officer (CIO or CBIO) as "Strategic Business Information Resource Steward"

Establishing Information Governance

Information Governance must be implemented naturally, with the ELT as the top Information Governance Team, in the same way it is the top governance team for financial management, business performance management, and human resources management.

In the Information Age, Information Resource Management and Information Quality Management must be added to the ELT as the top governance mechanism.

Any Information Governance mechanism that is made up of senior Leaders not a part of the ELT will fail. If an operational Information Governance Team is created, there must be at least two or three Executive Leaders from the top management team included as leading team members of this governance mechanism. Without this, and without addressing Information Quality as part of the ELT, the IQ transformation may fail.

Managing a Proof-of-Concept Project for Success

Perhaps the most important activity in the startup of an IQ function establishment is the Proof-of-Concept project. It is here you establish the value of the proactive Process Improvement approach to Information Quality Management.

Follow the "Critical Success Factors for Information Process Improvement Initiatives" in Chapter 7, in the Section "Step P4.1: Define Project for Information Process Improvement: Process Steps and Guidelines," under "Critical Success Factors for IQ Improvement Initiatives."

Summary

An effective IQ Management function cannot exist without having a fundamental Transformation from the Status Quo to a Culture of Continuous Information Process Improvement. The status quo management environment is the cause of the current degree of Poor Quality Information and the High Costs of Process Failure and Information Scrap and Rework.

The IQ transformation requires understanding and implementing the proven principles of Quality Management as implemented in the sound quality systems as described in Chapter 2, "The ABCs of the TIQM Quality System for Total Information Quality Management."

You learned about the IQMM maturity grid that outlines the five stages of IQ maturity and the characteristics and behaviors that must be established in each stage as a foundation for the next stage of maturity to be sustainable.

You learned why TQM and IQ implementation frequently fail, but not because of inherent flaws in TQM and TIQM principles and processes. Rather, they fail because of the many barriers that exist in the status quo management systems.

You learned the causes of failure in the Startup, Alignment, and Integration Phases of implementing TIQM and how you can prevent them from crippling your IQ environment implementation as a culture and habit of Continuous Process Improvement that leads to business excellence.

You learned about the various IQ Job Positions and their Accountabilities. You also learned about the Role Accountabilities for Information Quality required of various Business and Information Systems Job Roles.

You learned that the Executive Leadership Team has full accountability for Information Governance in the same way that it is accountable for governance of *financial and human resources*.

The Step-by-Step Guide to *Assessing Information Product Specifications and Information Architecture Quality*

"Creative thinking involves breaking out of established patterns in order to look at things in different ways."

Edward de Bono, *Lateral Thinking*

TIQM P1: Assess Information Product Specifications and Architecture Quality

The previous chapter described the cultural transformation and roadmap for implementing an Information Quality culture and environment. This is an ongoing and continuous journey to evermore increasing the processes of information development and information production. TIQM P1 is the first discrete process. P1 measures the quality of Information Product Specifications (data definition, valid values, and business rule specifications) data and the quality of Information Models representing the Enterprise Information Requirements and physical Database Design quality. Figure 4-1 illustrates this process in the context of TIQM in general.

TIQM P1 describes how to measure the Quality of Information Product Specifications (IPS). IPS includes data names and definitions; business rule specifications, also called validity rules or edit and validation rules; the set of valid values or range of values; Information Content format structure; and other characteristics that enable Business Professionals to understand the meaning of the Information they work with and to communicate clearly with each other across organizational boundaries. It also includes how to measure the quality of Information Models, which represent Enterprise Information Requirements and drive the design of databases that house the Enterprise's electronic information.

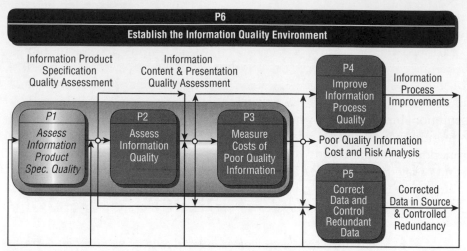

Figure 4-1: P1 Assess Information Product Specification Quality in the Context of TIQM.

Lack of correctly and clearly defined information causes *misinterpretation* that leads to wrong actions taken and wrong decisions made. Defects in Information Models and Database designs lead to failure to meet Enterprise Information needs. It furthermore creates high costs of maintenance and Information Scrap and Rework of maintaining disparately defined databases.

Overview

For information to have quality it must be correctly, completely, and clearly defined so that all Information Stakeholders understand the meaning of the information, the business rules that constrain it, and the valid values from which its content should come.

Key definitions:

- **Definition (*v*):** 1 — The act or process of stating a precise meaning; 2 — The act of making clear and distinct[1]

- **Definition (*n*):** 1 — (a) Stating the exact meaning (of words, etc.); (b) Statement that gives the exact meaning (of words, etc.)[2]

- **Communication (*n*):** 1 — A process by which information is exchanged between individuals through a common system of symbols, signs or behavior[3]

- **Productivity (*n*):** 1 — Efficiency, especially in industry, measured by comparing the amount produced with the time taken or the resources used to produce it[4]

- **Specifications (*n*):** 1 — A detailed, exact statement of particulars, especially a statement prescribing materials, dimensions, and quality of work for something to be built, installed, or manufactured[5]

Information does not just magically appear; it must be produced, just as physical products must be produced to meet *product specifications* through well-defined and controlled manufacturing processes. Products have "Product Specifications" to direct and control product quality. We must have correct, complete, and clear *Information Product Specifications* (IPS) for Information. IPS includes entity and attribute names, definitions, valid values, value formats for data storage and for presentation, business rule conformance, and unit-of-measure (for numerical and quantitative data). Information Producers need to know how to capture information with quality, and Knowledge Workers need to know how to interpret and apply the Information they receive.

If Knowledge Workers do not have a common understanding of the Information they work with, they can take wrong actions or make wrong decisions, diminishing productivity and increasing costs of Information Scrap and Rework.

Information Definition and Information Architecture as Information Product Specifications

Product specifications are "detailed, exact statements of particulars, especially a statement prescribing materials, dimensions, and quality of work for something to be built, installed, or manufactured."[6]

Similarly, there is a set of Information Resource Data (aka. metadata) that makes up the Information Product Specifications. Information Models represent the real-world Objects and Events that organizations need to know about and what Facts or Characteristics they need to know about those real-world Objects and Events to manage and perform the work of the Enterprise. Database designs have specific quality requirements to ensure the databases that house the enterprise knowledge are stable, flexible, and reused.

IPS Quality Characteristics are described in the next section.

Quality Characteristics of Information Product Specifications and Information Architecture

Several Quality Characteristics are required to provide a "detailed, exact statement of the information to be produced." Some of these are considered "Critical-To-Quality" (CTQ) — required for Information Producers to create and maintain quality data and for Knowledge Workers to retrieve and apply it effectively.

Five sets of IPS characteristics are required to define requirements and specifications for Quality Information to be captured, maintained, and applied. They include:

- ☑ Information Standards and Guidelines Quality
- ☑ Information Name Quality
- ☑ Information Definition Quality

☑ Business Rule Specification Quality

☑ Information Architecture Quality

The following represent Critical-to-Quality (CTQ) IPS quality characteristics.

Information Standards and Guidelines Quality

An organization's Information Standards and Guidelines represent the "Specification Guidelines" for creating the "Information Product Specifications." If these are faulty or if they are not followed, your data naming, definition, and business rule specifications will be deficient or poorly defined. Characteristics of Quality Information Standards include:

☑ Information Standards must be *Enterprise-Wide* standards. They are standardized across all business areas and business units in the same way that there is a single, standard General Ledger Chart of Accounts.

☑ Standards are business Stakeholder approved. Representatives of key Information Stakeholders across all business areas and business units are in agreement with the standards.

☑ Abbreviations are standardized across the enterprise. Abbreviations and acronyms used in data names must be documented in the Enterprise Business Term Glossary. Abbreviations should be a universal abbreviation from an authoritative source or an intuitive abbreviation agreed upon by representatives of all business areas.

NOTE A single term or abbreviation may represent one or more business terms in different domains or business contexts. These are allowed if they are clearly understandable within each context as to its specific business term in a given data name.

NOTE Synonym abbreviations may be required for the purpose of relating newly architected data to older legacy systems and databases and purchased application software. These should be temporary until legacy systems and databases are reengineered or redirected to Enterprise-Strength databases.

TIP Never attempt to standardize on obsolete applications or software package abbreviations. You may adopt international standards, such as ISO, or NIST or Industry Standard abbreviations for technical terms if they are stable AND are agreeable to a near consensus of business Information Stakeholders.

☑ Single object types. An entity type represents one and only one classification of real-world objects or events, such as Party (Customer) or Product in which each occurrence of the type is a unique real-world Entity with the same Attribute types required by the Enterprise. An Entity Type will have one single, unique, business-friendly name across the Enterprise.

☑ Correct object relationships. Guidelines specify relationships among object types that represent the actual relationships in the real world.

☑ Single fact types. An Attribute is a single fact type that represents a characteristic of a real-world object or event that the enterprise needs to know about. Attributes are *inherent* characteristics of the Object or Event represented. An Attribute will have one single, unique attribute name for an Entity Type.

☑ Standard names across all media. Labels (attribute names) are consistent across all media, such as the repository name of an entity type or attribute, label on a computer screen, column name in a report, and the data element name in a database file or table.

☑ Information Standards are applied in all new development and software package evaluations and in major application reengineering.

NOTE If "Information Standards are defined but not universally used, they are *NOT standards*" — they are only wishful thinking![7]

The objective of Information Standards and Guidelines is to increase communication effectiveness among Business and Information Systems Professionals, and to increase Business and Information Systems productivity.

Information Name Quality

Information names should be intuitive labels, recognizable by the Information Stakeholders that give a sense of the meaning of a business term, an object or event type, or a fact about an object or event. Imprecise naming leads to confusion, misinterpretation, and mistakes. Quality guidelines in naming should include:

☑ **Business Term Name quality:** Business terms represent concepts and classifications that are of interest to an enterprise, an industry (such as finance, manufacturing, or publication), or a function (such as accounting, actuarial, engineering, fabrication, legal, or Information Systems). Common terms may have different meanings in different domains just like English words may have different meanings in different contexts.

A business term is different from an attribute or data element name that must represent one and only one type of fact. Business terms are concepts that are inherent to the industry, such as manufacturing or banking or a functional discipline, such as accounting, auditing, or employee benefits. A business term may have different meanings in different domains of the business. The different homonyms, different meanings for the same business term name, must be identified for that single term name. This enables the business to understand the meaning of the term when used in different contexts. (See section "**Information Definition Quality**" on the next page.)

The business term name should be a commonly accepted name, an industry standard name, or an internally coined term with internal acceptance in a domain context, such as accounting, health and safety, manufacturing, or quality management, for example.

☑ **Entity Type Name quality:** Entity Type names are labels for the object or event classifications the enterprise needs to know about. The names should represent a singular classification of objects or events that the enterprise has an interest in. Unlike business term names, which may have different meanings, an entity type name should represent one and only one classification of objects or events, such as "Product," "Account," "Order," or "Party." A "Party" has two structural subtypes, "Person" and "Organization," or appropriate synonyms. The objects or events represented by one entity type or subtype name should share some common characteristics. Characteristics of "persons" are "person birth date," "family name" "given name," and "marital status," for example. Many of these characteristics will represent attributes and data elements that must be known about them for the business to carry out its mission effectively.

A single occurrence of an entity type, such as Person "John Adam Smith" may also play a specific "role," such as an "Employee" or "Customer" of an enterprise. Each of these classifications has specific common characteristics, such as "Employee hire date" or "Customer first service date."

☑ **Attribute Name quality:** An attribute name represents a fact about a real-world object classification (entity type), such as "person birth date," "family name" and "given name," or "Employee hire date" or "Customer first service date."

An attribute name may have a data value type label that indicates the type of data values held by this attribute. Standard data element types include ID (Identifier), date, code, name, currency amount, quantity, percent, length, height, weight, or number, for example.

To have quality, an attribute name must be a clear label that is intuitively indicative of a Characteristic all occurrences of an Entity Type. It must represent a single characteristic of a real-world object, that is, "Person, John Adam Smith," and be a unique attribute name for an entity type, that is, "Person given name" or "Person family name."

☑ **Standard attribute data value set specification.** The attribute has guidelines for the types of valid values, including:

☑ Range of values or discrete code values

☑ Complete code values with definition or description

☑ Business rule specifications that indicate correct value creation requirements, including code value creation and data formatting instructions

Information Definition Quality

Definitions of business terms, entity types, and attributes are critical for business communication. They are likewise critical for the information production of the data. If Knowledge Workers do not know the meaning of the data they are supposed to create, how can they know the right value to create?

Quality data definitions follow the lexicographic format, "A [*term being defined*] is a [*general class of which the term is a specialized class*] that [*phrase that differentiates membership in the specialized class from all members in the general class*]."

EXAMPLE "[An Employee is] a <u>Person</u> [general class as defined in the dictionary and / or in the Person entity type definition] who is employed by ABC company for wages or salary and benefits and who performs work in a defined ABC <u>Job Position</u> [what distinguishes an Employee from all Persons in the world]."

☑ **Business Term Definition quality:** Business terms must be defined so that the concept is clear within a specific domain of use. If a term has multiple definitions, the domain of use must be clearly specified for each unique meaning.

For example, the business term "Volume" may have meanings of "the amount of space occupied by a substance or object" (the physics concept) in the manufacturing production domain. "Volume" may also mean "one of a set of books" in the Information Center or Library domain. "Volume" may also mean "the loudness of sound, measured in decibels" used in the Health and Safety domain of an organization.

☑ **Entity Type Definition quality:** The definition of an Entity Type or Subtype must clearly and correctly define the objects represented by that classification of things or events. Because these represent collections of real-world things, persons or events, there must be a definition that differentiates between each unique classification (entity type or subtype).

For example, the definition of Customer must encompass *all* persons and/or organizations considered to be enterprise Customers. If there are different types or classifications of Customer, such as "Retail Customer" or "Wholesale Customer," each of these subtypes must have a definition that encompasses all, but no more than those Customers who are classified in each subtype.

Poor definition: "'Customer.' Information about people who buy our products."

This is one of many actual, poor definitions of "Customer" that I have seen. It is not a definition at all. Entity type definitions must define the classification of persons, organizations, or persons and organizations that qualifies them to be "Customers" — not state the obvious that we need to know "information" about them!

Better definition: "A 'Customer' is a person who has purchased or expressed interest in purchasing our products or services." Note that this includes "prospective Customers" as well.

☑ **Attribute Definition quality:** Attributes represent Characteristics of the Objects the Enterprise should know. They show up as "facts" about an occurrence of an entity type, such as the given name(s) of Customer Number 000123 is/are "John Adam" or the name of Product NN5120D is "The da Vinci Code Cryptex." Attributes represent Characteristics inherent to all occurrences of an object classification, such as Customer. Customers may be known in different states of existence, including "Prospective Customer," "Active Customer," and "Former Customer." All Active Customers (subtype) have a "Customer Begin Date" that should have a valid date value once a Prospective Customer becomes a purchasing Customer.

An Attribute definition should define the characteristic of the real-world Object represented. The definition should be of one and only one type of fact for occurrences of that type. Each occurrence will have its own unique value at a point in time.

The attribute definition:

☑ Follows the lexicographic formula for definitions.

☑ Is the correct definition of a Characteristic (fact type) of an Object or Event Type (Entity Type) that the Enterprise needs to know.

☑ Is a clear, noncircular definition (does not define a term with the term itself and is intuitive to the Information Consumers).

☑ Is a singular definition (defines one type of thing or one type of fact).

☑ Defines the real-world Object independently of how the Information may be used.

☑ Is inclusive of all occurrences.

Poor definition: "'Payment date' is the 'date of payment.'"

First, this does not specify what entity type this "payment date" describes. Is it a payment of an Invoice from a Customer? Secondly, if this is a payment on an Invoice (that is, "Invoice Payment Date"), there are many different dates that could be associated with a Payment. Is it the date the Customer wrote and dated the check? Is it the date the invoicing organization received the payment, entered it into the system, or the date the funds were actually transferred into an account? There is much ambiguity about both the name of the attribute and its meaning.

Better name and definition: "An 'Invoice Payment Received Date' is the date a Customer's Invoice Payment is received by the Company. For written checks, this is the date the envelope containing the check is received. For electronic payments, this is the date the Electronic Payment is received into the Company's bank account. For Electronic Payments, the Payment Received Date and Payment Deposit Applied Date are the same."

The preceding definition indicates there are two subtypes of payments, Physical Payments and Electronic Payments.

Business Rule Specification Quality

Business rules represent various types of policies, regulations, or other controls that may apply to business actions and the information that represents those business actions. Business rules must be complete, correct, and clear so that Information Producers who create information know the requirements and Knowledge Workers understand the constraints. Quality in business rule specification enables more effective software edit and validation rule execution and reasonability tests.

Business rule types include rules or policies that govern:

- ☑ Existence and state change (Offered Product becomes a Retired Product.)

- ☑ Dependency relationships (Life Insurance Policy Holder must have one or more Beneficiaries.)

- ☑ Derivation formula or calculation definition (Order item price equals the applicable item price, based on price-break quantity ordered, multiplied by the quantity of items ordered, less any discount program allowed.)

- ☑ Security classification (Clinical trial results can only be modified by the researcher who conducted the clinical trial.)

- ☑ Retention requirements (Employee tax withholding data must be retained for seven years or as per government requirements.)

- ☑ Legal, regulatory, privacy, health and safety, environmental, Consumer disclosure, or other regulatory compliance requirements. For example, Clinical trial results and clinical trial subject name must not be revealed to the researcher together.

Before entering a university, my son received instructions as to what he could bring with him to his dorm. These were business rules for a refrigerator, should he bring one:

Poor business rule specification: A refrigerator MUST meet the following specifications:

- 50 pounds
- 2.5 cubic feet
- 2.5 amperage draw

The ambiguity here is omnipresent. What does *"MUST meet"* "50 pounds" mean? Is it that it must weigh exactly 50 pounds? Probably not. This is probably a maximum limit. But does it mean 50 pounds empty, loaded, or the amount of weight of food it would hold? Does the 2.5 cubic feet define limits of the interior or exterior dimensions? Is the 2.5 amperage draw the exact amps it would draw or the upper limit?

Better business rule specification: *A refrigerator MUST meet the following specifications:*

- Does NOT weigh more than 50 pounds filled, AND
- Is NO larger than 2.5 cubic feet of interior space, AND
- Does NOT draw more than 2.5 amps of electricity

For more about additional characteristics of Information Product Specification Quality, please see Chapter 5, "Assessing Data Definition and Information Architecture Quality" in *Improving Data Warehouse and Business Information Quality.*[8]

Data Name and Definition Quality Characteristics

Establish the Critical-to-Quality (CTQ) Characteristics of IPS required for effective Business and Information Systems communication and productivity in which quality is required. At a minimum the components assessed should include:

- ☑ A data name (full and abbreviated) that is intuitive to the general Stakeholder Community in both the full name and abbreviated name if one exists

- ☑ **A Data Definition:** correctly, completely, and clearly defining the real-world object or event type or the Attribute of the Real-World Object or Event it describes

- ☑ **Data Name and Data Definition Consistency:** ("I see this data name and I think this definition; I see this definition and I think this data name.")

- ☑ **A Valid Data Value Set or Range:** that is specified correctly and understandably to the Stakeholders. Note that this is a measure of validity. Conformance to the valid values *does* not equate to *accuracy*.

- ☑ **Business Rules:** specify Information Integrity Requirements that are correct to the natural relationships in the real world or correct to the regulatory body or internal policy that dictates the rule

- ☑ **Calculation Formulas for Derived Data Attributes:** are correctly and clearly defined in a way the stakeholders can understand and agree with

- ☑ **A Format Standard for structured data values:** such as SSN, Phone Number, Street Address, or Product Code

☑ **Integrity Requirements such as Security, Confidentiality, prohibition of Information:** use for certain purposes, or disclosure to authorities that are correctly and clearly documented and made accessible to Stakeholders

Data Presentation Format Quality Characteristics:

☑ **Proper mode of presentation:** The information is communicated in the best mode (screen display, print output, audio, video, text message, for example).

☑ **Name consistency:** in different contexts, such as screen labels, report column headers, database data element names in query results

☑ **Correct presentation format template:** for formatted data such as dates, times, currency values, phone numbers, addresses, tax-ids, for example

☑ **Presentation objectivity that minimizes misinterpretation:** agreement of quantitative data and graphic representation, omission of explanatory data of apparent anomalies, omission of all data required for the task at hand, interpretive information that disagrees with the raw data

Information Architecture Quality Characteristics

Information Architecture Quality consists of Quality Characteristics of Information Models and Database Designs.

Information Model and Database Design Quality Characteristics

Both the Information Models and Databases are used by all processes, activities, and applications that require information specified in the Subject Information Models and housed in Databases.

General Quality Characteristics are:

☑ Operational Information Models and Databases are used directly by operational processes, activities, and application systems with no structural change. Only additive change is required for Entity Types with Attributes not required at the time of the original Information Model development.

☑ Reengineering of processes causes *minimal* impact on Information Models and Database Designs. Generally the only modifications required are to eliminate paper trail entity types or attributes that controlled paper trail processes that are eliminated by reengineering.

Information Models represent Enterprise Information Requirements as represented in a graphic Entity-Relationship or other standard Information Model Diagram that lists the Objects and Events (Entity Types) that the Enterprise needs to know about and the fact types, called Attributes, that the Enterprise needs to know. As such, the Information Models are vital components of the Information Product Specifications, and serve as the *specification* for Database Design.

The Information Model is similar to a Product "Bill-of-Materials" that specifies the component parts and materials required for the manufacture of a finished product. The Information Model, like the Bill-of-Materials, is used to design the physical Databases that will house the required data, from which the Enterprise's Information will be assembled for presentation to Knowledge Workers. Several Quality Characteristics are required to provide a Quality Enterprise-Strength Information Model, which is then used to develop Enterprise-Strength Record-of-Reference (RoR) Databases that can meet any Knowledge Worker's need for Information:

High-Level Business Information Model Quality

The high-level Business Information Model is a representation of the Resources of the Enterprise, and the fundamental classifications of Objects and Events the Enterprise needs to know about, and some of the major Facts the Enterprise needs to know about them.

Quality Characteristics include:

☑ Only one high-level Business Information Model exists for the Enterprise.

☑ The model is expressed in business terms.

☑ The model is understandable by the Enterprise Executives.

☑ Data names and definitions that conform to the name and Definition Quality Characteristics described earlier

☑ A model that is modeled by business resource or subject area, not department or functional business area. Business resources include both internal and external resources:

  ☑ People and Organization or Party Resources (Employee, Customer, Supplier, Business Partner)

  ☑ Financial Resources (GL Account, Payment, Invoice, Asset)

  ☑ Material and Parts Resources (Item, Material, Component)

  ☑ Product or Service Resources (Product, Bill-of-Material, Product-Price)

  ☑ Facilities and physical Assets (Asset, Facility, Equipment)

  ☑ Information Resources (Information Model, Database File, Application, Computer hardware, Software Application System)

  ☑ Accounts or Customer to Product or Service relationships; such as Insurance Policy (Customer to Insurance Product), Financial Account, Order and Sale

☑ External factors, such as regulation, economic condition, news

☑ Business Resource or Subject Areas represent *non-overlapping* business classifications of information. Entity types should be able to be classified in only one Business Resource Classification or Subject Area. If an Entity Type is listed in more than one Business Resource area, the areas may be functionally biased; in other words, data required by a Function or Business Area. Problems caused by a functional classification of "subjects" include:

   ■ Entity types may be defined functionally instead of inherently, such as Supplier and Vendor, Customer versus Account.

   ■ The same Entity Type may be inconsistently defined across different functional views.

   ■ Overlapping, Business Information Stewardship roles for synonyms; for example, one steward for Supplier and one steward for Vendor

☑ The model identifies and defines the most Fundamental or important Object Classifications or Entity Types, sometimes referred to as Business Entity Types.

☑ Fundamental Entity Types are documented with sample Attributes (not an exhaustive list) and occurrences and may include highly derived Attributes as Key Business Indicators, such as Customer-Lifetime-Value, Customer-Attrition-Rate, or Daily-Product-Sales-Amount.

☑ Sample Attributes include Key Business Indicators that are associated with the most fundamental Entity Types to document Strategic Information Requirements. For example, market-share-percent and total daily-product-sales-amount are derived attributes that describe Product at a point in time.

Operational Information Model Quality Characteristics

The detailed Operation Information Model (OIM) is a detailed Information Model that represents all *real-world* Objects and Events (entity types) that the Enterprise needs to know about, the nature of the relationships among the real-world objects and events, and a comprehensive list of characteristics (attributes) about the real-world objects and events that need to be known by the Enterprise.

■ **Operational Information Model Quality:**

   ☑ The Operation Information Model is a detailed Information Model driven from the Hi-level Subject Information Model to extend it with all detailed Entity Types and a comprehensive list of Attributes about the real-world objects and events required to be known by the enterprise.

☑ The Information Model Framework uses classifications of business resources that the enterprise needs to manage effectively as the basis of classifications of "information subjects" such as Party (with role types of Employee, Customer, Supplier, Business Partner), Product, Material (Parts, Components), Financial Resource, Facility and Equipment, for example.

☑ Inherent Relationships among Entity Types to other Entity Types that represent the correct relationships as exist in the real world that includes relationships of objects over time, not just at a point-in-time.

☑ Inherent Relationships of an Entity Type to its Attributes. Birth date, for example, is not an inherent characteristic of "Employee." A Person does not have a birth date because they are an Employee, but because they are a member of "homo sapiens," inheriting the characteristic of mammals that give birth to their offspring live. Birth date is an attribute of a Person, inherited by Employee, because an Employee is a Person.

☑ The OIM contains *all* Entity Types and all Attributes needed to be known by all Knowledge Workers who need information about the entities within that resource area.

☑ The Information Model contains the significant majority of all Attributes or Facts about real-world objects or events required by any Knowledge Worker to successfully perform their Value Work.

☑ The Information Model contains *all identified* Attributes Required to identify trends and patterns in Strategic or Tactical Databases, as are found in the Strategic (data warehouse) Databases and data marts. This is true for additional Attributes that may become known to Information Producers in their natural jobs, or for Attributes that must be identified by external third-party information brokers.

▪ **Entity-Type-to-Entity-Type Relationship:**

☑ Each Entity Type in the relationship represents a real-world classification of Objects or events that the enterprise needs to know about.

☑ Both Entity Types are defined clearly.

☑ The Relationship(s) between them is (are) defined clearly.

☑ The Relationships expressed in the model are the same that exist or may exist between the real-world objects and or events represented.

- **Attribute-to-Entity-Type Relationship:**
  - ☑ The Attribute is an inherent characteristic of this type.
  - ☑ All Occurrences of this Type (or Subtype) may contain a value for this attribute.
  - ☑ An Occurrence of this Type never needs more than one value for this attribute at a point in time for any process requiring this fact.
  - ☑ If processes need to know historical values of attributes that may change over time, such as name or address or product-price, these attributes are documented or modeled to illustrate the history requirement.
  - ☑ The Attribute does not contain more than one kind of fact to describe this Entity.
  - ☑ The Attribute describes only one Entity Type or Subtype. (Inheritance of attributes by subtypes is described in the next section.)
  - ☑ An Attribute that is derivable or calculable from other known facts is documented as derived. The Formula or Calculation of the Attribute is in the derived attribute definition. All base data used to calculate the derived data is defined in the model.

- **Entity-Type-to-Entity-Subtype Relationship:**
  - ☑ Each Entity Type or subtype is a meaningful object classification to the enterprise. At the topmost level, the generalized type may not be perceived by the business as a business classification of things. However, experience shows that business people involved in modeling of information can easily see the value and have no trouble modeling information by subtypes, or in reading subtype model hierarchies.
  - ☑ An Occurrence or member of a Subtype is also a member of any Super-Type in its hierarchy.
  - ☑ The relationship between occurrences of the type and subtype is always one-to-one. For example, a John Smith as a Person can only be related to one "John Smith" as a Customer or the one Employee "John Smith."
  - ☑ Each Type or Subtype has unique attributes or behaviors that cause it to be unique and therefore represented in the model. There are some exceptions to this in that the only attributes some subtypes may have are those inherited from the more general super-type. They may be modeled for communication purposes and balance.

☑ Each Subtype is in fact a *more specialized* classification of members of the Entity Type. For example, an Employee is a more specialized kind of Party who must also be a Person.

☑ All Attributes are *inherent characteristics* of the Type or Subtype with which they are first associated. Birth date is inherent to Person, not to the role of a Party as an Employee.

☑ An occurrence of a Subtype inherits *all* Attributes of all its ancestor super-types. This is a very important rule. The hierarchy is not precise if there are exceptions to inheritance. It should be noted, however, that for a given process not all attributes of a super-type are necessarily required for subtype occurrences. For example, Birthdate is an inherent characteristic of Person. It is a fact required for Customer and Employee subtypes, but does not need to be known about a Supplier Contact.

▪ **Entity Life-Cycle-State:**

☑ The Entity Life Cycle identifies the creation, or existence event, and the deletion, or archiving event.

☑ All Events that may affect or cause significant change to an Occurrence of this Type are identified. Significant change means that new attributes are known and some different business rules apply. For example, change of name or address is not a significant state change event unless new rules apply, such as in insurance policy coverage.

☑ The Life Cycle is defined in a way that a specific occurrence can exist in only one state at a point in time, as in the real world.

☑ *Every* State change is triggered by an identifiable business event.

☑ *Every* State change is associated with a process invoked by the business event.

☑ Each State *lists all* Attributes whose values are created or may be modified upon change to that state.

☑ Business rules governing the behavior of an occurrence in a given state are identified.

☑ The Attributes required to have valid values in a state will be ensured before the state transition event has been completed.

Operational Database Design Quality Characteristics

The Database Design represents the physical design specification of the physical database structure that houses enterprise data created or updated by Information Producers, and retrieved and applied by Knowledge Workers or application programs.

The Critical-to-Quality Characteristics of an Operational Database Design are:

☑ **Stability:** New applications and Knowledge Workers can access the database with no destructive change to the database structure. Only new data elements or database files are added to the design.

☑ **Flexibility:** Business Processes can be Reengineered without significant reengineering of the Database Design, meaning the database is designed independently of functional or business area–specific views of the information.

☑ **Reused:** For Operational Databases to be used by all applications and Knowledge Workers, they must be designed to implement all Attributes (fact types) required to support all Knowledge Workers. Reuse of Operational Databases without having to modify them indicates Quality Database Design. When different Business Areas can all share data from the same operational source, you eliminate the need for proprietary, departmental databases. Today's Information Technologies provide sufficient capability for transaction performance without having to implement uncontrolled, redundant databases. Quality Database Designs will:

  ☑ Implement the structure of the corresponding Enterprise-Strength Subject Information Model, such as Party (Customer) and Product.

  ☑ Not compromise Database Design for performance or other reasons from its corresponding Enterprise-Strength Subject Information Model, until all other types of performance improvement mechanisms are studied, designed, and implemented. This includes DBMS performance mechanisms, parallel processing and controlled replication, and redesign of application program logic to allow data access through in-memory tables rather than complex joins, for example.

  ☑ Implement Database Integrity Controls, except where they might preclude Information Producers from entering accurate or complete data, such as having an incomplete valid values list or, too small a field for long text values.

  ☑ Implement the Integrity Rules of the Relational Model if the DBMS is a relational database system.

☑ Implement triggers to test business rules not appropriate to be implemented at the DBMS level.

NOTE To implement business rules at the DBMS level, you must ensure that the integrity constraint is not violatable. If there are exceptions to the rule, those exceptions will never be allowed to be captured without modifying the database schema.

☑ Control replicated data where distributed databases are required for performance.

☑ Ensure replicated databases have identical data element names, definitions, valid value sets, and business rule specifications.

☑ Ensure operational database is used by the application system of immediate requirement (a new application is developed that requires this information), and is used by *all* subsequent application systems requiring information from this Business Resource or Information Subject Area.

☑ Ensure Strategic Databases do not need to transform data from its operational source into different valid value sets for the strategic database except for where data mining requires this for proper data analysis. Valid value sets for base data should remain identical between the Operational Record of Reference and the Strategic Record of Reference. Data may be aggregated into new derived attributes, but should be defined consistently with source data inputs that need summarization. They should only require date- and time-stamping of records from their Record-of-Origin or Record-of-Reference Database at its source.

The next section outlines the six process steps to assess Information Product Specifications and Information Architecture Quality.

TIQM P1 Process Steps: Assess Information Product Specifications and Architecture Quality

The purpose of this assessment is to measure the Quality of the Information Product Specifications, including data names, definitions, business rule specifications, valid value sets, and the Information Models and Database Designs.

The end purpose is to ensure that the Business and Systems Professionals can communicate clearly among themselves and across organizational boundaries and that the databases that house the Enterprise's Knowledge are stable, flexible, used, and reused effectively.

The process steps are illustrated in Figure 4-2.

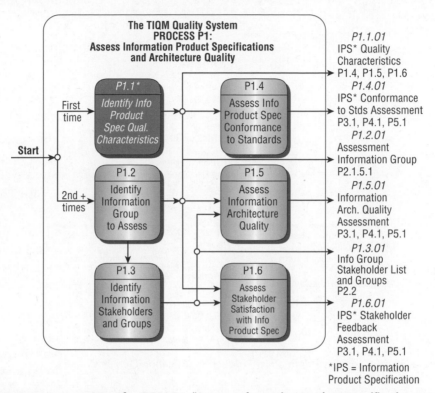

Figure 4-2: Process Steps for TIQM P1. "Assess Information Product Specifications and Architecture Quality."

Step P1.1: Identify Information Product Specification Quality Characteristics

This step identifies the set of Quality Characteristics that the organization should standardize for measuring Quality of all Data Definition and the Information Architecture that represents the Enterprise Information Requirements about a given Business Resource, also called an Information Subject Area.

This is a one-time activity that may be updated over time, based on the nature of the various Information Types required by the organization.

Objective of Step P1.1

The goal is to identify the Critical-to-Quality (CTQ) Characteristics, illustrated in Figure 4-3, for data definition and Information Architecture (Information Models and Database designs) that will enable efficient and standardized assessment of Information Product Specification (IPS) quality and to ensure that Data Definition and Information Architecture are correct, complete, clear, and structurally sound.

See Figure 4-3 that illustrates the process step, TIQM P1.1, participants, inputs, outputs and techniques and tools for this step.

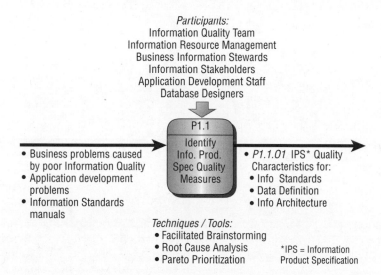

Figure 4-3: P1.1 Identify Information Product Specification Quality Characteristics.

Inputs to Step P1.1

- **Business problems caused by poor Quality Information:** Used to identify Root Causes of Information Product Specifications failure.

- **Application development, maintenance, and use problems caused by poor Quality Information:** Used to identify Root Causes of Information Product Specifications process failure.

- **Information Standards and Guidelines:** Used to identify Information Standards requiring Quality Assessment or requiring enhancement.

Outputs of Step P1.1

- *P1.1.O1:* Information Product Specification Quality Characteristics for:
  - Information Standards Quality
  - Data Name, Definition, and Business Rule Specification Quality
  - Information Architecture (Information Model and Database Design) Quality Characteristics

NOTE Use the section "Quality Characteristics of Information Product Specifications and Information Architecture" earlier in the chapter as your baseline and modify and/or extend it to identify CTQ IPS Quality Characteristics for your enterprise.

Participants and Roles in Step P1.1

Table 4-1: Participants and Roles in P1.1, Identify Information Product Specification CTQ Quality Characteristics.

PARTICIPANT	IQ ACTIVITY ROLE
Information Quality Team	Led by the Information Resource Quality Specialist, facilitates the discovery and documentation of the required Information Product Specification (IPS) CTQ Quality Characteristics.
Information Resource Management Team	Accountable for identifying and defining all Information Product Specification Attributes as part of the Information Resource data, and for establishing effective Information Standards. They develop Subject-Oriented Information Models that reflect the Enterprise Requirements for information about a specific Business Resource. They assist in identifying the CTQ (Critical-to-Quality) Information Product Specification Quality Characteristics.
Business Information Stewards	Subject matter experts who have been appointed to ensure the quality of the business Information Product Specification. Here, they assist in identifying the Critical-to-Quality Information Product Specifications Quality Characteristics to meet the needs of *all* Information Stakeholders.
Information Stakeholders	Information Producers and Knowledge Workers who create and who apply Information in their work. They assist in identifying the Critical-to-Quality Information Product Specifications Quality Characteristics to help them understand the meaning of Information and perform their Value Work effectively.

(continued)

Table 4-1 *(continued)*

PARTICIPANT	IQ ACTIVITY ROLE
Application Development Staff	Information Systems Professionals who capture requirements, design application systems, and who develop the systems. They assist in identifying the CTQ Information Product Specifications Quality Characteristics required for them to develop applications with quality.
Database Designers	Information Systems Professionals who translate Information Models into Enterprise-Strength Database designs. They assist in identifying the CTQ Information Product Specifications Quality Characteristics required to develop stable, flexible, and reused databases.

P1.1 Identify Information Product Specification Quality Characteristics: Process Steps and Activities

Note that this process step is conducted one time to identify Information Product Specifications CTQ Quality Characteristics that will be used by subsequent P1 Information Product Specifications assessments. These will be enhanced over time as the organization matures.

P1.1.1. Assemble the participants who represent all Information Stakeholder areas, led by the Information Resource Quality Specialist.

P1.1.2. Review the input documentation to identify Critical Information Resource data (metadata) about information that makes up the Information Product Specifications. Identify the Critical-to-Quality (CTQ) Information Product Specification attributes from the following lists and in the section "Quality Characteristics of Information Product Specifications and Information Architecture" earlier in the chapter.

P1.1.3. Identify any additional CTQ Information Product Specification Quality Characteristics that may be unique to your industry or business.

P1.1.4. Compile the list of CTQ Information Product Specification Quality Characteristics in your Information Resource Quality Standards and Guidelines in your Information Repository.

P1.1.5. Define the long-term and near-term Quality Standards and Guidelines for each of the Information Product Specifications Quality Characteristics.

Guidelines

You can find a comprehensive set of Information Resource Quality Characteristics (Data definition and information architecture) in *Improving Data Warehouse and Business Information Quality*, pages 87–118.[9]

At a minimum, the Information Product Specification Quality Characteristics should address the characteristics in the discussion under the earlier section, "Quality Characteristics of Information Product Specifications and Information Architecture."

Step P1.2: Identify Information Group to Assess

This step identifies a set of Entity Types and Attributes important to the Enterprise to measure its Information Product Specification Quality. This will generally be the data for a subsequent P2 Assessment of Information Content and presentation quality.

TIP Take a Pareto approach to selecting Information Groups based on importance to the enterprise and costs of process failure and Customer alienation. The information should be recognized as critical to the Enterprise by the Executives and where the degree and costs of poor quality are likely to be high. Follow TIQM Process P3.3 in Chapter 6 to develop estimates of costs of poor quality of various Information Groups and then to measure the direct costs of poor quality information.

Objective of P1.2

The goal is to select an important group of information for assessment where poor quality can cause significant process failure, and with it high costs of failure. The TIQM P1 Assessment of Information Product Specification Quality seeks to determine if the IPS quality enables correct, complete, and clear understanding of the meaning of data so that all Information Stakeholders understand the meaning of the information and that all processes that require the information can function properly.

Figure 4-4 illustrates the Process step to identify Information Groups to assess with inputs, outputs, participants and roles in P1.2.

Inputs to Step P1.2

- **Business problems caused by Poor Quality IPS Information:** As identified by Knowledge Workers
- **Application problems caused by Poor Quality IPS Information:** As identified by Business or Systems Professionals

This step analyzes the various Information Quality problems to develop Pareto Diagrams of relative importance and with Costs of Poor Quality Information to confirm them.

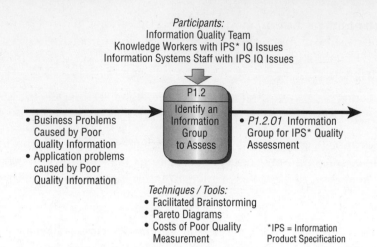

Figure 4-4: P1.2 Identify Information Group to Assess.

Outputs of Step P1.2

▪ *P1.2.O1* **Information Group for Information Product Specifications Quality Assessment:** The list of entity types and attributes to measure Information Product Specifications quality. See Figure 4-5.

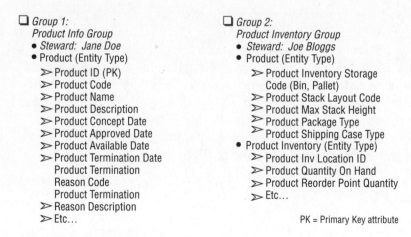

Figure 4-5: Sample Information Groups

Participants and Roles in Step P1.2

Table 4-2: Participant Roles in P1.2 Identify Information Group for Assessment.

PARTICIPANT	IQ ACTIVITY ROLE
Information Quality Team	Led by the Information Resource Quality Specialist, facilitates the identification of various Information Groups of information in which to conduct an Information Product Specifications Quality Assessment.
Information Resource Management Team	Accountable for identifying and defining all Information Product Specification Attributes and documenting them in the Repository or Data Dictionary. They are also responsible for development of the Information Model to be assessed.
Knowledge Workers with Information Product Specifications Quality Issues	Business Professionals or Managers who have identified existing Information Quality problems, either in content or in difficulties in understanding the meaning of the Information they require or share. Here they identify potential candidates for Information Product Specifications (and possibly content and presentation) Quality.
Information Systems staff	Information Systems Professionals who define requirements, design application systems, and who develop the systems or Database Designers who develop the physical databases. They assist in identifying potential Information Groups where significant issues exist.

P1.2 Identify Information Group for Information Product Specification Quality Measures: Process Steps and Activities

P1.2.1 Review existing documented IQ problems.

P1.2.2 Develop a survey to ask Business Management and Knowledge Workers to identify IQ problems you may not be aware of.

P1.2.3 Assemble the Managers and Knowledge Workers together to develop a relative significance of problems in the Information Product Specification or Content and Presentation Quality.

P1.2.4 If necessary, conduct a Cost of Poor Quality study. See Process Steps P3.2 "Calculate Information Production Capability Costs" and P3.3 "Calculate Poor Quality Information Costs."

P1.2.5 Brainstorm and plan a schedule to begin assessing the quality of the Information Product Specifications based on the relative importance, from most to next-most important.

TIP   Select and sequence the first three Information Groups to assess. After each Information Product Specifications assessment, study what you have learned. If there are systemic IQ issues with the Information Product Specification Quality, improve the Information Development and Data Definition processes.

Guidelines

The Information Groups should have cohesiveness among the entity types and attributes. The sample Information Groups in Figure 4-5 illustrate a group of descriptive information about Products that will be of broad interest to the Enterprise, while the second group illustrates Product Inventory with physical stacking patterns that will be of more limited interest, that is, to a smaller set of Information Stakeholder areas.

Step P1.3: Identify Information Stakeholders and Groups

This step identifies those Information Stakeholders who may participate in assessing the quality of the Information Product Specifications. Stakeholders participating in the assessments should not have been part of the Data Definition Team that defined the data to be assessed.

Objective of Step P1.3

The goal is to identify the "Stakeholders" of an Information Group, including internal and external Information Consumers and internal or external information producers.

The Information Consumers, as "Customers" of the Information are the ones who determine the Quality Requirements for the information. The Information Producers as the Suppliers of the Information must have a common understanding of the meaning of the Information they create. The Information Producers must also understand the Information Quality Requirements of their Customers and must have the expert Knowledge in the Information Product Specifications for the Information they produce.

Step P1.3 identifies the various Information Stakeholder groups (job roles) who create, update, and/or apply the Information Product Specifications (data name, definition, valid value set, and business rule specification) you are assessing. In the subsequent step P1.6, you will select specific individual Stakeholders from the different business areas to provide feedback as to the completeness, correctness, and clarity of understanding of the meaning of data to enable them to perform their processes effectively and efficiently.

Figure 4-6 illustrates the step for Identifying Information Stakeholders for assessing Information Product Specifications Quality.

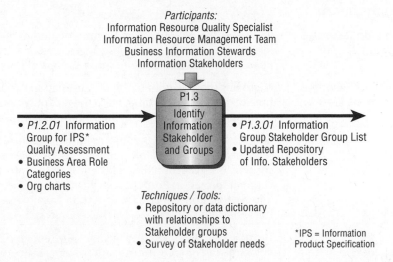

Figure 4-6: Step P1.3 Identify Information Stakeholder Groups and Stakeholders

Inputs to Step P1.3

- **P1.2.O1 Information Group for Information Product Specifications Quality Assessment:** Used to identify key Information Stakeholders by role that need to know the meaning of the Information in the Group to be assessed.

- **Business Area Role Categories:** Used to identify potential Stakeholders with interests in the Information Groups identified.

Outputs of Step P1.3

- **P1.3.O1 Information Group Stakeholder Group List:** Documents the stakeholders by business area and job position role

- **Updated Repository of Information Stakeholders:** Updates to the online repository of Stakeholder job position roles related to the Information Group.

Participants and Roles in Step P1.3

Table 4-3: Participant Roles in P1.3 Identify Information Stakeholders

PARTICIPANT	IQ ACTIVITY ROLE
Information Resource Quality Specialist	Facilitates the discovery and documentation of the Information Stakeholders by Business Area and Job Position or Role to the Information Groups of interest.
Information Resource Management Team	Maintains the documentation of Information Groups and the Stakeholders over time. Here they identify potential business Stakeholders in the Information Group selected.
Business Information Stewards	Require knowledge of the Information Stakeholders' relationship to various Information Groups to ensure continued satisfaction among them with the Information Group Information Product Specifications and with the Information Content and Presentation Quality as well. Here they assist to identify all Stakeholders.
Information Stakeholders	These known Business and Systems Stakeholders assist in identifying other Business and Systems Stakeholders in the Information to assess. The business Information Stakeholders may participate in information model-ing workshops or may also participate independently in the P1.6 Information Stakeholder Assessment of the Information Product Specifications Quality for informa-tion they did not define.

P1.3 Identify Information Stakeholders: Process Steps and Activities

P1.3.1 Assemble the IQ Team participants, including Subject Matter Experts (SME), led by the Information Resource Quality Specialist.

P1.3.2 Brainstorm who might be Stakeholders of the Information Group by business area and job position role. Differentiate between Information producer and Information Consumer roles.

P1.3.3 Document the Stakeholder roles to the Information Group in your repository.

NOTE The Business Information Stewards should take over the ownership of keeping their Stakeholder list current for each Information Group in their care.

Guidelines

Ensure that the Role relationships to the Information Groups are accessible on your intranet. This way, if roles are overlooked, incumbent Stakeholders can get in touch with the applicable Business Information Steward to update the Stakeholder list.

Step P1.4: Assess Information Product Specifications Conformance to Standards

This is the first of three assessments of Information Product Specifications Quality. This process is a formal technical assessment of conformance to well-defined Information Standards and Guidelines.

Objective of Step P1.4

To ensure the Information Product Specification process works properly by assessing Data Names and Definitions for compliance with meaningful Naming and Definition Standards that create a common, consistent business language.

Figure 4-7 illustrates Step P1.4.

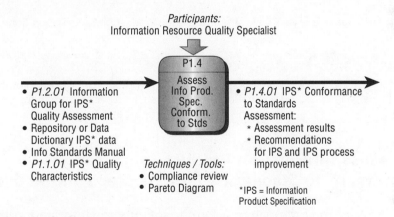

Figure 4-7: Step P1.4 Assess Information Product Specifications Process Step.

Inputs to Step P1.4

- **P1.2.O1 Information Group for Information Product Specifications Quality Assessment:** This identifies the entity types and attributes for Information Product Specifications Quality Assessment.

- **Repository or Data Dictionary Information Product Specification data:** This is the Information Group Information Product Specifications data to assess.

- **P1.1.O1 Information Product Specifications Quality Characteristics:** This is used to identify the Information Product Specification Quality Characteristics to assess.

Outputs of Step P1.4

- ▪ *P1.4.O1* **Information Product Specification Conformance to Standards Assessment:** Assessment results of Data Definition conformance to Information Standards and Guidelines. This includes the raw data of the conformance test results as well as Pareto Diagrams to represent the assessment results.

  - ▪ **P1.4.O1.F1** Business Term Conformance to Standards Assessment

  - ▪ **P1.4.O1.F2** Entity Type Conformance to Standards Assessment

  - ▪ **P1.4.O1.F3** Attribute Conformance to Standards Assessment

  - ▪ **P1.4.O1.F4** Business Rule Conformance to Standards Assessment

  - ▪ **P1.4.O1.F5** Information Product Specifications Assessment Pareto Diagram

Participants and Roles in Step P1.4

Table 4-4: Participant Roles in P1.4 Assess Information Production Specification Conformance to Standards.

PARTICIPANT	IQ ACTIVITY ROLE
Information Resource Quality Specialist	Conducts the Information Product Specification and Information Architecture Quality Assessment and produces the Assessment report and Pareto Diagrams

P1.4 Assess Information Product Specifications Conformance to Standards: Process Steps and Activities

P1.4.1 Review the Information Group to identify the Information Product Specifications to be assessed.

P1.4.2 Transfer the data names (in all forms), definitions, value sets or ranges, and the applicable business rule specifications onto the Information Product Specifications evaluation forms.

- ▪ For Business Term Assessment, use Business Term Conformance to Standards Assessment Form P1.4.O1.F1 for each business term. See Appendix A, Form P1.4.O1.F1 on the book's Web site. Follow the example in the Attribute Conformance to Standards in Figure 4-8 for an example.

- ▪ For Entity Type Assessment, use the Entity Type Conformance to Standards Assessment Form P1.4.O1.F2 for each entity type assessed. See Appendix A, Form P1.4.O1.F2 on the book's Web site. See Figure 4-8 for an example.

> **NOTE** TIQM Form numbers consist of the following format:
>
> **P1.4.O1.F1 where:**
>
> > **P1=The TIQM Process in which this Form is used.**
> >
> > **P1.4=The Step in the Process in which this Form is used.**
> >
> > **O1=The Output of the process step in which the Form is used.**
> >
> > **O1.F1=The number of the Template Form for this Output.**

- For Attribute Assessment use the Attribute Conformance to Standards Assessment Form P1.4.O1.F3 for each Attribute. See Form P1.4.O1.F3 for template on the book's Web site. Figure 4-8 represents a sample documented attribute for assessment. Figure 4-11 illustrates an example Pareto Diagram for attribute assessment results.

P1.4.3 Review the Information Product Specifications against the Information Product Specifications quality characteristic guidelines, established in P1.1.

P1.4.4 Document each Information Product Specifications Characteristic as fully compliant, partially compliant, or non-compliant with reason, as compared to the Information Product Specifications quality characteristic criteria in the Information Standards.

> **NOTE** Page 4 of 4 is intentionally omitted. See Form P1.O4.F3 on the book's Web site at www.wiley.com/go/IQApplied.

> **WARNING** This actual incident of overloading in "Gender Code" was introduced by the "enhancement" software provider to use gender code for its purposes. Do not allow external entities to introduce defects to your enterprise information architecture, no matter how "practical" they may seem to be.

P1.4.5 Develop Pareto Diagrams by error type in order by frequency of errors. See Figure 4-11 for an example.

> **NOTE** This is a technical compliance review that will involve evaluation of conformance to specific standards criteria and some subjective evaluation for certain guidelines criteria. The P1.4 Assessment will be augmented and confirmed by the P1.6 Assessment, which involves the Information Stakeholders and their subject-matter expertise to establish an information "Customer Satisfaction" evaluation.

TIQM® Quality System

Attribute Conformance to Standards Assessment

Attribute ID and Name:	E14A5: Person Gender Code	
Presentation Name(s):	Repository name:	Person Gender Code
	Abbreviated name:	Pers-Gndr-Code
	Screen name:	Gender
	Report name:	Gender
	Database element name:	Pers-Gndr-Code
	Document name:	Gender
Entity Type Attributed To:	Person	
Status and Version:	[X] Working; [ ] Complete; [ ] Recommended; [ ] Published; **Version =** V3	
	Working = Documentation may not be complete **Complete** = Fully documented	
	Recommended = Documentation ready for approval **Published** = Reviewed, approved and in use	
Assessed By:	Joan A. Smith	
Assessor Contact #:	+1 999-555-1212 JAS@company.com	
Date Assessed:	September 25	
Attribute Definition:	The sex of a person.	
Attribute Comments:	Codes include Male and Female and codes that define when the gender cannot be derived from a person's name.	
Attribute Valid Value Set and Code Value Definition:	[List complete set of finite data (code) values here, range of infinite values or examples of text or formatted values] 1 = Male 2 = Female 3 = Initials 4 = Unrecognizable 5 = Ambiguous	
Attribute Business Rules:	A change in Person Gender Code requires a change reason.	
Value Presentation Format:	Person gender code name (Male, Female, Initials, Unrecognizable, Ambiguous)	
Value Storage Format:	Person gender code value (1-5)	

Figure 4-8: Information Product Specifications Attribute Conformance to Standards Documentation P1.4.O1.F3 or an actual list of supposed "Valid Values"

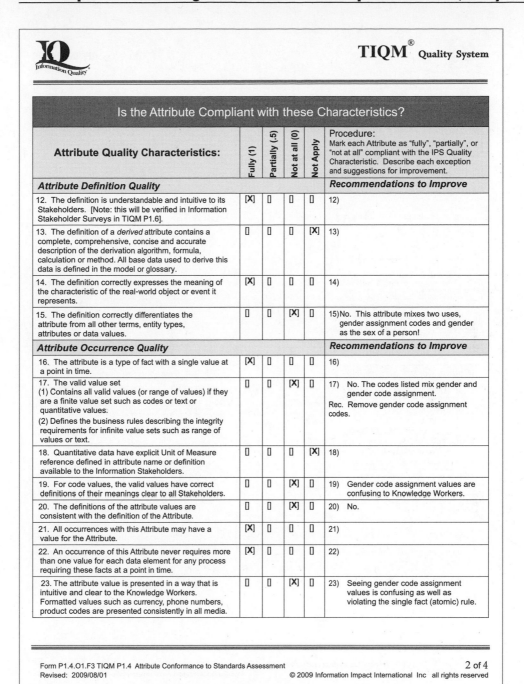

TIQM® Quality System

Is the Attribute Compliant with these Characteristics?				
Attribute Quality Characteristics:	Fully (1)	Partially (.5)	Not at all (0)	Not Apply	Procedure: Mark each Attribute as "fully", "partially", or "not at all" compliant with the IPS Quality Characteristic. Describe each exception and suggestions for improvement.
Attribute Definition Quality					***Recommendations to Improve***
12. The definition is understandable and intuitive to its Stakeholders. [Note: this will be verified in Information Stakeholder Surveys in TIQM P1.6].	[X]	▯	▯	▯	12)
13. The definition of a *derived* attribute contains a complete, comprehensive, concise and accurate description of the derivation algorithm, formula, calculation or method. All base data used to derive this data is defined in the model or glossary.	▯	▯	▯	[X]	13)
14. The definition correctly expresses the meaning of the characteristic of the real-world object or event it represents.	[X]	▯	▯	▯	14)
15. The definition correctly differentiates the attribute from all other terms, entity types, attributes or data values.	▯	▯	[X]	▯	15) No. This attribute mixes two uses, gender assignment codes and gender as the sex of a person!
Attribute Occurrence Quality					***Recommendations to Improve***
16. The attribute is a type of fact with a single value at a point in time.	[X]	▯	▯	▯	16)
17. The valid value set (1) Contains all valid values (or range of values) if they are a finite value set such as codes or text or quantitative values. (2) Defines the business rules describing the integrity requirements for infinite value sets such as range of values or text.	▯	▯	[X]	▯	17) No. The codes listed mix gender and gender code assignment. Rec. Remove gender code assignment codes.
18. Quantitative data have explicit Unit of Measure reference defined in attribute name or definition available to the Information Stakeholders.	▯	▯	▯	[X]	18)
19. For code values, the valid values have correct definitions of their meanings clear to all Stakeholders.	▯	▯	[X]	▯	19) Gender code assignment values are confusing to Knowledge Workers.
20. The definitions of the attribute values are consistent with the definition of the Attribute.	▯	▯	[X]	▯	20) No.
21. All occurrences with this Attribute may have a value for the Attribute.	[X]	▯	▯	▯	21)
22. An occurrence of this Attribute never requires more than one value for each data element for any process requiring these facts at a point in time.	[X]	▯	▯	▯	22)
23. The attribute value is presented in a way that is intuitive and clear to the Knowledge Workers. Formatted values such as currency, phone numbers, product codes are presented consistently in all media.	▯	▯	[X]	▯	23) Seeing gender code assignment values is confusing as well as violating the single fact (atomic) rule.

Form P1.4.O1.F3 TIQM P1.4 Attribute Conformance to Standards Assessment
Revised: 2009/08/01   2 of 4

Figure 4-9: P1.4 Information Product Specifications: Attribute Conformance to Standards Assessment Results (Form P1.4.O1.F3 Page 2)

IQ Information Quality   **TIQM**® Quality System

Are the Attributes Compliant with these Characteristics?					
Attribute Quality Characteristics:	Fully (1)	Partially (.5)	Not at all (0)	Not Apply	Procedure (Mark each Attribute as "fully", "partially", or "not at all" compliant with the IPS Quality Characteristic. Describe each exception and suggestions for improvement.)
Attribute Definition Quality					*Recommendations to Improve*
12. The definition of a derived Attribute contains a complete, comprehensive, concise and accurate description of the derivation algorithm, formula, calculation or method. All base data used to derive this data is defined in the model or glossary.	☐	☐	☐	☐	12)
13. The definition correctly expresses the meaning of the characteristic of the real-world object or event it describes.	☐	☐	☐	☐	13)
14. The Attribute is an inherent characteristic of the real-world object or event it describes.	☐	☐	☐	☐	14)
15. The definition precisely differentiates the Attribute from all other terms, entity types, Attributes, or data values.	☐	☐	☐	☐	15)
Attribute Occurrence Quality					*Recommendations to Improve*
16. The Attribute is a type of fact with a single value at a point in time for an occurrence.	☐	☐	☐	☐	16)
17. The valid value set: (1) Contains all valid values if they are a finite value set such as codes. (2) Defines the business rules describing the integrity requirements for infinite value sets such as range of values or text.	☐	☐	☐	☐	17)
18. For code values, the valid values have correct definitions of their meanings clear to all stakeholders.	☐	☐	☐	☐	18)
19. All occurrences of this Attribute may contain a value for each data element.	☐	☐	☐	☐	19)
20. An occurrence of this Attribute or subtype never requires more than one value for each data element for any process requiring these facts at a point in time.	☐	☐	☐	☐	20)

Figure 4-10: P1.4 Information Product Specifications Attribute Conformance to Standards Assessment Results (Form P1.4.O1.F3 Page 3).

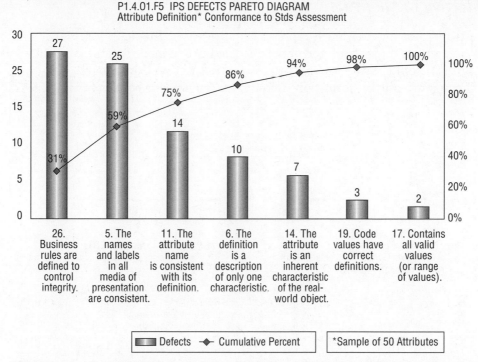

Figure 4-11: P1.4 Information Product Specifications Attribute Conformance to Standards Assessment Results Pareto Diagram (Form P1.4.O1.F5)

The Pareto Diagram lists the non-conformance defect counts in order of most frequent to least frequent. It is accompanied by a cumulative percentage of defects until all (100%) are accounted for.

NOTE The Information Resource Quality Specialist must be absolutely independent of the process that defined the data and must be objective to ensure an unbiased assessment.

P1.4.7 Identify recommendations for corrective maintenance and for Process Improvement as necessary. Document these in the assessment forms themselves P1.4.O1.F1, F2, and F3, respectively.

Step P1.5: Assess Information Architecture Quality

This second Information Product Specifications assessment measures the quality of an Information Model and its resulting Database Design.

Objective of Step P1.5

To ensure Information Models represent enterprise requirements for information within a given subject of information; and to ensure that operational database design is flexible, stable, and reused by all Information Consumers.

The step to Assess Information Architecture Quality can be seen in Figure 4-12.

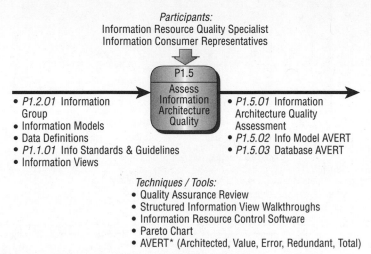

Figure 4-12: P1.5 Assess Information Architecture Quality.

Inputs to Step P1.5

- *P1.2.O1* **Information Group for Information Product Specifications Quality Assessment:** This identifies the Entity Types and Attributes for Information Model and Database Design Quality Assessment.

- **Hi-Level Business Information Model:** The Business Information Models to be assessed.

- **Detailed Operational Information Model:** The Business Information Models to be assessed.

- **Data Definitions:** The defined meaning of the data in the Model(s).

- *P1.1.O1* **Information Standards and Guidelines:** This identifies the Information Product Specifications Characteristics to Assess.

- *P1.5.I1.F1* **Subject Information Views:** Additional views of the Information Product Specifications to evaluate against the completeness of attributes identified and defined in the Information Model. See Form *P1.5.O1.F1* on the book's Web site.

NOTE These Subject Information Views must be independent and different Information Views from those used in the development of the Information Model, but within the subject of information in the model. See Template of an Information View Form (P1.5.I1.F1) on the book's Web site.

Outputs of Step P1.5

- *P1.5.O1.F1* **Information Architecture Quality Assessment:** Documents the results of the Information Model and Database Design Quality Assessment. Use Form P1.5.O1.F1 in Appendix A on the book's Web site.

- *P1.5.O2.F1* **Information Model AVERT Diagram:** Documents the degree of reuse of Entity Types and Attributes in the Information Model, illustrated in Figure 4-13. See Form P1.5.O2.F1 in Appendix A on the book's Web site.

- *P1.5.O3.F1* **Database AVERT Diagram:** Documents the degree of reuse of Operational Database Files and Attributes in the Database in Figure 4-16. See Form P1.5.O3.F1 Appendix A on the book's Web site.

Participants and Roles in TIQM P1.5

Table 4-5: Participant Roles in P1.5. Assess Information Architecture Quality.

PARTICIPANT	IQ ACTIVITY ROLE
Information Resource Quality Specialist	The Information Resource Quality Specialist conducts the Assessment of the Information Model and Database Design Quality with its report and Pareto Diagrams. This role also maintains the AVERT Diagram of Information Object Reuse by application system projects.
Information Consumer Representatives	These Information Producers and Knowledge Workers, who are independent of the teams that developed the Information Model and defined the information, participate in the Information Model and Database Design Assessment by developing additional Information Views of information they require to evaluate the completeness of the Information Model and Database design.

P1.5 Assess Information Architecture Quality: Process Steps and Activities

P1.5.1 Collect Information Model diagram to be assessed. There are two assessment scenarios to measure:

- A status quo, "legacy" Information Model that represents the old processes. This will document the status quo Information Modeling Process Quality.

- A recently produced Information Model that represents your current information modeling process quality. This represents a baseline for an architected approach to developing "Enterprise-Strength" Information Models and Database designs.

P1.5.2 Gather Information Model and Information Product Specifications Quality Characteristics to assess. These should be documented in the Information Standards, which Information Architects use to develop or modify Information Models.

P1.5.3 Identify additional Information Stakeholder representatives to develop additional Information Views of the subject of the Information Model to be assessed. An example Information View is shown in Figure 4-13.

INFORMATION VIEW:
Employee Training Transcript

Prepared by: *Diane Thomas*

☐ Process   ☐ Query   ☒ Report   ☐ Decision   ☐ KPI = Key Performance Indicator / CBI = Core Business Indicator
View name: *Employee Training Transcript*

Information Consumer for this Information: (Department/Role): *Managers*

What is the objective or use of this information: *To monitor staff development*

Frequency: How often would this query/report/process be produced or executed:
☐ Day   ☐ Week   ☐ Month   ☒ Qtr   ☐ Year   ☐ Demand   ☐ Other (explain)

What data is needed / included? (Attributes / Data Elements) | Description (or calculation/derivation if calculated or derived)

Employee Id/Name   *Course Description*   *Planned Completion Date*   *Actual Completion Date*

_____   _____   _____   _____

_____   _____   _____   _____

_____   _____   _____   _____

*Note: Attach sample format of the information (query/form/report)

Figure 4-13: P1.5 Information View Example "Employee Training Transcript"

NOTE To prevent bias, ensure that the Information Stakeholders selected were not part of the Information Modeling or Data Definition Team that developed the Information Model to be assessed. They may come from the same Business Areas as the Modeling Team members, but they should be unbiased by the work done to create the Model.

P1.5.4 Information Stakeholders develop additional Information Views. These will be used to identify if there are important Entity Types or Attributes missing from the model.

P1.5.5 Review the model for the following quality characteristics as outlined in the section "Information Architecture Quality Characteristics" at the beginning of this chapter:

- Entity Type-to-Entity-Type Relationship
- Attribute-to-Entity-Type Relationship
- Entity-Type-to-Entity-Subtype Relationship
- Entity-Life-Cycle-State

Guidelines for TIQM P1.5

Assess the intuitiveness of the Information Model to represent the real-world objects and events the organization needs to know to evaluate the Stability, Flexibility, and Reuse of the Information Model. Quality characteristics include:

- **Stability of the Information Model and Database design.** The model and design should NOT change as new products are added, unless there is a Strategic Enterprise Mission shift, such as moving from discrete manufacturing to process manufacturing. Basic changes to the Subject Information Model should be additive only — NO modification to the existing structure of the Subject Information Model or Database design.

NOTE If you must add attributes to the model and database design required for *current* operational or strategic processes, they are considered *defects* of fact-type completeness in the original Information Model and/or Database Design.

- **Flexibility of the Information Model and Database Design.** The model and design should have very little change if business processes are reengineered. The model and design should be non-dependent on the *way* in which processes are performed. For example, if you change your manufacturing production process, it should not require you to have to change your Information Models or Database Designs.

- **Reuse of the Information Model and Database design is High Quality.** The structure of the Information Model (that represents *enterprise* information requirements and the inherent relationships among the objects and events the enterprise needs to know about) and the database design should be reused across all operational processes of the enterprise unless there is a business reason for not sharing directly. For example, manufacturing production processes capture information required for quality management that may not be needed in the back-office or front-office processes.

Figure 4-14 illustrates an Information Model Quality Assessment result.

Only one standard (3) "driven from High-level Subject Information Model") was fully met, but only partial compliance with all other Characteristics.

P1.5.6 Review the additional Information Views to identify additional required entity Types, Attributes, or Relationships or correct Names, Definitions, or Relationships.

> **NOTE** The assessor should not make changes to the Information Model itself. All feedback should go back to the Information Modeling Team and the Information Architect responsible for the Information Model and the Business Information Stewards responsible for stewarding the information within their scope of work.

P1.5.7 Develop an AVERT spreadsheet that documents Data Development reuse and Scrap and Rework of Information Model components. See Figure 4-15 for an example of the patterns to look for in application development "quality," that minimizes the development of functionally biased Information Models.

Document the number and percent of Entity Types and Attribute Types (and Database files and Data elements) on a project-by-project control chart. Measure in the following categories:

- *Architected*: Entity Types and Attributes defined for the first time following quality Information Standards. Newly architected Entity Types and Attributes are considered "new" if they will replace obsolete legacy Entity Types and or Attributes.

> **NOTE** These Entity Types and Attributes are considered Quality, if future modeling projects within this Subject Area retain and use them with no modification or with only cosmetic modification, such as grammar that does not alter the definition.

- *Value:* Entity Types and Attributes reused *without* modification.

> **NOTE** The goal is to approach zero-defects by having the majority of your Entity Types and Attributes be reused without any modification or having to define them as new, Architected Attributes because of failure to discover them in the initial modeling project where Requirements were overlooked.

IQ Information Quality

TIQM® Quality System

Is the Architecture Compliant with these Characteristics?					
Information Architecture Quality Characteristics:	Fully	Partially	Not at all	Not apply	Procedure: Mark each Characteristic as "fully", "partially", or "not at all" compliant with the IPS Quality Characteristic. Describe each exception and suggestions to improve.
General Architecture Quality					**Recommendations to Improve**
1. Operational Information Models and Databases are used directly by operational processes, activities and application systems with no or insignificant structural change. Only additive change is required for entity types with attributes not able to be discovered at the time of the original Information Model development.	☐	[X]	☐	☐	1) Some entity types are redundant with ERP System files, whose processes are not able to be changed. Rec: Create enterprise model entity types as record-of-origin/reference.
2. Reengineering of processes causes minimal impact on Information Models and Database Designs. Generally the only modifications required are to eliminate paper trail entity types or attributes that controlled paper trail processes that are being eliminated by the reengineering.	☐	[X]	☐	☐	2) See number 1 above.
Operational Information Model Quality					**Recommendations to Improve**
3. The detailed Operational Information Model is driven from the Hi-level Subject Information Model.	[X]	☐	☐	☐	3)
4. Inherent relationships of an Entity Type to its Attributes. Birth date, for example, is not an inherent characteristic of "Employee." A person does not have a birth date because they are an employee, but because they are a member of "homo sapiens," inheriting the characteristic of mammals that give birth to their offspring live. Birth date is an Attribute of a Person, inherited by Employee, because an Employee is a Person.	☐	[X]	☐	☐	4) Some attributes are not inherent to the type associated with, but are inherent in the relationship of this entity type to another. Rec: Create an associative relationship entity type and associate the attributes to it.
5. The information model contains all entity types and a strong majority of all Attributes needed to be known by all Knowledge Workers who need Information about the entities within that resource area.	☐	[X]	☐	☐	5) 3 Entity types and 34 attributes were identified in post-model development review. Rec: Improve Information Modeling process to add more Information Views from broader representation of Stakeholders.
6. The Information Model contains the significant majority of all Attributes or facts about real-world objects or events required by any Knowledge Worker to successfully perform their Value Work.	☐	[X]	☐	☐	6) See # 5 above.
7. The Information Model contains *all identified* Attributes required to identify trends and patterns in strategic or tactical databases, as are found in the data warehouse databases and data marts. This is true for additional Attributes that may become known to Information Producers in their natural jobs, or for Attributes that must be identified by external third party Information Brokers.	☐	[X]	☐	☐	7) Includes about 90 % of all attributes. See number 5 above.

Figure 4-14: *P1.5.O1.F4.2* Sample Operational Information Model Quality Assessment, Page 2

- *Error*: Entity Types and Attributes had to be modified in order to be acceptable.

NOTE For all modifications, to Entity Types or Attributes, document the reason for the modification (poorly named, defined, business rule specifications, value sets, for other defects). See template Form *P1.5.O1.F4.2* on the book's Web site.

- *Redundant*: Entity Types and Attributes were defined in a modeling session, but they already existed in the earlier model iterations.

P1.5.8 Create an AVERT Reuse Diagram for Information Model Objects by projects over time. See Figure 4-15.

AVERT REUSE CHART									
Project Number: P0117			Completion Date: 9 April						
Project Name: Database Marketing			Project Manager: Kay Black						
Information Reuse by Application (AVERT) metrics (reuse over time)		Entity IPU		File IPU		Attribute IPU		Element IPU	
		Ent	Ent%	File	File%	Attr	Attr%	Elem	Elem%
A	1. *Architected:* Newly defined Objects (should go down)	58	36%	35	30%	247	40%	82	26%
V	2. *Value:* Objects Reused Without Change (should go up)	97	60%	13	11%	344	55%	121	38%
E	3. *Error:* Objects Modified (give reason) (should approach zero%)	5	3%	29	25%	24	4%	91	29%
R	4. *Redundant:* New but Redundant Objects (should approach zero%)	2	1%	40	34%	9	1%	21	7%
T	Total Information Product Units	162	100%	117	100%	624	100%	315	100%
	"Obsolete" legacy objects deleted (Should increase briefly, then decrease as objects are replaced)	Ent IPU		File IPU		Attr IPU		Elem IPU	

Figure 4-15: Sample *P1.5.O2.F1* Information Architecture AVERT Information Product Unit Reuse for Database Marketing Project

A. Count the number of Entity Types (58) and Attributes (247) that have been identified and defined new for the first time *and that have not been required in the past*.

V. Count the number of Entity Types (97) and Attributes (344) that are reused without any substantive modification. Only minor grammatical or format changes are required.

E. Count the number of entity types (5) and attributes (24) that had to be modified with a substantive (corrective) change. Document reason for the change (new business requirement or poor original definition).

R. Count the number of redundant entity types (2), and attributes (9) newly defined but found to be redundant with other entity types or attributes. Document the reason for the change (unaware of existing objects or original object so poorly defined it had to be scrapped).

T. Add the total number of entity types (162) in the A, V, E, R rows and place the total in the Entity IPU column (162); add the total number of attributes in the A, V, E, R, rows and place the total in the attribute IPU column (624).

NOTE The spreadsheet can calculate the percentage of each row.

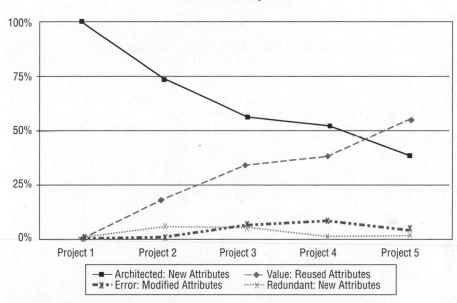

INFORMATION MODEL RE-USE QUALITY:
AVERT Redundancy Chart

Figure 4-16: Sample *P1.5.O2.F2* Information Model AVERT Diagram. Project 5 Is the Database Marketing Project.

P1.5.9 Update an AVERT Reuse Diagram for Database Objects by projects over time. See Figure 4-17 for an example of broken Database Design process.

A. Count the number of Database Files (35) and Data Elements (82) identified and defined new for the first time that have not been required in the past.

V. Count the number of Database Files (13) and Data Elements (121) that are reused without any substantive modification. Only grammatical or format changes are required.

E. Count the number of Database Files (29) and Data Elements (91) that had to be modified with a substantive (corrective) change. Document the reason for the change (new business requirement or poor original definition).

R. Count the number of redundant Database Files (40) and Data Elements newly defined (21) but found to be redundant with other Entity Types or Attributes. Document the reason for the change (unaware of existing objects or original object so poorly defined it had to be scrapped).

T. Add the total number of Database Files in the A, V, E, R rows and place the total in the File IPU column (117); add the total number of elements in the A, V, E, R, rows and place the total in the element IPU column (315).

NOTE The spreadsheet can calculate the percentage of each row.

Figure 4-17 illustrates Broken Data Definition and Information Modeling Processes.

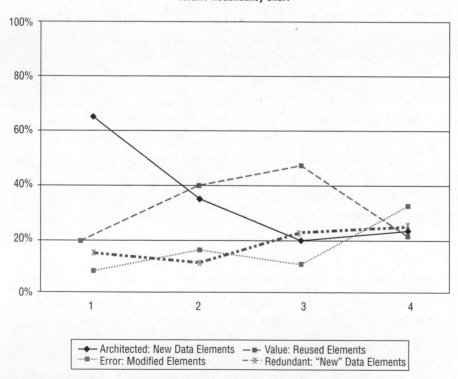

DATABASE RE-USE QUALITY:
AVERT Redundancy Chart

- ◆ Architected: New Data Elements
- ▪ Error: Modified Elements
- ▪ Value: Reused Elements
- ✳ Redundant: "New" Data Elements

Figure 4-17: Sample *P1.5.O2.F2* Database Reuse AVERT Diagram

The four projects in the AVERT diagram in Figure 4-17 illustrate a broken data development process. No application system was able to be developed with more than 50 percent of the data elements being reused without modification. Part of the problem includes ERP Software Files that are not Enterprise Strength, but are not able to be replaced, so redundant Database Files with redundant data in the ERP System.

For Process Improvements to eliminate the problems here, see Chapter 15, "IQ Applied to Information Management and Information Systems Engineering."

Step P1.6: Assess Stakeholder Satisfaction with Information Product Specification Data

Objective of Step P1.6

The goal is to ensure that the Data Definition Process is producing correct, complete, and clear definitions with the consensus of the Information Stakeholders, so they are able to create or apply information correctly and effectively.

Figure 4-18 provides a graphic of TIQM P1.6 with its Inputs, Outputs, Participants, and Techniques.

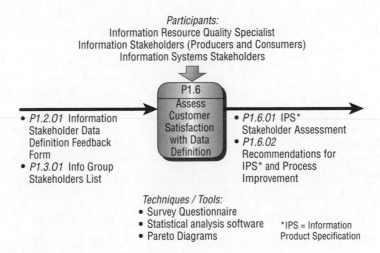

Figure 4-18: P1.6 Assess Stakeholder Satisfaction with Information Product Specification.

Inputs to Step P1.6

- **P1.2.O1. Information Group for Information Product Specifications Quality Assessment:** The set of information for Customer Satisfaction evaluation

- **P1.3.O1 Information Group Stakeholders List:** The list of Stakeholders from which feedback will be solicited

Outputs of Step P1.6

- *P1.6.O1.F1* **Information Product Specifications Stakeholder Assessment:** The results of each Information Stakeholder's Assessment.

- *P1.6.O2* **Recommendations for Information Product Specifications and Information Product Specifications Process Improvement:** Recommendations for enhancement of the data definition in the assessment or recommendations for improvement of the data definition process. A Process Improvement initiative should follow the Plan-Do-Check/Study-Act cycle as defined in TIQM Process P4 "Improve Information Process Quality" in Chapter 7.

Participants and Roles in TIQM P1.6

Table 4-6: Participant Roles in P1.6 Assess Stakeholder Satisfaction with Information Product Specifications

PARTICIPANT	IQ ACTIVITY ROLE
Information Resource Quality Specialist	Led by the Information Resource Quality Specialist, facilitates the P1.6 Information Stakeholder evaluation survey of the Information Product Specifications assessed.
Information Stakeholders	These Information Producers and Knowledge Workers, who are independent of the teams that developed the Information Model and defined the Information, participate in the Information Product Specifications IQ assessment by completing an Information Product Specifications Customer Evaluation survey, illustrated in Figure 4-21.
Information Systems Stakeholders, Including IRM, DB Designers and Application Development	Information Systems Professionals, who are independent of the teams that developed the Information Model and defined the information, provide a separate evaluation of the Information Product Specifications for the Information Group.

Step P1.6 Assess Stakeholder Satisfaction with Information Product Specification: Process Steps and Guidelines

P1.6.1. Identify 10 to 25 A-Priority (Critical-to-Quality) Attributes about the Information Group that are the most important to operational processes for Information Product Specification assessment.

TIP Separate the assessment of the technical material and part specification data and the descriptive material information (part or material description, price, for example) from the technical material information. There are different Stakeholders who depend on those two distinctly different Information Groups.

P1.6.2. Compile the data names, including abbreviations if any, definitions, valid value sets, and business rule specification on the "Information Stakeholder Information Product Specifications Assessment" Form. (See Template Form P1.6.O1.F1 on the book's Web site.) See Figure 4-19 for an example of documented Information Stakeholder form, ready for assessment.

TIP Use the Template Information Product Specifications Assessment Form P1.4.O1.F3 Attribute Conformance to Standards Assessment on the book's Web site and customize it if necessary, to gather Information Stakeholder feedback about the names and definitions, value sets, and business rules.

TIP Conduct this assessment on your own information first, then conduct it on other critical information.

P1.6.3. Select a sample of Information Stakeholders to evaluate the names and definitions, value sets, and business rule specifications for name appropriateness, definition accuracy, completeness, and clarity, as per the form.

P1.6.4. Send out the questionnaires with instructions ahead of the scheduled meeting and assemble the Information Stakeholders or conduct online meetings with the Stakeholders.

NOTE Ensure that the Stakeholders do not perceive the Assessment as a *people performance* measure. This assessment measures the effectiveness of the *information definition process – ONLY.*

P1.6.5. Compile the evaluation results and report them to key Stakeholders, Including Process Owners who might need to improve the Information Definition Process, if warranted. And of course, the feedback should be used to improve the actual definitions and business rule specifications as necessary.

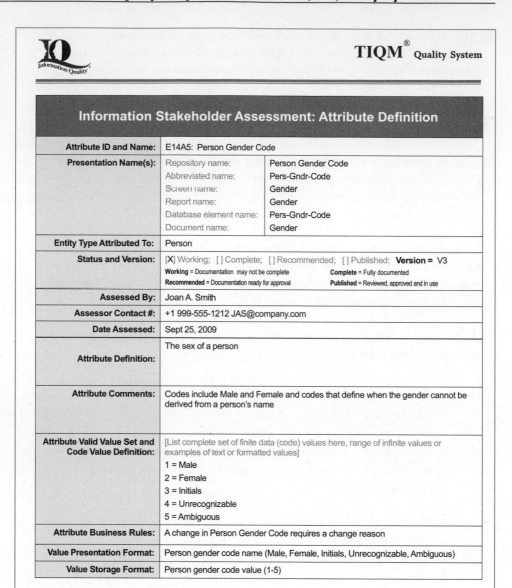

Figure 4-19: Sample Information Stakeholder Assessment Form for Attribute "Gender Code"

NOTE Ensure that the Stakeholders are NOT to look for the *perfect* definition, but the "I can live with it" definition. Minor tweaking is allowed, but major definition (content) change must go through the Information Definition Change Process.

If an item is rated "needs improvement," the assessor should identify the reason and suggest a possible improvement.

NOTE The goal is to have *complete, correct, clear, and consensus* definitions such that the enterprise can communicate clearly to eliminate process failure caused by *misinterpretation* of information.

TIP Use the first Attribute in the Information Group as a live practice opportunity for the first time assessors. Have people independently make their assessment of this Attribute. Then have people describe why they assessed the Characteristic the way they did. Use this as a teaching opportunity to ensure that the Stakeholders are comfortable with the assessment guidelines.

P1.6.6. Use the feedback to Improve the Information Definition Process, if warranted. Also use the feedback to improve the actual definitions and business rule specifications as necessary.

P1.6.7. Develop a Pareto Diagram of the Assessment results summary across the various Stakeholders for all data definition and specifications assessed. See Figure 4-20 for an assessment result of defect in IPS of "Customer Profile" Attributes by a Customer Information Stakeholder.

Because Information Consumers and Knowledge Workers are the "Customers" of Information, they are the ones to assess it for meeting their needs to accomplish their work or make their decisions. This critical assessment describes how well data is defined for and understandable to the Business Information Stakeholders who create the information and those who require the information in order to perform their work effectively.

NOTE If you have Poor Quality Data Definitions and Business Rule Specifications, call attention to the specific problems and identify Process Improvements. Poor Definitions and Quality Standards can cause *quality problems* in your internal processes and communications.

Figure 4-20 illustrates a sample Knowledge Worker assessment of the IPS for "Gender Code."

TIQM® QUALITY SYSTEM

Is the Attribute Compliant with these Characteristics?					
Attribute Quality Characteristics:	Satisfactory	Needs Improvement	Do not Know	Does Not Apply	**Procedure:** Mark each Attribute as "fully", "partially", or "not at all" compliant with the IPS Quality Characteristic. Describe each exception and suggestions for improvement
Attribute Quality					*Recommendations to Improve*
1. Business name is understandable and appropriate	[X]	[]	[]	[]	1)
2. The abbreviated names are understandable	[]	[X]	[]	[]	2) *Some are confusing* *Rec: Spell out "Gender"*
3. Data names in different contexts are consistent	[]	[X]	[]	[]	3) *Not consistent enough* *Rec: Spell out "Gender"*
4. The definition is complete, correct and clear	[X]	[]	[]	[]	4)
5. The name and definition are consistent	[X]	[]	[]	[]	5)
6. List of valid values, or codes is complete & defined clearly	[]	[X]	[]	[]	6) . *Some values displayed are NOT gender values.* *Rec: Remove extraneous gender values. NOT characteristics of person. "Unknown" is an acceptable code value.*
7. The code definitions, if any, are correct & understandable	[X]	[]	[]	[]	7) *See No. 6 above.*
8. The business rules are complete, correct and effective	[]	[X]	[]	[]	8) *No business rules defined*
9. This data has value to me in my area of responsibility	[]	[]	[]	[X]	9) *I do not need to know this.*
10. This data has value to the enterprise	[X]	[]	[]	[]	10)

Figure 4-20: Sample Information Stakeholder Assessment Results by a Knowledge Worker

Figure 4-21 illustrates the overall IPS Assessment of the Customer Primary Attributes for this IPS Information Stakeholder Assessment.

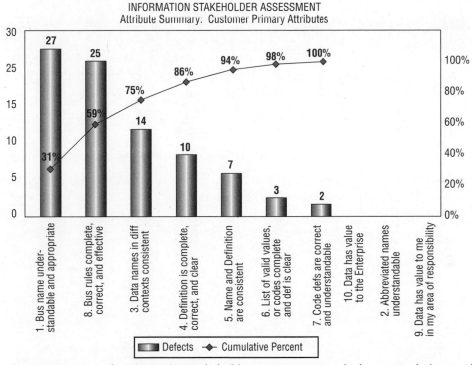

Figure 4-21: Sample Information Stakeholder Assessment Results by a Knowledge Worker

Summary: Information Product Specification Quality

To consistently deliver quality in the *Information Product*, you must ensure *quality* of the "Information Product Specifications." Knowledge Workers and Information Producers must have access to the Information Product Specification data to ensure they know the meaning of the data, its valid values, and the required business rules.

Both technical assessments of "Conformance to Standards" and Information Stakeholder assessments of "Meeting Customer Expectations" are required to ensure sound data names; definitions; valid value sets; and that business rules are correct, complete and clear.

If business terminology and information are not well-named, defined clearly and correctly with a consensus understanding, "what we got here is … a failure to communicate," as the Captain of Road Prison 36 (played by Strother Martin)

says in the movie, *Cool Hand Luke*. Business and Systems Professionals will "fail to communicate" effectively in their business interactions if Information Product Specifications are not *correct, complete, and clear.*

NOTE   "You cannot measure what is not defined." Paul Strassman

Furthermore, without clear definition of the meaning of data, its valid values, and its business rules for assuring its integrity, you cannot conduct the second TIQM P2 Assessment, "Assess Information Quality."

- If you do not know the *meaning* of the Information, you cannot measure its accuracy or validity.

- Data captured must be captured to conform to its product specifications.

- This requires Information Product Specifications to be correct, complete, and clear to all Information Stakeholders.

CHAPTER 5

The Step-by-Step Guide to *Assessing Information Quality*

> *"It ain't what you don't know that hurts you; it's what you know for certain that ain't so."*
>
> **Attributed to Mark Twain**

TIQM P2: Assess Information Quality

Whereas TIQM P1 assesses the quality of the "Information Product Specifications," TIQM P2 assesses the quality of the raw material of Information — Data — and the Finished "Information Product" as presented to Knowledge Workers or applied to work. See Figure 5-1 in relationship to other TIQM Processes.

Though you do not need to conduct a P1 to assess Information Product Specification data before you measure the Information Quality, you *must* know the meaning of the data to assess it properly based on Knowledge Worker expectations in order to measure the Critical-to-Quality Attributes.

Because IQ Assessment is a cost item, minimize the cost by:

- Measuring the right Information (Critical-to-Quality [CTQ]) to the business first
- Measuring the CTQ IQ Characteristics that meet Knowledge Worker CTQ requirements
- Minimizing the costs by using statistical sampling to reduce costs of assessment without compromising the integrity of the assessment

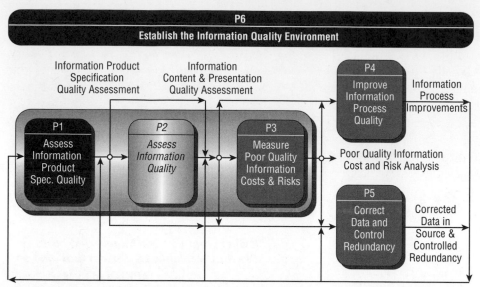

Figure 5-1: P2 in Context of TIQM

Overview

Grace Hopper, the highest-ranking woman ever to serve in the U.S. Navy and an early pioneer in computer science used to say, "One accurate measurement is worth a thousand expert opinions." This is precisely what we must do in measuring the Quality of Information. Follow the processes outlined here and you will have Accurate Measurement of the Critical-to-Quality IQ Characteristics that Knowledge Workers require.

MAIL ORDER COMPANY CALLS "EMERGENCY MEETING" AFTER AN ASSESSMENT FOUND 37 PERCENT OF NEW CUSTOMER RECORDS CREATED WERE DUPLICATE RECORDS

A major mail order catalog company had been complaining for years about their "problem" with duplicate Customers. I suggested to them they measure the order taking process where Customer records are created.

To their dismay they found more than a third of all "new" Customer records created were duplicates of Customer records they already had on file. The Executive VP of Marketing and Sales called an immediate "Emergency" meeting — the actual name of the meeting itself. This took place less than a week after the assessment results were known to address the problem. In less than a week after that meeting several stop-gap measures were implemented, followed by a formal Process Improvement that significantly reduced the duplicate Customer record problem.

To measure Information Quality you must know the meaning of the various Attributes for which data is captured, whose Quality can be measured via TIQM P1 as outlined in Chapter 4. If you have assessed Information Specifications Quality and made any required corrections that meet Knowledge Worker requirements, you are ready to measure the Quality of the Information Content and Presentation.

Information Quality Assessment is not just about measurement (for measurement's sake). Nor is IQ Assessment the measurement of data. Rather it is about ensuring that your processes are in control and consistently delivering the Quality of Information (the finished Information Product) that your Knowledge Workers require.

Key definitions include:

> *Control Chart:* A graphical chart for reporting process performance over time used to monitor whether a process is in control and producing consistent quality.

> *Statistical Process Control (SPC):* The application of statistical methods, including *Control Charts,* to measure, monitor, and analyze a process or its output in order to improve the stability and capability of the process, a major component of *Statistical Quality Control.*

> *Statistical Quality Control (SQC):* The application of statistics and statistical methods to assure quality, using processes and methods to measure process performance, identify unacceptable variance, and apply preventive actions to maintain process control that meets all Customer expectations. SQC consists of *Process measurement, Acceptance Sampling, Process Improvement*, and *Statistical Process Control.*

Our real purpose for measurement is to ensure our processes are in statistical control and delivering high Quality Information to all Information Stakeholders.

Information Quality Assessment Compared to Manufacturing Quality Assessment

The basis for Information Quality Assessment is derived from Product Quality assessment. Kaoru Ishikawa, the great Japanese Quality Guru, describes Assessment or Inspection of Manufacturing Quality in his book, *Guide to Quality Control.*

Figure 5-2 describes how Quality Control is applied to Manufacturing Process Improvement, along with my extrapolation of its counterpart of Quality Control applied to Information Process Quality.

Manufacturing produces tangible products, whether discrete goods such as television sets or automobiles, or process batches, such as soft drinks or refined gasoline (petrol). Information processes produce either discrete data such as a person's name and address or product price, or they may produce analog data such as temperature reading or chemical composition of a batch of gasoline.

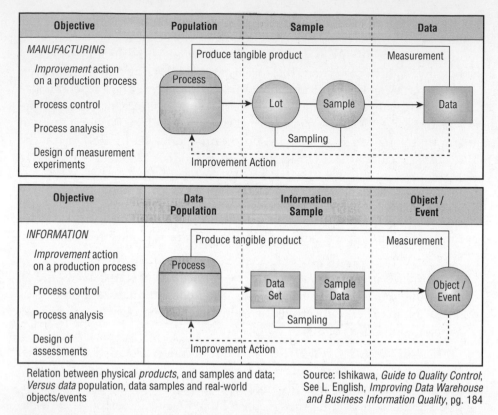

Relation between physical *products*, and samples and data; *Versus data* population, data samples and real-world objects/events

Source: Ishikawa, *Guide to Quality Control*; See L. English, *Improving Data Warehouse and Business Information Quality*, pg. 184

Figure 5-2: Comparison of Process Control Measurement in Manufacturing Processes to Process Control Measurement in Information Production Processes[1]

To measure Manufacturing Process Quality you sample Products produced from the process and compare them to the Process Specification Data defined to meet or exceed Customer requirements.

Information is the representation of facts needed to be known about objects and events of interest to the enterprise. To measure Information Process Quality, you compare the sampled data to the Characteristics of the Real-World Object or Event that the data represents. This measures Accuracy, the most important inherent IQ Quality. Although validity is important, assessing information to valid values and business rules is sometimes inadequate because data can conform to the valid value set and all business rules, but still *not* be Accurate.

Quality Characteristics of Information Content

Knowledge Workers have *numerous* Requirements for Information Content Quality and for Information Presentation Quality. Data content represents the raw material required to produce the finished "Information Products."

Major Critical-to-Quality (CTQ) Information *Content (data values)* Quality Characteristics include:

Definition conformance: Data values are consistent with the Attribute (Fact) definition.

Existence: Each process or decision has *all* the information it requires.

- ☑ **Record existence:** A *record* exists for every Real-World Object or Event the Enterprise needs to know about.

- ☑ **Value existence:** A given data element (fact) has a full value stored for all records that *should* have a value.

Completeness: Each process or decision has *all* the information it requires.

- ☑ **Value completeness:** A given data element (fact) has a full value stored for all records that *should* have a value.

- ☑ **Fact completeness:** Knowledge Workers have all the Facts they need to perform their processes or make their decisions.

Validity: Data values conform to the Information Product Specifications.

- ☑ **Value validity:** A data value is a Valid Value or within a specified range of valid values for this data element.

- ☑ **Business rule validity:** Data values conform to the Specified Business Rules.

- ☑ **Derivation validity:** A derived or calculated data value is Produced *Correctly* according to a specified Calculation Formula or set of Derivation Rules.

Accuracy: The data value *correctly* represents the Characteristic of the Real-World Object or Event it describes.

- ☑ **Accuracy to reality:** The data *correctly* reflects the Characteristics of a Real-World Object or Event being described. Accuracy and Precision represent the highest degree of *inherent* Information Quality possible.

- ☑ **Accuracy to surrogate source:** The data agrees with an original, corroborative source record of data, such as a notarized birth certificate, document, or unaltered electronic data received from a party outside the control of the organization that is demonstrated to be a reliable source.

Precision: Data values are correct to the right level of detail or granularity, such as price to the penny or weight to the nearest tenth of a gram.

Non-duplication: There is *only one* record in a given data store that represents a Single Real-World Object or Event.

Source Quality and Security Warranties or Certifications: The source of information (1) guarantees the *quality* of information it provides *with remedies for non-compliance*; (2) documents its certification in its Information Quality Management capabilities to capture, maintain, and deliver Quality Information; (3) provides objective and verifiable measures of the Quality of Information it provides in agreed-upon Quality Characteristics; and (4) guarantees that the Information has been protected from unauthorized access or modification.

Equivalence of redundant or distributed data: Data about an object or event in one data store is *semantically* Equivalent to data about the same object or event in another data store.

Concurrency of redundant or distributed data: The Information Float or Lag Time is acceptable between (a) when data is knowable (created or changed) in one data store to (b) when it is also knowable in a redundant or distributed data store, and concurrent queries to each data store produce the same result.

Currency: The "age" of the data is correct for the Knowledge Workers' purpose or purposes. Purposes such as inventory control for Just-in-Time Inventory require the most current data. Comparing sales trends for last period to period one-year ago requires sales data from the *respective periods*.

Quality Characteristics of Information Presentation

Knowledge Workers require different Content Quality Characteristics based on their need for that Information. Based on my work with dozens of clients, the major Information Presentation Quality Characteristics include:

Availability: The Characteristic of the Information being accessible when it is needed

Accessibility timeliness: The characteristic of getting or having the Information *when* needed by a process or Knowledge Worker

Presentation media appropriateness: The Characteristic of Information being presented in the right technology Media, such as online, hardcopy report, audio, or video. See Figure 5-3

Warning alerts in the airplane cockpits provide screens with color coding to identify the proximity of the plane to approaching "terrain" (mountains). As a plane gets close to the terrain, the color changes from green to yellow to red. If the terrain screen shows red, the terrain is about 30 seconds away from impact and warning lights flash and an audio warning message calls out, "Terrain! Pull up!" repeatedly.

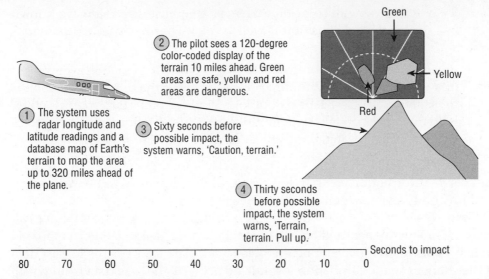

Green

② The pilot sees a 120-degree color-coded display of the terrain 10 miles ahead. Green areas are safe, yellow and red areas are dangerous.

Yellow

Red

① The system uses radar longitude and latitude readings and a database map of Earth's terrain to map the area up to 320 miles ahead of the plane.

③ Sixty seconds before possible impact, the system warns, 'Caution, terrain.'

④ Thirty seconds before possible impact, the system warns, 'Terrain, terrain. Pull up.'

| 80 | 70 | 60 | 50 | 40 | 30 | 20 | 10 | 0 | Seconds to impact |

Figure 5-3: New Warning System Gives Enough Time to Avoid Controlled Flight into Terrain[2]

Relevance: The Characteristic in which the Information is the right kind of Information that adds value to the task at hand, such as to perform a process or make a decision

Presentation Standardization: The Characteristic in which formatted data is presented consistently in a standardized or consistent way across different media, such as in computer screens, reports, or manually prepared reports

☑ **Structured Value Standardization:** Structured Attributes like dates, time, telephone numbers, tax ID numbers, product codes, and currency amounts should be presented in a consistent, standard way in any presentation. When numbers and identifiers are separated into natural groups, such as standard U.S. phone number formats [+1 (555) 999-1234], they are easier to remember and use.

☑ **Document Standardization:** Periodic Reports, such as Financial Statements, Annual Reports, and Policy and Procedure Manuals should have a standard format with a style sheet that presents the information in a consistent and easily read and understood format.

☑ **Signage Accuracy and Clarity:** Signs and other Information-Bearing Mechanisms like Traffic Signals should be standardized and universally used across the broadest audience possible.

Traffic signal lights are now standardized globally with red (stop), yellow (caution), and green (go) meanings. Furthermore, traffic signal lights have standard placement with red on top and green on bottom for those with color-blindness, so that meaning is always known from the light position as well as color. This message "redundancy" reduces error.

Presentation Clarity: The Characteristic in which Information is presented in a way that *clearly* communicates the *truth* of the data. Information is presented with clear labels, footnotes, and/or other explanatory notes, with references or links to definitions or documentation that clearly communicates the meaning and any anomalies in the Information.

Changes in data definition, valid value sets, or in business rule specification can cause information comparison across time boundaries to be misleading and invalid for comparison over time. See Figure 5-4.

Figure 5-4 illustrates one way to represent such changes in the rules for calculating unemployment and how to illustrate current unemployment compared to last year's data. It may not be possible to calculate adjustments to past data if the changes in the calculation formula do not have the base data from which to compare and normalize the recalculation of the previous time frame.

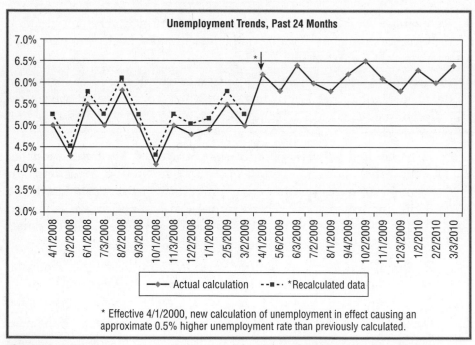

Figure 5-4: Illustration of Calculation Formula Change Notation for Better Trend Comparison

Another problem in Information Presentation is when Labels are *ambiguous* or *misleading*. For example, Figure 5-5 illustrates ambiguity in the label "Profit" of a mortgage report. "Profit" in this real-life example represented the "interest profit that would be realized if all mortgages were to be paid through to loan maturity." However, because very few mortgage loans are paid through maturity, this report is misleading.

Figure 5-6 illustrates a better way to present the "potential profit" by calculating the "net expected interest" based on the current payoff experience of mortgage Customers.

Monthly Mortgage Report							
Region	Branch	Num of On-Book Mort	Num of New Mort	Num of Paid Off Mort	Original Principal Amt (in 000s)	Outstanding Principal Amt (in 000s)	Profit (in 000s)
12		7,022	168	167	$1,260,660	$974,947	$5,317,699
	1201	908	12	31	$109,456	$87,565	$470,660
	1202	1,543	37	35	$219,631	$153,741	$900,486
	1205	289	12	18	$102,530	$92,277	$451,133
	1205	1,974	38	22	$348,273	$292,549	$1,480,159
	1206	851	16	19	$99,363	$66,573	$413,349
	1208	1,457	53	42	$381,408	$282,242	$1,601,912
22		6,164	193	182	$1,168,547	$907,537	$4,060,444
	2201	3,308	104	87	$535,155	$438,827	$2,033,589
	2204	2,856	89	95	$633,392	$468,710	$2,026,855
	. . .	. . .	. . .	. . .	. . .	. . .	. . .

Figure 5-5: Mortgage Report with Ambiguous Column Label "Profit"

Monthly Mortgage Adjusted Profitability Report									
Region	Branch	Num of On-Book Mort	Num of New Mort	Num of Paid Off Mort	Original Principal Amt (in 000s)	Outstanding Principal Amt (in 000s)	Max Interest Possible (in 000s)	Net Est Interest* (in 000s)	Monthly Interest Rec'd** (in 000s)
12		7,022	168	167	$1,260,660	$974,947	$5,317,699	$2,446,142	$9,408
	1201	908	12	31	$109,456	$87,565	$470,660	$216,503	$833
	1202	1,543	37	35	$219,631	$153,741	$900,486	$414,223	$1,593
	1205	289	12	18	$102,530	$92,277	$451,133	$207,521	$798
	1205	1,974	38	22	$348,273	$292,549	$1,480,159	$680,873	$2,619
	1206	851	16	19	$99,363	$66,573	$413,349	$190,141	$731
	1208	1,457	53	42	$381,408	$282,242	$1,601,912	$736,880	$2,834
22		6,164	193	182	$1,168,547	$907,537	$4,060,444	$1,867,804	$7,184
	2201	3,308	104	87	$535,155	$438,827	$2,033,589	$935,451	$3,598
	2204	2,856	89	95	$633,392	$468,710	$2,026,855	$932,353	$3,586
	. . .	. . .	. . .	. . .	. . .	. . .	. . .	. . .	. . .

*Based on current payoff experience
** Current Month Interest received

Figure 5-6: Corrected Label for Maximum Interest Possible and with New "Net Estimated Interest" Column

Presentation Objectivity: The degree to which Information is presented *without bias*, enabling the Knowledge Worker to understand the meaning and significance without misinterpretation

Numeric or Quantitative Data often requires Graphical Presentation. Objectivity means that the Graphical or Visual Presentation of the Information must not distort the *truth* as evidenced in the data.

For example, Figure 5-7 shows the difference in bias in a graphical presentation of a jewelry company's 2001 Annual Report.[3] The graph of five-year sales is plotted in the report (left graph) with a baseline of $1,000 (in millions). This biases the data, making it appear to show a three-fold growth in sales over five years.

The re-computed graph on the right presents a truthful picture of sales, plotted with a base line of zero, revealing the "truth" of a sixty-four percent (64%) sales growth. In the jeweler's 2001 Annual Report, the size of the increase as presented by the size of the column height "suggests" the 2001 net sales is 283% times the 1997 net sales. According to Edward Tufte, the jeweler's biased graph has a lie factor of 4.4 (283% / 64%), a four-fold distortion of reality.[4]

Presentation Utility: The degree to which Information is presented in a way Intuitive and appropriate for the task at hand. The Presentation Quality of Information will vary by the individual purposes for which it is required. Some uses require concise presentation, whereas others require a complete, detailed presentation, and yet others require graphic, color, or other highlighting techniques.

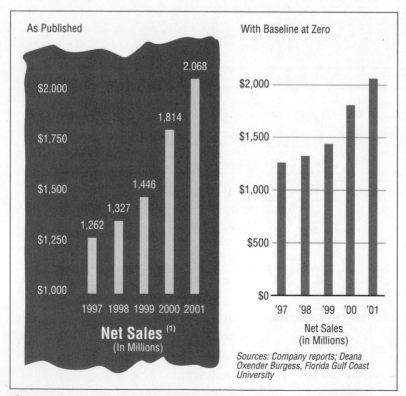

Figure 5-7: Jewelry Company Net Sales Report Bias versus Truthful

TIQM P2 Process Steps: Measuring Information Quality

This process conducts the actual Assessment of Information Content and Presentation Quality. The Knowledge Workers who require and apply Information in their work represent the internal Information "Customers." The end-Customers of your products and services make up the second set of Information Customers.

The assessment consists of eight steps, illustrated in Figure 5-8.

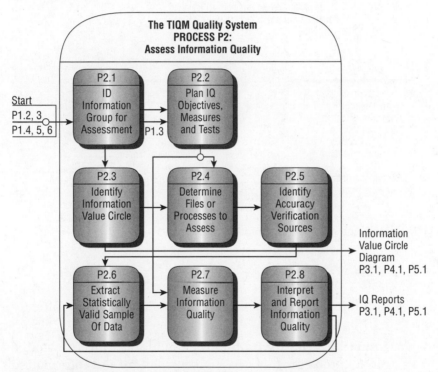

Figure 5-8: TIQM Process P2 Assess Information Quality Process Diagram with TIQM Process Inputs and Outputs to Other TIQM Process Steps

Step P2.1: Identify an Information Group for Quality Assessment

This step identifies a set of Information to measure its Quality, beginning with information *most important* with Quality Problems for the Enterprise. This Information Group will be assessed for Information Content and Presentation Quality.

NOTE This may be the same information as identified in the Information Group for Information Product Specification Quality assessment in TIQM P1.2.

Objective of Step P2.1

To identify a set of information where poor quality can cause significant *negative* impact to the enterprise and its Stakeholders. See Figure 5-9 for step P2.1

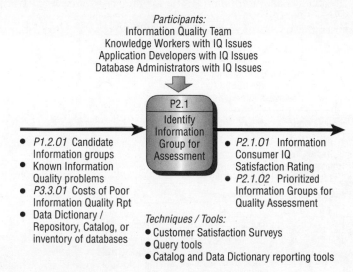

Participants:
Information Quality Team
Knowledge Workers with IQ Issues
Application Developers with IQ Issues
Database Administrators with IQ Issues

P2.1
Identify Information Group for Assessment

- *P1.2.01* Candidate Information groups
- Known Information Quality problems
- *P3.3.01* Costs of Poor Information Quality Rpt
- Data Dictionary / Repository, Catalog, or inventory of databases

- *P2.1.01* Information Consumer IQ Satisfaction Rating
- *P2.1.02* Prioritized Information Groups for Quality Assessment

Techniques / Tools:
- Customer Satisfaction Surveys
- Query tools
- Catalog and Data Dictionary reporting tools

Figure 5-9: P2.1 Identify Information Group for Assessment.

Inputs to Step P2.1

- *P1.2.O1* **Candidate Information Groups:** Information Groups already identified in P1 or P2

- **Known Information Quality Problems:** Any input from Knowledge Workers as to IQ problems that cause process failure and Information Scrap and Rework

- **Data Dictionary / Repository, Catalog, or Inventory of Databases:** Used to identify and document Information Groups

Outputs of Step P2.1

- *P2.1.O1* **Information Consumer IQ Satisfaction Rating:** See Form P2.1.O1.F1 TIQM P2.1 "Information Consumer IQ Satisfaction Rating" on the IQ Applied book Web site at www.wiley.com/go/IQApplied.

■ *P2.1.O2* **Prioritized Information Groups for Quality Assessment:** See an example of Information Groups with prioritized Attributes in Figure 5-10.

Participants and Roles in Step P2.1

Table 5-1 lists the participants and roles in P2.1.

Table 5-1: P2.1 Establish an Information Group for Quality Assessment Participant Roles.

PARTICIPANT	IQ ACTIVITY ROLE
Information Quality Team	Led by the Information Quality Specialist, facilitates the identification of various Information Groups of information in which to conduct an IQ assessment.
Knowledge Workers with Information Quality Issues	Business Professionals or Managers who have identified existing Information Quality problems, either in content or in difficulties in understanding the meaning of the information they require or share. Here they identify potential Candidates for Information Product Specification and Information Quality Assessments.
Application Developers & Administrators	Information Systems Professionals who experience IQ problems in their systems
Database Administrators	Information Systems Professionals who oversee Databases, who encounter IQ problems in their databases

Techniques and Tools for Step P2.1

Customer Satisfaction Surveys: Survey of Knowledge Workers to identify IQ issues that create significant Process Failure and Information Scrap and Rework. See Form P2.1.O1.F1 "Information Consumer IQ Satisfaction Rating" on the IQ Applied book's Web site at www.wiley.com/go/IQApplied.

IQ or Quality Issue Management software: Used to capture the IQ issues discovered and track them to a successful resolution

Catalog and Data Dictionary Reporting tools: To document Information Groups of data elements for assessment

Step P2.1: Identify an Information Group for Quality Assessment: Process Steps and Guidelines

P2.1.1 Review existing documented IQ problems.

P2.1.2 Develop a survey to ask Business Management and Knowledge Workers to identify IQ problems you may not be aware of. See Form P2.1.O1.F1 "Information Consumer IQ Satisfaction Rating" on the book's Web site.

P2.1.3 Conduct the survey among key Information Stakeholders.

P2.1.4 Assemble the Managers and Knowledge Workers together to develop a relative significance of problems in the Information Content and Presentation Quality.

Figure 5-10 illustrated a sample Information Group with CTQ attributes prioritized.

Data Element / Information Quality Classification	Accuracy Class	Complete Class	Validity Class
Customer ID	A	M	Uniq+Ck Dgt
Customer Family/Sur Name(s)	A	M	Nm+mrk
Customer Given/First Name(s)	A	M	Nm+mrk
Customer Middle Name(s)	A	OL	Nm+mrk
Customer Known-as Name	A	OH	Nm+mrk
Customer Personal Title	A	OL	VV,BR
Customer Formal Salutation	A	M	N/A
Customer Informal Salutation	A	M	N/A
Customer Telephone Number	B	M	F,BR
Customer Classification Code	B	OH	VV,BR
Customer Acquisition Source Code	B	OL	VV
Customer Acquisition Source Text	C	OL	N/A
Customer First Contact Date	C	OL	VDt, BR
Customer First Service Date	B	MS	VDt, BR
Customer Est. Annual Income	B	OH	VCur, F
Customer Head-of-House Code	B	OH	VV,BR
Customer Homeowner Code	B	OH	VV,BR
Customer Last Ver/Update Date	A	MS	VDt

Legend:
Accuracy class: A = High costs of poor quality; B = Med costs; C = Lower costs
Completeness class: M= Mandatory at create; OH= High; OL= Low; MS= Mandatory within Life Cycle State
Validity class: V = Valid value req'd; F = Format req'd; BR = Business Rule tests; N/A = Not Applicable

Figure 5-10: Example of Prioritized Information Group Attributes

P2.1.5 If warranted, conduct a Cost of Poor Information Quality study. See Process Step P3.3 "Calculate Poor Quality Information Costs" in Chapter 6.

P2.1.6 Brainstorm and plan schedule to begin assessing the content and presentation quality based on the relative importance, from most to next-most important.

TIP Select and plan the schedule for the Information Quality Assessments. There will be multiple kinds of IQ tests depending on how each Critical-to-Quality attribute is measured, as described in Step P2.2.

TIP Process Control IQ Assessments require regular measurements over time to ensure the process is in control or requires improvement. Process Control Assessment requires 20 to 30 IQ measurements over time to establish a Mean and Upper and Lower Control Limits.

Step P2.2: Plan IQ Objectives, Measures and Tests

To get an accurate assessment of your information, you must plan your objectives, and design your measurement tests, based on the CTQ IQ Characteristics Knowledge Workers require to perform their value work.

Objective of Step P2.2

To determine:

- The purpose for Information Quality assessment, such as:
  - An initial baseline assessment of a database
  - Process monitoring to ensure Information Process Quality Control
  - To identify data for data correction for a migration or data movement
  - To measure Information from an Information Broker or third party
- The Critical-To-Quality IQ Characteristics to assess
- To define the specific tests for each IQ characteristic to measure

Figure 5-11 illustrates the components of Step P2.2.

Inputs to Step P2.2

- *P2.1.O1* **Information Group for Quality Assessment:** The Information Group that will be measured
- *P2.3.O1* **Information Value Circle documentation:** Documentation as to data stores and/or processes to be measured
- *P3.3.O1* **Cost of Poor Quality Information Report:** This is used to prioritize various Information Groups and IQ characteristics, if you have conducted one.

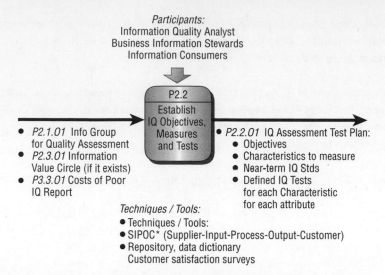

Participants:
Information Quality Analyst
Business Information Stewards
Information Consumers

P2.2
Establish
IQ Objectives,
Measures
and Tests

- *P2.1.01* Info Group
  for Quality Assessment
- *P2.3.01* Information
  Value Circle (if it exists)
- *P3.3.01* Costs of Poor
  IQ Report

- *P2.2.01* IQ Assessment Test Plan:
  - Objectives
  - Characteristics to measure
  - Near-term IQ Stds
  - Defined IQ Tests
    for each Characteristic
    for each attribute

Techniques / Tools:
- Techniques / Tools:
- SIPOC* (Supplier-Input-Process-Output-Customer)
- Repository, data dictionary
  Customer satisfaction surveys

Figure 5-11: P2.2 Establish Information Quality Objectives, Measures and Tests.

Outputs of Step P2.2

- *P2.2.01* IQ Assessment Test Plan:

  - **Assessment Objectives:** This establishes the purpose for the Assessment.

  - **IQ Characteristics to measure:** What Characteristics should be measured? Use Form P2.8.01.F1.3 IQ Characteristics Assessed Template. See all P2 Assessment Forms on the book website at www.wiley.com/go/IQApplied.

  - **Short-term IQ Standards expected:** What Quality near-term Target has been previously established for each IQ Characteristic?

NOTE Long-term IQ is zero-defects if defects create high costs of process failure.

  - **Defined IQ tests for each Critical-to-Quality IQ Characteristic for each attribute:** This describes the procedures for the IQ tests, such as Accuracy, Completeness, and Timeliness, on each Attribute.

Participants and Roles for Step P2.2

Table 5-2 illustrates roles and activities in Step P2.2.

Table 5-2: Participant Roles in P2.2 Establish Information Quality Objectives, Measures and Tests.

PARTICIPANT	IQ ACTIVITY ROLE
Information Quality Team	Led by the Information Quality Specialist, facilitates the definition of the IQ Assessment Objective, IQ Characteristics to measure, and defines the actual measurement processes and controls for assessment of the various IQ Characteristics.
Business Information Stewards	Subject Matter Experts who have been appointed to ensure the quality of the business Information Product Specification. Here, they assist in identifying the Critical-to-Quality IQ Characteristics to meet the needs of all Information Consumers.
Information Consumers	Knowledge Workers who apply Information in their work. They assist in identifying the IQ Characteristics and Quality Requirements for Information to Assess.

Techniques and Tools for Step P2.2

- **SIPOC (Supplier-Input-Process-Output-Customer):** A tool for capturing Information Consumer requirements in the information they require and the quality characteristics needed to accomplish the purposes requiring the information

- **Customer satisfaction surveys:** To collect required IQ Characteristics from "external" information stakeholders for Customer-facing Information

- **Repository, data dictionary:** To document the Information Quality Characteristics, measures, and tests for each Information Group

Step P2.2: Plan IQ Objectives, Measures and Tests: Process Steps and Guidelines

P2.2.1 Led by the IQ Specialist, assemble the Team of Business Information Stewards and Information Consumers, who are the "Customers" of the Information being assessed.

P2.2.2 Review any relevant documentation on the IQ issues known about the Information.

P2.2.3 Define the Objective for the IQ assessment, and the ongoing Quality Control Assessments conducted on a periodic basis.

Objectives include:

Baseline understanding of state of quality in a data store:

☑ Understand the state of quality produced by a current process (process capability).

☑ Understand effectiveness of a Process Improvement.

☑ Ensure quality of data movement and transformation processes for equivalence across multiple data stores.

☑ Preparation of data for a migration or conversion (data warehouse, new software or system)

☑ Other: _____

P2.2.4 Conduct a SIPOC across the information value/cost chain that creates the information in the selected Information Group. See procedure for how to conduct a SIPOC along with a template form on the IQ Applied book Web site at www.wiley.com/go/IQApplied.

P2.2.5 Conduct an end-Customer Satisfaction Survey with questions about IQ issues they may have with the organization's Customer-facing Information, such as products and product descriptions, Customer name and address information, billing information, order information, profile information, owner's or operations manuals, and assembly instructions, for example.

TIP **Conduct this survey as part of your regular Customer Satisfaction Survey mechanism.**

TIP **Failure to meet end-Customers' Expectations with Information can lead to lost Customers and their Customer Lifetime Value.**

P2.2.6 Identify the Critical-to-Quality IQ Characteristics for measurement. Various Knowledge Worker groups may have different Requirements for Quality in the Information they depend on, based on their unique needs.

TIP **See sections "Quality Characteristics of Information Content" and "Quality Characteristics of Information Presentation" earlier in the chapter.**

P2.2.7 Facilitated by the Business Information Steward, achieve a general consensus among the Information Consumers as to the Critical-to-Quality IQ characteristics.

P2.2.8 [IQ Specialist] then defines the IQ Assessment Test Plan defining the specific tests for each IQ characteristic for each attribute to be assessed. Following are guidelines for some of the CTQ IQ Characteristics.

Definition Conformance Test

Measurement test: Electronic or human inspection.

Test that the value of an attribute is consistent with the attribute's defined meaning, such as for the following data value type examples, short list only:

- **Date:** The value is consistent with a Gregorian calendar date.

- **Address:** The value is consistent with an address of the intended address type (street address, PO box, physical latitude, longitude), for example.

- **Code:** The meaning of the code value is consistent with the definition of the classification.

- **Quantity:** The value is an integer.

- **Currency Amount:** The presented value is consistent with the type and format of the specific currency:

  - **US$ or USD:** US$ 2,500.00 or USD 2,500.00

  - **Euro:** €

  - **Pound Sterling:** £

  - **Japanese Yen:** ¥

  - **Swedish Kroner:** SEK

- **Email Address:** The value has all components of an email address (person email name; @; organization name or short name (infoimpact, aol, gmail, icglink); domain (.arpa, .com, .net, .org, .gov, .mil, .info, .biz, .mobi, .co.uk, .eu, for example).

- **Dimension:** The value is a numeric value consistent with length, height, width. Other quantitative data includes volume, weight, loudness (decibels), speed, wattage, amperage, for example.

Existence and Completeness Tests

There are two types of Completeness in Information Content:

- **Record existence:** A record exists for every Real-World Object or Event that the organization needs to know about.

  It is difficult to "know what we do not know." Missing records on objects and events can be difficult to discover. Missing records can be caused by failing to record information that should be recorded, or deleting records that are still required to be known.

Missing records are sometimes found in "orphan" transaction records that are not related to a fundamental entity occurrence, such as an equity trade record that does not have a Customer or Account for which the trade is made.

When dealing with objects outside the capability of knowing, we often have to find reliable sources from which to compare our internal data. Recently, an Egyptian pyramid was "rediscovered." It had been originally found in 1842 by German archeologist Karl Richard Lepsius. However, it was lost again when shifting sands covered its remains.[5]

Measure the percent of missing records (that you have discovered and have added to the database) against the total of the unique existing records plus the missing records that have been discovered and added, such as new products acquired, but not listed in the product database.

▪ **Attribute value existence:** A value exists for every attribute that requires a value at a given point in time.

Measurement test: Electronic. Test for the presence of a value, and that the value is required for the attribute at the point in time of assessment.

▪ **Attribute value completeness:** An Attribute value is a full value representing all aspects represented by the attribute. For example, a street address must have all components of the street address, including thoroughfare number, name type, and pre- and post-directionals if they exist.

NOTE Certain Attributes are NOT required when a record is first created, but are required when there is a state change of a real-world object, such as when a Prospective Customer becomes a Purchasing Customer and they now have a "Customer-First-Service Date." Or, when a Product is retired and only now has a Product-Last-Available Date or when a planned product is now available for sale.

▪ **Completeness of optional attribute values:** A value exists for every optional attribute where a value provides *useful* and *valuable* information for at least one set of Knowledge Workers, even though it is not mandatory. For example, civic club membership of a Customer is not required to process orders for the Customer, but that may be valuable information for marketing to understand personal drivers and for product developers to understand Customer preferences.

NOTE Generally, optional attributes are not required for operational purposes, but may be important to understanding patterns and trends in Customer behavior, product experience, or economic trends. In essence, these attributes are required to support the strategic or tactical processes of the enterprise. In both these cases, a "missing" value is correct until an occurrence reaches the state of existence in which that value is required. For example, when a new product is in development, no Product price is required. However, once the product is officially available for sale, there must be a valid product price amount.

Measurement test: Electronic. Completeness is best measured by electronic means. Create assessment queries that test the required attributes for record creation, using an internal query language or by developing tests, sometimes called filters, in IQ Assessment software. Given the nature of the actual data value, it may be a "null," or may be represented by a blank or a zero or other "missing" indicator. These tests should also include state change values, applying a business rule test, to test if an entity is in a given state where one or more attribute values are required.

TIP Separate tests for mandatory completeness and optional completeness, for the impact on the enterprise processes are different. If having a value is *truly* optional, it is not an error to have a missing value unless the Attribute can add valuable Knowledge to certain processes.

NOTE Missing values in required Attributes cause operational processes to fail, but missing values in Strategic Attributes can cause missed opportunity.

Validity Tests

There are three types of validity to test:

- **Value Validity:** A value for an Attribute is one of the valid values (if a code) or within a range of values for quantitative or numeric information, such as salary amount is within the range for the job position (or level).

Measurement test: Electronic test, comparing the value to the set of valid values or range.

- **Business Rule Validity:** Data values conform to the specified *defined* Business Rules.

    Example: One manufacturer has business rules for changing the state of a "Placed Order" to an "Approved Order" when the following conditions are true (all business rules are met):

    1. The Order is a completed "Placed Order" (it has all attributes required to process the Order), **AND**

    2. The Customer has a Credit Status of "Credit Worthy," **AND**

    3. The Total-Order-Amount, plus the amount due on all outstanding invoices is not greater than the "Customer-Credit-Limit-Amount."

Measurement test: Electronic. Business Rule Validity is best tested using electronic tests, again coding them in a repository, business rules engine, or in an available query language or through filters you can create in IQ Assessment software.

NOTE Note that software tests for validity, measures validity, and only validity. Software validity tests can measure that a value is valid or not (given a valid value set or range). Software can also measure conformance to defined Business Rules.

NOTE Never report a validity assessment as an "Information 'Quality' Assessment" that may be misinterpreted as a measure of Accuracy. Accuracy requires a physical comparison of the data to the actual Characteristic Values of the Real-World Object or Event. This is described in the next set of IQ content measurements.

- **Derivation Validity:** A derived or calculated data value is produced correctly according to a specified calculation formula or set of derivation rules.

   To test derivation validity, construct a query to automate the calculation, independently from the source application that is calculating the data. This test must use the officially defined calculation formula, and execute it independently of the application program. If the two calculations agree, then the derived data is valid.

NOTE If the base values are Accurate, and the Calculation Formula is Correct and correctly performed, the resulting value is considered *Accurate*.

Accuracy Tests

   The data value correctly represents the characteristic of the real-world object or event it describes. To measure accuracy, you must compare the data to the physical characteristics of the real-world object the data represents, or by comparing the data to a recording of an event, to verify independently that the data was captured correctly and accurately.

- **Accuracy to Reality:** The data correctly reflects the Characteristics of a Real-World Object or Event being described. Accuracy and Precision represent the highest degree of *Inherent* Information Quality possible.

   Measurement test: Human inspection or highly calibrated measurement tool for measurement depending on the nature of the data Accuracy Verification Source.

   To measure Accuracy, you must compare the data to the physical Characteristic the data represents. This means comparing the data to the physical object, or person (where they can confirm the accuracy of certain data without bias), or by physically measuring Characteristics with high-precision, calibrated measurement devices. The tables with example accuracy to reality and accuracy to surrogate source are listed in Step P2.5 "Identify Accuracy Verification Sources."

- **Accuracy to surrogate source:** This compares data to what is expected to be an authoritative source, such as a credit card transaction file from a merchant provided to the credit card processor. However, the actual transaction captured in the Credit Card System could be handled correctly, but the price of the charged merchandise is *not* correct.

Measurement test: Electronic or human inspection.

The data agrees with an original, corroborative source record of data, such as a notarized birth certificate, document, or unaltered electronic data received from a party outside the control of the organization that is demonstrated to be a reliable source.

Precision Tests

- **Precision:** Data values are correct to the right level of detail or granularity, such as price to the penny or weight to the nearest tenth of a gram. However, producing optical fiber with a diameter variation of no more than ½ micron requires highly precise production and measurement equipment.

  Measurement test: Electronic or human inspection with or without calibrated measurement devices. This requires high-precision calibration of measurement tools or in calculations to sufficient decimal points to meet the most rigorous precision requirements of any Knowledge Worker.

Non-Duplication Tests

- **Non-Duplication:** There is *only one* record in a data store that represents a single Real-World Object or Event.

  Measurement test: Electronic *and* human inspection to corroborate the electronic match result.

  A major problem in many organizations with a proliferation of redundant systems and databases is that they have a huge problem with duplication or redundancy of records about their Customers and products or other Objects or Events of interest.

  Measuring duplication requires developing tests that can evaluate potential "Identity Attributes" likely to represent one person or one object. Identify all available and prospective "Identity Attributes" that can be used for duplicate matching. Ensure those Attributes are captured as a part of any create process for records of those types.

  Identity Attributes for persons include:

- Name (including name changes and aliases)

- Mother's maiden name

- Address (including former addresses with dates where possible)

- Phone numbers (including former numbers)

- Birth date

- Birth location (hospital, City, State (Province/Area), Country

- Various identification numbers (or partial), such as tax-ID, drivers license, self-created passwords and reminder words, for example
- Other potential Identity Attributes, such as organization memberships, physical characteristics, such as scars, tattoos, physical impairments, and biometric data (eye colors, hair colors, fingerprints, retina scans, DNA, facial image, for example). These are used where security or society requirements exist and privacy laws are not breached.

Timeliness Tests: The Information is available to the Knowledge Workers at a time acceptable for them to perform their work.

Measurement test: Human confirmation. The Information Consumers express satisfaction of time in which they receive required Information.

NOTE Information may be considered timely enough by Knowledge Workers who see only their own need for the information. Other Information Consumers further downstream may have their processes *fail* because the Information is not propagated to a database they can access on a timely basis. A better, more rigorous test is to measure the actual Information Float in the following measurement test.

Measurement test: Electronic record tracking. Monitoring software determines how long it takes to move data from source Record-of-Origin (paper document), electronic Record-of-Origin to a downstream data store from which Information Consumers have access to the Information. Measure the actual time of Information Float as one of the costs of data movement. This represents the amount of delay of accessibility by Information Consumers to data from their database as compared with the availability at the Record-of-Origin Database. See Figure 5-12 as an illustration.

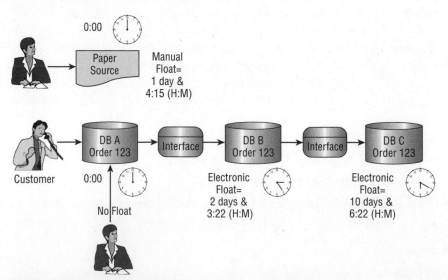

Figure 5-12: Information Float as a Measure of Timeliness

Consumers who can only access data in Database C must wait more than ten days for access to data that could be accessible immediately if they were able to have access to Database A. The operative question is what increased value could Knowledge Workers have if they had immediate access to Information in Database A?

NOTE There may be opportunity losses caused by excessive data movement to downstream Knowledge Workers. While certain operational processes may perform satisfactorily, there may be delays in access to Information that prevent Knowledge Workers from delighting their Customers or increasing their time-to-market in performing their work.

Warranty Tests

- **Source Quality Warranties, Certifications, and Integrity:** The source of information, whether internal or external:

    (1) Guarantees the Quality of Information it provides with *remedies* for non-compliance;

    (2) Documents its Certification in its Information Quality Management capabilities to capture, maintain, and deliver Quality Information;

    (3) Provides objective and verifiable measures of the Quality of Information it provides in agreed-upon Quality Characteristics;

    (4) Guarantees that the Information has been *protected* from unauthorized access or modification, and;

    (5) Has *Remedies* for non-compliance to agreed standards.

    Measurement test: Human inspection.

    For third-party Information Brokers that *sell* Information, expect or demand a *written warranty* for the Information and for that Warranty to be written into your contract with Information Brokers that *sell* Information. This warranty must contain *remedies* for when the quality in all Critical-to-Quality IQ characteristics is *not provided*.

    If the information is provided by Trade or Business Partners, or your Customers, then you will develop "Stewardship Agreements" for the information, and seek ways to make incentives for them to provide High Quality Information. Often, this will include your providing reciprocal Quality Information that adds *value* to your Trade Partners or Customers.

Equivalence of Redundant Data Tests

- **Equivalence of Redundant or Distributed data:** Data about an Object or Event in one data store is semantically equivalent to data about the same Object or Event in another data store.

    Measurement test: Electronic or human inspection.

Measure this by extracting a sample of data from a source data store, mapping its meaning to a downstream target data store that the data has been propagated to or has been created independently, to compare if they match. To do this, you must know the object that the attributes describe, and the semantic meaning of the data values. You map that to the target data store and compare or translate to evaluate if the data is semantically equivalent.

This can be tested with electronic tests if you are able to map cleanly the semantics of the data in the two data stores. For example, Gender code of M = Male and F = Female maps to data store 2 as 1 = Male and 2 = Female.

Step P2.3: Identify Information Value Circle

This process identifies all Activities of the life cycle from the originating create process to delivery to all Information Consumers, both internally and externally.

Objective of Step P2.3

To determine all business processes and applications, and all Information Producer roles that create or update information along with process interdependencies, processes that retrieve and present the Information, and Knowledge Worker (Information Consumer) roles that apply it. This is to identify points where defects may be introduced and where data Equivalence must be controlled. It also identifies where process failure will occur due to poor Quality Information.

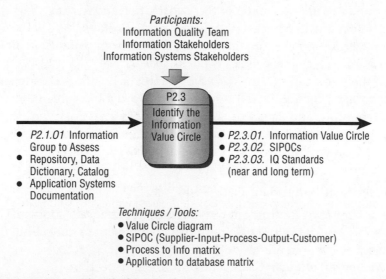

Figure 5-13: Step P2.3 Identify the Information Value Circle.

Inputs to Step P2.3

- *P2.1.O1* **Information Group to Assess:** Used to identify all applications that create, update, or retrieve the data and all databases that house it

- **Repository, Data Dictionary, Catalog:** Used to document the Information Groups and their dependencies on processes and Information Stakeholders

- **Application Systems Documentation:** Used to identify the specific processes (create, update, retrieve, delete) that impact the data

Outputs of Step P2.3

- *P2.3.O1* **Information Value Circle:** Graphic representation and description of the processes and applications that impact the information, their data stores, and Information Stakeholders' roles. This can be represented by a data flow or workflow diagram.

- *P2.3.O2* **SIPOC (Supplier-Input-Process-Output-Customer):** Individual SIPOCs for each of the Information Value Circle activities

- *P2.3.O3* **IQ Standards:** (near and long term)

Participants and Roles for Step P2.3

Table 5-3 describes the participants and roles in Step P2.3.

Table 5-3: P2.3. Identify Information Value Circle Participants and Roles.

PARTICIPANT	IQ ACTIVITY ROLE
Information Quality Team	Led by the Information Quality Specialist, facilitates the identification and documentation of the Information Value Circle for the Information Group to be assessed.
Information Stakeholders	Business professionals or managers who can identify processes they perform in the Value Circle
Application Developers and Administrators	Information Systems Professionals who can identify and document the application programs that create, update, retrieve, transform, and/or move the data
Database Administrators	Information Systems Professionals who can define the Databases that house the data within the Value Circle

Techniques and Tools for Step P2.3

- **Information Value Circle Diagram:** Any graphic to represent the component parts of the Information Value Circle, including Data Flow or Work Flow Diagrams.

- **SIPOC:** Used to document individual process steps within the Value Circle along with the information produced and the quality requirements for the produced information by the Information Consumers. See TIQM Forms and procedures on the book Web site at `www.wiley.com/go/TQApplied` for SIPOC Template and Procedures.

Step P2.3: Identify Information Value Circle: Process Steps and Guidelines

P2.3.1 Research and gather any current documentation about the Information Value Circle, including the business processes, databases, Information Producers, and Information Consumers in the Value Circle.

P2.3.2 Identify subject matter experts in all Information Stakeholder areas to identify and document the Information Value Circle or the missing components of the Value Circle. Document for each process within the Value Circle the:

- Process, or process step, definition

- Data store in which the data is created, updated, or retrieved

- Process performer business role (Call Center Representative, Insurance Agent, Internal Auditor), for example

- Information Stakeholder role (Information Producer, Information Transcriptionist, Translator, or Knowledge Worker)

- Interdependencies on other processes in the Value Circle

P2.3.3 Document the Value Circle and its components in the Enterprise Repository and Data Dictionary in a way that is accessible to all Information Stakeholders.

TIP Perform this process step once, and then update it as Process Improvement or reengineering initiatives are performed on it.

NOTE Be sure that all documentation is subject to change control, so you can ensure that specific definitions at a point in time can be determined.

P2.3.4 Analyze the SIPOC results to identify and prioritize the Critical-to-Quality IQ characteristics of the Knowledge Workers.

P2.3.5 Work with the Business Information Stewards and representative Information Consumers to establish long- and near-term Information Quality Standards for each CTQ Quality Characteristic for the various Data Elements.

P2.3.5.1 Group Attributes (Data elements) in logical groups by Information type (order and order item, Customer name and address, product descriptive information, for example) and by priority of attributes within each information type in terms of importance, and impact of defects:

- A priority = zero defect or near-zero defect required.
- B priority = minimal defect required.
- C priority = some defects are okay.

P2.3.5.2 Gather from the SIPOCs that Information Stakeholders created to identify the specific long-term Quality Requirements.

P2.3.5.3 After you conduct the first assessment and see the results, establish the near-term IQ standards for the Information Groups, along with a target date for Process Improvements to achieve that new, near-term standard. Work with the Business Information Stewards and representative Information Consumers to establish mutually acceptable Quality Standards.

NOTE The near-term IQ Standard must be mutually agreed to by the Manager of the create processes, and the downstream Information Consumer Managers whose processes depend on the Information.

NOTE The near-term IQ Standard must represent a "stretch-target" that requires change to accomplish. Otherwise, the process owner may *not* create meaningful and sustainable improvement.

Figure 5-14 illustrates an example of an Information Value Circle for "Customer Order."

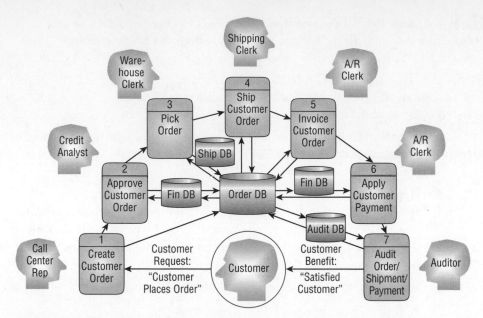

Figure 5-14: Sample Information Value Circle: Customer Order Value Circle

Step P2.4: Determine File or Process to Assess

To get the right Assessment Results, you must identify the right place to assess.

Objective of Step P2.4

To identify where data should be assessed to most effectively accomplish the objective for measurement.

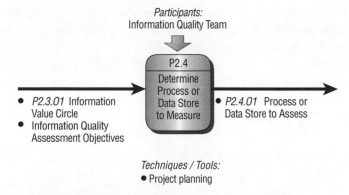

Figure 5-15: P2.4 Determine File or Process to Assess Process Step.

Inputs to Step P2.4

- ■ *P2.3.O1* **Information Value Circle:** Used to identify the source for assessment
- ■ **Information Quality Measurement Objectives:** Defines where to sample the Information for assessment.

Outputs of Step P2.4

- ■ *P2.4.O1* **Data Store or Process to Assess:** Identifies the place for sampling the Information for assessment.

Participants and Roles for Step P2.4

Participants and their roles are described in Table 5-4.

Table 5-4: Step P2.4 Identify Process or Data Store to Assess Participants and Roles.

PARTICIPANT	IQ ACTIVITY ROLE
Information Quality Team	Led by the Information Quality Analyst, identifies the process or data store to assess, given the assessment objectives.

Techniques and Tools for Step P2.4

- ■ **Project planning:** To determine the correct source from which to assess, given the assessment objectives

Step P2.4: Determine Process or Data Store to Assess: Process Steps and Guidelines

P2.4.1 Review the Assessment Objectives, as defined in P2.2.O1.

P2.4.2 Review the Information Value Circle, as documented in P2.3.O1.

P2.4.3 Select the Process or Data Store from which to assess the various IQ Assessment tests, as noted in Table 5-5.

Table 5-5: Source to Assess for an IQ Assessment, Based on Objectives

ASSESSMENT OBJECTIVE	WHERE TO ASSESS
1. Baseline understanding state of quality in a data store	Select the data store (database or file) in which the records are housed.
2. Understand the state of quality produced by a current process (process capability).	Identify the process that creates or updates the records in the record-of-origin. This may be:

2. (continued)

- Manually created on paper by the Information Producer.

- Electronically created with an application program by an Information Producer. Note that electronically created data must be sampled at the point of create, and before any corrective maintenance is performed. For data captured in a relational database, use the trigger feature to extract sample records on the insert or create action.

- Electronically created in an e-Business application program. Generally, this data represents transactions created by an e-Customer or e-Visitor. Sample the data directly from the Record-of-Origin Data Store into which the data is created. Ensure that no internal processes will have modified any of the original records.

- Captured via an embedded software routine by the measurement device. If the data is accessible and readable in the measurement device, take a sample from the device itself. If not, you must sample from the uploaded data from the device. If there are conversions of the data in the process of uploading it, you must ensure the data was not corrupted during the upload. You may have to work with the supplier of the device to develop the tests to confirm accurate transformation during the upload.

ASSESSMENT OBJECTIVE	WHERE TO ASSESS
3. Understand effectiveness of a Process Improvement	Reassess the process with the identical assessment tests as conducted on the process prior to the improvement.
4. Assure quality of data movement and transformation processes for equivalence across multiple data stores.	Sample data in the source data store, and identify the counterpart records in the target data store.

ASSESSMENT OBJECTIVE	WHERE TO ASSESS
5. Preparation of data for a migration or conversion (data warehouse, new software or system)	Identify the source data store and the target data store for conversion or migration. Sample records in the source data store; select the counterpart records in the target data store; and measure the equivalence of data.

Note: Migration and conversions to new software packages or new systems may also require additional Attributes not available in any source system that must be created. Also, there may be Attributes in the source system that are not required in the target software but that you still require for other processes. You must design the data store for those Attributes.

ASSESSMENT OBJECTIVE	WHERE TO ASSESS
6. Freeform and structured documents	Select the Document for IQ assessment and identify and select CTQ Facts in the Document to be assessed.
7. Graphics, drawings, schematics, graphs, floor layouts, etc.	Identify the specific graphic for IQ assessment. Sample from the components or the entire graphic to assess whether the proportions in the graphic Accurately represent the proportions of the Real-World Object represented. For example, a rectangle shape is drawn for something that is actually square.
8. Other: _____ _____ _____ _____	Determine the assessment source based on the preceding principles to the type of information and the assessment objective.

NOTE In establishing a process to measure, you must design the Process Tests to measure Information Quality consistently, so that your measurements are not skewed, comparing apples to oranges. For example, data for the trajectory and altitude of NASA's Mars Climate Orbiter were calculated in English units of measure, but the NASA Team entered them as metric figures, causing the Orbiter to crash on the backside of Mars.

Step P2.5: Identify Accuracy Verification Sources

The most critical IQ characteristic, Accuracy, is not able to be assessed electronically, except for derived data. For all other data, the accuracy will have to be compared to the real-world object the data represents or by observing the capture of event data or observing a recording of the event data capture and confirming accuracy of the captured data.

Objective of Step P2.5

To identify authoritative sources from which to verify information accuracy. Figure 5-16 illustrates the components of Step P2.5.

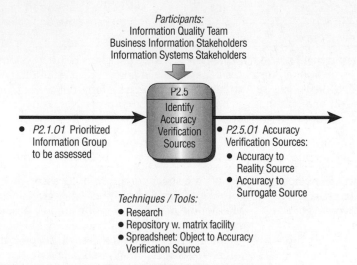

Figure 5-16: Step P2.5 Identify Accuracy Verification Sources

Inputs to Step P2.5

- ▪ *P2.1.O1* **Prioritized Information Group to be assessed**

Outputs of Step P2.5

- ▪ *P2.5.O1* **Accuracy Verification Source List**
  - ▪ Accuracy to Reality Verification Source
  - ▪ Accuracy to Surrogate Verification Source

Participants and Roles of P2.5

Table 5-6 represents the participants and roles in Step P2.5.

Table 5-6: P2.5 Identify Accuracy Verification Sources Participants and Roles.

PARTICIPANT	IQ ACTIVITY ROLE
Information Quality Team	Led by an Information Quality Specialist, identifies the Sources for Accuracy verification and documents them in the IQ Assessment process guidelines.

PARTICIPANT	IQ ACTIVITY ROLE
Business Information Stakeholders	Help identify sources for Accuracy Verification.
Information Systems Stakeholders	Help identify Information Broker sources for surrogate Accuracy Verification.

Techniques and Tools for Step P2.5

- **Research:** To identify sources from which to verify Accuracy to Reality and Surrogate to Reality for the Objects or Events assessed

- **Repository with Matrix facility:** To document the Accuracy to Reality Verification Source and any Surrogate to Reality Verification Source

- **Spreadsheet with Object to Accuracy Verification Source:** Use this if you do not have a repository with such capability

Step P2.5: Identify Accuracy Verification Sources: Process Steps and Guidelines

P2.5.1 Select Subject Matter Experts from the Information Stakeholders to research potential accuracy verification sources.

P2.5.2 Research and gather any documentation about potential Accuracy-to-Reality Verification sources.

P2.5.3 Research and gather any documentation about potential Accuracy-to-Surrogate sources.

P2.5.4 Select and document the most reliable verification sources for each object or event to be assessed.

- **Accuracy to reality:** This will be the object itself, or a recording or observation of an event.

- **Accuracy to surrogate:** This may be something that represents the Object or Event, such as original forms completed by a person or organization; legal documents, such as birth certificates, passports, or driver's licenses; or third-party information brokers. See Table 5-7 for a sample list of Accuracy verification sources.

Table 5-7 illustrates Accuracy Verification Sources for different types of Information.

Table 5-7: P2.5 Sample of Accuracy Verification Sources

ASSESSMENT OBJECT	ACCURACY TO REALITY SOURCE	ACCURACY TO SURROGATE SOURCE
Person: non-sensitive personal attributes such as, name, address, date of birth, telephone number, or tax-id number	The person, him or herself	Birth certificate, audited tax returns, deed of trust.
Person profile information, such as income, home value, buying behavior		Public records (will require recalculation based on age of data and market changes); Information Brokers
Person Address and Contact details	The person, her or himself	Postal Service authority; Information Brokers, such as Acxiom, or Credit Reporting Agencies
Medical Insurance Claim	Observation or video or audio recording of procedures of the medical encounter, or a second opinion diagnosis and treatment	Trained professional reviews Provider's Medical Records (provider's notes) of the Medical Encounter
Customer Order	Confirmation with order-placing Customer; observation or recording of order process	Customer-completed order form
Package shipping weights and dimensions	Measure of the product package itself with calibrated equipment	Third-party, independent measurement
Home Owners Insurance Application	Physical inspection of the property to confirm observable and measurable attributes, such as construction type and materials, distance to fire hydrant and fire station	Application document
Product Inventory	Physical inventory inspection	Not applicable
Vehicle Condition	Physical vehicle inspection	Information brokers, such as CarFax
Scientific Findings	Repeatable or reproducible measurements or split sample measurement	Not applicable
Bank account transactions	Recording of deposit and withdrawal transactions independent of the transaction processor	Person's checkbook transaction balancing

ASSESSMENT OBJECT	ACCURACY TO REALITY SOURCE	ACCURACY TO SURROGATE SOURCE
Latitude, Longitude, Altitude locations	Confirm at location with a calibrated GPS device with the appropriate precision	GIS Information Brokers
Equity Trade Transactions	Observation or recording of equity trade transactions independent of the Trader	Equity transaction documentation *that has been audited*
Product characteristics and features	Product characteristic measurement against product specifications; Product developer's documented concepts and features	Product developer's requirements and specifications
Product price	Current advertised price on label, shelf, or in advertisement (Note: label price may be overridden by sale ads.) (Note: Commercial product prices may be controlled by procurement agreements.)	Published price schedules for items within a timeframe, if any
Utility (water, gas, electricity, oil) consumption	Secondary, calibrated in-line meters to re-record consumption	Consumer feedback regarding meter readings (This only gives indication of a potential problem; leakage may occur and be undetected for some time.)

NOTE You must have a defined and repeatable process to be consistent in assessments across assessment events. Be sure to use the same verification source across all measurement events. If an Accuracy-to-Surrogate source seems to be unreliable, conduct an Accuracy-to-Reality on that surrogate source. It the source is found to be unreliable, replace it with another source. Document that you have changed sources to identify a source of variation in the IQ assessment results.

Guidelines

Be sure to conduct Accuracy-to-Reality in CTQ Information, as it is the most authoritative assessment of Inherent Quality in Information. You should conduct this in lieu of using surrogate third-party sources if you have control of access to the objects and events, and can record or observe the events, and access and measure or compare the data to the physical objects.

NOTE Neither Accuracy-to-Surrogate tests or Validity tests are an adequate substitute for physical Accuracy-to-Reality tests when you must know the truth.

Step P2.6: Extract Statistically Valid Sample of Data

Because Physical Accuracy tests can be expensive, going out to verify data against the Real-World Objects, Statistical Sampling of the data is critical to minimize the *costs* of the assessments without compromising the confidence in the assessment results. This can also be used for other assessments as well.

> **NOTE** Quality Assessment, whether Manufactured Products or Information, requires the elimination of bias in sampling and in the assessment process itself. Sampling requires techniques that ensure your sample is extracted according to statistical sampling methods, described in the following process steps.

Objective of Step P2.6

To select an appropriate number and mix of records to ensure the Quality Assessment of the sample *accurately* reflects the state of the total data population being assessed while minimizing the assessment costs.

Figure 5-17 illustrates the components of Step P2.6.

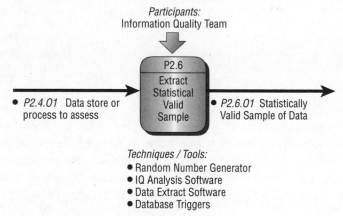

Figure 5-17: Step P2.6 Extract a Statistically Valid Sample.

Inputs of Step P2.6

- *P2.4.O1* **Database Files List for Quality Assessment:** The source from which to sample.

- **Processes that create this data**

Outputs of Step P2.6

■ *P2.6.O1 Statistically Valid Sample of Data:* This is the actual set of records to assess in a Secure Data Store that has not *corrupted* the data contents.

Participants and Roles for Step P2.6

Table 5-8 represents participants and roles in Step P2.6.

Table 5-8: Participants for P2.6: Extract a Statistically Valid Sample of Data.

PARTICIPANT	IQ ACTIVITY ROLE
Information Quality Team	Led by an Information Quality Specialist, calculates the sample size and extracts a valid sample using statistical methods.

NOTE The IQ Specialist must conduct the sampling and assessment in an absolute independent and unbiased way to ensure the integrity of the assessment.

Techniques and Tools for Step P2.6

■ **Random Number Generator:** Used to select records out of a total population to be sampled for assessment

■ **IQ Analysis Software:** Used to select records to sample or to sample an entire population of records

■ **Data Extract Software:** Internally developed sampling application

■ **Database Triggers:** Used to sample a record on insert or update, based upon the random sampling number generated

Step P2.6: Extract Statistically Valid Sample of Data: Process Steps and Guidelines

P2.6.1 Identify the total number of records in the full population of records. For data store assessment, use a simple record count query.

For process assessment, count the number of records created in a typical cycle of time to calculate an average number of records created in a day (week or month, depending on your natural cycle).

P2.6.2 Estimate the Standard Deviation of the total population of records by extracting a small sample (50 or 100 records) that will be used to calculate your sample size. If you have already assessed a sample using statistical techniques, use the Standard Deviation found in that sample. To calculate the Standard Deviation of the sample, use the formula:

$$s = \sqrt{(\Sigma d^2/(n-1))},$$

where:

s = the Standard Deviation of a sample;

d = the Deviation of an item from the mean or average;

n = the number of records in the sample;

Σ = "the sum of."

Calculate Standard Deviation Process Steps

1. Count the number of Records in the sample.

2. Count the number of Data Elements in all records that contain a defect of the IQ Characteristic measured.

3. Calculate the Mean (**x**) or average number of errors per record by dividing the total number of errors by the number of sampled records.

4. Calculate the Deviation (**d**) of each record by subtracting the mean number of errors from the actual number of errors in the record.

5. Calculate the Deviation squared (**d²**) for each record by multiplying the deviation by itself.

6. Calculate the sum of the deviations squared (**Σd²**) by adding all of the deviations squared together.

7. Calculate the Standard Deviation of the data sample (*s*) by dividing the sum of the deviations squared (**Σd²**) by the value of one less than the number of records in the sample (*n*-1) and taking the square root of the result.

Figure 5-18 represents a sample to illustrate the calculation of Standard Deviation in Table 5-9.

The example of a sample of records with inaccurate values marked contains 23 errors (defect in accuracy) found in 10 of the 50 records. To calculate the standard deviation, follow the calculation procedure in Table 5-9.

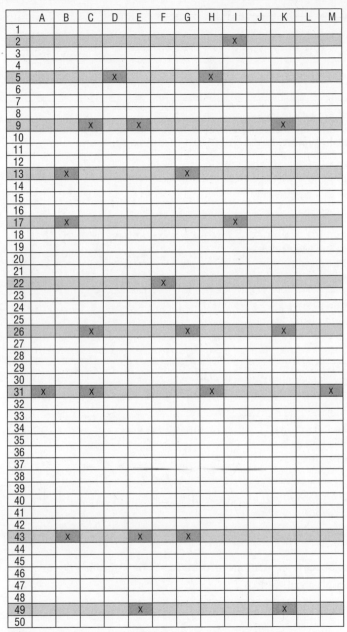

Figure 5-18: Sample of 50 Records with 23 NOT Accurate Data Values
Marked "X" in 10 Records with One or More Defects

Table 5-9: Example Calculation of the Standard Deviation of a Sample[6]

STANDARD DEVIATION CALCULATION STEPS	CALCULATION	RESULT
1. Count the number of records in the sample.	50 =	50
2. Count the number of data elements in all records that contain a defect of the IQ Characteristic measured.	23 =	23
3. Calculate the Mean (x) or average number of errors per record by dividing the total number of errors by the number of sampled records.	23 / 50 =	0.46
4. Calculate the Deviation (d) of each record by subtracting the Mean number of errors from the actual number of errors in the record.	Record 1 = 0 - 0.46 = Record 2 = 1 - 0.46 = etc.	-0.46 0.54
5. Calculate the Deviation Squared (d²) for each record by multiplying the deviation by itself.	Rec 1 = -0.46 x -0.46= Rec 2 = 0.54 x 0.54 = etc.	0.2116 0.2916
6. Calculate the Sum of the Deviations Squared (Σd²) by adding all of the deviations squared together.	0.2116 + 0.2916 + etc. =	50.4200
7. Divide the Sum of the Deviations Squared (Σd²) by the value of one less than the number of records in the sample (n-1).	50.4200 / (50-1) =	1.0290
8. Calculate the Standard Deviation of the data sample by taking the square root of the result.	√1.0290	1.0144

> **NOTE** For continuous process control monitoring, use the standard deviation of the previous sample assessed.

Calculate Sample Size

The formula for determining a statistical sample size is:

$$n = ((z \times s) / B)^2,$$

where:

n = the number of records to extract.

z = a Constant representing the Confidence Level you desire. How confident are you that the measurement of the sample is within some specified variation of the actual state of the data population? The confidence level is the degree of certainty, expressed as a percentage, of being sure about the estimate of the mean. For example, a 95 percent confidence level indicates that if you took 100 samples, the mean of the total population would be within the confidence interval (mean plus or minus the bound) in 95 of the 100 samples taken. There are statistical charts containing these constants. However, the three most-used confidence levels and their constants include those shown in Table 5-10.

Table 5-10: z Constant Values for Confidence Level Desired

CONFIDENCE LEVEL	z CONSTANT
99%	z = 2.575
95%	z = 1.960
90%	z = 1.645

s = an estimate of the Standard Deviation of the Data Population being measured. There is an inverse relationship between the degree of variation of errors within the data population and the sample size for analysis. The larger the variation, the smaller the sample size required to get an accurate picture of the entire population. The smaller the variation, the larger the sample size required. The fewer the errors, the more records must be sampled to find the defective records.

B = the Bound or the Precision of the measurement. This represents the variation from the sample mean within which the mean of the total data population is expected to fall given the sample size, confidence level, and standard deviation. If a sample (see Table 5-9) has a mean of 0.4600 errors per record, and a Bound of 0.0460, the mean of the total data population is expected to fall within a range of 0.4600 ± 0.0460, or from 0.4140 to 0.5060 errors per record, given the sample size, Confidence Level, and Standard Deviation.

NOTE If records of a given type, such as Order, are captured in separate locations, such as call centers or stores, you have a distributed population. Your sample should have a proportional representation of records from the distributed populations that together make a union of a single enterprise population. Your subsequent analysis may yield different patterns of error in the different strata of distributed sources.

> **NOTE** For ease of Statistical Process Control, select a Sample quantity above the calculated minimum sample size. It will keep your Quality Control Charts with the same Upper and Lower Control Limits.

Calculate Sample Size Process Steps

1. Define the confidence level you desire for the assessment (99%, 95%, 90%, or other) and put the z constant, from Table 5-10, in the sample size formula.

> **NOTE** An alternative to determining the bound is to set a fixed number of records to sample, such as 300, 500, 1,000, or 2,000 and a desired confidence level, and then let the bound be calculated in the sample size formula.

2. Calculate or select the Sample Size for the assessed Information Group: $n = ((z \times s) / B)^2$.

   2.1 Determine the Confidence Level (99%, 95%, 90%).

   2.2 Determine the Bound ± Variation from the Mean of a sample.

   2.3 Determine the Standard Deviation from a quick sample or from a previous calculation.

   2.4 Multiply the z constant times the Standard Deviation (s).

   2.5 Divide the result by the Bound.

   2.6 Square the result.

   2.7 Round up to the next whole number. This is the Sample Size to accomplish the Confidence Level.

Table 5-11 shows the calculation of a Sample Size based on the Standard Deviation in Figure 5-9.

Table 5-11: Example of a Calculation of Sample Size

SAMPLE SIZE CALCULATION STEP	CALCULATION	RESULT
1. Determine Confidence Level (99%, 95%, 90%) and the z constant.	95% Confidence, z = 1.960	1.960
2. Determine the Bound, expressed as a percent ± of the mean of a sample).	Bound = 10% of mean = 0.10 * 0.46 =	± 0.046
3. Take the Standard Deviation from a quick sample or a previous assessment in which the Standard Deviation was taken and plug that into the Sample Size Calculation.	s = 1.0144	1.0144

SAMPLE SIZE CALCULATION STEP	CALCULATION	RESULT
4. Multiply the z constant by the s standard deviation.	(z * s) = 1.960 * 1.0144	1.9882
5. Divide the result by the Bound (0,046).	(1.9882 / 0.046) =	43.22
6. Square the result.	43.22 * 43.22 =	1,867.97
7. Calculate the sample size by rounding the result to the next highest number (even if the fraction is less than 0.5).	1,867.97 =	1,868

NOTE For ease of Statistical Process Control, select a Sample Quantity above the calculated minimum sample size. It will keep your Quality Control Charts with the same Upper and Lower Control Limits.

P2.6.4 Implement a mechanism to execute the random number generator in the sampling process.

TIP If you wish to extract a given *percentage* of records from a population, use a random number generator from 0 to 1, where 0 = no sampling, and 1 = 100% sampling. If your percentage is five percent of the records, set r = to 0.05 (5% of 1) and select record where r ≤ 0.05.

TIP If you wish to extract a given *number* of records from a population, determine the number of records to be extracted out of the total population and calculate the percent of sampled records out of the total population. If, for example you wish to select 300 records out of a population of 2,200 records (say the average number of orders per day), then 300 / 2,200 = 13.64%. Use a random number generator from 0 to 1, where 0 = no sampling, and 1 = 100% sampling. If your percentage is 13.64%, set r = to 0.1364 (13.64% of 1) and select record where r ≤ 0.1364. This is especially important if you want to collect the same number in a sample. There will be some variation in the number sampled, based on the variation in the number of orders taken per day.

- For originating application programs that create data into a relational database with trigger capability, set a random number generator routine that will calculate whether or not a record will be selected on record insertion.

- For paper documents where information is first created, count and number each paper document individually. Based on the number of documents in the total population, calculate your Sample Size. Develop a random number generation routine or use sampling software to calculate a number that will achieve your calculated Sample Size.

P2.6.5 Isolate the sampled records in a controlled data store or paper record, or photocopied image of the source creation document.

▪ For electronic records, write them to the Sample Database before the record is confirmed and updates can be made.

NOTE **For integrity of the assessment process, the chain of custody of the sampled records or paper documents must be controlled to prevent tampering with or altering the electronic records or paper documents. For electronic records, you must prevent updates to any of the sampled records. For paper records, you must prevent alteration of the information collected.**

P2.6.6 Document the Controls in the Chain of Custody of the Sampled Records to be assessed that prevents alteration or updates to the data once it has been extracted for assessment.

▪ For original electronically created data, you must ensure that:

1. The Information Producers are not aware of the timing of the sampling for IQ Assessment. This will *bias* their information production activities.

2. The sampling process ensures a statistical random sample (each record has equal likelihood of being selected) that ensures the minimum number of records given the standard deviation of a quick sample or previous assessment sample.

3. The process has not been modified in any way from the currently defined procedures, equipment, and personnel.

4. The records have *not* been altered since record creation.

5. The records sampling process did not introduce errors into the sampled records.

6. The data store into which the sampled electronic records are stored did not corrupt the data, such as by truncating data values, mapping data to incompatible data types (such as variable to fixed size or numeric to alphanumeric or scientific notation), having inconsistent format with the source database, or treating missing values differently.

▪ For information created on paper documents, ensure that:

1. The records could *not* have been altered by someone since record creation. Erasures or Strike-Outs are evidence of alteration. Seek to find out the original values and reason for change, or else reject the record.

2. Treat Erasures or Strike-Outs as corrections to an original value.

3. The records sampling process did not introduce errors into the sampled records, such as pulling a paper record that was not selected by the random number generator.

4. Any photocopying made of the actual documents did not introduce errors into the copy, such as missing parts of the data at the edges of the document or being too light, failing to reveal data or erasures, or too dark, obscuring the readability of the data.

P2.6.7 Make the data available to the assessment process, again, controlling the chain of custody to assure no alteration in the data.

NOTE Without the assurance of Sound Statistical Methods to Sample data and without assurance of the Integrity of the Chain of Custody of the Sampled data, you can lose credibility of any Assessment result.

Step P2.7: Measure Information Quality

This process step conducts the actual measure of Information Quality.

Objective of Step P2.7

To measure a data sample against specific IQ Characteristics in a controlled way to determine process reliability (quality) or variation and to discover the kind and degree of defects

Figure 5-19 lists the components of Step P2.7.

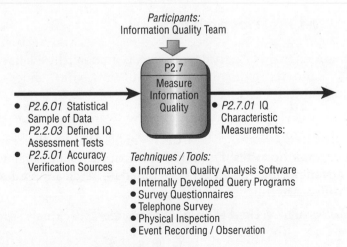

Figure 5-19: P2.7 Measure Information Quality.

Inputs to Step P2.7

P2.6.O1 Random Sample of Data: The data records or documents to be assessed

P2.2.O1 Defined Business Rules and Measures: The specific IQ Characteristics and Assessment tests to be executed, such as Completeness, Accuracy, Validity, Presentation Intuitiveness, for example

P2.5.O1 Data Accuracy Verification Source List: The sources used to ensure the Accuracy (to Reality and to a Surrogate Source)

Outputs of Step P2.7

P2.7.O1 IQ Characteristic Measurements: The results in the form of "Vital Statistics" of IQ Quality Measurement for each IQ Characteristic for the sample of data

Participants and Roles in Step P2.7

Table 5-12 represents participants and roles in Step P2.7.

Table 5-12: P2.7 Measure Information Quality Participants and Roles.

PARTICIPANT	IQ ACTIVITY ROLE
Information Quality Team	Led by an Information Quality Specialist, conducts or oversees the execution of the Assessment Tests.

Techniques and Tools for Step P2.7

- **Information Quality Analysis software:** Commercially available software used to Validate Conformance to Valid Values or Business Rules and non-duplication of records

- **Internally developed Query programs:** Software routines created by internal staff to Validate Conformance to Valid Values or Business Rules

- **Survey Questionnaires:** Developed for individual persons to verify the Accuracy of personal data or transaction data being assessed, which they can confirm without bias

- **Telephone survey:** Used to verify Accuracy of individuals as to data they can confirm without bias

- **Physical Inspection:** Used to measure Accuracy of Real-World Physical Objects, Locations, Facilities, or Equipment

- **Event Recording (or Event Observation):** Used to measure Accuracy of Real-World Events, such as equity trades, banking transactions, orders, or airline reservations made over the phone or in person

- **Spreadsheets:** Used to capture Assessment Results

Step P2.7: Measure Information Quality: Process Steps and Guidelines

Step P2.7.1 Review the design of the IQ Assessment tests as defined in P2.2.O3.

Step P2.7.2 Execute the IQ Assessment tests in a way that is totally *independent and unbiased.*

> **NOTE** Ensure that you are testing an as-is process without alteration. If there have been "adjustments" made in the process by people that know you are conducting the assessment, they may vary their behavior, giving you a false reading of the actual process performance.

> **NOTE** Ensure that the Information Producers are not aware of the sampling time period.

> **TIP** Ensure that you do not introduce bias in the Assessment by seeking to interpret the data. You must measure the data *without bias* as to the comparison of the data to the defined business rules or the Attributes of the Real-World Objects or Events the data represent.

> **NOTE** Do *not* mix Assessment of different IQ Characteristics into one Assessment Test result. Test Value Completeness, Validity (Values and Business Rules), Non-duplication, and Accuracy in separate tests. Test Presentation Quality by getting Information Customer Satisfaction in the way Information is provided and presented to them.

Step P2.7.3 As you conduct each Assessment Test, capture the Assessment "Vital Statistics" in each IQ Characteristic measured:

- Total number of Records assessed
- Total number of Data Elements assessed
- Total number of Defects identified (by individual IQ Characteristic)
- Total number of Sampled Records with one or more defects
- Mean Number of Defects per Record
- Average Number of Defects per Record with one or more errors

In the example in Figure 5-18, there were:

- Fifty (50) Records in the sample
- Each Record had 13 Data Elements assessed
- Twenty-three Errors in all records
- Ten of the 50 Records contained one or more errors

Table 5-13 illustrates the calculation of the IQ Vital Statistics in the Accuracy Assessment conducted of the preceding sample. You will conduct this for each content IQ Characteristic measured, such as Value Completeness, Validity, Accuracy to the Real-World Object.

Assessments of other Characteristics, such as Non-duplication, will be different.

Table 5-13: IQ Vital Statistics of Content Assessment (Accuracy Here)

IQ VITAL STATISTIC	CALCULATION	RESULT
Total Records in sample	=	50
Total Data Elements per record in assessment	=	13
Total Defect Opportunity (number of records times the number of data elements)	50 * 13 =	650
Count of all Data Elements with a Defect	=	23
Count of Records with one or more defects	=	10
Total Defect percent	23 / 650 =	3.5384%
Defective Record percent	10 / 50 =	20%
Mean Defect per total record	23 / 50 =	0.46
Std Deviation = $s = \sqrt{(\Sigma d^2 / (n - 1))}$	$\sqrt{(50.4200/49)} =$	1.0144
Mean Defect per Defective Record count	23 / 10 =	2.3
DPMO (Defects Per Million Opportunities)	3.5384%*1,000,000 =	35,384

These vital statistics will be used in calculating Quality Control Charts in the next TIQM Step P2.8. See Table 5-9 for the steps to calculate standard deviation.

Guidelines for Step P2.7

To measure Accuracy of the selected facts, compare the data Value for each Fact to the Characteristic of the Real-World Object the Fact represents. For Accuracy of a product price, compare the product price to the price of the product established by the product manager for the applicable time period. Measure the "Shipping" Weight, by taking samples of the product, as packaged, and weigh each package to determine if the *actual* shipping Weight of the Package is within Specifications of that product's shipping weight.

Step P2.8: Interpret and Report Information Quality

This step translates the raw data of the Assessment into actionable Graphics and Recommendations for next steps.

Objective of Step P2.8

To communicate the state of Information Quality in a way that:

- Enables Knowledge Workers to know their Information's Reliability.
- Provides feedback to Information Producers and Managers on how well their processes are performing.
- To identify Processes that Require Improvement based on the impact of defects and to facilitate Root-Cause analysis
- Figure 5-20 shows components of reporting in P2.8.

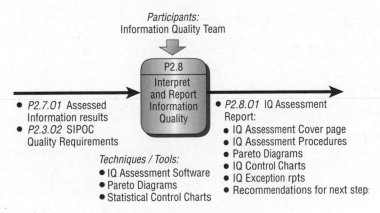

Figure 5-20: P2.8 Interpret and Report Information Quality.

Inputs to Step P2.8

- **P2.7.O1 Assessed Information Results:** The raw data of the Assessments used to Interpret and Present the Graphic Representations and Next Steps based on P2.3.O2 SIPOC Quality Requirements

▪ **P2.3.O2 SIPOC Quality Requirements:** Used to determine recommendations for next steps based on measured results

Outputs of Step P2.8

P2.8.O1 **IQ Assessment Report:**

- ▪ **IQ Assessment cover page:** Introduces the assessment formally.

- ▪ **IQ Assessment procedures:** Describes the controls used to assure the assessment was controlled and unbiased.

- ▪ **IQ Vital Stats by IQ Characteristic:** To document the actual findings of the Assessment

- ▪ **Pareto Diagrams:** To describe Defect Types by Frequency or Impact

- ▪ **IQ Control Charts:** To describe Process Capability over time

- ▪ **IQ Exception Reports:** To identify data to correct

- ▪ **Other reports or charts as warranted:** As needed for unusual requirements

- ▪ **Recommendations for next steps:** Suggested Process Improvement Initiatives and one-time data correction initiatives as may be required

Participants and Roles for Step P2.8

Table 5-14 represents the participants and roles in P2.8.

Table 5-14: P2.8: Interpret and Report Information Quality Participants and Roles.

PARTICIPANT	IQ ACTIVITY ROLE
Information Quality Team	Led by an Information Quality Specialist, analyzes the Assessment results in the various IQ Characteristics and identifies the significance and next steps based on the Assessment Results and the Requirements of the Information Consumers.

Techniques and Tools for Step P2.8

- ▪ **IQ Assessment software:** Purchased or internally developed Software used to Assess Validity, Completeness, Conformance to Business Rules. These may have acceptable reporting capabilities for the applicable assessment tests.

- **Pareto Diagrams:** To represent Defect Types in priority sequence
- **Statistical Control Charts:** To report Process Performance *over time*

Step P2.8: Interpret and Report Information Quality: Process Steps and Guidelines

TIP Be sure to differentiate between major and minor error types, as illustrated in the following real-life story.

FAILURE TO REPORT IQ BY SIGNIFICANCE CAN LEAD TO MISTRUST

I attended a Senior Management presentation by a new IQ Team. The IQ analyst presented the results of their recent (and first) IQ assessment of their Customer information. She proudly announced that a serious problem existed in their Customer information with 57 percent of the Customer records having one or more errors in them.

A Senior Manager asked her if that figure was for major errors like wrong addresses or did it also include minor errors like inconsequential spelling of an organization name. She had to confess to the latter, without having the segmentation between the two. The look on the Executive's face clearly revealed that he could not trust the assessment!

Process steps include:

P2.8.1 Collect all Assessment Results produced in Step P2.7.O1.

P2.8.2 Draft the Assessment Procedure Summary, describing the Assessment Procedures, the IQ Assessment Vital Statistics, the IQ Characteristics Assessed, using Form P2.8.O1.F1.2 and 3 on the IQ Applied book Web site at www.wiley.com/go/IQApplied, or an alternative to establish the credibility of the various assessments. See Figures 5-21, 5-22, and 5-23 for documenting IQ Assessment procedure and findings and recommendations in IQ Characteristics assessed.

P2.8.3 Select the right reporting technique for each IQ Characteristic assessment result. For example, use Form P2.8.O1.F1 forms for the Vital Statistics for each IQ content characteristic assessed. Use P2.8.O1.F1.5 for Equivalence of redundant data and P2.8.O1.F1.6 for Timeliness Assessment. See Figure 5-24 for an example Vital Statistics for an Accuracy Assessment.

IQ Assessment Cover Letter

Information Group:	Customer Order and Order Item
Assessed By:	CCE
Assessment Date:	Aug 18,

Background

The Information Quality Team has assessed the following information group by assessing the data contained in the listed source files and databases or produced by the listed business processes. This assessment covers data created or updated during the period indicated.

File(s) or Database(s) Sampled & Assessed:	Customer Order Fulfillment DB
Process(es) Sampled and Assessed:	Customer Order Create, Pick, Ship, Invoice, Apply Payment;
Start Date/Time From:	July 1, 12:00:00 am
End Date/Time To:	July 31 11:59:59 pm

IQ Assessment Approach

The quality of the information assessed is the responsibility of the process manager or managers of the respective information process or processes. The Information Quality Assessor's responsibility is to express an opinion on the data's reliability based on our assessment.

We have conducted this assessment in accordance with generally accepted statistical sampling procedures and internally developed assessment process specifications found in the *Total Information Quality Management Processes and Guidelines* Section TIQM P1. *Assess Information Quality*. The accompanying attachments document:

- Assessment Findings and Recommendations for next actions
- The specific Procedures used for this IQ assessment
- Vital Stats for Accuracy and Validity assessments
- Specific Pareto Diagrams of defect types and Quality Control Charts of current process quality

General IQ Assessment Conclusions

Our detailed Findings and Recommendations on the next page.
In our opinion, according to customer surveys of expectations of this information, we reached the following general conclusions with respect to the assessed information and information processes:

1. There are significant problems with Order placement and order items that require immediate attention to the processes because of the downstream process failures and Information Scrap and Rework.

2. There is excessive information float in the Order Fulfillment Value Circle that prevents timely access to product replenishment and financial analysis that requires attention for it is causing waste in financial float.
Specific recommendations follow in the next pages.

Sincerely,

CCE

The Information Quality Team

Figure 5-21: IQ Assessment Cover Letter Example

TIQM® Quality System

IQ Assessment Findings and Recommendations

Information Group:	Customer Order, Order Item
Assessed By:	CCE
Assessment Date:	Aug 18,
Page:	1 of 1

IQ Assessment Findings and Recommendations

In our opinion, according to Customer surveys of expectations of this information, we found the following findings and make the following recommendations based upon the Knowledge Workers' information requirements:

1.	1A. Finding: There are significant problems with Order placement and order items. 1B. Recommendation: :Conduct a Cost-of-Poor Quality Information analysis followed by a PDSA Process Improvement initiative on the Order placement process. 1C. Recommendation: Once the Process Improvement has been made, take corrective action to correct errors in Order Fulfillment Customer databases.
2.	2A. Finding: There is excessive information float in the Order Fulfillment Value Circle that prevents timely access to product replenishment and financial analysis. 2B. Recommendation: Conduct a PDSA Process Improvement initiative on the Order Fulfillment Value Circle to improve tImellness of information.
3.	3A. Finding: 3B. Recommendation:
4.	4A. Finding: 4B. Recommendation:
5.	5A. Finding: 5B. Recommendation:
6.	6A. Finding: 6B. Recommendation:
7.	7A. Finding: 7B. Recommendation:
8.	8A. Finding: 8B. Recommendation:
9.	9A. Finding: 9B. Recommendation:
10.	10A. Finding: 10B. Recommendation:
11.	11A. Finding: 11B. Recommendation:
12.	12A. Finding: 12B. Recommendation:

Form P2.8.01.F1.2 IQ Assessment Recommendations Form
Revised: 2009/01/30

1 of 1

Figure 5-22: IQ Assessment Findings and Recommendations Example

IQ Information Quality — TIQM® Quality System

IQ Characteristics Assessed

Information Group:	Customer
Assessed By:	CCE
Assessment Date:	Aug 18
	Background
	See IQ Characteristics in Chapter 5, "Step-by-Step Guide to *Assessing Information Quality.*" Headings "Quality Characteristics of Information Content" and "Quality Characteristics of Information Presentation."
File(s) or Database(s) Sampled & Assessed:	Customer Order Fulfillment DB
Process(es) Sampled and Assessed:	Customer Order Create, Pick, Ship, Invoice, Apply Payment;
Start Date/Time From:	July 1, 12:00:00 am
End Date/Time To:	July 31 11:59:59 pm

Assessed			IQ Characteristics Assessed
Yes	**No**	**N/A**	**Content Characteristics**
[]	[]	[]	Definition Conformance
[]	[]	[]	Record Existence
[]	[]	[]	Value Existence
[X]	[]	[]	Value Completeness
[X]	[]	[]	Accuracy and Precision to Reality
[]	[]	[]	Accuracy and Precision to Surrogate Source
[X]	[]	[]	Value Validity
[X]	[]	[]	Business Rule Validity
[]	[]	[]	Derivation Validity
[X]	[]	[]	Non-Duplication
[X]	[]	[]	Redundancy Equivalence
[]	[]	[]	Source Quality Warranties or Certifications
Yes	**No**	**N/A**	**Presentation Characteristics**
[]	[]	[]	Availability
[X]	[]	[]	Accessibility Timeliness
[]	[]	[]	Presentation Media Appropriateness
[]	[]	[]	Relevance
[]	[]	[]	Value Format Standardization
[]	[]	[]	Document Standardization
[]	[]	[]	Signage Standardization
[]	[]	[]	Presentation Clarity, Objectivity and Utility
[]	[]	[]	Other 1:
[]	[]	[]	Other 2
[]	[]	[]	Other 3:

Form P2.8.O1.F1.3 IQ Characteristics Assessed
Revised: 2009/08/01

1 of 1

Figure 5-23: IQ Characteristics Assessed Example page

TIQM® Quality System

IQ Assessment Results Vital Statistics	
Information Group:	Customer Basic Information
Assessed By:	CCE
Assessment Date:	25-Sep
File(s) or Database(s) Sampled & Assessed:	Customer Master DB
Process(es) Sampled and Assessed:	Customer Create in OF Process
Start Date/Time From:	1 August Midnight
End Date/Time To:	31 August 11:59:59pm

IQ Vital Stats and Assessment Results		
Information Group:	*Customer Basic Information*	
IQ Characteristic:	*Accuracy to Reality*	
Vital Stats	*Formula*	*Result*
Sample Record Count	" = Record Count"	50
Sample Attribute Count	" = Data Element Count"	13
Total Defect Opportunity	" = Rec Count * Data Element Count"	650
Total Defect Count	" = Total Count of Defects"	23
Mean Defects / Record	" = Tot Defect count / Record count"	0.46
Confidence Interval	" Mean ± 10% of mean"	0.414 - 0.506
Confidence Level		95%
Standard Deviation	$" = \sqrt{\Sigma d^2 / (n-1)}"$	1.0144
Total Defect Percent	" = Defect Count / Tot Opportunity"	3.5385%
DPMO	" = Defect percent * 1,000,000"	35,385
Total Defective Record Count	" = Count of Defective Records"	10
Percent Defective Records	" = Defective Rec Count / Rec Count"	20.00%

* Notes: Enter data into the blank fields in the Result column; Shaded fields contain calculations

Figure 5-24: Vital Statistics for Accuracy Assessment Example Page

Figure 5-25 represents an Equivalence of Redundant Data assessment.

IQ Information Quality

TIQM® Quality System

IQ Assessment Results
Vital Statistics

Information Group:	Customer Order Information
Assessed By:	MM
Assessment Date:	18-Jul
File(s) or Database(s) Sampled & Assessed:	Order Record-of-Origin DB to Shipping Order DB
Process(es) Sampled and Assessed:	Order Update Activity
Start Date/Time From:	June 1 12:00am
End Date/Time To:	June 30, 11:59:59 pm

IQ Vital Stats and Assessment Results

Information Group:	Order Information	
IQ Characteristic:	*Equivalence*	
DB1: Order Record-of-Origin DB	DB2: Shipping Order DB	
Vital Stats	*Formula*	*Result*
Sample Record Count	" = Record Count"	1,000
Sample Attribute Count	" = Data Element Count"	12
Total Defect Opportunity	" = Rec Count * Data Element Count"	12,000
Total Defect Count (Not Equivalent)	" = Total Count of Defects"	3,397
Percent Not Equivalent	" = Percent NOT Equivalent"	28.3%
Record Count in DB1 Missing in DB2	" = Record count in DB1 NOT in DB2)"	132
Percent Records Missing in DB2	" = Percent Missing in DB2"	13.2%

* Notes: Enter data into the blank fields in the Result column; Shaded fields contain calculations

Form P2.8.O1.F1.5 IQ Characteristic Assessment Vital Stats Template-Equivalence
Revised: 2009/08/01
1 of 1

Figure 5-25: Vital Statistics for Equivalence of Redundant Data Assessment

Figure 5-26 illustrates the Vital Statistics for a timeliness assessment.

IQ Information Quality

TIQM® Quality System

IQ Assessment Results Vital Statistics	
Information Group:	Order and Order Item Financials
Assessed By:	JRJ
Assessment Date:	18-Jul
File(s) or Database(s) Sampled & Assessed:	Order Create and downstream databases
Process(es) Sampled and Assessed:	Order Fulfilment
Start Date/Time From:	June 16 / 12:00:00am
End Date/Time To:	June 16 11:59:59pm

IQ Vital Stats and Assessment Results		
Information Group:	*Order and Order Item Financials*	
IQ Characteristic:	*Timeliness*	
Vital Stats	*Formula*	*Result*
Sample Size	" = Record Count"	100
Paper Record of Origin Date/Time	" = Paper Record Date/Time"	N/A
Mean Electronic Record of Origin Date/Time	" = Average Date/Time of all records"	June 16, 2:47pm
Mean Electronic Date/Time avail to 1st KWs	" = Available to Credit Analysts"	June 17, 8:00am
Information Float to 1st KWs	" = Information Float to Credit Analysts"	18H:13M
Mean Electronic Date/Time avail to 2nd KWs	" = Available to Whse Clerk"	June 17, 12:32pm
Information Float to 2nd KWs	" = Information Float to Whse Clerk"	22H:26M
Mean Electronic Date/Time avail to 3rd KWs	" = Available to Shipping Clerk"	June 17, 6:42pm
Information Float to 3rd KWs	" = Information Float to Shipping Clerk"	28H:55M
Mean Electronic Date/Time avail to 4th KWs	" = Available to A/R Clerk (Invoice)"	June 18, 8:00am
Information Float to 4th KWs	" = Information Float to A/R Clerk"	37H:13M
Mean Electronic Date/Time avail to 5th KWs	" = Available to A/R Clerk (Pmt)"	July 11, 12:02pm
Information Float to 5th KWs	" = Information Float to A/R Clerk"	25D:17H:15M
Mean Electronic Date/Time avail to 6th KWs	" = Available to Auditor"	July 17, 8:00am
Information Float to 6th KWs	" = Information Float to Auditor"	31D:13H:13M
Mean Electronic Date/Time avail to 7th KWs	" = Available to Data Whse"	Aug 1, 8:00am
Information Float to 7th KWs	" = Information Float to Data Whse"	45D:21H:13M
Mean Electronic Date/Time avail to 8th KWs	" = Available to Fin Data Mart"	Aug 2, 8:00am
Information Float to 8th KWs	" = Information Float to FinData Mart"	46D:21H:13M
Mean Electronic Date/Time avail to 9th KWs		
Information Float to 9th KWs		
Mean Electronic Date/Time avail to 10th KWs		
Information Float to 10th KWs		

* Notes: Enter data into the blank fields in the Result column; Shaded fields contain calculations

Figure 5-26: Vital Statistics for a Timeliness Assessment, Measuring Information Float Across a Value Circle

Figure 5-27 illustrates a Non-Duplication assessment.

TIQM® Quality System

IQ Assessment Results Vital Statistics		
Information Group:	[Insert name of Information Group Assessed here]	
Assessed By:	[Insert name of IQ Assessor here]	
Assessment Date:	[Insert date of assessment here]	
File(s) or Database(s) Sampled & Assessed:	[Insert name of database sampled and assessed here]	
Process(es) Sampled and Assessed:	[Insert name of process assessed here]	
Start Date/Time From:	[Insert start date and time of data sampling here]	
End Date/Time To:	Insert end date and time of data sampling here]	

IQ Vital Stats and Assessment Results		
Information Group:	*[Insert Information Group Assessed here]*	
IQ Characteristic:	*Nonduplication*	
Vital Stats	*Formula*	*Result*
Sample Record Count	" = Record Count"	10,000
Data Store Record Count	" = Total Record Population Count"	12,116,219
Duplicate Record Count	" = Duplicate record count in sample"	3,723
Percent Duplicate Records	" = Percent duplicates"	**37.2%**
Duplicate Records in Total Population	" = % in sample * total record count"	4,510,868
Unique records with one or more dups	" count of sample recs w. 1+ dups"	3,581
Percent unique Rec's w. 1+ duplicates	" = % unique w 1+ duplicates"	**35.8%**
Percent unique Rec's w. 1+ duplicates in Pop	" = % unique * Total Population"	**4,338,818**

* Notes: Enter data into the blank fields in the Result column; Shaded fields contain calculations

Form P2.8.O1.F1.7 IQ Characteristic Assessment Vital Stats Template-Nonduplication   1 of 1
Revised: 2009/08/01   © 2009 Information Impact International Inc   all rights reserved

Figure 5-27: Vital Statistics for a Non-Duplication Assessment

■ Summary Charts and Pareto Diagrams for identifying Defect Types, such as Inaccurate Values in the various data elements in one Pareto, Missing Data in another Pareto, and Invalid Values, or Non-conformance to Business Rules in yet another Pareto. See Figure 5-28 for an example of a summary chart.

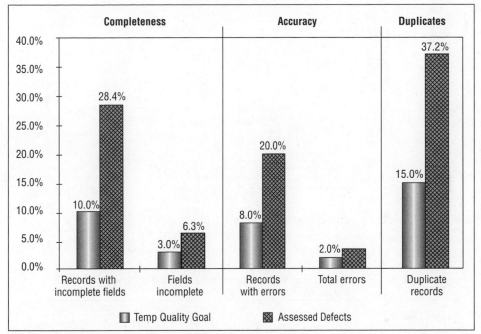

Figure 5-28: Summary Chart of Critical IQ Characteristics

Summary charts should be exploded into meaningful Pareto Diagrams, by error type or data elements in error, as illustrated in Figure 5-29.

The number at the top of each column represents the number of defects of that type found. The cumulative percentage graph represents the cumulative percent of errors of each type from most frequent to least frequent.

A more useful Pareto, however, is the "Impact Pareto," where you weight the different defect types by actual cost of process failure downstream and Information Scrap and Rework, or by relative estimated impact on process failure downstream.

Figure 5-30 is an illustration of an Impact Pareto Diagram by costs or impact of error type.

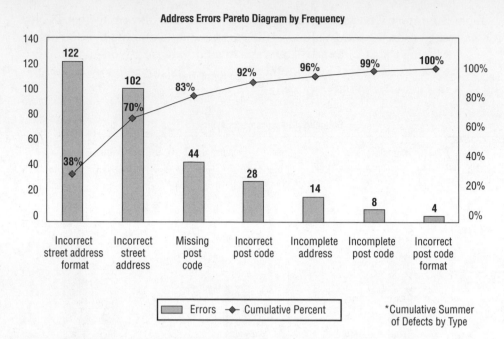

Figure 5-29: Frequency Pareto Diagram of Defect Types in Address Records

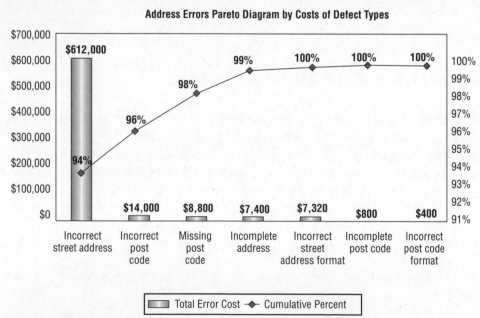

Figure 5-30: Address Errors Pareto Diagram by Costs of Defect Types

Table 5-15 provides the raw data and its calculation of an Impact (Cost of Poor IQ) Diagram as presented in Figure 5-30.

Table 5-15: Calculation of an Impact Pareto by Costs of Defect Types

A	B	C	D	E	F
ERROR COUNT	ERROR WEIGHT COST/ERR	WEIGHTED RESULT	ERROR TYPE	TOTAL ERROR COST/YR	SAMPLE PERCENT OF POPULATION
122	$0.60	$73.20	Incorrect street address format	$7,320	1%
102	$60.00	$6,120.00	Incorrect street address	$612,000	1%
44	$2.00	$88.00	Missing post code	$8,800	1%
28	$5.00	$140.00	Incorrect post code	$14,000	1%
74	$1.00	$74.00	Incomplete address	$7,400	1%
8	$1.00	$8.00	Incomplete post code	$800	1%
4	$1.00	$4.00	Incorrect post code format	$400	1%
382				$650,720	Total
		(A×B)		(C÷F)	

NOTE The Impact Pareto should drive your Process Improvement Initiatives.

P2.8.4 Develop Statistical Quality Control Charts for Critical-to-Quality Characteristics, such as Accuracy, for critical information processes.

The p Chart is used for Defective Products or Records produced by a current process. The example Control Chart in Figure 5-31 illustrates a p Chart of Insurance Applications with errors and missing (required) information in insurance applications, monitored on a daily basis. Below the p Chart we illustrate the calculation for this Control Chart that is appropriate for any Attribute (discrete) data.

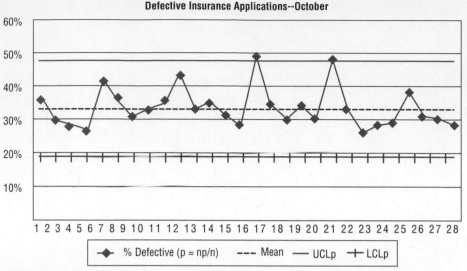

Figure 5-31: Example of a p Control Chart Illustrating an Out-of-Control Insurance Application Create Process

The most popular Attribute data Control Chart is the p Chart, which describes the fraction (percent) of Defective Records produced.

- The calculation steps for the p Chart in Figure 5-31 are:
- k = number of samples (subgroups) = 30.
- n = # records sampled (each sample) = 100.
- np = # defective records = 999.
- p = Σnp / Σn = 999 / 3000 = 0.333 (33.3%).
- CLp = p ± 3 * √p(1-p)/n *(p Chart calculation)*.
- UCLp = 0.333 + (3 * √((0.333 * (1 - 0.333)) / 100)).
- UCLp = 0.333 + (3 * √((0.333 * 0.667) / 100)).
- UCLp = 0.333 + (3 * √(0.2221 / 100)).
- UCLp = 0.333 + (3 * √ 0.002221).
- UCLp = 0.333 + (3 * 0.0471).
- UCLp = 0.333 + 0.141 = 0.474.
- LCLp = 0.333 - 0.141 = 0.192.

In the forthcoming chapter 7, "The Step-by-Step Guide to *Improving Information Process Quality*," we describe TIQM Process P4, and we illustrate the results of a simple improvement on this process.

Figure 5-32 illustrates various Control Chart Calculations based on type of data.

Attribute Data Control Chart Formulae

Type Control Chart	Sample Size	Central Line	Control Limits
Fraction defective	Variable, usually ≥50	For each subgroup: p=np/n For all subgroups: $\bar{p}=\Sigma np/\Sigma n$	$UCLp = \bar{p} + 3\sqrt{\dfrac{\bar{p}(1-\bar{p})}{n}}$ $LCLp = \bar{p} - 3\sqrt{\dfrac{\bar{p}(1-\bar{p})}{n}}$
p Chart			
Number defective	Constant, usually ≥50	For each subgroup: np=# defective units For all subgroups: $n\bar{p}=\Sigma np/k$	$UCLnp = n\bar{p} + 3\sqrt{n\bar{p}(1-\bar{p})}$ $LCLnp = n\bar{p} - 3\sqrt{n\bar{p}(1-\bar{p})}$
np Chart			
Number of defects	Constant	For each subgroup: c=# defects For all subgroups: $\bar{c}=\Sigma c/k$	$UCLc = \bar{c} + 3\sqrt{\bar{c}}$ $LCLc = \bar{c} - 3\sqrt{\bar{c}}$
C Chart			
Number of defects per unit	Variable	For each subgroup: u=c/n For all subgroups: $\bar{u}=\Sigma c/\Sigma n$	$*UCLu = \bar{u} + 3\sqrt{\dfrac{\bar{u}}{n}}$ $*LCLu = \bar{u} - 3\sqrt{\dfrac{\bar{u}}{n}}$
U Chart			

np = # defective units
c = # of defects
n = sample size within each subgroup
k = 3 of subgroups

* This formula creates changing control limits. To avoid this, use average sample sizes n for those samples that are within ± 20% of the average sample size. Calculate individual limits for the samples exceeding ± 20%.

Source: Goal/QPC: *The Memory Jogger II*, 1994, p. 39
Goal/QPC: *Six Sigma Memory Jogger II*, 2002, p. 78

Figure 5-32: Control Chart Calculations for Attribute Data

P2.8.5 Analyze the patterns in the Control Chart to see if the process is in control. Figure 5-33 identifies seven conditions that illustrates a process out of control.

P2.8.5.1 Analyze the process mean to determine if it is aligned with Knowledge Worker requirements.

Figure 5-33 identifies seven conditions that illustrate out of control processes.

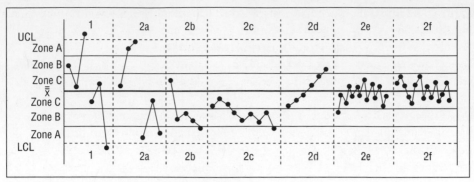

Source: Lloyd S. Nelson, Director of Statistical Methods, Nashua Corporation,
New Hampshire, as cited in Goal/QPC: *The Memory Jogger II*, 1994, p. 46, or *The Six Sigma Memory Joggen II*, p. 85.

Figure 5-33: Out-of-Control Condition Indicators

The process is considered Out-of-Control if any of the following conditions is true:[8]

1. One or more points fall outside of the control limits

2. When the Control Chart is divided into zones, as shown in Figure 5-33:

    2a. Two points, out of three consecutive points, are on the same side of the average in Zone A or beyond

    2b. Four points, out of five consecutive points, are on the same side of the average in Zone B or beyond

    2c. Nine consecutive points are on one side of the average

    2d. There are six consecutive points, increasing or decreasing

    2e. There are fourteen consecutive points that alternate up and down

    2f. There are fifteen consecutive points within Zone C (above and below the average)

    P2.8.5.2 If the process is Out-of-Control, establish a Process Improvement initiative to identify the Root Cause or Causes and eliminate them first. See "TIQM P4 Improve Information Process Quality" in Chapter 7.

TIP If a process is Out-of-Control, it must be stabilized and brought In Control before you can Improve the Process to Reduce Variation. Root Causes of Out-of-Control processes are Special Causes, that is, they do not come from the normal variation in the process itself.

P2.8.6 Analyze the process mean to determine if it is aligned with *all* Knowledge Worker requirements.

NOTE A process may be completely in control, according to the Control Charts, but the data may not meet the Knowledge Workers' needs. This may mean the process is performing according to Process Specifications, but the Process Specifications do not satisfy Knowledge Worker Requirements. You will need to conduct a Root-Cause Analysis to identify the failure and Improve the Process.

TIP IQ defects do not follow a normal bell curve. There is no optimum center line of errors like there is an optimal value for the diameter of optical fiber. IQ defects follow the "Smaller is best" Poisson curve. In other words, the closer we get to zero defects relative to cost of quality and cost of poor quality, the higher the quality of information. See "TIQM P3 Measure the Costs and Risks of Poor Quality Information" in Chapter 6.

P2.8.7 Create a timeliness report, if a CTQ Characteristic by measuring the Information Float of when Information is captured inside the organization, on paper or electronically. Capture the time that electronically propagated data is loaded into a downstream database where Knowledge Workers need to access it. Process Steps include:

P2.8.7.1 Date and timestamp any paper document at its point of receipt or creation.

P2.8.7.2 Date and timestamp electronic records that are created.

P2.8.7.3 Date and timestamp the records as they are propagated to one or more downstream databases.

P2.8.7.4 Calculate the Information "Float" or delay between the time the data was created on paper until created into the electronic Record-of-Origin Data Store.

P2.8.7.5 Calculate the Information "Float" or delay between the time the data was first created electronically and to when it reaches the data store of each set of Knowledge Workers who need it. See Figure 5-26.

P2.8.8 Analyze the results of other IQ Assessment Tests you performed to learn what those tests tell you as to meeting Information Consumer Requirements.

P2.8.9 Determine recommendations and next steps based on all IQ Assessment results.

P2.8.6.1 Begin the documentation of the recommendations and next steps, using the template TIQM Form P2.8.O1.F1.2 on the book website at www.wiley.com/go/IQApplied.

NOTE Do *not* recommend specific Improvements to a Process in the report, based on your Assessments alone. You must always Analyze Root Cause using Cause-and-Effect Analysis with the Information Consumers who perform the process to identify and confirm the Root Causes. Only once you know the Root Cause(s) can you then define Improvements to Eliminate the cause of Defects.

P2.8.6.2 Analyze each IQ Characteristic Assessment result against the Information Consumer SIPOCs of IQ Requirements in each IQ Characteristic assessed. Is the Quality currently being Produced consistently meeting all Knowledge Worker and external end-Customer Expectations? If not, establish a Process Improvement initiative to address and eliminate the Root Cause of the Defects.

P2.8.6.3 Identify processes that are meeting all Knowledge Workers' Requirements, as compared to the SIPOCs of IQ Requirements. No actions are required for these processes.

NOTE Ensure that all Assessment Sampling, Assessing, and Reporting Accurately represent the true state of Process Quality. If not, document in the report the shortcomings and recommendations for preventing them in the future.

P2.8.4 Identify processes that are NOT meeting all Knowledge Workers' Requirements as compared to the SIPOCs of IQ Requirements. Next steps will be to establish a Process Improvement Initiative to identify Root Cause or causes and to Identify and Implement Improvements following the Plan-Do-Check/Study-Act cycle defined in Chapter 7, "TIQM P4 Improve Information Process Quality."

P2.8.5 Once all Assessments have been analyzed and recommendations developed, create the cover letter for the formal Assessment Report, using the template P2.8.O1.F1, "IQ Assessment Cover Letter" found on the book's web site at www.wiley.com/go/IQApplied.

Summary

With these rigorous assessments, two possible outcomes emerge:

1. Your Processes are In Control and meeting Information Consumers' Requirements, or

2. Your Processes require Improvement to Eliminate the causes of Defects identified in the Assessment.

If the assessment outcome is the second one, you should conduct TIQM P3 "Calculate Costs of Poor Quality Information" in Chapter 6 to establish the Business Case for a Process Improvement. Then conduct an Information Process Improvement Initiative (TIQM P4, "Improve Information Process Quality") in Chapter 7 to eliminate the costs and waste of the current defective process.

The Step-by-Step Guide to *Measuring Costs and Risks of Poor Quality Information*

*"Quality is free, but it is not a gift. What costs money are the unquality things —
all the actions that involve not doing jobs right the first time."[1]*

Philip B. Crosby

The Costs of Poor Quality Information, evidenced by the process failure, recovery from the process failure, and the ensuing Information Scrap and Rework establishes the business case for investing in Total Information Quality Management (TIQM).When you measure the extent of missing, inaccurate, untimely, or duplicate data, it is not the number of defects but the costs and consequences of those defects on process failure and Customer alienation that are important.

This chapter describes how to measure both the direct costs and the lost and missed opportunity costs so that Executives and Change Sponsors can feel the pain and costs of maintaining the status quo. This chapter further describes how you can measure the Return on Investment (ROI) of your Process Improvements (TIQM P4) described in the next chapter.

TIQM P3. Measure Poor Quality Information Costs and Risks

Figure 6-1 illustrates the relationship between measuring the costs of poor quality and the other TIQM processes.

By assessing Information Product Specification Quality (TIQM P1) and Assessing Information Quality (TIQM P2), you establish the extent of IQ problems. By measuring the Costs of Poor Quality Information (TIQM P3), you translate the extent of the IQ problems into the lost currency value, in terms of both the direct costs of Information Scrap and Rework and lost and missed opportunity in the form of Customer Lifetime Value (CLTV).

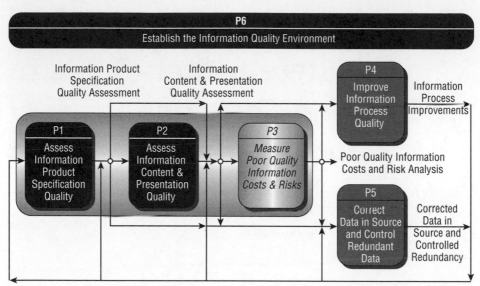

Figure 6-1: TIQM Process 3: Measure Poor Quality Information Costs and Risks in the Context of TIQM.

The outcome of P3 directs Process Improvement Initiatives, followed by data corrective maintenance initiatives, where defective data in the sources is contaminating operational and business intelligence retrieval processes.

TIQM P3. Measure Poor Quality Information Costs and Risks Overview

TIQM Process P3 measures the cost of the recovery from failure, waste, and Information Scrap and Rework (IS&R) caused by defective information throughout the various Value Circles within the enterprise. This process also measures the opportunity costs in terms of missed or lost CLTV and the failure to accomplish the mission of the enterprise.

Overview

This process describes how to measure the Costs of Poor Quality Information, in terms of the failure of the downstream processes and the costs of the resources (Employee and Customer time, money, equipment, and facilities) consumed in IS&R.

The Economics of Information Quality Management

Often management has a misconception that the costs of a proactive IQ Management System increase the costs of doing business. However, every sound, proactive Quality Management System has proven that implementing an effective Quality Management System that addresses Process Improvement to prevent defects and costs of failure returns a profit. Figure 6-2 illustrates the economics of a *reactive* IQ Management System based on an "Inspect and Correct" philosophy. This model is now obsolete and is replaced with a new, proactive model, illustrated in Figure 6-3.

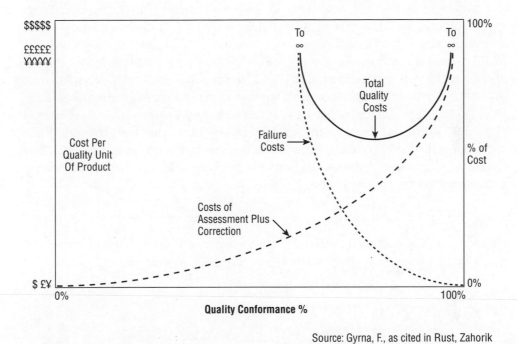

Source: Gyrna, F., as cited in Rust, Zahorik
and Keiningham, *Return on Quality*

Figure 6-2: Old Cost of Quality Model for the "Inspect and Correct" Approach[1]

There are three reasons to measure the Costs of Poor Quality Information. They include:

1. To determine the real business impact of Information Quality problems

2. To establish the business case for Information Process Quality Improvement Initiatives

3. To provide a baseline for measuring the effectiveness of Information Process Improvement Initiatives

This chapter describes how to measure the Costs of Poor Quality Information and how to measure the ROI of Process Improvement Initiatives.

In the earliest days of Manufacturing Quality, the Quality Management Model was to inspect items to prevent defects from getting to Customers. Defective products cause Workers to have to perform "Scrap and Rework" to bring defective products up to quality standards or scrap them if they were too costly to repair. *This model presumes that quality activities* increase *costs*. Without an effective process to follow for designing Quality into the production processes, this became a self-fulfilling prophecy. However, as the quality profession matured, it became clear that when one focused on Defect Prevention and Designing Quality Into the Processes, the total costs of quality actually decreased as variation (defects) in the processes was reduced.

The same misconception exists today in Information Quality. Organizations that conduct only data profiling and data cleansing, (i.e., "information inspection and correction") find that thoughtful management will reject the high costs of reactive data correction — and rightfully so. When data quality is only "inspect and correct," you pay more for Scrap and Rework that does *NOT* solve the root problem. On the other hand, organizations that have adopted the habit of Plan-Do-Check/Study-Act (or Six Sigma's Define-Measure-Analyze-Improve-Control) cycle of Continuous Process Improvement have found that the new model for costs of quality, illustrated in Figure 6-3, does in fact reduce the Costs of Poor Quality Information, by attacking and eliminating the Root Causes of broken processes that create the defects.

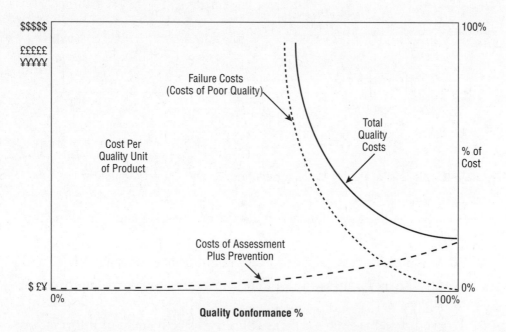

Source: F. Gyrna, "Quality Costs" in *Juran's Quality Handbook*

Figure 6-3: New Cost of Quality Model for the "Design-Quality-into-Processes" Approach[2]

Here, the total quality costs go *down* as you *invest* in defect prevention. By investing in defect prevention and error-proofing processes (dashed line), the costs of failure and IS&R (dotted line) go down dramatically, reducing the total costs of quality significantly (solid line).

Categories of Costs of Quality

Measuring the Costs of Poor Quality Information is quite simple. You simply measure the value of the resources that are consumed in recovery from process failure and the IS&R that is performed that is caused by Poor Quality Information. So the process is simply identifying and counting the value of the resources (people time, money spent, materials consumed, costs of facilities and equipment used). Then extrapolate the total costs, based on the frequency of defects, into an annual Cost of Poor Information Quality that can be compared to your annual operating revenue (budget in government or not-for-profits).

Quality Management has generally adopted a three-category Costs of Quality (COQ) framework. This includes:

1. **Costs of Failure and Information Scrap and Rework**
    There are two types of failure:

    - **Internal failure:** This is when process failure and defects are discovered within the organization before they *directly* affect the Customer.

NOTE The Customer and other Stakeholders are always affected by Quality Failure — they pay higher prices to cover the costs of the Information Scrap and Rework.

    - **External failure:** Here, the defective information directly affects the Customer in the form of a misspelled name, a wrong address, the wrong item delivered, or the misapplication of a payment or deposit, for example.

NOTE The consequences of External Failure are much higher than those of Internal Failure, for you now risk Lost and Missed Opportunity, measured in lost or missed Customer Lifetime Value.

2. **Costs of Inspection or Assessment**
    Costs of inspection are the costs you incur to measure and find the Information Quality problems. There is no value added by the inspection. It tells you that you have a broken process and the extent of the problem. Activity-Based Costing (ABC) would count this activity as "cost-adding," not "value-adding."
    The goal of assessment is to minimize costs by effective statistical sampling to reduce costs without decreasing the confidence interval.

3. **Costs of Prevention**

Prevention is how you eliminate the costs of failure, by designing quality in and error-proofing the processes to prevent failure and Information Scrap and Rework.

Costs of prevention include:

■ Administrative costs of managing the Information Quality function

■ Costs of Process Improvement activities

■ Education to help Employees learn how to improve their processes

Cost Categories of Failure and Information Scrap and Rework

Major cost categories consist of direct costs and opportunity costs.

Direct Costs

Direct costs are the value of all resources consumed in activities such as Information Scrap and Rework activities or Process Improvement activities, including:

■ **People time:** Cost of people time spent in recovery from failure and Information Scrap and Rework, such as time spent resending an ordered item when an incorrect item was sent, or time on the phone to ameliorate complaints

■ **Money expended:** Direct monetary payments to Customers or fines paid for non-compliance

■ **Materials consumed:** Materials wasted because of manufacturing defects caused by Poor Quality Information, or wasted catalogs sent because of multiple Customer records

■ **Facilities and equipment used:** Costs of overhead for facilities and equipment required to perform or support work

■ **Information services used:** The costs of overhead for information services if not included in other resources cited previously

NOTE Some organizations have people time costs with only benefits loaded. Other organizations may have facilities, equipment, and information services loaded into the hourly rate for all employees. Understand from the Finance Department what is loaded into the various cost figures, so you neither overstate nor understate the true costs of poor quality information.

Opportunity Costs

Opportunity costs include missed or lost value caused by Poor Quality Information. They include:

- **Missed Customer Lifetime Value:** Missed revenue or profit caused by:
  - Sub-optimized business decisions caused in part by defective, missing, or untimely information
  - Missed revenue, for example, from address errors that cause promotion campaigns to fail to reach the target audience, or sending multiple catalogs to one household instead of to unique prospects, or by making sub-optimized decisions on strategic or tactical initiatives
- **Lost Customer Lifetime Value:** Lost revenue or profit caused by loss of Customers alienated in part by Poor Quality Information, such as the misspelling of their name, sending the wrong item, sending an item to the wrong address, misapplying a deposit or withdrawal, or not observing their contact preferences

The Opportunity Costs of Poor Quality Information are often far greater than the direct costs of failure and Information Scrap and Rework.

Objectives

To identify and measure the waste and missed and lost opportunity caused when defective information causes process failure and Information Scrap and rework

Process Steps: P3. Measure Poor Quality Information Costs and Risks

Process TIQM P3 is the Business-Case Measurement. This process quantifies the costs and losses caused by Poor Quality Information and the ROI from Information Process Improvements.

Here, we describe the process steps and activities to measure:

P3.1 Business objectives and drivers, including Key Performance Indicators (KPI), which if affected by Poor Quality Information, could cause business failure.

P3.2 Costs of ownership of information and systems development (acquisition), maintenance, and operations

P3.3 Direct Costs of Poor Quality Information

P3.4-6 Opportunity costs and losses and potential risks caused by Poor Quality Information

P3.7 ROI of Process Improvements

Figure 6-4 illustrates the process steps to measure the Costs of Poor Quality Information, including costs of ownership of information production processes, and direct and opportunity costs of poor quality. Also included is the step to measure the ROI of Process Improvements.

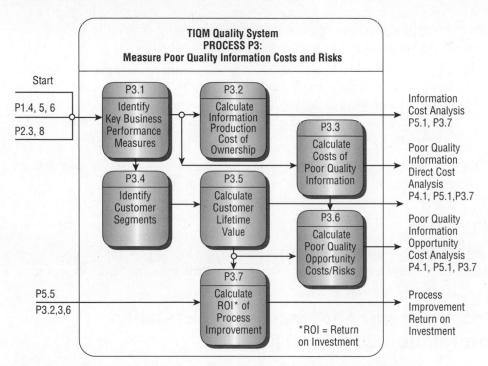

Figure 6-4: TIQM P3. Measure Poor Quality Information Costs and Risks.

Step P3.1: Identify Key Business Performance Measures

This step identifies the specific Key Performance Indicators that indicate the success or failure to accomplish the Enterprise Mission. They are key for Executives to ensure that the enterprise is effective in its aim or purpose for existence. Understanding how Poor Quality Information compromises the ability of the Enterprise to accomplish these Key Performance Indicators is impetus for management to address proactive Process Improvements to increase business effectiveness.

You must be able to translate the Costs of Poor Quality Information into a description of how it prevents the organization from achieving its Key Performance Measures, to get and sustain top management involvement and leadership in Continuous Information Process Improvement activities.

Objective

To identify the basis for costing Poor Quality Information and valuing Quality Information and to understand the KPIs that Poor Quality Information can sub-optimize or cause to fail. Step P3.1 illustrates the components for Identifying KPIs.

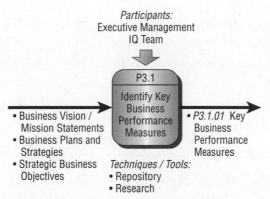

Figure 6-5: P3.1 Identify Key Business Performance Measures.

Inputs to Step P3.1

- **Business Vision/Mission:** The Business Vision and Mission represent the Value Proposition of the end-Consumers and Stakeholders of the Enterprise. If the mission is not achieved, all Stakeholders are hurt.

- **Business Plans and Strategies:** Strategic business initiatives are the bold moves that enable us to accomplish the Mission. Look for how Poor Quality Information can prevent the strategy from succeeding.

- **Strategic Business Objectives:** It's important to outline the key business objectives and Key Performance Measures that measure the important outcomes that lead to Enterprise effectiveness.

Outputs of Step 3.1

P3.1.O1 **Key Business Performance Measures:** Documented Key Performance Indicators that can fail or be sub-optimized by Poor Quality Information

Participants and Roles in P3.1"Identify Key Performance Measures"

Table 6-1: Step P3.1 Participants and Their Roles

PARTICIPANT	IQ ACTIVITY ROLE
Executive Management	Establishes the Key Performance Indicators and sets strategic initiatives for the enterprise to accomplish the mission.
Information Quality Team	Document the Key Performance Indicators measures as a component of analyzing the Costs of Poor Quality Information.

Techniques and Tools for Step P3.1

- **Repository:** A database to house information about the Information Resources of the enterprise
- **Research:** Analysis to discover KPIs and their calculations

Step P3.1: Identify Business Performance Measures — Process Steps and Guidelines

Process steps in P3.1 include:

P3.1.1 List all documented Key Business Performance Indicators. Typical Performance Measures include, some or many of the following:

- ☑ Accomplish mission.
- ☑ Increase profits or surplus.
- ☑ Reduce costs.
- ☑ Reduce cycle time.
- ☑ Increase product/service quality.
- ☑ Increase Customer Satisfaction.
- ☑ Increase Employee Satisfaction.
- ☑ Increase productivity.
- ☑ Increase market share.
- ☑ Increase Shareholder value.
- ☑ "Personal" drivers of Executive Sponsors

P3.1.2 Document how each Key Business Performance Indicator is calculated.

P3.1.3 Determine which Key Business Performance Indicators are *vital* to actual enterprise performance (the Vital Few versus the Useful Many).

P3.1.4 Identify what Information Groups are required to calculate each performance measure.

P3.1.5 Describe generally how Poor Quality Information can hamper the accomplishment of, or skew, each measure.

TIP **Understand how Executives see performance effectiveness.**

1. **Be sure to note the critical performance measures regularly reviewed by Executives.**

2. **Be sure to document the Enterprise Standard Calculations Formula for the measures.**

3. **Be sure to document the change management procedure for if and when performance measure calculations change.**

Step P3.2: Calculate Information and Systems Costs of Ownership

This step measures how well the enterprise creates effective automated business processes that enable Knowledge Workers to perform their work efficiently and effectively, and how well the enterprise designs its knowledge bases in a way that delivers Quality, Just-in-Time Information to its Knowledge Workers.

The Value Proposition for the development of Information Systems and databases derives from the Resource Management Life Cycle, which is used to manage all enterprise resources and is shown in Figure 6-6.

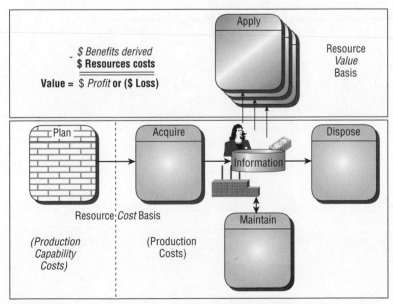

Figure 6-6: The Universal Resource Management Life Cycle

A process that plans for the acquisition, application, maintenance, and disposition of resources to maximize the value derived from the application of the resource, relative to the cost of acquisition, maintenance, and disposition of the resource, should manage every resource of the enterprise. This applies to information resources as well as to financial, people, materials, and facilities resources.

The Value Proposition is that information has value when it is applied by Knowledge Workers when they perform their work or by automated processes that make decisions such as to open a water valve when a fire is detected, or to buy shares of an equity on a buy authorization by an equity purchaser or to execute a "sell" order on the dropping of the price to a sell trigger point.

Objective

To identify what percent of Information Systems development, maintenance and operations is value-adding and what percent is cost-adding in order to improve Information Systems and business productivity and effectiveness.

See Figure 6-7 for components of Calculating Information and Systems Costs of Ownership.

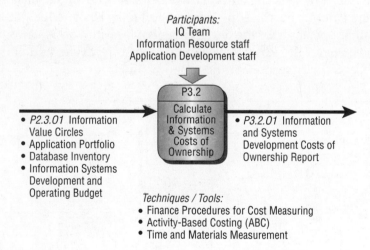

Figure 6-7: P3.2 Calculate Information and Systems Costs of Ownership.

Inputs to Step P3.2

▪ *P2.3.O1* **Information Value Circles:** These Value Circles identify processes downstream that may fail because of Poor Quality Information produced by the source information capture process

- **Application Portfolio:** Documentation of all applications that perform automated processes
- **Repository or Database Inventory:** Documentation of all database files and other data stores that capture, maintain, and deliver critical business information

Outputs of Step P3.2

- *P3.2.O1* **Information and Systems Development Costs of Ownership Report:** Documentation of costs of ownership of information and systems objects over their useful lifetime, such as five years or ten years, based on your organization's financial accounting principles

Participants and Roles for Step P3.2 "Calculate Information and Systems Costs of Ownership"

Table 6-2: Step P3.2 Participants and Their Roles

PARTICIPANT	IQ ACTIVITY ROLE
Information Quality Team	Led by the Information Resource Quality Specialist; facilitates the definition of the costs of ownership of Information and Systems Engineering, including development and operational costs.
Information Resource Management Staff	Assist in documenting the costs of Information Modeling and Database Design, including Scrap and Rework.
Information Systems Development Staff	Assist in documenting the costs of systems components (data-create programs, data movement programs, report programs, etc., including Scrap and Rework).

Techniques and Tools for P3.2

- **Finance Procedures for Measuring Costs:** These are the official costing formulas and procedures for measuring capital expenditures and operating costs.
- **Activity-Based Cost Accounting (ABC):** This measurement method calculates the costs by category (capital investment, value-adding activity, cost-adding activity).
- **Resource Life Cycle Management:** This tool helps identify the Infrastructure, Value, and Cost basis of the Information Resources:

- **Infrastructure investment:** The first Enterprise-Strength, sharable Database File of a given Entity Type, such as Customer or Product information. The controlled replication of databases for performance or backup purposes is an investment. These should be sharable by any application or Knowledge Worker requiring information about Customers or Products. In addition, infrastructure investments include the first Enterprise-Strength Customer and Product creation and maintenance application programs.

    These are part of the infrastructure because you must have a database to house information for accessing by other applications, and you must have application programs that create and maintain the data for other applications to have access to accurate, complete, up-to-date information.

- **Value-adding basis:** All non-redundant applications that retrieve information from the Enterprise-Strength Record-of-Origin/Record-of-Reference Databases are value-adding. They retrieve information and use it to perform work or to support decisions. The value of information is realized when it is applied to create value for the end-Customers. Value-adding applications include:

    - Non-redundant application programs that retrieve information to perform a process or take an action, such as to turn on a sprinkler system on detection of a flame or smoke

    - Non-redundant application programs that answer a query

    - Non-redundant application programs that produce a standard or ad hoc report

    - Non-redundant data analysis programs that analyze patterns or trends

    - Decision support programs that enlighten decisions

    - Decision support programs that generate Key Performance Indicators

NOTE Some application programs have both infrastructure and value-adding aspects. For example, one application program may retrieve Customer data in order to create an Order record with one or more Order-Item records. Use the ratio of the number of data elements retrieved (Value basis) to the number of data elements created (infrastructure, if not redundant) to determine what percent is infrastructure as opposed to Value basis.

- **Cost-adding basis:** All applications that duplicate work or store data redundantly and redundant databases (second through *n*th Customer or Product databases) are cost-adding. Because Information is the only *non-consumable* resource the enterprise has, it is a cost to maintain the data in multiple, redundant, and usually disparately defined databases that are a waste of money to create, maintain, and use in the operational environment. Cost-adding components include:

- Redundant application programs that create or maintain the same type of data (Customer or Product)
- Redundant operational databases that house data in a separate data store. The data is available elsewhere.
- Applications that move data from one operational database to another are cost-adding. You already have the data in one database — access it from there.

Step P3.2: Calculate Information and Systems Costs of Ownership: Process Steps and Guidelines

Process steps in P3.2 include:

P3.2.1 Identify the repositories and sources documenting application systems and databases.

P3.2.2 Count the number of application programs in your production portfolio, including purchased software packages as well as internally developed applications and applications that may be developed and operated by outsourcing or offshore organizations.

P3.2.3 Determine the relative percent of application programs that create only, retrieve only, or perform a combination of retrieving some data for the purpose of creating other data. This allows you to properly allocate portions to Infrastructure versus Value versus Cost-adding categories. The example in Figure 6-8 illustrates that the average percentage of attributes retrieved (application or value-adding) in the sample is 25 percent, while 75 percent of attributes are either created or updated (acquisition).

TIP To calculate the relative percentage of a program that both creates or updates, and retrieves data, take a statistically valid random sample of 30 to 50 programs that retrieve some data and create other data. For example, an Order Entry program will retrieve Customer and Product data and then create an Order. Count the number of fields that are either created or updated in a program, then count only the number of fields that are retrieved. See Figure 6-8.

P3.2.4 Count or estimate the number of database tables and other data stores in the production environment. This provides a quick inventory of how many database tables or other data stores exist.

Program Number	Attributes Retrieved Count	Attributes Created/ Updated Count	Total Attributes	Percent Attributes Retrieved
OF 110	15	33	48	31%
OF 122	5	26	31	16%
AP 205	4	28	32	13%
AP 333	8	32	40	20%
HR 210	7	19	26	27%
HR 722	7	33	40	18%
CS 105	15	28	43	35%
CS 224	8	37	45	18%
AR 333	15	38	53	28%
AR 452	9	3	12	75%
Total	93	277	370	**25%**

Figure 6-8: Calculating Percent of Retrieved Data versus Created Data

P3.2.5 Determine the number of unique, Record-of-Origin/Record-of-Reference database files (infrastructure) versus the number of *redundant* database files (cost-adding).

P3.2.6 Determine the total Information Systems annual budget for development and maintenance of applications and databases, including acquisition of purchased software and hardware over the typical life of applications, such as 5, 7, or 10 years. This excludes production operations and operations support. The figures represent the resource planning costs, not the cost of operating the applications and databases. See the example in Figure 6-9.

NOTE Use net present value when calculating past years' budgets. If actual budget data is not available, use reliable estimates.

Guidelines

P3.2.7 Count the number of *Infrastructure components*:

- Total unique, Enterprise-Strength database files: (200)
- Enterprise-Strength create application programs: (300)
- No strategic interface applications were counted.

P3.2.8 Count the number of *Value basis components*:

- Total retrieve and retrieve-equivalent programs: (300)

A	B	C	D	E	F	G	H	I
2		Information and Systems Costs of Ownership Worksheet Example						
3		Cost Category	Total Count	Relative Weight Factor*	Average Weighted Units	Total Dev & Maint Costs**	Total Costs by Cost Category	% of Costs
4	*Infrastructure Basis:*							
5		Enterprise unique DB tables / files	200	0.75	150	$3,061,200		
6		Enterprise reusable create programs	300	1.5	450	$9,183,600		
7		Unique strategic interface programs						
8		Total infrastructure expenses					$12,244,800	24%
9	*Value Basis:*							
10		Total retrieve equivalent programs+	300	1.00	300	$6,122,400		
11		Total value-adding expenses					$6,122,400	12%
12	*Cost-Adding Basis:*							
13		*Redundant create/update programs*	*400*	*1.50*	*600*	*$12,244,800*		
14		*Redundant retrieve programs*	*100*	*1.00*	*100*	*$2,040,800*		
15		*Interface Pgms (ETL, EAI, EII, SOA)*	*400*	*1.00*	*400*	*$8,163,200*		
16		*Redundant database tables / files*	*600*	*0.75*	*450*	*$9,183,600*		
17		*Total cost-adding expenses*					*$31,632,400*	*63%*
18		**Lifetime Totals *****	**2,300**		**2,450**		**$50,000,000**	**100%**
19		Cost per weighted unit = (H18/F18)	$20,408			(G=F*E19)		

Notes:

*   Determine relative development effort avg weight of each category (retrieve pgm=1.0).

\+   For programs that retrieve some information & create/update other information, determine the percent of retrieve only attributes and percent of create/update attributes (e.g., to retrieve customer and product information to create an order).

*** Based on 2,300 application programs and database files in portfolio and $50 million in development / maintenance costs over 10 years.

Figure 6-9: Calculating Information and Systems Costs of Ownership by Infrastructure, Value Basis, and Cost-Adding Basis

P3.2.9 Count the number of *Cost-adding components*:

- Total redundant create/update programs: (400)
- Total redundant, overlapping retrieve programs: (100)
- Total interface programs: (400)
- Total redundant databases and files: (600)

P3.2.10 Determine the relative weighting factor for the development of the various components. Use the relative amount of time and cost as a value of 1. The effort to develop a database file may be less than that, so here we use a 0.75 weight factor. Create programs require editing and validation, so they have a weight factor of 1.50, which means that they take one and a half times as much effort as it does to develop a retrieve program.

P3.2.11 Create a column chart to illustrate the lifetime cost of information production in the infrastructure, value-basis and cost-adding basis. See Figure 6-10.

P3.2.12 Use this as a basis to make improvements to the Information and Application Development processes.

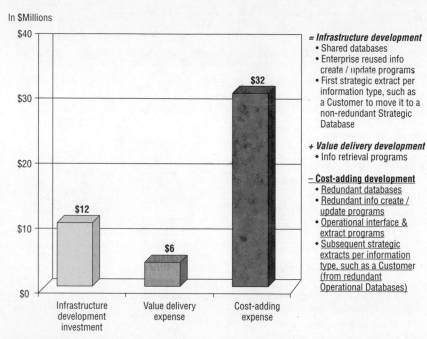

Figure 6-10: Reporting Information Costs of Infrastructure, the Value Basis, and the Cost-Adding Basis

Step P3.3: Calculate Direct Costs of Poor Quality Information

This step measures the direct costs of process failure caused by Poor Quality Information and the resulting direct costs of "Information Scrap and Rework."

Objective

To quantify — in bottom-line currency figures — the tangible, direct Costs of Poor Quality Information to establish the business case for Total Information Quality Management. See Figure 6-11 for Step components.

Inputs to Step 3.3

P2.1.O2 **Priority Information Group:** The defective information causing process failure and Information Scrap and Rework

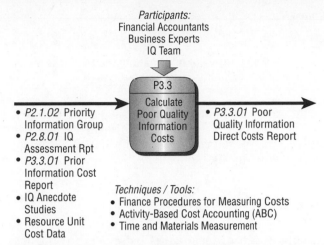

Figure 6-11: TIQM Process P3.3 Calculate the Direct Costs of Poor Quality Information.

P2.3.O1 **The Information Value/Cost Circle:** Used to identify the downstream processes that are failing because of Poor Quality Information

P2.8.O1 **IQ Assessment Report:** Used to identify the nature and frequency of information defects

P3.3.O1 **Prior Direct Costs of Poor Quality Information Report:** Prior cost measurements to analyze changes in costs of poor quality

Outputs of Step 3.3

P3.3.O1 **Direct Costs of Poor Quality Information Report:** Report of the quantified direct Costs of Poor Quality Information with descriptions of methods, assumptions, costing figures and formulas, and identification of gaps, unknowns, or anomalies in the results

Participants and Roles for Step 3.3 "Calculate Direct Costs of Poor Quality Information"

Table 6-3: P3.3 Participants and Participant Roles

PARTICIPANT	IQ ACTIVITY ROLE
Information Quality Team	Led by an Information Process Improvement Facilitator; leads the measurement of the direct Costs of Poor Quality Information assessment.
Finance Staff	Establish and confirm the procedure and formulas or rates for calculating direct costs of activities and resources.

(continued)

Table 6-3 *(continued)*

PARTICIPANT	IQ ACTIVITY ROLE
Business Information Stewards	Help identify the information and business areas where Costs of Poor Quality Information are high.
Affected Knowledge Workers	Information Consumers whose processes were hampered by Poor Quality Information participate in Time and Materials Analysis to measure their time in IS&R to calculate Costs of Poor Quality Information.

Techniques and Tools for Step P3.3

- **Finance Procedures for Measuring Costs:** Get the official costing figures and procedures for measuring capital expenditures and operating costs and ROI.

- **Activity-Based Cost Accounting (ABC):** This measurement method calculates the costs by category (capital investment, value-adding activity, cost-adding activity).

- **Time and Materials Measurement:** This tool is used by Knowledge Workers to measure their time in three categories:

  - **System imposed time,** such as staff meetings or project reporting

  - **Value-adding work,** such as capturing Customer orders, filling orders, invoicing orders, and the like that is a part of their normal job description

  - **Cost-adding work,** such as when information defects cause them to have to hunt for information or perform workarounds, along with direct costs of compensation and or materials consumed in the Scrap and Rework

Step P3.3: Calculate Direct Costs of Poor Quality Information — Process Steps and Guidelines

Process steps in P3.3 include:

P3.3.1 Document approved guidelines for measuring the direct costs of resources for time and materials measurement to measure IS&R. This includes:

- **Cost of people time:** What rate per hour is the official cost for people time? There may be multiple rates for people time based on job classification.

- **Cost of facilities, equipment, and overhead:** If these are not loaded into *people time*, establish them as an additional overhead cost based on people time spent in Information Scrap and Rework.

- **Cost of specific resources or materials:** Specific resources consumed in recovery from a process failure and in Information Scrap and Rework (IS&R) will be specific to each type of IS&R activity, such as a replacement product shipped, or costs of duplicate item catalogs sent to one household or resent to a Customer who did not receive one. Each item will have its own accounting costs for material not counted in people time.

P3.3.2 Translate this to an annualized cost for one Full-Time Equivalent (FTE) by multiplying the hourly rate by 2080 hours per year or its equivalent in different cultures. At a rate of $60 per hour times 2080, this would equate to $124,800 per FTE per year.

If 100 people spend an average of 35 percent of their time in IS&R activities, then the equivalent FTE in IS&R is 35 (100 (people) times 35% = 35 FTE). Multiplying 35 FTE by $124,800 determines that $4,638,000 is wasted in IS&R.

> **TIP** Any measurement of people time and materials must follow approved guidelines set by the Finance Department. Otherwise, any calculations may be challenged or rejected.

P3.3.3 Develop a plan to measure direct Costs of Poor Quality Information. This includes:

P3.3.3.1 From the Information Value Circle, identify the Knowledge Workers dependent on the information.

> **TIP** Identify about 30 to 50 different business process areas across *all* business areas to get a statistical and representative sample of business process areas across the enterprise. This will ensure that you have a basis for extrapolating the costs across all business process areas in your final estimate of the Costs of Poor Information Quality across the enterprise, based on actual cost measurements of the studied areas.

P3.3.3.2 Have managers select four to six Knowledge Workers from each affected business process area, in which Knowledge Workers are performing the same type of work, for measuring normal processes and failed processes to calculate IS&R.

> **TIP** Ensure that the selected Knowledge Workers represent all age, gender, and length of experience variations in their area. This helps ensure that the measurements will be representative. Having only the most or least experienced personnel will bias the results and skew the average times recorded.

NOTE Measurement of the normal, status quo process will allow an average cost of transaction from which to quantify the Cost-of-Ownership of the status quo process. This will be compared to Cost-of-Improved process for determining Return on Investment of Process Improvements, described in step P3.7.

P3.3.4 Measure five to ten normal (no quality problem) transactions, including the time interval between transactions from each person to get a baseline of the average time to perform their work when no IQ problems exist.

P3.3.5 Measure the same number of transactions where IQ problems cause the process to fail.

    P3.3.5.1 Document the nature of the rework or workarounds to handle the failed transactions caused by Poor Quality Information. Measure the additional time required to perform the Information Scrap and Rework or Work-arounds.

    P3.3.5.2 Document all monetary or materials costs incurred in the recovery and Scrap and Rework.

P3.3.6 With the same, or different, individuals conduct a week-long Time and Materials documentation of how much time each selected Knowledge Worker spends in three categories of work:

- **Value Work:** The defined responsibilities in the Worker's job description that add value for the Customer, unless the defined responsibilities are Information Scrap and Rework, such as resending an item, because the first one sent was the wrong item, and finding and fixing bad addresses that come back as undeliverable mail, for example

- **System-Imposed Time:** This includes time in staff meetings, project status meetings, and time reporting

- **Information Scrap and Rework:** The time spent recovering from process failure and Information Scrap and Rework caused by defective information of any kind, *whether defined in the employee's job description or not*. This includes documenting the costs of any non-people resources, such as cost of the resent item, direct compensation to an unhappy Customer, and cost of postage and catalogs sent to the same Customer as a result of duplicate records

TIP Each person should record his or her times over a full week of work. Different individuals should measure their time over various weeks within a month to get the different demand periods. For example, if you have four people measuring their time, assign each to a unique week of the month to get all variations from month startup through month end. This facilitates a more representative and accurate measurement.

P3.3.6.1 Knowledge Workers record the beginning and ending times for each time block in which they are performing their (1) Value Work, (2) system-imposed work, or (3) IS&R work, during their designated week. See Figure 6-12 for an example of time monitoring and comparing before and after transaction times.

TIP Be available during the startup of P3.3.6.1, as Knowledge Workers will have questions as to what is IS&R versus Value Work. Note that some IS&R work is actually written tasks for certain job positions. This defined IS&R work should be documented in the IS&R category, not the Value Work category.

P3.3.6.2 Knowledge Workers record any questions or comments about their time reporting.

P3.3.6.3 The IQ Team resolves questions and ensures that the tasks fit the criteria of (1) Value Work, (2) system-imposed work, or (3) IS&R work. Make adjustments as required.

TIP Technically, seasonal demand periods such as the holidays and promotional rush times in the retail sector as well as slack times like that during February in the same sector should both be represented. Peak demand and additional part-time staff introduce new variables that should be accounted for. If you are not able to conduct this analysis during peak time periods, you may extrapolate using measured data and factoring in higher error rates during peak times from known experience. Document all assumptions made.

P3.3.7 The IQ Team consolidates all direct Costs of Poor Quality Information into a Poor Quality Information Direct Costs Report. See Figure 6-13.

Step P3.4: Identify Customer Segments

Step P3.4 is a required step for the measurement of lost and missed opportunity.

Objective

To identify meaningful groups of Customer Segments to be valued. This provides a Customer Segment to establish Customer Lifetime Value (CLTV). See Figure 6-14.

Inputs to Step P3.4

Customer segment lists and definitions: Customer segments identified by your Marketing and Sales management

Information Scrap and Rework Time & Materials Worksheet

Employee Name:	Department:				Tel Extension:							
Date:	Day of week:											
						Cumulative Totals:	$150.00	8.00		4.25	0.50	3.25
										FOR IQ TEAM USE ONLY		
Tot Time / Act Num	Activity Description	Activity Class*: Value Work	System Impos'd Time	Info Scrap & Rework	Start Time	Stop Time	Other Resources Consumed in Information Scrap & Rework	Est / Act Resource Costs	Knowledge Worker Comments or Questions	Time in Value Work	System Imposed Time	Time in Scrap & Rework
1	Place Customer calls	X			8:30 AM	9:45 AM				1.25		
2	Chased missing tel numbers			X	9:45 AM	10:30 AM						0.75
3	Staff Meeting		X		10:30 AM	11:00 AM					0.50	
4	Place Customer calls	X			11:00 AM	11:35 AM				0.58		
5	Lunch	N/A			11:35 AM	12:35 PM			no time counted			
6	Handle Customer Complaint			X	12:35 PM	1:05 PM	Gave $50 Credit	$50.00				0.50
7	Place Customer calls	X			1:05 PM	1:50 PM				0.75		
8	Handle Customer Complaint			X	1:50 PM	2:20 PM	Gave $25 Credit	$25.00				0.50
9	Place Customer calls	X			2:20 PM	3:30 PM				1.17		
10	Update personal Cust DB			X	3:30 PM	4:15 PM						0.75
11	Sent replacement item			X	4:15 PM	4:30 PM	Item cost & Shipping ($75)	$75.00				0.25
12	Place Customer calls	X			4:30 PM	5:00 PM				0.50		
13	Chased missing tel numbers			X	5:00 PM	5:30 PM						0.50
14												
15												
16												
17												
18												
19												
20												

Legend: *Value Work: The work in your job description that adds Value to the Enterprise and its Customers

*System Imposed Time: Time imposed by not adding value, eg Staff meetings; training; project status rpts

*Information Scrap & Rework: time spent in recovering from Failure of Poor Quality Information and Finding & Fixing it, Rework, Work-Arounds, etc.

Additional Comments:

Figure 6-12: Information Scrap and Rework Time and Materials Worksheet Example

Subscription Company: Annual Costs of Poor Quality Information	
Direct Costs:	
People time and materials costs	$23,535,360
Annual vendor costs for data correction	$8,257,375
Annual Direct Costs of Poor Quality Information (20.1% of $155 million operating revenue)	**$31,792,735**

Figure 6-13: Poor Quality Information Direct Costs Report

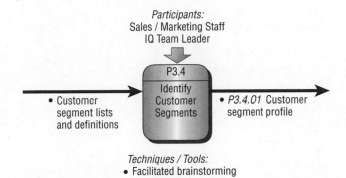

Figure 6-14: P3.4 Identify Customer Segments.

Outputs of Step P3.4

P3.4.O1 **Customer Segment profile:** The list and profile description of all relevant Customer Segments for valuation

Participants and Roles for Step 3.4 "Identify Customer Segments"

Table 6-4: P3.4 Participants and Participant Roles

PARTICIPANT	IQ ACTIVITY ROLE
Information Quality Team	Led by the Information Process Improvement Facilitator, works with Marketing and Sales and Finance staff to determine the Customer Segments for CLTV calculation.
Marketing and Sales staff	Identifies and defines the profiles for different Customer Segments.
Finance staff	Establishes the rules for calculating Customer Lifetime Value (CLTV).

Techniques and Tools

Facilitated brainstorming: Used to determine the Customer Segments and their profile description, and to determine the rules for calculating CLTV

Step P3.4: Identify Customer Segments — Process Steps and Guidelines

Process steps in P3.4 include:

P3.4.1 Collect the Customer Segments that exist from Marketing and Sales. For example, airlines have frequent flier programs with elite status based on level of air travel. Examples of frequent flier segments are Platinum, Gold, Silver, Frequent Flier, and Casual Flier.

P3.4.2 Verify and document the profile description for the different categories and calculations, if any, that determine membership in a given Customer Segment.

For example, the airlines have variations on frequent flier classifications as segments:

- **Platinum:** 100,000+ miles or points a year
- **Gold:** 50,000+ miles or points a year
- **Silver:** 25,000+ miles or points a year
- **Frequent Flier:** Frequent Flier card holder up to 25,000 miles points a year
- **Casual Flier:** Periodic fliers

Step P3.5: Calculate Customer Lifetime Value

Customer lifetime Value (CLTV) is the most useful measure of lost and missed opportunity caused by Poor Quality Information. This step describes how to calculate CLTV if your organization has not yet established CLTV valuation.

Objective

To establish a meaningful hard measure of Customer lifetime Value with which to measure lost and missed opportunity caused in part by Poor Quality Information. See Figure 6-15 for the steps to calculate CLTV.

Figure 6-15: P3.5 Calculate Customer Lifetime Value.

Inputs to Step P3.5

P3.4.O1 **Segmented Customer Profile:**

Sales history database(s)

Outputs of Step P3.5

P3.5.O1 **Segmented Customer Lifetime Value table**

Participants and Roles for Step 3.5

Table 6-5: P3.5 Participants and Participant Roles

PARTICIPANT	IQ ACTIVITY ROLE
Information Quality Team	Documents or facilitates the development of Customer Lifetime Value valuation for the purpose of measuring opportunity Costs of Poor Quality Information
Finance staff	Establish and confirm the procedure and formulas or rates for calculating CLTV.
Marketing and Sales staff	Defines the Customer Segments and their profiles.

Techniques and Tools

- **Stratified sampling:** Used to extract random samples of Customers by Customer Segment for developing CLTV

- **Data extract tools:** Used to extract sales history data for the sample of segmented Customer records for calculating CLTV
- **Spreadsheet:** Helpful for developing the overall calculation of CLTV

Step P3.5: Calculate Customer Lifetime Value — Process Steps and Guidelines

Process steps in P3.5 include:

P3.5.1 Confirm the formula for calculating Customer Lifetime Value for your organization. If you do not have one, the following steps will lead you to develop a meaningful CLTV valuation.

P3.5.2 Confirm that you have access to the Customer sales or Customer sales history database to extract sales data over the defined lifetime of a Customer relationship.

NOTE Use the accepted duration for the CLTV calculation, such as five years, seven years, ten years, or another. Commercial Customers' organizations may have 20 years or longer duration.

P3.5.3 Using a sample of 1,200 first-time Customers from five years earlier, randomly extract 200 Customers per month from each month during the year. If you start in the middle of the year, such as July, extract random samples through June of the next year.

TIP If you have multiple Customer segments, use stratified samples for each segment to valuate.

P3.5.4 For all Customer segment samples, extract the sales revenue for all sampled Customers each year in a spreadsheet or CLTV software application.

P3.5.5 Use net present value for normalizing value and costs if your organization requires it.

P3.5.6 Aggregate the total sales revenue over the lifetime period.

P3.5.7 Calculate the individual CLTV revenue by dividing the total cumulative total revenue by 1,200, or the total number of Customers sampled in the first year.

TIP While many organizations use sales revenue as the CLTV, it is more accurate to translate that to net present *profit*.

P3.5.8 Determine the costs of goods sold and costs of Customer acquisition and retention for the net operational costs in order to determine net present profit. There are three figures to capture:

- Costs of goods sold in the first year
- Costs of Customer development and acquisition in the first year
- Costs of Customer retention or relationship management in the second and subsequent years

P3.5.9 Aggregate the total net costs over the lifetime period and calculate the net present value.

P3.5.10 Subtract the total net present value costs from the total net present value sales revenue to calculate the net profits.

P3.5.11 Divide the total net present profit by the total number of Customer records sampled and tracked to establish the CLTV, as illustrated in Figure 6-16.

P3.5.12 Divide the last Period Cumulative CLTV by the number of periods in the Customer Lifetime to get an annual or periodic average annual value. In the example in Figure 6-17, the average annual or periodic value is $2,708 \div 5 = \$541.60$ per year over a 5-year period. See Figure 6-16 for an example CLTV calculation.

P3.5.13 Repeat this for all relevant Customer segments.

P3.5.14 To develop a single, blended CLTV for multiple Customer segments, take the annual or periodic value per year for each segment times the percent of Customers in that segment to get a weighted average. This makes it easier to calculate opportunity Costs of Poor Quality Information. See Figure 6-17.

NOTE If you use the annual sales revenue as your CLTV number, be sure to make it clear that the figure represents revenue and not profit.

Use this blended CLTV to measure missed and lost opportunity as the result of Poor Quality Information.

Customer Lifetime Value Calculation: Customer Segment 1					
	Period 1	Period 2	Period 3	Period 4	Period 5
Revenue	**2005**	**2006**	**2007**	**2008**	**2009**
New Customers	1,200				
Repeat Customers		822	675	449	321
Retention Rate		69%	56%	37%	27%
Average Period Sales	$1,537	$1,683	$1,056	$1,116	$1,022
Total Revenue	$1,844,400	$1,383,835	$712,500	$501,253	$327,911
Discount Rate	0.66	0.73	0.81	0.90	1.00
Net Present Value Revenue	$2,794.545	$1,895,664	$879,630	$556,948	$327,911
Cumulative Revenue	$2,794,545	$4,690,210	$5,569,839	$6,126,787	$6,454,698
Customer Lifetime Revenue	**$2,329**	**$3,909**	**$4,642**	**$5,106**	**$5,379**
Expenses					
Cost of Goods Sold %	35%	35%	35%	35%	35%
Costs of Goods Sold Amount	$645,540	$498,342	$249,375	$175,439	$114,769
Customer Acquisition Cost %	26%				
Customer Acquisition Costs	$479,544				
Customer Relationship Cost %		6%	6%	6%	6%
Customer Relationship Costs		$83,030	$42,750	$30,075	$19,675
Total Costs	$1,125,084	$567,372	$292,125	$205,514	$134,444
Discount Rate	0.66	0.73	0.81	0.90	1.00
NPV Costs	$1,704,673	$777,222	$360,648	$228,349	$134,444
Profits					
NPV Profit	$1,089,873	$1,118,442	$518,981	$328,599	$193,467
Cumulative NPV Profit	$1,089,873	$2,208,315	$2,727,296	$3,055,895	$3,249,363
Customer Lifetime Value	**$908**	**$1,840**	**$2,273**	**$2,547**	**$2,708**

Figure 6-16: Example Calculation of Customer Lifetime Value (CLTV)

Customer Segment	Segment Annual CLTV	Segment Percent	Segment CLTV amt.
1	$541.60	14%	$75.82
2	$510.26	23%	$117.36
3	$429.92	28%	$120.38
4	$232.76	35%	$81.47
Blended Average CLTV Profit per year over a 5-year Lifetime		100%	**$395.03**

Figure 6-17: Example Calculation of Average Annual Blended CLTV per Year over a 5-Year Period

Step P3.6: Calculate the Opportunity Costs of Poor Quality Information

Poor quality information often causes more missed and lost opportunity value than the direct Costs of Poor Quality Information.

Objective

To establish the relative importance of information to the business, and to be able to measure the Missed and Lost Opportunity Costs of Poor Quality Information. See Figure 6-18 for the steps to calculate the Opportunity Costs of Poor IQ.

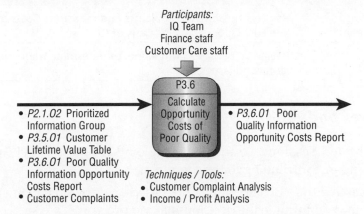

Figure 6-18: P3.6 Calculate Opportunity Costs of Poor Quality Information.

Inputs to P3.6

P2.1.O2 **Prioritized Information Group:** The Information Group for which Poor Quality Information Opportunity Costs are being measured

P3.5.O1 **Customer Lifetime Value Table:** The profit or revenue figure to be used to calculate Lost and Missed Opportunity, whether by Customer segment or as a blended figure for all Customer Segments

P3.6.O1 **Poor Quality Information Cost Report:** Prior opportunity cost reports from previous studies to analyze trends

Customer Complaints: Actual recorded Customer Complaints, recordings, or written verbatim Customer conversations. These are reviewed for presence of IQ issues as part of the complaint

Outputs of P3.6

P3.6.O1 **Poor Quality Information Opportunity Costs Report:** The report analyzing the Lost or Missed Opportunity caused by Poor Quality Information

Participants and Roles for Step 3.6 "Calculate Opportunity Costs of Poor Quality Information"

Table 6-6: Step P3.6 Participants and Their Roles

PARTICIPANT	IQ ACTIVITY ROLE
Information Quality Team	Reviews Customer Complaints and measures Costs of Missed and Lost Opportunity in terms of CLTV.
Customer Care staff	Reviews Customer Complaints to determine frequency of IQ-related issues.

Techniques and Tools:

- **Facilitated Sessions:** To analyze Complaints for those with IQ problems causing or contributing to the complaint
- **Research:** Study of failed initiatives based on decision making requiring information input to the decision-making process

Step P3.6: Calculate Opportunity Costs of Poor Quality Information — Process Steps and Guidelines

There are three types of opportunity costs incurred by organizations. They are:

- **Lost Customer Lifetime Value:** This is the revenue and profit lost when Customers have Complaints about your organization. For our purposes, we look at Complaints that have IQ issues as a cause or a component of the cause.

- **Missed CLTV in Operations:** These costs are attributed to IQ issues that prevent or minimize CLTV, such as when duplicate catalogs are sent to the same household, preventing the additional catalogs from going to prospective Customers, or incorrect addresses that create undeliverable mail.

- **Missed CLTV in Flawed Decisions:** These costs are the result of poor decisions based on poor quality, missing, or untimely information.

Process steps in P3.6 include:

P3.6.1 Calculate lost CLTV caused by Poor Quality Information:

The message in the e-Satisfy TARP retail study requires organizations to resolve complaints quickly — on the Customer's timetable — rather than at your convenience. But the real message is to prevent the situations that cause Customer complaints in the first place.

P3.6.1.1 Collect the Customer Complaints and analyze what percentage of them have IQ issues as part of the cause of the complaints.

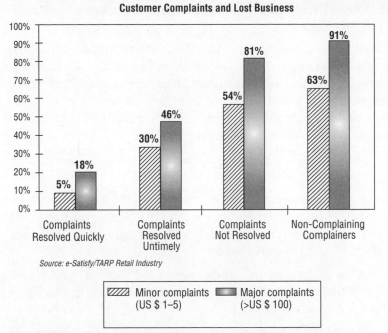

Customer Complaints and Lost Business

Source: e-Satisfy/TARP Retail Industry

Minor complaints (US $ 1–5) Major complaints (>US $ 100)

Figure 6-19: Customer Complaints in Retail and Lost Business

HOW MANY CUSTOMER COMPLAINTS HAVE IQ ISSUES AS A COMPONENT?

One major European Bank found that 100 percent of their Complaints had IQ issues as a component when considering data definition, content, and presentation quality issues.

One not-for-profit organization found 61% of their Complaints had IQ issues associated with them.

P3.6.1.2 Measure the revenue and profit in the year before the Customers made a Complaint caused by IQ issues, or use your calculated average annual CLTV.

P3.6.1.3 Measure the revenue and profit in the year after their complaint, or use the loss of the CLTV resulting from their defection. See Figure 6-19.

NOTE You may want to analyze the Customer revenue and profit from Customers, grouped by strong revenue and profit versus those with deceasing or terminated revenue. This will give you a pattern of identifying the complainers who do *not* tell you of their complaints, but tell their complaints to others.

P3.6.2 Calculate missed CLTV caused by Poor Quality Information in operational activities.

P3.6.2.1 Analyze the IQ issues in name and address data and other Information Groups that can cause communication problems with Customers, including sub-optimizing mail or email marketing campaigns. These include duplicate catalogs or mailings, undeliverable addresses, obsolete addresses, and other issues that prevent catalogs or items from reaching their intended recipient.

P3.6.2.2 Calculate the response rate of purchases or orders of those in the *profiled* mailing.

P3.6.2.3 Calculate the response rate of purchases or orders of those in the *mishandled or misdirected* mailing. There will be some residents who will have moved, with new occupants having moved in. They may have responded to the promotion.

P3.6.2.4 Based on the difference in response from the profiled group and the mishandled or misdirected group, calculate the difference in first-time Customer response.

P3.6.2.5 Calculate the rate of Missed Opportunity in CLTV in operational activities, such as misdirected mail and in absence of a unique, qualified prospect because of duplicate catalogs being wasted on one household. See Figure 6-20.

Missed Opportunity Costs	
Catalogs mailed	1,092,431
• Duplicate addresses (15.3%)	167,142
• Wrong/missing address (20.7%)	226,131
• Total catalogs "scrapped"	393,273
• Costs per catalog	$2.61
Non-recoverable direct costs	$1,026,443
Response rate of target Customers	1.5%
Response rate of "missed" Prospects	0.4%
Missed Customer Opportunity Rate	1.1%
Misdirected & duplicate catalogs	393,273
Missed first time Customers	4,326
Customer Lifetime Value "per Customer" per year	$395.03
Missed Customer annual profit	$1,708,901
5–year Total Missed Opportunity	$8,544,505

Figure 6-20: Measuring Missed Opportunity in Operational Processes

P3.6.3 Calculate Missed CLTV caused by Poor Quality Information in strategic and tactical activities (decisions).

P3.6.3.1 Identify decisions that affected strategies and tactics where the outcomes were sub-optimized. Examples include new product failure in the marketplace, sub-optimized or failed investments, failed mergers or acquisitions, inaccurate Business Performance Indicators.

P3.6.3.2 Analyze decisions that affected strategies and tactics that were sub-optimized. Analyze decisions where known or unknown Information Quality issues contributed to the failure or sub-optimization.

P3.6.3.3 Quantify the Missed Opportunity in each sub-optimized decision affected by Poor Quality Information.

HOW MANY CUSTOMER COMPLAINTS HAVE IQ ISSUES AS A COMPONENT?

A major global bank misinterpreted a risk code. They subsequently lost over $600 million when the company they invested in failed.

A major bank acquired a successful subprime lender for over $2 billion and assumed its $1 billion debt. After two years, they failed to capitalize on their acquisition. They ended up closing all its branches and took a nearly $3 billion write-off. They had failed to conduct a thorough due-diligence analysis of the lender's books and data.

P3.6.4 Compile the opportunity costs and the direct costs into a single Costs of Poor Quality statement. See Figure 6-21.

Subscription Company: Annual Costs of Poor Quality Information	
Direct Costs:	
People time and materials costs	$23,535,360
Annual vendor costs for data correction	$8,257,375
Annual Direct Costs of Poor Quality Information	**$31,792,735**
Opportunity Costs:	
Lost opportunity: IQ-related complaints (60.1%)	$1,840,767
Lost opportunity: Est. non-complaining complainers with IQ-related complaints (3 X complaints)	$5,522,301
Auto subscription declines missed opportunity	$2,940,000
Non-deliverable mail & monthly bill missed opportunity	$95,731
Annual Direct Costs of Poor Quality Information	**$10,398,799**
Total Annual Costs of Poor Quality Information (27.2% of $155 million operating revenue)	**$42,191,534**

Figure 6-21: Total Annual Costs of Poor Quality Information (Direct and Opportunity Costs) in a Not-for-Profit Subscription Organization

This arms you with the "data" you need to establish an imperative to implement a Culture of Continuous Process Improvement, starting with the most urgent and critical IQ issues that threaten the health of your enterprise.

Once you have improved the critical processes, you should follow Step P3.7, which will enable you to quantify the ROI of the Process Improvements.

Step P3.7: Measure the ROI of Information Process Improvements

This process establishes the value of Process Improvement, which prevents the recurrence of the Root Causes of *broken* information processes that cause downstream process failure and high costs of Information Scrap and Rework.

Objective

To quantify — in bottom-line currency figures — the ROI of Information Process Improvement, and to raise awareness of the importance of Information Quality Management as a core competency.

Figure 6-22 illustrates the Process step to calculate the Return-on-Investment of Process Improvements.

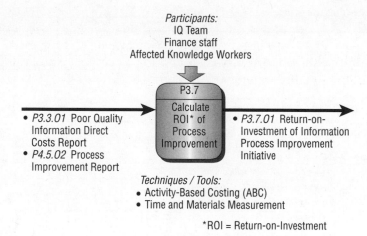

Figure 6-22: P3.7 Calculate ROI of Process Improvement.

Inputs to P3.7

P3.3.O1 Poor Quality Information Direct Costs Report: Analysis of Direct Costs of Poor Quality Information in process prior to improvement

P4.5.O1 Process Improvement Report: Documentation of the Process Improvement, including reduction of incidence and costs of Information Scrap and Rework.

Outputs of P3.7

P3.7.O1 **Return on Investment of Process Improvement Initiative:** Recalculation of the costs of ownership and ROI of the improved process

Participants and Roles for Step P3.7 "Measure the ROI of Information Process Improvements"

Table 6-7: P3.7 Participants and Participant Roles

PARTICIPANT	IQ ACTIVITY ROLE
Information Quality Team	Led by the Information Process Improvement Facilitator, usually the Process Owner; leads the measurement of the Direct Costs (and possibly the Opportunity Costs) of Poor Quality Information assessment in the improved process and for calculating the ROI of a Process Improvement.
Finance staff	Establish and confirm the procedure and formulas or rates for calculating direct costs of activities and resources and the formula for calculating ROI of the Process Improvement.
Affected Information Producers	Information Producers measure their cycle time in the improved process to calculate a new cost of ownership.
Affected Knowledge Workers	Calculate the new time spent in Information Scrap and Rework as reduced in the Process Improvement to calculate the reduction in waste.

Techniques and Tools

- **Finance Procedures for Measuring Costs:** Get the official costing figures and procedures for measuring capital expenditures and operating costs and ROI.

- **Activity-Based Cost Accounting (ABC):** This measurement method calculates the costs by category (capital investment, Value-adding activity, Cost-adding activity).

- **Time and Materials Measurement:** This tool is used by Knowledge Workers to measure their time in three categories:

  - System imposed time, such as staff meetings or project reporting

  - Value-adding work, such as capturing Customer orders, filling orders, invoicing orders, and the like, that is a part of your normal job description

  - Cost-adding work, such as when information defects cause you to have to hunt for information, or perform workarounds, along with direct costs of compensation and or materials consumed in the Scrap and Rework

Step P3.7: Measure the ROI of Information Process Improvements: Process Steps and Guidelines

This step measures the new state of quality in the process improved. This step will be conducted once the defined improvement has been implemented, procedures have been rewritten, training has taken place, and controls have been put into place to sustain the gain so that the process is in control. Process steps in P3.7 include:

P3.7.1 IQ The Team measures the costs of the new, improved process to get an average time per transaction for comparing to the previous status quo process. Where Poka Yoke (Error-Proofing) techniques have been applied, there may be some additional time required in the process. Follow the process steps in Step P3.3.

INSURANCE COMPANY SAVED THOUSANDS A YEAR BY IMPROVING AUTO INSURANCE APPLICATION PROCESS

Insurance company A had an auto insurance application from which it took an average of 11.1 minutes to enter data electronically. An average of 540 auto policy applications were processed daily, times 250 working days a year, which equaled 135,000 policies processed per year.

The quality of the process was deficient, however, with 34 percent of auto policy applications being defective, with one or more fatal errors or omissions. Annual Information Scrap and Rework (IS&R) time averaged 42 minutes × 45,900 defective policies = 32,130 hours, the equivalent of 15.5 FTEs per year. Their cost of people time is $75 per hour, or $156,000 per year per FTE, including overhead and equipment. 15.5 FTEs × $156,000 = $1,162,500 per year in direct people costs in IS&R caused by the defective auto insurance policy application process.

DIRECT COSTS:

- 34% defective policies/year = 34% × 135,000 policies = 45,900 defective policies.
- 45,900 defective policies/year × 42 minutes = 32,130 hours / 2080 = 15.5 FTE.
- 15.5 FTE × $156,000/yr = per FTE = $2,418,000 in direct costs per year in IS&R.

OPPORTUNITY COSTS:

- Errors caused underwriting mistakes leading to losses of $3,465,000 in claim overpayments (22% were overpaid by $350, with one-third of policies filing claims).
- Alienation of policy holders caused cancellations of 18% per year with losses of $850 premium per policy = 135,000 × 18% = 24,300 × $400 = $20.7 million in lost premium.

PROCESS IMPROVEMENTS TO THE PROCESS:

- Increased the auto insurance application process to 12.2 minutes, or by 10.5%.
- Reduced defective applications to 4.2 percent or 5670 policies/year (4.2% × 135,000 policies).

NOTE Sometimes, however, non-value-adding steps are eliminated and the actual improved process time is less than the original transaction times.

P3.7.1 Information Producers document their time and materials spent in the three categories as outlined in Step P3.3 to calculate the new rate of direct costs of the improved process. See Figure 6-23.

As-Is Process Time Measurement				Improved Process Time Measurement				
Tran Num	As-is Time (Min)	As-is Time (Sec)	Total Tran As-is (in Sec)	Tran Num	Improved Proc Time (Min)	Improved Proc Time (in Sec)	Improved Time Total (in Sec)	Diff in Tran Times
1	9	22	562	1	9	54	594	
2	12	5	725	2	13	5	785	
3	8	44	524	3	10	22	622	
4	10	15	615	4	12	31	751	
5	9	12	552	5	12	24	744	
6	14	37	877	6	11	13	673	
7	9	8	548	7	11	37	697	
8	12	15	735	8	12	13	733	
9	11	44	704	9	15	19	919	
10	13	12	792	10	13	33	813	
Mean Time	10	Mean As-is Sec	663.4		10	Improved Mean (Sec)	733.1	Diff (Min)
	Count	Mean (Min)	11.1		Count	Mean (Min)	12.2	1.2
							% increase	10.8%

Figure 6-23: Time Measurement of the As-Is, Unimproved Process and the Improved Process Time

P3.7.2 Knowledge Workers, who require the information produced by the improved process, document the time and materials they expend in the same three categories (Value Work, System-Imposed Time, and Information Scrap and Rework).

NOTE This waste of time and materials should be able to be reduced significantly based upon the rate of defect production in the original status quo process. If you do not get the cost reduction you expected, the Process Improvement may have failed to have a positive impact. If true, go back to TIQM Process P4 to study and analyze why the improvements failed.

P3.7.3 Document the amount of time spent performing the as-is unimproved process.

P3.7.4 Document the amount of time in the downstream areas where poor quality causes failure. Document people time and rate. Document opportunity costs or losses. See Figure 6-24.

Line Item	Expense Category	Five Year Cost of Ownership of As-Is Process: Creating Auto Insurance Application Policies				
		Year 1	Year 2	Year 3	Year 4	Year 5
1	Process Auto Ins Policy (11.1 minutes; $75/hr) 135,000 apps/yr	$1,873,125	$1,873,125	$1,873,125	$1,873,125	$1,873,125
2	Cost of Poor IQ (34% Defects=42 min=(15.5 FTE* $156,000/yr)	$2,418,000	$2,418,000	$2,418,000	$2,418,000	$2,418,000
3	Claims over pmt: $350ea of 22% of 135,000 (of claims)	$10,395,000	$10,395,000	$10,395,000	$10,395,000	$10,395,000
4	Lost Oppor: Lost Premium 18% x 135,000 x $850	$0	$20,655,000	$20,655,000	$20,655,000	$20,655,000
5	Cost of Poor IQ: (N/A)	$0	$0	$0	$0	$0
6	Cost of Poor IQ: (N/A)	$0	$0	$0	$0	$0
7	**Annual Cost of Poor IQ**	**$12,813,000**	**$33,468,000**	**$33,468,000**	**$33,468,000**	**$33,468,000**
8	**Accumulated Costs of Poor IQ**	**$12,813,000**	**$46,281,000**	**$79,749,000**	**$113,217,000**	**$146,685,000**
9	**Annual Costs of Ownership**	**$14,686,125**	**$35,341,125**	**$35,341,125**	**$35,341,125**	**$35,341,125**
10	**Total 5-Yr Costs of Ownership**	**$14,686,125**	**$50,027,250**	**$85,368,375**	**$120,709,500**	**$156,050,625**

Figure 6-24: Five-Year Costs of Ownership of As-Is Process "Create Auto Insurance Policy"

Figure 6-24 captures the Costs of Poor Quality Information in the Auto Insurance Application Create process. Following is an explanation of the process:

- **Line 1:** Average time to create an auto insurance application is 11.1 minutes. The cost of people time is $75/hour per Employee/Agent. There are 135,000 defective auto insurance applications per year with 34 percent of them being defective.

- **Line 2:** The cost of finding and fixing defective applications is 42 minutes per defective application.

- **Line 3:** 22 percent of the defective applications cause overpayment with an average overpayment of $350 per application.

- **Line 4:** Problems with the defective applications cause a defection rate of about 18 percent of Customers per year.

- **Lines 5 and 6:** Not applicable. These would be used to document other categories of costs.

- **Line 7:** The Annual costs of poor quality per year

- **Line 8:** The annual costs of ownership each year

- **Line 9:** The aggregated Costs of Poor Quality Information over a five-year lifetime.

P3.7.5 After the improved process has been stabilized and put in under control, return to measure the defective records produced by the current (improved) process. There should be a marked difference in error rates.

P3.7.6 Go to the downstream areas whose processes had failed because of the existing rate of defects, and measure any direct Time and Materials costs in ongoing IS&R activities.

P3.7.7 Document the one-time costs of Process Improvement and amortize it over the five-year (or your life cycle) life of the application and Process Improvement. Figure in the additional costs of time of error-proofing in the process itself as part of the cost of production of the information.

P3.7.8 Calculate the profit in the form of eliminated costs of Information Scrap and Rework and opportunity costs reclaimed. See Figure 6-25 for an example.

Line Item	Expense Category	Year 1	Year 2	Year 3	Year 4	Year 5
	Five Year Cost of Ownership of Improved Process and 5-Year ROI: Creating Auto Insurance Application Policies					
1	Process Auto Ins Policy (12.2 minutes; $75/hr) 135,000 apps/yr	$2,058,750	$2,058,750	$2,058,750	$2,058,750	$2,058,750
2	New Poor IQ (5.1% Defects=42min= (0.051*135,000*$75*(42/62)	$361,463	$361,463	$361,463	$361,463	$361,463
3	Claims over pmt: $350ea of 0.023% of 135,000 (of claims)	$1,086,750	$1,086,750	$1,086,750	$1,086,750	$1,086,750
4	Lost Oppor: Lost Premium 2.4% x $135,000 x $850	$0	$2,754,000	$2,754,000	$2,754,000	$2,754,000
5	Cost of Poor IQ: (N/A)	$0	$0	$0	$0	$0
6	Cost of Poor IQ: (N/A)	$0	$0	$0	$0	$0
7	**Status Annual Cost of Poor IQ**	**$14,686,125**	**$20,947,088**	**$85,368,375**	**$120,709,500**	**$156,050,625**
8	**Improved Costs of Poor IQ**	**$3,506,963**	**$6,260,963**	**$12,521,925**	**$18,782,888**	**$25,043,850**
9	**Saved Costs of Ownership**	**$11,179,163**	**$14,686,125**	**$72,846,450**	**$101,926,613**	**$131,006,775**
10	**Total 5-Yr Savings of Process Improvement**	**$11,179,163**	**$14,686,125**	**$72,846,450**	**$101,926,613**	**$131,006,775**

Figure 6-25: Costs of Ownership and ROI on Process Improvement (Auto Insurance Policy Creation)

Figure 6-25 captures the reduced Costs of Poor Quality Information in the Auto Insurance Application Create process as the result of an Information Process Improvement. Following is an explanation of the process:

- **Line 1:** The time for the auto insurance application process increased to 12.2 minutes. Cost of people time is $75 per hour. Defects decreased to only 5.1 percent of auto policy applications. These still average 135,000 policy applications per year.

- **Line 2:** With the new defective application rate of 5.1 percent, the annual costs of the Information Scrap and Rework are 42 minutes times 5.1% times 135,000 applications per year.

- **Line 3:** Total costs of claims overpayment has been reduced to 2.3 percent of policies. Overpayment average is still $350 per claim.

- **Line 4:** Customer attrition was reduced to 2.4 percent, reducing lost premiums to about $1 million per year.

- **Line 5 and 6:** Not applicable here.

- **Line 7:** The cost of poor IQ in the status quo process (before Process Improvement).

- **Line 8:** The aggregated costs of poor quality per year for five years.

- **Line 9:** The saved costs of Process Improvement, aggregated.

- **Line 10:** The total 5-year savings of Process Improvement.

So what do you do with the savings? See Figure 6-26.

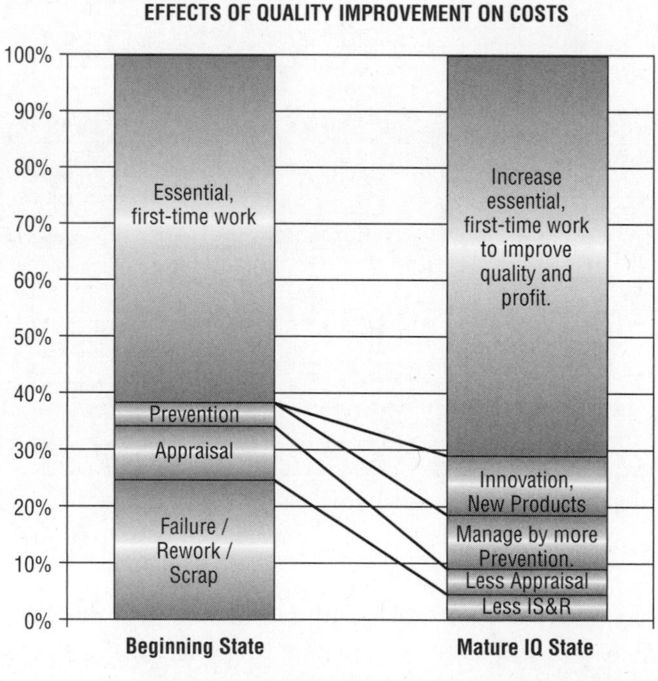

EFFECTS OF QUALITY IMPROVEMENT ON COSTS

Source: Gyrna, "Quality and Costs," Juran & Godfrey, Juran's Quality Handbook, 5th ed.

Figure 6-26: Effects of Process Improvement on Business Effectiveness

By freeing up the majority of the time formerly spent in recovery from information failure and Information Scrap and Rework, you can invest in your Value Work and increase innovation in new products and innovation to retain your valued Customers.

Summary

You have learned how to:

- Understand your enterprises Key Business Performance Indicators that will tell you the important Business Results Executives expect.
- Measure the Total Costs of Ownership of your Information and Information Systems capabilities.
- Measure the direct Costs of Poor Quality Information by measuring the amount of people time consumed in recovery from failure and Information Scrap and Rework, along with other resources, such as financial compensation, material waste, and equipment and facility costs in Information Scrap and Rework.
- Calculate Customer Lifetime Value and Measure the missed and lost CLTV as opportunity Costs of Poor Quality Information.
- Measure the Return on Information Process Improvement Initiatives over the life of the improvement.

Armed with a positive Return on Investment, you should see Management becoming much more involved in your IQ Initiatives and providing a visible call to action and resources to drive the IQ Culture forward.

The Step-by-Step Guide to *Improving Information Process Quality*

*"If you keep doing what you always did,
you'll keep getting what you always got"[1]*

Jackie "Moms" Mabley

Introduction to Improving Information Process Quality

It is this process — Improve Information Process Quality — that gives an organization the right to call its practice Information *Quality* or Information *Quality* Management.

Organizations that address only the "Inspect and Correct" processes should **not** use the term "Quality" in their business area or function name.

TIQM P4 enables an organization to achieve "Business Effectiveness through Information Effectiveness" when performed as a habit by everyone in the organization. Note that:

- Assessment is a *Cost of Poor Information Quality* that forces us to measure to find broken processes.

- Data correction is only one *Cost of Poor Information Quality* caused by defective information processes. Other costs include direct costs and opportunity costs to recover from process failure caused by defective information.

> ## NEW TIQM P4 "IMPROVE INFORMATION PROCESS QUALITY" AND TIQM P5 "CORRECT DATA AND CONTROL DATA REDUNDANCY"
>
> For those of you who are familiar with my first book, *Improving Data Warehouse and Business Information Quality (IDW&BIQ)*, I have an important change to announce:
>
> The original TIQM P4 "Improve Information Product Quality" *(IDW&BIQ)* is now TIQM P5 "Correct Data and Control Data Redundancy," Formerly, TIQM P4, "Information *Product* Improvement: Data Reengineering and Cleansing."
>
> The original TIQM P5 "Improve Information Process Quality" in *IDW&BIQ* is now TIQM P4, "Improve Information Process Quality," and is positioned above the parallel process of TIQM P5, "Correct Data and Control Data Redundancy," as illustrated in Figure 7-1.
>
> This is intentional in that the "Improve Information Process Quality" process is the core competency of a real Information Quality System. P5, now "Correct Data and Control Data Redundancy" is the Cost of Poor Quality Information. It is *Muda* (Japanese word for "waste"). Every penny you spend in P5 is waste because the information production processes do *not* have quality *designed in* to prevent defects.

If an organization performs only Assessment and Data Correction activities, it is *NOT* performing Information Quality Management. Rather it is stuck in a self-defeating mode of "Inspect-and-Correct." It is throwing good money after bad by reactive waiting until poor quality data causes process failure and then fixing the consequences. By designing quality *into* the process to prevent defective information, you avoid the process failure and recovery costs caused by the defects.

The only means of eliminating these costs of Information Scrap and Rework is through designing quality into the processes that create, update, deliver, and present information to the Knowledge Workers who require it to perform their processes effectively and efficiently to accomplish the Enterprise Mission and to delight its end-Consumers.

Not only is this process the Value Proposition and the core competency of a Quality Management System, it is also downright fun!!! People in the organization have *fun and fulfillment* when they Improve Broken Processes and eliminate the waste, process failure, and the costs and drudgery of data correction. They take pride in their work, and spread the gospel of Continuous Process Improvement among their peers.

In this chapter, we describe the step-by-step approach to conducting effective Information Process Improvement.

Improving Information Process Quality

TIQM begins and continues with the umbrella process of TIQM P6, "Establish the Information Quality Environment," that inculcates the principles of Total Information Quality Management. Because Information Quality Management is not just a set of projects, it is a culture of caring for Information Consumers and a habit of Continuous Information Process Improvement involving everyone in the enterprise.

- TIQM P6 provides for the awakening, education, and training to transform management so they can dismantle the barriers to Information Quality and to empower everyone to take part in the Information Quality revolution.

- Processes TIQM P1 and P2 measure to find broken Information and Information Production Processes that need improvement. P3 measures the Costs of Poor Quality Information to establish the priority of Process Improvements.

- TIQM P4 "Improve Information Process Quality" is performed to *improve* or *design quality into* an Information Process.

- Once processes are improved, TIQM P3.7 is performed to measure the Return-on-Investment.

- Then required data correction (TIQM P5) should be performed as a one-time event for existing defective data.

Figure 7-1 illustrates the process P4 "Improve Information Process Quality" in context.

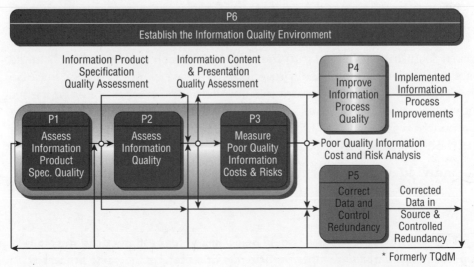

Figure 7-1: TIQM P4 Improve Information Process Quality in Context of TIQM

TIQM P4: Improve Information Process Quality

Improving defective processes and designing quality into new processes represents the core competency of an Information Quality Culture. The Plan-Do-Check/Study-Act and its Six Sigma variation of Define-Measure-Analyze-Improve-Control processes represent *the* Value Proposition for Total Information Quality Management. Without an effective Process Improvement Capability, an organization will squander its money, throwing it away in recovery from process failure and on data inspection and correction, called "Information Scrap and Rework." Making TIQM P4 a habit is what legitimizes the label "Information Quality Management."

PROCESS IMPROVEMENT RESULTS IN HEALTH CARE

Dr. Blan Godfrey recently described the turn-around improvement in hospitals that have implemented rigorous quality improvement actions. Hospitals that used to have 23 infections per day are now reporting "number of days since last infection." And when they find an infection, they send a Team to interview the physician, nurse, and all other people involved so they can identify the cause and implement preventive measures.

Like this example, the objectives of TIQM P4 are simple: Identify and eliminate the Root Causes of broken information processes that create defective information. This eliminates the causes and costs of process failure and Information Scrap and Rework, and eliminates Customer alienation caused by Poor Quality Information.

Four Categories of Information Process Improvements

Improvement initiatives fall into four categories, each of which may have its own set of project management procedures and governance protocol. Because Process Improvement initiatives involve improving and error-proofing processes to eliminate defects, they invariably (when performed correctly, based upon documented waste and Costs of Poor Quality Information) will yield a positive Return-on-Investment. The four categories of improvements are:

1. **Individual Improvements:** Everyone should be empowered to improve their own process procedures where it affects their own work, but does not impact others.

NOTE Improved procedures should be evaluated for best practices and standardized and shared with other participants who perform the same processes.

2. **Departmental Process Improvements:** Improvements affect processes that do not cross organizational boundaries and can be sponsored by a single Process Owner. Business Process Owner and beneficiary are the same.

NOTE Make it easy for these Process Improvement Initiatives to be conducted. Managers who are accountable for the quality of the information produced by their processes are accountable for the quality to meet their downstream peer managers' information requirements. Do NOT over-govern these initiatives.

3. **Cross-Organizational Process Improvements:** Business Process Reengineering Events and Kaizen Events that cross organizational boundaries that require Executive sponsorship and cross-organizational participation

NOTE Major Information Process Improvement Initiatives are the most political among middle management precisely because they are cross-organizational, demanding Horizontal Management around the Information Value Circles. These initiatives require an Executive Leadership Sponsor who can mediate across the organizational boundaries.

4. **Systemic Business System Improvements:** Business Management Systems, Performance Measurement Systems, and environmental enhancements that influence how work is performed

NOTE Systemic improvement initiatives must be championed and sponsored by the CEO, because these improvements challenge and change the Performance Measures that cause *negative* behavior. Measures of *speed* of information production *without* a measure of the costs of ownership caused by defects also cause Information Producers to work without care about downstream process failure. Performance measures such as these drive negative management and employee behavior.

TIP Seek to eliminate unnecessary procedural activities and red tape for the various categories of Improvement Initiative governance. The goal is to conduct Process Improvements — *NOT* to govern the Process Improvement Process. Allow Knowledge Workers and Information Producers to identify broken processes, and empower them to improve them with minimal approval steps. This can cause improvement initiatives to get bogged down and become a disincentive for identifying and solving real problems.

TIQM P4 Process Steps: Improve Information Process Quality

Here are the steps to Improve Information Process Quality. Process steps are diagramed in Figure 7-2 and described on a step-by-step basis in the rest of the Chapter.

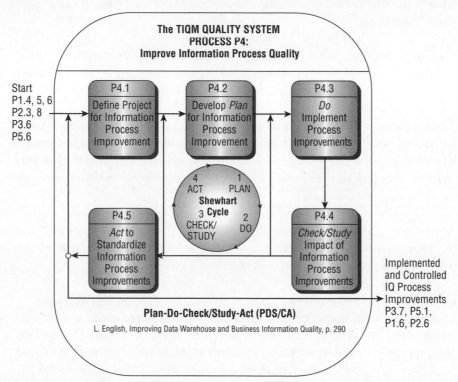

Figure 7-2: TIQM Process P4 Improve Information Process Quality Diagram with TIQM Process Inputs and Outputs to Other TIQM Process Steps

Step P4.1: Define Project for Information Process Improvement

This step establishes a formal project for an Information Process Improvement initiative.

Objective of Step P4.1

To establish Information Process Improvement Initiatives to eliminate the causes and costs of defective information by identifying the Root Causes and implementing

Poka Yoke (a Japanese term that means Error-Proofing Error Prevention Techniques) to eliminate the causes of defects.

See Step P4.1 in Figure 7-3 for components of the step.

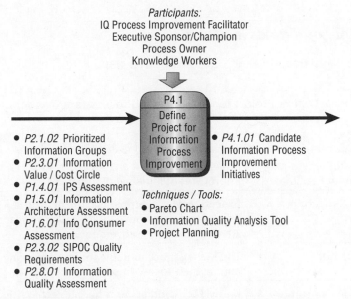

Figure 7-3: P4.1 Define Project for Information Process Improvement

Inputs to Step P4.1

P2.1.O2 **Prioritized Information Groups:** Specific Information where High Quality is required

P2.3.O1 **Information Value/Cost Circle:** Identifies the Information Production Process and interdependent Consumer Processes

P1.4.O1 **IPS Assessment:** Identification of defective information product specification requiring Process Improvement

P1.5.O1 **Information Architecture Assessment:** Identification of defective Information Models and/or Database designs requiring Process Improvement

P1.6.O1 **Information Consumer Assessment:** Identification of failure to meet Information Consumer Information Quality Requirements

P2.3.O2 **SIPOC Quality Requirements:** Defined Information Consumer Requirements for Information Quality where Process Improvement is required

P2.8.O1 **Information Quality Assessment:** IQ Assessment results of a Process requiring Improvement

Outputs of Step P4.1

P4.1.O1 Candidate Information Process Improvement Initiatives: Project plan for Process Improvement

Participants and Roles in Step P4.1

Table 7-1 lists participants and IQ Roles in this step.

Table 7-1: P4.1 Define Project for Information Process Improvement Participants and Roles.

PARTICIPANT	IQ ACTIVITY ROLE
Information Process Improvement Facilitator	Along with the IQ Team, identifies Process Improvement Initiative or initiatives.
Executive Sponsor or Champion	Executive who champions a major Process Improvement Initiative, or CEO who sponsors Cultural Transformation Improvements
Process Owner	The Manager accountable for implementing and maintaining the Process Improvements
Information Consumers	Knowledge Workers or other Subject Matter Expert Information Consumers affected by Poor Quality Information help identify Information and Requirements for Improvement. They will confirm the deficiencies in the Information Quality and will assist in identifying Root Causes and defining improvements to prevent recurrence of defects.
Information Producers	Process Improvement Team members who *perform* the process to be improved, both the actual Information Content Producers as well as the Transcriptionists who enter data into the databases. They will identify Root Causes and identify Process Improvements. In addition to the Information Producers who are experts at the job, you want newly hired Producers and Information Producers of other information who are not ingrained in the status quo process. They bring a new dimension to seeing the causes and seeing breakthrough thinking improvements.

Techniques and Tools for Step P4.1

- **Pareto Chart:** Pareto analysis used to identify potential improvement initiatives based on defect frequency or impact

- **Information Quality Assessment and Data Profiling Software:** Used to identify types of problems leading to projects for improvement
- **Project Management:** Used to manage the initiative for success

Step P4.1 Define Project for Information Process Improvement: Process Steps and Guidelines

This process step creates an Information Process Improvement Initiative, following your organization's project management protocol or protocols. Activities include:

P4.1.1 Identify candidate broken Information Processes and select Information Process for improvement.

TIP This may be the same Information as identified in the Information Group for Information Product Specification Quality in TIQM P1.2 or TIQM P2.1.

P4.1.2 Identify the Process Owner or owners. Multiple processes may be involved, such as the business processes and the application systems process that have different Process Owners' accountabilities for implementing the Information Process Improvements.

P4.1.3 Identify the Facilitator for the Information Process Improvement Initiative.

TIP Process Owners should facilitate the Process Improvement Initiative because they have accountability for the process results. Sometimes a neutral IQ Process Improvement Facilitator, knowledgeable in the Plan-Do-Check/Study-Act Cycle or the TIQM Six Sigma Define-Measure-Analyze-Improve-Control counterpart will Co-facilitate Root Cause Analysis (RCA) and Process Improvement definition.

P4.1.4 Identify the Information Producers and other pertinent personnel who can identify defect causes and improvements to eliminate causes. This always includes Information Producers, Transcriptionists and Translators, Information Agents, and other Subject Matter Experts in the process being improved.

P4.1.5 Develop the *project* plan for conducting the Information Process Improvement steps of the Plan-Do-Check/Study-Act cycle.

TIP The Gantt chart will contain all of the steps of P4, including P6.7 measuring the ROI of the Process Improvement.

Critical Success Factors for IQ Improvement Initiatives

Here is a checklist of Critical Success Factors for selecting Information Process Improvement initiatives:

- ☑ Process Improvement Initiative will solve a critical Business Problem Visible to Executives.
- ☑ Business case that is achievable with given resources
- ☑ Funding is provided.
- ☑ IQ Initiative Sponsor/Champion with *authority and willingness* to drive the Improvement Initiative and remove barriers
- ☑ IQ Improvement Team understands and meets Executive Sponsor expectations or re-focuses expectations if unrealistic.
- ☑ Process Owner with Accountability, *willing to implement* the Process Improvements
- ☑ Process Improvement Facilitator has Process Improvement skill and experience.
- ☑ Active involvement of Subject Matter Experts (SMEs) who are the Information Producers to identify Root Causes and define improvements
- ☑ Ability to measure IQ and Costs of Poor Quality before improvement
- ☑ Ability to measure IQ and reduction of costs to calculate Return-on-Investment

Step P4.2: Develop Plan for Information Process Improvement

Whereas Step P4.1 establishes the *project* plan for the improvement, P4.2 establishes the *Process Improvement* plan, consisting of:

1. Analyzing and identifying Root Cause or Causes
2. Defining Improvements that will *prevent recurrence* of the cause and its defects

Objective of Step P4.2

To eliminate *business problems* caused by Poor Information Quality by identifying and eliminating the Root Causes and error-proofing the information processes to prevent recurrence of causes of the broken process.

Figure 7-4 illustrates the inputs, outputs, participants and techniques and tools for Process P4.2.

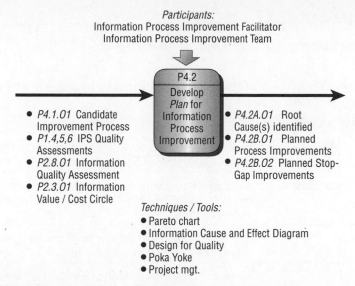

Figure 7-4: P4.2 Develop Plan for Information Process Improvement.

Inputs to Step 4.2

P4.1.O1 **Candidate Improvement Process:** The Information Process selected for improvement

P1.4,5,6 **IPS Quality Assessments:** Assessments of Information Product Specification data if this is an Information Resource Process requiring Improvement

P2.8.O1 **Information Quality Assessment:** Assessments of Information Quality if this is an information production process

P2.3.O1 **Information Value Circle:** The Value Circle of process activities where improvements will be made

Outputs to Step 4.2

▪ *P4.2A.O1* **Root Cause(s) Identified:** Identified Cause or Causes of the Effects to be eliminated

▪ *P4.2B.O1* **Planned Process Improvements:** Defined Improvements designed *to eliminate* the Cause or Causes and incidents of the Effect

▪ *P4.2B.O2* **Planned Stop-Gap Improvements:** Temporary defect prevention techniques to precede major reengineering improvements that require significant time for design and implementation, used to slow down defects until formal improvements can be implemented

Participants and Roles in P4.2

Table 7-2 describes the Participants and Roles in Step P4.2.

Table 7-2: P4.2 Develop Plan for Information Process Improvement Participants and Roles.

PARTICIPANT	IQ ACTIVITY ROLE
Information Process Improvement Facilitator	Facilitates Root-Cause Analysis and defined Process Improvements for trial implementation.
Executive Sponsor or Champion	Executive who champions a major Process Improvement Initiative, or CEO who sponsors Cultural Transformation Improvements
Process Owner	The Manager accountable for implementing and maintaining the Process Improvements
Knowledge Workers	Subject Matter Expert Information Consumers affected by Poor Quality Information help identify information and Information Quality Requirements.
Information Producers	Process Improvement Team members who perform the process to be improved and who will identify Root Causes and identify Process Improvements

Techniques and Tools for Step P4.2

- **Pareto Chart:** Pareto analysis used to identify potential Improvement Initiatives based on defect frequency or impact
- **Information Cause and Effect Diagram (Ishikawa-English Diagram):** Used to identify and document potential Root Cause or Causes of specific Information Effects and the Business Effects caused by the Information Effect
- **Design for Quality:** Techniques for Designing Quality into a process to meet specific Requirements
- **Poka Yoke:** Techniques used for Error-Proofing processes
- **Project Management:** Used to manage the initiative for success

Step P4.2 Develop Plan for Information Process Improvement: Process Steps and Guidelines

The first part of this step identifies Root Causes to eliminate by defined Process Improvements. The second part of this step defines improvements to eliminate the Causes of the Information Effect (defects) to prevent the losses from them.

P4.2.1: Analyze and Confirm Root Cause(s) of the Information Effect (Defective Information)

This step identifies and ensures that the real Root Causes of the broken information process are identified. Steps include:

P4.2.1.1 Create a Cause-and-Effect Diagram (Ishikawa-English Diagram) to list all possible causes and identify actual Root Cause(s) of the specific Information Effects (defects) analyzed.

P4.2.1.2 Understand and describe the *Information* Effect clearly in the Information Effect box. This is classification of the Information Quality problems resulting from the broken process.

P4.2.1.3 Identify the *Business* Effect that the Information Effect causes. The elimination of the Information Effect causes will also eliminate the negative Business Effects resulting from the defective information.

NOTE Although the IQ function focuses on preventing IQ problems, the real goal is to eliminate the negative effects on the Business caused by those IQ problems. In essence, when you focus on eliminating the business problems — that the Business Management cares about — you will sustain *management commitment* and championship of the IQ Value Work.

P4.2.1.4 Facilitated by the IQ Process Improvement Facilitator, begin brainstorming potential causes of the defined Information Effect from the Information Producers. Be sure to have a Cause-and-Effect Diagram visible to all participants. Use Figure 7-5 as a tool to stimulate ideas.

P4.2.1.5 Classify causes into the one of the six Categories of Cause as illustrated in Figure 7-5, Information Cause and Effect Diagram.

The classifications of causes are referred to as the six "M's":

- **Materials:** Includes the Data itself, its Presentation (handwritten, file transmitted, oral communication, the forms the data comes in, the definition of the data, the labels of the data elements)

- **Methods:** The defined or undefined processes, written, or procedures followed or not followed, process steps, exception handling guidelines, for example

- **Machines:** The Technology Components such as Application Software and Hardware, Information Models and Database designs, the Network, Computer Terminals, Workstations, Laptops where Information is captured, manipulated, or transformed and moved

- **Manpower (Human):** Error-inducing conditions or error-likely situations that cause "Human Error," such as "typos," transpositions, or missed entry. Human Error must always be traced back to Root Causes.

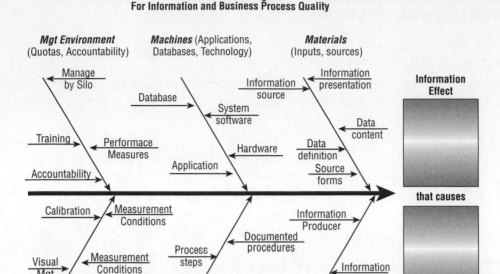

Cause-and-Effect Diagram*
For Information and Business Process Quality

*Also called an Ishikawa-English Diagram

Figure 7-5: Information Cause and Effect Diagram with Components of Cause, Also Called an Ishikawa-English Diagram

NOTE Human Error is *NOT* a cause of Poor Quality Information. Human Error is *CAUSED* by Error-Likely Situations and Error-Inducing Conditions, such as having to multitask, meet quotas, or handwrite data in too small of a space, for example.

- **Measurement:** Measurement processes inherent in the defined process, such as Embedded Systems in healthcare equipment that Monitors Vital Signs or in taking Measurement in Manufacturing or Chemical Processes

- **Management and Environment:** Corporate Values, *counter-productive* Performance Measures, lack of Accountability, Culture of Productivity by Speed, Quota systems, Ranking of employees, poor work conditions (noise, inadequate technology)

> **NOTE** Organizations that are immature in their current state of IQ Management will find that many Root Causes come from the Management and Environment cause category.

P4.2.1.6 Seek understanding of the causes identified. The only valid question during the cause discovery process is, "What do you mean by?" Seek to define the causes, but do NOT critique or challenge a cause. Even unlikely-seeming causes may be right on target.

> **NOTE** Avoid thinking or talking about Improvements or "solutions" during the cause discovery process. It will take the process off-target and possibly cause you to mis-identify the real Root Causes.

P4.2.1.7 As the free-association discovery of causes slows, seek to dig deeper from the "precipitating cause" to a Root Cause, by asking "why?" for each of the obvious *precipitating* causes.

> **NOTE** Generally, the actual Root Causes cannot be isolated during the RCA brainstorming.

P4.2.1.8 Conduct further measurement or design-of-experiments to isolate the Root Cause(s). For the most complex causes, use design-of-experiments to isolate and confirm the Root Cause(s).

> **NOTE** Failure to get to the actual Root Cause or Causes will make your recommended Process Improvements sub-optimized at best or fail outright at worst.

P4.2.2: Define Improvements Designed to Eliminate the Root Causes and Therefore Eliminate the Information Effect

The second part of P4.2 is to identify Process Improvement techniques to eliminate the Root Cause or Causes and prevent the defects.

P4.2.2.1 Understand the nature of the Root Cause or Causes. The poka yoke or error-proofing technique will be commensurate with the nature of the cause.

P4.2.2.2 For each Root Cause, match all possible preventive techniques.

P4.2.2.3 Evaluate each possible preventive technique until the best ones are found.

Table 7-3 illustrates causes, both Precipitating and Root Causes, in order to isolate the real Root Cause or Causes.

Table 7-3: P4.2B Potential Defect Prevention Remedies for various Effect Causes

CAUSE TYPE⁺	CAUSE	DEFECT PREVENTION REMEDIES
Legend: **PC =** **RC =**	**Precipitating Cause** **Root Cause**	
RC	Mgt & Env: Lack of Quality Culture	Establish the Costs of Poor Quality Information in both direct and opportunity costs in ability to accomplish the enterprise mission, and the value of Process Improvements with positive Return-on-Investment.
RC	Mgt & Env: Lack of Management Accountability	Establish Management Accountability, with training, so they know how to accomplish Information Quality.
RC	Mgt & Env: Manage down silos versus across Value Chains	Educate Executives as to Information-Age management as an Orchestra Conductor managing the enterprise as a single system of interdependent components — NOT independent units.
PC	Mgt & Env: Work space noisy	Implement noise-reduction techniques.
RC	Mgt & Env: Lack of understanding Knowledge Worker Requirements in Value Circle Design	Reengineer process design process to identify cross-organizational Knowledge Worker requirements dependent on the process being designed.
RC	Mgt & Env: Lack of emphasis on training	Evaluate and measure training for effectiveness. Redesign Training as necessary.
RC	Measure: Failure to maintain device calibration	Establish regular preventive device calibration scheduling.
PC	Measure: Used the wrong measure device	Error-proof the selection of Measurement Device for Attribute Measured.
RC	Machines (IT): Lack of enterprise-wide information management	Establish Enterprise-Wide Information Management as a *business function* and reengineer Information Management, Information Modeling, and Database Design process for Enterprise-Strength Information Management.

CAUSE TYPE+	CAUSE	DEFECT PREVENTION REMEDIES
PC	Machines (IT): Disparately defined information models and databases	Reengineer Information Management, Information Modeling, and Database Design process for Enterprise-Strength Management.
PC	Methods: Absence of a designed process	Define the process with Error-Proofing and Checklists as necessary.
RC	Methods: Have informal process definitions.	Define a rigorous process for developing process procedures.
PC	Material (Information): Customers miskey information in Web forms.	Redesign forms to Error-Proof them, such as calculating and testing credit-card numbers for Check Digit Validity.
PC	Human: Lack of knowledge of procedures	Provide Training, or redesign existing training.
PC	Human: Misread the measurement device	Provide Training in how to calibrate and use measurement devices.

P4.2.2.4 Ensure the preventive measure or measures that are recommended will be effective prevention of the Root Cause of the Information Effect addressed. The prevention will be implemented in a controlled way for evaluation in P4.3, and will be measured for effectiveness in P4.4 and rolled out into all production areas in P4.5 if the improvements are effective.

Guidelines

The identification of causes will identify both Precipitating Causes, as well as potential Root Causes. You must continue to ask "why?" to get back from Precipitating Causes to the Root Causes.

NOTE Any improvement that addresses elimination of the *precipitating causes only* will be suboptimized at best, and will fail outright at worst. Sometimes you will have to go back and observe and reassess the processes in Root Cause Analysis Step P4.2.2.8 to confirm that the identified cause is a real Root Cause. Other times, you may have to *design and conduct* a Design of Experiments to isolate the actual Root Cause.

Step P4.3: Do Implement Information Process Improvements

Step P4.3 implements the suggested Improvements in a *controlled* way to test, study, and verify the *efficacy* of the Improvements.

Objective of Step P4.3

Ensure the effectiveness of the defined Process Improvements in a controlled way so that the improvements meet expectations and do not introduce negative side-effects.

Figure 7-6 lists the participants and their roles in Step P5.3.

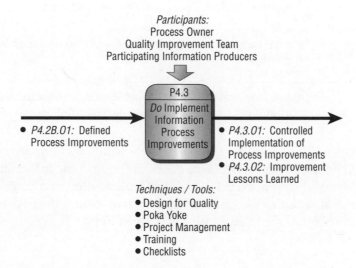

Figure 7-6: P4.3 Do Implement Information Process Improvements Step.

Inputs to Step P4.3

- *P4.2.2.O1* **Defined Process Improvements:** The defined improvements to be tested in a real, but controlled environment

- *P2.3.O1* **Information Value Circle:** Graphic representation and description of the processes and applications that impact the information, their data stores, and Information Stakeholders' roles. Used to identify where the improvements are to be made.

- *P2.3.O2* **SIPOC Chart (Supplier-Input-Process-Output-Customer):** Individual SIPOC Charts for each of the Information Value Circle activities. Used to identify the Information Quality requirements of the Information Consumers.

Outputs of Step P4.3

- *P4.3.O1:* **Controlled Implementation of Process Improvements:** Improvements implemented in a controlled environment for study to ensure they meet expectations

- *P4.3.O2:* **Improvement Lessons Learned:** Lessons Learned through the implementation of the Process Improvements

Participants and Roles in P4.3

Table 7-4 lists the participants and roles in Step P4.3.

Table 7-4: P4.3 Do Implement Information Process Improvement Participants and Roles.

PARTICIPANT	IQ ACTIVITY ROLE
Process Owner	Oversees the implementation of the Process Improvements in a controlled environment.
Quality Improvement Team	Assists in the implementation of the Information Process Improvements.
Participating Information Producers	Executes the newly improved process in the controlled environment.
Other subject experts	Other subject experts, such as Systems Analysts, Programmers, Information Management Staff, when their expertise is required for system design, programming, or database reengineering

Techniques and Tools for Step P4.3

- **Design for Quality:** Techniques for designing quality into processes

- **Poka Yoke:** Techniques for Error-Proofing processes

- **IQ Software Preventive Techniques:** These techniques allow information creation applications to access Business Rule and Edit and Validation routines. These will assist in ensuring Validity of the created data.

- **Business Rules Engines:** Also used to allow Business Rules to be fired for data create applications

- **Training:** For ensuring Information Producers understand how to perform the newly improved process

- **Checklists:** Tool to ensure all aspects of a process have been performed and completed correctly
- **Project Management:** For managing the controlled improvements for success

Step P4.3 Do Implement Information Process Improvements: Process Steps and Guidelines

P4.3.1 Define the requirements for the controlled implementation of the defined Process Improvement. This includes the Control Mechanisms to ensure the process will be implemented in a way that does not induce bias. This includes such controls as:

- Implement software edits and validation results in a test environment against appropriate test data.
- Implement training for a representative mix of Information Producers who represent different age groups, experience levels, locations, and other variable factors.
- Implement screen designs, form designs, and report designs with a representative sample of Information Producers (Data Capture designs) and Knowledge Workers (information delivery).
- Implement new Performance Measures in a select, representative group of managers in a Proof-of-Concept approach. This will require training in the IQ principles and the provision of resources and training to their staff to be able to provide the quality expected in the performance measure for Information Quality.

TIP For complex improvements involving multiple improvement components, such as a form design and a procedure modification, implement and measure each component independently and as a whole to ensure multiple improvements do not conflict and cause failure or negative side-effects. If the overall improvements fail, this will identify which component or components were the cause.

P4.3.2 Develop the plan for implementing the improvements, in such a way as to control the environment to simulate the real production environment.

TIP Software improvements in the application systems should be tested in the software test environment first. Then they should be incorporated in the overall Process Improvements implemented in the production environment.

P4.3.3 Determine the optimum time to measure the controlled, improved process. This will reveal whether or not the improvement measures were effective. If the Assessment is too soon after implementation, the process may not have become stable. If too late after implementation in which the improvement is not effective, time and resources will be wasted.

TIP Measure the process soon after implementation to ensure the improvements appear to be working. To measure the effectiveness of the improved process, allow time for the process to have stabilized and achieve a stable state of IQ. For example, to measure the effectiveness of enhanced training, you must allow enough time after the training (four to five weeks) to determine that the training became part of the Information Producers' habit.

Step P4.4: Check/Study Impact of Information Process Improvement

Step P4.4 confirms whether the Process Improvement worked effectively.

Objective of Step P4.4

Confirm the effectiveness of the defined Process Improvements in a controlled way to ensure that the improvements meet Knowledge Worker Expectations and have not introduced Negative Side-Effects.

Figure 7-7 illustrates the components of Step P4.4.

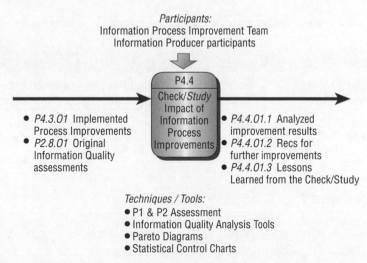

Figure 7-7: P4.4 Check/Study Impact of Information Process Improvement

Inputs to Step P4.4

- *P4.3.O1* **Implemented Process Improvements:** Documentation of the Process Improvements
- *P2.8.O1* **Original Information Quality Assessments:** Used to understand the current state of Quality

Outputs of Step P4.4

- *P4.4.O1.1* **Analyzed Improvement Results:** The assessment results of a P1 "Assess Information Product Specification and Architecture Quality" (see Chapter 4) or a P2 "Assess Information Quality" (see Chapter 5) depending on the process improved
- *P4.4.O1.2* **Recommendations for Further Improvements:** If the improvements are *not effective*, identify the Root Cause of the improvement failure along with recommendations for corrective adjustments in the planning or implementation of the improvements
- *P4.4.O1.3* **Lessons Learned from the Check/Study:** Documentation of the Root Cause(s), adopted Improvements, and Lessons Learned from the study of the controlled improvements to the process

Participants and Roles in Step P4.4

Table 7-4 illustrates the participants and roles in Step P4.4.

Table 7-5: P4.4 Check/Study Impact of Information Process Improvement Participants and Roles.

PARTICIPANT	IQ ACTIVITY ROLE
Information Process Improvement Team	Analyzes the controlled Process Improvement results, Root Cause if not successful, and Lessons Learned.
Information Producer Participants	Share their experiences in the Process Improvement and analysis of any Root Cause if not successful and share their Lessons Learned.

Techniques and Tools for Step 4.4

- **P1 and/or P2 Assessment:** These assess the degree of quality in the various Critical-to-Quality IQ Characteristics tested.

- **Information Quality Analysis Tools:** To assist in conducting the Electronic tests, such as Completeness, Value Validity, Business Rule conformance, Non-duplication, and redundant data Equivalence

- **Pareto Diagrams:** Used to report the Assessment Measurements in a priority sequence

- **Statistical Process Control Charts:** To measure process control over time

Step P4.4 Check/Study Impact of Information Process Improvements: Process Steps and Guidelines

This process step conducts a TIQM P1 or TIQM P2 assessment, depending on whether the improvement is to an information production capability process, such as improving information modeling or a business information production process, such as order entry, inventory management, market to Customer, or apply payment.

P4.4.1 Follow the TIQM P1 "Assess Information Product Specification and Information Architecture Quality" in Chapter 4, or TIQM P2 "Assess Information Quality" in Chapter 5.

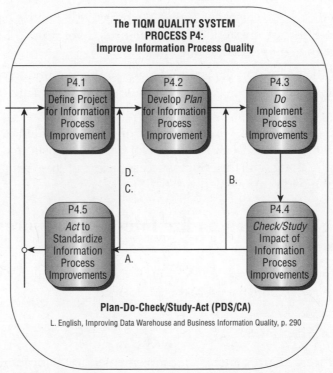

Figure 7-8: Procedure for When Improvements Do Not Accomplish the Objective

> **NOTE** The process of assessment of the controlled, implemented improvement should be identical in both method and conditions as the original assessment processes, so as to NOT introduce bias into the newly improved process assessment results.

P4.4.2 Follow the TIQM P3.7 "Calculate ROI of Process Improvement" in Chapter 6 to establish the economic value of the improvement.

P4.4.3 Confirm that the improvements accomplished the objectives and that no Negative Side-Effects (new process variation) were introduced into the process. See Figure 7-8.

P4.4.4 Did the improvements accomplish the objectives with no Negative Side-Effects? If yes, follow A to P4.5 and Act to Standardize the Improvements and roll them out across the enterprise.

P4.4.5 If no, did the Team implement (Do) the improvements properly? No? Then follow B to P4.3 and re-implement.

P4.4.6 If yes, ask, did the Team plan properly? If no, follow C to P4.2 and re-plan. The Root Cause may not have been identified correctly or the suggested improvements did not eliminate the Root Cause.

P4.4.7 Did the improvement accomplish the objective, but introduce a Negative Side-Effect or unintended consequence? If yes, follow D to P4.2 and re-plan to eliminate the side effect(s).

P4.4.8 Did the new improvements solve the problem with no new Negative Side-Effects? Follow A to P4.5 and act to standardize the Process Improvement and roll it out across the enterprise.

P4.4.9 Document the Lessons Learned from the controlled improvement implementation. Document the Root Causes of unsuccessful improvements, along with the critical success factors of the re-implemented or re-planned improvements.

Step P4.5: Act to Standardize Information Process Improvements

This process puts the Process Improvements in Control and rolls out the improvements to all places where the process is performed.

Objective of Step P4.5

To ensure Process Improvements are implemented in all locations where the process is performed and to ensure the process remains in control.

Figure 7-9 illustrates the components of Step 4.5.

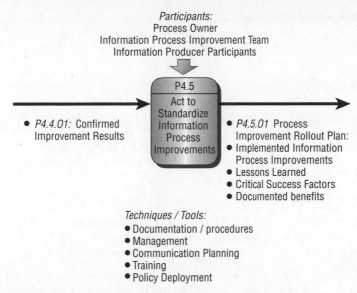

Participants:
Process Owner
Information Process Improvement Team
Information Producer Participants

P4.5
Act to Standardize Information Process Improvements

● *P4.4.O1:* Confirmed Improvement Results

● *P4.5.O1* Process Improvement Rollout Plan:
● Implemented Information Process Improvements
● Lessons Learned
● Critical Success Factors
● Documented benefits

Techniques / Tools:
● Documentation / procedures
● Management
● Communication Planning
● Training
● Policy Deployment

Figure 7-9: P4.5 Act to Standardize Information Process Improvements.

Inputs to Step P4.5

▪ *P4.4.O1* **Confirmed Process Improvement Results:** Verification that the Process Improvements worked without introducing Negative Side-Effects

Outputs of Step P4.5

▪ *P4.5.O1* **Process Improvement Rollout Plan:** This is used to ensure that all aspects of the rollout to other parts of the business are successful and repeatable:

▪ **Implemented Process Improvements:** The improvements are implemented correctly and are operating in control.

▪ **Recorded Lessons Learned:** Knowledge acquired during the improvement initiative planning, controlled implementation, checking on the improvement effectiveness, and implementation across the enterprise

▪ **Critical Success Factors:** The factors that contributed to and ensured the success

▪ **Documented Benefits:** In the form of Return-on-Investment over the "Cost-of-Ownership" within your organization

Participants and Roles in Step P4.5

The participant roles and responsibilities in Step P4.5 are listed in Table 7-6.

Table 7-6: P4.5 Act to Standardize Information Process Improvements Participants and Roles.

PARTICIPANT	IQ ACTIVITY ROLE
Process Owner(s)	Accountable for the rollout of the verified improved process to all execution points
Information Process Improvement Team	Facilitates the implementation across the enterprise to ensure correctness of implementation.
Information Producer Participants and other Stakeholders across the enterprise	Become trained in the improvements, the new process procedures, error-proofing techniques, form or screen design changes, or others whose procedures are changed by the improvements.
Information Consumers	Confirm whether the improvements are meeting their IQ Requirements.

Techniques and Tools for Step P4.5

- **Documentation/procedures:** Used to standardize the process or procedure execution
- **Change Management:** To ensure P4.5 is implemented properly across all environments
- **Communication Planning:** Used to plan the messages and prepare the Information Producers for the new procedures
- **Training:** New processes require unlearning of old habits and learning and inculcation into the new processes.
- **Policy Deployment:** A management approach to achieve Customer Satisfaction by focusing on a few Critical-to-Quality issues and establishing goals from the top down to the Workers, such that meeting a Manager's goal requires meeting goals for the organization level below

Step P4.5 Act to Standardize Information Process Improvements: Process Steps and Guidelines

This step ensures the improved process is implemented properly across the enterprise.

P4.5.1 Develop the project plan and schedule for rolling out the improvements to all processes requiring them.

P4.5.2 Develop the Communication Plan for preparing each process execution point to be ready and trained for the improvement rollout.

P4.5.3 Translate the developed process definition and procedures into the Enterprise Standard Process and Procedure formats.

P4.5.4 Follow all change management procedures for changes to:

- Process definition, including Data Capture and entry procedures
- Application design and coding
- Required data movement and transformation programs
- Information Model and data definition
- Database Design enhancement

P4.5.5 Rollout Process Improvements to each process execution point as scheduled. For each implementation, document:

- Procedures implemented, including local variations
- Process changes required
- Training experience
- Problems encountered and addressed
- Lessons Learned and Critical Success Factors identified

Guidelines for Effective Improvement Implementation

A Critical Success Factor for Root Cause Analysis calls for ensuring participants in the process have been included in identification of Root Causes and Process Improvement definition. If remote Teams have minimal participation in the original Root Cause Analysis and Improvement definition, ensure they are involved in the trial of the improvements in the controlled implementation. Listen to their experience and consider additional improvements they suggest. Note that this may become a subsequent Information Process Improvement Initiative that may take the quality to a new level.

TIQM Six Sigma DMAIC

For IQ practitioners who follow Six Sigma, Table 7-7 illustrates the sequence of TIQM processes and steps within the Six Sigma DMAIC phases.

Table 7-7: TIQM Processes and Steps Mapped to Six Sigma Phases and Steps

SIX SIGMA DMAIC PHASES AND STEPS*		TIQM PROCESSES AND STEPS+	IQ PROCESS/STEP ACTIVITY
D.	Define Phase	P4.1	Define Project for IQ Improvement:
		P2.2	Plan Objectives; Conduct SIPOC.
M.	Measure Phase	P1	Assess Information Product Specification Quality.
		P2	Assess Information Quality.
		P3	Measure Poor Quality Information Costs.
A.	Analyze Phase	P4.2.2.1	Plan Information Quality. Improvement: Conduct Root Cause Analysis; Confirm Root Cause identification.
I.	Improve Phase	P4.2.2.2	Plan Information Quality. Improvement: Define Process Improvements.
		P4.3	Do Implement Information Process Quality Improvements.
C.	Control Phase	P4.4	Check/Study Improvement Results.
		P4.5	Act to Standardize Information Quality Improvements.
		P2.2	Plan new IQ Objectives: Monitor new process.

*Source: Pande, et. al. *The Six Sigma Way*; +English, *Improving Data Warehouse and Business Information Quality*

Note: In this book, process P4 is called P5. P4 is the permanent new process number.

Best Practices in Information Quality

Over time, experience shows us that as practices become defined, some of them emerge as Best Practices, some are marginal, and some, in fact, are counter-productive.

Document Best Practices and the beneficial results they accrue. Also document counter-productive practices and their negative consequences.

The following describes Best Practices in a number of areas proven in real-world experience in the following:

- **Management and Environment**
- **Business Procedures**

- **Procedure Writing:** This is also addressed in Chapter 14, "Information Quality Applied to Document and Knowledge Management."

- **Data Creation and Maintenance**

- **Information Presentation**

- **Information Management and Information Systems Engineering:** This is addressed in Chapter 15, "Information Quality Applied to Information Management and Information Systems Engineering."

- **Information Resource Management:** This is addressed in Chapter 15, Section "Best Practices for Information Management Quality."

IQ Best Practices: Management and Environment

These Best Practices are critical to the sustainability of an effective Information Quality culture. They require a fundamental management transformation of the status quo.

- **Create an Information Quality Vision Statement that directly ties to the enterprise Mission and Vision Statement.** Executive Leadership must always see how IQ Management *increases* the ability of the Enterprise to accomplish its Mission effectively and meet its true value objectives and performance measures.

TIP Not all Enterprise Performance Measures are Critical Success Factors of the Enterprise. In fact some are counter-productive to the accomplishment of the Enterprise. For example, accomplishment of quotas with no measure of the Quality and Costs of Ownership may provide a false sense of accomplishment. Performance measures must be in sync with Customer Delight and Lifetime Value.

- **Create Information Policies that implement sound guidance for managing information as an enterprise resource.** This includes:
  - Planning for Information at a *Strategic* level.
  - Creating Information Models that are Enterprise-Strength and translating them into Enterprise-Strength Database Designs.
  - Implementing Management Accountability for Information.
  - Providing *training* for Management, Information Producers, and Knowledge Workers.
- **Define and implement the Information Process Improvement Cycle (Plan-Do-Check/Study-Act) as a core competency.**
  - Coach and Educate Executives in their new roles in the Information Age.

- The Executive Leadership understands its role in making Information Quality happen, organizes itself to make IQ happen, and *communicates* to Staff why change is required.

- Executive Leaders are held *accountable* for Information Quality produced by the processes in their control to meet all internal and external Information Consumer Requirements.

- Provide training for all Information Producers and Information Consumers. This includes:

  - Knowing who their Downstream Information Customers are

  - Knowing what Processes require the information

  - Knowing the Costs of Poor Quality Information

  - Knowing how to identify Root Causes and Improve their Processes following the Plan-Do-Check/Study-Act cycle

  - Empowering Staff to Improve their Processes.

- **Define Information Quality Accountability statements for Managers and Information Producers' job descriptions.** IQ accountability means meeting or exceeding their downstream Information Customers' Requirements for Information Quality.

  - Seek Employee suggestions for Information Process Improvements and involve Information Producers in Information Process Improvement Teams. When people improve their own processes, they have a new *pride in ownership* of the improved processes. The participants in the Improvement definitions are eager to implement their Improvements because they defined them. Improvements suggested by external personnel will often be received with some resistance, as "not-invented-here."

  - Provide new Employee Orientation on Information Management Principles and Information Stewardship (accountability) for Customer delight and Business Mission accomplishment. Organizations that rally all personnel in the Mission of the Enterprise that is focused on the Customers are more highly motivated and productive.

  - Provide formal Information Quality training for Employees and Managers in how to identify IQ issues and how to conduct Root Cause Analysis, Information Process Improvement, and SIPOC (Supplier-Input-Process-Output-Customer) analysis to understand IQ requirements of their Information Consumers.

  - Develop a habit of documenting and *sharing knowledge* about all Information Process Improvements, Root Causes, and the ROI of the Improvements.

Best Practices: Business Procedures

These best practices address *effectiveness* in the processes and procedures Information Producers and Knowledge Workers follow to perform their work. The purpose of procedures is to ensure that processes are Repeatable and Reproducible and process performers perform their work with consistent quality.

- **Don't accept bad data — send it back to the originator.** Provide immediate feedback — positive and negative, so Information Producers and Management understand there are problems they must address.

- **Don't force Knowledge Workers to create private databases or reports.** Provide access to the Record-of-Reference Database designed to meet all Knowledge Worker Requirements or via *controlled* replication.

- **Develop a data update process that empowers *any* Knowledge Worker to correct data or communicate data corrections to the Process Owner.** This should be performed by updating data in the Record-of-Reference Database directly or communicating required updates to the accountable Process Owner.

- **Understand your Customers as Information Consumers and seek out their Expectations for the Information you share with them.** Ensure your Customer Feedback Process gathers information about the satisfaction of the Information you provide them, and how well you communicate with them based on their Expectations, written or oral.

- **Use timely points of contact with Customers and Volatile Data Sources to Verify data Accuracy and Keep Information Current.** This requires maintaining a last verified/updated date in records about objects that are subject to Information Quality decay.

- **For complex procedures, use checklists to ensure all information is collected and verified properly.** Checklists represent the "measure twice" Principle of the Carpenter to ensure you have performed each component of a process and captured all the data and verified it before completing the process.

- **When writing periodic reports such as project reports, emails, or forms to collect information, use "clean" templates.** Do *NOT* use previously completed documents or forms for new correspondence, email, or forms, because you may fail to replace previous data from the old document. Information from the previous document can easily be overlooked and left in the current report as inaccurate values that were true for the previous report.

- **Verify Third-Party–provided Information with Independent Sources who can corroborate it.** In the same way you assess information you create, you must also assess Third-Party Information to ensure it meets *your* IQ Requirements.

- **Develop contracts with Warranties for Information Quality purchased from Information Brokers.** Ensure there are *remedies or compensation* for defects in purchased information. If you find 20 percent Defective Information in the information you buy, you should receive at least a 20 percent refund of the money you paid for it, plus handling charges for having to find it and call it to the attention of the Information Broker.

- **Develop easy-to-follow Information Capture and Maintenance Procedures:**
  - Use standard guidelines.
  - Observe training of new Information Producers.
  - Observe process execution in the Gemba, which means "The 'real place' where the Value Work takes place, such as where products are produced or where Information is learned."

Best Practices: Procedure Writing Guidelines

The Best Practices in Procedure Writing Guidelines error-proof written procedures to minimize misinterpretation and failure to perform procedures correctly.

These best practice guidelines are addressed in Chapter 14, "Information Quality Applied to Document and Knowledge Management."

Best Practices: Information Creation and Maintenance

These best practices address effectiveness in the processes and procedures capturing, creating, and maintaining information. These best practices are addressed in Chapter 15, "Information Quality Applied to Information Management and Information Systems Engineering" in the section "Best Practices for Information Creation and Maintenance."

These are the processes that "acquire" the *raw material* of data that will be captured and maintained and to be accessible to all Knowledge Workers to perform their Knowledge Work.

Best Practices: Presentation Quality

Information Creation and Maintenance Best Practices address effectiveness in the processes of capturing, creating, and maintaining information. Presentation Quality Best Practices address the processes that retrieve the raw material of data and assemble it into useful Information as presented to Knowledge Workers to perform their Knowledge Work.

- **Before developing a report or a screen design that will present information to Knowledge Workers, ensure you understand their Requirements.** Keep asking the question, "What do you mean by … ?" until you hear confirmation, and both parties can repeat the meaning, and you know you have a *consensus* of understanding of the best and correct way to deliver the Information to the prospective Knowledge Workers.

- **Design for Information Consumer(s).** Understand how they use Information and how they need to see it, hear it, sense it, or apply it to perform an action, such as to trigger an automatic purchase or sale of a stock or mutual fund.

- **Ensure Clarity and Objectivity.** Information must *always* be presented in a way that is *intuitive and easy* for any Knowledge Worker in a given role to interpret it correctly and apply it correctly, such as to take a *right* action or to make a *correct* decision.

- **Use the "Who, What, Why, Where, When, How" Checklist to ensure all pertinent Information.** When we fail to gather *all* of the Information, we run the risk of missing information, especially in event or meeting announcements that can lead to omissions of location of the event, date or time of the event, what preparation is needed, and what the agenda is, for example. This wastes people's time and keeps them from performing their Value Work.

- **Intuitive, standard, "correct" data names, labels, terms.** *Unclear, inappropriate labels* for data cause failure of interpretation of the meaning of the data that leads to misunderstanding and *misuse* of the data.

- **Data Definition must be available, Standardized among Representatives of all Information Stakeholders.** Information Producers and Knowledge Workers alike need to know the *meaning* of the Information, its Valid Values and Business Rules that constrain it.

- **Provide Help and access to Definitions.** Make it easy for Information Stakeholders to access the meaning of Business Terms in an Enterprise Glossary and the meaning of data in their Databases that should be accessible in an Information Repository or Dictionary.

- **Ensure Quality across multimedia (printed and online).**

- **Ensure Information is Presented Completely and Objectively.**

- **For Quantitative Information, use the *right type* of graphical device, chart, or diagram.** Do not use a column chart when you should be using a line chart or cluster chart.

- **Intuitive Presentation Format in context:** This includes:

  - Information should be "Minimalist" and concise, with drill down as needed.

  - Order sequence of data and linkage should be logical, such as linear time sequence, or general to specific.

  - Presentation Type: may balance graphic with text.

- **"Unstructured" data should be *Structured*.**

  - Use Information Mapping to *"chunk"* meaningful groups.

  - Use intuitive idea presentation sequence.

  - Ensure Reading difficulty is three grade-levels lower than the intended audiences' education.

- **Conduct a "Usability Test" of the Information Presentation with Representative Information Consumers.**

- **Make it easy for the Customer to provide Feedback**

- **Provide Abstracts and/or Executive Summaries for Reports, Articles, Studies, Experiments, or Presentations.** These provide a quick synopsis for the readers to help them determine whether the document is *relevant* to their work and mission.

- **Use meaningful Names, Titles, Keywords, or Meta tags.** This helps people find information in your intranet.

- **Provide a Legend for Labeling Components and Footnotes or Links to explain Anomalies.** Explanations of unexpected patterns, trends, or data values need to have the context to *interpret* them properly.

- **Identify the Source from which the Information comes.** Ensure that Knowledge Workers know where the Information comes from, so they know what confidence to ascribe to it.

- **Assessment of sampled data must describe the Population sampled, Sample size, Confidence level, and Sampling technique applied to establish credibility.**

Best Practices: Information Systems Engineering

These best practices address Information Systems that capture, maintain, and present information to the Knowledge Workers. Information Systems are to the Information-Age intangible Information Products what the manufacturing equipment is to the Industrial-Age tangible products.

These best practices are described in Chapter 15, "Information Quality Applied to Information Management and Information Systems Engineering."

Best Practices: Information Management

Best practices for Information Management as a Strategic Enterprise Resource are described in Chapter 15, "Information Quality Applied to Information Management and Information Systems Engineering." See Section "Best Practices in Information Management Quality."

Best Practices for Document and Knowledge Management are found throughout Chapter 14, "Information Quality Applied to Document and Knowledge Management."

Summary

Key points of Improving Information Process Quality include the following Lessons Learned:

- Process Improvements do not just happen. They must be planned to truly resolve the problem cause.

- To truly resolve the problem you must discover and eliminate the Root Cause or Causes.

- Those who Improve Processes should be the ones who Perform them. They know the problems, and given an opportunity, they will identify the Causes and define Improvements that eliminate the cause.

- Process Owners who are *accountable* for the Quality of the Information should facilitate the Process Improvement Initiatives on the processes for which they are accountable. They are accountable for Quality to meet their downstream Information Consumers' Requirements.

- Processes must be put In Control once improved. They will not stay in control without being Error-Proofed and monitored.

- You should measure the Costs of Poor Quality before Improvement, and then measure the Return-on-Investment following the Improvement. This confirms the Business Case for IQ and the sustainability in the Information Quality Environment.

CHAPTER 8

The Step-by-Step Guide to *Data Correction and Controlling Data Redundancy*

"In the U.S.A. about a third of what we do consists of redoing work previously 'done.'"

Joseph M. Juran[1]

Introduction to Data Correction and Controlling Data Redundancy

In the early days of Quality Management in manufacturing, Quality was considered to be Quality Assurance, that is, you *inspected* the products as they were produced and pulled *defective* products off the assembly line to Rework them, or Scrap them if they were *too* defective to fix.

As Quality Management *matured*, it became clear that you could achieve *sustainable* Quality only by *designing* Quality Into the Processes that produce the products.

The phrase "Scrap and Rework" represents a Cost of Poor Quality. The popular Japanese word for Scrap and Rework is *Muda*, which literally means "waste." The same is true for Poor Quality Information produced by processes. You cannot sustain Information Quality by *inspecting and correcting* defects. Information *Muda* is something you must eliminate or minimize as an activity.

Unfortunately, during the early days of establishing and maturing your IQ Capabilities, you will encounter preexisting defective data that has already been created by defective processes. If that data is required by current business processes, you will have to spend time and money to correct it so future use by processes won't fail.

There are *right* and *wrong* ways of conducting data correction or "Information Scrap and Rework." We explore that in TIQM Process P5, "Correct Data and Control Data Redundancy."

NEW TIQM P4 IMPROVE INFORMATION PROCESS QUALITY AND TIQM P5 CORRECT DATA AND CONTROL DATA REDUNDANCY

For those of you who are familiar with my first book, *Improving Data Warehouse and Business Information Quality (IDW&BIQ,* Wiley 1999), I have an important change to announce:

The original TIQM P4 Improve Information Product Quality *(IDW&BIQ)* is now TIQM P5 "Correct Data and Control Data Redundancy."

The original P5 Improve Information Process Quality in *IDW&BIQ* is now TIQM P4 "Improve Information Process Quality" and is positioned above the parallel process, P5 Correct Data and Control Data Redundancy, as illustrated in Figure 8-1.

This is intentional to show that the "Improve Information Process Quality" process is the core competency of a real Information Quality System. P5, now "Correct Data and Control Data Redundancy," is the Cost of Poor Quality Information. It is *Muda* (Japanese word for "waste"). Every penny you spend in P4 is waste because the information production processes do not have quality designed in to prevent defects.

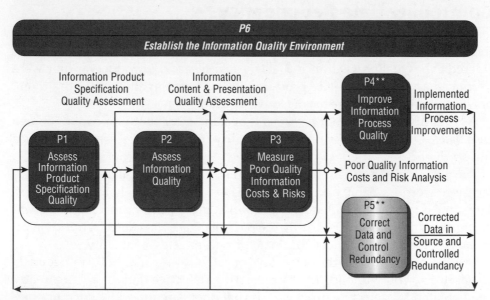

** Note: The Processes P4 and P5 are changed from my 1st book to increase focus on Process Improvement
          as the TIQM core competency

Figure 8-1: TIQM Process Diagram with P5, Correct Data and Control Redundant Data in Context.

The Sound Way to Correct Data Defects and Control Data Movement and Redundant Data

Correcting data is a *costly waste* of time, materials, facilities, and equipment, including the Information Consumers' time and money. Poor Quality Information comes from *defective* Information Processes. Your ultimate goal is to eliminate the *need* for data correction by *designing quality into* the processes that create and maintain data, to prevent defects that must be corrected. Continuous Information Process Improvement eliminates the *Causes* of defective information processes and the costs of ongoing data correction.

The sound way to address data correction is to minimize it by Designing Quality In to prevent the Root Causes of the defective information.

The following scenario represents how most organizations address Information Quality today.

Out-of-Control Information Create Processes

If you don't design quality into information-producing processes, there will always be a significant degree of error in created Information, with a cascading effect on Information Quality as data is *propagated* from one database to another, as shown in Figure 8-2.

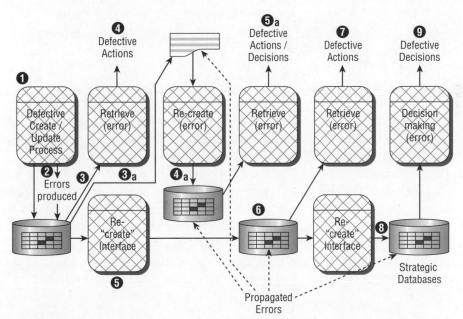

Figure 8-2: Uncontrolled Processes and Cascading Poor Quality Information

In an immature organization, errors will be routine in Information Processes, as there is no comprehension of error-proofing techniques. These processes may even be in control, with a known variation of errors. These scenarios will exist:

1. A broken process creates defects.

2. Defects and quality data get stored in the Record-of-Origin Database.

3. Processes retrieve the defective Information.

    3a. Reports from the defective source data may be used to enter data into another, often proprietary, Database to support other Knowledge Workers.

4. Knowledge Workers using *defective* Information take incorrect actions, such as charging the wrong price, misspelling a Customer's name, or sending a Customer the wrong item.

5. Errors are propagated to the new database.

6. Actions taken or decisions made from the propagated errors cause processes and decisions to *fail* or be *sub-optimized* at best.

7. Errors get propagated to other databases.

8. Errors are extracted from the propagated data.

9. Decisions made are *sub-optimized* as determined by the extent of errors.

10. Defects are propagated to the Strategic Databases (data warehouse).

11. Defects used in decision-making *sub-optimize* the decisions as determined by the nature and degree of error.

Hidden Information Factories as a Reaction to Poor IQ

Organizations in IQMM Awakening Stage 2 may see Knowledge Workers take data correction matters into their own hands when they require Accurate Data to perform their jobs properly, if they do not get accurate data from their Information Producers.

Often Knowledge Workers, unable to wait for systems support or Information Producers to capture data correctly, will become their own IQ Team, *correcting* data in their own *proprietary* databases. In the same way that manufacturing quality saw assembly line workers create their own "Hidden Factories" of parts, so also do Information Consumers often have to create their own "Hidden Information Factories" of *correct* Information they need to perform their work.

The scenario is:

1. Knowledge Workers in Business Area 2 cannot trust the data in Business Area 1's database.

2. Knowledge Workers create their own database with extracts from Business Area 1.

NOTE Not all errors may be corrected, depending on how well Knowledge Workers are able to get back to the source of knowledge.

3. Knowledge Workers develop their own processes for keeping the data they need current and correct to the best extent possible.

4. With increased Quality of Information, Knowledge Workers are better able to perform their defined work *properly*.

Several problems beset this data correction approach:

▪ Business Area 2's Knowledge Workers are not able to perform their Value Work until they correct the data. Data correction adds Cost, not Value.

▪ This creates an "unnatural" accountability for IQ created by Business Area 1. Here Business Area 2 has to take on *accountability* for correcting Business Area 1's defective Information.

▪ Data correction costs are *sub-optimized* because not all other dependent Information Stakeholders benefit from the corrected data in Business Area 2's private, proprietary database.

▪ Other downstream Information Consumers may also conduct data correction efforts that lead to further inconsistencies across the Information Value Circle.

▪ Because some Information cannot be corrected after initial creation, errors will still *cause actions or decisions to fail*.

Because data correction activities can introduce new Information Defects, they must be conducted following the controlled procedures described here.

Data Correction for the Data Warehouse Only

Many organizations apply the following approach: Fix data mainly as it is prepared for loading into a data warehouse. Concern for solving Information Quality problems in Gemba (the source of where data originates) is missing. The mindset is that Information is a *compartmentalized* resource. Quality of Information at the source is irrelevant, unnecessary, or "out of scope" for the data warehouse initiatives. See Figure 8-3 for the scenario.

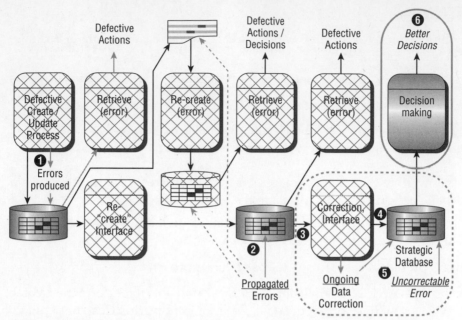

Figure 8-3: Sub-optimized Data Correction for the Data Warehouse Only

This scenario for data correction is as follows:

1. Broken processes create errors at the source, but data correction at the source of data is rejected as out-of-scope. The false thinking is that "we only need to correct data as it comes into the data warehouse."

2. Errors are propagated from Record-of-Origin Database to Record-of-Reference Database that feeds the data warehouse.

3. Massive, costly data correction activity is implemented, using software that looks at reference databases to correct discovered errors, *often* introducing errors and *often* failing to identify errors.

4. Corrected data is propagated to the data warehouse along with undiscovered and uncorrectable errors.

5. Uncorrectable errors will be propagated to the data warehouse without being able to be corrected.

6. Better — not necessarily optimal — decisions are able to be made, but only for Knowledge Workers using the data warehouse.

NOTE Not all errors may be corrected depending on the capability of the software and access to correct data values.

NOTE   Data correction software has limitations. Often, as much as 10 percent of the results of data "cleansing" will be false negatives (identification of "correct" data that are in fact wrong) and will be false positives (identification of "not correct" data that are in fact correct).

Problems Caused by Correcting Data Downstream Only

The problems in this approach include:

- *No after-the-fact* data correction initiative will be able to correct *all* errors, let alone do so *cost-effectively*:
  - The cost to correct data is often *10 times as much* or more as the cost required to capture data *accurately* at the point of creation.
- It *sub-optimizes* the cost of correction — only downstream Knowledge Workers benefit.
- *Processes* using the defective data at the source *still fail*.
- A new IQ problem is created — *inconsistency:*
  - Queries from the two databases will *NOT* match.
  - Drill-down processes will *NOT* balance.
  - Knowledge Workers will stop trusting data.
  - Defective data in the source *can subsequently corrupt* the downstream database with false positives and false negatives.

Data correction can introduce additional errors such as assigning a wrong gender code based on a person's name because it is common to one gender. Data correction must be done only when appropriate and under the guidelines stated here.

Automated defect detection is based on "validity checks" *only*. However, valid values can be "wrong." For example, an item price may be numeric and within the valid range for the product type but may be the wrong price for the item).

Optimized Process Improvement at the Source with One-Time Data Correction at the Source with Controlled Data Propagation

The *only appropriate* way to treat data correction is *as a one-time activity* for data in any given database. But you must correct data only *after* you have Improved the Defective Creation Process of the source data and improved the data propagation process so that it is in control. See Figure 8-4.

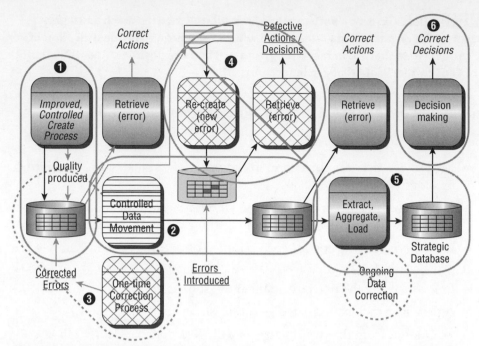

Figure 8-4: Optimized Process Improvement and One-Time Data Correction for All Knowledge Workers

This scenario includes:

1. Plan and execute a Process P4 Improve Information Process Quality *first* to stop the defects from occurring. This analyzes and discovers the Root Cause, so the Improvement will *prevent* reoccurrence of the defects.

2. Implement controls in the processes that extract, transform (if necessary), correct, and load data to error-proof them.

3. Conduct a planned, *one-time data correction* activity on the data in the source database. Ensure that all Knowledge Workers accessing data from this source or downstream Record-of-Reference databases or Strategic (business intelligence) Databases will have Quality Information as well.

4. Eliminate "Hidden Information Factories," and redirect access to the authoritative Record-of-Reference Databases.

5. Because all applicable processes are *error-proofed* and *in control*, the propagation of data to the Strategic Databases is in control and likely to meet all Knowledge Worker needs.

6. Design decision support processes to present Information to each group of Knowledge Workers in a way that is *intuitive and unbiased*, so Knowledge Workers can use the Information correctly and in a timely way.

Optimized Information Management That Eliminates the Waste Caused by Data Redundancy and Data Propagation

This represents the *highest maturity* of the Enterprise in the Information Age. The organization is maximizing the value of its Information in Enterprise-Strength Shared Databases. See Figure 8-5.

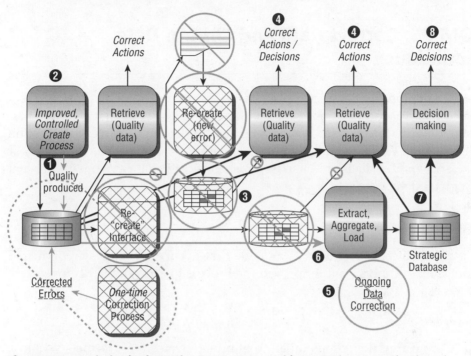

Figure 8-5: Optimized Information Management with Enterprise-Strength, Shared Databases, and Minimal IQ Issues

1. The Record-of-Origin Database is designed as an Enterprise-Wide Sharable Database, Subject by Subject (Customer, Product, Order).

2. The Create process is Error-Proofed and minimal errors are created.

3. *Unnecessary, redundant* Databases are eliminated along with the corresponding propagation and transformation processes.

4. Knowledge Workers are able to access data from a *single shared* database, designed to meet all Knowledge Workers' Knowledge Requirements.

5. No ongoing data correction is required to move data into the Strategic Databases (data warehouse).

6. No "extract, transform, and load" process is required to transform data for the Operational Data Store (ODS), for it shares the same data element

format, structure, valid values, and business rules. Aggregation is required only for summarized data.

7. Strategic Databases have few defects or errors.

8. Knowledge Workers' actions and decisions are *optimized* because they have the *correct* Information, presented *intuitively without bias*.

TIQM P5. Correct Data and Control Data Redundancy

Please remember that correcting data is *not* a value-adding process. It is a cost of Poor Quality Information. Quality Management tells us that we must first Design Quality Into the Processes that create, update, and deliver Information to Knowledge Workers and processes so that they can take the *right* action or make an *optimized* decision. Then we must correct the data as a one-time event for a given data store.

Overview

Treat any data correction activity as a one-time event after you have conducted a Root Cause Analysis and Improved the Process to Prevent the Recurrence of Defects.

Key terms:

Containment: Actions taken to eliminate Defective Products within a process by inspecting and removing the Defective Products (Scrap)

Corrective Maintenance: Actions taken to remove or Fix a Defect or Defective Product *after* it has been Produced or Created (Rework)

Scrap and Rework: Actions taken to *remove or fix* Defective Products *after* they have been produced and *mitigating* the problems caused by the Defective Products

Information Scrap and Rework: Actions taken to *remove or fix* Defective Information after it has been produced and *mitigating* the problems caused by the Defective Information

Preventive Maintenance: Actions taken to remove the *Causes* of defects or unacceptable variation by *improving and error-proofing* processes to *prevent* defects or unacceptable variation from being produced

Objectives

There are six major objectives for data correction:

- Correct Errors and Information Defects in operational source Databases that *cause processes to fail*.

- Correct Errors in Data provided by Third-Party Brokers or Business Partners to prevent retrieval and application processes from failing.

- Prepare and transform data required for conversion to new Information Systems or purchased Software Package Databases.

- Consolidate and transform data required by *mergers and acquisitions*, where data must be "integrated" (transformed or consolidated) into an Enterprise Database.

- Prepare and correct data *required for data mining* for decision analysis, where errors and omissions will cause the analysis to fail.

- Correct and transform data in the Source Database(s) prior to propagating them to a Strategic Database (data warehouse).

Avoiding Pitfalls

Do not rely on data correction for solving the Information Quality problems in your organization. Your core competency must be TIQM Process P4 Improve Information Process Quality.

- Conduct a Data Correction Activity *as a one-time event* for any given data store, *after* you have identified Root Causes and Improved and Error-Proofed the Defective Process.

- Always correct data in its Source Data Store and *propagate the corrections* to any required, redundant Data Stores. The reasons are:

  - Processes using data from the source *will continue to fail*.

  - Correction of data in a downstream data store creates a new IQ issue — *inconsistency of data from source to target*. Provenance (data lineage) is lost; queries from source to target *will not match*, causing the questioning of both values.

  - Defective data left in the source *will eventually corrupt data* in the downstream data store when it is propagated.

  - This *sub-optimizes money spent to correct* the data. You will end up having to spend additional money to correct the data at the source when the pain is felt there.

Process Steps: Correct Data and Control Data Redundancy

The TIQM P5 process overview diagram for data correction and control of data movement is represented in Figure 8-6.

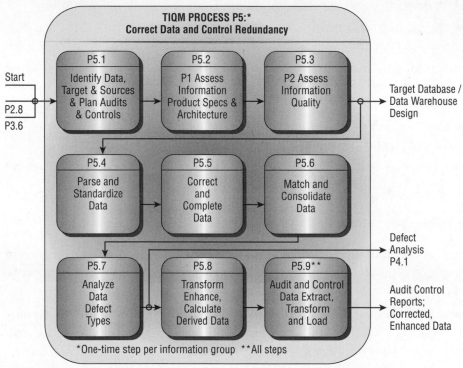

Figure 8-6: P5. Correct Data and Control Data Redundancy Process Steps

This process should be conducted one time only for a given data store or Information Group where IQ issues are causing processes to fail.

Step P5.1: Identify Data, Target, and Sources and Plan Audits and Controls

As always, the key to Quality Management is Continuous Improvement of the Information Processes. TIQM calls for solving Business Problems using the Pareto approach — solving *the most significant and troublesome information problems first* and then moving to the next most significant issues.

Here, you identify the most significant IQ issues to identify Critical-to-Quality (CTQ) Information. Improve the Defective Process *first*, ensure the Create process *is in control*, and then correct the Defective Data *as a one-time activity*.

Objective of Step P5.1

To determine which Information Groups and Record-of-Origin Databases or Files require Data Correction to prevent ongoing Process Failure from Defective Information use.

Figure 8-7 illustrates the participants, inputs, outputs and techniques, and tools in Step P5.1.

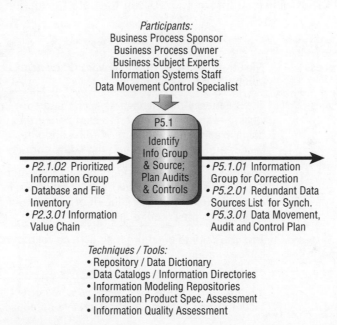

Figure 8-7: TIQM P5.1. Identify Information Group and Source Data; Plan Audits and Controls for Data Movement.

Inputs to Step P5.1

P2.1.O2: Prioritized Information Group

Data dictionary/repository, catalog, or inventory of databases

P2.3.O1: Information Value Circle with processes requiring the defective information

Outputs of Step P5.1

> *P5.1.O1:* Information Group for Correction
>
> *P5.2.O1:* Redundant Data Source and Targets List for Synchronization
>
> *P5.3.O1:* Data Movement, Audit and Control Plan

Participants and Roles in Step P5.1

Participants and roles in Step P5.1 are described Table 8-1.

Table 8-1: P5.1. Establish an Information Group for Data Correction Participants and Roles.

PARTICIPANT	IQ ACTIVITY ROLE
Business Process Sponsor	The Strategic Information Steward (Executive Leader) of the information to be corrected.
Business Process Owner	The Business Area Manager is Accountable for Information Quality requiring correction to eliminate errors to prevent downstream process failure. He/she appoints a Project Leader and Team for the one-time data correction effort.
Business Subject Experts	Business Subject Experts identify data to be corrected, and who knows the data, and who will participate in correcting errors, either in terms of content or in the definition of the information they require or share.
Application Systems Managers and Developers	They participate in automating data correction routines that can be made.
Information Modelers and Database Administrators	Information Systems Professionals who correct Information Model errors and reengineer defective databases
Data Movement Control Specialist	Plans audits and control routines for controlling data movement, ensuring correct data transformation, if required, and ensuring adequate data controls for data movement.

Techniques and Tools for Step P5.1

Repository/ Data Dictionary: Used to store Information Resource Data (IRD), including Data Names, Definitions, Valid Value sets, Business Rules, and Processes creating, updating, retrieving, and deleting data. The key to effective Information Management is to have accessibility to Information Models and Data Definitions for all Stakeholders.

Data Catalogs/Information Directories: Same as above

Information Modeling Repositories: Used to store graphic Information Models; they will also have data definition and other IRD data.

Information Product Specification Assessment (TIQM P1): Used to identify and measure the quality in Data Definition, Valid Value sets, Business Rule Specification, and Information Model and Database Design

Information Quality Assessment (TIQM P2): Used to identify and measure data Accuracy and for capturing Accurate data values for correction

Step P5.1: Process Steps and Guidelines

1. Identify Critical Information from a Source Data Store where existing defects and omissions are causing process failure and high costs of Information Scrap and Rework.

2. Identify the process or processes that are creating or updating the data that may be the cause of the defects.

3. Conduct a TIQM P4 Improve Information Process Quality Initiative to Error-Proof and put the Process In Control before you start data correction activities.

Guidelines for Step P5.1

- Apply the Pareto approach with your Business Subject Experts to address the highest-priority data first.

- Improve the process first to prevent the *continued production of defects*.

NOTE This minimizes the costs of the data correction based on the rate of defective data currently created.

- Plan the Audits and Controls to ensure that data required to be propagated is extracted, transformed properly, if necessary, controlled, and loaded properly into the Target Data Store. See Step P5.9 for the Audit and Control Step.

- Plan the data correction activities as a *one-time event* for the data in the source database.

- Plan the Audits and Controls necessary to ensure that processes that transform and propagate the data are In Control.

Step P5.2: Conduct TIQM P1. Assess Information Product Specifications and Architecture Quality

This is TIQM P1, as outlined in Chapter 4. Follow the steps in TIQM P1 to provide an accurate picture of how well the data requiring correction is defined and how well the Information Model(s) and database(s) are architected.

> **NOTE** Often, data with quality problems also has Poor or No Definition, leaving the Knowledge Workers and Information Producers alike to speculate on its meaning. A necessary part of Information Scrap and Rework is to rework and redefine the meaning of the critical Information.

Objective of Step P5.2

Ensure that you have a correct and complete Definition of the data, its Business Rule Specifications, and Valid Value Sets as well as the Quality of the Information Architecture. This is required before you conduct the data correction.

Figure 8-8 assess the quality of the Information Product specifications data to ensure you know the meaning of the data.

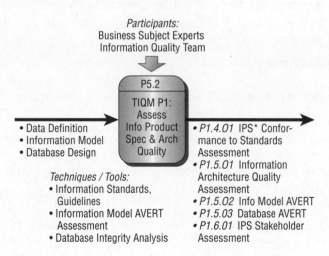

Figure 8-8: P5.2 (TIQM P1). Assess Information Product Specification and Information Architecture Quality.

Inputs to Step P5.2

Refer to Chapter 4, "The Step-by-Step Guide to *Assessing Information Product Specification and Information Architecture Quality*," for Inputs to all respective IPS assessment steps.

Outputs of Step P5.2

See Chapter 4 for the Outputs of respective IPS assessment steps.

Participants and Roles in Step P5.2

See Chapter 4 for Participants and Roles in the respective assessment steps.

Techniques and Tools for Step P5.2

See Chapter 4 for Techniques and Tools for the respective assessment steps.

Step P5.2: Process Steps and Guidelines

See Chapter 4, "The Step-by-Step Guide to *Assessing Information Product Specification and Information Architecture Quality*" for Process steps.

Guidelines for P5.2 in the Context of Data Correction

- Because the purpose of the Information Product Specification Assessment is data correction, you must ensure that you have correct, complete, and clear Data Definition, Valid Value Sets, and Business Rule Specifications.
- Poor quality Information Models and Database Designs require reengineering to eliminate the structural integrity problems of the Information Model and the physical Database Design.

See Chapter 4, "The Step-by-Step Guide to *Assessing Information Product Specification and Information Architecture Quality*" for process step details.

NOTE Defects in Data Naming, Definition, Business Rule Specification, and Valid Value Sets, and poor quality of Information Models and Database Designs are caused by broken processes. They ultimately must be improved and error-proofed to avoid Poor Quality Information Product Specifications and Information Architecture Design in future initiatives.

Step P5.3: Conduct TIQM P2. Assess Information Quality

Conduct an Information Quality Assessment (TIQM P2), as outlined in Chapter 5, "The Step-by-Step Guide to *Assessing Information Quality*." This will focus on the Quality of the Information Content, the data as found in the Databases and as presented to Knowledge Workers.

Objective of Step P5.3

To discover the accurate and complete values in order to correct the defective data in the source Data Store

Figure 8-9 illustrates the components of TIQM Step P5.3.

> **NOTE** Because data correction is an expensive part of the *Cost of Poor Information Quality*, it *should* be conducted as a one time event *after* you identify Root Causes and Improve the Defective Process and put it In Control.

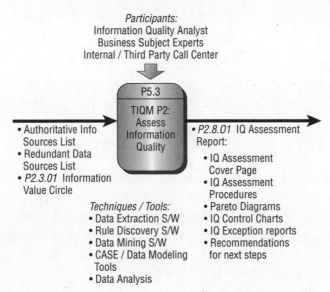

Participants:
Information Quality Analyst
Business Subject Experts
Internal / Third Party Call Center

P5.3

TIQM P2:
Assess
Information
Quality

• Authoritative Info
  Sources List
• Redundant Data
  Sources List
• *P2.3.01* Information
  Value Circle

• *P2.8.01* IQ Assessment
  Report:

  • IQ Assessment
    Cover Page
  • IQ Assessment
    Procedures
  • Pareto Diagrams
  • IQ Control Charts
  • IQ Exception reports
  • Recommendations
    for next steps

Techniques / Tools:
• Data Extraction S/W
• Rule Discovery S/W
• Data Mining S/W
• CASE / Data Modeling
  Tools
• Data Analysis

Figure 8-9: P5.3 TIQM P2: Assess Information Quality for Data Correction.

Inputs to Step P5.3

See Chapter 5, "The Step-by-Step Guide to *Assessing Information Quality*" for the Inputs to the respective Assessment steps.

Outputs of Step 5.3

See Chapter 5 for the Outputs of the respective assessment steps. The P2.8.O1 Exception Report(s) are the most important for the Data Correction activities.

Participants and Roles in Step P5.3

See Chapter 5 for Participants and Roles in the respective assessment steps.

Techniques and Tools for Step P5.3

See Chapter 5 for Techniques and Tools for the respective assessment steps.

Step P5.3: Process Steps and Guidelines

See Chapter 5 "The Step-by-Step Guide to *Assessing Information Quality*" for process steps and guidelines for the respective steps.

> **NOTE** Because this Assessment is in the context of a data correction activity, you must capture not just the fact of and percent of defects but also the *accurate and complete data values* for data correction activities and *identify and confirm duplicate entities* (Customers, products, event transactions) for consolidation or duplicate elimination.

> **NOTE** Do not correct data while you are conducting your accuracy assessment. It will interfere with your assessment, and it may prevent you from capturing the correct values for later corrective maintenance. This is especially true if you are assessing Customer information directly with the Customer.

Step P5.4: Parse and Standardize Data

Standardized Information is critical to effective communications across different Business Areas. This step parses data and puts it into Standard Formats for reengineering the databases.

Objective of Step P5.4

To standardize data into atomic values, and to standardize the formats and data values to increase business communication and to facilitate data correction activities (see Figure 8-10).

Inputs to Step P5.4

Assessed Data

P2.8.O1: **IQ Exception Report:** Identification of Inaccuracies with Correct Values Identified

Assessed Data Valid Value Sets and Rules: The Validity tests applied

Data Anomalies: The potential errors identified in the assessment

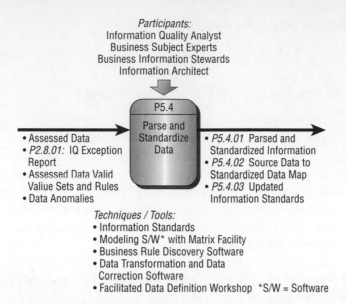

Participants:
Information Quality Analyst
Business Subject Experts
Business Information Stewards
Information Architect

P5.4

Parse and
Standardize
Data

- Assessed Data
- *P2.8.01:* IQ Exception Report
- Assessed Data Valid Valiue Sets and Rules
- Data Anomalies

- *P5.4.01* Parsed and Standardized Information
- *P5.4.02* Source Data to Standardized Data Map
- *P5.4.03* Updated Information Standards

Techniques / Tools:
- Information Standards
- Modeling S/W* with Matrix Facility
- Business Rule Discovery Software
- Data Transformation and Data Correction Software
- Facilitated Data Definition Workshop   *S/W = Software

Figure 8-10: P5.4 Parse and Standardize Data for Information Management Control

Outputs of P5.4

P5.4.O1: **Parsed and Standardized Information:** Data definitions that have been standardized at the atomic level; used to reengineer databases and to identify potential duplicate records

P5.4.O2: **Source Data to Standardized Data Map:** Used to propagate data from unstandardized to standardized redundant data store

P5.4.O3: **Updated Information Standards:** Used to reengineer Information Models, Database designs, and Application Systems

Participants and Roles in P5.4

Participants and roles in Step P5.4 are described Table 8-2.

Table 8-2: P5.4. Parse and Standardize Data Participant Roles.

PARTICIPANT	IQ ACTIVITY ROLE
Information Quality Analyst	Leads and conducts the IQ Assessment to identify Correct and Complete Data Values for data correction activity.
Business Subject Experts	Identify the IQ Characteristics to assess and verify or define the proper Business Rules for assessing Validity.

PARTICIPANT	IQ ACTIVITY ROLE
Business Information Steward	Ensures the Completeness, Correctness, and Clarity of the Data Definition, Valid Value Sets, and Business Rule Specification.
Information Architect	Develops the Information Model and attributes to support the standardized data parsed from overloaded attributes.

Techniques and Tools for Step P5.4

- **Information Standards:** Used to guide the standardization process. Often these will be updated with the various data correction initiatives as overloaded data elements are discovered.

- **Modeling Software with Matrix Facility:** Used to document the nonstandard data to standardized data that is correctly named and defined

- **Business Rule Discovery Software:** Used to find patterns in the data that lead to standardization and atomic data values

- **Data Transformation and Data Correction Software:** Used to electronically parse the data into atomic-level facts

- **Facilitated Data Definition Workshop:** Used to ensure that data is identified, named, and defined in a standard way, that is correct, complete and clear

Step P5.4: Process Steps and Guidelines

1. Identify the data elements that require parsing. These will include data elements that have been overloaded like Person Name, Address, and Product Code such as Catalog Code or VIN (vehicle Identification Number).

This enables better matching for duplicate records and creates a more stable database design when data is in an atomic format. See Figure 8-11.

Pers ID	Person Name	. . .
101	Mr. John A. Smith, Jr.	. . .
. . .		. . .
525	J.A. Smith	. . .

⇒

Pers ID	Person Name					. . .
101	Mr.	John	A	Smith	Jr.	. . .
. . .						. . .
525		J	A	Smith		. . .

Prod Num	Product Code	. . . UOM
210	PENA77Bu	. . .
211	PENA75Bl	. . .

⇒

Prod Num	Product Code					UOM
	Mfr #	Item #	Type	Size	Color	
210	Pentel	Pencil	Autom	0.7 mm	Blue	Ea
211	Pentel	Pencil	Autom	0.5 mm	Black	Ea

Figure 8-11: Two Examples of Parsing and Standardizing Data

The first example is a parsing of data components without modification, only mapping each component to its unique Attribute field. The second is an extrapolation of the encoded meaning embedded in a product code into its atomic attributes, decoded into meaningful values in standardized, atomic-level Attributes.

> **TIP** Maintain the free-form data values as captured for person names, addresses, or other free-form textual information. In the event of parsing errors, you have the original data as provided.

2. Use this to develop tests for duplicate matching where duplicate records are common. See TIQM Process P5.6 later in this chapter for guidelines.

3. Use this also to revisit and reengineer your operational Information Model and Database Design, if required.

> **TIP** For more on Name and Address Parsing to support international name and address requirements, see Chapter 9, "Information Quality Applied to Customer Care."

Step P5.5: Correct and Complete Data in the Source

From the IQ Assessment and documentation of the P2.8.O1: Exception Reports, you can conduct data correction work.

Objective of Step P5.5

To correct information errors to the highest quality *feasibly* possible, minimizing process failure from the current level of information defects. Figure 8-12 illustrates the process to correct data, including the inputs, outputs, and techniques and tools to enable data correction and control data movement.

Inputs to Step P5.5

Defective Data Files: Actual data to be corrected and or completed

Data Documentation (Definition): To ensure understanding of defined meaning of data and data values and business rules for correlation and derivation correctness

P5.4.O2: **Source Data to Standardized Data Map**: Identifies the standard formats from the *source* Data Store and to the *target* Data Store

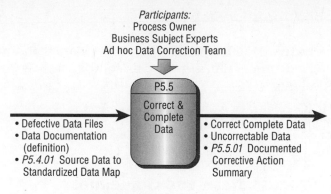

Figure 8-12: P5.5. Correct and Complete Missing Data.

Outputs of Step P5.5

Corrected, Completed Data in Source Database: Data corrected in its source database

Uncorrectable, Rejected Data in Exception File: Data that cannot be corrected

P5.5.O1: **Documented Corrective Action Summary:** Summary of data correction activities and results

Participants and Roles in Step P5.5

Participants and roles in Step P5.5 are described Table 8-3.

Table 8-3: P5.5. Correct and Complete Missing Data Participant Roles.

PARTICIPANT	IQ ACTIVITY ROLE
Process Owner	Ensures data is corrected to meet downstream Stakeholders' needs as much as possible.
Business Subject Experts	Correct data that cannot be corrected electronically.
Business Information Steward	Ensures the Completeness, Correctness, and Clarity of the Data Definition, Valid Value Sets, and Business Rule Specification.
Ad Hoc Data Correction Team	Conducts the data correction activities electronically or manually.

Techniques and Tools for Step P5.5

- **Data Corrective Maintenance Software:** Software that can correct certain data fields from valid *reference* data sources, such as postal data for address validity
- **Physical IQ Accuracy Assessments:** The Accuracy Assessments made by the Call Center or by others is used to identify Accurate Values for updating the database files.

Step P5.5: Process Steps and Guidelines

1. Correct inaccurate data and fill in missing data as gathered during the TIQM P2 IQ Assessment from the Exception Reports of correct values.

NOTE Data must be corrected, and missing data completed in the source first, as long as data is used from that data store and where use will cause processes to fail. If data is corrected in a downstream target data store, the data will be out of sync with the source data, creating a "data Equivalence" problem.

TIP The Information Producers should make the corrections to the data. They are accountable for the data they create, so they should correct their own data or participate with those who do the data corrections.

2. As an alternative, you may seek a third party to conduct the updates to correct the data.

TIP I recommend this *only* if you have a reliable source that you trust and if it is cost-effective, and you have a *Warranty* for the quality of the data they correct.

NOTE Data that has been corrected and has had missing values provided gives you a greater ability to find potential duplicate entities (person, product, organization, for example).

Guidelines for P5.5 and P5.6

All data corrections (as described in steps P5.5 and P5.6) must be:

- Corrected in the *Source* if the data is still being used from the source and there are no legal or regulatory prohibitions against changing the data there or in the Operational Record-of-Reference if the source is no longer used and must not be altered

- Updated through the *authorized* application that maintains the Information at the source to avoid redundant (and potentially error-prone) programming of data integrity rules

- Synchronized across *all redundant* databases to maintain consistency. The real solution to this is to design quality into the Operational Database Design so that the database *supports all* Operational Information Stakeholders and *all operational* applications requiring the Information

- Performed in transit to the target if done at the time of conversion for one-time conversion efforts (Data correction performed before the final switchover to a new application must be done at the source as stated above.)

- Corrected first at the source unless restricted as stated above, then propagated to the target so there is *consistency* from source to target for ongoing propagation of Information (e.g., to a Strategic Database such as a data warehouse or a downstream legacy application or software package data structure)

- Audits and controls to ensure the transformation, as indicated in this section, if it is possible to correct at the Originating Source or the Record-of-Reference Database. If some processes require corrected information, while others require the original, defective data as captured, design the database to house the original and corrected versions of the data or is provided in a parallel database.

Step P5.6: Match and Consolidate Data

Matching and consolidation of duplicate records for objects is required when multiple Information Producers are creating data of the same type. This is especially true in types of data such as Customer, Supplier, Product, and other common types of master data.

Objective of Step P5.6

To create a single authoritative electronic *Occurrence* of Reference to represent a *single* Real-World Object or Event. See Figure 8-13 for the TIQM P5.6 process step to Match and Consolidate data.

Inputs to Step P5.6

- **Input Database Files:** Files analyzed for potential duplicate records. Files will be analyzed internally first. Then files will be analyzed against other files to identify cross-database duplicate records.

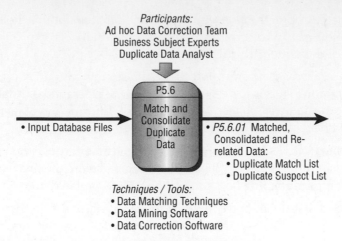

Participants:
Ad hoc Data Correction Team
Business Subject Experts
Duplicate Data Analyst

P5.6

Match and Consolidate Duplicate Data

• Input Database Files

• *P5.6.01* Matched, Consolidated and Re-related Data:
  • Duplicate Match List
  • Duplicate Suspect List

Techniques / Tools:
• Data Matching Techniques
• Data Mining Software
• Data Correction Software

Figure 8-13: P5.6. Match and Consolidate Duplicate Data.

Outputs of Step P5.6

- ▪ *P5.6.O1:* Matched, Consolidated, and Re-related Data:
    - ▪ **Duplicate Match List:** Duplicates that were consolidated
    - ▪ **Duplicate Suspect List:** Records that are suspected of being duplicates but not yet confirmed

Participants and Roles in Step P5.6

Participants and roles in Step P5.6 are described Table 8-4.

Table 8-4: P5.6. Match and Consolidate Data Participants and Roles.

PARTICIPANT	IQ ACTIVITY ROLE
Ad Hoc Data Correction Team	Led by the data correction project leader, develops match and de-duplication logic or software to identify and consolidate duplicate records.
Business Subject Experts	Identify potential Business Rules and Criteria for Identifying potential duplicate records.
Business Information Steward	Ensures the Completeness, Correctness, and Clarity of Data Definition, Valid Value Sets and Business Rule Specification for preventing duplicate record creation.
Duplicate Data Analyst	Skilled in techniques for identifying and preventing duplicates and defining consolidation rules

Techniques and Tools for Step P5.6

▪ **Data Matching Techniques:** Techniques for identifying potential duplicate records

▪ **Data Mining Software:** Data Mining tools have the ability to identify *patterns* in records that are *close matches*, when query software cannot find duplicates with even a small discrepancy in spelling.

▪ **Data Correction Software:** Software that can test for *potential duplicate matches* based on the various algorithms

Step P5.6: Process Steps and Guidelines

1. Develop a process for duplicate matching to prevent future duplicate occurrences that includes multiple tests for identity matching.

2. Identify potential Identity Attributes for each Entity Type subject to potential duplicate occurrences. These may include the following:

   ▪ **Person (Customer):** Given Name, Known-As Name(s), Aliases, Family Name (current and previous or maiden), Address (and previous addresses), Tax ID numbers (last four digits), other Identity numbers such as Driver's License Number, Birth Date, Mother's Maiden name

   ▪ **Organization (Supplier, Business Partner):** Legal Entity Name, Doing Business As Name, Common Name, Short Name, Inception Date, Registration Jurisdiction.

   ▪ **Product (Supply item):** Product Code, Product Supplier, SKU (Stock Keeping Unit), Unit of Measure

   ▪ **Transactions (Payment, Wire Transfer, Order, Sale):** Customer ID, transaction attributes

3. Develop Business Rules and matching logic to identify potential duplicate occurrences. These will be included in *real-time tests* for defect prevention or in batch mode to identify duplicate occurrences in the databases.

4. Develop software routines in existing duplicate-matching software or in your own internal routines.

NOTE Because data correction and consolidation are "Information Scrap and Rework" activities, you should do them only once for a given data store. Conduct the P5.6 Step after you have improved the broken process and implemented Process Improvement to Error-Proof the Process against duplicate occurrences.

TIP Use the Identity matching logic to test for duplicates in the Create process — not just for data batch data correction and duplicate matching and consolidation.

Guidelines for Step P5.6

All data corrections (as described in steps P5.5 and P5.6) must be:

- *Corrected in the Source* if the data is still being used from the source and there are no legal or regulatory prohibitions to keep you from changing the data there, or in the operational Record-of-Reference if the source is *no longer used* and must not be altered.

- Updated through the *authorized* Application that maintains the information at the source to avoid redundant (and potentially error-prone) programming of data integrity rules.

- Synchronized *across all redundant* Databases to maintain consistency. The real solution to this is to Design Quality into the Operational Database Design so that it is sharable across all Operational Applications.

- Performed in transit to the target if done at the time of conversion for one-time conversion efforts (data correction performed before the final switchover to the new application must be done at the source as stated previously).

- Corrected *first at the source* unless restricted as stated earlier, then *propagated to the target*, so there is Consistency *from source to target* for ongoing propagation of Information (e.g., to a Strategic Database such as a data warehouse or a downstream legacy application or software package data structure).

- Audited and Controlled to ensure that all transformations are performed *correctly* and that data is correctly propagated at the originating source or Record-of-Reference Database.

- If some processes require *corrected information*, while others require the *original, defective data* as captured, Design the Database to house the original *and* corrected versions of the data, or design a parallel database for the corrected data.

Step P5.7: Analyze Defect Types

This provides Lessons Learned from "Information Scrap and Rework" initiatives. These lessons can be applied to new processes to prevent defects that exist in the current, status quo processes.

Objective of Step P5.7

To leverage the Knowledge of the *data correction work* to discover patterns of errors, to identify Information Process Improvement Opportunities, and to incorporate Error-Proofing into new Process Designs.

Quality Management expects us to document Lessons Learned from our experiences. TIQM Step P5.7 in Figure 8-14 describes how to analyze patterns of defects that can help you design quality into new processes before their implementation.

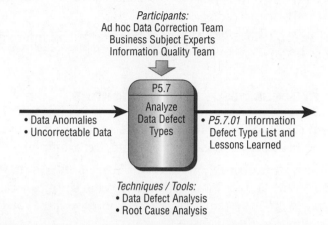

Figure 8-14: P5.7. Analyze Data Defect Types and Lessons Learned.

Inputs to Step P5.7

Data Anomalies (Defect Types): Used to study and Identify Root Causes in order to identify Error-Proofing Techniques for new process designs

Uncorrectable Data: Used to discover causes and correct data values

Outputs of Step P5.7

P5.7.O1: **Information Defect Type List and Lessons Learned:** Used to analyze and identify Root Cause or Causes to Identify Error-Proofing Techniques for new process designs

Participants and Roles in Step P5.7

Participants and Roles in Step P5.7 are described Table 8-5.

Table 8-5: P5.7. Analyze Defect Type Participants and Roles.

PARTICIPANT	IQ ACTIVITY ROLE
Ad Hoc Data Correction Team	Led by the Data Correction Project Lead, seeks to identify defect types and Root Causes for future Error-Proofing.
Business Subject Experts	Seek to discover Lessons Learned to prevent the Causes of the Defects that resulted in expensive corrections.
Information Quality Team	Documents the Lessons Learned for sharing with others.

Techniques and Tools for Step P5.7

- **Data Defect Analysis:** Type of analysis that examines Information Defects and their patterns
- **Root Cause Analysis:** Seeks to identify Root Causes of Information Defects to prevent Recurrence.

Step P5.7: Process Steps and Guidelines

1. **Document each type of Information Defect for each type of Information:** (Customer, Product, Transaction, Location, for example)

2. **Use Ishikawa-English Diagrams to identify and isolate Root Causes of the different Defect Types:** (Missing data, duplicate data, errors in procedure, errors in system logic, etc.) Do not stop until you discover and isolate originating Root Cause(s).

3. **From the P4 Process Improvement, revisit the Root Cause and identify other processes that may have the same Root Causes:** Establish Process Improvement Initiatives for these processes.

4. **Document them and post them on the IQ Team's company Intranet:** to share Lessons Learned across the Enterprise

Step P5.8: Transform, Enhance, and Calculate Derived Data

This step makes any required transformations, enhances the data as necessary, and calculates any derived data required for either the source or the target data store.

Objective of Step P5.8

To successfully map and propagate the corrected and consolidated, transformed, enhanced, and derived data to the target data store. Figure 8-15 illustrates the important step of accurately transforming and enhancing data and calculating derived data to increase the value of your information resources.

Inputs to Step P5.8

- *P5.6.O1:* **Matched, Consolidated and Re-related Data:**
  - **Duplicate Match List:** List of records matched and consolidated
  - **Duplicate Suspect List:** List of records with potential duplicates not confirmed
- *P5.8.O1:* **Data Map of Source Data to Target:** Updates to Source-to-Target Mapping of Data Movement Control

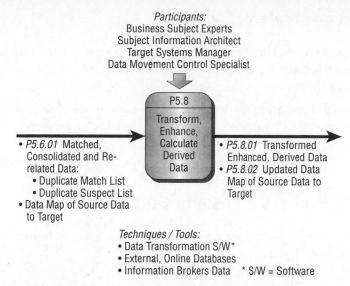

Participants:
Business Subject Experts
Subject Information Architect
Target Systems Manager
Data Movement Control Specialist

P5.8
Transform,
Enhance,
Calculate
Derived
Data

• P5.6.01 Matched,
  Consolidated and Re-
  related Data:
  • Duplicate Match List
  • Duplicate Suspect List
• Data Map of Source Data
  to Target

• P5.8.01 Transformed
  Enhanced, Derived Data
• P5.8.02 Updated Data
  Map of Source Data to
  Target

Techniques / Tools:
• Data Transformation S/W*
• External, Online Databases
• Information Brokers Data   * S/W = Software

Figure 8-15: P5.8. Transform, Enhance, and Calculate Derived Data.

Outputs of Step P5.8

- *P5.8.O1:***Transformed/Enhanced/Derived Data:** Data to propagate to the target data store.

- *P5.8.O2:* **Updated Data Map of Source Data to Target:** Data Mapping Enhancements of Information from the Source Data Map to the Target Data Map and Data Transformations, if any

Participants and Roles in Step P5.8

Participants and roles in Step P5.8 are described Table 8-6.

Table 8-6: P5.8. Transform, Enhance, and Calculate Derived Data Participants and Roles.

PARTICIPANT	IQ ACTIVITY ROLE
Business Subject Experts	Ensure that Business Rules for Transformation, Enhancement, and Calculation are specified properly.
Subject Information Architect	Ensures that any modifications to the Information Model, Data Definition, and Database Design are made.
Target Systems Manager	Ensures that any Application System Modifications are made to handle the new data.
Data Movement Control Specialist	Ensures whether data movement is required and if so, that data transformations and calculations have been performed properly.

Techniques and Tools for Step P5.8

- **Data Transformation Software:** Used to implement Transformation Rules for data that is defined differently or with *different* Valid Value Sets across different databases

- **External Information Brokers or Online Databases:** Source of Information *external* to the Enterprise that is required for augmenting Enterprise Information to support specific trend analysis or decision support. Some external data may be required for operational source databases.

Step P5.8: Process Steps and Guidelines

1. First, determine if data transformation and movement to redundant databases are required.

   Poor reasons for data redundancy:

   - **Convenience for a *downstream* Business Area:** Electronic data is the *only non-consumable resource* the Enterprise has. Redirect access to the authoritative Record-of-Origin or Record-of-Reference Database.

   - **Poor design of existing database:** Redesign the Database to support *all* Knowledge Workers who require Information an Enterprise-Strength Subject Database.

   - **Information *hoarding* by the source Business Area:** Politely remind the Process Owner (Business Area Manager) that Information is an Enterprise Resource, not "owned" by that Business Area or Manager.

   - **Information from the Record of Origin must be propagated to a purchased Software Package data structure:** Is this software package *really required and value-adding*? Most application software packages are poorly designed and do not contain *all* Attributes required by all Knowledge Workers for the Information subject at hand.

CAUTION Any time that data must be moved from one data store to another, you increase your non-value-adding costs of Information Management, Application Development, and Maintenance, and you increase the points of defect introduction to your Information.

CAUTION The goal of TIQM here is to reengineer your critical Operational Databases on a Subject-by-Subject basis to be Enterprise-Strength, supporting any and all Information Stakeholders. Subjects might include, for example: Party (Customer, Supplier, Employee, Business Partner), Product, Financials, Operating transactions (Order, Deposit, Equity Trade), Facility, and Location.

2. If the data movement is required (with or without transformation) follow these steps. See Figure 8-16 for an example:

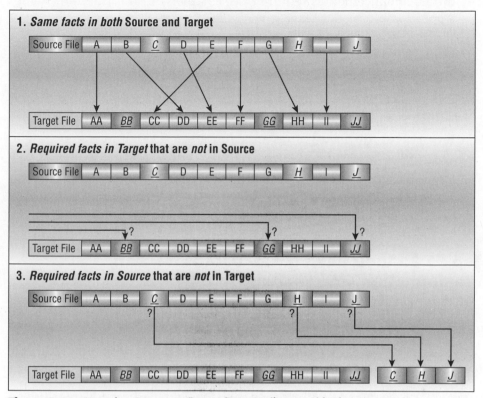

Figure 8-16: Mapping Source to Target Data Attributes with Three Scenarios

2.1 **Identify Attributes in the Source Data Store and the Target Data Store that do *NOT* have to be transformed.** These attributes can be moved without modification. See Figure 8-16.

2.2 **Determine which Attributes require *some transformation*, such as different domain value sets.** (DB1 Gender codes 1 = Male, 2 = Female, and 3 = unknown) transformed into DB2 as (Gender codes F = Female, M = Male, and U = Unknown)

2.3 **Identify Attributes required in the Target Database that are *not* in the source database.** Identify how to create or capture the Attributes required in the target, so they can be populated to the target.

2.4 **Identify the Attributes that exist in the Source Database but are *not* required in the Target Database.** You must find a way to keep these if they are still required for business processes, generally in an Enterprise-Strength Subject Database.

3. Develop transformation logic to transform values from the source to the target.

4. If data enhancement is required, see Chapter 15, "Information Quality Applied to Information Management and Information Systems Engineering," section "Information Broker-Provided Information."

5. Develop Audit Controls to ensure the transforms are performed properly and get the right results.

6. Ensure that data received from Third Parties is defined Correctly and Clearly and are Understandable by Knowledge Workers.

7. Ensure that the Data Values are Accurate and Complete according to Accuracy Assessments against the Real-World Objects or Events.

8. Determine the optimum propagation schedule for the data based on Knowledge Worker needs.

9. Measure the outcomes of all data movement activities.

Step P5.9: Audit and Control Data Extraction, Transformation, and Loading

Audits and Controls ensure that data is Extracted, Transformed, and Loaded correctly so that Knowledge Workers have access in a timely way.

Objective of Step P5.9

To ensure that the right data is extracted from the right file, properly transformed according to the defined transformation specification, and loaded properly into the right data elements in the Target Data Store.

This step addresses the audit and control aspects of data correction and control of data movement. See Figure 8-17.

Inputs to Step P5.9

- **Corrected, Consolidated, Transformed, and Enhanced Data to Load:** Data that has been corrected and prepared for propagating to a downstream data store.

- **Source Information Definition and Business Rule Specifications:** Data defined and specified Correctly, Completely, and Clearly.

- **Target Data Definition and Business Rules:** Business Rules have Clear, Accurate Specifications, so Knowledge Workers can ensure that the Rules are Correct and Information Systems Developers can encode them in the data movement logic.

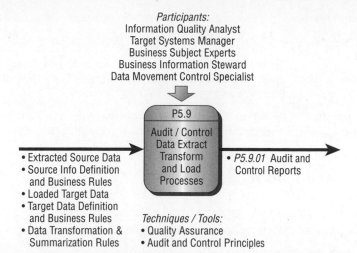

Participants:
Information Quality Analyst
Target Systems Manager
Business Subject Experts
Business Information Steward
Data Movement Control Specialist

P5.9

Audit / Control
Data Extract
Transform
and Load
Processes

• Extracted Source Data
• Source Info Definition
  and Business Rules
• Loaded Target Data
• Target Data Definition
  and Business Rules
• Data Transformation &
  Summarization Rules

• *P5.9.01* Audit and
  Control Reports

Techniques / Tools:
• Quality Assurance
• Audit and Control Principles

Figure 8-17: P5.9. Audit and Control Data Extract, Transform, and Load Processes.

▪ **Data Transformation and Summarization Rules:** Business Rules for deriving other data have Clear, Correct, and Complete Calculation Specifications to accurately calculate the resulting derived data.

Outputs of Step P5.9

▪ *P5.9.O1:* **Audit and Control Reports:** Documentation that indicates whether or not the data movement was successful, with counts and control totals of data handling, and exception reports, if any, of anomalies in the process

▪ **Successfully propagated data:** The data propagated correctly to the target

Participants and Roles in Step P5.9

Participants and roles in Step P5.9 are described Table 8-7.

Table 8-7: P5.9. Audit and Control Data Extraction, Transformation, and Loading Participants and Roles.

PARTICIPANT	IQ ACTIVITY ROLE
Information Quality Analyst	Leads the development of IQ audit controls for data propagation.
Target Systems Manager	Ensures that the target application system will support the propagated data.
Business Subject Experts	Review and ensure that proper business rules are created for data transformations.

(continued)

Table 8-7 *(continued)*

PARTICIPANT	IQ ACTIVITY ROLE
Business Information Steward	Ensures the Completeness, Correctness, and Clarity of the Data Definition, Valid Value Sets, and Business Rule Specification changes.
Data Movement Control Specialist	Develops the programs or mechanisms to implement the Audits and Controls for Data Movement activities.

Techniques and Tools for Step P5.9

- **Quality Assurance:** Structured review to ensure that audit and control mechanisms are properly specified, implemented, and tested
- **Audit and Control Principles:** Guidelines for developing controls for data transformation and movement

Step P5.9: Process Steps and Guidelines

1. **Develop record count controls to ensure proper record handling.** Note that this is done well in ETL (Extract, Transform, and Load) software. See Figure 8-18 for an example of the "Order Record" Count.

   This example illustrates Record Count Controls:

   1.1. Identify an independent count of Records to Input into a process.
        Total Count of Records expected = 11,200

   1.2. Count the *number* of Records as they are input into the process.

   1.3. Identify the control data for record handling:

   - Unchanged records passed = 11,050.
   - Changed records passed = 115.
   - Consolidated records passed (in this example) = 12.
   - Total count of records passed to the next step = 11,177.
   - Duplicate records not passed (in this example) = 15.
   - Rejected records not passed (in this example) = 2.
   - Total count of records handled = 11,177 + 15 + 8 = 11,200.

   The result is that the Record Count Audit balances.

2. **Develop Control Total Count routines to test for content handling.** Most ETL software does *NOT* do this at all. Figure 8-19 illustrates the Control Total for "Order Amount" Total.

*ECTL = Extract, Correct, Transform & Load

Audit Record in:	Record Count In:	Record Counts Out:		
		Unchanged records out:	11,050	
		Modified/corrected records out:	115	
		Consolidated records out:	12	
		Actual records passed to next step:		11,177
		Duplicate records not out:	15	
		Rejected records not out:	8	
11,200	11,200	Reconciled record count out:		11,200

Balance   Balance

Audit Detail ▷──── Audit ────◁ Fact Table

Figure 8-18: Audit Controls for Propagated Data: Record Counts

This example illustrates Control Totals and Content controls:

2.1. Identify an independent Order Amount Total of records to input into a process.

- Total Order Amount expected = $410,000.00.

- Total Order Amount passed to next step = $395,775.55.

- Order Amount Corrected and passed to next step = $10,400.30.

- Total Order Amount for records passed = $406,175.85.

- Total Adjusted for Order Amount not passed to next step = -$1,318.08.

- Total Rejected records Order Amount not passed = -$6,042.23.

- Total Order Amount handled = $410,900.00.

The result is that the Order Amount Control Total audit balances from input to output.

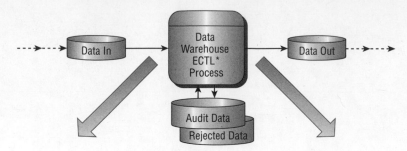

*ECTL = Extract, Correct, Transform & Load

Audit Record in:	Control Total In:	Control Total Out:		
		Unchanged total out:	$395,775.55	
		Corrected total out:	$10,400.30	
		Actual total passed to next step:		$406,175.85
		Adjusted total not out:	−$1,318.08	
		Rejected total not out:	$6,042.23	
$410,900.00	$410,900.00	Reconciled total out:		$410,900.00

Balance   Balance

Audit Detail ▷━━━ Audit ━━━◁ Fact Table

Figure 8-19: Audit Controls for Propagated Data: Control Totals

3. **Develop an Audit Trail Record or Attribute Group to identify IQ Assessment or Correction activities for one or more Attributes in a record.** This will assist Information Producers in documenting when they correct data in the normal course of doing business or when they verify with a Customer that they have the correct address and contact details, for example.

Audit Attributes are shown in Table 8-8.

Table 8-8: IQ Audit Attribute Codes and Descriptions

RECORD ELEMENTS	AUDIT ID	IQ CODE	QUALITY ACTION DESCRIPTION
...	...	AV	Accuracy Verified to Real World Object or Event Recording/Observation
...	...	AS	Accuracy Verified to Surrogate
...	...	VV	Value Validity Verified
...	...	BV	Business Rule Validity Verified
...	...	CA	Corrected to Authoritative source

RECORD ELEMENTS	AUDIT ID	IQ CODE	QUALITY ACTION DESCRIPTION
...	...	CS	Corrected to Surrogate source
...	...	CV	Corrected to Valid value
...	...	CE	Corrected to an Estimate
...	...	ER	Error - Not Corrected
...	...	QX	Questionable, Suspect
...	...	UA	Unaudited

Strengths and Weaknesses of Data Correction Software

Data cleansing *sic*. ("Data Correction" or "Information Scrap and Rework") software has strengths and weaknesses in performing data correction actions.

Strengths of Data Correction Software

Strengths of Data Correction Software include:

- Automates tedious work.
- Handles high volumes of data.
- Implements multiple business rule tests.
- Reports on frequency of identified errors.
- Applies changes to data from reference tables of supposedly correct data.

Weaknesses of Data Correction Software

- Data Correction Software is a Cost of Poor Quality Information. Every bit of money spent in data correction is wasted money because data defects could have been prevented at the source by applying error-proofing techniques to eliminate the causes of the defects in the processes.
- Data Correction Software is *subject* to false positives and false negatives at a rate of about 10 percent each:
  - False Positives are records incorrectly identified as having errors.
  - False Negatives are records incorrectly identified as correct that actually have errors.
- Data Correction Software has to be continually tweaked to keep its routines current.

- Data Correction software is generally quite expensive.

- Data Correction Software is often weak on Global (International) Name and Address Information.

- Data Correction Software cannot match native data to accurate values. It must match it to valid values and values assumed to be correct. For example, the software may assume that a valid postal address is a correct address, but the party associated with the address may no longer be at that address.

Summary

You have learned that:

1. Data Correction is the *equivalent* of manufacturing "Scrap and Rework." Every dollar, euro, pound sterling, or yen spent in data correction is "Information Scrap and Rework" that is incurred because quality and error-proofing techniques were not designed into the information processes that create, maintain, and present information.

2. When you conduct data correction, you should improve the offending, *defective process first* to stop the current rate of error production. Then conduct the data correction activity as *a one-time event* for data within a database *after* you have improved the processes.

3. You should not embed Data Correction Software into a mainstream operational process. Instead, implement Error-Proofing Techniques to *prevent* defects from occurring in the process in the first place.

Part

III

Information Quality Applied to Core Business Value Circles

The objective of Part III is to help IQ and business professionals learn how to apply TIQM processes to core Enterprise Business Processes or Value Circles. The purpose is not to define these processes for your organization; but to understand the IQ issues within these Value Circles, how to apply those quality principles, processes, and methods to measure the quality of critical information; and how to design quality into the processes to prevent defective information and the business process failure it causes.

The chapters in Part III include:

Chapter 9: **Information Quality Applied to Customer Care:** *"Prospect-to-Valued-and-Valuable-Customer."* This chapter addresses the Quality of Information required to sustain a relationship of loyalty with your end-Customers.

Chapter 10: **Information Quality Applied to Product Development:** *"Product-Idea-to-Product-Retire."* This chapter addresses the Quality of Information required to Innovate new Products and Services and to understand Customer Requirements.

Chapter 11: **Information Quality Applied to Supply Chain Management:** *"Forecast-to-Satisfied-Customer."* This chapter addresses the Quality of Information required to ensure that the entire Supply Chain is managed Effectively and Efficiently.

Information Quality Applied to Customer Care: *"Prospect-to-Valued-and-Valuable-Customer"*

"It costs 4-5 times as much to develop a new Customer relationship as to maintain a relationship with existing, happy Customers"
US Dept of Commerce

"Cutting corners is the quickest way to go out of business"
Dominic Walsh, London Times, 10/27/2008

Introduction to Information Quality in Customer Care

This chapter on Information Quality in Customer Care is the first of the IQ Applied chapters precisely because the Customer is the second-most important Stakeholder to any organization, next to its Employees. Organizations must focus on the Needs, Requirements, and Expectations of its Customers to succeed in accomplishing its Mission, let alone to become World-Class.

I originally entitled this chapter "IQ Applied to Marketing and Sales," but I rejected that precisely because of the severe *lack of care* for the individuals and organizations who are the lifeblood of any successful organization—their Customers. Customer Value does not come from exploitation of those who fund the organization by buying products and services, nor does it derive from unscrupulous behaviors such as up-sell, bait-and-switch, misrepresentation, and fraud. The sub-prime and variable-rate mortgage schemes that led to the 2007–2009 real-estate crisis and financial meltdown in the U.S. and around the world that were foisted on gullible and unsuspecting homebuyers by lenders who knew that the rate increases were going to cause payment failure. The tragedy is the suffering and loss incurred by the Consumers and their Neighbors whose homes lost value as well.

This has mushroomed into a national and international crisis, requiring government interventions not seen since the Great Depression of the 1930s.

No organization can survive in the long term if it takes an *exploitative* attitude toward its purchasing Customers.

Organizations that value their Customers will have them at the center of all major Value Circles.

Many organizations exploited the concept of "Customer Relationship Management (CRM)," using it mostly for cross-selling or up-selling. This made it more a practice of "customer relationship Manipulation, with a little "c" customer and little "r" relationship, and Big "M" Manipulation!" This type of CRM was destined to fail because Customers are savvier today to exploitative tactics.

Here we describe how to develop and nurture a mutually satisfying relationship from *"Prospect-to-Valued-and-Valuable Customer"* through Quality Customer Information and Business practices.

NOTE Although this chapter is about Customers specifically, the principles and best practices apply to all Party Types, such as Organization and Person and Party Roles, such as Customer, Employee, and Supplier or Trade Partner.

Categories of Customer Information

Quality principles must be applied to three critical categories of Customer information:

- **Customer name, identity, and profile information:** This includes all components of a personal name and identity information, such as a Social Security number (last 4 digits in the USA), a national insurance number or equivalent, or a driver's license number. In Criminal Justice and National Security, other identity information is required, such as FBI IDs, and Interpol IDs, as well as Biometric Identity Attributes like scars, marks, and tattoos, fingerprints, retina scans, facial imaging, and DNA.

- **Customer address and contact information:** This includes a full postal address, email addresses, and telephone and mobile phone numbers, with effective dates and times for the way(s) in which you communicate with them.

- **Customer experience and interaction information:** This includes Information about Customer interactions, inquiries, Complaints, and Product Experience over the life of their relationship. IQ problems can alienate Customers, driving them away. Failure to understand Complaints and or product failures leads to *lost business*, as well as incorrect assignment of warranty accountability and costs.

Customer Information Stakeholders

There are many Customer Information Consumers and Stakeholders throughout the enterprise. Failure to provide Quality *Information* through its Value Circle will cause Marketing Campaigns, Order Fulfillment, Financial Management, and Customer Care processes to fail, often with catastrophic results.

Internal Information Stakeholders

Many within the organization require Customer Information to perform their jobs toward the accomplishment of the enterprise Mission. See Table 9-1 for their Customer Information interests.

Table 9-1: Internal Information Stakeholders and Customer Information Interests

INTERNAL INFORMATION STAKEHOLDERS	INFORMATION INTERESTS
Engineers for Physical Products	Require Customer Requirements Information to design products or components to meet Customer Quality Expectations.
Manufacturing Personnel	Require Product Specifications in order to translate Product Quality Requirements into Process Quality Specifications to produce or assemble components or material into other components or finished products that meet Customer Quality Requirements.
Quality Management Personnel	Quality Requirements to ensure Quality is Designed In and achieved in the various Processes of development, production, and delivery
Actuaries for Financial Products	Market, demand, and Customer Requirements to create new services, such as financial, insurance, or investment products
Contract Officers	Name and address information to develop formal relationships with Trading Partners
Sales Representatives or Agents	Name, address, and privacy and contact preference information to develop relationships with Customers to be able to stay in touch on an appropriate basis
Marketers	Prospect and Customer name, address, and profile, preference, and contact preference information for customized marketing campaigns
Accounts Receivable Staff	Name, identity, and address information for analyzing risk and invoicing and payment application

(continued)

Table 9-1 *(continued)*

INTERNAL INFORMATION STAKEHOLDERS	INFORMATION INTERESTS
In Criminal Justice, Law Enforcement, and Healthcare	Physical Identity Information to ensure that they have the right person of interest
Every Employee Who Is a Touch Point with Customers	Customer insight information. Each touch point with a Customer is a "Moment of Truth"[1] point in which the Customer has an interaction with an organization that makes an impression, positive or negative, about the organization.

External Information Stakeholders

Likewise, many external Stakeholders require Customer and Customer-related Information. See Table 9-2 for their Customer Information Interests.

Table 9-2: External Information Stakeholders and Their Customer Information Interests

EXTERNAL INFORMATION STAKEHOLDERS	INFORMATION INTERESTS
End-Consumers	People who buy and use your products and services, whether buying directly from you or your agent, distributor, or retail outlet care that you understand their Requirements for the products or services, and that you protect the confidential information they provide you.
Trade Partner Buyers and Distributors, Retailers, or Agents	A source of end-Customer feedback, they care to see their Customer Lifetime Value increase.
Supplier Sales Representatives or Agents	End-Customer Product Requirement and Preference Information and Customer Feedback and Complaint Information
Regulatory Authority Compliance Personnel	Regulation compliance and conformance, such as "Truth in Advertising," "Truth-in-Lending," and "Sarbanes-Oxley," information to ensure that Customers and other Stakeholders are being treated properly
Information Brokers Who May Add Value to Customer Information	Personal and Organizational Information to correct for sale or to *add* Attributes to enable organizations to better understand their Customers
Credit Reporting Agencies	Credit and payment history

The Customer Care Value Circle: "Prospect-To-Valued-and-Valuable-Customer"

The Customer Care Value Circle, "Prospect-To-Valued-and-Valuable-Customer," is required to find prospective Customers, develop a mutually beneficial relationship, and maintain and increase value to the Customer. Figure 9-1 illustrates this Value Circle.

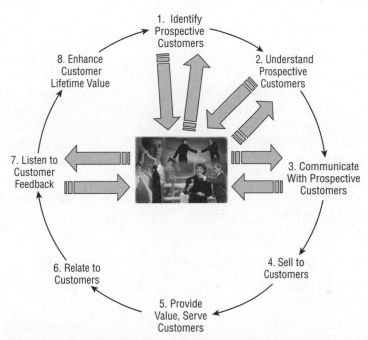

Figure 9-1: Customer Care Value Circle: "Prospect-to-Valued-and-Valuable-Customer"

DISCLAIMER

The purpose of this chapter *IS NOT* to teach you how to perform Marketing and Sales, provide Customer Care, and analyze Customer behavior.

The purpose *IS* to guide you through the processes of measuring and improving the Quality of the Information Processes that create, maintain, and deliver *Information* about Customers so you can have successful Customer relationships that are valued by you and valuable to you.

You learn how to apply quality principles to Product and Customer Relationship Processes so you can improve the Customer Lifetime Value across the, "Prospect-to-Valued-and-Valuable-Customer" Value Circle.

The following describes the Value Circle processes with their general activities, quality methods, and the IQ issues that can cause process failure.

1. Identify Prospective Customers

This process seeks to understand those who are *candidates* to become Valuable Customers based on their demographics and other characteristics that make them interested in your products or services.

Process Activities

For every organization that has products or services, there will be a general target audience of prospective Customers. In the past, organizations took a product-centric approach where they thought of their products and how to sell them.

However, successful organizations today must take a new Customer-centric approach, thinking first of the prospective Customer audience and of their Customers' needs in the products and services they offer. These organizations are replacing *Marketing* with Customer Care and *mass* communication with *personalized* communication.

Organizations are only as successful as their ability to *delight* their Customers. Process activities include:

- Identifying the right Markets and the right Customer Segmentation
- Identifying sources of prospective Customer Information
- Developing communications across all channels that will draw prospective Customers to you
- Conducting focus groups for your products and services to identify potential Customer Segmentation Characteristics

Common Information Quality Issues

Common Information Quality issues include:

- Prospective Market to Customer Segment mismatch
- Duplicate prospect or Customer records
- Lack of understanding of the *Synergy* between product or service mix and prospective Customer interests
- Failure to capture all Attributes (facts you need to know) that can be *valuable* for Customer understanding
- Lack of understanding of Customer Relationships, both organizational and personal

- Out-of-date data in third-party and purchased data
- Inaccurate or missing Profile Information that identifies likely prospective Customers

2. Understand Prospective Customers

This process seeks to understand the needs and Expectations of the prospective Customers and degree of synergy with products and services. This is described in Chapter 10, "Information Quality Applied to Product Development: "Product-Idea-to-Product-Retire," in the section "Applying Information Quality to *Customer Requirement Information*."

Process Activities

1. Conduct Quality Function Deployment (QFD) sessions with prospective and existing Customers to identify Customer Requirements. See Chapter 10, section, "Applying Information Quality to *Customer Requirement Information*."

Common Information Quality Issues

- Missing or incomplete Customer Information capture
- Duplicate Prospective Customer or Customer records
- Lack of consistency (Equivalence) of Customer Information across multiple Customer data stores

3. Communicate with Prospective Customers

This process includes all activities that make up a touch point with Customers, from direct marketing mail, email, the Web site, Internet cookies, Call-Center out-bound calls, Call-Center in-bound calls, catalogs, and newspaper fliers or advertisements.

Process Activities

1. Develop purpose of contact with a Customer Value Proposition.
2. Plan communication.
3. Perform the communication in a medium and contact method of choice to the Customer.
4. Evaluate Customer feedback from communication.

Common Information Quality Issues

- Inaccurate Customer Profile Information
- Inaccurate or missing Customer Contact Preference Information
- Duplicate communication due to duplicate Customer records

4. Sell to Customers

This process is not just a money-making activity. Here you provide something of Value (product or service) to Customers that helps them to be successful with why they do business with you.

This process simply exchanges your goods and/or services in exchange for payment or other consideration from the Customer. This is an important touch point with your Customer. Poor Customer Care, Service, or *Negative body language* will harm your reputation.

Process Activities

1. Provide multiple channels for selling and interaction. Let your Customers determine their preferred channel.

2. Provide pleasant, helpful service in the selling event in person, via phone, and via electronic contact.

3. Where personal relationships are involved, ensure you align the items or services you promote to your Customer's demonstrated requirements.

NOTE Minimize undue efforts to up-sell to Customers. Stop if you feel resistance. They must be the lead for any add-on purchases.

Common Information Quality Issues

- Incorrect or missing Pricing
- Incomplete or missing Product Information
- Poor Assembly Instructions
- Insufficient or unreasonable Product or Service Warranty
- Poor Product Information, Web site, or Catalog Design

5. Provide Value; Serve Customers

This process before, during, or after a sale or acquisition transaction is another important touch point.

Process Activities

1. Provide knowledgeable help to Customers as they search for, evaluate, and select products or services.

2. Answer queries honestly and patiently. "The Customer is always right."

3. Handle Customer Complaints or concerns with *special* care.

Common Information Quality Issues

- Failure to keep Customer Product and Service Histories
- Failure to capture and *learn* from Customer Complaints

6. Relate to Customers

This process maintains communications with Customers in accordance with Customer preferences.

Process Activities

1. Create and capture Customer Contact Preference types (mail, email, telephone, catalog) and contact times.

2. Understand Customer Profile and Product/Service Requirements.

Common Information Quality Issues

- Failure to capture correct Customer contact details
- Duplicate Customer records
- Too frequent or too infrequent contact based on Customer need

7. Listen to Customer Feedback

This process analyzes Customer contact and feedback information.

Process Activities

1. Capture *vital* Information about Customer Experiences, both positive and negative.

2. Regularly analyze both individual Customer Experiences and aggregate Customer Experience patterns and trends.

3. Empower Employees to document observed Customer Complaints if Customers do not want to write their Complaints down.

Common Information Quality Issues

■ Incomplete/missing Complaint or Customer Experience observations

■ Bias in capturing Complaint or Experience observations

8. Enhance Customer Lifetime Value

This process is simply the end-result of providing *real* Customer Care to the people who pay the bills at your organization.

Process Activities

1. Keep focused on the *changing needs* of your Customers.

2. Keep evaluating Customer Complaints and Experiences.

3. Keep involving Customers in new Product Focus Groups.

Common Information Quality Issues

■ Lack of process to capture and keep Customer Experience Information current

■ Bias in *interpretation* of Complaint and Experience Information

2. Understand Customers [Better]

This process brings us back to understanding our Customers and their needs better, leading us to improve products and services that more effectively meet Customer needs.

Process Activities

1. Improve Customer Knowledge.

2. Identify new Products or Services based on Customer needs.

3. Identify Improvements to existing products.

Common Information Quality Issues

Same IQ issues as found in Chapter 10, "Information Quality Applied to Product Development: *'Product-Idea-to-Product-Retire.'*"

- Failure to transform Customer Product Quality Requirements into Product Specifications that ensure that the functionality and capability of the products meet Customer Requirements and Expectations
- Failure to ensure that the product can be manufactured at the expected cost within the expected timeframe with the required quality

Information Quality in the *"Prospect-to-Valued-and-Valuable-Customer"* Value Circle

We will analyze four major groups of information where quality is paramount:

1. Customer Name and Identity Information, including international name information
2. Customer Address and Contact Information, including international address information
3. Customer Profile and Demographic Information
4. Customer Experience, Feedback, and Complaint Information

Information Quality Issues and Costs in Customer Name and Identity Information

This section discusses five major Information Quality issues in the "Prospect-to-Valued-and-Valuable-Customer" Value Circle.

Poor Quality in Customer Name and Identity Information

Errors in name spelling, in salutation or professional designations, and in identity information communicate that the Customer is not important to the organization. See Table 9-3 for common IQ issues and the Costs of Poor Information Quality.

Table 9-3: IQ Issues and Costs in Poor Quality Customer Name/Identity Information

IQ ISSUES	COSTS OF POOR INFORMATION QUALITY
Name misspelling	Alienation of Customer and lost business
Duplicate Customer records	Lack of ability to know Customer Lifetime Value; inability to consolidate Customer records, losing touch

(continued)

Table 9-3 *(continued)*

IQ ISSUES	COSTS OF POOR INFORMATION QUALITY
Inaccurate and missing identity information	Losing contact with your Customers; inability to prevent duplicate Customer records from being created; failure to identify persons-of-interest in Justice and National Security work
Unsecured Customer records	Identity Theft of Customer Information with Customer Harm and cost of recovery; also loss of reputation and Customer Lifetime Value

PERSONAL INFORMATION ERRORS MAKE ORGANIZATIONS LOOK UNPROFESSIONAL AND UNCARING

Receiving a letter from an IQ software provider addressed to me as "Miss Larry English" speaks volumes about its broken processes.

Most recently I became "Marry English" according to my Starwood Preferred Guest Card!!! See Figure 9-2.

Figure 9-2: My Recently Issued "Starwood Preferred Guest" Card

Costs of Poor Quality in Customer Name and Identity Information

- Errors in Name Spelling and in Salutation or Professional Designations can cause a negative "Moment of Truth" in which Customers determine that you do not care about them, taking their business elsewhere.

- Errors or omissions in other Identity Attributes can lead to *losing contact* with your Customers or the inability to prevent duplicate Customer records from being created.

- Not knowing the cultural norms for name and address information can create embarrassment and legal liability. Currently in Germany, only German and European Union Ph.D.s and medical doctors can use the honorific "Dr." in front of their names. Doctors and those with Ph.D.s from other countries may not use the designation "Dr." Violators are subject to a year in prison. In March 2008 state education ministers recommended amending the law to allow U.S. citizens with a doctorate or medical degree to be addressed as "Dr."[2]

- Customers' Name Information is subject to decay, as when by marriage or other reasons their names changed. Inability to maintain current name information leads to loss of contact with an individual and lost business.

- Errors and omissions in Identity Information in Criminal Justice and national security can result in wrong convictions or acquittals with harm done to society that cannot be recovered or repaid.

AIRLINES FACE $35,000 FINES OVER MISTAKEN TERRORIST IDS

The U.S. Transportation Security Administration (TSA) is threatening to fine airlines for each instance of incorrectly telling passengers they are on a terrorist watch list. TSA says that airlines have not developed proper processes to ensure they do not misidentify innocent Customers as terrorists.[3]

BROKERAGE FIRM FINED $1 MILLION FOR CUSTOMER DATA VIOLATIONS

"The SEC alleged that from October 2003 to June 2005 the E*Trade Financial will pay a second $1 million penalty for its failure to comply with anti-money laundering rules. They failed to properly document and verify the identities of more than 65,000 Customers as required by several rules, including the U.S. Bank Secrecy Act."[4]

NOTE You can find more information about the USA Patriot Act, the Financial Crimes Enforcement Network, and regulatory fines at www.FINCEN.gov.

Customer relationships are another key part of Customer information. Individuals have multiple relationships, such as household or professional associations that link them together. This process of connecting these people or company entities together is known as house-holding.

Organizations can have a legal structure of divisions and/or subsidiaries that need to be known. This information is needed for multiple purposes such as to be able to aggregate and quantify the total credit risk exposure for the whole relationship. The linkage data itself is a common source of definition quality and data maintenance issues.

> **NOTE** This problem also applies to all Party information, including contact personnel within an organization's Customers, Suppliers, and Trade Partners as well as your own Employees.

Poor Quality in Customer Address and Contact Information

Errors or omissions in Address and Contact Information causes you to lose contact with Customers and Prospective Customers, misdirect mailings and catalogs or marketing campaign material.

Costs of Poor Quality Information in Customer Address and Contact Information

Errors or omissions in Address and Contact Information cause you to send items to the *wrong* address or call the *wrong* person. This harms the organization's credibility and ability to interact with the Customer.

This in turn can lead to losing them and their Customer Lifetime Value.

Unique Quality Issues in International Name and Address Information

Errors in the Name and Address Information of your International Customers leads to poor communication with, and understanding of, those Customers; Customer loss; and sub-optimal exploitation of that market.

Costs of Poor International Name and Address Information Management

- All costs of poor quality national Customer Name and Address Information apply equally to international Customer Name and Address Information.

- Widely varying postal and telecommunication systems can lead to the inability to communicate with your Customers if you do not understand the *cultural and language* intricacies of the Requirements.

- Customers claim *ownership* of their names, addresses, and personal data. These can have strong cultural significance for them. Failure to take this into account, such as printing a "state" when a country has none, or printing addresses in the wrong format, increase the chance of an unhappy "Moment of Truth," when Customers decide to take their business elsewhere.

POOR INFORMATION QUALITY AND A LACK OF UNDERSTANDING OF A FOREIGN MARKETPLACE CAN BE EXPENSIVE

Microsoft released Windows 95 with its time zone maps not showing Jammu-Kashmir as being wholly in India, an offense under Indian law. The software was banned while corrections were made, causing large losses in sales.

In 2003, a U.K. utility's broken billing processes prevented it from timely billing of Customers, many of whom changed suppliers, costing the company £13 Million (US$19.5 million).

A credit card company sent an offer in 2002 to a person who died in 1973.

A mailshot was sent to inhabitants of Amsterdam offering them cheap flights to an event happening in Amsterdam!!!

Reports suggest that US$1 billion intended for victims of Hurricane Katrina went astray through fraud, exacerbated by poor Information Quality measures. Money for damaged property was paid to prison inmates. One person used 13 different Social Security numbers, 12 of which were invalid, to claim compensation for 13 addresses of which only eight existed.

Inaccurate or Missing Diacritical Marks

Diacritical marks in non-English languages affect both pronunciation and word meaning. In German, for example, "schwül" with the umlaut means humid or sultry, but "schwul" (no umlaut) means homosexual.

Duplicate Customer Name and Address Information

Errors in the combination of name and address information leads to duplicate Customer records being created.

Costs of Duplicate Customer Records

- Duplicate Customer records create excess direct costs in all forms of contact and interaction with the Customers, from duplicate mailings, outbound phone calls, and email communications.

    Duplicate Customer records within a database and duplicate (and disparate) Customer records across databases are common and serious Information Quality problems in many organizations. Duplicate Customer record rates of 25 percent to 35 percent are not uncommon.

    Duplicate Customer records impact calculations like sales per Customer and Customer Lifetime Value.[5] See Chapter 6, "The Step-by-Step Guide to *Measuring the Costs and Risks of Poor Quality Information*," Step P3.5 "Calculate Customer Lifetime Value," for how to measure Customer Lifetime Value.

Duplicate Customer records further cause you to:

- Mail multiple statements, flyers, or catalogs.
- Misunderstand the total credit risk exposure of the relationship.
- Provide the wrong level of service.
- Create Customer dissatisfaction due to incorrect information.
- Fail to follow Customers' contact preferences, driving them away.
- Fail to understand the demographics or psychometrics of a Customer.
- Have Scrap and Rework to find, merge, and de-duplicate records.
- Scrap and Rework for downstream Knowledge Workers whose processes fail duplicate Customer records.

- Costs of *matching and de-duplication* of records that are potentially the same individual or organization

- Opportunity costs of *lost business* when two different individual Customers have their records consolidated into one

This makes an organization look disorganized and wasteful, resulting in potential lost Customer Lifetime Value.

How to Measure Customer Information Quality

First, conduct an assessment of the quality of Customer Information data definition quality, TIQM Process P1, "Assess Information Production Specifications and Information Architecture Quality," described in Chapter 4. Specific steps include P1.4, "Assess Information Product Specifications Conformance to Standards," and P1.6, "Assess Stakeholder Satisfaction with Information Product Specification Data."

Follow the process steps in "Assess Information Quality," TIQM Process P2, described in Chapter 5. In this chapter, I describe challenges and tips for measuring Customer Name, Identity, and Address information.

Identify a Set of Information for Measuring Quality (TIQM P2.1)

Follow TIQM P2.1 in Chapter 5. The specific information you will measure here are the specific attributes that make up Customer Name, Identity, and Address Groups.

Plan IQ Objectives, Measures, and Tests (TIQM P2.2)

Follow TIQM P2.2 in Chapter 5. The measure of this information is accurate and complete spelling of the Customer's given name, salutation, prefix, suffix, known-as-name, surname or family name, and accurate and complete identity information, such as birth date, and Social Security, Tax-ID or National Insurance Number if your organization requires it for financial or government reporting. Otherwise capture the last four digits to assist in preventing duplicate Customer records.

> **NOTE** The real Identifier for you Customers, should be a single Enterprise-defined ID Number that does not have any embedded meaning in it, (that is, you do not have facts you need to know embedded in the Customer ID Number). We recommend that your Customer ID Number have a Check-digit for integrity of keying it to minimize keying transpositions from attaching records to a wrong Customer. This applies to all "Parties", not just Customers.

Identify the Customer Value Circle (TIQM P2.3)

Follow TIQM P2.3 in Chapter 5, to document the Value Circle for Customer Life Cycle to identify current processes that may introduce errors. This is especially important if there are multiple create processes for a Customer.

Determine Data Store or Process to Assess (TIQM P2.4)

Follow TIQM P2.4 in Chapter 5. To measure the current process, measure the process that first captures the data, whether electronically or on paper.

In the case of Customer Name, Identity, and Address information, the Information Store will be the first place the information is captured, an electronic data store or the paper document or form.

Identify Accuracy Verification Sources (TIQM P2.5)

Follow TIQM P2.5 in Chapter 5 for how to identify the correct sources to verify *Accuracy* of the Information. This is the most critical inherent Quality Characteristic for any Information. The verification source of *most* Customer Information will be the individual Customers themselves. Some attributes cannot be verified by the Customers without bias, however. For example, knowing their current home valuation will require an assessment of comparable home sales to determine home value. Annual earnings will require evaluation of their employers' internal payroll checks or verification of the relevant tax authority, such as the U.S. Internal Revenue Service, Canada Revenue Agency, or the U.K. Inland Revenue.

Extract a Statistically Valid Sample of Data (TIQM P2.6)

Follow TIQM P2.6 in Chapter 5. For organizations with a single defined process for creating and maintaining Customer records, you will sample from the Record-of-Origin data store (paper or electronic) to determine the Quality of the data in the data store. You will select a sample of records from the current process to measure process capability.

For organizations with multiple channels and *different* Customer processes and databases for those channels, you will need to take representative samples from each strata (channel). Usually, the processes are different for capturing Customer Information in the different channels because there is often no enterprise-wide standard for capturing Customer Information. When Divisions are segmented by Product Line, there will be duplicate Customer records if Customers conduct business with different Divisions.

If Customer Information is created by different processes, you must take a proportional sample of each stratum of Customer records and measure and report them as unique subsamples. Some processes may be well in control with satisfactory IQ, whereas others are Out-of-Control and require Improvement.

NOTE Eliminate bias in sampling by ensuring the sample is selected outside of the knowledge and control of the Information Producers. If they are aware that measurement is being performed, the Producers may pay attention to Quality during the sampling period, and then return to status quo behavior afterwards.

Measure Information Quality (TIQM P2.7)

Follow TIQM P2.7 in Chapter 5. When measuring current and ongoing process control, you must eliminate bias. To measure accuracy:

- Ensure you are comparing the data to a true Real-World Object, Person, or Observation or Recording of an event as an authoritative Accuracy-to-Reality source.

- Avoid interpreting the data as you assess it.

- Avoid correcting the data in the source during assessment. This is the duty of the originating source area.

Interpret and Report Information Quality (TIQM P2.8)

Follow the process steps in TIQM Process P2.8 in Chapter 5 for developing your analysis and recommendations based on your assessment compared to the Information Consumer stated Requirements.

Use the template forms as found in the IQ Applied Book Web site for the Assessment Report.

How to Improve Customer Name, Identity, and Address Information Process Quality

Having assessed Customer Information Quality, you will have identified which process or processes are broken and require improvement. If the processes are not achieving Customer Satisfaction, you need to *improve* the processes. Follow the TIQM P4 steps in Chapter 7 "The Step-by-Step Guide to *Improving Information Process Quality*."

Define Project for the "Create Customer Information" Process Improvement (TIQM P4.1)

Follow TIQM P4.1 in Chapter 7 to define one or more initiatives to improve the prospective processes for capturing Customer Name, Identity, and Address information that are broken:

- Identify the Business Process Owner, who will be *accountable* for facilitating the Improvement Initiative and for implementing necessary process improvements.

- Select the Process Owner to lead the Information Process Improvement initiative. In some cases, you may also involve a neutral Process Improvement Facilitator to co-lead the Process Improvement Initiative if required.

- Identify all participants, as described in P4.2: "Develop Plan for Information Process Improvement Participants and Roles." See Tables 9-1 and 9-2 in this chapter for Customer Information Stakeholders.

NOTE There may be different processes involved in the preceding information requiring improvement. Be sure to separate them into discrete initiatives, focusing on the specific culpable process.

NOTE Follow your organization's procedure for establishing an improvement initiative like this. You may have different procedures based on whether this will be a minor Kaizen Event of incremental improvement or a major project requiring several months to Reengineer the Process, Application Programs, and Databases.

Develop a Plan for a "Customer Information" Process Improvement Initiative (TIQM P4.2)

Follow TIQM P4.2.1 in Chapter 7. This step is the most important step of the Process Improvement initiative. Here you will analyze and isolate the Root Cause or Causes and define suggested Improvements that will seek to eliminate the cause and incidents of defects in the Information.

Follow the step activities in TIQM P4.2.1 to develop a Cause-and-Effect Diagram (Ishikawa-English Diagram), and facilitate the discovery of the Root Cause or Causes. See Figure 9-3 for an example Cause-and-Effect Diagram for Duplicate Customer problems.

The Information Effect of high rate of duplicate Customer records result from a broken Customer Information Capture process that allows duplicates. But the real effect to solve is the business effect of wasting money on duplicate mailings, *improper* contact because of multiple records across different divisions, with alienation of Customers and potential lost business.

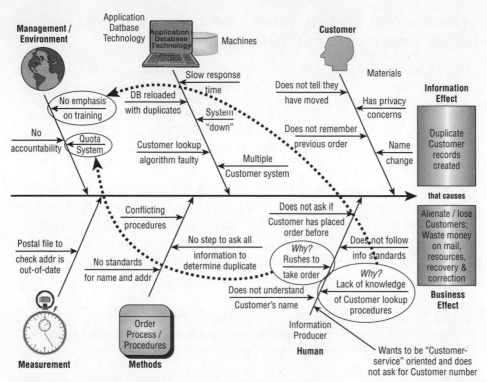

Figure 9-3: Duplicate Customer Cause-and-Effect Diagram

The causes follow the classic six categories (six Ms): Manpower (Human), Methods, Materials, Machines, Measurement, and Management and Environment.

In this example, there are two apparent Human Factor (Manpower) causes of "lack of knowledge of Customer lookup procedures" and "rushes to take orders," without capturing all data. However, when you ask why these causes occur, you find Root Causes that go back to Management and Environment. The first is a lack of emphasis on training. The second is quotas that emphasize speed over quality.

This indicates sound training and challenging the performance measures of a quota system as Improvements to prevent cause of duplication effects.

Define Improvements to Eliminate the Root Causes and Therefore Eliminate the Information Effect (TIQM P4.2.2)

Follow TIQM P4.2.2 in Chapter 7 to define error-proofing controls to prevent recurrence of the duplicate Customer records effect. See Table 9-4 for considerations for improvements based on cause.

Table 9-4: Duplicate Customer Root Causes: Process Improvement Considerations

DUPLICATE CUSTOMER ROOT CAUSES	PROCESS IMPROVEMENT CONSIDERATIONS
1. **Machines:** Multiple source databases where Customer records are created	1. Establish a single Enterprise-Strength Record-of-Origin Customer database. With all Customer records in a single database, it is much easier to test for duplicates at the create point.
2. **Mgt & Environment:** Lack of emphasis on training	1. Develop and implement enhanced training for Information Producers to understand the Attributes required for Duplicate Matching and to ensure they capture the data accurately to enhance the lookup algorithm.
3. **Machines:** Not all attributes are captured to effectively identify duplicates.	See Root Cause 4.
4. **Machines:** No process, or defective process for designing Enterprise-Strength Information Models and Database Designs	1. Define Information Requirements, Information Model and Database Design processes to address Enterprise Information Models and Databases. Then redesign the Customer Database and System to capture as many Identity Attributes as capability allows.
5. **Measurement:** Faulty duplicate matching algorithm	1. Enhance the duplicate matching algorithm with soft matches, true phonetic matches, multiple Identity Attributes, and historical data such as address changes and name changes.
6. **Source Information:** Purchased names and addresses have duplicates in them or are obsolete data.	1. Develop Warranties with Information Brokers and Third-Party Providers. Test the records for duplicates within the provided file and with your current and historical Customer database(s).
7. **Human:** Order Takers rush to take the orders.	1. See Root Cause 10.
8. **Human:** Order Takers do not look to see if a Customer is on file.	1. Note that this is a precipitating cause. Understand why.
9. **Mgt. & Environment:** Lack of accountability in Call Center management.	1. Eliminate quotas and Measure Cost of Ownership caused by defective information captured and duplicate Customer records created.
10. **Mgt. & Environment:** Call Center staff has quotas for how many orders placed.	1. Implement Accountability for Information Quality in Call Center Manager's job description as part of a plan to implement Accountability in *ALL* Management. Note: This requires time for training and resources to enable the capability to deliver quality.

Best Practices for Duplicate Customer Record Prevention

- Capture as *much* Identity Attribute information as you can to aid the match routines. The more Attributes and partial Attributes, such as the last four digits of a Tax Id Number, the better the ability to match duplicate records.
- Develop and conduct "close matches" with match attributes, such as:
  - Correlated data elements
  - Abbreviations compared to spelled-out names
  - Known-as names compared to given names or aliases
  - Organization Names compared to common, abbreviated or "Doing-Business-As Names"
  - Phonetic matches, such as "John" and "Jon," "Jean" and "Gene"
  - Partial match on Tax ID Numbers, such as the last four digits of the U.S. Social Security number or a Tax ID Number
  - Historical data, such as *former* Names and Addresses
- Develop close match tests across the applicable attributes.
- Develop *relative weights* for match criteria as you gain experience on the correlation of Attributes.
- Extract and identify potential duplicate occurrences.
- Verify and select duplicates for consolidation.
- Capture Attributes that are *stable over time*, such as mother's maiden name.
- Retain *historical values* and *original* (including erroneous values) for future matching.
- Test for duplicates at *point of data capture*.

NOTE It is far better to test and prevent duplicate records than to capture the duplicate with another record and then have to try to discover the duplicates *after* the point of knowledge acquisition.

Do Implement Information Process Improvements (TIQM P4.3)

Follow Step P4.3 in Chapter 7 for how to implement the suggested improvement(s) in a *controlled* way to test, study, and verify efficacy of improvements.

Duplicate Customer records require improvements in the organization culture, process, and the applications that do electronic tests to identify potential duplicate individuals or organizations.

In this example, if lack of training is the Root Cause, you evaluate and *improve the training* with respect to Attributes used in the duplicate Customer *lookup* procedures. Develop a *refresher training* course, based on the *lookup* procedures.

NOTE Be sure the procedures are optimal for duplicate matching. Then develop the training material to reinforce following the procedures.

Select a representative sample of Call Center staff or Information Producers to go through the training. Then put them back out in their jobs.

Check and Study the Impact of Information Process Improvements (TIQM P4.4)

Follow Step P4.4 in Chapter 7 to analyze results of implemented improvement.

Assess the *Quality* of the newly trained Team, immediately to see if the training has made a difference. Again, in the example of lack of emphasis on training, reassess the duplicate create rate of the Call Center staff who took the training. After four or five weeks, when the training *should have* taken effect, measure the results of their new Customer records. Conduct independent match analysis to discover whether the rate of duplicates has dropped, increased, or stayed the same.

If the duplicate results "increased or stayed the same," conduct a Root Cause Analysis to find out why the improvement did not work.

Act to Standardize Information Process Improvements

Once it is confirmed that the improvements met the expectations without introducing Negative Side-Effects, follow TIQM Step P4.5 in Chapter 7, "Act to Standardize Information Process Improvements."

This step provides the improved process to all Information Producers. So, if training is the improvement, you schedule and deliver training to all other Information Producers, scheduled as required.

Best Practices in International Customer Information Quality

Your Customers claim ownership of their personal information: Name, Address, Contact, and Identity Information. They place a high value on it and expect you to do the same. Best Practices need to be followed to ensure not only that this Information is gathered, stored, and manipulated in ways that enable you to make optimal use of them; but that, in a Customer-centric manner, you show respect to your Customer through these best practices with this data. This allows the building of a profitable relationship and dialog with the Customer.

Best Practices will ensure that the Customer Name, Address, Contact, and Identity Information is:

- In existence
- Accurate
- Complete
- Current
- Non-duplicate
- Consistent
- Relevant

To achieve this, follow the Best Practices described next.

Knowledge of Customer Nationality, Language, Norms, Culture, Address Characteristics

Understand how Name and Address Systems work, what components they contain, and how they are put together, both in your native country and for international data. Only through knowledge will you be able to design Systems and Databases to recognize and correctly manage each part of the data.

Customer Information Model and Database Design

Your Customer Information Model and Database Design must capture all Critical-to-Quality Name and Address Attributes. Address Line 1 is *not* an Attribute. That is an Information Presentation output on a label or envelope.

Once you have identified the many atomic and quasi-atomic Attributes, you design your application system to parse the Name and Address data into their respective data elements in the database.

Name Information, for example, will parse into Form-of-Address (Mr., Mrs., Dr.), First Given Name, Middle Name(s), and Family or Surname(s). Postal Address will parse into Thoroughfare Name, Type, Directional and Type, House or Building Number, and Building Sub-number. Contact and Identity information will be processed and stored in Identity Records and Types. Telephone Number consists of a Country Code, an Area Code, and a Subscriber Number. Because each can change separately from the other (individually, such as the Subscriber Number, or as a range, such as the Area Code), they should be stored and maintained in *separate atomic* Data Elements in a Database.

This general rule can also be applied to Addresses, but if you require International Names and Addresses, more than 100 atomic Data Elements are potentially required to store all Address components. When designing a Database to store Name and Address Information, two aspects should always be uppermost in your consideration: the needs of your Customer and the needs of your processes.

For example, a Thoroughfare Type ("Avenue") and a Thoroughfare Name ("of the Americas") are always found written as a unit in the Address: "Avenue of the Americas". You would only need to consider storing these components in separate fields if one of your processes required searching, matching, or listing in a manner excluding the Thoroughfare Type.

You must ensure Information Producers have the Information and Training required to *recognize and split* these components during data capture (for every country and every language). If you split these components, capture enough information to allow the information to be correctly reconstructed (such as their relative positions, which can differ within countries, such as "Avenue of the Americas" and "Fifth Avenue"). Generally it is best to maintain components in atomic Data Elements that can be concatenated as a unit in Addresses, such as Thoroughfare Name with Thoroughfare Type and Place Name with Suffixed Sorting Code. Those components that are used operationally: A Postal Code for searching, or a Building Number for de-duplication, for example, should be stored separately.

Table 9-5, first published in *Practical International Data Management* by Graham Rhind,[6] documents the Data Elements required to hold all International Name and Address Information for an output Postal Address Block. This level of detail is more than most companies require, though extra information such as language codes and maiden name would be required for other company internal processes and information uses.

Table 9-5: Required Attributes for International Name and Address Quality

DATA ELEMENT	EXAMPLE CONTENTS	EXAMPLE COUNTRY	EXPLANATORY NOTES
Form of Address	Mr., Herr, Mme, Señora	USA, Germany, Spain / Spanish	For Salutation
First Given Name	Graham, John	USA, UK	Identity matching
Middle Given Name(s)	Fitzgerald, Pat	USA	Identity matching
Preposition(s)	van de, de la	The Netherlands, France, Mexico	Separated to allow correct name sorting

(continued)

Table 9-5 *(continued)*

DATA ELEMENT	EXAMPLE CONTENTS	EXAMPLE COUNTRY	EXPLANATORY NOTES
Main Family/ Surname Full Islamic Names other than Given Name	Rhind, Smith; Jafar Mohammed ibn Musa al-Khwarizmi	The Netherlands, USA Middle East	Used for matching and de-duplication
Other Family / Surnames	Martinez	Spain, Spanish-speaking America	Identity matching
Known As Name or Calling Name	Bert	The Netherlands; USA	Dutch people often have a different known-as name than their given name.
Full Initials	A.G.L.M.	The Netherlands	Required for output on an envelope for a Dutch person
Seniority	Junior, Senior, III	USA	
Academic / Professional Designation(s)	Dipl. Ing., Ph.D.	UK, Germany	
Company Name	B.B.C.	UK, USA	Identity matching
Company Type	Inc., Ltd, GmbH, S.A.		Identity matching
Full Company Name	B.B.C. Ltd		Identity matching
Sub-Building, Japanese/Uzbek Sub-Building Indicator and Number	Room 17, #15	Japan, Uzbekistan, UK, USA	Location finding
Building Name, Japanese Area 1 Indicator, Uzbek Building Indicator	Station House, Marunouchi	Japan, Uzbekistan, UK	Location finding
Japanese/Korean Line 1 Number, Uzbek/Taiwan Building Number	7-4	Japan, Korea, Uzbekistan/Taiwan	Location finding

DATA ELEMENT	EXAMPLE CONTENTS	EXAMPLE COUNTRY	EXPLANATORY NOTES
Full Street Address, Japanese Area 2 Indicator, Taiwanese Thoroughfare 1 Indicator & Number	High Street, chome	Japan, Taiwan	Location finding
Thoroughfare Name Component	High		Sometimes parsed off to allow improved matching and de-duplication
Thoroughfare Type	Street, Avenue, Lane, rue, calle (correct casing)		
Thoroughfare Type Position Indicator	Before, After Thoroughfare Name		Required to ensure correct printed format on output (*Avenue* of the Americas or Fifth *Avenue*)
Thoroughfare Directional	N, S, E, W, NE, North, South, etc.		
Thoroughfare Directional Type	Before, After Thoroughfare Name		
Japanese Line 2 Number	2	Japan	
House Number Prefix	Km	Italy	
House Number	23		For matching, de-duplication and postal address validation.
House Number Suffix, Second Number in House Number Range and all following characters	bis, hs, 2° D-17, a-12b		Location finding

(continued)

Table 9-5 (continued)

DATA ELEMENT	EXAMPLE CONTENTS	EXAMPLE COUNTRY	EXPLANATORY NOTES
Post-Thoroughfare Address String, Japanese Area 3 (Ward), Urban District, Uzbek District Indicator and Number, Taiwanese Thoroughfare 2 Indicator and Number	Farm Road Industrial Estate, Naku-ku, Urb. San Juan, Col. Acapulco		Location finding
Settlement (1),	Ewelme	UK, South Africa	Location finding
Settlement (2), Taiwanese Section Indicator and Number	Benson	UK, Thailand, Taiwan	Location finding
Postal Town, Japanese Area 4	Oxford, Nagoya-shi	UK, Japan	Location finding
Street Address Postal Code	OX9 7RR	UK	Location finding
Sorting Code	Cédex, 18	France	Location finding
Province / County / State / Prefecture / Island name / Part of Territory / Governorate / Emirate Name	Oxfordshire, MI, CA, AICI, Gozo	UK, Italy, USA, Canada, Australia, Japan, Malta, Hong Kong, Oman, Panama, Puerto Rico, United Arab Emirates	Location finding
Post Delivery Type Indicator	P.O. Box, Private Bag, Post Restante		Location finding
Postbox or Other Delivery Type Number Prefix	N-	Bahamas	Location finding
Postbox or Other Delivery Type Number	12		Location finding
Postbox or Other Delivery Type Number Suffix	B		Location finding

DATA ELEMENT	EXAMPLE CONTENTS	EXAMPLE COUNTRY	EXPLANATORY NOTES
Postbox or Other Delivery Type Postal Code	3200 AA		Location finding
Postbox or Other Delivery Type Settlement, Post Office Name where Postbox is Situated	Bloemfontein, CAUSEWAY BAY POST OFFICE	South Africa, Hong Kong	Location finding
Postbox or Other Delivery Type Postal Town	Amsterdam		Location finding
Postbox or Other Delivery Type Sorting Code	Cédex, 18	France	Location finding
Large-Organization Postal Code Holder	12938	USA, Sweden, Germany	Location finding
Country Code	GB, D, USA		Location finding

Some Customers prefer to provide you with a "vanity" address, for example, one which shows a residence being in a neighboring, possibly more prosperous, district, or having a more pleasant-sounding street address. If so, the database should hold both the vanity address for communication and the correct postal address for processing and operational purposes. The *key* for quality communication is that you use the Name and Address Information as given by the Customer.

There is no maximum number of lines for postal addresses, though more than seven lines (including the country name) is rare; and postal services rarely insist that a certain address element appears on a specific line number in each address block. More important is the relative position of the elements, such as placing the postal code on the final line of the block and before the place name, and the format, such as ensuring the place name is uppercase. The output format may also vary according to delivery type, for example to a physical street address or to a mailing address, such as a post office box.

Tables 9-6 to 9-17 show some typical, but not exhaustive, ways in which the address elements from Table 9-5 may typically be output for a number of countries, for a physical Street Address, and for a Mailing Address, illustrating the wide range of formats used globally. Note that some text, such as the "z.H." ("for the attention of:" in the German example) and punctuation, are output automatically on the basis of country and language and are not required to be stored in the database, and that some information, such as a Country Name, can be derived from the Country Code. Not all elements will exist for every address in a country, so those data elements would be empty and not used. We illustrate this in some examples following each table. Where lines are empty, other lines will move up on output to take their place.

Table 9-6: Proper Postal Address Format for the USA

LINE NO.	USA ADDRESS LINE FORMATS	
Addr Line 1	[Form of Address] [First Given Name(s)/Initials] [Family Name] [Seniority] [Academic/Professional Title]	
Addr Line 2	[Company Name] [Company Legal Type]	
Addr Line 3	[House Number] [Thoroughfare Number] [Directional, and Type] [Thoroughfare Name and Type] [Sub-Building Indicator(s)]	[Postal Delivery Type] [Postal Delivery Type Number]
Addr Line 4a	[Second Street Address String], (if any) else 4b	
Addr Line 4b	[Postal Town] [Postal Code] [State] (if no Second Street Address String)	
Addr Line 5	[Country Name (derived from Country Code)]	
Addr Line 6	Not Applicable	
Addr Line 7	Not Applicable	

NOTE If mailing from the U.S. to inside the U.S., no Country name is required.

Table 9-7: US Postal Service Address Output Examples

DR S HOLMES SR, PHD
2978 W MAIN ST # 12
MINNEAPOLIS MN 23976-4542
USA

DR S HOLMES SR, PHD
PO BOX 142
MINNEAPOLIS MN 23976-2846
USA

Table 9-8: Proper Postal Address Format for Germany

LINE NO.	GERMANY ADDRESS LINE FORMATS	
Addr Line 1	[Company Name] [Company Legal Type]	
Addr Line 2	[z.H] [Form of Address] [Family Name] [Academic/Professional Title]	
Addr Line 3	[Thoroughfare Name and Type] [House Number] [Sub-Building Indicators]	[Postal Delivery Type] [Postal Delivery Type Number]

LINE NO.	GERMANY ADDRESS LINE FORMATS
Addr Line 4a	[Second Street Address String] (if any, else 4b)
Addr Line 4b	[Postal Code] [Postal Town]
Addr Line 5	[Country Name (derived from Country Code)]
Addr Line 6	Not Applicable
Addr Line 7	Not Applicable

Table 9-9: German Address Examples

Bäcker Meyer GmbH
z.H. Dipl Ing. Herr Mirgel
In der Raste 10
53001 BONN
GERMANY

Bäcker Meyer GmbH
z.H. Dipl Ing. Herr Mirgel
Postfach 52 83 71
53009 BONN
GERMANY

Table 9-10: Proper Postal Address Format for France

LINE NO.	FRANCE ADDRESS LINE FORMATS	
Addr Line 1	[Form of Address] [First Given Name] [Family Name] [Academic/Professional Title]	
Addr Line 2	[Company Name] [Company Legal Type]	
Addr Line 3	[Building Name]	[Postal Delivery Type] [Postal Delivery Type Number]
Addr Line 4	[House Number] [Sub-Building Indicators] [Thoroughfare Name and Type]	
Addr Line 5	[Second Street Address String]	
Addr Line 6	[Postal Code] [Postal Town] [Sorting Code]	
Addr Line 7	[Country Name (derived from Country Code)]	

Table 9-11: French Address Examples

M. Jean DUPONT
Boulangerie du Pain SA
Bâtiment Rose
25 bis rue Emile Zola
ZI Villeras
91190 GIF SUR YVETTE CEDEX
FRANCE

M. Jean DUPONT
Boulangerie du Pain SA
BP 176
91190 GIF SUR YVETTE
FRANCE

Table 9-12: Proper Postal Address Format for Russia

LINE NO.	RUSSIA ADDRESS LINE FORMATS	
Addr Line 1	[Company Name] [Company Legal Type]	
Addr Line 2	[Family Name] [First Given Name] [Middle Given Name(s)/Initials]	
Addr Line 3	[Thoroughfare Name and Type] [House Number][,] [Sub-Building Indicators]	[Postal Delivery Type] [Postal Delivery Type Number]
Addr Line 4	[Second Street Address String]	
Addr Line 5	[Postal Town] [Region]	
Addr Line 6	[Postal Code]	
Addr Line 7	[Country Name (derived from Country Code)]	

Table 9-13: Russian Address Examples

Moscow Bakery OOO	Moscow Bakery OOO
Ivanova Jelena	Ivanova Jelena
prospekt Tverskaya 9, appart. 187	P.O. Box 827
MOSCOU	MOSCOU
103009	103012
RUSSIA	RUSSIA

Table 9-14: Proper Postal Address Format for Sweden

LINE NO.	SWEDEN ADDRESS LINE FORMATS	
Addr Line 1	[Company Name] [Company Legal Type]	
Addr Line 2	[Form of Address] [First Given Name] [Middle Given Name(s)/Initials] [Family Name] [Academic/Professional Title]	
Addr Line 3	[Thoroughfare Name and Type] [House Number] [Sub-Building Indicators]	[Postal Delivery Type] [Postal Delivery Type Number]
Addr Line 4	[Second Street Address String]	
Addr Line 5	[Postal Code] [Postal Town]	
Addr Line 6	[Country Name (derived from Country Code)]	
Addr Line 7	Not Applicable	

Table 9-15: Swedish Address Examples

Seglarrestaurangen AB	Seglarrestaurangen AB
Fru Inger Lilja	Fru Inger Lilja
Vasavagen 3	Box 9
582 20 LINKOPING	582 27 LINKOPING
SWEDEN	SWEDEN

Seglarrestaurangen AB
Fru Inger Lilja
582 99 LINKOPING
SWEDEN

NOTE The last example for large organization postal code holders, no postal addressing details are required before the postal code and postal town line.

Table 9-16: Proper Postal Address Format for Brazil

LINE NO.	BRAZIL ADDRESS LINE FORMATS	
Addr Line 1	[Company Name] [Company Legal Type]	
Addr Line 2	[Form of Address] [First Given Name] [Middle Given Name(s)/Initials] [Family Name] [Academic/Professional Title]	
Addr Line 3	[Thoroughfare Name and Type] [House Number][,] [Sub-Building Indicators]	[Postal Delivery Type] [Postal Delivery Type Number]
Addr Line 4	[Second Street Address String]	
Addr Line 5	[Postal Code] [Postal Town] [-] [State Code]	
Addr Line 6	[Country Name (derived from Country Code)]	
Addr Line 7	Not Applicable	

Table 9-17: Brazilian Address Examples

Gingierman Bakery S/A	Gingierman Bakery S/A
Sr. Manuel Paes de Carvalho	Sr. Manuel Paes de Carvalho
Rua São Luis 3, 2º andar	Caixa postal 76
12003-213 BELÉM – PA	12003-298 BELÉM – PA
BRAZIL	BRAZIL

For full information on postal formats and other critical cultural information, please refer to the *Global Source Book for Address Data Management* by Graham Rhind.[7]

Best Practices for International Name and Address Information Processes

- Ensure that the Information Model contains *all* Attributes for Address Types you communicate with, and that the Database correctly holds all Data Elements from which to parse Name and Address into and to format a *proper mailing* Address as required. If you are planning global operations, have global business partners, or are involved in Merger and Acquisition activity, you must design to handle International Name and Address Information.

- Data should be parsed into Atomic or Semi-Atomic Data Elements so you can use key elements, such as Postal Code, Thoroughfare Name, and House Number, in processes such as matching duplicate occurrences and to generate correct postal formatted addresses on envelope or package labels.

- Data Elements should be designed so it is easy to parse Name and Address Information into the correct Attributes and Formats, and then to be able to map them to a *proper* Delivery Address.

- Standardization is key. Develop standard formats and input masks in forms and train input staff to follow standard formats and guidelines. Even if a format is found to be incorrect, it is easier to correct standardized data at a later stage to achieve quality.

- If you work with International Organizations and Individuals, design your system to support data written in different writing systems, such as alphabetic or pictogrammic, written in different code pages, with different diacritical marks (accents) and written in different directions on the page. Often data has been *transliterated* (written in a different alphabet than its original form). Because there are few officially sanctioned transliteration systems, this often makes data difficult to compare with other transliterations or the original.

- The *key to managing* different languages is to understand the issues involved in advance and to make maximum use of available technology. Though technology cannot yet support all languages, using Unicode, asking the Customers for their *preferred language*, making them aware of the *languages* that you are able to support, and using available information such as code-page and language settings on the Customers' computers and in their browsers will all *reduce errors* from different language and script use.

BE CAREFUL WHAT YOU WISH FOR IN INTERNATIONAL COMMUNICATIONS

John Yunker[8] recounts the tale of a professional society who wanted to expand their subscriber base beyond those with a moderate grasp of English. The marketing director duly translated the society's membership form into Chinese.

The first completed Chinese form arrived within a few weeks. Naturally, it had been completed in Chinese. None of the staff could read Chinese, and their membership database was not enabled to allow the entry of Chinese double-byte characters. Revenue and a Customer were lost due to being ill-prepared.

- *Always* standardize Customer data according to the cultural norms of the Customer if the Customer will see their data, such as in credit reports or contact preference.

- *Capture and store data in full* rather than abbreviating it. Abbreviations do not translate well. They can mean different things to different people in different cultures. Operationally, data written in full is easy to abbreviate. Once abbreviated, data may not be able to be transformed back to its full state. For example, "*ST*" in an address could mean "*Saint*" or "*Street.*"

- *Allow punctuation* in your data. This makes the data more readable for Customers, and it makes sense operationally. Commas show lists; full stops show abbreviations. This is useful for parsing data.

- Store and present data *in mixed-case*. It is more pleasing and readable to the Customer, and there is no good operational reason not to.

- Use *uppercase data* for matching and searching. This can be programmed to be done in memory, leaving the data in its correct state in the database.

NOTE ▪ Beware that uppercasing some letters *with diacritical marks* will result in the loss of that mark because not all code-pages contain uppercase equivalents of lowercased marked characters. Once a diacritical mark has been lost, it is *almost impossible to restore it automatically*.

- *Always use diacritical marks*. For speakers of most languages they are an important aspect of being able to understand and read text, and incorrect or missing marks don't just make a text less readable, they can change the meaning of the text in negative ways that can rebound very badly upon you.

CRITICAL DIACRITICAL MARKS MAKE ALL THE DIFFERENCE

1. The Spanish word "año" (with a tilde) means "year," but the same spelling without the diacritical mark, "ano," means "anus." Can you imagine how it would feel to receive a birthday invitation for a twelve-year-old's birthday to celebrate his or her twelve anuses!!!

2. In Hungarian, the word Tőke (double acute accent) means capital (as in money), but the word Töke (with an umlaut) means testicles.

3. Norwegian: "Se og Hør" means "Look and Listen," but "Se og Hor" means "Look and Adultery."

- *Always use local-language forms,* particularly of place names. Some companies still think it normal to store place names such as Köln as Cologne and Milano as Milan, and go to a great deal of expense to do this. There is no reason to do this and it guarantees you will annoy your Customers.

- *Use full stops* when writing Acronyms or Abbreviations such as B.B.C. Operationally, this allows your systems to see that this is an abbreviation and, for example, to leave the data in uppercase. No system can recognize that BBC is an abbreviation and not a word. If you wish to present such data without full stops, you can easily program it this way.

- Use *numeric fields* to store only data required in calculations. Storing telephone number and postal code data in numeric fields causes loss of required leading 0s.

Customer Information Validation, Error-Proofing, and Correction

- *Validate and correct* the Address, Contact, and Identity Information with the Customer at the point of discovery. Validate that the telephone number contains the *correct number of digits* for the country concerned, that a bank account number passes validation tests, and that addresses are valid postal addresses and correctly formatted.[9]

Figure 9-4 illustrates an error-filled Name and Address Label.

G Hind
Rugulieisgracht 88
Amsredam
Netherlands
1017-lv   1st class
netherlands

Figure 9-4: Validation During Data Capture Prevents Major Information Quality Problems and Improves the Chances That Your Communication to the Party Arrives.

The problems in the Address in Figure 9-4 are numerous:

- Given Name is an initial instead of full given first name, "Graham," and represents missed knowledge.
- Family Name is an not correct: correct value is "Rhind"
- City name "Amsredam" is misspelled: correct value is "Amsterdam."
- Country name "Netherlands" has been written twice in the same address, in the wrong place in one case, incorrectly cased in the other, and in both cases abbreviated; it should be "The Netherlands"
- Thoroughfare name "Rugulieisgracht" is not correct; the correct value is "Reguliersgracht"
- Thoroughfare number, "88," is the *only* correct part of the address
- Postal code is incorrectly cased and formatted; the correct value is "1017 LV"
- The address block contains extraneous information that will cause problems for automated mail systems: "1st class"

- The world and its systems are dynamic to a surprising degree. Ensure that the tables and masks used for validation *are up-to-date*. Ensure that a staff member has accountability to keep this current.
- Do *not* attempt to standardize *personal* names. This can destroy *accuracy* and your relationship with your Customer. Names are highly personal and have huge varieties of spellings, punctuation, casing, and diacritical marks that you must capture accurately.
- Do not assign "Gender" from a name, especially when International data is included. Names are not often assigned exclusively to only males or females even within one country, and a name usually assigned to one gender in one country and language is often assigned to the other gender elsewhere: Jan, Jean, Nicola, and so on.
- Ensure that *all name and address data is verified* before a record is created. Use creative ways to verify information, such as having the providing party repeat numbers backward to you, or you repeat data back in a non-standard way, such as repeating numbers given as "one-two-three-four" (1234) as twelve-thirty-four. This makes people stop and think. Sometimes it is appropriate to repeat data back with an error in it intentionally, to see if the provider sees and corrects it.
- Capture data electronically where possible, to allow electronic validation at the point of entry. Validation upon entry also allows a dialog with your Customer or the data-entry staff during creation to ensure maximum accuracy.
- If data is captured on paper, either by the person filling out a form, or an Information Producer capturing Information about the Customer, have

the Information Producer verify information before leaving the presence of the Party. Then have the Information Producer transcribe the information electronically. Errors missed in manual verification are best corrected by the person who captured the information because they are the actual source.

- If a separate Data Transcriber enters data electronically, have them capture it as soon as possible and provide feedback to the Information Producers if validation errors are found that they cannot correct.

- If you have periodic contact with your Customers, verify correctness of information subject to decay at appropriate intervals; six to nine months, for example. Verify all critical attributes are still correct. Some organizations verify Customer Information at every contact point.

- If you have infrequent contact with large volumes of Customers, periodically verify your volatile data with the Customer to maintain accuracy and to prevent data decay over time.

- Subscribe to *updates from postal authorities*, telecommunications providers, or *reliable information brokers* for updates to dynamic data, such as new or changes to thoroughfare names or address numbers, postal codes, or to telephone area codes or prefixes. Names, addresses, address systems, telephone numbers, telecommunication systems can change often in our dynamic world.

Error-Proofing Customer Information Capture Design

Capture Customer data with *real-time error-proofing* techniques and tools. Figure 9-5 illustrates the optimum way to ensure Quality Customer Information. The scenario follows:

1a. Information comes in to a Call Center or in person with an insurance broker.

2a. The Call Center Rep verifies accuracy by asking leading questions to confirm accuracy of name spellings, and verify address and telephone numbers at the point of capture.

2b. The software application invokes defined Edit and Validation rules for Valid Values, Business Rules, and Correlation and Reasonability Tests to ensure Correctness of Information.

Alternatively:

1b. Data comes in from a Web Customer Information capture screen.

2b. With no Information Producer interacting with the Customer, the software application invokes Edit and Validation Rules for Valid Values, Business Rules, and Correlation and Reasonability Tests are applied.

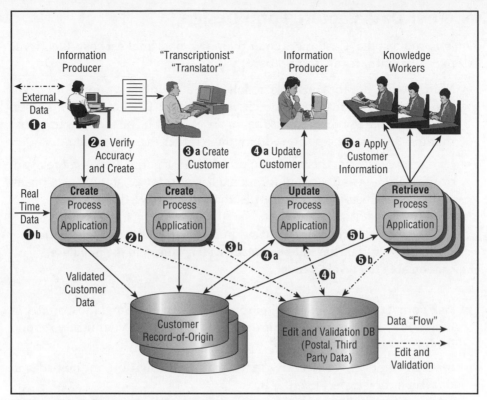

Figure 9-5: Customer Data Create Process with Real-time Edit and Validation and Accuracy Verification

Alternatively:

3a. The Information Producer, such as the insurance Broker, passes a paper document with the data captured to a "transcriptionist" who will enter the data into the Customer database.

3b. The software invokes the Edit and Validation Rules.

4a. A Customer calls in for additional interaction. The Producer will re-verify the Accuracy of the Information "on file" and updates changed data as necessary.

4b. The software invokes the Electronic Edit and Validation Rules, and informs the Information Producer of anomalies, if any.

5a. Knowledge Workers apply Name and Address Information in Marketing Campaigns, Billing, and in Product Recall announcements, for example, accessing data from the Record-of-Origin Customer database.

5b. The software assembles the Name and Address Information into the *correct mailing name and address format* for delivery. Test Edit and Validation Rules here to ensure data is current with postal and other standards.

Customer Data Capture Form Design

When you request that Customers enter their own data, make it easy. Electronic Customer data entry forms should be:

- Multilingual, as far as possible, to take into account the various languages spoken in the countries in which you operate. The language a person speaks is often not the same as that of the country he or she lives in at that moment. Ask for the preferred language rather than assuming it.

- Dynamic. *Do not ask* Customers to provide Information that is *not* relevant or which they cannot provide, such as asking for a "state" or a "postal code" from Customers in countries that do not have them.

NOTE Customers in countries with new postal code systems, or where the existence of the system has not been made widely known to the populace, may not be able to provide a code.

- Ask your Customers first for their preferred Language and the Country in which they reside, and program your input form to dynamically rebuild itself in a way that ensures:

  - Customers are asked only for relevant information, in the order in which they expect to enter it.

  - Input Masks and Edit Validations to verify the data at the point of data capture.

NOTE Make a data element required *only if every* Customer is able to provide that information. Commonly, Data Capture Forms insist, for example, on a postal code and still, too often, for a state, which locks out large numbers of people.

Postal code *	
*Required field	

Figure 9-6: Asking for Data That the Customers Cannot Provide Alienates Them, Reduces Response, and Creates Defects in Your Databases.

It is better to allow an optional field, with Edits to Require a Value *where* the values exist. See Figure 9-7.

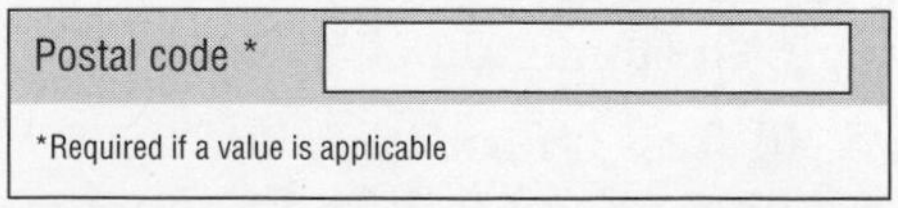

Postal code *	
*Required if a value is applicable	

Figure 9-7: Design Data Capture Where Values Apply to Most, with Only a Few Where Values Are Not Applicable.

NOTE This data capture design in Figure 9-7 does not *force* people to enter an invalid value if they have no postal code in their country. Also note that the data entry space is *closer* to the data label of the Attribute to be captured. This reduces error of entering data in a wrong space where multiple data fields are required.

NOTE The best design asks for data only that is relevant and required, with screens generated and presented to the Customer only when the data is knowable and required.

▪ Do not use drop-down lists except when the list of options is small, exhaustive, and complete. Drop-downs are commonly used for forms of address (Mr, Mrs, and so on) and job titles. In neither case is it possible to add every possible form of address to the drop-down list.

Figure 9-8 illustrates poor drop-down list that does not have a comprehensive list of Form of Address Titles.

Figure 9-8: Drop-downs Such As These Leave Customers Frustrated if they have Other Forms of Address Frustrated, such as *Professor, Lord, Engineer, Sir, Colonel, Reverend*.

▪ Ensure that drop-down lists are *up-to-date*. How many companies keep up with the ever-changing names of countries—how many still have Yugoslavia in their lists, or Serbia and Montenegro?

As the world changes, you must keep data *subject to decay, current*. See Figure 9-9 for obsolete Country information.

Figure 9-9: Your Systems Need to Keep Up with a Changing World.

The country "Serbia and Montenegro" has not existed since June 3, 2006 when Montenegro declared its independence and Serbia acknowledged that the two republics were independent and sovereign countries.[10]

TIP ISO and other standardized country codes require time to create as the political landscape continues to change. It is best to maintain your own country codes with your defined Country ID to prevent delay in your ability to create mailings in a timely manner, and, assignable when you come to know of a country code change, with cross reference to ISO or other standard codes to populate when they become available. This prevents you from having to create artificial codes and then having to change them when you get the official codes.

NOTE Use your codes for your internal use, and the standardized codes for information exchange.

- Do not allow a default value to fields or have drop-downs default to the first item on a list rather than to an empty value. This will guarantee biased results.

Figure 9-10 illustrates how default values bias data capture.

Figure 9-10: Fields Containing Default Values Will Lead to Skewed Information

- Be very careful and culturally neutral when choosing field labels. Use descriptive labels and describe clearly the data you are looking for. Does the label "Title" mean "Job Title," "Form of Address," or "Academic/ Professional Title"? Does "Position" mean "Job Title," "Job Function," or "Job Hierarchy Level"?

- Provide the Customers access to Data Definition of Data Elements, so they are clear as to what you need them to provide. This is especially the case if your form is not translated into each language. A recent market research study in a single country asked for the respondents' "Title." Six percent provided their job title instead of the required form of address — a significant effect on the quality of the data gathered.

- Avoid *locally specific or non-universal* labels, such as "ZIP Code," and *culturally loaded* labels, such as "Christian name."

Figure 9-11 illustrates how generic or culturally loaded Fields cause problems.

- Ensure that the fields are long enough to contain your Customer's data. The longest place name in your country might be 30 characters or so, but the longest in the world has *163 characters*; people's names and job titles can be long and complicated; the longest country name at the time of writing has *52 characters*. If in doubt, leave more space than might be required or use a variable-length data element. This will greatly aid your Information Quality, prevent Customer irritation, and prevent Poor Quality caused by *abbreviating or truncating* the data.

Title
Mr
First Name
Surname
Position
Mr
Mrs
Dr
Ms
Professor
Please Specify

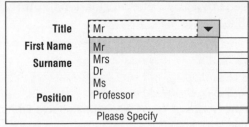

Figure 9-11: Non-specific Field Labels ("Title", "Position"), Culturally Loaded Field Labels ("First name" or "Surname"), and Incomplete drop-down Fields Contribute to Poor Quality.

Figure 9-12: illustrates how fields of insufficient length cause truncation errors and alienate your Customers.

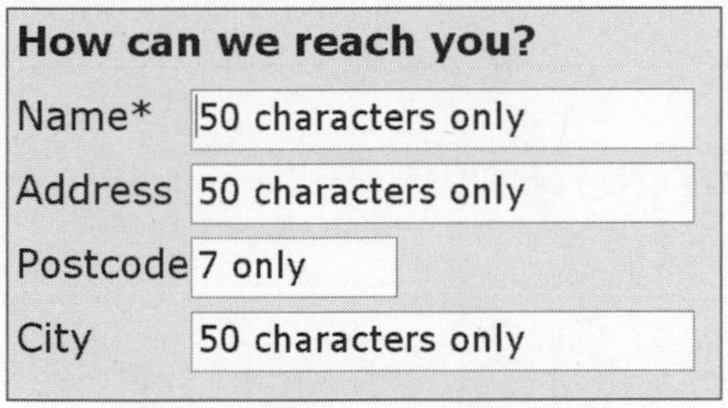

How can we reach you?
Name* 50 characters only
Address 50 characters only
Postcode 7 only
City 50 characters only

Figure 9-12: "How can we reach you?"

Limiting field sizes to save space causes data to be truncated causing downstream process failure. This form could not even accept a U.S. ZIP+4 code.

Check the spelling on your form! It is astounding how many forms are posted with spelling errors and typos. See the "Address" label in Figure 9-13.

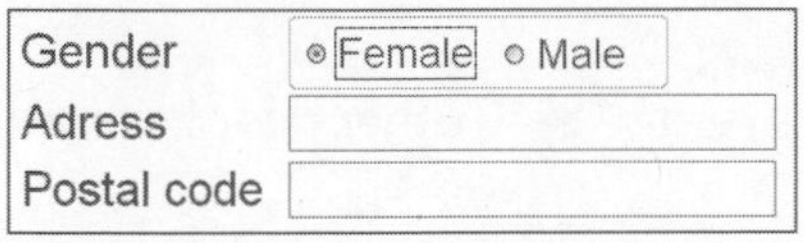

Gender
Female
Male
Adress
Postal code

Figure 9-13: Check the Spelling On Your Data Collection Forms

Finally, ensure that Business Subject Matter Experts are involved in the design of data collection forms. Forms can be added simply and quickly to Web pages, and usually are added by technical staff without any reference to the organization's information requirements. *Resist the urge to gather information until quality has been designed into* the forms and processes. Design to *delight* rather than *annoy* your Customers.

Designing quality and cultural sensitivity into the Information Capture Forms will bring your Customers back. See Figure 9-14.

Select your country of departure	Netherlands
Select your language of preference	English

Figure 9-14: Adjusting Input Forms to the Norms of Your Customers Reduces Errors and Builds a Good Relationship with Them and Increases Their Trust in You.

ADDRESS VERIFICATION AT SCHNEIDER NATIONAL

While 20 to 40 percent or more of many organizations' Customer Addresses contain errors, Schneider National maintains less than one percent error in its Customer shipping addresses. How? It *verifies* the delivery address with each Customer Order. With this practice, there is *no address decay* over time with respect to shipping orders.

Best Practices in Customer Experience and Interaction Information Quality

How you care and relate to your Customers will spell the difference between enterprise success and failure.

If you retain nothing else from this chapter, remember the statistics in Figure 9-15.

This study, conducted by e-Satisfy/TARP of the retail industry found there is a direct — and strong — correlation between Customer Complaints and lost business. Summary conclusions are:

- Only four percent of retail Customers who have a Complaint will tell the organization.

- Customers with a Complaint will tell on average 8–10 other people about their experience.

- Variables in the Complaints make a difference in saving or losing a Customer:

  1. The size of the Complaint in value. Minor Complaints were valued at US$5.00 or less. Major Complaints were US$100.00 or more.

  2. How the organization addressed the Complaints:

     - Resolved quickly, on the Customers time table
     - Resolved slowly, on Company's time table

- Complaints not resolved
- Complainants not telling you their Complaints (approximately 96 % of Customers with Complaints)

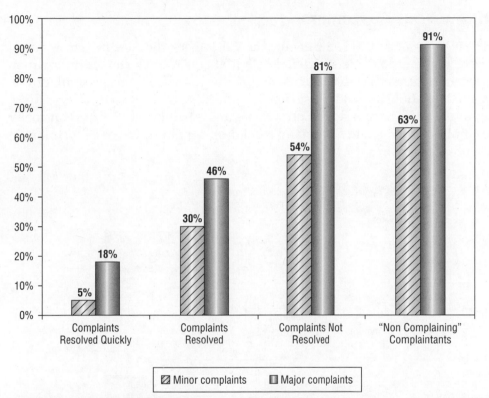

Figure 9-15: How Many of Your Customers with Complaints Will Not Buy from You Again?[11]

The retail experience measured by TARP:

- Minor Complaints resolved quickly saw a 5% attrition.
- Major Complaints resolved quickly saw nearly one out of five defect.
- Minor Complaints that were resolved, but not in a timely manner saw a Customer loss of 30 percent.
- Major Complaint's not resolved quickly saw nearly one-half of the complainants go elsewhere.
- Minor Complaints with no resolution saw a 54 percent Customer loss.
- Major Complaints not resolved led to a loss of eight out of ten Customers.
- Non-complaining Complainants with minor Complaints saw a loss of 63%, nearly two-thirds.
- Non-complaining Complainants with Complaints of US$ 100 or more saw nine out of ten go elsewhere.

> **NOTE** It is imperative that all organizations have a mechanism to identify, document and analyze Customer Complaints. To not do so, will jeopardize your ability to delight your Customers on a sustainable basis.

Know Your Customers

The *more* you need to know about your Customers, the *more* Information you need to gather to understand and delight them. Your Customer Information Model and Database Designs must support the Knowledge you need to cultivate a *caring* relationship with Customers.

You need to have a set of Entity Types and Attributes to capture Customer Complaint events and Complaint resolution similar to the one illustrated in Figure 9-16.

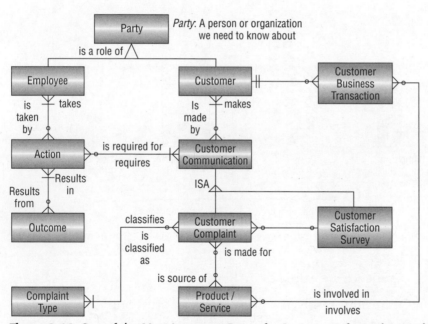

Figure 9-16: One of the Most Important Parts of a Customer Information Model and Database Design: a Customer Complaint Model

Best Practices in Customer Care

- Remember that without Customers, you are out of business.
- Define and implement a comprehensive set of Customer Values, such as Customer Satisfaction, Privacy, and Security of their *private* Information.

- Earn your Customers' *trust* by treating them as you would want them to treat you. This requires you to understand their needs for your Products or Services.

- Deming's Point 1 of quality states that we must "create constancy of Purpose for Quality of Product and Service." "The *obligation* to the Customer never ceases."

- Treat Employees as you want your Employees to treat your Customers. "The obligation to the Knowledge Workers never ceases."

- The only way the Enterprise can truly *know* its Customers is through managed, quality, and shared Customer Information available to all Customer-facing personnel.

- Learn and document everything you can about the Customers and their needs.

- Become Stewards of Quality Information for your own internal "Customers."

- Use *every reasonable point of contact* to verify Customer knowledge and capture all feedback, from Complaints to kudos. Maintain data *corrections* and *updates* along with last verified/updated data.

- Empower Employees to correct Customer data online as they discover errors or communicate correct Customer data they come to know.

- Empower Employees, train them, and involve them in Information Process Improvement Initiatives.

- Make Customer Contact and Complaint data available to all Employees who deal with Customers.

Best Practices in Customer Information Quality

- Define all Attributes about Customer and Customer Relationships that you require to be able to understand and delight your Customers.

- Ensure the data is defined consistently to meet all Customer Information Stakeholders' Needs to achieve Customer Satisfaction.

- Ensure the correct spelling of Customer's names, as this creates a strong relationship.

- Capture the pronunciation of the Customer's names if you have personal contact with Customers. This is often more important than name *spelling*.

- Capture Customer data at the Business Event of Information Discovery.

- Automate *data capture directly* where feasible. For example, use Customer Frequent Flyer, Shopper, or Guest cards to scan in for efficient data capture.

- Capture all Attributes about Customers that are required for all downstream Knowledge Workers' Requirements. Remember the Customer Value Circle with its many Stakeholders.

- Train Information Producers and *required* Transcriptionists well so they know the *meaning* of the data, Valid Values, and Business Rules to capture the data correctly.

- Ensure Information Producers know their Information Customers and the uses and costs of their data.

- Capture and share Complaints and Employee exit interviews, actions, and Lessons Learned.

- Implement data Defect-Prevention Techniques in Information capture.

- Allow a value of "Unknown" when facts are not known.

- Creatively *repeat vital information* given orally.

- Confirm correct spelling; do not assume you know it.

- Don't automatically use *default spell check options*.

- Allow Customers to *update their* information.

- Capture and maintain *historical* Customer data for *duplicate* Customer record tests.

- Capture Attributes for Customers that do not change to provide finer Customer identity.

- Develop easy-to-follow data capture procedures. See the section "Applying Quality to Technical, Procedural, and Documentation Writing" in Chapter 14: "Information Quality Applied to Document and Knowledge Management."

  - Use standard guidelines.

  - Observe *training of new* Information Producers. Listen to the questions the Information Producers have. Is the training adequate?

  - Observe process execution in the workplace (Gemba). Observe their work to see if the trainees are able to apply their learning. Verify this in an assessment after four or five weeks of applying the training.

- Create a single update process or procedure to update required redundant copies, if the redundancy is truly required.

- Maintain *frequent contact* with Customers for currency of volatile data.

- Create a "last verified date" Attribute for Customer data.

- Use points of contact to verify Customer knowledge and capture observed Complaints.

- Make Customer Contact and Complaint data available to all Employees who deal with Customers.

- Use Customer Complaint data for *Product Development*.

- Create Attributes for "do not contact" and honor them.

- If acquiring mailing lists, *match against your* "do not mail/contact" Attributes, and refrain from contact.

- If purchasing Prospect Information, *get a Warranty* for an acceptable (to you) level of quality.

- Create a process and empower any Employee to *correct inaccurate data* directly or communicate to a source who can.

- Maintain and update an audit trail for each Information Group.

- Measure Information Quality, provide feedback, and Improve Processes to *prevent defect recurrence*.

- Implement Management Performance Measures and Accountability.

- After implementing a PDCA process, Management Accountability, and Training, charge back costs of Information Scrap and Rework to the *originating unit*.

- Provide Customer-focused Warranty or Guarantee with respect to the Products and Services you provide them. Provide them a Warranty as to the Quality of the Information you provide them and to the *security* of their Information you maintain about them.

Summary

Customers can be sensitive about personal information. Manage it carefully.

- Among all your Stakeholders, your Customers are the *most important* for your ability to stay in business.

- How you treat your Customers will determine their "Customer Lifetime Value" (CLTV).

- To create a Value Proposition for your Customers, you must understand their Needs and Expectations for the Products and Services you offer. They are looking to you to satisfy those needs. If you cannot deliver to meet their expectations, do not expect them to remain "loyal" to you.

- To understand their Needs and Expectations, you must capture Attributes about the Customers that will tell you what they need.

- You must *protect* your Customers' Private and Proprietary Information to Prevent Identity Fraud that can bring high cost of remediation to you, but will be devastating to your Customers.

- Capture and maintain Quality Information by *staying in contact* and empowering your Customer-facing staff to keep their data current and accurate.

CHAPTER 10

Information Quality Applied to Product Development: *"Product-Idea-to-Product-Retire"*

"Simply put, if you understand Customer Requirements better than your competitors, you'll grow."

A Global Chemical Company

Introduction to Information Quality in Product Development

Every organization provides products[1] or services to its Customers or constituents, whether a corporation, a not-for-profit organization or a government agency. This chapter addresses Information Quality in the Product Development Value Circle, "Product-Idea-to-Product-Retire." A critical success factor for organizations is to ensure they develop products and services that meet or exceed Customer expectations. This chapter addresses the first part of the Supply Chain, that is the Conception of product ideas, to discovery of Customer Requirements, to the Engineering, Design, and Development of the processes that manufacture or deliver the products and services.

In Chapter 11 we examine the operational Supply Chain Management Value Circle, "Forecast-to-Satisfied-Customer," which includes Forecasting Demand, Customer-Order Management, Production Scheduling, Order Fulfillment, Shipping, In-Use Servicing, and Product Disposition.

Product Development or "Production Capability,"(Covey)[2] is the ability to identify products through the development of the capability to produce, deliver, and service the products throughout their product lifetime. This chapter describes Quality Principles applied to information to support the identification of potential products, Customer Requirements for the products, and product and Process

Specification required to produce Products and Services that meet or exceed Customer Requirements and Specifications, including product retirement and disposal. This critical topic directly affects the success of the enterprise. Any enterprise that does not provide products that meet the needs of its Customer market is doomed to fail.

Quality Information about Customer needs and expectations is paramount in evaluating product concepts and developing them into Customer-beneficial, profitable Products.

This chapter addresses the information and Quality of Information:

- Required to understand the Requirements and Expectations of the end-Consumers of products and services, so that the organization develops products and services that satisfy or delight the Customer in the assembly, use, and servicing or maintenance of the products and services provided to the Customer

- Required by internal personnel to plan, design, produce, and deliver products and services

- Required to evaluate effectiveness of products and services and determine if and when products require enhancement, redesign, or retirement

What Information is required to support and optimize The Product Development Value Circle, "Product-Idea-to-Product-Retire"?

Categories of Product Development Information Requiring Quality

Quality principles must be applied to two critical categories of Information in Product Development:

- **Product Concept Information**, including Customer Requirements, needs, and Expectations, along with Customer Feedback and Complaint or Warranty claim information about existing products, and direct observation of product use

- **Product Engineering or Design Specifications and Product Manufacturing Process Specification and Bill-of-Materials (BOM) Information**, such as parts, product or part dimensions, chemical formulations, and work or assembly instructions. It is not enough to "know" the Customer Requirements. The Customers' *Product* Requirements must be translated into *Process* Specifications that enable the process to produce the products or deliver services that meet the Customer Requirements.

Product Development Information Stakeholders

There are many Information Consumers and Stakeholders throughout the interdependent Supply Chain Business Partners and within an enterprise. They all assume important roles as Information Consumers and/or Information Producers. Failure to provide high-Quality *Information* through the Value Circle will cause product development processes to fail, sometimes with catastrophic results.

Internal Information Stakeholders

Within the organization, Information Stakeholders include those shown in Table 10-1.

Table 10-1: Internal Information Stakeholders and Their Information Interests

INTERNAL INFORMATION STAKEHOLDERS	INFORMATION INTERESTS
Engineers	Require Customer Requirements Information to design Products or Components to meet Customer Quality Expectations.
Manufacturing personnel	Require Engineering Specifications in order to translate product Quality Requirements into Process Quality Specifications to produce or assemble components or material into other components or finished products that meet Customer Quality Requirements.
Quality management personnel	Quality Requirements to ensure that Quality is designed in and achieved in the various processes of development, production, and delivery
Service product developers	Market, demand, and Customer Requirements to create new services, such as financial, insurance, or investment "products"
Catalogers	Require Specifications to create Product Information to share with Customer Trading Partners.
Contract officers	Contract and Product Information to develop formal relationships with Trading Partners
Procurement staff	Supply information and pricing to order goods or supplies from Suppliers.
Sales representatives or agents	Product and pricing information to develop relationships with Customer buyers to understand their Requirements and for selling goods and services that will meet their and their end-Consumer Requirements

External Information Stakeholders

Information Stakeholders outside the enterprise include those shown in Table 10-2.

Table 10-2: External Information Stakeholders and Their Information Interests

EXTERNAL INFORMATION STAKEHOLDERS	INFORMATION INTERESTS
End-Consumers	The first and last people in the Supply Chain, whose needs and expectations, including Information Requirements, must be met by the end products and services, including Requirements Conformance, Assembly and Operating Instructions, Warranty, Service and Disposal Information
Trade partner buyers	Product feature and Quality Specifications; price information to purchase products or materials
Supplier sales representatives or agents	Supply materials and Quality Requirements to produce the organization's products
Supplier product catalogers	Product Specification Information compared to Product Quality Requirements
Regulatory authority compliance personnel	Regulation Compliance and Conformance Information
Communities in which the enterprise resides	Economic and environmental impact information
Shareholders	Business and financial performance information

The Product Development Value Circle: *"Product-Idea-to-Product-Retire"*

The Product Development Value Circle, *"Product-Idea-to-Product-Retire"* is required to standardize product development from a concept through launch to eventual retirement and disposal. Figure 10-1 illustrates this Value Circle.

Figure 10-1: Product Development Value Circle: *"Product-Idea-to-Product-Retire"*

DISCLAIMER

The purpose of this chapter *IS NOT* to teach you how to develop new products.

The purpose *IS* to guide you through the processes of measuring and improving the Quality of the information processes that create, maintain, and deliver *information* about new product ideas and about Customer Requirements for those new products, so your new products are successful in the marketplace.

You learn how to apply Quality principles to product and Customer Requirements so that you can improve the product development Value Circle, "Product-Idea-to-Product-Retire."

Dr. Deming is correct when he says, "the Consumer is the most important part of the production line."[3] Because the Consumers are the ones who "pay the bills," they are the key Stakeholders who matter when *report cards* are generated.

Quality is not an engineer's determination, nor a marketer's determination, nor a manager's determination. It will always be the Customers who have the final say.[4] The best way to ensure that you delight the Customer is to ensure that you design your products and services around the needs and Requirements of the end-Consumers. This is why the Consumer is at the *center* of the "Product-Idea-to-Product-Retire" Value Circle.

It is too late to start thinking about Customer Satisfaction after you have designed and produced your products and services. The proactive organization will seek to understand Customer Requirements and design Quality into the products to meet or exceed those Customer requirements.

But the internal Information Consumers are at the heart of the Value Circle as well, for they must have Quality Information to produce the products and provide services that meet their end-Consumer expectations.

Many organizations today have shifted their emphasis from the end-Consumer to the Shareholder. While Shareholders have a stake in the success of the enterprise, they are only "lending" money to the company on the promise of seeing their "investment" grow. But that invested money is not a gift. Decisions made for the benefit of the Shareholders may lead management to make short-term decisions that put the long-term success of the enterprise in jeopardy.

The message is clear: Stay focused on your Customers and delight them.

Provide the same focus on your Knowledge Workers — who perform the real Value Work — without whom you cannot delight the Customers.

"Product-Idea-to-Product-Retire" Value Circle Processes

Quality must be designed into today's Products and Services if the organization *values* its Customers and their Lifetime *Value*. In order to design Quality into the processes that produce products, you must have *accurate* and *complete* information about the Consumer's Quality Expectations for those Products. This includes the Quality of Information associated with the products and services that you develop, deliver, and maintain. The eight Product-Idea-to-Product-Retire Processes[5] include:

1. Product Concept Creation
2. Customer and Business Requirements Analysis
3. Product Concept Development
4. Product Design and Development
5. Production Process Design and Product Launch
6. Product and Service Production and Delivery

7. Product Consumption and Feedback

8. Product Enhancement, Redesign, and Retirement and Disposal

Table 10-3 describes the Quality tasks associated with each process and the Quality methods or tools relevant to the process.

Table 10-3: Product-Idea-to-Product-Retire Value Circle Processes, Quality Assurance Requirements, and Quality Methods

PRODUCT-IDEA-TO-PRODUCT-RETIRE VALUE CIRCLE PROCESSES	QUALITY ASSURANCE TASKS	PRODUCT DEVELOPMENT QUALITY METHODS
1. Product Concept Creation	Ensure that new technology and/or ideas are robust for downstream development.	Idea brainstorming, Robust technology development
2. Customer and Business Requirements Analysis	Ensure that the new product/service concept you come up with has the right functional requirements, which satisfy Customer needs.	Quality Function Deployment (QFD)
3. Product Concept Development	Ensure that the new concept can lead to sound design, free of design vulnerabilities Ensure the new concept to be robust for downstream development.	Taguchi Method/Robust TRIZ (Theory of Inventive Problem Solving) Axiomatic design Design of Experiments (DOE) Simulation/optimization Reliability-based design
4. Product Design, Prototyping and Development	Ensure that the designed product (design parameters) delivers desired product functions over its useful life. Ensure that the product design to be is robust for variations in the manufacturing, consumption, and disposal stages.	Taguchi Method/Robust Design Design of Experiments (DOE) Simulation/optimization Reliability-based design/ testing and estimation
5. Production Process Design and Product Launch	Ensure that the manufacturing process is able to deliver the designed product consistently.	Design of Experiments (DOE) Taguchi Method/Robust Design Troubleshooting and diagnosis

(continued)

Table 10-3 (continued)

PRODUCT-IDEA-TO-PRODUCT-RETIRE VALUE CIRCLE PROCESSES	QUALITY ASSURANCE TASKS	PRODUCT DEVELOPMENT QUALITY METHODS
6. Product and Service Production and Delivery	Produce designed product with a high degree of consistency, free of defects.	Statistical Process Control (SPC) Troubleshooting and diagnosis Inspection
7. Product Consumption and Feedback	Ensure that the Customer has a Satisfactory Experience in consumption.	Quality in after-sale service Customer Satisfaction Evaluation
8. Product Enhancement, Redesign, Retirement and Disposal	Ensure that products continue to meet Customer needs with trouble-free and safe product disposal.	Service Quality Customer Care

The following describes the Value Circle Processes with their general activities and Quality methods, and the IQ issues that can cause process failure.

1. Product Concept Creation

This Process creates potential product or service ideas within the scope of the organization's mission. Product ideas may come from product developers, end-Consumers' suggestions or technological innovations.

Process Activities

Every successful product or service must have a need and a concept that can fulfill that need. Sometimes breakthrough product ideas are conceived in the light of new or emerging technologies. These breakthrough ideas must be converted into product ideas that require the developers to "create" a need in the marketplace. "Quality" is irrelevant if there is no perception of need among the prospective Customers for the product concept.

The objective of product or service Idea Creation is to identify things that have the potential to become products and services. Product ideas must satisfy an identified or potential need in a market.

Process Quality Methods

- Idea brainstorming
- Robust technology development
- Customer Feedback, suggestions, and product evaluations

Common Information Quality Issues

This process captures the Information that will enable you to *evaluate* Product ideas and their viability. This includes the completeness, accuracy, and precision of:

- Prospective market (Customer segments)
- Estimate of market demand
- Ability and technology to develop the product concept
- Ability and technology to provide capacity of production and delivery
- Estimates of costs versus prospective return
- Real or potential competitive products

The viability of various products will be assessed in the next process, "Customer and Business Requirements Analysis."

2. Customer and Business Requirements Analysis

This Process identifies the Customer Requirements and Business Requirements for the conceived Product. You must accurately understand the Customer's stated and unstated Requirements for the product, from iPods with music as a virtual product to household appliances with controls designed in for convenience and to prevent Consumer error and accidents.

Process Activities

The Customer and Business Requirements and analysis phase seeks to identify the features, functions, Quality Requirements, Expectations, and Customers' Needs for the Product concept being considered.

The key Quality tool for this phase is "Quality Function Deployment" (QFD), used to discover end-Customer and business Requirements for product Quality. QFD is also useful for capturing end-Customer and Business Information Quality Requirements. Key steps in the process are:

1. Identify Customer needs and wants.
2. Translate the "Voice of the Customer" into Functional and *measurable* product Requirements.
3. Develop a business feasibility study, including product Quality Characteristics and Specifications.
4. Translate the product specs into Process Specifications.

USING INFORMATION TO ERROR-PROOF PRODUCTS AGAINST CONSUMER ERRORS

My wife and I recently bought a new front-loading washer/dryer combination in our move to replace high-energy-consuming appliances with environmentally friendly ones. The LG model washer has various wash/spin cycles based on the various wash-load groups, such as permanent press, cotton, among others. There is a range of settings that you can select — but the washer is programmed to prevent you from selecting settings that are harmful to the intended wash load, such as setting the wash load of "delicates" to a water temperature setting of hot/cold or extra hot/cold for the wash/rinse cycle, which could damage delicate fabrics. See Figure 10-2 for a picture of the control panel. This is an example of "poka yoke," Japanese for the error-proofing of processes to prevent mistakes.

Increasingly, Information is a component of Products and Services that add value from the Customer's perspective.

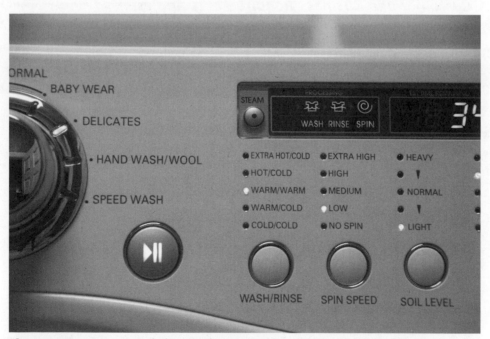

Figure 10-2: LG Tromm Clothes Washer Control Panel with Quality Designed in to Prevent Errors That Could Damage Delicate Fabrics

Process Quality Methods

- **Quality Function Deployment (QFD)**
- **Voice of the Customer (VOC):** Part of QFD that captures Customer Requirements in their actual words
- **Voice of the Business (VOB):** Part of QFD that captures the organization's Requirements to develop the product effectively and with high Quality

Common Information Quality Issues

Issues here involve the correct design of QFD sessions, in which Customers participate in the Requirements definition and design phases of product development. Issues include:

- Bias in the Requirements and Information Gathering Process used to identify real need and requirements
- Bias in the Customer participant sampling, in which a representative sample of the market is not achieved
- Misidentification of correct Features and Functional Requirements important to the Customers along with the Quality Characteristics and weightings for the product. Are the functional Requirements and Quality Characteristics valid for the population represented by the sample?
- Missed discovery of previously unstated Customer Expectations (completeness of Information)
- Failure to verify that the Business Requirements (for Product and Information Quality) are consistent with the VOC requirements. If not, production to the business Requirements may not achieve Customer satisfaction, and the product may fail in the marketplace.

Use QFD to understand the Customer Requirements for Product Information and Information Quality. This includes Assembly Instructions, Owner's Manual, Maintenance Requirements and Instructions, Warranty data and Warranty Claim Instructions, and Product Disposal Guidelines.

3. Product Concept Development

The product idea is now translated into a Product Concept with Features and Requirements that may be producible.

Process Activities

In process 3, you translate the product concept, using VOC and VOB, into a high-level product concept, which includes the *purpose* and *intended use* of the Product along with a Value Proposition. The high-level product concept is then translated into a Product Definition with Product Quality Requirements defined to ensure that the product meets the intended purposes and Customer expectations. Activities include:

1. Develop a high-level concept, including the purpose, general use and value proposition.

2. Develop a product definition with base-level functional requirements.

3. Design concept generation, evaluation, and selection processes.

4. Develop the system, architecture, information, and organizational design.

5. Develop a model or simulation of the initial design.

Process Quality Methods

- Design of Experiments (DOE)
- Taguchi Method of Quality Engineering or Robust Design
- TRIZ, the acronym for the Russian method translated as the Theory of Inventive Problem Solving, also known as TIPS
- Standardize-Do-Study-Act Cycle
- Axiomatic Design
- Simulation and Optimization
- Reliability-based Design, Testing, and Estimation

Because there are *multiple* Requirements for Products, several design techniques exist to optimize the CTQ requirements, such as Design for Serviceability and Design for Reliability, in general called DFX or Design for X, with the variable being Serviceability or Reliability, for example. Several of these methods with their description reference are cited in Table 10-4.[6]

Table 10-4: Design for X Methods Reference

X PRODUCT/PROCESS	DFX	REFERENCE
Assembly	▪ Boothroyd-Dewhurst DFA	O'Grady and Oh[7]
	▪ Lucas DFA	Sackett & Holbrook[8]
	▪ Hitachi AEM	Huang[9]
Fabrication	▪ Design for Dimension Control	Huang[10]
	▪ Hitachi MEM	Arimoto et al.[11]
	▪ Design for Manufacturing	Boothroyd et al.[12]

X PRODUCT/PROCESS	DFX	REFERENCE
Inspection and test	▪ Design for Inspectability ▪ Design for Dimension Control	Huang[13]
Material logistics	▪ Design for Material logistics	Foo et al.[14]
Storage and distribution	▪ Design for Storage and Distribution	Huang[15]
Recycling and disposal flexibility	▪ Design for Ease of Recycling	Beitz[16]
Environmental repair	▪ Design for Environmentalibility ▪ Design for Reliability and Maintainability	Navichandra[17] Gardner and Sheldon[18]
SERVICE		
Cost	▪ Design for Whole Life Costs	Sheldon et al.[19]
Service	▪ Design for Serviceability	Gershenson and Ishii[20]
Purchasing	▪ Design for Profit	Mughal and Osborne[21]
Sales and marketing	▪ Design for Marketability ▪ QFD	Zaccai[22]
Use and operation	▪ Design for Safety ▪ Design for Human Factors	Wang and Ruxton[23] Tayyari[24]

Common Information Quality Issues

- ▪ Failure to transform Customer Product Quality Requirements into Product Specifications that ensure that the functionality and capability of the products meet Customer Requirements and Expectations
- ▪ Failure to ensure that the Product can be manufactured at the expected cost within the expected timeframe with the Required Quality

4. Product Design, Prototyping, and Development

Process 4 models and prototypes the Product or Service Scenarios. Design principles call for developing exact, detailed Functional and Quality Requirements.

Product design calls for the Specification of Material Requirements and Properties such as dimensions, material composition, and part Specification.

Service design requires process definition, organization design, outcomes Specification, service delivery medium, and service delivery Quality Characteristic Specification.

Process Activities

1. Develop exact, detailed functional requirements.
2. Develop an actual implementation to satisfy the functional and Quality Requirements (design parameters).
3. Build prototypes of the product.
4. Conduct process testing, adjustment, and validation with prospective Customers.
5. Install the manufacturing process and equipment.
6. Validate the process and product design.
7. Identify ongoing product (or service) servicing requirements.
8. Define the process for product servicing.
9. Prototype and verify the product servicing process.
10. Formalize the servicing process.
11. Provide training in product servicing.

Process Quality Methods

- Design of Experiments (DOE)
- Taguchi Method of Quality Engineering or Robust Design
- TRIZ or TIPS
- Standardize-Do-Study-Act Cycle
- Axiomatic Design
- Simulation and Optimization
- Reliability-based Design, Testing, and Estimation

Common Information Quality Issues

- Incomplete or inaccurate definition of functional and Quality Requirements (design parameters)
- Inaccurate or imprecise product measurement data as compared to required Critical-to-Quality (CTQ) requirement Specifications

UK RETAILER OPENS NEW STORES IN HONG KONG WITH MASSIVE OVERSTOCKS AND SHORTAGES

A major retailer in the UK opened retail stores in Hong Kong with early sales producing significant overstocks in its large sizes of clothing and significant shortages in the smaller sizes of clothing. The cause? Not understanding that its Asian Customers are smaller in stature than their British counterparts. They had stocked the stores using the company's standard British body-size distribution!

ERROR IN SPECIFICATION OF HUBBLE SPACE TELESCOPE LENS COSTS $700 MILLION TO REPAIR[25]

"The diameter of the telescope's 2.4-meter (94-inch) main mirror was too flat near the edge by about one fiftieth the width of a human hair."[26] This small error was enough to cause the lens to fail to focus properly, causing 85 percent of the light to be focused incorrectly. This, in turn, caused the telescope to see only one tenth as far into space as it was "designed" to. The manufacturing process ground the lens exactly as specified, but this was a very expensive product Specification error!

5. Production Process Design and Product Launch

This finalizes the production process design, using the Standardize-Do-Study-Act (SDSA) cycle to ensure that the process is defined and designed to produce the Nominal Values in the CTQ Specifications. This produces Products or Services that *meet or exceed* Customer Requirements.

Process Activities for Manufacturing

1. Transform the Product Quality Specifications into Process Specifications. This means ensuring that the process is able to produce the Products to meet the Nominal Values in all CTQ Characteristics.

2. Evaluate the technology (manufacturing equipment) for capability to deliver the necessary product Quality.

3. Calibrate or retool equipment to meet Nominal Value production. An effective Calibration System will have the following:[27]

   - Traceability documentation
   - Proper calibration labels
   - Uncertainty budgets

- Calibration interval procedures
- Good scheduling practices
- Environmental conditions and parameter management
- Calibration management software support
- Documented calibration training and procedures
- Continuous Process Improvement

4. Finalize the manufacturing process design using SDSA.

5. Conduct process testing, adjustment, and validation.

6. Install and calibrate manufacturing equipment to meet Nominal Values for Quality Characteristics.

7. Conduct and adjust final process design.

8. Provide manufacturing process training to the production staff.

Process Activities for Service Delivery

1. Finalize the service delivery process design (SDSA).

2. Conduct service delivery testing, adjustment, and validation.

3. Implement the service delivery process.

4. Ensure service delivery Quality Characteristics are consistently met.

5. Provide service delivery process training to the delivery staff.

Process Quality Methods

- Design of Experiments (DOE)
- Taguchi Method of Quality Engineering or Robust Design
- Troubleshooting and Diagnosis
- Quality Inspection

Common Information Quality Issues

- Incomplete, inaccurate, or unclear process definitions and work instructions
- Incomplete, inaccurate, or imprecise process and product measurement results
- Inaccurate, incomplete, or unclear product physical storage and stacking pattern instructions
- Inaccurate, incomplete, or unclear Hazardous Materials Handling information specified in the Material Safety Data Sheets (MSDS)

6. Product and Service Production and Delivery

This process represents the full-scale manufacturing or service delivery.

Quality management in this process ensures the conformance of products or services delivered to meet the Requirements and Expectations of the Customers and end-Consumers.

Process Activities for Manufacturing

1. Regular measurement of Quality Characteristics of Requirements and Specifications

2. Use Statistical Process Control (SPC) Charts to measure the Critical-to-Quality Characteristics.

3. Ensure conformance with all Quality Requirements of Component Parts or Materials and the Finished Products.

Process Quality Methods

- Statistical Process Control Charts
- Troubleshooting and Diagnosis
- Inspection of CTQ Characteristics
- Pareto Diagrams of Nonconformance areas
- Plan-Do-Check/Study-Act applied to Nonconformance Discoveries
- Root Cause Analysis to identify the *causes* of defects to eliminate

Process Activities for Service Delivery

1. Regular measurement of Service Delivery outcomes

2. Capture Customer Satisfaction data in key Service Delivery requirements.

3. Ensure Customer Satisfaction for all Vital Expectations and Requirements.

Use the tools identified above.

Common Information Quality Issues

- Intuitive Assembly Instructions and Owner's Manual information
- Intuitiveness and ease of use of products
- Unclear and or biased Customer-satisfaction form questions
- Inaccurate measurement of Process and Product Quality Characteristics

7. Product Consumption and Feedback

This *vital* process enables end-Consumers to share their experiences about your Product and Service Quality. The Customer-focused Organization will have designed Quality into their Products and Services, so the Customer Feedback should not produce undesirable surprises, except in the most unusual circumstances. Customers always have the final say. If they walk away from your Products or Services, they will take with them their wallets and will share Complaints with others.

Process Activities

1. Get *frequent* and *regular* Feedback from your Customers as to their Satisfaction with your Products and Services

2. *Act* on what you *learn* from your Customers

Process Quality Methods

- Quality in After-Sale Service
- Customer Satisfaction Evaluation and Action

Common Information Quality Issues

- Bias in Customer Satisfaction Form Questions (See Chapter 14 "IQ Applied to Document and Knowledge Management")
- Incompleteness of Customer satisfaction surveys
- Inaccurate interpretation of Customer Satisfaction Surveys
- Inaccurate or incomplete Warranty Claim data
- Inaccurate Process and Product Measurement data in CTQ Requirements

8. Product Enhancement, Redesign, Retirement and Disposal

When the product is offered to the marketplace, it will thrive or languish subject to the market reception. As we have seen with vacuum tubes, pneumatic automobile tires, manual and electric typewriters, and video cassette recorders, many products and components become obsolete or are displaced over time as innovation and technology advance.

Customer experience determines product success. If a product or service does not meet Customer needs consistently, management must make a choice: minor enhancement, redesign, or retirement of a product or service.

Products with hazardous materials, such as batteries or pesticides, must have clear guidance on how to recycle or dispose the materials in an environmentally and personally safe way. This is critical information that addresses the needs of society and the local community.

Process Activities

There are three scenarios here for Product Management:

1. The Product needs *minor* improvements that keep the product competitive or add *minor* functionality. This requires a small project version of the Value Circle, beginning with Process 2, "Customer and Business Requirements Analysis." Modifications to original Requirements must be verified and implemented with Quality.

2. The Product needs *major redesign* to meet market changes. This requires a major project beginning with Process 2. Generally, this results in a new Product that replaces the now-obsolete Product. If Product Safety is the driving factor in redesign, external regulations and oversight will be required.

3. The Product is *no longer profitable* (not needed) in the marketplace and will be retired. If a Product is retired, the disposal of Products in inventory must be addressed. Hazardous materials in the Product, if any, must be disposed of in an environmentally friendly way. The evolution of computing technology has seen semiconductors replace magnetic core RAM, which replaced transistors, which replaced vacuum tubes, which replaced mechanical relays — all in the space of 60 years.

Process Quality Methods

- Service Quality
- Customer Care
- Materials Reuse, Recycling, or Disposal

Common Information Quality Issues

- Inaccurate or incomplete Requirements data related to the decision to enhance, redesign, or retire a product or service
- Inaccurate, incomplete, or unclear Hazardous Materials Handling and Safety data, required for *safe* handling and *proper* disposal

Information Quality in the *"Product-Idea-to-Product-Retire" Value Circle*

We will analyze two major groups of information where Quality is paramount:

1. Customer Requirement Information for a Product
2. Business Product and Process Specification Information for a Product

Information Quality Issues and Costs in Customer Requirement Information

Major Information Quality issues in the "Product-Idea-to-Product-Retire" Value Circle include:

Issue: Poor Quality Information as to Need and Customer Requirements for a Product

The Research and Development organization may overreach and generate ideas that are not on the radar of the marketplace. Some ideas may be simply "before their time." Other ideas may be generated in the absence of confirmation by prospective end-Consumers. Sound Product ideas may be conceived but with Poor Quality in gathering and understanding the Customer's Needs and Expectations for the Product.

Costs of Poor Quality Information in Conceived Product Need/Demand

- Loss of investment in the development of a Product not needed by the market if it is a failure, and diminished revenue
- Underestimating the demand, resulting in loss of opportunity because of insufficient inventory and inability to deliver to meet demand

Issue: Lack of Understanding of End-Consumers' Requirements and Expectations for a Conceived Product

Costs of Poor Quality Information about End-Consumers' Requirements and Expectations for a Conceived Product

- Failure to identify real Customer Requirements and the Quality Characteristics required by them, leading to poor Quality design and failure in the marketplace
  This, in turn, leads to dissatisfied Customers and lost business.

Issue: Poor Quality Information about the Ability of the Enterprise and Its Suppliers to Produce and Deliver the Conceived Product

Costs of Poor Quality Information about Internal Enterprise and Supplier Production Capability

- Inability or diminished ability to deliver the Products by launch date and during Product offering, causing *lost* sales and Customer Dissatisfaction

SMITH CORONA GOES BANKRUPT *TWICE* MAKING UNNEEDED PRODUCTS

After more than a century of innovation in typewriter technology, Smith Corona came to an ignominious demise. It had failed to recognize and negotiate the Information Age revolution of the computer and word processing paradigm shift. Smith Corona's final innovations of its first Personal Word Processor in 1985 and "the world's first Laptop Personal Word Processor" in 1989 could not match the word processors that ran on personal computers. In its press release of its final bankruptcy, CEO Martin E. Wilson says, "Despite tremendous efforts over the past five years, it became clear that Smith Corona could no longer continue to operate as a stand-alone business. … The new Product sales that would have alleviated our financial constraints did not materialize."[28] This was a sad demise for a company that made high-Quality typewriters, but in attempts to update what it calls its "ink on paper heritage," it introduced a new series of Products and services it hopes will compete on the world market.[29] Obviously, its "hopes" did not materialize. The world market voted "no!" And Smith Corona is no more!

Issue: Poor Quality Product Engineering and Manufacturing, Specification and Requirements Data (BOM)

Costs of Poor Quality Information about the Product Engineering and Manufacturing Specification (BOM)

- High costs of Scrap and Rework, high Warranty costs and decreased Customer Satisfaction, and Lost Business

COMPLEX WIRING TANGLES AIRBUS JUMBO PRODUCTION, COSTING IT LOST BUSINESS

Complexity in the wiring of the jumbo double-decker Airbus A380, now two years behind schedule, has caused Customer cancellations of a number of plane orders, including a FedEx cancellation of 10 A380s; they will now buy, instead, 15 Boeing 777 aircraft from its major competitor.[30] In Airbus's second announcement of delays, Airbus's parent company, European Aeronautic Defence and Space (EADS), cut its future profit forecasts by $2.5 billion and saw its share price fall 26 percent in one day.[31] Airbus also lost orders from other major airlines.

Issue: Poor Quality Information as to the Quality of the Offered Product and the Customer Experience (Complaints, Warranty Claims, and Feedback) with the Product

Costs of Poor Quality Information about Product Quality as Experienced by the end-Consumers

- Failure to identify Product problems early in the Customer experience with loss of Customers before remediation

---

FIRESTONE FAILED TO SHARE CUSTOMER COMPLAINT DATA WITH FORD

In a videotaped deposition, a Ford Explorer wheel engineer testified that he learned Firestone was withholding Customer Complaint information from the automaker.[32]

This tragic scenario of poor-quality tires not fit for high-temperature conditions coupled with high center-of-gravity SUVs caused more than 200 deaths and 700 injuries as a result of tire separation and SUV rollover accidents. The direct costs to Firestone from the recall are well over $1 billion and the loss of its major Customer, Ford, just before they were to celebrate a 100-year business partnership anniversary!

Issue: Poor Quality Information as to When to Improve, Innovate, or Retire a Product

Costs of Poor Quality Information as to Need for Product Improvement, Enhancement, or Retirement

- Incomplete, inaccurate Warranty and Customer Feedback data could prevent an organization from understanding when to enhance or retire a substandard Product, costing it sales and incurring subsequent higher costs to improve or replace the Product, along with the high costs of inventory and disposal of unsold inventory.

Applying Information Quality to *Customer Requirement Information*

We shall examine how to measure Information Quality in two major sets of information in the Product-Idea-to-Product-Retire Value Circle and how to improve the processes that produce the information:

1. Lack of *complete and accurate* Product Requirement and Expectation information, called "Customer Requirement Information"

2. Inaccurate or imprecise Product Engineering and Manufacturing Process Specification and Bill-of-Materials (BOM) based upon Customer Requirements, called "Product Specification Information."

How to Measure and Improve *Customer Requirement Information* and *Customer Requirement Information* Process Quality

The first rule of Quality is "the Customer is *always* right." The second rule is "if the Customer is wrong, go back to the first rule." Customer Requirement Information consists of Customer Needs, Requirements, and Expectations for a specific Product planned for the marketplace.

Organizations that start and end their Product development life cycle with the Product concept will generally fail in the marketplace. Good ideas will not meet Customer Needs and Expectations unless they are designed to meet them and *tested* for conformance.

The most important input into Product development is the Customer input.

Customer Requirements through Quality Function Deployment

Quality Function Deployment (QFD) is a very effective tool for gathering Customer Requirements and Expectations for a given Product, whether Consumer goods, such as an automobile, or in services, such as online banking. Yoji Akao introduced QFD in Japan in 1966 to proactively involve the Customer in the design of Products. This led to the *maturing* of Quality Management by moving from Quality Control of Requirements as understood by Production to ensuring that there was Quality Control of Requirements that were *critical* to the *Customers* as captured in the Voice-of-the-Customer (VOC).

In Chapter 15, we illustrate how to apply QFD to involve Information Stakeholders in Information Systems Design and in Information Requirements gathering for Enterprise Information Model development and Database Design.

QFD is a set of specific methods for ensuring Quality throughout each process of the Product Development Value Circle, from Product/Service concept and Customer Requirements through Design and Manufacturing or Service Delivery and Product Enhancement or Redesign. QFD involves capturing the VOC to:

- Identify and understand their Requirements for the Product.
- Translate the VOC into Quality Specifications for the Product or Service.
- Translate the Product Quality Specifications into Production Process, Formulation Specifications or Service Requirement Specifications.
- Ensure Quality at each process of Product Development to provide Quality that satisfies Consumers.[33]

QFD consists of involving end-Customers in the development of the Requirements, Features and Capabilities of Products they will (may) be using. QFD seeks to gather the VOC as *verbatim* statements of Customer needs, Requirements, and Expectations and translating this into Requirements and Specifications that can be engineered and manufactured to.

A critical part of QFD is identifying the *relative* importance of each Customer Requirement to identify the *vital few* or Critical-to-Quality (CTQ) Requirements from the more peripheral Requirements.

Next you create Voice of the Business (VOB) to determine Enterprise Requirements and its capability to produce the Product or deliver the Service with the required Quality.

How to Measure the Quality of QFD Information Gathering Forms: Correctness, Completeness and Clarity

To ensure Quality of VOC information, you must ensure the Quality of the questionnaire or Requirements Information collection devices. The questions must be phrased clearly and distinctly to identify the nature, form and response requested from prospective Customers.

> **BY DEFINITION THE VOC VERBATIM STATEMENTS ARE ACCURATE**
>
> **Statements may be subject to *different interpretations*, so you must ask questions in ways that are simple and clear, so you can interpret the Customer Verbatim statements correctly. This enables you to ensure that your interpretation of the requirement is the same as the prospective Customer's and to create more accurate Product Requirements statements.**

A TIQM P1 Assessment of Information Product Specification Quality will help you ensure that your forms do not cause confusion and misinterpretation of terms or questions you present or ask of your Customer participants. This minimizes the potential for receiving faulty information from the participants.

Follow the baseline assessment steps in Chapter 4 "Assessing the Quality of Information Product Specification and Information Architecture Quality" (TIQM P1). Here are some tips for this assessment applied to Product Quality Requirements Specification.

Identify Information Product Specifications Quality Measures (TIQM P1.1)

See Chapter 4. The critical Quality Characteristics here are Correctness, Completeness, and Clarity of communication. The most important measure is that the Customers *accurately* understand the descriptive Product Information along with any Assembly and Product Use and Safety Instructions. The VOC Verbatims should provide you with their Quality Requirements and Expectations provided for a given Product by Customers. Specific measures include:

- Intuitive Business Term Names and Correct, Complete, and Clear definition
- Clarity in written Definitions and Specifications
- Wording of Definitions, Questions, and Instructions is intuitive, understandable, and helpful.

- High *relevance* of Descriptive Information about the Product to the Customer Segment(s)
- Complex Product or Service Concept Information is presented in a way that illuminates, such as from a (1) general concept or abstract to (2) a more specific description to (3) the most detailed information.

Assessing Customer Satisfaction with Data Definition (TIQM P1.6)

Customer Satisfaction Assessment steps include:

1. Develop the QFD form to gather information.

2. Identify a representative set of prospective Customers, using statistical sampling techniques, to solicit Feedback about the QFD *form design*, questionnaire and option wording, or general information about the Product concept.

3. Use statistical sampling to be sure that you do not have a bias in the Prospective Customers selected.

This will enable you to ensure the Quality of the Information-Gathering devices for the QFD VOC sessions.

To ensure the Quality of the Information gathered from the Prospective Customers, you can conduct an Information Quality Assessment to reconfirm the original Verbatim responses with the individual QFD participants. See the step: "Measuring Information Quality (Accuracy, Criticality, and Relevance) of Customer Requirements Information" (TIQM P2.7), later in this chapter.

The purpose of the P1.6 Assessment is to ensure that your QFD participants understand clearly the *kind* of Information you need and can give you actionable Customer Verbatim statements that lead you to identify their real Requirements accurately.

Identifying a Set of Information for Measuring Quality (TIQM P2.1)

The specific Information you will measure here is the Function, Feature, and Quality Requirement Information gathered from the QFD participants.

Planning IQ Objectives, Measures and Tests (TIQM P2.2)

The measure of this "soft" Information is clear and correct statements of Quality Requirements and Expectations Required for the Product.

There are "no wrong answers" in the Voice of the Customer. However, you must ensure that you truly understand the Requirements of the Customers and their *relative* importance.

To ensure understanding, ask, "What do you mean by?" questions. This will enable you to ensure that you have an *accurate understanding* of the Customer's input and requirements.

Determining Information Store or Process to Assess (TIQM P2.4)

In the case of gathering Customer Requirements and Expectation Information, the Information Store will be the collected Customer Verbatims or VOC statements.

Identifying Accuracy Verification Sources (TIQM P2.5)

See Chapter 5, "The Step-by-Step Guide to *Assessing Information Quality*," Step P2.5 for how to identify the correct sources to *verify* the Accuracy of the Information. This is the most critical inherent Quality Characteristic for any information. The verification source of the VOC Verbatims is the individual Customer participants.

Extracting Statistically Valid Sample of Data (TIQM P2.6)

Because you will have a relatively small sample of Customers involved in the QFD initiative, you will want to use *all* Information gathered from all Customer participants, a 100 percent sample of the total population of QFD participants. The Critical Success Factor is for you to select a *Statistical* random Sample.

Measuring Information Quality (Accuracy) of Customer Requirements Information (TIQM P2.7)

To measure VOC Accuracy, you can ask the Customer to confirm the importance with which they rate given Attributes individually. The process of verification of understanding a declarative requirement statement is simple. Ask, "What do you mean by ... ?" Look out for words that are *ambiguous* in the context of the Requirement Statement. For example, "The coffee must be hot, but not too hot." This must be translated into a temperature range in order to control consistency. What is different about this IQ assessment is that you assess the Customer Verbatims on the spot with the Customers themselves. Once you have clarity in the Requirements statements, you will have the participants evaluate the *importance* of the various Requirements to prioritize them as to their relative importance to the participants' perceived satisfaction.

You can also use statistical evaluation of individual Attribute Satisfaction Performance to overall Product Satisfaction. The goal is to identify the Vital Few Quality Attributes that correlate highly to overall Product Satisfaction.

The statistical evaluation provides the highest reliability when measuring the Product Attribute (Requirement) Quality because it eliminates bias. From this, you can infer that individual Attributes that rate High Satisfaction are more important than those that rate Low Satisfaction compared with overall Product Satisfaction.[34] Figures 10-3 and 10-4 illustrate Attribute Performance Satisfaction versus *overall* Product Satisfaction. Figure 10-3 reveals a Low Revealed Importance, with Figure 10-4 showing Attributes where Satisfaction of *individual* Attributes correlates *highly* with overall Product Satisfaction. The Attributes with a *correlation* to overall Product Satisfaction should be considered Critical-to-Quality (CTQ) Attributes.

LOW REVEALED IMPORTANCE

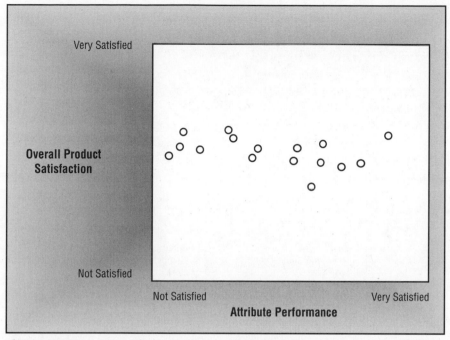

Figure 10-3: Low Revealed Importance of Individual Requirement Attributes[35]

HIGH REVEALED IMPORTANCE

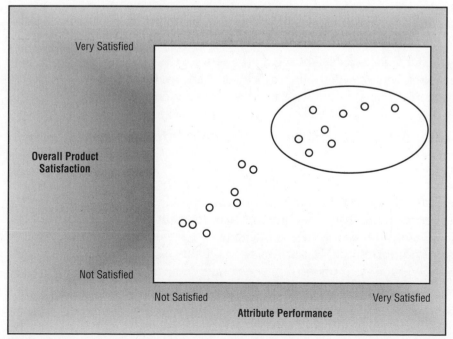

Figure 10-4: High Revealed Importance of Individual Requirement Attributes[36]

This evaluation identifies the Critical-to-Quality Requirements of the Customers with minimal bias. Figure 10-5 describes the Klein Grid of Customer Needs, which, to characterize the Stated *versus* Revealed importance of Requirements, identify high-impact Requirements and "hidden" Requirements in which *breakthrough* opportunities may be found.

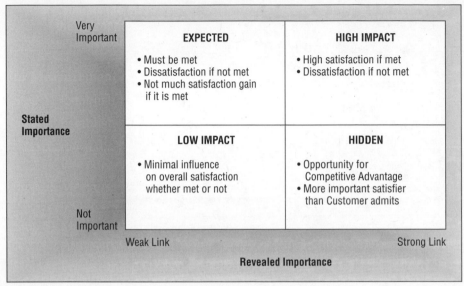

Figure 10-5: Klein Grid of Customer Needs[37]

Interpreting and Reporting Information Quality (TIQM P2.8)

Report the relative importance of individual Quality Requirement Attributes using Cluster Charts, as represented previously, to the Product Design Teams. This enables them to weight the respective Features, Functions, and "Quality Requirements" based on unbiased Customer experience and evaluation.

How to Improve "Customer Requirement Information" Process Quality

If new Products have had Quality problems based on early Customer experiences, Complaints, and Warranty Claims, you need to address Quality of the process that gathers Product Requirements Information from your Customers. A major Chemical manufacturer understands the need for accurate Customer requirement information. Describing their Quality Management System, they say, "Simply put, if you understand Customer Requirements better than your competitors, you'll grow."

▪ **Customer experience, Product Warranty and Claim, and Customer Complaint Information:** Information about the Product Guarantees, Recalls, Customer Inquiries, Product Experience, and Customer Feedback (Complaints, Suggestions, Employee observations of Customer Experience). IQ problems here can alienate Customers, causing them to go elsewhere. Failure to understand Complaints and/or Product Failure can lead to Lost Business, as well as incorrect assignment of Warranty accountability and costs.

- ▪ Product Warranty period is overly long, increasing costs of Product failure

- ▪ Product Warranty does not cover sufficient time for Customer Product life, causing post-Warranty Failure and unhappy Customers

- ▪ Ignoring Customer Complaints and Suggestions or employee-observed Customer problems or satisfaction, causing Missed Opportunities for improvement and *increased* business (or reduction in lost business)

- ▪ Warranty Claims with insufficient data to determine *exact* Cause of Product Failure or abuse

Define a Project for the "Gathering Customer Quality Requirements" Process Improvement (TIQM P4.1)

Follow TIQM P4.1 in Chapter 7 for establishing an Improvement project. Review your process for gathering Customer Requirements for new Products. Do the results deliver Customer Satisfaction, the first time, every time? If not, you need to improve the *process*.

Do you maintain a Knowledgebase of Information on the Product Experience in the marketplace relative to the early Customer statements of Features, Functions, and Quality Requirements? If not, begin one.

If you do have one, but you are unhappy with your Customer Experience (dissatisfaction) with new Products, you should improve the *process*. If it is not improved, the process will continue to sub-optimize the Quality of the Products you develop, robbing you of profit as a result of failure to achieve Customer Satisfaction because of not understanding Customer Requirements and Expectations in the first place.

Plan a "Customer Quality Requirements Gathering" Process Improvement (TIQM P4.2)

The first part of planning is to analyze and identify the Root Cause or Causes of missing, unclear, incorrect, or misinterpreted Quality Requirements. Follow TIQM P4.2.1 "Analyze Root Causes of the IQ problem" in Chapter 7. Analysis of the Root Causes requires understanding the needs and expectations of the Customers and facilitating the identification of precipitating causes and to drill down to the Root Causes.

Identify and Confirm the Root Causes of Faulty Customer Quality Requirements Information (TIQM P4.2.1)

Root Causes can include:

- Lack of gathering Customer Quality Requirements and Expectations Information

- Poorly wording questions that do not solicit Requirements or that yield poorly considered, and potentially irrelevant, requirements

- Bias of Customer input caused by *poorly worded* questions for Requirements capture or solicitation

- Misinterpretation of Customer Verbatims, translating them into "Specifications" that do not represent real Customer Requirements

- Failure to identify *dependent* relationships of Quality Requirements to features and functions that deliver them

- Management or Product developer bias that "we know better than the Customer" what Customers need without gathering Customer Requirements or observing actual Customer Product use and Feedback

- The Product Developer is too close to existing Products and unable to see breakthrough Product ideas.;

See a possible Cause-and-Effect Diagram in Figure 10-6.

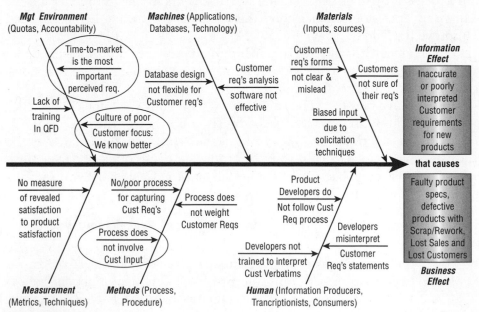

Figure 10-6: Cause-and-Effect Diagram for Poor Quality Customer Requirements Capture

Remember that these are suggestive Root Causes. For your situation, you must define your Information Effect and Business Effect clearly and determine with your Information Producers the potential causes and then ask, "Why?" until you get back to the *Root Cause*. In many cases, you must *observe or design* Experiments (DOE) to isolate the Root Cause.

Identify Preventive Actions for Faulty Customer Quality Requirements Information (TIQM P4.2.2)

Based on actual, isolated Root Causes, design possible *Preventive* Actions, which may include:

- Learn and implement QFD for your Product Development Process. This addresses the activities of Quality assurance throughout the Product Development Value Circle, whose aim is to address Customer Satisfaction.

- Incorporate an appropriate selection of prospective Customers in the Voice of the Customer

- Ensure that the questionnaires are *not biased* toward a preconceived internally desired result. An example is biasing a Product concept toward the manufacturer's priorities of speed and low cost, rather than Customer priorities.

- Ensure that the Customer Verbatims represent *accurate* Requirements by confirming them through "what do you mean by" questions, or better yet through statistical analysis of *individual* Feature and Requirement Attribute Performance Satisfaction and overall Product Performance Satisfaction, as described in the section, "Measuring Information Quality (Accuracy) of Customer Requirements Information (TIQM P2.7)" earlier in this chapter.

- For additional information on intuitive and clear document design and development, see Chapter 14, "Information Quality Applied to Document and Knowledge Management."

A Quality Chart or a "House of Quality" (HOQ) can be used to capture Customer Requirements as "Demanded Quality" and the Features, Technology, and Quality Capabilities that satisfy Quality Requirements. The Requirements are weighted as to importance, and they can be evaluated. See Figure 10-7, a House of Quality identifying Quality Characteristic Requirements for a flip chart, to illustrate a completed HOQ.

This HOQ represents a complete analysis of a QFD to define Customer Quality Requirements, as represented in the VOC from Customer's Verbatims to Product Specs to Engineering Specs to Manufacturing Process Specs. This allows you to prioritize Requirements and identify positive and negative or neutral correlations among Requirements.

A. The Customer's Quality Requirements are identified in the left-hand Rectangle labeled "Demanded Quality."

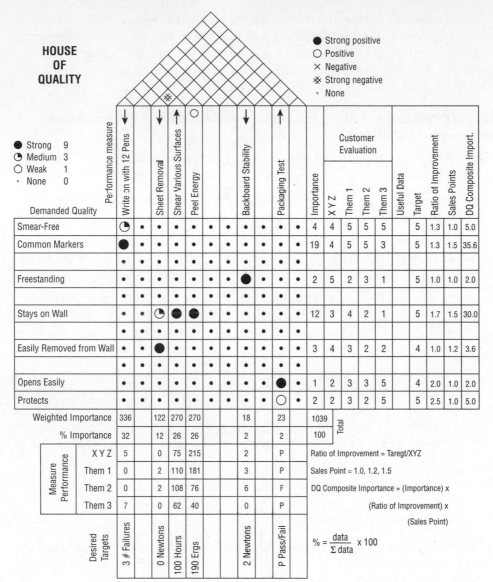

Figure 10-7: Example of a House of Quality for Flip-Chart Pad Quality Requirements[38]

B. Performance Measures are described in the upper-center rectangle.

C. The matrix of these columns and the Demanded Quality rows illustrates how strongly the Performance Measure captures the Quality Requirement.

D. The Desired Target Measures are captured at the very bottom rectangle for each Performance Measure.

E. The *relative importance* of each Quality Characteristic is established in the center rectangle below the matrix of Quality Characteristic and Performance Measure.

F. The Demanded Quality composite importance is calculated on the extreme right of the House of Quality.

The QFD and HOQ enable you to understand the Customer Quality Requirements and prioritize them, identify Product Feature Performance Measures that correlate to the Requirement, and evaluate them in a *controlled* process.

Applying Information Quality to *Product Quality Specification Information*

Tips for Measuring Product Quality Specification IQ

Measuring the Quality of Product Quality Specifications requires two kinds of assessments:

▪ Measure the Quality of the Product Quality Specification Information *Definition* (TIQM P1), and

▪ Measure the Accuracy and other Information Quality Characteristics (TIQM P2) of Product Quality Specification *Information* Content and Presentation.

How to Measure Product Quality Specification IQ and Improve the Product Quality Specification Process

Only *after* you understand accurately your Customer's Quality Requirements and Expectations can you translate these into Product Feature, Function, and Quality Specifications.

In manufactured Products, you have two sets of Specifications:

▪ Engineering (or Design) Product Specifications

▪ Manufacturing (or Production) Process Specifications

From an Information Quality perspective as well as a Customer perspective, the Engineering and Manufacturing Specifications must be defined to meet or exceed the Customer Expectations without adding undue costs to the Product. If you design and produce Products that meet the *Nominal Values* in the respective Quality Characteristics, the Products should consistently meet or exceed Customer Expectations.

The Taguchi Loss Function teaches us that there is a Nominal (or Optimum) Value for Design and Production of each Quality Characteristic. Failure Mode Event Analysis (FMEA) enables the identification of the Mean Time to Failure (MTTF) and Mean Time Between Failure (MTBF). This can help you measure the costs associated with failure based on Variation from the Nominal Value. FMEA also enables you to identify the Accuracy and Precision of Quality Attribute Nominal Values, as you will see in the IQ Assessment process (TIQM P2).

In QFD, the QFD Team must translate the Customer Requirements into Product Specifications that can be measured in a way that ensures that, when produced Products conform to the Specifications, they will also meet Customer expectations.

How to Measure the Quality of the Product Quality Specification Definition

In a TIQM P1 Assessment of Information Definition Quality, you look for Correct, Complete, and Clear Definition of the Product Quality Characteristics and their Nominal Values. That way, Product Developers know how to calculate them *accurately* to the right Precision, and assembly-line Workers or Producers know how to produce or assemble them to the Nominal Values.

Follow the baseline assessment steps in Assessing the Correctness and Clarity of Business Information Definition (TIQM P1)[39] in Chapter 4. Here are some tips for applying this assessment to Product Quality Specifications.

Identify Information Definition Quality Measures

The critical Quality Characteristics for Product Quality Specifications are Accuracy *and* Precision, Completeness, and Clarity for Design and Production conformance. Key measures include:

- Intuitive Business Term Names and the Correct, Complete, and Clear Definition of Product Quality Specification Characteristics. Critical Product Attributes include the following. The term "Item" or "Material" could be substituted for the term "Product" in this list:
  - Product Name
  - Product Identifier (or Product Code)
  - Product Description
  - Product Bill of Material (BOM)
  - Product Feature Name
  - Product Feature Definition
  - Product Feature Attribute Specification Name (such as, length, height, weight, diameter, color, or chemical composition, among others)

- ▪ Product Feature Attribute Specification Definition
- ▪ Product Feature Attribute Specification Value Type (Nominal, Smaller-the-Best, or Larger-the-Best)
- ▪ Product Feature Attribute Specification Unit of Measure (UOM) (such as, meter or foot, kilogram or pound, Color RGB Code or spectrum color code or sound frequency, or hardness scale or chemical formula, for example)
- ▪ Product Feature Attribute Specification Type Nominal Value
- ▪ Product Feature Attribute Specification Type Upper Limit Value
- ▪ Product Feature Attribute Specification Type Lower Limit Value

- ▪ Completeness of Product Quality Specifications as compared with Customer Requirements
- ▪ Clarity in written Definitions and Specification Description
- ▪ Intuitive screen and report design for both novice and experienced Knowledge Workers
- ▪ Help mechanisms that are intuitive and helpful
- ▪ Relevance of Product Quality Specification Information to meet *all* Knowledge Workers' needs for each to successfully perform his or her work

Identify a Set of Information to Assess Definition Quality (TIQM P1.2)

Take the QTC Characteristics (Attribute Specifications) listed previously that have a high correlation to Product Characteristic Quality Satisfaction as compared to overall Product Performance Satisfaction and their subsequent Quality Specification data. See TIQM P1.2 in Chapter 4.

Assess Information Definition Technical Quality (TIQM P1.4)

Measure conformance of Data Names and Definitions of Terms or Data Elements compared to Enterprise Information Standards, Formats, and Name and Definition Clarity and Correctness Requirements. See TIQM P1.4 in Chapter 4.

Assessing Product Information Stakeholder Satisfaction with Data Definition (TIQM P1.6)

The most important measure is that of the Product Information Stakeholders' Satisfaction with the Definition to enable them to perform their respective work effectively. The Information Stakeholders will include Product Design Engineers and Manufacturing Production Engineers to verify the Correctness and Completeness of Definition, and to Verify the Correctness and Precision of the Valid Value domain, especially in arithmetic or scientific data.

The Process activities include:

1. Use the Data Definition Quality/Value Assessment Form described in Chapter 4 (TIQM Step P1.6) for Stakeholders to rate their evaluation of definition Quality

2. Identify a set of Information Stakeholders who depend on Product Information to solicit Feedback. Ensure that you have representatives from all parts of the Product Development Value Circle to *prevent bias* caused by lack of representation across the Value Circle.

3. Collate and analyze the results of your surveys. Establish a Process Improvement initiative. See Chapter 7, "The Step-by-Step Guide to *Improving Information Process Quality*," (TIQM P4) when Process Improvement is required.

How to Measure Accuracy and Other Product Quality Specification Information Quality Characteristics (TIQM P2)

The second assessment is an assessment of the accuracy of selected Product Information. Follow the general steps in "Measuring Accuracy and Other Information Quality Characteristics" in Chapter 5. Here are tips for Product Information Quality measurement.

Identify a Set of Information for Measuring Quality (TIQM P2.1)

Select a set of 10 to 15 Critical-to-Quality Product Specification Attributes to measure for Accuracy. For manufactured goods, these may include the Product component's size, weight, material thickness, or chemical composition as required to achieve Customer Satisfaction, as discovered in the QFD Requirements gathering.

Plan IQ Objectives, Measures, and Tests (TIQM P2.2)

There are two major objectives for assessment:

1. Degree of Accuracy and Precision of the Requirements Specification Nominal Values and Specification Limits compared with the Engineering Design and Manufacturing Process Specifications

2. Degree of Accuracy capability of the Manufacturing Processes to achieve the Nominal Values in Product production

The IQ Characteristics to measure are Accuracy and Precision of the Nominal Values of the Product Feature Specification Nominal Values of the CTQ Attributes, based on their importance to the Customers' Satisfaction. This will be a Physical Accuracy Assessment, measuring the Products that have failed or services with Complaints to evaluate the actual measures of the failed products or services compared to the Nominal Values for Product Production or Service Delivery.

Identify the Information Value Circle (TIQM P2.3)

In order to understand process capability, you must understand the Processes that make up the "Product-Idea-to-Product-Retire" Value Circle, This Value Circle defines all Processes from the Product Concept to Product Requirements to Process Specification Requirements to Product Production and ultimately Product Retirement and Replacement. Document this Value Circle using a Value Circle format,[40] or use data flow or work flow diagrams. Also see the discussion of TIQM P2.3 in Chapter 5.

Determine Information Store or Process to Assess (TIQM P2.4)

For the "Product-Idea-to-Product-Retire" process capability, you will select the Process that produces Product Specification data. Select the Product Specification data produced by the current Product Specification process.

Identify Accuracy Verification Sources (TIQM P2.5)

See Chapter 5 "The Step-by-Step Guide to *Assessing Information Quality*," Step P2.5 for how to identify the *correct* sources to Verify the Accuracy of the Information. For Product Quality, Characteristic Information will be verified in the MTBF analysis of the Products and the actual measures of the Critical-to-Quality Attributes, and the costs incurred in the Product failure.

The Accuracy Verification Sources of optimal Nominal Value are the measurements of the MTBF of Products that conform to the Nominal Value compared to the MTBF of Products that vary from the Nominal Value for CTQ Attributes.

Remember that you are measuring the Accuracy and Precision of the Nominal Value for each CTQ Quality Characteristic Specification.

There are two assessments here:

1. The correlation of the Quality Specification data to the Customer Requirements. Are the Nominal Values for CTQ Attributes consistent with the Customer Requirements for the Product or Product Feature?

2. The Accuracy and Precision of the Nominal Value for the Critical-to-Quality Attributes. The Accuracy of the Nominal Value is determined by the inverse correlation of Products that met the Nominal Value to the costs of Product (or Feature) failure. The costs of failure should be *lowest* in the Products closest to the Nominal Values.

Extract Statistically Valid Sample of Data (TIQM P2.6)

For this assessment of the Accuracy and Precision of the Nominal Value, you must select failed Products and services to measure the CTQ Characteristics that failed. Select an adequate statistical sample of failed Products or service delivery over an appropriate timeframe of service in order to measure the frequency and cost of failure. Compare to the distance from the Nominal Values of the features.

The items must be selected randomly to ensure an unbiased assessment result. See Chapter 5 "The Step-by-Step Guide to *Assessing Information Quality*," Step P2.6: Extract Statistically Valid Sample of Data" for how to determine the size of a sample for your Confidence Level.

Measure Information Quality in the Selected IQ Characteristics (TIQM P2.7)

Measure the Accuracy of the Specification's Nominal Value by comparing the rate and costs of failure correlated to the actual manufacturing Nominal Value for the failed Product Features.

Use FMEA and Mean Time To Failure (MTTF) to measure the Accuracy, or precision, of the Nominal Values for Product Quality Attributes. For example, handles for automobile doors must operate properly over the expected life of the vehicle. Determining an "average" number of door openings, the door handles can be opened and closed by robots to simulate the number of openings/closings that should take place during that lifetime without failure. If you selecting samples of door handles that represent Nominal Values of material or construction, and some that represent various deviations above and below the Nominal Values, the MTTF should be the longest for those that equal or are closest to the Nominal Values. If handles that conform to higher or lower than the Nominal Values perform the best, the original expected Nominal Value is not Accurate and should be adjusted.

Many Quality Attributes will conform to a bell curve in which the "Nominal-Is-Best" Specification value applies. This is represented in Figure 10-8.

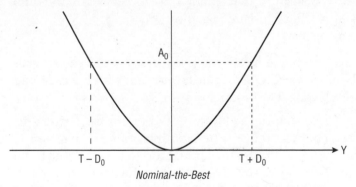

Figure 10-8: Nominal-the-Best Target Specification Value[41]

If the Nominal Value *is* the best value, the Products made with conformance to the Nominal Value will perform the best. By measuring failed Products and comparing the Actual Produced Value to the Nominal (target) Value, one can compare the failure rate at various Actual Values of each Product to the failure rate of Products conforming to the Nominal Value. See Figure 10-9.

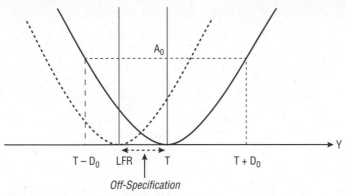

Figure 10-9: Inaccurate Nominal Value Specification Based on MTTF

If you find that the Target Value is not the true Nominal Value, you will need to correct the Nominal Value and recalibrate the equipment as necessary to achieve it. Before you do this, however, you should conduct a Plan-Do-Check/Study-Act improvement initiative to ensure that you have found and eliminated the Root Causes of the Variation. The Root Cause could be in the Specification Process or in the Production Process.

It should be noted that not all Quality Characteristics and Variations are centered around a normal distribution (bell curve). Some Quality Characteristics conform to "Smaller-the-Better" (see Figure 10-10) such as amount of greenhouse gases emitted from an engine, or inaccurate data values in a Product record, or "Larger-the-Better" (see Figure 10-11) such as the heat resistance of the Space Shuttle heat shield tiles.

Interpret and Report Information Quality (TIQM P2.8)

- Report the data in the form of number or percent of defects measured. Use a statistical Quality Control Chart of the process measured over time. See Chapter 5, "The Step-by-Step Guide to *Assessing Information Quality*," TIQM Process Step P2.8. "Interpret and Report Information Quality."

- Communicate Assessment Reports to Engineers, Product Developers, and Production Control Specialists who calibrate the Production equipment so that Quality Teams can analyze and implement the proper Improvements.

How to Improve Product Quality Specification Process Quality

Once you have ensured that you have understood the Customer's *real* Requirements and expectations, and once you have ensured that you have translated those Requirements into measurable Product Specifications that can be manufactured to, you should be on the right track for satisfying Customers.

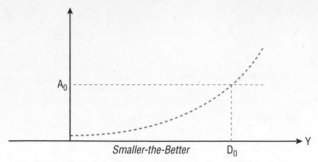

Figure 10-10: Smaller-the-Better Quality Loss Function[42]

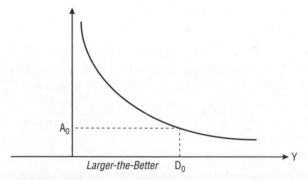

Figure 10-11: Larger-the-Better Quality Loss Function[43]

Remember that Customers can be fickle in a rapidly changing world with new technologies and new options coming at them at an ever-accelerating pace.

Define a Project for Product Quality Specification Process Improvement

Follow TIQM P4.1 in Chapter 7 to establish an Improvement Initiative. The specific process addressed here is "Define Product Feature Quality Specifications." This also applies to "Define Production Process Quality Specifications."

Follow your organization's normal project planning procedures to establish a Process Improvement initiative and:

1. Identify the Process Owner who is accountable for the process and for implementing improvements.

2. Identify those who are part of Information Production (Information Producers, Transcriptionists, or Translators), such as Product Developers, Design Engineers, and Product Catalogers who will participate in the Root Cause Analysis and Process Improvement definition activities.

3. Identify and assign a Process Improvement facilitator (Process Owner).

Develop the project plan for conducting the Process Improvement activities of the Plan-Do-Check/Study-Act cycle. See Chapter 7, TIQM P4.1 for general guidelines.

Plan a Product Quality Specification Process Improvement

The first part of planning (TIQM P4.2) is to analyze and identify the Root Cause or Causes of the problem you seek to solve, such as "out-of-date content." See TIQM P4.2.1 "Analyze Root Causes of the IQ Problem" in Chapter 7. Analysis of the Root Causes requires understanding the needs and expectations of the Customers and facilitating the identification of *precipitating* causes to drill down to and isolate the Root Causes.

Identify Causes of Poor Product Quality Specification Information

TIQM P4.2.1 walks you through this. Examples of (Root) Causes include:

- Lack of attention to Information as an integral component of the Product Specification
- Specification and Machine Calibration are in *incompatible* units of measure.
- *Lack* of Management Accountability for Product Specification data
- *Lack* of a Change Control Procedure for Product data
- *Lack* of Engineer's or Product Developer's understanding of Customer needs
- Production control lacks the ability to translate Specifications to equipment Calibration.
- Defective process for capturing Customers' Requirements and Expectations
- Defective process for translating Customers' Requirements into Product Specifications
- Lack of engineering knowledge necessary to translate Customer Requirements into specific Engineering Requirement Specifications with Accurate Nominal Values
- Defective process for translating Product Specifications into Process Controls
- Production equipment cannot be calibrated to *proper precision*.
- Product Catalogers *misinterpret* the Engineering Specifications and Nominal Values.
- Computer-Aided Design (CAD) software lacks the capability to capture the Specification Values with *appropriate precision*.
- Artificial deadlines to get the Product to market, result in neglecting to discover Customer Requirements and Expectations.

See Figure 10-12 for how these potential causes would look on a Cause-and-Effect Diagram. Use an Ishikawa Diagram to define the IQ Effect (problem) and to collect, analyze, identify, and confirm the applicable Root Cause or Causes.

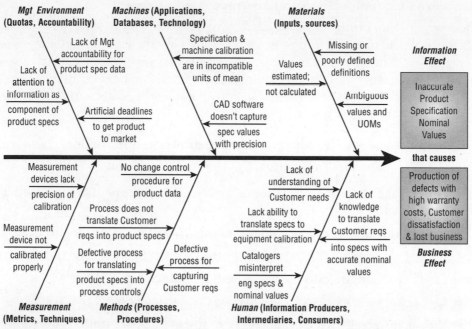

Figure 10-12: Cause-and-Effect Diagram for Poor Product Specification Information

NOTE These are illustrative Causes based on actual Root Cause Analysis. Each defect type may have different causes within different organizations. Ensure that you conduct a rigorous Root Cause Analysis to ensure that you understand and isolate the real Root Causes of the defects in your Product Specification data. Resolving the wrong "Root Cause" will sub-optimize your Process Improvement at best, and cause it to fail at worst.

The second part of planning is to define Process Improvements that eliminate the cause of defects described in the IQ effect. See TIQM 4.2B "Define Process Improvements to Prevent Recurrence of the Defects" in Chapter 7.

Identify Preventive Actions for Product Quality Specification Information Defects (TIQM P4.2.2)

Preventive actions include:

- Managers of Product Developers must be held *accountable* for the Quality of Product developers' and Product Quality Specification Information.

Once Managers have accountability written into their job descriptions and are *held* Accountable for Information Quality, and once training and resources are provided to Product Developers, then they may also be *held* accountable for their Information.

▪ Product Developers should use QFD to identify Customer Requirements and translate them into Product Quality Characteristic Specifications, and verify them in prototypes.

▪ Quality assurance tests should be put in place to ensure the Quality of:

  ▪ Customer Quality Requirements

  ▪ The correlation of Product Engineering Specifications to Customer Requirements

  ▪ The correlation of Process Specifications to Engineering Specifications to ensure that Products are produced to conform to valid Product Specifications. This involves analysis of MTTF to ensure the Correctness and Precision of Nominal Values for Quality Characteristics.

  ▪ Customers' Experience with the Products

To improve Product Specification and Production Quality to prevent losses, there are two major approaches:

▪ The first is to find processes that are producing Products "off-target," and Improve the Requirements Specification and/or the Production Process to hit the Nominal Value consistently. This is illustrated in Figure 10-13.

▪ The second is to find Processes that have wide *variability* and reduce the sources causing variation, as illustrated in Figure 10-14.

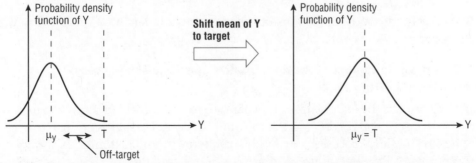

Figure 10-13: Reduce Quality Loss by Improving Mean Performance to Nominal Value.[44]

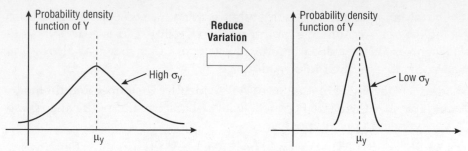

Figure 10-14: Reduce Quality Loss by Reducing Variation.[45]

Do Implement "Product Quality Specification Process" Improvements (TIQM P4.3)

The "Do" activity implements the Product Quality Specification Process improvements in a controlled way. Steps include:

1. Define or enhance your Product Quality Specification Process. Ensure that it is a complete and instructive process definition.

2. Identify a mix of Product Engineers or Developers for the *controlled implementation* of the "Improved" Process.

3. Provide Training to the Product Developers who will be testing the new Process.

4. Have the Product Developers follow the new Process for the next new Products on which they work.

5. Have the Product Developers keep detailed notes as they follow the Process. This should include ease of use comments, description of any gaps, Lessons Learned from the new Process, and Critical Success Factors they may have identified.

Next, you will study the results of the *controlled* implementation of the new Process for its *effectiveness*.

Check and Study Impact of Product Quality Specification Process Improvements (TIQM P4.4)

You can compare the experiences of the "improved" Product launches and experience of those developed using the original Process. This will require time to see the Production Process go through a cycle to gather Customer Experience at the points of Product failure — if any — in the new Product launches.

The key metrics will include:

▪ Customer Satisfaction with the new Products

▪ Rigor of the Product Quality Specification Process to improve the definition of the Nominal Values to enable zero-defect Product Production in the first pass

Act to Standardize "Product Quality Specification Process" Improvements (TIQM P4.5)

This formalizes the new *standardized* process for Product Quality Specification and rolls it out to all Product development.

Document the Knowledge you have gained from each IQ Process Improvement initiative:

- Lessons Learned from the Root Cause Analysis

- Critical Success Factors learned from the Process Improvement "Do" implementation

- Lessons Learned from the final "Act" to put the process in control and roll it out to the rest of the enterprise

NOTE Measure the Cost of Poor Information Quality, before you make Improvements (TIQM P3.3-6) *and* afterwards (TIQM P3.7, see Chapter 3) to document your Return on Investment. This helps you confirm the value of your IQ improvements and sustain management support.

BEST PRACTICES

WORLD'S FIRST COMPUTER-ON-A-CHIP COMPANY STANDARDIZES BILL-OF-MATERIAL (BOM) AND SAVES MONEY WHILE INCREASING EFFECTIVENESS

The Problem: The world's first computer-on-a-chip company grew at an accelerated rate by demand. Its growth got stymied by an out-of-control Bill-of-Materials (BOM) process, trying to represent thousands of permutations of form, fit, and function into a 25-digit part number. With no standardized BOM structure, engineers began introducing many non-form, -fit, and -function attributes, such as "where manufactured," into the part number without control. Different groups cobbled together loosely managed standards such as using the 13th position of the part number to mean something specific that was different from what others used it for.

The Best Practice: Management realized that they needed to design and control Product information. A new Product structure blueprint needed to be highly specified; in addition to providing structure for Product manufacturing, it also became used to drive policy, help in decision making, and serve as a standard guide to reconstruct the backbone of the company.

How They Did It: Management created a nonpartisan, cross-organization volunteer Team, founded on the idea that they must establish true Requirements for the life cycle of the Product and all its parts. This blueprint would guide all future reconstruction and use. Representatives from every part of the organization

(continued)

WORLD'S FIRST COMPUTER-ON-A-CHIP COMPANY STANDARDIZES BILL-OF-MATERIAL (BOM) AND SAVES MONEY WHILE INCREASING EFFECTIVENESS *(continued)*

participated in the definition of the Product structure (Bill-of-Materials). The following list describes the magnitude of the change required:

- **Cross-functional Information Design Teams**
- **Standard definitions and business rules for the top 80 percent of the entities and attributes that had to be signed off on by *value chain* Executives**
- **Standard conceptual and detailed Information Models had to be signed off by *value chain* Executives.**
- **Executive agreement for all current and future efforts to manage Product structure information to adopt the new design and policy**
- **Governing processes used to control yearly funding of reconstruction efforts**
- **Governing processes to control disparate attempts to resolve Product structure issues**
- **Multiyear programs to migrate planning systems one at a time**
- **Multiyear programs to migrate execution systems one at a time**
- **Cross-functional governing Teams to judge ongoing compliance with the design**
- **Educational classes on the new processes, polices, and governing models**

KEY LEARNINGS:

- **Master data, such as your company's Product structure, is used horizontally across the many parts of the company. Build an Enterprise-Strength, cross-functional set of design Requirements with all the key Stakeholders (including terms, definitions, business rules, and authorized sources).**
- **Large efforts to redesign your company's master data will require a governing process that will outlast organizational policy. You need senior Executive support and policy written at the same level as the company's security, hiring, or financial policies.**
- **The design must be widely known and accepted across the Enterprise.**
- **To try to solve silo organization problems, turn independent efforts into incremental efforts, following the single master design for your master data.**
- **Quality master data does not come from *after-the-fact, reverse engineering* efforts to homogenize or harmonize disparate sources. It ultimately comes from good solid cross-functional designs and a means to realize the ultimate sources with the least amount of time and money.**

Conclusions and Benefits: This truly Enterprise approach to Enterprise Information enabled us to use advance planning solutions for long- and short-term planning, and align supply-and-demand efforts across the Supply Chain, as well as create a cleaner view of the Product from the Customer's perspective. It helped not only the top-line financial numbers but also the bottom-line profit by reducing the number of systems and processes required to handle the old, obsolete embedded-meaning part numbers. The company has even worked with a large enterprise resource planning (ERP) company to redefine their master data efforts to include an extendable enterprise design. This approach can be applied to all master data. This Fortune 500 Company is now redesigning other master data subjects such as Customer, Supplier, and Employee. The model has helped to redefine transactional data, especially in the area of planning transactions such as forecasting, planning, and scheduling.

True High-Quality Information does not happen by accident or mutate from a poor design in the first place. Design quality in now, and you will reap the benefits of highly Productive data for years to come.

ASTON MARTIN CREATES "COST TO KNOWLEDGE RATIO"

Aston Martin creates a "Cost to Knowledge Ratio" to identify the number of items built from the first time it receives information that there is an issue to when the issue is resolved.

In order to reduce Warranty liability and increase Customer satisfaction, Aston Martin developed a process called the "Cost to Knowledge Ratio" to minimize its cost to knowledge ratio, that is, the number of units built from when it first receives data identifying an issue to when the issue is resolved. The formula is:

$$\text{Cost to Knowledge Ratio} = \frac{\text{Number of Units at Risk}}{\text{Cost of Each Repair}}$$

- A low ratio is characteristic of a system that has *interdependent* data. The knowledge is inherent within the data layer so that the total business cost is a function of the reporting delay.

- A high ratio is characteristic of a system that has *disparate* data. The total business cost is a function of the time and resource required to understand the significance of the data. The knowledge is inferred from the data during post-Warranty acceptance processing.

The ratio indicates how efficient the overall Warranty process actually is by taking into account the delay caused by both visible and hidden business processes. Where the ratio is consistent across issue categories, the data

(continued)

ASTON MARTIN CREATES "COST TO KNOWLEDGE RATIO" *(continued)*

content quality for these categories has been optimized relative to the business Warranty process even though the business process itself may not have been optimized.

Optimizing the business process for Warranty cost management requires consistent and repeatable issue categorization at the point of data entry, translating the technician's knowledge into a standardized data set that meets the Knowledge Worker's Information Quality expectations. To achieve this, the interface must first impart the Knowledge Worker's data content Quality Requirements to the technician by controlling the claim content and detail. The data itself then becomes the control by which the technician is guided to assign the correct category.

With consistent and repeatable issue categorization, the business's confidence in what the data actually represents increases. Aston Martin Warranty achieved cost reduction through reduced time lines and informed decision making.

Summary

Now that you have the capability to identify and capture Customer Quality Requirements for Products and Services and can define Quality Specifications that will achieve Customer Satisfaction in the Product Experience, we tackle the challenges of Supply Chain Value Circle "Forecast-to-Satisfied-Customer," in the next chapter.

Information Quality Applied to Supply Chain Management: *"Forecast-to-Satisfied-Customer"*

> *"Our social mission as a manufacturer is only realized when products reach, are used by, and satisfy the customer"*
> **Konosuke Matsushita**[1]

Introduction to Information Quality in the Supply Chain

This chapter focuses on the Forecasting, Production Scheduling, Production, Delivery, In-use Service, and Product Disposition in Supply Chain Management.

Supply Chain Management can be very complex when there are many independent entities or trading partners involved. This is further complicated by the many logistic and external factors and variables that can cause failure or sub-optimization.

The Supply Chain is an end-to-end set of activities that begins with requests or Requirements for Products and services from or for end-Consumers and ends with satisfied — or unsatisfied — Customers. From the beginning request, the Production work must be scheduled and controlled from materials and components until the Finished Product is produced. Delivery Processes move the Product to various Trading Partners until the finished Products and services get delivered to the end-Consumer.

Information Quality problems with Information exchanged among Trading Partners cause Supply Chain Management to fail. Problems caused by disparately defined Information and incompatible Information Models cause miscommunication throughout the Supply Chain.

Uncontrollable variables, such as weather events, economic downturns or upturns, political events, and union work stoppages that shut down assembly lines or transportation, can cause disruption in the overall Supply Chain. Many of those variables are not captured because there is not a "natural" process within the organization to capture such information, or it is ignored because it is not perceived as important. However, this Information is critical to plan for, and avert problems in the delivery of Products and services. Information Brokers who specialize in various types of externally created or observed events may be a source for purchase.

Key definitions include:

> *Supply Chain:* The distribution channel of a Product, from sourcing to delivery to the end-Consumer (also known as a Value Chain but called 'a Value Circle'), and is typically comprised of multiple companies that coordinate Supply Chain activities

> *Supply Chain Management:* The oversight and coordination of materials, finances, and Information within and among companies as they move in processes from Supplier to manufacturer to wholesaler to retailer to the end-Consumer through service and to Product disposal

The Supply Chain Value Circle: *"Forecast-to-Satisfied-Customer"*

The Supply Chain is called different things in different organizations, such as "Order-to-Cash," "Quote-to-Cash," or "Promise-to-Delivery." However, we will refer to it as *"Forecast-to-Satisfied-Customer"* for two reasons. First, it puts the rightful focus on the *end-Customer,* without whom you would not be in business, and secondly, it is a Value Circle that must benefit the Customer — not just the Enterprise and its Shareholders.

The *"Forecast-to-Satisfied-Customer"* Value Circle continues the *"Product-Idea-to-Product-Retire"* Value Circle, managing the operational planning, Production, distribution, and Customer-satisfaction experience of the business. Figure 11-1 illustrates the Supply Chain in a multi-tier manufacturing through retail to Consumer environment.

DISCLAIMER

The purpose of this chapter *IS NOT* to teach you how to manage the Supply Chain.

The purpose *IS* to guide you through the processes of measuring and improving the Quality of the Information processes that create, maintain, and deliver *Information* about Forecasting Demand, Logistics, In-use service, Warranty and Customer feedback.

You learn how to apply Quality Principles to the Supply Chain so that you can improve the Supply Chain Value Circle, *"Forecast-to-Satisfied-Customer."*

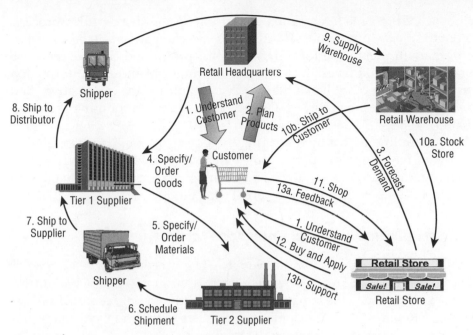

Figure 11-1: "Forecast-to-Satisfied-Customer" Value Circle

Because much Information is exchanged among the Trading Partners, there is a critical need to manage the Information *across enterprise boundary lines*; that is, to manage the *extended* Enterprise.

The most significant barrier to Enterprise effectiveness and efficiency comes when the Enterprise allows its divisions or organization units to operate as *independent* Entities with no regard as to how the units are inter-dependent on each other for Enterprise effectiveness. When organization units set *departmental goals*, the goals invariably become *department-centric*, often *disassociated* with the Mission or aim of the Enterprise and the needs of the end-Customers. When organization units ignore or minimize the capture of Information required for their downstream organization units, the "enterprise" Value Circle begins to fail.

Downstream organization units must create their own Information-capture processes if their upstream Information-Supplier departments fail to capture the additional Information when they are at the natural point of Knowledge Capture. For example, Marketing needs a marketing channel, a promotional campaign to which a Customer responded to, along with the Customer's age (birth date), marital status, and household income for future marketing campaigns. The Call Center, however, may not capture it because of their Order volume goals. Finance on the other hand, requires financial Information about Orders and Sales.

With a volume goal or quota, the Call Center may not see it as its responsibility to capture the additional — and *seemingly* unnecessary birth date, marital status, and household income Information to perform the "Order capture" process. Without the *profile* Information, future marketing campaigns will be less effective, or marketing must perform the additional profile and channel response Information while Finance has to acquire the financial and risk Information externally at higher costs than if the Call Center captured the Information. And if the Product Price is not correct, Financial Billing and Accounting Processes will fail.

The bottom line is that by managing the Enterprise on a department-by-department basis forces departments — inadvertently or consciously — to compete against each other, rather than working together in synergy or as an ensemble, to compete against the external competitors!

The External Supply Chain: Enterprise Interdependency

The Enterprise must get its internal Supply Chain in control to be an *effective* Business Partner in the larger "extended-enterprise" Supply Chain. We address Information Quality in the Supply Chain for the Products or Services from the Customer's Requirements to originating Suppliers to the end-Consumers' use and Customer support and Product disposal.

Supply Chain Management is a virtual necessity for every business and not-for-profit organization to accomplish its work and achieve its Mission, whether delivering physical Products or intangible Services or Information. It is a reality that no organization is a truly *standalone entity*, existing in and of itself. Virtually all commercial, governmental, and not-for-profit institutions are interdependent on other organizations to survive and thrive. Some organizations extract or acquire raw materials. Others may "process" raw materials into usable components or materials that are combined into components (possibly by yet another organization) for their Customers. Those organizations may assemble the materials with other components into "Finished" Products. These Products ultimately get shipped to retailers, dealers, or end-Consumers. And at the same time yet other organizations provide services for distribution, training, office supply, or Product or equipment repair or maintenance in support of an organization's core processes or Value Circles.

This chapter addresses the Information and its Quality to support the operational activities in the Supply Chain "Forecast-to-Satisfied-Customer" required to:

- Forecast, Schedule, and Produce Products and Services to meet Demand;
- Distribute and Deliver Products and Services to the Retailer or to the Customer;

- Maximize the Customer Experience in the assembly, use, servicing, maintenance, support, and Product disposition through the life of the Products and Services;

- Enable internal personnel to plan, produce, and service Products and Services;

- Evaluate *effectiveness* of Products and Services and;

- Determine Product enhancements, replacement, or retirement.

Supply Chain Interdependencies and the Value-Add Proposition

Figure 11-2 illustrates the *interdependencies* of Internal Business Areas within an Enterprise or Business Partners in the Supply Chain.

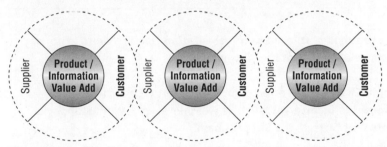

Figure 11-2: The Interdependencies of Business Areas or Business Partners in a Supply Chain

Each organization participates in roles as Supplier and/or Customer from the originating Supplier organization to the end-Consumer of the Product. Within an organization, there is an "internal" Supply Chain as a manufacturer's Product moves through the Production processes in specific workstations or business areas. Each Production process has internal Suppliers (the preceding process or processes) and internal Customers (the receiving process or processes). All processes are *interdependent* on each other to produce the "Product" with Quality. Each process in the Supply Chain is the "Customer" of the preceding process, completes its Value-Adding work, and becomes the Supplier for the next process.

Each organization is a link in the macro Supply Chain. Each link must operate properly, adding Value and providing its end result to its immediate Customer throughout the Value Circle until the end-Customers receive Quality Products and services.

U.S. HOME CONSTRUCTION SUPPLY CHAIN SEVERELY DEPRESSED BY THE SUB-PRIME MORTGAGE MELTDOWN IN 2007

Lenders that had become addicted to offering mortgages featuring low initial rates of interest that skyrocketed after a few years or even a few months have triggered a tsunami of mortgage defaults and home foreclosures that "set the stage for borrowers to default in massive numbers and lenders to take a bath." The July 2007 foreclosure rate due to defaults was double that of the year before.[2]

This in turn has caused the homebuilding industry to face excess Supply and lowered Demand as lenders tossed stacks of high-risk applications in the wastebasket after seeing default rates soar.

"A number of investment firms had strongly touted 'bundled' mortgage funds containing a high percentage of sub-prime loans. Now, those once-popular funds are tanking as investors realize there is no way to place a value on the underlying mortgages."[3]

NOTE This is a problem of Information Presentation Quality. There is no way to understand the value or risk of the "investment."

NOTE The Supply Chain can be affected by events not within the actual Supply Chain processes themselves, such as weather events, work stoppages, or political events that "affect" the Supply Chain.

Internally, each business area or workstation involved in the internal Supply Chain must also perform its work with Quality from the Supplier business area or workstation to its Customer business area or workstation. Defects introduced in any business area or workstation diminish the Quality of the Finished Product.

Quality occurs in the Supply Chain when all *interdependent* Customers-turned-Suppliers (both organizational Customers and internal Business Areas or Workstations) perform their work by adding *Value*, eliminating defects, and by minimizing cost-adding activities *from the perspective of the end-Consumer.*

Cost-adding-only activities reduce the Quality of the Product while increasing costs that must ultimately be paid by the end-Consumer. Any reduced Quality from these activities can cause Warranty Failure and *dissatisfaction* among both downstream Business Areas or Workstations and end-Customers, reducing Customer Lifetime Value throughout the Supply Chain.

The Supply Chain begins and ends with the end-Customer. You must understand Customer Needs and Expectations for a given Product idea in order to develop Products, Services — and Information — that Meet or Exceed their Expectations. The Supply Chain Value Circle does not end with delivery. You must continue with follow-up Support, Service, Product Maintenance, Warranty Service, and Product Disposition as necessary. You also need *active listening* to Customer Feedback to identify their needs for improvements to Products and Services.

Each pairing of Entities in the Supply Chain Value Circle represents a Supplier-Customer pair. But, it is not enough to just meet one's immediate Customer needs. Every organization in the Supply Chain must develop and deliver their Components, Materials, Support, Service and for example, that meet the stated Requirements and unstated Expectations of the end-Consumer for all organizations within the Supply Chain to be successful and remain competitive. Therefore, the end-Consumer must always be placed in the center of the Supply Chain Value Circle.

While difficult in complex or hazardous material cases, the Supply Chain must be managed and controlled for the benefit of the end-Consumers, as well as for the other Stakeholders of Employees, Investors, and Communities.

DEADLY GERMS AND TOXINS MISHANDLED BY HIGH-SECURITY LABS

From 2003 to 2007, "U.S. laboratories that handle the world's deadliest germs and toxins have had more than 100 accidents and missing shipments ... and the number is increasing as more labs do the work."[4]

While regulators say the public has not been at risk from these incidents, the truth is that some of the toxins and germs can cause illnesses that have no cures. The 72 substances, called "select agents," represent germs and toxins responsible for some of the world's worst medical tragedies for humans and animals. This is but one category of materials that must have zero defects in handling and shipping.

The number of incidents has doubled from 2004 to 2007, and at the same time the number of labs that handle these "select agents" has doubled as well, increasing the risk to the public.

A GAO report says, "No single federal agency ... has the mission to track the overall number of these labs .... Consequently, no agency is responsible for determining the risks associated with the proliferation of these labs."[5]

It is of little use for Suppliers to delight their purchasing retail Customers if the Products fail to meet *end-Consumer expectations*. Unhappy end-Customers and lost sales cascade all the way back to the beginning of the Supply Chain.

Categories of Supply Chain Information Requiring Quality

There are several categories of Information in the Supply Chain to which Quality principles must be applied:

- **Customer Product Requirements:** Information about your Customers' Quality Needs and Expectations for your Products. If you have missing or inaccurate understanding of Customer Requirements, your Products can disappoint, losing Customers. This set of Information is addressed in Chapter 10, "Information Quality Applied to Product Development: *"Product-Idea-to-Product-Retire."*

▪ **Product Engineering and/or Design Specifications, Product Manufacturing Specifications, and Bill-of-Materials (BOM):** Information that provides the Specifications, Product Structure, and Procedures for the manufacture of Products. This is also treated in Chapter 10.

▪ **Forecast (projected sales) and Demand (Orders or Sales):** Information that projects your Customers' expected purchases (Forecast) of your Products and records their actual orders and purchases (Demand). High Forecasts cause you to over produce and increase costs of inventory. Low Forecasts cause you to have shortages when Demand exceeds Inventory, with missed sales or increased costs of rush orders for Suppliers and accelerated Production costs. Inaccurate Order Information, such as wrong Items, Quantities, or UOM discrepancies increase complaints, returns, and alienated Customers.

▪ **Supplier Component or Material and Competitor Product Information:** Information your Suppliers provide about their Products and Materials along with Order Lead Times. Errors in Accuracy, Precision, or Interpretation in their description, lead time, and specs can cause failure in your Products or Product delivery. What else is sold as alternatives to your Products? Lack of Knowledge can cause *missed or lost* Opportunities. But what you do know about Competitor Products can help you to know how to market your Products, or what you need to improve to better compete in the marketplace.

▪ **Order, Logistics, and Inventory Information:** Information about quantity-on-hand, on-order, and location. Logistics Information addresses the location and movement of Products and/or materials. Overstated Inventory numbers can cause unexpected stock-outs and higher costs of rush orders or missed sales, whereas understated Inventory numbers increase Costs of Inventory and Scrap due to shelf-life expiration. Inaccurate location information leads to increased costs of hunting, finding, and moving items.

▪ **Product and Package Measurement Information:** Information about the dimensions, weights, stacking patterns of Product packages or cases. Inaccurate information increases the costs of storage, sub-optimizing transportation caused by over, under or odd-sized packaging that can lead to damaged Products.

▪ **Product and Promotional Marketing and Owner or Instruction Manual Information:** (Note: These categories of Information are treated in Chapter 14, "Information Quality Applied to Document & Knowledge Management,") Section "Applying Quality to Technical, Procedural, and Documentation Writing."

Supply Chain Information Stakeholders

Throughout the different organizations and within any single organization, there are many Information Stakeholders in roles of Information Consumers and/or Information Producers. Failure to provide Quality Information can cause the Supply Chain processes to fail, sometimes with catastrophic results.

Internal Information Stakeholders

Internal Information Stakeholders and their Information interests are found in Table 11-1:

Table 11-1: Internal Information Stakeholders and Their Information Interests

INTERNAL STAKEHOLDERS	INTERNAL STAKEHOLDERS' INFORMATION INTERESTS
Engineers	Customer Requirements Information to design Products or Components. They create Product Feature Quality Specifications to meet Requirements.
Manufacturing Personnel	Product Requirements and Process Specifications and Process Controls to make or assemble components or material into other components or finished Products
Quality Management Personnel	Quality Requirements to ensure Quality is designed in and achieved in the various processes of development, Production, and Delivery
Service Product Developers	Market, Demand, and Customer Requirements to create new services, such as financial, insurance, or investment "Products"
Catalogers	Product Information that they create for sharing with Customer Trading Partners so they can evaluate and select the right materials for their Products
Contract Officers	Contract and Product Information to develop formal relationships with Trading Partners for buying raw materials and selling Products
Procurement Staff	Supply Information, contract terms, and Supply pricing to order goods or supplies from Suppliers
Sales Representatives or Agents	Customer, Product and Pricing Information for understanding Customer Requirements in order to sell the *right* goods and services to Customers
Marketers	Product Feature and Differentiator Information to advertise and promote Products and assess emerging Customer Requirements, along with sales and Customer feedback Information to evaluate Marketing Campaigns

(continued)

Table 11-1 *(continued)*

INTERNAL STAKEHOLDERS	INTERNAL STAKEHOLDERS' INFORMATION INTERESTS
Accountants	Cost and Sale Price Information to establish margins in Production and sales
Warehouse Staff	Stack patterns, packaging Requirements, shelf life, and material safety information, required for worker safety and to prevent damage
Transportation Drivers	Material Safety Information, to understand proper handling and disposition

External Information Stakeholders

External Information Stakeholders and their Information Interests are cited in Table 11-2.

Table 11-2: External Information Stakeholders and Their Information Interests

EXTERNAL INFORMATION STAKEHOLDERS	INFORMATION INTERESTS
End-Consumers	The first and last people in the Supply Chain, whose needs and expectations, including their Information Requirements, must be met by the end Products and Services. These include Requirements conformance, Assembly and Operating Instructions, Warranty, Service, and Disposal Information.
Trade Partner Buyers	Product Description, including Features and Differentiators, Quality, and Price Information to purchase Products or materials that meet their end-Consumers' needs
Supplier Sales Representatives or Agents	Supply Materials and Quality Requirements to produce Products for your Customers to meet their Expectations
Supplier Product Catalogers	Product Specification Information of their Products compared to your Customers' Requirements to ensure Products meet Customer expectations
Logistics Partners	Shipment pick-up and delivery address, times, routing Requirements, and container Requirements to move the materials or Products accurately and efficiently
Regulatory Authority Compliance Personnel	Industry, applicable regulation Requirements, compliance inspection results, and conformance Information

EXTERNAL INFORMATION STAKEHOLDERS	INFORMATION INTERESTS
Communities in which the Enterprise Resides	Economic and environmental impact Information to ascertain the organization's social and environmental Stewardship
Shareholders	Business and Financial Performance Information to make buy or sell decisions

Applying Information Quality in the Supply Chain requires a focus on both internal and external Customers and their Information Requirements. Without Quality Requirements to execute the Supply Chain processes from planning for Production, the processes may fail. This will decrease Customer satisfaction with the Products or Services through their expected lifetimes.

"Forecast-to-Satisfied-Customer" Value Circle Process Activities

Every Value Circle begins and ends with the Customer. From a Product idea, you must understand the Customer Requirements and Expectations in order to develop Products, Services — and Information — that meets or exceeds their Expectations.

It is of little use for a Supplier to delight its *purchasing* Retail Customer if the Products or services fail to meet the retailer's (now in the role of Supplier) end-Consumer expectations. Lost Sales and Customers cause the retailer to reduce their purchases from their immediate Supplier, cascading all the way back to the most upstream Supplier.

The "Forecast-to-Satisfied-Customer" Value Circle includes the following 13 Processes. The processes are described following the list, along with the Information Requirements and IQ issues within each process. The processes include the following:

1. Understand Direct- and end-Customer Product and Information Needs and Expectations.
2. Plan and Develop Products to Meet Customer Expectations.
3. Forecast Product Demand.
4. Specify or Order Goods from Tier 1 Supplier(s).
5. Tier 1 Supplier(s) Specifies and Orders Goods from Tier 2 Supplier(s).

6. Tier 2 Suppliers Schedule Shipments to Tier 1 Supplier.

7. Tier 2 Supplier Ships to Tier 1 Supplier (Tier 2's Customer).

8. Produce Finished Goods.

9. Shipper Delivers to Retailer Warehouse or Distribution Center.

10. Distributor or Warehouse Stocks Store, or Ships to Consumer.

11. Customer Shops and Evaluates Product.

12. Customer Buys Product — or Not.

13a. Customer Provides Feedback, Complaint, or Compliment.

13b. Supplier Supports Customer.

1. Supplier Understands Customer and (end-Consumer) [Better].

1. Understand Direct- and End-Customer Product and Information Needs and Expectations

Organizations, at both an Enterprise level and at a local level, must understand their Customers' Needs and Expectations of the Products they offer. While this will develop over the life of the Customer Relationships, it is critical to understand this as part of the "Product-Idea-to-Product-Retire" Value Circle.

> **NOTE** This and the following process are critical processes in the Supply Chain. How to apply IQ principles to Customer Requirements Information Quality are addressed in Chapter 10.

2. Plan and Develop Products to Meet Customer Expectations

> **NOTE** See Chapter 10 for how to apply IQ principles to Product Specification Information Quality to meet Customer Requirements.

3. Forecast Product Demand

This process seeks to understand accurately the quantity of Products to produce or make available for sale to optimize the Production cycle. Its goal is to minimize the problems caused by:

- Over-Production with its additional cost of unsold inventory or lost revenue in liquidation sales or disposal

- Under-Production with its lost opportunity in sales and costs of rush Production or delivery

- Mismatch in Forecast data definition, such as Unit-of-Measure (UOM), Product Specification optimum values, and Forecast quantity differences, can lead to inaccurate Forecasts.

Process Activities

Once you have Products defined and can produce them, the challenge is to *accurately* Forecast Product Demand and ensure you and your Suppliers have the *capacity* to deliver throughout the critical links in the Supply Chain.

Accurate Forecasts require careful understanding of the variables that influence Demand, both internal *and* external to the organization, such as weather conditions and labor actions.

Common Information Quality Issues

- Inaccurate or untimely projections from your Customers of their Forecast of Demand for their Products, along with the algorithms and methods for Forecasting can cause you to over-produce, increasing costs of inventory and disposal, or under-produce, causing shortages with costs of rush shipments and Customer alienation.

- Inaccurate history of Customer's past Product purchases prevents you from correcting inaccurate Forecasts based on known variables.

- Inaccurate or untimely economic, climatic, political, and other factors that influence Consumer behavior, such as concerns about the economy and Supplier behavior in the Supply Chain (labor issues and materials' availability, for example) can cause errors in calculated estimated Demand for Products.

- Inaccurate understanding of Consumer Requirements and Consumer Experience with prior and current Product purchases can cause you to mis-estimate actual Demand, with costs of over- or under-Production.

- Inaccurate Bill-of-Materials and Requirements for component materials can cause Supply order errors of materials that do not conform to your and your Customers' Requirements.

- Inaccurate Supplier *lead times* for materials or components can cause Production failure with materials arriving too late or too early.

- Inaccurate *shelf life* of Materials and Products leads to shelf-life expiration and costs of disposal that can cause unhappy Customers and Lost Business.

4. Specify or Order Goods from Tier 1 Supplier(s)

An organization must define its Product Specifications that it will produce, including the Bill-of-Materials (BOM) for the materials and components from which it will produce its Products. This requires a clear understanding of its Suppliers of Materials or Components, along with the lead times required to get the various Supply items from its Suppliers so that it minimizes inventory, yet *prevents* inventory shortages through Just-in-Time Inventory management.

Process Activities

Before you place your first order for materials, you must:

1. Clearly define your own Product Information, including BOM, Materials Requirements, UOM, and other pertinent Product Information.

2. Understand the Materials or Component Specifications from your Suppliers.

3. Agree on a mapping of your Product Information Model and your Suppliers' Materials Information Models so that you have an accurate mapping of the Information to be exchanged.

4. Plan and schedule your order with your immediate (Tier 1) Suppliers, in parallel with Process 3 "Forecast Product Demand." Because many manufacturers subscribe to Just-In-Time (JIT) Manufacturing, the planning, scheduling, and ordering of materials are Critical-To-Quality (CTQ). Information about lead times for order and delivery are critical to the effectiveness and efficiency of the process. Errors here can cause major failure and disruption of the Supply Chain.

If your Tier 1 Suppliers must resource materials from their (Tier 2) Suppliers for your orders, more complexity exists in the order-Production cycle.

Common Information Quality Issues

- Inaccurate or incomplete product Bill-of-Material (BOM)
- Inaccurate Customer Product Requirements and expectations that cause faulty Supplier orders
- Inaccurate or imprecise Supplier Product Specifications that do not match your Product Specifications, which causes your Production process to fail
- Inaccurate Production Capacity and Cycle Information that sub-optimizes Production scheduling
- Inaccurate or incomplete Tier 2 Suppliers' Material or Component lead times that causes untimely material deliveries

- Inaccurate or incomplete Supplier lead time for order of various materials or components that causes untimely material deliveries

- Inaccurate or incomplete Material Shelf-Life for materials and components that causes scrap and expired materials

- Inaccurate or incomplete Hazardous Material and Material Handling Requirements and Instructions that cause accidents or injury to persons or harm to the environment

- Inaccurate or untimely Customer delivery date, time, and location Requirements that alienate Customers

5. Tier 1 Supplier(s) Specifies and Orders Goods from Tier 2 Supplier(s)

Even as you specify *your* Orders for Materials from your Suppliers, your Suppliers must also schedule *their* Orders with *their* Suppliers as necessary to meet your order needs.

Process Activities

In some cases, the Suppliers will have components in inventory, produced to anticipate orders, based on current Forecasts. In other cases, Suppliers will have a JIT (Just-In-Time) Model and will produce component parts for direct shipment to Customers on a real-time basis. The process described in Process 4 applies here to a Tier 1's Suppliers.

Common Information Quality Issues

- Poorly defined product Bill-of-Materials (BOM) leads to Product Production failure.

- Material Order Information derived from poorly defined BOM and quantities leads to ordering inappropriate materials causing loss of Product Quality or higher Quality materials with higher costs than required.

- Lack of accurate Customer Product Requirements leads to ordering *sub-optimum* materials that causes defects.

- Mismatch in Product Specifications with Customer Requirements causes ordering *wrong* materials.

- Inaccurate Supplier Lead Times for order of various materials can cause scheduling problems in Production.

- Missing or inaccurate batch or lot numbers can prevent the ability to trace *defective* materials discovered after Product failure.

- Inaccurate material Shelf-Life can cause losses of shelf-life expiration from inventory.

- Inaccurate Hazardous and Material Handling Requirements and Instructions may cause problems in shipping of materials.
- Lack of *accurate* Customer delivery time Requirements may cause your Supplier orders to be scheduled inappropriately, causing you to miss your Customer's delivery Requirement.

6. Tier 2 Suppliers Schedule Shipments to Tier 1 Supplier

Tier 2 Suppliers provide Supply materials, parts, or components to their Customer (a Tier 1 Supplier). There can be many tiers in a complex Supply Chain.

Process Activities

This process provides the planning and logistics scheduling to ship its Products to its Customer (Tier 1 Supplier). This may be carried out through its fleet of delivery vehicles or through a third-party transportation provider.

Common Information Quality Issues

- Inaccurate Information about transport *vehicle or container* availability and location
- Inaccurate *driver or pilot schedule* or availability Information
- Inaccurate Vehicle Type match to Load and Material Requirements, such as refrigeration, enclosed trailer, or flatbed trailer, for example
- Inaccurate Pick-up and Delivery date and time, address and exact location, routing and directions
- Inaccurate projected travel route, Forecasted weather, and other conditions that may affect ship time
- Inappropriate Stacking Pattern for materials in shipment or in inventory that can cause damage to materials in storage or in transit
- Inaccurate Estimated Mileage and/or Travel Time Requirements and Restrictions in pick-up to delivery
- Inaccurate or incomplete permits

7. Tier 2 Supplier Ships to Tier 1 Supplier (Tier 2's Customer)

This process performs the logistics of shipping the materials from Supplier pick-up point to Customer delivery point.

Process Activities

Tier 2 Suppliers use their shipping capability or a third-party logistics organization to get the materials to their Customer. This includes:

- Determining the Shipment Method and Conveyance Type
- Matching a specific "box" (Trailer or Container box) to the Cab or Ship
- Matching the Conveyance Equipment to the Requirements for the Materials, such as liquid chemical, refrigeration, enclosed or open-bed
- Inaccurate Time-of-Delivery, especially in JIT environments, can disrupt Production schedules
- Scheduling the equipment and driver/pilot
- Calculating the route and estimating times to meet Pick-up and Delivery Requirements; scheduling a single conveyance for multiple pick-ups and deliveries from different pick-up and delivery entities complicates this.
- Handling any tariff or inspections in transit
- Handling any ownership changes in materials in transit
- Securing the materials in the containers to prevent damage
- Inventorying and ensuring the pick-up is from the right location, for the right items and quantities
- Inventorying and ensuring that the right items and quantities are delivered to the right location at the right time

Common Information Quality Issues

- Inaccurate availability and location information of *transport vehicle or container* causes hunting for the equipment, delaying material pick-up and delivery.
- Inaccurate or missing information about *drivers or pilots* transporting the shipment can cause delays in pick-up and delivery.
- Inappropriate vehicle conveying the shipped goods can be the *wrong type or size* of vehicle for the materials to be shipped. For example, sending a flat-bed trailer when a box-trailer is required, or sending a box trailer when a refrigeration trailer is required. These can cause damage to goods shipped or rescheduling delay of getting the right vehicle.
- Inaccurate scheduled pick-up and delivery date and time, and pick-up location can *cause delays* (late pick-up) and possible *missed delivery times*, or can cause a waste of time and equipment (early pickup).

- Inaccurate or missing actual *pick-up and delivery date and time, or location and routing* can prevent analysis of effectiveness of shipping logistics.

- Inaccurate shipment route, shipping lane, weather and other conditions that affect ship method and delivery time allowed that can cause delays and miss delivery Requirements, increasing costs and alienating Customers.

- Inaccurate or missing *stacking pattern* for materials in shipment or inventory can cause damage and loss of materials or Products.

- Errors in *actual mileage and times, pick-up to delivery notations*, conditions, and comments can cause mis-payment to drivers or fines for exceeding driver time allowed.

- Errors in material *ownership, ownership changes, and liability* during shipping can cause delays in delivery, with possible fines or penalties.

- Inaccurate transit time, driver time, standing time, inspection times, and locations can cause possible fines.

- Lack of *traceability* or Chain-of-Custody control and documentation of critical items, materials, or persons in transit, sometimes called Movement Information, can cause loss of material with short shelf-life or inability to use material in which contamination might be introduced. For example, evidence samples taken in criminal cases can be thrown out of court if documentation of Chain-of-Custody Control cannot be guaranteed.

8. Produce Finished Goods

This process represents the final manufacturer or provider of end-Consumer goods or services in the Supply Chain. Products and services produced or provided become finished goods and services to the end-Consumer. One more distribution and delivery point may exist to get goods to retail stores or directly to the Consumers.

Process Activities

This process produces the finished Product or delivers the service that the end-Consumer will receive and use. The activities are the same as for Tier 1 and Tier 2 Suppliers except the Product produced here will be the finished Product for the end-Consumer.

Common Information Quality Issues

- Mismatch of Customer Requirements and Product Specifications will continue to cause Production of defective Products, which will create Customer dissatisfaction.

- Inaccurate Customer Order Information for Products or Specifications for Materials will cause defective Production in Make-to-Order Products.

- Poor Information for Production Scheduling that can cause Production delays or Errors in Production, creating defects that alienate Customers

- Errors in Component Parts can cause assembly line *shut-down* and costs for start-up.

- Faulty Batch or Lot Documentation for Traceability and Recall possibility can cause Customer dissatisfaction should Products fail, but may be unable to be identified with a voluntary or mandated recall.

- Faulty Production Inspection information can release defective Products to Customers, again causing Customer dissatisfaction.

- Inaccurate or incomplete Packaging Requirements that can lead to higher costs of packing or Product damage in storage or transit

9. Shipper Delivers to Retailer Warehouse or Distribution Center

The Shipper here could be the manufacturer's own distribution capability or a third-party Logistics Provider.

Process Activities

The planning, scheduling, and delivery are the same as in Process 7, except the recipient is a distribution center or a warehouse from which retail delivery will be made or from which end-Consumer orders are shipped.

Common Information Quality Issues

NOTE Refer to "Common Information Quality Issues" in Process 7. "Tier 2 Supplier Ships to Tier 1 Supplier (Tier 2's Customer)," because they are the same.

10. Distributor or Warehouse Stocks Store, or Ships to Consumer

This process is the final logistics move to the retail store shelves or shipment of items to the end-Consumers.

Process Activities

There are two types of processes here. The first is the stocking of retail stores. The second is shipping of items to the end-Consumers themselves through telephone, mail, or e-tail (electronic) orders.

Activities for Retail Store Delivery

The IQ Requirements for the retail stores and outlets are the same as Process 9 "Shipper Delivers to Retailer Warehouse or Distribution Center" except that the delivery is to a retail store or outlet.

Common Information Quality Issues in Retail Store Delivery

The IQ issues are the same for delivering to the warehouse or distribution center, with the caveat that some items may be delivered and stocked on store shelves directly. Other items may be stocked on an on-Demand or scheduled basis. In addition to the IQ issues cited in Process 7 (and 9), other retail store delivery IQ issues include:

▪ Inaccurate Shelf Location Information about store shelves can cause misplacement of items.

▪ Inaccurate Shelf Item Shelf stocking patterns can sub-optimize the placement or volume of items stocked.

▪ Inaccurate *placement* of or old item discount coupons can *decrease* sales.

> **NOTE** Also refer to "Common Information Quality Issues" in Process 7, "Tier 2 Supplier Ships to Tier 1 Supplier (Tier 2's Customer)."

Activities for End-Consumer Delivery

Here the warehouse or distribution center packs items for shipment and sends them to a Customer via commercial or postal delivery carriers, based on shipping method and instructions from the end-Customer.

Common Information Quality Issues in End-Consumer Delivery

▪ Inaccurate or missing Customer Name and Address details, including Delivery Instruction Information, can cause final delivery to go astray, causing Customer calls and excess costs of finding and re-routing the shipment.

▪ Inaccurate or missing Pick-up and Delivery Date and Time and location and routing can prevent Customer *tracking* of Shipments and Customer dissatisfaction in delivery delays.

11. Customer Shops and Evaluates Product

This is a critical, but often overlooked, activity. To the extent possible you want to discover what the prospective Customers Experience as they consider your Products and Services. Some key observations:

▪ What do Customers do when they shop?
▪ What do Customers look at when they pick up a package?
▪ Why do Customers put the items back?
▪ What causes Customers to put items in their shopping cart?

- What happens when the Customers get to the checkout stand?
  - Do they purchase all items?
  - Do they put some items back?
  - Do they find pricing errors?
  - Do they have a friendly and courteous checkout experience?

These are all critical pieces of Information that help sellers understand their Customers — if the sellers would take time to observe, capture, and analyze Information about Customers' behavior with various Products.

Process Activities

Retail store shoppers will shop for and evaluate Products from within the choice of the store and from other purchase sources, determining which — if any — is the right Product for them based on their Experience and the Information made available to them at the time of evaluation or purchase.

Some activities retail store staff can perform include:

1. Observe Customer behavior, without appearing to be intrusive.

2. Document questions Customers ask about various Products and communicate them to Product development or purchasing staff and to the Product Suppliers.

3. Discover what Customers were looking for in their evaluation of items, specifically what they sought but did not find.

4. Hold focus groups of typical Customers to discover the Information or Characteristics they look for in certain kinds of Products.

NOTE For consideration of IQ in e-Business, please see Chapter 13, "Information Quality Applied to Internet and e-Business Information: 'e-Surfer-to-Satisfied-e-Customer."

Common Information Quality Issues

- Unclear or confusing Product Information on the Package and in the Owner's Manual and Assembly Instructions can create frustration in Customers who are not experts in the Products.

- Unclear descriptions of Product Functional Features, look and feel, emotional and status Characteristics and brand reputation, cost-of-ownership perception and warranty, among other Customer Requirements and expectations can alienate and lose sales.

- Higher Product prices relative to perception of Value can alienate Customers and lose sales.

- While these last two issues are not purely IQ issues, other Customer irritations, such as *lack of attention by a clerk*, or *too much unwanted attention by a clerk*, can alienate Customers and lose sales.

- When Customers get items home or have them delivered, and find after opening them that they do not meet the *expected* Features and Functions or the items do not meet Quality Expectations, they will have experienced a mismatch between the package or promotional description of the Product. This causes Returns, Costs of handling the returns, and also potential lost business.

12. Customer Buys Product — or Not

This Customer process is *vital* to retailers. As important as, if not more than, the Customers' purchases of one or more items, is their decision to *not* buy something. But I rarely see retail store staff seeking to ask Customers why they did not buy an item they were considering but ultimately rejected.

Even when a Customer brings back an item, requesting a refund or exchange, many stores do not capture sufficient detail to identify the Critical-to-Quality Requirements that led to the return.

Process Activities

These activities are performed by the Customer:

1. Purchases Product.

2. Opens purchased Product.

3. Studies and evaluates it, especially if packaged in a way that makes it hard to evaluate in the store.

4. Makes decision to try the Product. Note that sometimes the "in-home" evaluation will lead the Customer to say, "This is not the right Product," and return it, untried.

5a. Uses the Product with a satisfactory experience.

5b. Uses the Product with an *unsatisfactory* experience during its lifetime and *returns it* if under warranty or disposes of it if out of warranty.

6. Communicates likes and dislikes to the retailer, hopefully.

Common Information Quality Issues

- Lack of Customer Feedback and Product evaluation conclusions, preventing effective improvement of Products and their potential increased sales

- Failure to capture Customer's *perception* of missing Quality Characteristics
- Failure to have retail staff capture their observations of Customer complaints, especially when the Customers are so frustrated that they will probably not file a formal complaint with the store

13a. Customer Provides Feedback, Complaint, or Compliment

This is *vital* Information, and should be captured whenever and *wherever* Customer feedback is provided.

When Customers volunteer Information, capture it immediately and provide it to merchandisers. Capture negative feedback (missing features, poor warranty, wrong colors, and so on), as well as positive feedback ("I love this feature of the Product..."). Both of these kinds of feedback messages should be logged into your Knowledge Base by Product, Service, and other categories of learning.

You should create a defined process for enabling any touch point to Customers to capture and document any Feedback Customers provide. Often, busy people will not stop to complete organizations' pre-printed Customer Comment Forms, but may share that Information orally if asked by empathetic personnel.

Process Activities

This important process should include the following steps:

1. Observe Customer Feedback or Complaint.
2. Capture Customer Feedback or Complaint if you are asked — do not make Customers fill out a complaint form.
3. Clarify Feedback or Complaint to ensure accurate *understanding*.
4a. Resolve Complaint *immediately* (on the Customer's timetable) and to their satisfaction based on the situation.
4b. Ensure Customer the feedback *will be* addressed.
5. Get Customer contact details if the Customer wishes to hear outcomes.
6. Forward Feedback to appropriate personnel.
7. Perform all Promises or Commitments made to the Customer on a *timely* basis.

Common Information Quality Issues

- Not providing easy access for Customers to share feedback and complaints with you *prevents accurate* Information about their needs and Expectations in your Products and Services as well as in how they wish to be communicated with.

- Failing to capture Customer Feedback and Complaints prevents you from knowing your Customers' Expectations in the Products and Services provided.

- Failing to *communicate back with* Customers to resolve Complaints or *thank them* for helpful suggestions that enable you to improve your processes

Make it **Easy** for your Customers to provide feedback, especially feedback as to where you need to improve. Many organizations and managers shy away from getting the proper feedback to improve their Customer Experience and increase sales the most effective way — by *meeting or exceeding* Customer Expectations.

13b. Supplier Supports Customer

Whether in a B2B, B2C, G2G, or G2C,[6] your organization cannot prosper without providing ongoing support for the Products and Services you provide throughout the life cycle of the Products or services. For example:

- Automobile dealers generally offer Servicing for the Vehicles they sell.

- Automobile manufacturers offer Warranties on Vehicles they manufacture.

- Automotive Suppliers provide Warranties on their Component Parts to the manufacturer.

- Automobile Insurers provide accident Insurance and support their Customers with prompt and satisfactory *claim handling* in the event of an accident.

- Government agencies support their constituents in their various missions, such as when local Building Code Inspectors ensure the builder's work *conforms* to local building codes, when the Environmental Protection Agency ensures that companies comply with Environmental Regulations, or when the IRS offers help to taxpayers in *filling out the appropriate tax forms correctly*.

Process Activities

This process provides support to the Customer in the *use and maintenance of a Product throughout its lifetime*, including during and after Warranty coverage along with disposition, especially when Products contain hazardous materials. The first point of support comes from the retailer or e-tailer through whom the Consumer purchased the Product.

For complex problems, retail support may give way to *expert support* from the manufacturer to sort out the cause and provide resolution.

Use approaching Product Warranty *expiration dates* as a Customer touch point to capture feedback on Customer Experience where appropriate. This will enhance the Customer Experience if it is perceived as a genuine interest in the Customer and not just a "marketing" call.

Common Information Quality Issues

- Not handling Customer Product Warranty claims *on a timely basis* can alienate and drive Customers away.
- Inaccurate or missing Product use conditions can prevent you from identifying key Quality Requirements in Product Enhancement.
- Inaccurate Information about Product *failure causes* can lead you to make wrong improvements and have continued Quality problems.
- Inaccurate Batch or Lot Information prevents identifying those who may have defective Products subject to a Product Recall.
- Customer-*unfriendly* terms and conditions in complaint handling or in replacing a recalled item can *alienate* and drive away Customers.

1. Supplier Understands Customer and (end-Consumer) [Better]

The Supply Chain closed-loop has now come full circle, and with design and Quality Control, the result is — should be — a satisfied Customer, or we now understand our Customer Requirements better — identifying and seizing opportunities for improvement. This process provides you with additional insight into your Customers by collecting Information throughout the Supply Chain, especially the Customer Experience with Products and Services. This enables you to better understand your end-Consumers' Expectations and Needs and better relate to them in the Customer-Supplier *partnership*.

Process Activities

This process clarifies and expands on the end-Customers' Requirements for your Goods and Services based on their Experiences with Products and how your Customers wish to be related to. The application of this knowledge should enable you to improve the processes that produce and deliver the Goods and Services to one's purchasing Customers and increase their Customer Lifetime Value.

Common Information Quality Issues

- Inaccurate or missing Sales History for clients keeps you from understanding their needs and increasing Customer-Lifetime Value.
- Inaccurate or missing Customer Feedback, Complaint, or Warranty Claim Information causes failure to understand Customer needs or identify trends in Customer Requirements for new Products.

- Inaccurate Customer Lifetime Value and its variation over time prevents you from optimizing marketing campaigns.
- Inaccurate or incomplete Product Quality and Customer Feedback Information can cause you to *fail to identify* required improvements.

Next we describe how to measure and improve Information Quality in the Supply Chain Value Circle *"Forecast-to-Satisfied-Customer."*

Applying Information Quality to Various Information Groups in the Forecast-to-Satisfied-Customer Value Circle

Here we address applying Quality Principles and Processes to Measure and Improve various processes within the *"Forecast-to-Satisfied-Customer"* Value Circle.

Forecast-to-Satisfied-Customer Information Groups

We will address Quality management assessment and improvement of these categories of Supply Chain Information (Information Groups):

- **Forecast (Projected Sales) and Demand (Orders or Sales) Information**
- **Supplier and Competitor Product Information**
- **Order, Logistics, and Inventory Information**
- **Product Package Measurement Information**
- **Product, Marketing, and Promotional Information and Owner or Instruction Manual Information. Treated in Chapter 14, "**Information Quality Applied to Document and Knowledge Management," Section **"**Applying Quality to Technical, Procedural, and Documentation Writing."

Information Quality Applied to Forecast and Demand Information

Here we discuss the IQ issues, costs, and causes of poor Quality Forecast and Sales Information. We describe how to measure and improve the process Quality of Forecast, Order and Sales Information.

Applying Quality to Forecast and Demand Information

Forecasts can come from three sources:

- Customers' estimates of their Customers' future purchases
- Third-party Information Brokers who gather sales Information from retailers or other sources
- Internal staff estimates of projected orders or sales based on past experience

Achieving Accurate and Complete Forecast Information requires working with Customers as well as with third-party Information Brokers that provide sales and or Forecast Information to manufacturers or retailers in addition to your own internal staff's estimates.

Forecast and Demand IQ Issues and Costs

Forecast Information is by definition imprecise, but the degree of imprecision can spell the difference in the bottom line being *black or red*, and — more importantly — Customers being *happy or not*.

Information that projects your Customers' expected purchases (Forecast) of your Products and records their actual orders and purchases (Demand). Inaccurate Forecast Information causes either over-Production and increased costs of inventory or under-Production and costs of missed sales and rush orders and Production scheduling due to outages.

Table 11-3 lists various IQ issues and the Costs of Poor IQ they create.

Table 11-3: Common Information Quality Issues and Costs in Product Forecast and Demand Information

IQ ISSUES	COSTS OF POOR INFORMATION QUALITY
Forecast estimates higher than Demand	Increased costs of manufacturing, inventory, and cost of inventory disposition
Forecast estimates lower than Demand	Increased stock-outs and costs of rush orders to offset stock-outs that lead to loss of credibility and lost business, with stock-outs causing missed opportunity and inaccurate Forecasts based on actual "sales"
Mismatch in Forecast data definition, such as Unit-of-Measure (UOM) and Forecast quantity differences	Can lead to inaccurate Forecasts with the costs specified in the preceding Costs of Poor Quality.

How to Measure Forecast Information Process Quality

The major objective for measuring Forecast Information accuracy is to ensure you are producing the right quantity of Products — not more not less — that should be sold in a given time period, thereby minimizing waste and costs of over-Production or under-Production. Are the Forecasting processes (both internal and within your Customers) producing accurate sales projections within acceptable precision limits?

In the near term, you will need to measure the Accuracy and Precision (*uncertainty or margin of error*) of Customer and third-party Forecasts to discover which, if any, processes are broken, their causes, and how to make improvements, if required.

Your long-range Requirement is to gather history of Forecast Information, by source, as compared to actual sales (Demand) in the Forecast period. A most critical set of Information that you must gather, acquire, or estimate are the external factors that can influence actual Demand for Products. These factors include weather events, economic conditions, elasticity to price, source conditions, labor actions, and political events, among others.

Both data mining and dimensional data analysis will lead you to identify the variables that influence Demand and to continually refine the accuracy and precision of Forecasting based upon the heuristics learned from studying the impacts of those variables.

There are three distinct groups of Information to assess:

- Product *Forecast* Information by time period, which is the estimate of projected orders and/or sales in a given period

- Product *Sales* Information by time period, which is the actual orders and or sales in a given period

- Product *Demand* Information by time period, which is the actual orders and or sales in a given period plus the back-orders and or sales that were missed because of stock-outs, less the returns during the time period. Note that some organizations include returns in the Demand figures, and seek to discover the cause of return.

How to Measure the Quality of Forecast and Demand Information Definition (TIQM P1)

To assess Information Definition Quality of Forecast and Demand Information, you will assess the correctness, completeness, and clarity of the data names and definitions to ensure there is accurate consensus of the meaning of the Attributes about the Products that your Supplier provides to you. This measures the Quality of the "Information Product Specification" Information. The names should be meaningful and definitions must be correct, complete, and clearly understood with consensus among all Forecast Information Stakeholders.

Manufacturing staff or service delivery goals are to avoid over-Production or the need for rush Production, and marketing goals are to fill orders that meet Customer Product or service delivery Requirements.

Follow the baseline assessment steps in Chapter 4 "The Step-by-Step Guide to *Assessing Information Product Specifications and Information Architecture Quality*" (TIQM P7). Here are some tips for this assessment applied to Forecast and Demand Information.

Identify Information Definition Quality Measures (TIQM P1.1)

The critical Quality Characteristics here are Correctness, Completeness, and Clarity of communication to ensure that respective Supplier and Buyer Attributes are compatible and to prevent misunderstanding and process failure as a result.

Information definition Characteristics include:

- Intuitive Business Term Names and Correct, Complete, and Clear Definitions
- Clarity in written Attribute (Data Element) Definitions and Specifications
- Complete Specification of Valid Values with clear meanings of each Attribute Value, including variables affecting Forecast and Demand
- Accurate, Complete, and Clear Specification of the Formulas to calculate Product Forecast, Sales, and Demand
- Clear and explicit Unit-of-Measure codes in all contexts of Numeric or Quantitative Information

Identifying Forecast Attributes to Assess Definition Quality (TIQM P1.2)

Develop a Pareto Diagram based upon importance of the various Information groups based on the costs and impacts of poor Quality. Identify the A-priority or zero- or near zero-defect Information as the first category to measure, followed by the B-priority or next-most Important Information as the second tier to measure.

There are two types of prioritization: (1) the Attributes required to best estimate Forecast, and (2) specific Products that are the most significant to have the most precise estimates.

See TIQM Process P3.3 to estimate the impacts of poor Quality, and to measure the costs to confirm the relative priority.

This should include the Forecast Models used, and their Formulas, assumptions, limitations, and Variables that affect the Forecast.

Identifying a Set of Information Stakeholders of Forecast Information (TIQM P1.3)

Identify representatives from each of the different Information Consumer areas that require Forecast Information to perform their work. You should include representatives of those who create Forecast Information, because they must have a clear understanding of the meaning of the "Information Product Specification" Information and its importance, so they know how to capture and maintain it correctly. See Table 11-1: "Internal Information Stakeholders and Their Information Interests" at the beginning of this chapter for critical, internal Stakeholders. External Stakeholders include your Customers whose staff creates Forecast Information.

The representatives you select here will participate in the Information Stakeholder feedback sessions in a subsequent "Information Product Specification Assessment step (TIQM P1.6) to assess the correctness, completeness, and clarity of the data definition.

Assessing Forecast Information Product Specification Technical Quality (TIQM P1.4)

This assessment measures the Information Product Specification (IPS) Information, that includes data names, definitions, and business rules for conformance to enterprise Information Standards, Formats, and Name and Definition Clarity and Correctness. See the assessment guidelines in Chapter 4. Business Rules are critical for Forecasting, to understand the factors that influence Demand for Products and services.

Assessing Forecast Information Model and Database Design Quality and the Forecast Model Effectiveness (TIQM P1.5)

There are two sets of Information Models and Database Designs to assess, as well as assessing the Forecast Model that consists of the formula and weightings of the various Variables used to estimate the Forecast of Product Demand:

- The Forecast *Information* Model that should identify all the factors that influence Demand and that contain the actual Forecasts for Products from all sources

- The Order and Sales *Information* Models and Databases. This Information will be used to assess the accuracy and precision of Forecast Information from your various sources.

Assess the intuitiveness of the Information Model to ensure it represents the Real-World Objects and Events the organization needs to know to maximize the ability to Forecast Demand as accurately as possible. See Process P1.5 in Chapter 4 for the basic process step description with tips. Quality Characteristics include:

- Stability of the Information Model and Database Design. The Forecast Information Model and Database Design will have a tendency to change more than other Information Models, because Forecasting is dependent on many factors, many of which are not easily knowable. Its development will be iterative based upon Design of Experiments to understand the interactions of the variables and their influence on Demand. The goal is having completeness of Attributes that influence Demand.

- Flexibility of the Information Model and Database Design. The Model and design should have very little change if business processes are reengineered. The Model and design should be non-dependent on the *way* in which Forecasting is performed. The Model should allow for experimentation in refining the Forecasting process.

- Reuse of the Information Model and Database Design is high. Quality in the structure of the Forecast and Order and Sales Information Models (that represents *Enterprise* Information Requirements and the inherent relationships among the objects and events the enterprise needs to know about) and the Database Design should be usable directly by all Enterprise Stakeholders, including Manufacturing, Manufacturing Production scheduling, and Marketing and Sales.

Assessing Customer "Satisfaction" with Data Definition of Forecast Information (TIQM P1.6)

The most important measure is the Information Stakeholders' "satisfaction" with the Data Names, defined Meanings, set of Valid Values and Value Definitions, and Specification of the Business Rules describing the way in which the Forecast variables should influence Demand. Step activities include:

Step 1. Identify 10 to 25 Forecast attributes that are the most important to Forecasting and Production scheduling and marketing and sales processes (TIQM P1.6.1).

TIP Assess the Forecast Information and Forecast Model separately from the Order and Sales Information. Use the Order and Sales Information in TIQM Process P2, "Assess Information Quality," to measure the accuracy of the Forecast Information after you have measured the Information Product Specification Information Quality.

Step 2. Compile the Information Names, including abbreviations if any, definitions, Valid Value sets, and Business Rule Specification on the "Information Resource Quality Assessment" form (TIQM P1.6.2).

TIP Use the template "Information Product Specifications Quality/Value Assessment Form," on the book's Web site at www.wiley.com/go/IQApplied, to gather Information Stakeholder feedback about the names and definitions, value sets, and business rules. This assessment will measure the Stakeholders' individual perceptions of how well the Business Rule Specifications affect the Forecast of Product Demand.

TIP Conduct this assessment on your internal Forecast Information Definitions first, then conduct it on your Suppliers' Forecast Information Definitions.

Step 3. Select a sample of Information Stakeholders, including Production scheduling personnel, Customer Representatives who create Forecast Information, and third-party reps as well, to evaluate the Names and Definitions, Value sets, and Business Rule Specifications for Name Appropriateness, Definition Accuracy, Completeness, and Clarity, as per the form (TIQM P1.6.3).

Step 4. Send out the questionnaires with instructions ahead of the scheduled meeting and assemble the Information Stakeholders or conduct an online meeting with the Stakeholders over your intranet (TIQM P1.6.O1.F1).

Step 5. Compile the evaluation results and report them to key Stakeholders, including process owners who might need to improve the Information definition process, if warranted. And of course, the feedback should be used to improve the actual definitions. Business Rule Specifications for Forecasting will come through *experimentation* to test Forecast assumptions to refine the Forecasting Model (TIQM P1.6.5).

Step 6. Use the feedback to improve the Information definition process, if warranted. Also use the feedback to improve the actual Definitions and Business Rule Specifications as necessary (TIQM P1.6.6).

TIP If your Customers' Forecast Information definitions and Business Rule Specifications are lacking, call attention to the specific problems, and at the same time offer to work with them to help them improve. Poor definitions and Quality Standards can be difficult to reconcile to the attributes in your own Information Model, which can cause Quality problems in your own Forecasting processes.

Measuring Accuracy (Precision) of Forecast and Demand Information Quality (TIQM P2)

The second assessment is an assessment of the Accuracy and Precision of Forecast Information. Follow the general steps described in Chapter 5, "The Step-By-Step Guide to *Assessing Information Quality*." Tips for Forecast Information Quality Assessment follow here.

> **TIP** Conduct separate assessments of Forecast Information by source. One will be of your internal Forecasts. Your Customers may provide Forecasts of their probable orders, which you may use based on your experience to create your own Forecasts. Other Forecasts may be produced by third-party Information Brokers. The processes used in each of the sources will be unique and will produce variations (errors) independent of each other.

Identifying a Set of Forecast Information for Measuring Accuracy (TIQM P2.1)

Select the set of Forecast Information that may include:

- Forecast Sales Quantity:
    - For a Product, item, SKU (Stock Keeping Unit),
    - During a time frame or sales or product production period,
    - From a Customer, Production facility, or distribution center,
    - Using all Forecast variables (weather events, work stoppages, economic conditions, and so on),
    - Applying a Forecast Model calculation formula

Sometimes you have rolling Forecast projections, such as from 90-days out, 60-days out, and 30-days out, each of which should be more precise than the previous one.

Planning IQ Objectives, Measures, and Tests for Forecast Information (TIQM P2.2)

This step defines your business objective for measuring Forecast IQ, the specific Quality Characteristics you will measure, and the tests for actually conducting the assessment of each Quality Characteristic.

Step 1. Establish an IQ Assessment objective. See the first paragraph in the section "How to Measure Forecast Information Process Quality."

Step 2. Identify the specific Quality Characteristics to assess. This should include Accuracy, Completeness, and Timeliness of the Forecast Information:

▪ **Accuracy:** To measure Accuracy of Forecast Information, compare the Forecast for a Product for a specific time period to the actual orders and sales (Demand) that are made for that Product during that period.

▪ **Completeness:** To measure Completeness of the Forecast Information, compare the coverage of all of the (Customer) Forecasts that you get with the Forecasts that you need to have in order to have confidence in your own internal Forecasts for all Products your are analyzing.

▪ **Timeliness:** To measure Timeliness, measure the percent of Forecasts you get within the time required to schedule, produce, and/or deliver the Products to meet Customer Requirements.

Step 3. Define the specific measurements to accurately assess the conformance to each Quality Characteristic.

For example, to measure accuracy of Forecast Information, you will take the Forecasts for specific Products in their Forecast period, and compare them on a period-by-period and source-by-source basis once the final Demand figures are calculated. Demand = sales plus backorders minus returns and warranty scrap, depending on how your Demand quantity is calculated. See an example assessment diagram in the discussion of interpreting and reporting accuracy results, later in this section.

Identifying the Information Value Circle (TIQM P2.3)

If it has not been documented before, define the process and process steps of Forecasting internally for your organization. Your measures must measure the IQ Characteristics specified previously, along with any others that the Knowledge Workers require for their processes to perform properly.

> **NOTE** You will not perform this step on your Customers' Forecasting processes. This is a step your Customers *should* perform on their Forecasting process. Your measurement of Customer Forecast accuracy will measure the effectiveness of the Customer Forecasting process.

Determining Information Store or Process to Assess (TIQM P2.4)

This will be the Forecasting process itself, based upon the Forecast Information produced, as compared to the actual sales amounts.

NOTE Low Forecasts can lead to loss of sales as compared with actual Demand because of low Production and stock-outs. You will need to revise your Demand (what Customers actually order or want) upward based on stock-outs and backorders.

Identifying Accuracy Verification Sources (TIQM P2.5)

See Chapter 5 "The Step-by-Step Guide to *Assessing Information Quality*." Step P2.5 will lead you to the fact that the authoritative source to measure Forecast Information accuracy is the Actual Sales figures for the time of Forecast projection, adjusted as necessary as indicated in the preceding note.

Extracting Statistically Valid Sample of Forecast Data (TIQM P2.6)

Begin with the most problematic Forecast problems to sample. It may be by Customer or by your internal Forecasts of Products, aggregated from all Forecast information.

Measuring Forecast Information Quality in Selected IQ Characteristics (TIQM P2.7)

This step executes the specific measurements as defined in TIQM P2.2.2. You should measure the process effectiveness of each Forecast source (Customer, third party, and your own internal Forecast process).

- **For Accuracy**: Compare the Forecast quantity to the actual Demand quantity. You will need to document how you estimated or calculated the adjusted "Demand" figures in your IQ Assessment report.

- **For Completeness**: Identify all missing Forecast figures compared to actual Demand.

- **For Timeliness**: Determine whether the Forecasts you received were made in time for you to successfully schedule Production without incurring costs of rush orders from your Suppliers or costs of overtime to fill the orders. This is a yes or no result.

Interpreting and Reporting Information Quality of Forecast Information (TIQM P2.8)

Report the information in the form of number or percent of defects measured. Use a statistical Quality Control Chart of the process measured over time. See Chapter 5, "The Step-by-Step Guide to *Assessing Information Quality*," Process Step P2.8, "Interpret and Report Information Quality."

For Forecast Accuracy, track the Forecasts and the actual adjusted Demand (sales plus missed sales due to stock-outs) and the Variation among them. See Figure 11-3.

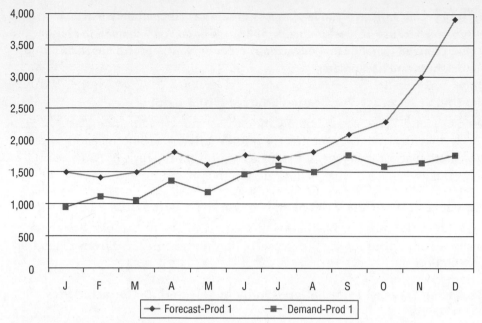

Figure 11-3: Forecast Versus Demand Tracking to Measure Forecast Accuracy

Note that the Forecasted sales are consistently higher than actual Demand (sales) indicating higher costs of inventory and handlings.

Communicate the Assessment result to Production schedulers to alert them to the results in the event Production scheduling adjustments may be required. Communicate Assessment results in an appropriate format and time to each Forecast source (Customer, third party, and internal Forecasters) to evaluate the need for Process Improvements.

Use the Quality Control Chart to document the Forecast Process Capability over time as compared to actual Sales.

How to Improve Forecast and Demand Information Process Quality (TIQM P4)

The assessments conducted in the preceding sections should give you an indication of if and where your Forecast processes may be broken. If the current Forecast processes (multiple processes in Customer organizations and internal within your organization) are causing process failure, waste, and Product and Information Scrap and Rework, you, or your Customers, need to improve the respective defective Forecast processes.

If your Order and Sales processes are broken, you may under-report Orders or Sales that cost you lost revenue, or overcharge your Customers.

Use the Plan-Do-Check/Study-Act cycle described in TIQM P4 "Improve Information Process Quality" in Chapter 7. You may also use TIQM Six Sigma and apply the DMAIC (Define-Measure-Analyze-Improve-Control) steps that implement the same TIQM processes, but in a slightly different way. See the TIQM Six Sigma DMAIC mapping in Chapter 7, in the section "TIQM Six Sigma DMAIC."

TIP Measure the costs of IQ problems in Forecast Information *before* you conduct a Process Improvement. This becomes a baseline for measuring the effectiveness of the improvement. Once the process is Improved and In Control, you should measure the reduction in the costs of failure and Information Scrap and Rework, and in manufacturing Scrap and Rework by the improved process. This establishes the ongoing value of Process Improvement. See TIQM P3, "Measure Poor Quality Information Costs and Risk," in Chapter 6.

Defining a Project for Forecast Process Improvement (TIQM P4.1)

This process step creates a Process Improvement Initiative, following your organization's project management protocol. Activities include:

- Identify the Forecasting Process requiring improvement. For example, this may be the organization's Forecasting process, or that of one or more of its Customers who provide Forecast Information for their own purchases.

- Identify the Facilitator for the Process Improvement. This should be the Process Owner of the Forecast process.

- Identify the Information Producers and other pertinent personnel who can identify defect Causes and Improvements to eliminate causes. This always includes the Forecasters of Product Demand.

- Develop the project plan for conducting the Process Improvement activities of the Plan-Do-Check/Study-Act cycle.

Planning for a Forecast Process Improvement: Root-Cause Analysis (TIQM P4.2.1)

The first step of "Plan" Process Improvement (TIQM P4.2.1) is to brainstorm and discover the Root Causes of the negative Information Effects and the negative Business Effects caused. With your Information Process Improvement Facilitator and the Forecast Process Improvement Team, brainstorm likely Root Causes on a Cause-and-Effect diagram to analyze and confirm the Root Causes of inaccurate Forecasts. See how to conduct a Root-Cause Analysis session in Chapter 7, Step TIQM P4.2.1.

Root Causes can include, but are not limited to, those listed on the Cause-and-Effect diagram in Figure 11-4.

The identification of causes will identify both precipitating causes, as well as potential Root Causes. You must continue to ask "why?" to get back from precipitating causes to the Root Causes.

TIP   Any improvement that addresses elimination of the precipitating causes *only* will be *suboptimized*. Sometimes you will have to go back and observe the processes to confirm that a cause is the true Root Cause. Forecasting is a complex process with many variables, requiring many designed experiments to identify the impacts of the interactions among the variables.

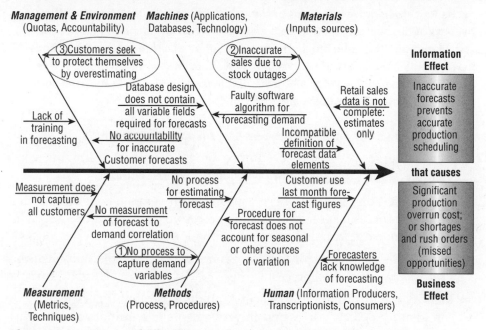

Figure 11-4: Cause and Effect Diagram for Defective Forecast Information

Planning for a Forecast Process Improvement: Defining Improvements to Prevent Defect Root Causes (TIQM P4.2.2)

Preventive actions include:

Table 11-4: Forecast Root Causes and Potential Improvement Considerations

INACCURATE FORECAST ROOT CAUSE	PROCESS IMPROVEMENT CONSIDERATIONS
1. No process to capture Demand variables (Figure 11-4)	Establish projects to analyze variables that influence Demand and study the impact of their interactions on Demand to improve the formula and process for calculating Forecasts.
2. Inaccurate Demand (orders and sales) due to stock outages (Figure 11-4)	If Forecasts are understated, identify the variable(s) and adjust the formula to minimize stock-outs.

INACCURATE FORECAST ROOT CAUSE	PROCESS IMPROVEMENT CONSIDERATIONS
3. Customers seek to protect themselves by overestimating (Figure 11-4)	This seems acceptable to some Customers, but it ends up driving up the costs to you in overproduction. Help them understand that you will have to pass on costs if excessive Forecasts cause you waste in overproduction. Prevention techniques include: ▪ Provide training to Customers to help them understand how it increases their costs increase. ▪ Define with your Customers a common Forecast process that includes all applicable variables that influence Demand. ▪ Provide training to Customers to help them understand how to perform the new Forecast process to increase Forecast Accuracy.

"Do" Implement Forecast Process Improvements in a Controlled Way to Study Effectiveness (TIQM Step P4.3)

First define Improvements to your internal Forecast process and implement it in a controlled way to record the results to study the impact of the Improvements.

It will take some iterations to fine-tune it. The goal here will not be *absolute* accuracy, but a *precision* of Accuracy that will minimize costs and problems of overproduction or underproduction. After a successful trial internally, turn to two or three of your Customers and help them implement this in a controlled way to test it for their own Demand.

Check and Study Impact of the Process Improvements on the Forecast Process and its Results (TIQM Step P4.4)

In this process step you study the effectiveness of the improvements on Forecast accuracy. A key observation point is to ensure you do not introduce Negative Side Effects that decrease Forecast accuracy or create new problems.

Ensure this by comparing the actual and adjusted sales to the Forecast from your newly defined or improved Forecast process.

Study the Forecast and Demand results to assess the increase in effectiveness of the process definition.

Once you feel comfortable with your internal results, go back to step P4.3 to implement them for your test-case Customers.

Act to Standardize the Forecast Process Improvements (TIQM Step P4.5)

Once your have an *effective* Improvement, put the Process In Control with actions to *standardize* the Improvements and roll the process out to the other Customers. See the general description of this process step in Chapter 7. Depending on the magnitude and distribution of the implementation your "Act" plan needs to include:

- Project roll-out plan by unit, division, country, facility, and so on

- Communication and training plan, so that people will be aware of what is coming, how it affects them, how to prepare, and the training they will receive to be able to perform the new process and use the equipment and system effectively

- Statement of preparatory work that must be done before the implementation, including:

  - IQ assessment of any Information that will need to be updated, enhanced, or migrated to new data stores

  - New Information required to be created or captured prior to implementation or at the time of implementation

  - Determination of what to do with existing Information that *may no longer* be required for the new process, but *is still* required for other processes

- Implementation of new equipment and software for the new or improved process

- System and stress testing of the new process with equipment and software

- IQ assessment of sample Information created or modified by the new process

- Study and elimination of variation of the tested process

- Establishment of Statistical IQ monitoring of CTQ Forecast Attributes, Variables, and Formulas to ensure the process stays stable and in control to meet all Production Schedulers' and Marketing and Sales' Requirements

Information Quality Applied to Supplier and Competitor Product Information

Manufacturers must know critical Information about the Supply Materials that are required to produce their Products to meet Customers' Expectations. You must also know your Competition and their core competing Products to understand their niche and strengths and weaknesses in the marketplace.

A major challenge in Supply Chain Management is communicating Information among Trading Partners when each organization has different "languages" (data names and definitions).

Applying Quality to Supplier and Competitor Product Information

Faulty Information about Suppliers' Products can cause failure in their or your Manufacturing processes. Failure to understand the competition can lead to missed opportunities for improvement.

Supplier and Competitor Product Information Quality Issues

Common IQ issues and their costs in the Supply Chain failure include those listed in Table 11-5.:

Table 11-5: Information Quality Issues and Costs in Supplier Product Information

IQ ISSUES	COSTS OF POOR INFORMATION QUALITY
Inaccurate, ambiguous, or unclear Product data names and definitions in Supplier Product Information	Can cause mismatch to your Product components and materials, causing costs of Production failure and Product Scrap and Rework.
Mismatch in Data Definitions and Database Designs within an organization and across Trading Partners	Can cause confusion as to what Parts or Materials are right for your Products.
UOM mismatch or ambiguity	Wrong quantities received or shipped
Product *label* and Product *ingredient* mismatch	Can violate Truth-in-Advertising laws with fines, and could harm Consumers with further fines.
Lack of Standards for exchanging Information	Can lead to increased incidences of miscommunication and mismatch of parts to Products.
Errors in *mapping* Supplier to buyer organization Product Information	Can cause confusion as to what Parts or Materials are right for your Products, which can cause Production *failure* and Product Scrap and Rework.
Inaccurate Order Item Lead Times for materials or components	Can cause *rush orders or missed schedules* for Production and lost opportunity.
Inaccurate or complex Bill of Material (BOM) Information	Can cause Production errors and Product Scrap and Rework.
Mismatch of Engineering Specs to Manufacturing Specs or Errors in either	Can cause defect production and Product Scrap and Rework or Product failure in use with increased Warranty costs and decreased Customer Satisfaction.
Inaccurate batch or lot identification for recalls	Can increase the costs of Product *recalls* and potential *legal liability*.

(continued)

Table 11-5 (continued)

IQ ISSUES	COSTS OF POOR INFORMATION QUALITY
Inaccurate Quality Characteristics and Specification information with mismatch to your Quality Requirements	Can cause Product *failure in consumption* and lost Customers.
Ordering or Supplying the wrong items	Can cause costs of *returns and re-ordering* and possible *delays* to your Customers.
Product failure caused by mismatch in Supplier material Quality in Product Specifications	Can lead to increased Scrap and Rework and Product *failure* in Customer use, resulting in lost or decreased business.
Inaccurate Batch or Lot identification for potential recalls	Can cause increased costs of *identifying* failure Cause and handling a required or voluntary recall.
Lack of, or inaccurate, Information about Competitor's Products	Can cause missed opportunity by not having competing Products or by not being able to communicate your Products' *differentiating features* or where you to need to improve your Products.
Inaccurate Kanban (see the following note) quantities for assembly line components	Higher quantities can cause more handling and waste of time; lower quantities can cause unexpected stock-outs and rush replenishment, slowing down the Production line.

CAUTION Kanban: The Japanese word for "signboard," "shop sign," or "chit," it is a card used for Demand pull in Just-In-Time (JIT) Inventory Management that is attached with a specific quantity of parts to provide at a point in the Production line; such that when the parts are used, the Kanban card is returned to the parts source as an order for more. Errors in quantities or location point can break the JIT cycle, costing time and cause Production Failure.

How to Measure Supplier Product Information Quality

Assess and ensure the Quality of Supplier Product Information Definition (TIQM P1), and measure the accuracy and other IQ characteristics of content and presentation Quality (TIQM P2), by following the respective steps in Chapter 4, "The Step-by-Step Guide to *Assessing Information Product Specifications and Information Architecture Quality*," and Chapter 5, "The Step-by-Step Guide to *Assessing Information Quality*."

How to Measure the Quality of Supplier Product Information Definition (TIQM P1)

Follow the baseline assessment steps in Chapter 4, "The Step-by-Step Guide to *Assessing Information Product Specification and Information Architecture Quality*" (TIQM P1). Following are some tips for this assessment applied to Supplier and Competitor Product Information.

Identify Information Definition Quality Measures (TIQM P1.1)

If you have not identified and standardized the basic Information Definition Quality Characteristics by now, review steps TIQM P1.1 and TIQM P2.2 in Chapters 4 and 5 and seek to establish a standard set. These Quality Characteristics should be the same for assessment of all discrete Information types.

One group of Product Attributes are those that are descriptive of your Suppliers' Products or Materials, including Product Name, Description, Feature, Feature Descriptions, and Costs.

The second group of Product Attributes includes the Technical Information related to Engineering and Manufacturing Specifications for Product Quality. The critical Quality Characteristics here are Completeness, Accuracy, and Precision, such that the Supplier Parts and Materials can be evaluated to meet your Product Quality Requirements and that you can produce Products that meet the Quality Requirements of your Customers. Chapter 4 describes how to measure and improve your internal processes that create and maintain Product Specification information, both Internally and with Business Partners.

Identifying Supplier Product Information Attributes for Definition Quality Assessment (TIQM P1.2)

Develop a Pareto Diagram based upon importance of Supplier Product Attributes and the costs and impacts of poor Quality. Identify the A-priority or CTQ attributes and create an Information Group as the first set of Attributes to measure, followed by the B-priority or near-CTQ information as the second-tier Information to measure. See TIQM Process P3.3 in Chapter 6 for how to estimate the impacts of poor Quality, and how to measure the actual direct and opportunity Costs of Poor Quality to confirm the relative priority.

The Supplier's Product Information includes, but is not limited to, the following attributes:

- Supplier Product ID
- GTIN (Global Trade Item Number)
- Supplier Product Description
- Supplier Product ID to (your) Product ID relationship

- Supplier Product Feature ID
- Supplier Product Feature Description
- Supplier Product Cost Amount
- Supplier Product Cost-Break Quantity
- Supplier Product Order UOM
- Supplier Product Order Lead Time
- Supplier Product Batch (or) Lot Number
- Supplier Product Net Weight
- Supplier Product Stack Pattern Code
- Supplier Product Shelf Life Expiration Date (if any)
- Supplier Product Quality Assurance Rating
- Product Component Kanban Quantity at Assembly Line Point
- Other Attributes as determined by your Requirements, such as GTIN Package Information, described in Section 6.5

Identifying Supplier Product Information Stakeholders (TIQM P1.3)

Identify representatives from each of the Supplier Product Information Stakeholder business areas as listed in the Internal and External Stakeholder lists in Tables 11-1 and 11-2.

The representatives you select here will participate in the Information Stakeholder feedback sessions in a subsequent Definition Assessment step (TIQM P1.6).

Assessing Supplier Product Information Definition Technical Quality (TIQM P1.4)

The Information Resource Quality Specialist should assess Technical Definition Quality Characteristics as described in TIQM Step 1.4 in Chapter 4.

NOTE Eliminate bias by ensuring the assessment is made by an independent assessor who was not part of the definition activities.

NOTE These assessed Entity Types and Attributes should be documented in an enterprise-wide Information Resource Repository or Data Dictionary and in an Enterprise-Wide Glossary of Business Terms available to any Knowledge Worker or Information Producer who may need to reference Terms and Attributes (Data Elements) to understand their meaning.

Assessing Supplier Product Information Model and Database Design Quality (TIQM P1.5)

Assess the Quality of your internal Supplier Product Information Model. This should be a subset of your Product Information Model first.

Then assess the Information Models and Databases or Files that your Suppliers provide to you with their Material and Part Information.

Are the Information Models intuitive to the real world? Are the Models compatible with one another for Information exchange? See Process P1.5 in Chapter 4 for the basic process step description with tips. Quality Characteristics include:

- The Information Model and Database Design are *stable* to accommodate new applications and Knowledge Workers *with only additive changes*, with no structural changes.

- The Information Model and Database Design is *flexible* to support process *reengineering with minimal structural change*. Typically, "paper-trail" entity types and files go away.

- The Information Model and Database Design is reused by *all* operational Knowledge Workers and applications requiring Information from them for all operational processes.

NOTE   Your Supplier Product Information Stakeholders must be able to easily understand the meaning of the Product or Material Information from the Suppliers and relate that Information to your internal Product Information. The information should closely approximate an "apples-to-apples" comparison of the Information. If data definitions are confusing, there are probably significant IQ problems in the Supplier's information itself.

Assessing Customer "Satisfaction" with Data Definition of Supplier Product Information (TIQM P1.6)

Follow steps TIQM P1.6.1–P1.6.6. Step activities include:

Step 1. Identify 10 to 25 A-priority (CTQ) Attributes about Supplier Product Information that are the most important to operational and business processes (TIQM P1.6.1).

TIP   Separate the assessment of the *technical* Material and Part Specification information and the *descriptive* Material Information (Part or Material description, price, for example) from the technical Material Information. There are different Stakeholders who depend on those two distinctly different Information groups.

Step 2. Compile the Data Names, including Abbreviations if any, Definitions, Valid Value sets, and Business Rule Specifications on the "Information Product Specifications Quality/Value Assessment" form (TIQM P1.6.2) in Chapter 4. Customize this for your organization if necessary.

> **TIP** Conduct this assessment on your own Product Information *first*, then conduct it on your Suppliers' Product Information.

> **TIP** If your Suppliers' Information Resource Data Definitions and Business Rule Specifications are lacking, call attention to the specific problems, and at the same time offer to work with them to help them improve. Poor Definitions and Quality Standards can be difficult to reconcile to the Attributes in your own Information Model, which can cause Quality problems in your own production processes.

Measuring Accuracy and Other Product Supplier Information Quality Characteristics (TIQM P2)

The second assessment is an assessment of the Accuracy of selected Supplier Product Information. Follow the general steps described in Chapter 5 "The Step-by-Step Guide to *Assessing Information Quality*." Following are tips for Supplier Product Information Quality measurement.

> **TIP** Likewise, conduct this assessment on your own Product Information *first*, then conduct it on your Suppliers' Product Information.

Identifying a Set of Information for Measuring Quality (TIQM P2.1)

You will probably select the same 10 to 25 A-priority, QTC Supplier Product Attributes for which you measured "Information Product Specifications" Quality.

The Supplier's Product Information should be Accurate and Precise to the Quality Characteristics you have specified.

Planning IQ Objectives, Measures, and Tests (TIQM P2.2)

Establish your objectives for the IQ Assessment. Why are you measuring? See the fundamental objectives in Step TIQM P2.2 in Chapter 5. One objective should be regular process measurement to ensure the Quality of the Supplier Products conform to their Specifications and that they are consistent with your Quality Requirements for your Products.

Determine the CTQ IQ Characteristics to measure, such as Completeness, Accuracy, Validity, Timeliness of availability, and others, based on importance and impact to processes the Knowledge Workers perform.

If the same data resides in multiple databases, you will also need to measure the Equivalence of the data across the different Databases to ensure the processes of data movement are In Control.

Identifying the Information Value Circle (TIQM P2.3)

In order to understand process capability, you must understand the processes that make up the Information Value Circle that creates the Product Information. Information on TIQM P2.3 "Identify Information Value Circle" can be found in Chapter 5, "The Step-By-Step Guide to *Assessing Information Quality*." Document this Value Circle using a Value Circle format, the Information Value/Cost Chain from my earlier book or other Process or Information Work Flow Model.

> **NOTE** You will not perform this step on your Supplier's Information processes. You receive their Information as a "Finished Product."

Determining Information Store or Process to Assess (TIQM P2.4)

For your internal Product Information, this will be the originating source of (1) Product Information for internal and Customer use, and the originating source of (2) Production Control Product information that manufacturing requires for assuring Quality Control within your Production processes.

Each Supplier will provide you with a file containing their Product (Materials, Components, or Finished Products) Information that you require for Ordering and Production or Distribution and Sales. Consider this assessment as a measurement of their Supplier Product Information Delivery Process.

If you have multiple Suppliers providing the same Materials or Components, you assess the Information separately from each Supplier. This will help you evaluate relative performance of the various competing Suppliers, both in the form of Information Quality and Product or Materials Quality.

Identifying Accuracy Verification Sources (TIQM P2.5)

See Chapter 5 "The Step-by-Step Guide to *Assessing Information Quality*," Step P2.5 for how to identify the correct sources to *verify* the Accuracy of the Information. This is the most critical inherent Quality Characteristic for any Information, especially for CTQ Product Attribute Specification values.

For Production Control Information, the Products produced represent the Accuracy Verification Source for the Production Quality Characteristics, such as Size Dimensions, Material Composition, and Weight, for example, that will be compared to samples of the actual Supplier Products to ensure conformance of the Products to the Specifications.

Extracting Statistically Valid Sample of Data (TIQM P2.6)

Follow Step TIQM P2.6 "Extract Statistically Valid Sample of Data" in Chapter 5 to determine the number of records required to be sampled for your confidence level, which you need in your assessment results. Extract the records using a technique that ensures a statistical (unbiased) sample.

Measuring Information Quality in the Selected IQ Characteristics (TIQM P2.7)

To measure Accuracy of the selected Facts, compare the data Value for each Fact to the measured Characteristic of the real-world Object the fact represents.

> **NOTE** Avoid bias in the accuracy measurement by ensuring you use measurement processes and devices that are calibrated, controlled, repeatable, and reproducible. To measure Product weight, use a calibrated scale with a common Product placement on the scale and in a room with constant and consistent temperature and humidity.

Interpreting and Reporting Information Quality (TIQM P2.8)

Follow Process Step P2.8, "Interpret and Report Information Quality," in Chapter 5, and communicate assessment results to all key Information Stakeholders.

BEST PRACTICE: HEALTH INSURANCE ORG. ISSUES IQ REPORT CARDS

A Health Care Insurance provider issues "report cards" to its Health Care Providers, providing feedback on the Completeness, Validity, and Timeliness of their provided Information. By showing each Provider their scores along with the other (unnamed) Providers, Information Quality improved significantly over time, reducing error-rates by more than 60 percent.

BEST PRACTICE: AISIN SEIKI MANUFACTURING PLANT IN JAPAN USES JIT FOR PRODUCTION OPTIMIZATION

In the space of a high school basketball court, Aisin Seiki's mattress production area produces mattresses of 750 different colors, styles, and sizes per day on seven dedicated assembly lines. How can they do this in such a small space? By using Just-In-Time manufacturing principles and kanban as a method of JIT inventory control.

"Except for the quilting machines, the machines in each line are laid out in order of processing. Major processes include spring-coil forming, spring-coil assembly, multi-needle quilting, cutting, flange-sewing, padding, border-sewing, tape-edge sewing, and packaging. Each process connects to the next, allowing no room to plan extra work-in-processes. Only one work piece at a time flows between the processes. The quilting process makes only one piece of cloth for one mattress at a time. Each work piece moves through the workstations while being processed. Twenty minutes after the weaving machine starts weaving the mattress cover, the mattress is completed and ready to be shipped to "one of their 2,000 furniture store Customers."[8]

Having good Information about their Production processes and their Customer orders enables them to schedule Production efficiently, eliminating waste of inventory through their JIT and the kanban system of just-right quantity of materials and parts in the Production line. Thanks to Masaaki Imai for this example, cited in his excellent book, *Gemba Kaizen*.[9]

How to Improve Supplier and Competitor Product Information Quality

The improvement of a Trade Partner's Product Information requires cooperation among the Trading Partners. Improvement of processes outside of one's control and authority presents its own set of problems.

How to Improve Supplier Product Information Process Quality (TIQM P4)

The Assessments conducted in the preceding section should give you an indication of if and where your Supplier Product processes may be broken.

Use the classic Plan-Do-Check/Study-Act cycle described in TIQM P4 "Improve Information Process Quality," in Chapter 7. You may also use TIQM Six Sigma and apply the DMAIC (Define-Measure-Analyze-Improve-Control) format, which implements the same TIQM processes, but in a slightly different way. See the TIQM Six Sigma DMAIC mapping in Chapter 7, "The Step-by-Step Guide to *Improving Information Process Quality*," in Table 7-7 "TIQM Processes and Steps Mapped to Six Sigma Phases and Steps."

> **CAUTION** As always, measure the costs of IQ problems in Supplier Product Information *before* you conduct a Process Improvement. This becomes a baseline for measuring the effectiveness of the Improvement. Once the process is Improved and In Control, measure the reduction in the Costs of Failure and Information Scrap and Rework, and in Manufacturing Scrap and Rework by the improved process. This establishes the ongoing value of the Information Process Improvement. See TIQM P3, "Measure the Costs of Poor Quality Information," in Chapter 6.

Defining a Project for Supplier Product Process Improvement (TIQM P4.1)

This process step creates an Information Process Improvement Initiative, following your organization's project management protocol. See TIQM P4.1, "Define Project for Information Quality Improvement," in Chapter 7.

Planning for a Supplier Product Information Process Improvement: Root-Cause Analysis (TIQM P4.2.1)

The first step of "Plan" Process Improvement (TIQM P4.2.1) is to define the "Effect," that is, the IQ issue requiring improvement, such as "Supplier Product cost schedules are not current." Secondly, you brainstorm and discover the Root Causes of the negative effects. See how to conduct a Root-Cause Analysis session in Chapter 7, Step TIQM P4.2.1.

Root Causes can include, but are not limited to, those in Table 11-6, along with considerations for Process Improvements.

The identification of causes will identify both precipitating causes, as well as potential Root Causes. You must continue to ask "Why?" to get back from precipitating causes to the Root Causes.

> **NOTE** Any improvement that addresses elimination of the *precipitating causes only* will be suboptimized. Sometimes you will have to go back and observe the processes to confirm that a cause is a real Root Cause. Supplier Product Information management is a complex process of sharing and interpreting disparate Information provided by Suppliers.

> **NOTE** Do not think about improvements to the process until you fully understand the real Root Causes. Otherwise, you can bias your Improvement, based on the current process definition.

Planning for a Supplier Product Information Process Improvement: Defining Improvements to Eliminate the Root Causes (TIQM P4.2.2)

Preventive actions include those listed in Table 11-6.

Table 11-6: Defective Supplier Product Information Root Causes and Potential Improvements

INACCURATE SUPPLIER INFORMATION ROOT CAUSE	PROCESS IMPROVEMENT CONSIDERATIONS
No map of your Products' BOM to your Supplier Components and Materials	Ensure early that your Suppliers must have clear *mapping* of your Supplier Product Information Model the respective Information for mapping. Provide them with a template for Product Information mapping.
Supplier Product Information lacks clear definition.	Caused by lack of Information Definition Guidelines or by Failure to treat Information as a Product. Help the Suppliers improve their own Information Model and Definition Processes.
Suppliers do not understand importance of your Information Requirements about their Products and Materials and do not make Improvements.	This seems acceptable to some Customers, but it ends up driving up the potential to buy and use the *wrong* materials, causing your Products *to be defective*. Help them understand that you will have to pass on costs of improving their Definitions so you can use their Information. Prevention techniques include: ▪ Provide *training* to Suppliers to help them understand how it decreases their total costs if they provide Clear and Accurate Product Information.

INACCURATE SUPPLIER INFORMATION ROOT CAUSE	PROCESS IMPROVEMENT CONSIDERATIONS
	▪ Define with your Customers a common Supplier Product Information Definition Process that increases clear and correct definitions.
	▪ Provide *training* to Suppliers to help them understand your needs for Information about their Products and Materials.
	▪ Provide *benefits back to* Trade Partners for implementing Process Improvements and higher IQ levels, including providing Value-Added Information back.

"Do" Implement Supplier Product Process Improvements in a Controlled way to Study Effectiveness (TIQM Step P4.3)

First define *Improvements* to your internal Product Information process and implement it in a controlled way to record the results to study the impact of the Improvements.

The goal of this Improvement is to ensure your internal and external Customers *clearly understand* what they need to know to apply your Information about your Products and Materials. After a successful trial internally, turn to two or three of your Suppliers and help them implement this in a controlled way to test it for their own Demand.

Check and Study Impact of the Process Improvements on the Supplier Product Information Process and its Results (TIQM Step P4.4)

In this process step you study the *effectiveness* of the Improvements on Supplier Product Information Clarity and Accuracy. Ensure you do not introduce Negative Side-Effects that create new IQ problems.

Study the impact the Product Information Process Improvement makes on the needs of your internal Knowledge Workers and external Customers.

Once you feel comfortable in your internal results, go back to step 4.3 to implement in your test-case Suppliers.

Act to Standardize the Supplier Product Process Improvements (TIQM Step P4.5)

Once your have an *effective* Improvement, put the process In Control with actions to *standardize* the Improvements and "Control the Gains" (keep the improvements "In Control") and roll the process out to the other Suppliers.

Best Practices in Supplier Product Information Quality

Best practices include the following:

BEST PRACTICE: AERA ENERGY WRITES IQ STANDARDS INTO INFORMATION SUPPLIER'S CONTRACTS

Aera Energy LLC, a California oil and gas production company, writes Information Quality Standards into its contracts with its Information Suppliers. When Aera Energy began that practice in the late 1990s, within three months of the new contracts, the error-rates dropped 50 percent.

BEST PRACTICE: AERA ENERGY ALLOWS ITS INFORMATION SUPPLIERS TO ATTEND AERA ENERGY'S INFORMATION QUALITY TRAINING

Aera Energy does not just expect Information Quality from its Information Suppliers — it encourages them to send representatives to Aera Energy's IQ training. After one training session, I spoke with a Supplier representative who had attended the training to ask him how it went. He showed me a list of thirteen things he said he could take back to improve their Information processes.

Tips for Measuring and Improving Competitor Product Knowledge

The more accurate your knowledge about your competitor's Products, the better you are able to position your competing Products or find areas in which to improve your existing Products.

Please know, however, that you must not lock yourself into detailed analysis of their Products, for you must always be thinking about your Customers' needs *for tomorrow*. Focusing on today *can prevent you* from seeing how to innovate tomorrow's "Breakthrough" Products that are not yet in the minds of your competitors.

TIP Do not try to over-analyze your Competitors' Products. Focus on your Customers and their Needs and what you can do *to delight them* in the long haul.

TIP Most *Breakthrough* Innovation comes not by *incremental* Improvement, but by creative thinking and innovation that applies technological breakthroughs or radical process design. Overly fixating on Competitors' Products may cause you to miss the *Breakthrough Innovations* that dramatically change the competitive market, such as the quartz crystal movement watches that completely transformed the watch industry in the late 1960s, and the MP3 players that are transforming the music media players from CDs to music on Demand.

Best Practices for Competitor Product Knowledge

> **HEALTHCARE INSURANCE PROVIDER REGULARLY ASSESSES CUSTOMER SATISFACTION WITH ITS INFORMATION — NOT JUST ITS HEALTH SERVICES**
>
> A major Healthcare Insurance Provider uses independent third parties to conduct Satisfaction Surveys of its Customers and its *Competitors'* Customers to identify how well they compare. The surveys include questions about its Customers' Satisfaction with the *Information they provide*, such as the regular and custom reports — not just its healthcare insurance services. This allows the provider to understand which processes it needs to improve from a competitive perspective.

Information Quality Applied to Order, Logistics, and Inventory Information

Here we discuss the IQ Issues, Costs, and Causes of Poor Quality Logistics and Inventory Information. We describe how to *measure and improve* the Process Quality of Order, Logistics, and Inventory Information.

Applying Quality to Order, Logistics, and Inventory Information

Logistics and Inventory processes are required for an organization to know where and how much Products and Materials it has and when and where it needs to be moved from and to.

Like Forecasting, Logistics requires *coordination and collaboration* among Business Partners, throughout all tiers of Suppliers and Distribution Channels to end-Customers.

The Logistics of moving Materials and Products can be outsourced or provided by internal logistics departments.

Achieving Accurate and Complete Logistics and Inventory Information requires working with Suppliers and Customers as well as with third-party Transportation Providers to get Materials and Products to where they need to be when they need to be there.

Logistics and Inventory IQ Issues and Costs

Logistics and inventory Information is critical for an organization to get both Raw Materials and Finished Goods from where they are to where they need to be, on a timely basis, especially in the JIT Production world.

Inaccurate Logistics Information causes Production delays and high costs of rescheduling or unhappy Customers who do not get their goods on their time Requirements. This *can lead to lost* Customers and Fines or Penalties for *late* shipments along with *increased costs of* rush Orders or Deliveries.

Table 11-7 lists Logistics IQ Issues and Costs of Poor Quality Information.

Table 11-7: Information Quality Issues and Costs in Product Logistics and Inventory Information

LOGISTICS IQ ISSUES	COSTS OF POOR QUALITY INFORMATION
Order form design ambiguity	Causes errors in order capture.
Order errors (Item ID, quantities, Unit-of-Measure or Price)	Causes wrong Shipments, Quantities, or Prices resulting in Returns and unhappy Customers.
Logistics scheduling errors	Causes missed pick-ups or deliveries with costs of delays, and possible spoilage of short shelf-life items such as produce or fresh food.
Inaccurate Addresses or *poorly worded* Directions	Causes Products and Materials to go to the wrong place, resulting in *increased* transportation costs, penalties, and missed Production or Customer deliveries.
Timeliness, completeness, and accuracy of *Cargo Ownership* during transit	Can cause delays to port-of-entry or destinations that may change.
Inaccurate Inventory Location and Quantities	Causes *increased* cost of Inventory (overstocks) or *surprise* Outages and costs of rush orders.
Inaccurate Pick-up or Delivery times	Leads to driver waiting and *increased costs* of transportation.
Imprecise GPS Information of Trailers or Containers	Increases *driver time to find trailers or containers*, with the potential of missed pick-up and delivery times, leading to cost of time and penalties for late pick-up or delivery.
Inaccurate Case Sizes and Weights	*Sub-optimizes* transportation containers or trailers, *increasing transport costs* per item.
Scheduling wrong container type (refrigeration required, enclosed, flat-bed, for example)	Can *increase* loss of perishable items, or *increased costs* of container (more expensive than required); secondary costs, failure to optimize use of containers, and damage to shipped items.
Missing or inaccurate Road or Route Information	Causes delays or re-routing extra transport time.

LOGISTICS IQ ISSUES	COSTS OF POOR QUALITY INFORMATION
Inaccurate mileage from point-to-point	Can cause delays in pick-up or delivery, or cause drivers longer times beyond their limits to meet schedule.
Hidden Factories of Items without updating Inventory	Causes increased costs of Inventory, as Hidden Factory quantities are not accounted for.
Failure to use FIFO in perishable Items	Causes higher costs of Scrap of expired shelf-life items.
Improper Packaging Specifications	Can *cause damage* to packaged items.
Wrong Stack Pattern	Can *cause damage* to goods and Scrap or Rework.
Inaccurate Material Handling Safety Instructions	Can *cause injury* to Employees and Customers.
Logistics Schedule Changes	Causes *going to wrong locations* for pick-up and/or delivery, or *timing mismatches* and late or overly early delivery times when Customers may not be prepared to receive shipments.
Inaccurate Kanban Quantities for Assembly Line Materials	Higher quantities cause more handling and waste of time; lower quantities can cause unexpected stock-outs and rush replenishment, slowing down the Production line.

How to Measure Logistics Information Process Quality

While Logistics Information is very important in Production scheduling, it is essential to JIT or Lean manufacturing organizations where availability times can be measured to within the minute.

In the near term, you will need to measure the precision of Customer and third-party Logistics to discover which, if any, processes are broken, their causes, and how to make improvements, if required.

Your long-range Requirement is to gather history of Logistics Information, by source, in terms of Order Accuracy, Shipment Pickup and Delivery timing, Shrinkage or Breakage costs, and Reliability. A most critical set of Information that you must gather, acquire, or estimate are the *external factors* that can influence actual Demand for Products. These factors include weather events, economic conditions, source conditions, labor actions, and political events, among others.

Both data mining and dimensional data analysis will lead you to identify the variables that influence Demand and to continually refine the precision of Logistics based upon the heuristics learned from studying the impacts of those variables.

There are three distinct groups of attributes addressed here:

- **Product Logistics (Inventory, Materials, and Product Movement) Information.** This is required to ensure that Just-In-Time Production and delivery needs are met.

- **Product Sales, Returns, Scrap, and Warranty Information.** The Critical Quality Characteristics here are Accuracy, Completeness, and Clarity of communication.

- **Product Returns Information.** Most important is to understand the reason (cause) for the returns, whether it's the return of material to your Suppliers or your Customers' returns of Products purchased from you.

How to Measure the Quality of Order, Logistics, Inventory, and Movement Information Definition (TIQM P1)

To assess Information Definition Quality of Logistics and Inventory Information, you will assess the Correctness, Completeness, and Clarity of the Data Names and Definitions to ensure there is Accurate and Consensus of the *meaning* of the Attributes about the Products that your Supplier provides to you. This measures the Quality of the "Information Product Specification" Information. The Names should be Meaningful and Definitions must be Correct, Complete, and Clearly understood between Manufacturing staff and Marketing and Sales.

Manufacturing staff or Service Delivery goals are to avoid overproduction or the need for rush Production, and Marketing Goals are to fill Orders that meet Customer Product or Service Delivery Requirements. Logistics goals are to get the *right* Goods to the *right* place at the *right* time, without damage.

Follow the baseline assessment steps in Chapter 4 "The Step-by-Step Guide to *Assessing the Quality of Information Product Specifications and Information Architecture Quality*" (TIQM P1)[10]. Here are some tips for this assessment applied to Internet documents and Web content.

Logistics Information to assess includes:

- Customer Orders and Order Items
  - Customer order date and time
  - Customer name and address
  - Customer order item ID, quantity, and unit of measure
  - Customization Specifications as required
  - Customer order shipping address and directions
  - Customer order requested delivery date and time

- Orders to Suppliers and Supplier order items
  - Supplier order date and time
  - Supplier order Employee name and address
  - Supplier order item ID, quantity, and unit of measure
  - Supplier customization Specifications as required
  - Supplier order shipping address and directions
  - Supplier order requested delivery date and time
- Containers or trailers available
- Container or trailer GPS location coordinates
- Drivers or Pilots available
- Scheduled pick-up date and time
- Pick-up contact, address, and directions
- Scheduled delivery date and time
- Delivery contact, address, and directions
- Actual pick-up date and time
- Damaged goods observed at pick-up
- Actual delivery date and time
- Damaged goods observed at delivery
- Container or trailer scheduled
- Container or trailer used
- Container or trailer tare weight (weight empty) and gross weight (sum of the weight of the goods and the weight of the container or trailer)
- Delivery route scheduled
- Delivery route taken with reasons for detours, if any
- Inspection point dates and times and results
- Pick-up, transport, and delivery problem descriptions, if any
- Product movements from point-to-point in transit or in warehouse to manufacturing to assembly line point

Identify Logistics Information Definition Quality Measures (TIQM P1.1)

The critical Quality Characteristics here are Accuracy, Completeness, and Clarity of communication to ensure that logistics Information Attributes are Correct, Complete, and Clear to ensure efficient movement of Materials and Products on a timely basis.

Information definition Characteristics include:

- Intuitive Business Term Names and Correct, Complete, and Clear Definitions

- Clarity in written Attribute (Data Element) Definitions and Specifications

- Complete Specification of Valid Values with Clear meanings of each Attribute value

- Accurate, Complete, and Clear Specification of Business Rules that constrain data values, or data or record relationships

- Accurate, GPS Location data of Trailers or Containers, or of Products for shipment, including in-transit data where required

- Accurate Manifest Information about cargo Items in transit

- Data Value Format Guidelines for "structured" data such as Product Codes. This is especially important in translation to Bar Codes and RFIDs (Radio Frequency Identifiers).

- Unit-of-Measure Codes are clear and explicit in all contexts of Information usage.

Identifying Logistics Information Attributes to Assess Definition Quality (TIQM P1.2)

Develop a Pareto Diagram based upon importance or an Information group of logistics data and the costs and impacts of poor Quality. Identify the A-priority or CTQ information as the first category to measure, followed by the B-priority or near-CTQ information as the second tier to measure. See TIQM Process P3.3 to estimate the impacts of poor Quality, and to measure the costs to confirm the relative priority.

Identifying a Set of Information Stakeholders of Logistics Information (TIQM P1.3)

Identify Representatives from each of the different Information Consumer areas that require Logistics Information to perform their work. You should include representatives of those who *create* Logistics Information, as they must have a clear understanding of the meaning of the "Information Product Specification" Information and its importance, so they know how to capture and maintain it correctly. See Table 11-1 near the beginning of this chapter for a listing of the Internal Stakeholders of Forecast and Demand Information. External Stakeholders include your Customers whose staff creates Logistics Information.

The Representatives you select here will participate in the Information Stakeholder feedback sessions in a subsequent Definition Assessment step (TIQM P1.6).

Assessing Logistics Information Definition Technical Quality (TIQM P1.4)

See the assessment guidelines in Chapter 4. A critical component for Logistics is the effectiveness of the Business Rules and Formulae that are used to understand the factors (Variables) that influence Demand for Products and Services.

Assessing Logistics Information Model and Database Design Quality (TIQM P1.5)

There are two sets of Information Models and Database Designs to assess:

- The Logistics Information Model that should identify all the Factors that influence Demand and that contain the actual Logistics for Products from all sources.

- The Order and Sales (including Returns) Information Models and Databases. This information will be used to assess the Accuracy and Precision of Logistics Information from your various sources.

Assess the Intuitiveness of the Information Model to ensure it represents the Real-World Objects and Events the organization needs to know to maximize its ability for Logistics Demand as effectively as possible. See Process P1.5 in Chapter 4 for the basic process step description with tips. Quality Characteristics include:

- The Information Model and Database Design are *stable* to accommodate new applications and Knowledge Workers with only *additive* changes, and with no structural changes.

- The Information Model and Database Design is *Flexible* to support process reengineering with *minimal* structural change. Typically, "paper-trail" entity types and files go away.

- The Information Model and Database Design is Reused by *all* operational Knowledge Workers and applications requiring them for operational processes.

This is a technical assessment performed by a Specialist in Information Resource Quality that measures the Quality of the Information Resource Models and Databases Designs. The next assessment will be an assessment of Completeness, Correctness, and Clarity of the Logistics Data Definitions.

Assessing Customer "Satisfaction" with Data Definition of Logistics (TIQM P1.6)

The most important measure is that of the Information Stakeholders' *Satisfaction* with the Data Names, Defined Meanings, set of Valid Values and Value Definitions, and Specification of the Business Rules describing the way in which the Logistics Variables influence Demand. Step activities include:

Step 1. Identify 10 to 25 Logistics Attributes that are the most important to Logistics and Production scheduling and marketing and sales processes (TIQM P1.6.1).

Step 2. Compile the Data Names, including Abbreviations if any, Definitions, Valid Value Sets, and Business Rule Specifications on the "Information Product Specifications Quality Assessment Form" (P1.6.O1.F1).

TIP Use the template Stakeholder Evaluation Form on the book's Web site at www.wiley.com/go/IQApplied and customize it if necessary, to gather Information Stakeholder Feedback about the Names and Definitions, Value Sets, and Business Rules. Is there a consensus of satisfaction with the names and defined meanings of terms, entity types, and attributes, and in the business rule Specifications?

TIP Conduct this assessment on your internal logistics Information Definitions first, then conduct it on your Suppliers' logistics Information Definitions.

Step 3. Select a sample of Information Stakeholders, including Production scheduling personnel, Customer reps who create logistics Information, and third-party reps as well, to evaluate the Names and Definitions, Value Sets, and Business Rule Specifications for name appropriateness, Definition Accuracy, Completeness, and Clarity, as per the form (TIQM P1.6.3).

TIP Ensure you have appropriate representation from all business areas that require or create the logistics Information. Timing issues and the interdependencies among Stakeholder business areas require accurate and timely communications.

Step 4. Send out the questionnaires with instructions ahead of the scheduled meeting and assemble the Information Stakeholders or conduct an online meeting with the Stakeholders over your intranet (TIQM P1.6.4).

Step 5. Compile the evaluation results and report them to key Stakeholders, including Process Owners who might need to improve the Information Definition Process, if warranted. And of course, the feedback should be used to improve the actual definitions. Business Rule Specifications for Logistics will come through experimentation to test Logistics assumptions to refine the Logistics Model (TIQM P1.6.5).

Step 6. Use the feedback to improve the Information Definition Process, if warranted. Also use the feedback to improve the actual Definitions and Business Rule Specifications as necessary (TIQM P1.6.6).

TIP If your Customer's Logistics Information definitions and business rule Specifications are lacking, call attention to the specific problems, and at the same time offer to work with them to help them improve. Poor definitions and Quality Standards can be difficult to reconcile to the attributes in your own Information Model, which can cause Quality problems in your own logistics processes.

Now that you have a clear assessment of the meaning of the Logistics Information, measure the Accuracy and other critical Quality Characteristics of the data and Information Presentation.

Measuring Accuracy of Logistics Information Quality (TIQM P2)

The second assessment is an assessment of the accuracy of Logistics Information. Follow the general steps described in Chapter 5 "Measuring Accuracy and Other Information Quality Characteristics." Following are tips for Logistics Information Quality measurement.

TIP Conduct separate assessments of Logistics Information. One will be of your internal Logistics. Your Logistics Information are your schedules for Production and movement of Products and Materials within your warehouses, manufacturing facilities, and to your distribution centers or retail units. The other Logistics Information you depend on is that of your Suppliers who are scheduling from their Suppliers, if any, to their manufacturing and distribution centers to your receiving points. Everyone in the total Supply Chain is interdependent on each other to increase value and decrease waste in the *movement* of Materials and Products to the end-Consumers.

NOTE The Supply Chain does not end with the receipt of the Products or services delivered to the end-Consumers — it continues through the life of the Product or service, and its servicing, to its end of life or end of use and disposition.

Identifying a Set of Logistics Information for Measuring Accuracy (TIQM P2.1)

Select the set of CTQ Logistics attributes that may include:

- Customer Orders and Order Items
- Orders to Suppliers and Supplier Order Items
- Containers or Trailers available
- Container or Trailer GPS Location Coordinates
- Drivers or Pilots available
- Scheduled Pick-up Date and Time
- Pick-up Contact, Address, and Directions
- Scheduled Delivery Date and Time
- Delivery Contact, Address, and Directions
- Actual Pick-up Date and Time

- Damaged Goods observed at Pick-up
- Actual Delivery Date and Time
- Damaged Goods observed at Delivery
- Container or Trailer scheduled
- Container or Trailer used
- Container or Trailer Tare Weight (weight empty) and Gross Weight (sum of the weight of the goods and the weight of the container or trailer)
- Delivery Route Scheduled
- Delivery Route Taken with reasons for detours, if any
- Inspection Point Dates and Times and Results
- Pick-up, Transport, and Delivery Problem Descriptions, if any
- Product Movements from Point-to-Point in Transit or in Warehouse to manufacturing to assembly line point

The measurement of Accuracy of Logistics Information compared to Orders and Planned Movements will increase your ability to improve the Logistics and Movements of Components and Materials, and finished Products and Services.

Planning IQ Objectives, Measures, and Tests for Logistics Information (TIQM P2.2)

This step defines your business objective for measuring Logistics IQ, the specific Quality Characteristics you will measure, and the tests for actually conducting the assessment of each Quality Characteristic.

Step 1. Establish IQ Assessment objective. The major objective for measuring Logistics Information accuracy is to ensure moving Supplies, Inventory, and finished Products from where they are to where they need to be throughout the Supply Chain efficiently to eliminate waste of excess inventory, or stock-outs and rush shipments. Are the Logistics processes (both internal and within your Suppliers) maximizing your Production and Delivery processes to meet your Customers' Expectations?

Step 2. Identify the specific Quality Characteristics to assess. This should include Accuracy, Completeness, and Timeliness of the Logistics Information, as well as the Accuracy of Item Movement Pick-up and Delivery Times.

- **Accuracy:** To measure Accuracy of Logistics Information, such as if actual pick-up and delivery dates and times are accurate to within an acceptable variation of scheduled pick-up and delivery dates and times

- **Completeness:** To measure Completeness of the Logistics Information, such that you know where any item is in any shipment in any container at any point in time

- **Accuracy of Pick-up and Delivery Addresses and Times:** To measure Accuracy of the pick-up and delivery times, confirm manually recorded times with independent conformation or automated time recording with calibrated clocks, depending on precision Requirements.

VALID POSTAL ADDRESSES CAN CAUSE LOGISTICS PROCESSES TO FAIL

In logistics, the process of getting a tractor, trailer, and driver to a pick-up location will fail if the postal address is different from the pick-up or delivery location. Pick up and delivery addresses are physical loading or unloading docks that often require physical directions for the drivers. Using postal addresses can also cause discrepancies in shipping distances, a factor in transportation costs. The pick-up delivery addresses must allow for instructions and landmarks to guide the drivers.

TIP Sometimes, packages will not have their bar codes or RFIDs read properly, and their location is not known until the next location scan point. This can cause problems if transportation vehicles are in accidents, and it will not be able to be determined if items are on board or not. Find and fix Root Causes of missing location Information at any required location point in the Supply Chain.

- **Timeliness:** To measure Timeliness, ensure that you get all Logistics Information at a time you require to know the state of items, and and that you can deliver the Information to your Customers as requested.

- **Equivalence:** To ensure that the Information in any redundant data store is consistent with each other

Step 3. Define the specific measurements tests to Accurately Assess the Conformance to the Quality Characteristic

Identify and Define your Forecast-to-Satisfied-Customer Information Value Circle (TIQM P2.3)

If they have not been documented before, define the process and process steps of your Supply Chain both internally for your organization and across your Supplier, distributor, and Customer organizations. Each process can have failure that cascades through the subsequent processes.

NOTE You will not perform this step on your Suppliers' Logistics processes. This is a step they should perform on their Logistics processes. You may work with all your Business Partners in measuring and improving the overall Supply Chain processes for the benefit of the end-Consumers.

Determining the Logistics Information Store or Process to Assess (TIQM P2.4)

This will be the originating databases or data stores in which Logistics Information is first captured. If the Information is modified in this originating data store or moved to another data store and modified, you need to measure any changes to ensure they are correctly modified and are traceable back to the source data.

CAUTION If a package actual delivery date and time is earlier than the actual package pick-up date and time, you have an error somewhere.

Identifying Accuracy Verification Sources (TIQM P2.5)

See Chapter 5, "The Step-by-Step Guide to *Assessing Information Quality*." Step P2.5 will lead you to the fact that the *authoritative source* to measure Logistics Information Accuracy is the Actual Sales figures for the time of Logistics projection, as adjusted as necessary for the preceding note.

TIP To measure Accuracy of GPS locations of Containers, Packages, or Tractors, use a highly calibrated GPS device and at a specific physical location of a Container or Package, compare the installed GPS location coordinates with those of your calibrated and more precise GPS device.

Extracting a Statistically Valid Sample of Logistics Data (TIQM P2.6)

Begin with the most problematic Logistics Information problems to sample. It may be by Customer or by your internal Logistics of Products, aggregated from all Logistics Information.

Measuring Logistics Information Quality in Selected IQ Characteristics (TIQM P2.7)

This step executes the specific measurements as defined in TIQM P2.2.2. You should measure the process effectiveness of each Logistics source (Supplier and your internal Logistics processes).

TIP The key to effective IQ assessment is to ensure you perform the assessment in a way that *minimizes bias* in the measurement. Measurement must be made at a time and in a way that is outside the knowledge of the Information Producers, and in a way that does not corrupt the actual data values, and in a way that there can be no update of Information after the Information was created. This measures Accuracy (or validity) of the originating create process.
    See Chapter 5 for a discussion of general principles for conducting the assessment in a way that is "repeatable" and "reproducible."

To minimize bias:

- **For accuracy**: This means comparing the *actual* Pick-up and Delivery dates and times with automated GPS tracking, or barcode scanning that can be verified by observers of the Pick-up and/or Delivery events.

SOME AIRLINES REPORTED FAULTY ON-TIME FLIGHT ARRIVAL DATA

Shortly after the U.S. Department of Transportation (DOT) mandated flight arrival Information, it conducted an inspection to assess the accuracy of the arrival time Information. The DOT sent out inspectors to observe arrival times of 372 flights for ten airlines at eight airports. Airlines that had planes equipped with an Aircraft Communication Addressing and Reporting System (ACARS) had a 40-percent error rate of arrival times, compared with inspectors' observed times. The errors were due to the reporting touch-down time — not gate arrival time. Of the airlines whose gate agents reported arrival times manually, the error rate was 59 percent as compared to the inspectors' observed times. The airlines that reported manually had an anomaly of flights arriving 14 minutes after scheduled arrival time, the latest time a flight could arrive and still be considered "on-time." This indicates a bias in arrival-time reporting because of the Requirement to report the information publicly — and whereby flyers may make travel decisions. Biased reporting has been significantly reduced due to periodic, unannounced accuracy assessments by the DOT since the late 1990s.[11]

- **For Completeness**: This means determining where location or package Information is missing.
- **For Timeliness**: This means ensuring that pick-ups and deliveries were on dates and times that were acceptable to all parties.

Interpreting and Reporting Information Quality of Logistics Information (TIQM P2.8)

Report the Information in the form of number or percent of defects and defective records measured. Use a statistical Quality Control Chart of the process measured over time. See Chapter 5, "The Step-by-Step Guide to *Assessing Information Quality*," Process Step P2.8, "Interpret and Report Information Quality."

For Logistics accuracy, track the logistics events in their scheduled and actual dates and times. Look for ways to improve and reduce time and costs of movements and inventory. See "Best Practices in Logistics Information Quality" at the end of this section.

TIP See the IQ Assessment templates in Chapter 5, "The Step-by-Step Guide to *Assessing Information Quality*," TIQM Process Step 2.8, "Interpreting and Reporting Information Quality."

> **NOTE** Always use assessment Information to identify which processes to improve to eliminate waste, such as overstocks, delays in movements, inaccurate locations (from or to) that require moving again, inaccurate Product weights that increase transportation costs, and Information Scrap and Rework of defective and missing Information.

How to Improve Logistics and Inventory Information Process Quality (TIQM P4)

The preceding assessments should give you an indication if and where you or your trade partners' logistics processes may be broken. If the current logistics processes (multiple processes in Customer organizations and internal within your organization) are causing process failure, waste, and Product and Information Scrap and Rework, you, or your Customers, can use the classic Plan-Do-Check/Study-Act cycle described in TIQM P4 "Improve Information Process Quality" in Chapter 7. You may also use TIQM Six Sigma and apply the DMAIC (Define-Measure-Analyze-Improve-Control) format, which implements the same TIQM processes, but in a slightly different way. See the TIQM Six Sigma DMAIC mapping in Chapter 7, Table 7-7, "TIQM Processes and Steps Mapped to Six Sigma Phases and Steps."

> **CAUTION** Before you improve the Logistics, or any other process, measure the Costs of IQ problems in logistics Information *before* you conduct a Process Improvement. This becomes a *baseline* for measuring the effectiveness of the improvement. Once the process is improved and in control, you should measure the *reduction* in the costs of Failure and Information Scrap and Rework, and in Manufacturing Scrap and Rework by the improved process. This establishes the ongoing Value of Process Improvement. See TIQM P3, "Measure the Costs of Poor Quality Information," in Chapter 6.

Defining a Project for Logistics Process Improvement (TIQM P4.1)

This process step creates a Process Improvement Initiative, following your organization's project management protocol. Activities include:

4.1.1. Identify the Logistics *process* requiring improvement. For example, this may be the organization's Logistics Process, or that of one or more of its Customers who provide Logistics Information for their own purchases.

4.1.2. Identify the *Process Owner*, who is accountable for the logistics process to be improved, and who is responsible for implementing improvements to meet all Information Consumers' IQ Requirements.

4.1.3 Identify the facilitator for the Process Improvement Initiative. This should be the Process Owner. An IQ IPI facilitator may co-facilitate.

4.1.4 Identify the Information Producers and other pertinent personnel who can *identify* defect Causes and Improvements to eliminate causes. This always includes the Information Producers, Transcriptionists, Translators, and others whose processes create or update the defective Information.

4.1.5 Develop the project plan, based on your organization's project management procedures for conducting the Process Improvement Initiative.

TIP Improvement Initiatives may fall into two categories: major and minor. Each may have its own set of project management procedures and governance protocol. Because Process Improvement Initiatives involve improving and error-proofing processes to eliminate defects, they invariably (when performed correctly, based upon documented waste and Costs of Poor Quality Information) will yield a positive Return on Investment.

NOTE Seek to reduce *unnecessary procedural activities and red tape* for minor improvement initiatives. Allow people to easily identify broken processes, and enable them to improve them with minimal approval steps that can cause improvement initiatives to get bogged down and become a disincentive for identifying and solving real problems.

Planning for a Logistics Process Improvement: Root-Cause Analysis (TIQM P4.2.1)

The first step of "Plan" Process Improvement (TIQM P4.2.1) is to brainstorm and discover the Root Causes of the negative effects. With your Process Improvement facilitator and the Logistics Process Improvement Team, brainstorm likely Root Causes on a Cause-and-Effect diagram to analyze and confirm the Root Causes of the inaccurate Logistics Information or other studied Logistics IQ problems. See how to conduct a Root-Cause Analysis session in Chapter 7, Step TIQM P4.2.1.

Root Causes can include, but are not limited to, those listed on the Cause-and-Effect diagram in Figure 11-5.

The identification of causes will identify both precipitating causes, as well as potential Root Causes. You must continue to ask "Why?" to get back from precipitating causes to the Root Causes.

If the Process Improvement Team is not able to determine the cause definitively, you must go and measure the process against the different potential causes to identify the specific Root Cause or Causes. You may have to conduct one or more Design of Experiments to isolate the actual Root Cause.

NOTE Any improvement that addresses elimination of the precipitating causes only will be suboptimized. Sometimes you will have to go back and observe the processes to confirm that a cause is a real Root Cause. Logistics is a complex process with many variables, potentially requiring Design of Experiments to identify the impacts of the interactions among the many causal factors.

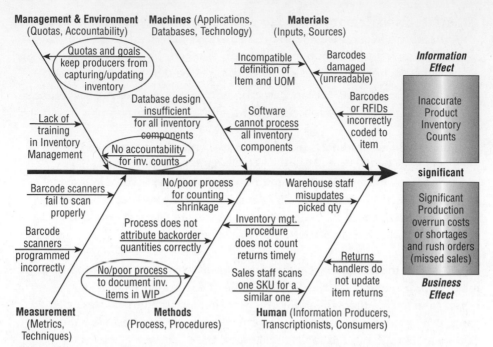

Figure 11-5: Cause-and-Effect Diagram for Defective Inventory Information

TIP Avoid finger pointing or blame assignment as you seek to discover the causes of the "broken processes" — not broken people. The causes will always be in the process itself or in the management environment that influences how processes are performed.

Planning for an Inventory Process Improvement: Defining Improvements to Prevent Defect Root Causes (TIQM P4.2.2)

See the general description of Process TIQM P4.2.2 in Chapter 7. Preventive actions or considerations include those shown in Table 11-8.

Table 11-8: Logistics Root Causes and Potential Improvement Considerations

INACCURATE INVENTORY ROOT CAUSES	PROCESS IMPROVEMENT CONSIDERATIONS
1. Material: Barcodes damaged and unreadable	1. Ensure the barcode label creation process is not causing the damage. If so, identify the cause and error-proof the label production process. For example, the labels may be too thick for the printer, causing the labels to tear. Backing on labels may be difficult to separate and cause a tear. 2. Place barcode labels in places less likely to be damaged and where readers can access clearly.

INACCURATE INVENTORY ROOT CAUSES	PROCESS IMPROVEMENT CONSIDERATIONS
2. Material: Incompatible definition of item and UOM	1. Ensure there is clear and precise definition of when and how to count items, and when and where to use the item SKU count and when to extend the inventory count by multiplying the UOM times the quantity of cases or packs. 2. Ensure that all uses of numeric values are associated with clear labels that unambiguously identify the meaning of the values. 3. Ensure all staff are properly trained in the use of quantities and UOMs.
3. Process: No or poor process for counting shrinkage	1. Define or improve the process definition for all activities associated with inventory count updating. Involve all actors who are involved in creating and updating of inventory information. 2. Define all business rules required to handle all aspects of inventory quantities and the locations and movements of the inventories.
4. Process: Does not attribute backorder quantities correctly.	Same as 3.
5. Process: No or poor process to document inventory items in WIP	Same as 3.
6. Process: Inventory management procedure does not count returns in a timely manner.	Same as 3.
7. Technology: Database design insufficient for all inventory components	Conduct a Product Information Model review to ensure the Inventory Entities and Attributes in the Model (and Database Design) reflect the required information to manage inventory accurately and on a timely basis. This includes inventory quantities in each bin or stack of items, order quantities and adjustments, back-order quantities and adjustments, return quantities, and quantities of items completed in WIP areas. Also, you must know about items Scrapped, Reworked, or forgiven when replacement items are provided to Customers. Make all updates necessary to the Product Information Model and Database Design to house all necessary inventory Information.

(continued)

Table 11-8 (continued)

INACCURATE INVENTORY ROOT CAUSES	PROCESS IMPROVEMENT CONSIDERATIONS
8. Technology: Software cannot process all inventory components or difficult to use.	Redesign the software to process all inventory information properly. Define and implement all approved business rules for counting inventory. Ensure that every process that makes adjustments to inventory counts handles the adjustments correctly, incrementing and decrementing the proper inventory counts accurately.
8. Measurement: Barcode scanners fail to scan properly.	Analyze the cause of scanner failure. Is it mechanical failure? Software failure? Improper use of scanner? Barcode error? (See causes 1. and 2.)
9. Measurement: Barcode scanners are programmed incorrectly.	1. See cause 8.
10. Human: Returns handlers do not update item returns.	1. Find out why. Lack of knowledge of update procedures? Faulty procedures? No procedures at all? Then go review and improve them. (See causes 3–6) 2. Lack of training? (See cause 14.)
11. Human: Warehouse staff mis-updates picked quantities.	1. Find out why. Lack of training? (See cause 14.) System screen designs not intuitive or hard to use? (See cause 8.)
12. Human: Sales or warehouse staff scans the wrong SKU for a similar one.	1. Why? Lack of training? See cause 14. 2. Staff pressed for quotas or speed scan a convenient SKU instead of the correct inventory item? (See cause 13.) 3. Poor systems design? 4. Lack of accountability for inventory counts? (See cause 15.)
13. Mgt Environment: Quotas and goals keep Producers from capturing or updating inventory correctly.	1. Measure the costs of ownership of the processes based upon speed first and accuracy and completeness last. Management must see how their performance measures are a false sense of Productivity and increased Scrap and Rework for all. See TIQM Process P3, "Measure Poor Quality Information Costs and Risk" in Chapter 6, "The Step-by-Step Guide to *Measuring the Costs and Risks of Poor Quality Information.*"

INACCURATE INVENTORY ROOT CAUSES	PROCESS IMPROVEMENT CONSIDERATIONS
14. Mgt Environment: Lack of appropriate training in inventory management	1. Review training materials and update and enhance them as necessary. Involve training development staff and subject experts in development or enhancement of training.
	2. After improving the training material, test its effectiveness by measuring the performance of those who take it and a control group of those who have not taken the training.
15. Mgt Environment: No accountability in management for inventory counts	1. Why? Information is perceived as a by-Product and not a valued Product and resource of the enterprise. Ultimately, you will need to implement accountability for every manager (first) in their job descriptions. Then, with training and providing the resources necessary to perform Information work effectively, accountability can be written into Information Producers and Knowledge Workers' accountabilities.
	2. In the short term, you can develop Stewardship contracts between Information Producer managers and their downstream Information Consumer managers. Accompanying these contracts and accountability, every Stakeholder must have training in IQ principles, processes, and techniques for improving and error-proofing processes.

TIP If you have business partners with best practices in logistics, involve them in your Process Improvement definition initiative.

"Do" Implement Logistics Process Improvements in a Controlled Way to Check Effectiveness and Study Lessons Learned (TIQM Step P4.3)

See the TIQM Process Step P4.3 in Chapter 7 for guidelines and how to manage the controlled, proof-of-concept Process Improvement. It is critical to conduct this PoC improvement in a way to ensure its success in your early improvement initiatives while you are seeking to gain management commitment and demonstrate tangible business value of IQ management.

First define improvements in your internal Logistics Process and implement it in a controlled way to record the results to study the impact of the improvements.

It may take some iteration to fine tune it. The goal here will not be zero defects, but a precision of accuracy that will minimize costs of overproduction or underproduction, Information Scrap and Rework, and Stakeholder alienation. After a successful trial internally, turn to two or three of your business partners and help them implement this in a controlled way to test it for their own logistics processes.

Check and Study Impact of the Process Improvements on the Logistics Process and its Results (TIQM Step P4.4)

In this process step you study the effectiveness of the improvements on logistics accuracy. Observe the results to ensure you do not introduce negative side effects that create new problems.

Do this by comparing the actual and adjusted sales to the logistics from your newly defined or improved logistics process.

Study the logistics and inventory results to assess the increase in effectiveness of the process definition.

Once you feel comfortable in your internal results, go back to step 4.3 to implement in your test-case Customers.

Act to Standardize the Logistics Process Improvements (TIQM Step P4.5)

Once your have an effective and sustainable improvement, put the process in control with actions to standardize the improvements and roll the process out to all Stakeholders.

Best Practices in Logistics Information Quality

SCHNEIDER NATIONAL IMPROVES ITS CUSTOMER'S ORDER SCHEDULING PROCESS, SAVING TIME AND MONEY

Schneider National, Inc., the nation's largest truckload carrier had trouble with Customer Transportation Orders' Logistical Information being unreliable, and frequently modified less than 24 hours prior to Shipment Pick-up Time, causing driver and truck scheduling problems. Schneider's Process Improvement Team conducted an analysis of their Customer Order Process, involving 7-8 of the Customer's key Knowledge Workers, ranging from Manufacturing to Customer Care across organizational lines. The joint Schneider-Customer Team was able to improve the order process and put it in control, eliminating the waste generated by the unreliable process. Because their Customer's Stakeholders were involved in the analysis and process improvement, the new process was readily accepted and performed.

The improvement benefited both Schneider National and their Customer.

> ## SCHNEIDER NATIONAL, INC. IMPROVES ITS TRAILER LOCATION PROCESS, WITH A MULTI-MILLION DOLLAR SAVINGS POTENTIAL
>
> Because of network communication costs, Schneider National, Inc., a national transportation company, conducted "trailer (box) searches" by sending a signal via satellite to its trailers once a week to "ping" the GPS location of each trailer used for Customer Shipments. By experimenting they found that their frequency of gathering GPS location information was not appropriate in delivering the type of Information Accuracy required. GPS location information four or more days old meant the trailer probably had been moved to a new location. By increasing the frequency of the box search from four days to between two and three days, Schneider increased the likelihood that the trailer was indeed where the information said it would be. The multi-million dollar savings potential was well over the increased costs of the more frequent box searches.

Information Quality Applied to Package Measurement Information

Here we describe how to measure and improve the process Quality of package measurement Information. Poor Quality Package Measurement Information causes *Under- or Over-Sizing of Package containers*, *under- or over-stated* weights and other errors that increase the costs of storage and transportation. It can further cause damage to Products if the packaging is not sufficiently strong for stacking, storage, and or shipping.

Measuring Accuracy of Product Package Measurement Information Quality (TIQM P2)

Package Measurement Information is important to minimize the space in both *retail* packages and *shipping* packages, to minimize cost of packaging and shipping.

To measure Accuracy and Precision of Package Measurement Information, you will conduct a physical assessment of sample packages for the same *packaged* Products, comparing the *actual package* weights and dimensions to the published standard weights and dimensions for that packaged Product. The packages sampled should be for a single packaged Product type as identified with a unique Global Trade Item Number (GTIN). Follow the general steps described in Chapter 5, "Step-By-Step Guide to *Assessing Information Quality*," in the section about Measuring Accuracy and Other Information Quality Characteristics.

Identifying a Set of Logistics Information for Measuring Accuracy (TIQM P2.1)

Select the set of Package Measurement attributes that may include:

- Case or Package GTIN
- GTIN Item Description
- Package Description
- Package Weight Unit of Measure
- Net Content Nominal Weight (if applicable)
- Net Content Weight Specification Limits (if applicable)
- Package Gross Weight Nominal Value (if applicable)
- Package Gross Weight Specification Limits (if applicable)
- Package Dimension Unit of Measure
- Package Length (Depth) Nominal Value and Specification Limits
- Package Width Nominal Value and Specification Limits
- Package Height Nominal Value and Specification Limits

Planning IQ Objectives, Measures, and Tests for Package Measurement Information (TIQM P2.2)

This step defines your Business Objective for measuring Product Package Measurement Information IQ, the specific Quality Characteristics you will measure, and the Tests for conducting the Assessment of each Quality Characteristic.

Step 1. Establish IQ Assessment objective. The major objective for measuring package measurement Information accuracy is to ensure the weights and dimensions of the sampled packages for a specific GTIN Product are within an acceptable variation of the weight and dimension Specifications that minimizes costs of Logistics. Conversely, your second objective is to ensure that the defined measurement nominal values and Specification Limits are accurate to the actual Product packages produced.

Step 2. Identify the specific Quality Characteristics to assess. This should include Accuracy and Precision of the sampled package measurements to conform to the package measurement Specifications, falling within the dimension Specification Limits.

Identifying the Package Measurement Process Value Circle (TIQM P2.3)

Document the Package Measurement Value Circle to understand the process activities and Information Stakeholders' requirements.

Determining the Package Measurement Process to Assess (TIQM P2.4)

The process measured is the process that establishes the package weights and measures that are to be shared with trading partners.

> **NOTE** This assessment also measures the degree to which the physical packaging process conforms to the specified nominal values within its Specification Limits.

Identifying Accuracy Verification Sources (TIQM P2.5)

See Chapter 5 "The Step-by-Step Guide to *Assessing Information Quality*." Step P2.5 will lead you to the fact that the authoritative source to measure Logistics Information accuracy is the Actual Sales figures for the time of Logistics projection, as adjusted as necessary for the preceding note.

For Product package measurement Information, the accuracy source will be the sampled packages.

> **TIP** To measure Accuracy and Precision of Product Package Measurement Information, you compare the Nominal Value and Specification Limits to the *actual* measured values of the sample Product packages.

Extracting Statistically Valid Sample of Logistics Data (TIQM P2.6)

The selection of sampled packages must be conducted as randomly as is possible for a set of physical objects. You must have the broadest representation of actual packages to avoid sample bias.

> **TIP** To minimize bias, select samples from all types of sources, including random samples from multiple lots or batches and random samples from multiple pallets or bins or from store shelves from multiple stores.

Measuring Logistics Information Quality in Selected IQ Characteristics (TIQM P2.7)

This step executes the specific measurements as defined in TIQM P2.2.2. You should measure the process effectiveness of each Logistics source (Supplier and your internal Logistics Processes).

> **NOTE** The key to effective IQ assessment is to ensure you perform the assessment in a way that *minimizes bias* in the measurement. Measurement must be made at a time and in a way that is *outside the knowledge* of the Information Producers, in a way that does not corrupt the *actual information values*, and in a way that *there can be no update of information* after the information was created. This measures accuracy (or validity) of the originating create process. See Chapter 5 for a discussion of general principles for conducting the assessment in a way that is "repeatable" and "reproducible." To minimize bias:

- **Ensure your measurement area has a controlled environment that is consistent across all measurements made. This includes controlled temperature and humidity.**

- **Standardize a measurement procedure that at least adheres to the guidelines published in the GDSN Package Measurement Rules for consistency,[12] but may be more rigorous depending on your organization's Requirements.**

- **Calibrate the measurement equipment or device to ensure it is accurate to the appropriate precision. Use the same measurement equipment or device to ensure consistency of measurement.**

For Measurement of Non-Consumer Trade Items:[13]

Step 1. Establish the *natural base* of the package.

Step 2. Establish *standard measurement points* for the package.

Step 3. Place the package with the base *on a smooth surface in a specific location.* Use a *jig to control the placement to ensure uniformity* in measurement.

Step 4. Measure the width of the package and record the results. If measurements are *recorded manually*, double-check them.

Step 5. Measure the length (depth) and height and record the results. If measurements are *recorded manually*, double-check them.

Step 6. Weigh the package on a *calibrated* weigh scale and record its gross weight. If the weight is *recorded manually*, double-check the figure and precision.

For Measurement of Consumer Trade Items:

Step 1. Establish *the front* of the package.

Step 2. Establish *standard measurement points* for the package.

Step 3. Place the package on a *smooth surface in a specific location* with the front facing you. *Use a jig to control the placement* to ensure uniformity of measurement.

Step 4. Measure the width of the package and record the results. If measurements are *recorded manually*, double-check them.

Step 5. Measure the length (depth) and height and record the results. If measurements are *recorded manually*, double-check them.

Step 6. Weigh the package on a calibrated weigh scale and record its gross weight. If the weight is *recorded manually*, double-check the figure and precision.

How to Improve Product Package Measurement Information Process Quality (TIQM P4)

It is *not enough* to simply correct inaccurate Product package measurement information in your database and your trade partners' database. You must identify the *Root Causes* and *improve the process* to prevent defective package measurement information in the process that creates and maintains it.

See Table 11-9 for example Root Causes and Considerations for Process Improvement.

Table 11-9: Product Package Measurement Error Root Causes and Potential Improvement Considerations

INACCURATE PRODUCT PACKAGE MEASUREMENT ROOT CAUSES	PROCESS IMPROVEMENT CONSIDERATIONS
1. Process: Package weights and measures not kept up-to-date with Product changes	1. Enhance Product design process to re-measure and recalculate the Nominal Values.
2. Process: Package weights and measures are calculated without sample measurement.	1. *Define* a process for Product sample measurement before assigning nominal values.
3. Technology: Software does not calculate weights and measures appropriately.	1. Software calculations must be corroborated by physically measuring sampled Product packages as described in a previous section, "Measuring Accuracy of Product Package Measurement Information Quality."
4. Technology: Data does not contain all components for correct calculation.	1. Same as number 3.
5. Measurement: Equipment is not as precise as is required.	1. Replace with *more precise* equipment.
6. Source: Weights and dimensions of components are inaccurate.	1. Improve the process for measuring the *component parts*, as described in the section, "Measuring Accuracy of Product Package Measurement Information Quality."
7. Human: Information Producers did not follow strict procedures for measuring Product packages.	1. Provide *training and follow-up* to ensure procedures are followed.
8. Human: Information Producers fail to measure in a standard way, getting invalid measurements.	1. Ensure process is *clearly defined* and Producers follow them.

(continued)

Table 11-9 *(continued)*

INACCURATE PRODUCT PACKAGE MEASUREMENT ROOT CAUSES	PROCESS IMPROVEMENT CONSIDERATIONS
9. Human: Staff measures the wrong Products.	1. Find out why. Lack of training? (See cause 14.) System screen designs not intuitive or hard to use? (See cause 8.)
10. Human: Information Producers rush to measure, making errors.	1. Review *performance measures* and ensure speed is *not* inappropriately rewarded over accurate work.
11. Human: Staff measures the *wrong* Product packages.	1. Ensure the process confirms that the Product package measures are correct with the sampled packages.
12. Mgt. Environment: Measurement conditions are *variable across measurements*.	1. Standardize the process to ensure a *constant and stable environment* exists for measurements.
13. Mgt. Environment: Staff rewarded for speed over Quality work	1. Review performance measures and ensure speed is *not* inappropriately rewarded over accurate work.
14. Mgt Environment: Lack of appropriate training in the package measurement process	1. Review *training materials, update and enhance* them as necessary. Involve training development staff and subject experts in development or enhancement of training. 2. After improving the training material, test its effectiveness by measuring the performance of those who take it and a control group of those who have not taken the training.
15. Mgt Environment: *No accountability* in management for Product package measurement Information	1. Why? Information is perceived as a by-product and not a valued Product and resource of the enterprise. Ultimately, you will need to implement *accountability for every manager* (first) in their job descriptions. Then, with training and providing the resources necessary to perform Information work effectively, accountability can be written into Information Producers' and Knowledge Workers' accountabilities. 2. In the short term, you can develop stewardship contracts between Information Producer managers and their downstream Information Consumer managers. Accompanying these contracts and accountability, every Stakeholder must have training in IQ principles, processes, and techniques for improving and error-proofing processes.

Best Practices in Product Package Measurement Information Quality

REGIONAL RETAIL CHAIN IMPROVES PRODUCT PACKAGE SIZE AND WEIGHT ACCURACY: MAXIMIZES ITS DISTRIBUTION AND REDUCES TRANSPORT COSTS

A regional retail chain conducted accuracy assessments of its packaged Product weights by selecting a sample of the shipping cartons and found that on average the actual weights were about 0.75 pounds heavier than the stated packaged Product weights. Obsolete information was caused by failure to re-weigh Products when the Product Specifications were modified over time. By correcting the weights and improving the process to capture the correct weights by weighing samples, it increased utilization of nearly 20 percent more capacity of its shipping containers. This reduced the number of shipments — and shipping costs of suboptimized shipments considerably.

MANUFACTURER IMPROVES PRODUCT PACKAGE SIZE AND WEIGHT ACCURACY: SAVES OVER $2 MILLION PER YEAR FOR ONE PRODUCT LINE ALONE

A manufacturing firm discovered by IQ assessment that every Product's weight in one Product line was overstated. Information Quality decay was the precipitating cause. Failure to keep Product Specifications up-to-date was the Root Cause. Once the information and process were updated, the company saw transportation costs decrease by more than $2 million per year on the one Product line. Expected savings when other Product lines are updated are estimated at up to $3 million more.

Summary

You have learned some critical places in the "Forecast-to-Satisfied-Customer" Value Circle where Information Quality is vital to the effectiveness of Forecasting, planning, production, delivery, servicing, and disposal of products and is critical for the success of the enterprise. When you continually delight Customers, you retain them, deepen their loyalty, and increase their Customer Lifetime Value.

CHAPTER 12

Information Quality Applied to Financial and Risk Management: "Budget-to-Profit"

"Making decisions that focus on quarterly profit-and-loss statements without understanding Customer needs is a guaranteed way to enterprise failure."

Larry P. English

Introduction to Information Quality in Financial and Risk Management

This chapter on *Information Quality in Financial Management* describes how to measure and improve *Financial and Risk Management Information*. The goal is to ensure that the organization is fiscally responsible, and has an accurate and clear understanding of the Value derived from its spending and investment. This chapter also addresses the Quality of Compliance Information to ensure that it is being a good Steward for *all* of its Stakeholders.

Financial resources are used to acquire other resources, for example, to hire and pay Employees, build or lease facilities, purchase equipment to develop products and services for the Customer. Financial Information represents the organization's income and expenses and its asset and liability position as well as its Financial health.

Without accurate Financial Information, Strategic and Tactical Planning is hampered and operational activities can be disrupted.

Figure 12-1: The Importance of Accurate Expense and Time Reporting

Categories of Financial and Risk Information

Quality principles must be applied to three critical categories of Financial Information:

- **Budget Planning, Financial Management Accounting, and External Financial Reporting Information:** This includes, Budget Account Codes and General Ledger Account Codes, and Budget Information. This also includes actual revenue and expense allocation information to enable the company to analyze the effectiveness of its investments and expenditures. *External Financial Reporting* includes Information the organization reports on its fiscal health to its Stakeholders, including statutory and regulatory reporting for public companies as required by the Securities and Exchange Commission in the United States, International Financial Reporting Standards in many other countries, and other regulatory reporting requirements.

- **Risk Management Information:** This includes Information such as Credit rating and history, organizational Executive Leadership Team strength, S&P (Standard and Poor's) Rating, as well as Risk Factors, such as home construction material and location for insurance underwriting that enables the organization to understand the Risk of management decisions.

- **Audit and Compliance Information:** This includes Information about the organization's ability to meet minimum Requirements to assure the public and other Stakeholders that it is being a good Steward to all. Examples include: Sarbanes-Oxley, the Fair Credit Act Reporting (U.S.), The USA PATRIOT Act, and similar legislation around the world and Basel II for Financial Institutions.

Financial Information Stakeholders

There are many Financial Information Consumers and Stakeholders throughout the Enterprise. Failure to provide High-Quality *Information* through the Financial Value Circle will cause Budgeting, Capital expenditures, and Financial transaction (invoices, payments, and deposits), Accounting, Fraud Detection, and Regulation Compliance processes to fail, sometimes with catastrophic results.

Internal Information Stakeholders

Within the organization, Financial Information Stakeholders include those shown in Table 12-1.

Table 12-1: Internal Information Stakeholders and Their Information Interests

INTERNAL INFORMATION STAKEHOLDERS	INFORMATION INTERESTS
CEO and CFO	Responsible and accountable for the management of the Enterprise's Financial Resources, the CFO requires accurate, complete, and timely Financial Information to meet internal and external Financial Management Analysis and reporting. Under Sarbanes-Oxley regulation, the CEO and CFO must sign off on Financial Statements, attesting that they represent the financial health of the Enterprise accurately with no *material errors* in its Financial Position.
Accountants	Accountants require accurate information about all transactions to ensure that the Financial Reports are accurate.
Internal Auditors	Internal Auditors require access to information and processes to conduct broad and comprehensive internal verification (audits) of Financial Information and the processes that create, update, or delete Financial Information, ensuring that effective Controls are in place.
Contract Officers	Contract Officers require Information, Policies, and Procedures to create Contracts, update contract details, cancel contracts, and administer contracts. In this role, they rely on a wide variety of Financial Information.
Budget Planners and Finance Departments	Finance Departments have direct Accountability for much of the Financial Information and Financial Statements. They regularly set the Budgets and Forecasts, and work with management on a regular basis to ensure accurate Financial Tracking and Planning and to provide management and External Financial Reports.

(continued)

Table 12-1 (continued)

INTERNAL INFORMATION STAKEHOLDERS	INFORMATION INTERESTS
Financial Analysts	Analysts mine and analyze Financial Information or combine it in new ways to create Business Intelligence. For example: Analysts advise the CEO about the right price to offer for a potential acquisition.
Risk Analysts	Risk Departments require Financial and Decision-making Information to determine the Risks the organization faces, at an Enterprise level or at a decision level. For example, they forecast the overall Credit Risks for all Loans on the books or the total expected Insurance Losses. This type of Financial Information is used to determine and set aside adequate Reserves to cover forecasted losses.
Actuaries and Underwriters	Actuaries trained in math, statistics, and Accounting set Premiums based on Life Expectancy and other Risk Factors for Life Insurance Contracts, Annuities, and Warranty Periods for Products.
	Underwriters make the approval decisions on loans or insurance contracts, possibly requiring additional terms and conditions or denying a loan or insurance application.
Accounts Receivable staff	Receivables staff require accurate information about Product Prices and Orders to properly Invoice and Collect Payments from Customers. Responsible for ensuring that monies are received and processed properly from the sale of goods and services.
Accounts Payable staff	Payables staff are responsible for correctly paying Suppliers for materials and services provided. They are responsible and accountable for paying the company's bills correctly per agreed upon terms. Double payments are a common concern.
Department and Line Managers	Managers develop budget requests for their units for resources necessary to accomplish departmental *and* Enterprise goals. They require accurate financial and other information to make business decisions consistent with the budget, business plan, and Risk temperament.
Compliance Managers	Compliance Departments assist Management in understanding and achieving Compliance with Laws and Regulations. As mentioned earlier, regulations such as Basel II, Sarbanes-Oxley, and the USA PATRIOT Act have Financial Information Requirements.

External Information Stakeholders

External Information Stakeholders and their Information interests are found in Table 12-2:

Table 12-2: External Information Stakeholders and Their Information Interests

EXTERNAL INFORMATION STAKEHOLDERS	INFORMATION INTERESTS
External Auditors	External Auditors require Financial Accounting Information to ensure that reports *accurately* represent the financial health of the Enterprise. External auditors are used, especially for publicly traded companies, to do an independent verification of the integrity of financial information as related to the financial health of an organization.
External Financial Analysts and Stock Brokers	These Stakeholders require accurate Financial Information about publicly traded companies to issue "Buy, Hold, or Sell" recommendations for Investors. Financial reports and analysis require *accurate* Financial Information to understand the financial health of an entity.
Government and Governmental Agencies	The federal governmental organizations such as the Federal Reserve use financial information to determine the health of the economy and where to set the Federal Funds rates and manage the money supply with the goal of having a healthy economy while keeping inflation low.
National and Local Government Tax Authorities	Tax authorities ensure that proper taxes are being withheld and paid.
Suppliers and Business Partners	Suppliers, such as a Parts Supplier to a manufacturing company, use their Customer's financial information to determine payment terms, such as "payable in 30 days," "cash in advance," or "cash on delivery."
Organizational Customers	Customers receive the benefits of High-Quality Information. For example, a Brokerage company with accurate monthly statements or a utility with accurate meter readings and, therefore, accurate monthly bills.
Employees' Families	Employee families want assurance that the financial position of the Enterprise and their pensions and retirement programs are on a sound footing.
Investors	Investors want assurance about the financial position of the Enterprise they invest in to see their investments grow.
Competitors	Competitors look at each other's public Financial Information to understand their competitive position and to help set strategies for growth and acquiring market share, and to select ways to achieve competitive advantage.

(continued)

Table 12-2 *(continued)*

EXTERNAL INFORMATION STAKEHOLDERS	INFORMATION INTERESTS
Creditors	Creditors want assurance that the financial position of the Enterprise is sound and their *loans* will be repaid.
Neighborhood Communities	Communities want assurance that the financial position of the Enterprise will keep the economy of their neighborhood *growing*.
Regulatory Investigators and Agencies	Regulators want assurance that the Enterprise will do good by its Stakeholders, mentioned above.

The Financial and Risk Management Information Value Circle: *"Budget-To-Profit"*

The Financial and Risk Management Information Value Circle: *"Budget-To-Profit,"* is required to ensure that money is spent wisely and decisions are made soundly for the benefit of all Stakeholders. Figure 12-2 illustrates this Value Circle.

Figure 12-2: "Budget-to-Profit" Value Circle

"Budget-to-Profit" Value Circle Processes

The *"Budget-to-Profit"* Value Circle must be addressed as a holistic Value Circle, centered around all Stakeholders. It begins by understanding the purpose of the Enterprise, its Mission and Value Proposition for its Customers, the needs of all Stakeholders, and the products needed to accomplish its Value Proposition.

1. Understand Mission, Customers, and Products

Before you can develop a budget, you must understand the Value Proposition of the Enterprise to the Customer, the needs of the Customer and the capability of the products to deliver value to the Customer.

1. Understand Mission Process Activities

1.1. **Executive Leadership Team:** Develop a shared understanding of the purpose, Mission, Vision, and the Value Proposition for Customers.
1.2. **Managers and staff:** Understand the big picture and how their work is integral to the accomplishment of the aim of the Enterprise and to the delight of their Customers, both internal and external.
1.3. **All Employees:** Understand, capture, and maintain the Critical-to-Quality (CTQ) Information required to realize the Mission.

Common Information Quality Issues

Information Quality issues here include a lack of accuracy or completeness, or inadequate:

- Understanding or acceptance of the Enterprise Mission and Vision
- Understanding of internal and external Customer Requirements
- Understanding of Product, Service, and Information Quality necessary to meet Customer Requirements
- Understanding of *critical* Information required to realize the Mission

Regardless of what part of the Enterprise one works in, all Employees should share a common vision of the purpose of the Enterprise and understand the needs of both internal and external Customers, along with their role in delighting the Customers.

2. Analyze Risk

There are various kinds of Risks affecting the "Budget-to-Profit" Value Circle:

- **Strategic Risk (for a business):** The current and prospective impact on earnings or capital arising from adverse business decisions, improper implementation of decisions, or lack of responsiveness to industry changes. An Information Broker company that collects and sells information without investing in Information Quality *will lose market share* to a Competitor that does.

■ **Credit Risk:** The Risk of loss from a debtor's non-payment of a loan or other line of Credit (either the principal or interest (coupon) or both). An Information Quality example is the recent subprime crisis, where many loans were set up with *inaccurate* Information, which resulted in record high default rates.

■ **Market Risk:** The Risk that the value of an investment will decrease because of moves in financial markets such as changes in stock prices, interest rates, foreign exchange rates, or commodity prices

■ **Operational Risk:** The Risk of loss resulting from inadequate or failed internal processes, people, and systems, or from external events.[1] Operational Risks can be further defined as a measure of the link between a firm's business activities and the variation in its business results[2]

■ **Fraud:** Defined as deceit, trickery, or breach of confidence, perpetrated for profit or to gain unfair or dishonest advantage,[3] Fraud is a type of operational Risk and must be considered, especially for Financial Products and Services, internal or external to the organization.

UK BANK LOST £90 MILLION ($145 MILLION) BECAUSE OF DATA ERRORS

A UK bank lost £90 million because of errors in a computer model that caused inaccurate valuation of a Risk manager's investment positions.

THE BIGGEST INTERNAL FRAUD INCIDENT BY A STOCK TRADER

Reported in the *New York Times*, Jan 25, 2008: "Société Générale, one of the largest banks in Europe, was thrown into turmoil Thursday after it disclosed that a rogue Employee executed a series of 'elaborate, fictitious transactions' that cost the bank more than €5.47 billion ($7 billion), the biggest loss ever recorded by a single trader."

NICK LEESON AND BARINGS BANK

Nick Leeson, a rogue trader at Barings, engaged transaction trades far above his trading authority that resulted in the total collapse of Barings Bank. ING in a major coup, purchased Barings Bank, her Majesty, Queen Elizabeth's personal bank, for £1 (US$2.00)!!!

▪ **Reputation Risk:** The Risk that a firm's goodwill or public perception *will be tarnished*, resulting in potential lost sales and the need to spend money to reestablish its reputation. For example, when a company has a breach of their Customers' *personal* Information, Customers may lose trust in the firm, damaging its reputation. Many such incidents have occurred recently.

These definitions overlap and some Risks are linkable correctly to more than one Risk type. A Risk caused by a person may also have an impact on a firm's reputation. For the purposes here, this overlap is not a problem, but if these categories are used to assign actual financial losses, they require agreed-on and *clearly defined* Business Rules across the Enterprise.

Organizations considering Mergers and Acquisitions (M&A) must consider a variety of information issues and Risks to make sure that they know what they are getting. Steve Sarsfield says in M&A, the "Cash flow is audited and examined with due diligence, but information assets are often only given a hasty passing glance."[4] Duplicate Customer records indicate a lack of Customer knowledge and Customer Lifetime Value or Product Mix Synergy in a merger. For due diligence, analyze the accuracy of all critical information.

MAJOR BANK WRITES OFF NEARLY $3 BILLION IN FAILED ACQUISITION

A major bank acquired an apparently successful subprime mortgage lender. It did not conduct adequate due diligence. After two years, it closed all 97 branches and took a $2.9 Billion write-off.

Insist on assessing the Accuracy, Completeness, and Non-duplication of the Information of the company you seek to acquire or merge with. Bring in your Team, or hire a third party to examine the information. Look at the Customer, Inventory, Sales, Supply Chain, and other critical indicator information.

2. Analyze Risk Process Activities

2.1. **Conduct Risk Assessments using *Qualitative* Methods.** This gives you the big picture of potential Risks.

2.2. **Measure Expected Risks Using *Quantitative* Methods.** Mathematical models measure potential Risk given various scenarios.

2.3. **Create and Execute Risk Reduction and Risk Management Improvement plans.** Define and design appropriate Risk mitigation mechanisms.

2.4. **Measure Actual Risk Incidents, such as Accidents or Warranty Costs.** For a product such as an automobile, the Warranty Costs are realized Risks. For loan companies and banks, defaulted on loans are realized Credit Risks.

2.5. Design Effective and Efficient Controls in Processes to Reduce Risks. A Risk in its original state is considered an *Inherent* Risk. A Control reduces the Risk, and the remaining Risk is called the *Residual* Risk. For example, verifying a Credit application through one or more Credit Bureaus is a Control to ensure this Risk is verified. A low score on a Credit Report results in a higher down payment, higher interest rate, or Credit rejection.

2.6. Detect and Prevent Fraud Risk. For example, use effective Fraud Detection *algorithms* to quickly identify and disable a Credit card if a fraudulent pattern is detected.

Common Information Quality Issues

- **Credit Risk Scoring Models use dozens of Attributes to *quantify* the Risk for a given Customer and Loan Request.** Accuracy of Credit Attributes directly impacts lender and borrower alike. For Consumers, the FICO (Fair Isaac & Co) score is a key data item. FICO seeks to determine the likelihood that Credit Customers will pay their bills. Errors in FICO scores caused by data errors have resulted in lawsuits and eventually legislation giving Consumers specific rights to view their FICO scores and *challenge and change errors* in the supporting data. Recent studies of the three Credit Rating Agencies reveal that 25 percent of individual Credit reports have *material errors or omissions* that can materially affect a Credit rating, causing Credit denial.[5]

- **Identity Theft is a Risk based on fraudulent misuse of name, address, and Personal Identity Information.** This type of fraud has a horrific impact on the victims. Organizations must provide high protection of information that can lead to the theft of the identity of its Customers or Stakeholders.

- **Poor Information Architecture Design Processes result in multiple Disparate Databases.** Multiple Customer databases cause a variety of problems such as combined statement errors or incorrectly measuring Credit Risk, and extending Credit to a Customer who is in default on another product. Many organizations struggle with architectural complexity. It happens for a variety of reasons such as mergers, projects that never realized their full multi-phase plan, or inadequate management oversight. The Root Causes of this are *managing* the Enterprise *up and down the functional Business Areas*, and not having a process that develops Information Models that support *all* Information Stakeholders in the Enterprise. See Chapter 15, "Information Quality Applied to Information Management and Information Systems Engineering," for how to overcome this.

3. Plan Budget to Meet Enterprise Mission

Planning is required to accomplish the Mission economically. Organizations must fund the resources acquired to do so.

3. Plan Budget Process Activities

3.1. **Understand the Enterprise Mission and your unit's Value Proposition for it:** Without a clear understanding of the Enterprise's purpose and how individual work enables accomplishment, a business unit may inadvertently spend money in ways that cause other internal processes to fail.

3.2. **Develop Budgets:** To accomplish the Value Proposition

3.3. **Manage Capital Planning:** To maximize strategic use of capital equipment or facilities

3.4. **Manage Resource Allocation:** To utilize resources (money, staff, and equipment) effectively, continually evaluating resource application effectiveness, defined in Activity 8

3.5. **Manage cash flow:** To minimize waste

3.6. **Manage Financial Risk:** To avoid catastrophic failure or losses

3.7. **Acquire, maintain, and deploy fixed assets:** Maximize the value of capital assets.

3.8. **Evaluate unit performance toward Mission accomplishment:** Continual evaluating of resource application effectiveness

Common Information Quality Issues

- A *most significant* IQ problem Root Cause in Financial Management is managing to the *quarterly or annual Financial Statements* instead of to the Mission Statement. Focus on short-term gains in order to increase share price can sacrifice the long-term health of the Enterprise. Deming is right that management has two problems, those of today and those of tomorrow. If Management focuses on today's problems and compromises its ability to achieve its long-term Mission, it may very well *sacrifice the financial health* of the Enterprise and its Stakeholders.

NOTE Managers should NOT attempt to "smooth-out" their financial expenditures and income for Financial Management purposes. There is natural variation in income and expenditures that should be monitored for trends and patterns. "Smoothing" prevents the organization's ability to recognize and exploit those variations.

- Asset Management requires high quality Asset Information, including Quantity, Location, Value, Depreciation, and perhaps Condition. A common problem is not keeping an accurate Asset Inventory.

- Quantifying Financial Risk is key for banks, insurance companies, and many other organizations as well as in merger and acquisition transactions. In part, the subprime crisis of 2007–2009, was the result of many mortgage loans that were set up with insufficient risk analysis resulting in record high loan defaults.

4. Spend/Invest According to Plan

Here you apply financial resources to build infrastructure, hire and develop staff, buy materials, produce products and services, and develop and delight Customers in ways that effectively accomplish the Mission of the Enterprise.

4. Spend/Invest Process Activities

Process activities for Spend/Invest According to Plan include:

4.1. **Review Mission and My Unit's Value Proposition to It:** The Mission statement describes what an organization is and what it must accomplish to be successful and effective. The Value Proposition is the unique capabilities, service, or product that the organization provides to its Customers.

4.2. **Create, Manage, and Control Forecasts:** The forecast is the future financial plan. It is the expected financial position over time based on projected revenues, expenses, and other Financial Information such as the Value of Investments and sales over time.

4.3. **Manage Cash Flow:** This is the management of cash as it moves into and out of the business such that sufficient cash exists for ongoing operations.

4.4. **Manage Investments:** This includes the oversight and buy, sell, and hold decision processes for invested assets.

4.5. **Manage Security Master Database:** The creation, updating, or deletion of securities' data records in an Enterprise-Security Master Database. The notion of a Master Database pertains to having a single place to manage key information that allows for syndication or use by multiple systems and databases within the organization. Benefits include less labor to keep information updated with improved quality.

4.6. **Manage and Process Accounts Payable:** The oversight, Accounting, and processing of payments for goods and services received

4.7. **Manage Supplier (Party) Master:** The creation, updating, or deletion of Supplier records in the Party Database

4.8. **Manage Employee reimbursements:** The process of providing payments to Employees for things like travel, supplies, or other incidentals

4.9. **Empower Human Resources:** Allow trained Employees to make decisions (that support the organization's Vision, Mission, and Values) at the lowest level of the organization possible. Benefits include lower costs and faster decisions.

4.10. **Evaluate Unit Performance and Results to Mission:** Creating balanced scorecards and Key Performance Indicators enables Employees, management, and Stakeholders to see organizational progress toward goals and to make adjustments as needed.

Common Information Quality Issues

- When sufficient funds are no longer available, managers often put the expenses in an Account Code where funds are available, skewing the analysis of where money is actually spent or income earned.

- Failure to adequately define and maintain accurate Project-Tracking Information can skew the true purpose of the spending or investment.

CLIENT BOOKS "BOOK COSTS" AS CONSULTING FEES

Because they were over budget in their book and journal expense Code, a company bought several of my books but asked me to charge the cost as the equivalent amount of consulting time, skewing their actual expenditures.

- If amounts require more "paperwork," managers may use a workaround.

STATE GOVERNMENT ENTITY COSTS ITSELF $1,000 MORE TO AVOID EXTENSIVE PROCEDURE

I was asked to conduct a training session for the Department's staff. The fee and expense amount was over the manager's spending authority for a single item, so he asked me to conduct this as a "public seminar" with a per-student fee to be charged to the attendee business unit. They advertised it to external organizations as well. However, the costs for the seminar ended up being $1,000 more than if they had paid my in-house training fee! The additional costs my company accrued to handle it this way neutralized the additional revenue!!!

- Direct financial payments or billing processes often have *duplicate payment problems*. Many Information Quality Management initiatives have achieved direct business benefits by looking for duplicate invoice payments.

Causes include people, system, and process, from internal or external fraud or both. "According to the ACFE, the median loss attributed to billing schemes was \$130,000." "Mark Van Holsbeck, director of Enterprise Network Security for Avery-Dennison, estimates that corporations have a duplicate payment rate of 2% of total purchases."[6]

- The Basel II accord, described in detail later, rewards financial firms that have accurate information and accurate forecasting and modeling of loan default rates by reducing the capital reserves required for loans.

- Lack of maintaining Information Role Accountabilities current an accurate is an issue in work-flow applications. The systems route work based on role-to-person mappings. Out-of-date information from organizational changes, departures, or hiring, for example, causes the work flow to break down, producing Information Quality issues and process failures.

5. Deliver Value to Stakeholders

An organization keeps Customers coming back with increased Customer Lifetime Value when it continually delights them. To delight purchasing Customers, the organization must satisfy its Employees. This means providing training and resources so that they can do their jobs properly to delight the Customers and end-Consumers. Investors are Stakeholders, but not the most important. The Customers and end-Consumers are the bill payers. Investors make "loans" to the organization in expectation of profit on their "investment."

There is a *direct* correlation between Customer Satisfaction and Share value. Making decisions that focus on quarterly profit-and-loss statements without understanding Customer needs is a guaranteed way to Enterprise *failure*.

5. Deliver Value to Stakeholder Process Activities

5.1. **Deliver Value to Customers and end-Consumers:** Value is providing *high-quality* Products or Services for the price paid.

5.2. **Deliver Value to Employees and Families:** Fair pay for *high-quality* work, empowerment, pride of workmanship, security in employment, and growth

5.3. **Deliver Value to Suppliers and Business Partners:** Fair pay for *value-added contribution*

5.4. **Deliver Value to Communities:** Ensure good *Stewardship* of economic value and environment, and community service.

5.5. **Deliver Value to Regulatory Agencies:** Abide by the *spirit and letter* of the Regulations for the benefit of all Stakeholders.

Common Information Quality Issues

- **Multiple (duplicate) Customer records:** Duplicate Customer records causes undercalculation of Customer Lifetime Value, which in turn distorts budget requirements. See how to calculate Customer Lifetime Value in Chapter 6, "The Step-by-Step Guide to *Measuring the Costs and Risks of Poor Quality Information*," Steps, P3.4 "Identify Customer Segments," and P3.5 "Calculate Customer Lifetime Value."

- **Inaccurate Credit Rating of Customers:** Increased Risk of payment problems

- **Defective Customer Create and Update Process:** Creating duplicate Customer records, *not capturing all required* Information — only "mandatory" Information, or capturing the wrong information, prevents you from knowing your Customers as well as you require. See Chapter 9 "Information Quality Applied to Customer Care: *Prospect-to-Valued-and-Valuable-Customer*," for how to provide high-quality Customer and Customer Care Information.

Customer Information as part of "Know Your Customer Information" is a *regulatory requirement* within the USA PATRIOT Act and in similar legislation in many countries. While this isn't financial information in the form of currency, it is essential information for conducting business and running operations. Various laws require it in the Financial Services Industry for control of business operations such as billing, statement mailing, regulatory compliance, and cross-selling.

Important Customer Information includes items such as found in Section 326 of the "Impact of the USA PATRIOT Act on National Security," near the back of this Chapter. See also, Chapter 9, "Information Quality Applied to Customer Care: *Prospect-to-Valued-and-Valuable-Customer*," for how to Measure and Improve Customer Information Quality.

6. Account for Income and Expenses

This process documents your income and expenses. This is required to maintain fiscal stability and ensure the financial health of the Enterprise.

6. Account for Income and Expenses Process Activities

6.1. **Create and maintain Chart of Accounts:** The hierarchical list of Financial Accounts that is used by the Enterprise

6.2. **Post income and expense amounts in the *proper* Account Codes in one's budget:** Postings, called journal entries, are business transactions and their monetary values in the Accounting System. Correct identification and usage of Account Codes is essential for accurate financial reporting.

6.3. **Place Order to Pay processes:** Includes requisitions, authorizations, Accounting transactions, ordering and receipt of materials or services, and invoicing and payment activities

6.4. **Reconcile and Validate transactions:** Validation is a method or system to verify that transactions adhere to business rules. Reconciliation ensures that two sets of financial information correspond.

Common Information Quality Issues

- Posting expenses or incomes in the *wrong* Accounts because the applicable budget amount in the correct Account was *insufficient*

- Failure to follow standard, applicable Accounting Business Rules

- **Insufficient reconciliation process:** Reconciliation is a common control process for Financial Information. Reconciliation quickly identifies when something is wrong with financial information; for example, reconciling a checkbook ledger to the bank statement. When they don't match, people find and fix errors iteratively until the two are reconciled. This type of process happens thousands of times in large organizations in support of maintaining the accuracy of financial information. While it is a necessary step, Reconciliation is a "normal" form of *waste and Rework*. If all Financial Information were gathered, entered, and moved between systems perfectly, Reconciliation would not be needed. Reconciliation is an important step to find gaps to be researched and resolved. From the financial Information Quality practitioner's perspective, the reconciliation process is a source of great value, for it highlights opportunities to find information problems, trace them to their Root Cause(s), and ideally improve the process to eliminate the source of the error in the future. Without reconciling financial information, you Risk material errors that will propagate to produce key financial statement errors or decision support system errors. Examples include:

  - Errors in Information captured at the receiving dock, such as actual items received disagreeing with the manifest

  - Errors in Billing and Payment Information

  - Errors in Orders, such as wrong Items, Quantities, or Prices

  - Errors in Tax Rates or the Formulas to calculate taxes

7. Audit Financial Results

This provides assurance that all financial transactions are properly understood so that management can ensure that the Enterprise is in good financial health.

7. Audit Financial Results Process Activities

7.1. Plan the Audit: Develop a plan for conducting a Financial Audit.

7.2. Identify the Processes and Artifacts to be tested: Specify the target processes, information, and auditing tests.

7.3. Conduct the Audit tests: Conduct the audit tests.

7.4. Review and Refine the Findings based on their importance: Ensure the correctness of audit findings and conclusions.

7.5. Identify Corrective Actions, if any: Determine the corrective and preventive actions required.

7.6. Publish the Audit results: Notify all required Stakeholders of the findings and results.

7.7. Verify that Corrective Actions are completed: Ensure that the corrective and preventive actions were made and are sustainable.

Common Information Quality Issues

- Auditors will carefully check system access controls. The information about who should have access and who is authorized to grant access and the processes to remove access when people terminate or change roles

- Auditors will look for data Integrity Controls when Information is moved from system to system. Are adequate controls in place to ensure that data integrity is maintained? How are errors detected and handled? If they find insufficient controls around *critical* Business Information, Auditors "write up" the deficiencies. Some Audit Departments implement ongoing automated Information Quality tests to ensure that controls continue to work effectively.

- Auditors may check for adequate Information Quality Policies for *critical* Information as well as management oversight to ensure that Employees are following policies. They check to make sure that new Employees have *adequate* training to perform data entry and other process duties correctly, looking for adherence to defined processes. Audit findings may be published when the actual process does not match the defined process. Auditors look for critical processes, such as "Create Customer," "Record an Inventory Movement," or "Pay Invoice."

- Auditors categorize their findings from a Risk-based point of view. They will be harsh on findings about *material* impacts to Financial Information and Information Process Defects *that directly affect* Customers.

8. Analyze Return-on-Investment (ROI)

This activity measures the value delivered on the investments made.

8. Analyze ROI Process Activities

8.1. **Manage Asset Inventory:** Track asset location, movement, and use.

8.2. **Manage Asset Valuation:** Measure asset value based on appreciation or depreciation.

8.3. **Manage Product Master:** Track product inventory location and quantity and measure costs and profit on sales of goods.

8.4. **Calculate Cost of Goods Sold:** Determine the costs to provide goods and services.

8.5. **Calculate Customer Acquisition and Retention Costs:** Calculate your marketing and sales, and overhead costs.

8.6. **Calculate the Profit/Loss:** Calculate your Profit and Loss by period.

Common Information Quality Issues

- **Inaccurate Inventory Processes:** Cost in overhead or rush deliveries
- **Inaccurate Asset Valuations:** Cause loss in amortization.
- **Poor Product Definition or poor Bill-of-Material (BOM) maintenance:** May cause defective product manufacturing with increased warranty costs.
- **Inadequate management of Product Information during the new Product Development process:** May miss Customer's real requirements.
- **Duplicate Customer records:** Skew Customer Lifetime Value.

9. Report to Stakeholders and Regulators

External financial reporting is required by external auditors, regulators, external financial analysts, and investors for their due diligence.

9. Report to Stakeholders and Regulators Process Activities

9.1. **Identify which reports are required:** Identify reports and reporting requirements.

9.2. **Collect and Standardize Information needed for reports:** Assess material financial information for external reporting.

9.3. **Prepare reports:** Translate assessment results into report format.

9.4. **Review and Approve reports:** Ensure Quality and Accuracy.

9.5. **Publish reports:** Deliver reports to required recipients.

TWO UNITS OF E*TRADE FINANCIAL FINED $1 MILLION

The Securities and Exchange Commission fined E*Trade Financial $1 million dollars for Customer data violations. The units failed to properly document and verify the identities of more than 65,000 Customers as required by several rules, including the U.S. Bank Secrecy Act. From January 2003 to May 2007, the authority said, the units failed to provide necessary automated tools to detect suspicious trading activity.[6]

Common Information Quality Issues

- **Source errors in Financial Information Postings:** Errors or omissions in financial transactions, such as wrong amounts in revenue/expense Codes

- **Different Answers from two or more analysts** *to the same business question*: Disparate databases used or different query calculations

- **Transformation Errors:** Global companies conduct business in multiple currencies. The correct currency must be used for local reporting and a different currency for global reporting. Improper transformation between currencies will cause *inaccuracies*. Fortunately, reconciliation or other controls identify these issues for correction and Rework

- **Inadequate Validation Processes:** No or inadequate verification of source financial information, calculation algorithms, or required calculation changes

- **Complex Report Design:** Report design fails to apply *standard Accounting protocol*. This is more problematic for global companies that must adhere to many local reporting requirements that differ by country.

- **Inadequate Definitions:** Data definitions are not clear, leading to *misinterpretation or improper valuation* of assets. A recent example is inadequate definition of how to value Collateralized Debt Obligation assets when the market became frozen and existing asset valuation definitions failed.

1. Understand Mission, Customers, and Products [Better]

This takes us full circle with knowledge gained and Lessons Learned from the operations of the Enterprise.

Information Quality Applied to the "Budget-to-Profit" Value Circle

We will analyze three major Information Groups of Financial Information:

- Financial Management Accounting and External Financial Reporting Information
- Risk Management Information
- Audit and Compliance Information

Applying Information Quality to Financial Management Accounting and External Financial Reporting

Major Information Quality issues in the "Budget-to-Profit" Value Circle can affect both internal and external Stakeholders. Poor budget planning and poor allocation of income and expense posting can lead to errors in spending or income allocation that results in a poor understanding of the Financial Position.

Financial Management Accounting & Reporting Information Quality Issues

Common IQ issues and their costs in Financial Planning failure include:

Table 12-3: IQ Issues and Costs in Financial Management Accounting Processes

IQ ISSUES	COSTS OF POOR INFORMATION QUALITY
Inaccurate, ambiguous, or unclear Chart of Accounts Definitions	Leads to *misinterpretation and wrong* Accounting figures, that can result in *incorrect decisions.*
Estimation Errors in Budget Amounts or Time periods	Leads to *overfunding or underfunding* with subsequent reallocation from other Cost Centers.
Entering data that requires judgment	Leads to *incorrect assignment of costs* to General Ledger Accounts.
Interpretation of complex Accounting rules	Leads to *inaccurate* asset valuation.
Global difference in Accounting definitions and standards	Leads to geographic *variation* and dual reporting .
Lack of transparency into actual IT costs	Leads to extra costs by storing information in multiple places with high costs of information movement programs.

External Financial Reporting Information Quality Issues

Common IQ issues and costs of External Financial Reporting failure:

Table 12-4: Information Quality Issues and Costs in External Financial Reporting

IQ ISSUES	COSTS OF POOR INFORMATION QUALITY
Improper currency translation	Inaccurate Risk calculation and *under- or overestimating* cash reserve needs
Improper asset valuations	Inaccurate Risk calculation and *under- or overestimating* cash reserves needs
Counterparty issues	*Inability to rate the Risk* of the total exposure
Errors that result in restatements	Drop in stock price because of a *loss in confidence* in predictable reporting
Regulator-identified IQ issues	*Fines and costs of* specialized consultants to make improvements

How to Measure the Quality of Financial Management Accounting and Reporting Information

By definition, Budget Planning Information is an estimate. The real measurement of budget "accuracy" is the precision of the estimates and in the tangible results of the expenditures to accomplish the Mission effectively.

Budget plans change in a dynamic world. Customer Requirements change, economic conditions change, and new opportunities emerge, requiring budget changes.

External Financial Reporting Information is *not* an estimate as Budget Planning is. External Financial Reporting Information must be *accurate and precise* to the point that it does not contain a "material" *error* that fails to reflect the true Financial Health of the Enterprise. Accuracy assessment must be conducted against the posting of financial transactions and of the auditing of those financial transactions. Serious fines can be levied for inadvertent or known material errors.

How to Measure the Quality of Budget Codes Definition

Follow the baseline assessment steps in Chapter 4 "The Step-by-Step Guide to *Assessing Information Product Specifications and Information Architecture Quality*" (TIQM P1).[8]

Here are some specific tips for this assessment applied to Budget Code Information.

Identify Information Definition Quality Measures

If you have not identified and standardized the basic Information Definition Quality Characteristics by now, review steps TIQM P1.1.1 through steps TIQM P1.1.5 in Chapter 4 and establish a standard set. These Quality Characteristics should be the same for assessment of all discrete Information Types.

One group of Budget Planning Attributes consists of General Ledger Budget Codes and Cost Center Codes. Are the Attribute Names and Definitions Correct, Complete, and Clear?

You must also measure the correlation of your base Attributes and the Attributes required for external Financial Reporting. Do they correlate? Do you apply the *correct* Business Rules for *calculating* Information reported externally as required by the applicable Regulators?

Identify Financial Management Accounting Information Attributes for Definition Quality Assessment

Follow TIQM P1.2 in Chapter 4 to identify Critical-to-Quality (CTQ) Attributes. Develop a Pareto Diagram based upon the importance of the Budget Planning Attributes and the *costs and impacts* of poor quality. Identify the A-priority or Critical-to-Quality (CTQ) Attributes, and create an Information Group as the first set of Attributes to measure, followed by the B-priority, or near-CTQ, information as the second tier information to measure. See TIQM Process P3.3 in Chapter 6 for how to estimate the impacts of poor quality, and how to measure the actual Direct and Opportunity Costs of Poor Quality to confirm the relative priority.

Budget Planning Information includes, but is not limited to, the following attributes:

- Budget Codes
- Budget Code Classification (revenue or expense)
- Cost Center Codes
- Organizational Hierarchy
- Prior Period Income and Expense Amounts
- Future Period Forecasts
- Forecast Period Key Assumptions and Business/Economic Factors
- Income Report Category
- Expense Report Category
- Financial Report Period
- Special Conditions
- Asset Number
- Asset Name and Definition

- Asset Valuation Type
- Asset Valuation Type Depreciation Schedule
- Asset Valuation Amount
- Asset Valuation Formula and Rules

Identify Financial Management Information Stakeholders

Follow TIQM P1.3 in Chapter 4 to identify representatives from each of the Financial Management Information Stakeholder Business Areas in the Internal and External Stakeholder lists in Tables 12-1 and 12-2.

The representatives you select here will participate in the Information Stakeholder feedback sessions in a Definition Assessment step (TIQM P1.6) in Chapter 4.

Assess Financial Management Information Definition Technical Quality

The Information Resource Quality (IRQ) Specialist should assess Technical Definition Quality Characteristics as described in TIQM Step 1.4 in Chapter 4. This step assesses the Quality of the Data Names, Definitions, Valid Value Sets, Value Formats, and Business Rule Specifications. This is essentially a Conformance to Information Standards Assessment.

> **NOTE** Eliminate bias by ensuring that the assessment is made by an independent IRQ Specialist who was *not* part of the original Data Definition process.

> **NOTE** These assessed Budget Codes should be documented in an Enterprise-wide Management Accounting Handbook available to all Managers.

Assess Financial Information Model and Financial Database Design Quality

Follow TIQM P1.5 in Chapter 4 to assess the Technical Quality of your internal Financial Resource Information Model and Database Design.

Is the Information Model intuitive to the real world? See Process P1.5 in Chapter 4 for the basic process step description with tips. Quality Characteristics include:

Assess the Technical Quality of your external Financial Reporting Information Model.

- Is the Information Model accurate to the Real World and to the reporting standards from your regulatory authority?
- Is the Model comprehensive so that it contains *all* Object Types and Object Characteristics of the required Financial Information?
- The Financial Information Model and Database Design are *stable* to accommodate new Applications and Knowledge Workers with only *additive changes*, no structural changes. Structural changes are very costly to make.

- The Financial Information Model and Database Design are *Flexible* to support process reengineering with minimal structural change. Typically, "paper-trail" Entity Types and Files go away.

- The Financial Information Model and Database Design are *Reused* by *all* operational Knowledge Workers and applications requiring them for operational processes.

- The Internal Financial Information Model maps well to the External Reporting Information Model with a minimal set of transformations required.

NOTE Your Budget Planning Information Stakeholders must be able to easily understand the meaning of the Budget Codes to develop an accurate projection of their spending and/or income. If Code definitions are confusing, they may cause incorrect budget allocations.

NOTE Your Internal and External Financial Reporting Information Stakeholders must be able to easily understand the meaning of the Financial Reporting Codes to provide an accurate report of income and/or spending. If Code definitions are confusing, they may cause inaccurate reporting that may be subject to serious fines or penalties.

NOTE Budget and Account Codes need to have flexible reporting relationships. Products may be sold by multiple divisions or companies. You must be able to roll revenue and expenses appropriately without double-counting them.

Assess Customer "Satisfaction" with Data Definition of Financial Management Information

Follow steps TIQM P1.6.1–P1.6.6 in Chapter 4. Step activities include:

Step 1. Identify 10 to 25 A-Priority (CTQ) Attributes about Budget Planning and Management Accounting Information that are most important to operational and management processes (TIQM P1.6.1) in Chapter 4.

TIP Focus on Budget Codes and General Ledger Accounts as well as the Financial Transactions and their Definitions. Are they Clear and Correct to use for planned spending or income?

Step 2. Compile the Data Names, including Abbreviations if any, Definitions, Valid Value sets, Business Rule Specifications on the "Information Product Specifications Quality/Value Assessment" form (TIQM P1.6.2.I1) in Chapter 4. Customize this form if necessary.

TIP Conduct this assessment within your own department first, then, conduct it on an Enterprise level next.

NOTE The purpose of this assessment is to ensure that Managers are able to apply Income and Expense Amounts to the right Account Codes for *Management Accounting* purposes. This enables more accurate Financial Analysis of the financial health of the Enterprise.

Measuring Accuracy and Other Budget Planning and Management Accounting Information Quality Characteristics

The second assessment is an assessment of the accuracy of selected Budget Planning and Reporting Information. Follow the general steps described in Chapter 5 "Step-by-Step-Guide-to *Assessing Information Quality*." Here are tips for Budget Planning Information Quality measurement.

TIP Likewise, conduct this assessment on your own department's Budget Information first, then, conduct it across the Enterprise.

Identify a Set of Budget Planning Information for Measuring Quality

You will probably select the same 10 to 25 A-priority, CTQ Budget Planning Attributes for which you measured "Information Product Specifications" Quality. Follow TIQM P2.1 in Chapter 5.

Plan IQ Objectives, Measures, and Tests

Establish your Objectives, Measures, and Assessment Tests following TIQM P2.2 in Chapter 5. The real objective is to assess how well the Budget Estimates compare with the Actual Income and Expenditures to accomplish the Enterprise Mission. This will always be a soft measure, as priorities will change during the fiscal year.

The important measures are Completeness, Accuracy, and Timeliness of Budget Information. Did we omit Income or Expense Categories for needed funds, and how closely did we *estimate* Income and Expenses compared with actual Income and Expenses.

NOTE Zero defects are *not* required here. The key is to ensure that estimates are good enough to manage and control the processes and the Enterprise effectively to accomplish its Mission. Changes to the budget estimates do not automatically mean errors. As competition and economic conditions change, so must the allocation of funding change to meet the challenges.

> **NOTE** As Budget Estimates require adjusting during the fiscal year, document the changes along with the *reason* for them. Retain the original budget estimates along with the updated estimates throughout the year.

Identify the Information Value Circle

Follow TIQM Step P2.3 in Chapter 5. In order to understand process capability, you must understand the processes that make up the Information Value Circle that creates the Budget Information. Document this Value Circle using a Value Circle format as illustrated in Chapter 5, "The Step-by-Step Guide to *Assessing Information Quality*," Figure 5-14, or in the Value Chain format in my first book,[9] or another Process or Information Work Flow model.

> **NOTE** This should be the Enterprise budget planning life cycle.

> **NOTE** For external reporting, you will follow the External Reporting Rules provided by the Regulatory authority for your Enterprise.

Determine Information Store or Process to Assess

Follow (TIQM P2.4) in Chapter 5. The Budget Planning Cycle is the process being assessed.

> **NOTE** This is a soft measure. Remember that "close" is the goal (it does not have to be precisely "on budget" but "near budget") as defined by the Finance Department.

> **TIP** To measure the Precision of your Forecast, use a "Forecast Accuracy" technique that measures your Budget compared to the Forecast over a three-to-five-year period to confirm the appropriateness of your budgeting. Simply maintain the budget figures and your actual expenditures over the determined time period.

Identify Accuracy Verification Sources

Follow TIQM P2.5 in Chapter 5, "The Step-by-Step Guide to *Assessing Information Quality*." The assessment of the Accuracy of the Budget Plan compares the *Actual* Income and Expenses to the *Planned* Income and Expenses.

Accuracy of Financial Transactions compares the Information with a Recording or Observation of the *original data capture,* or an independently confirmed Financial Transaction.

Extract a Statistically Valid Sample of Data

Follow Step TIQM P2.6.1 "Extract Statistically Valid Sample of Data" in Chapter 5 to determine the *number of records necessary* to sample for the *Confidence Level* you need in your assessment results. Extract a sample of Business Units that represent the variety of organizational entities, from various Profit Centers and Cost Centers.

Sampling does not apply for External Financial reporting. This must be a full Financial Statement for the applicable Reporting Period.

Measure Budget Planning Information Quality

Follow TIQM P2.7 to measure the Accuracy of the selected Financial Results by comparing the *actual* income and *expenses* to the *planned* income and expenses.

Measure Completeness. Identify Income or Expense Codes with no amounts in the Budgeted Income and Expense Codes where actual expenditures existed.

> **NOTE** Note that missing information in an Income or Expense Code is not necessarily an error. It may just be that no Financial Transactions were made in these categories.

Interpret and Report Budget Planning Information Quality

Follow Process TIQM Step P2.8. "Interpret and Report Information Quality" in Chapter 5, "The Step-by-Step Guide to *Assessing Information Quality*," and communicate the assessment results to all key Information Stakeholders.

If there are significant and costly problems as a result, initiate an Information Process Improvement Initiative, described in the next section.

How to Improve Management Accounting and Reporting Process Quality

The improvement of Budget Planning Information requires cooperation among the Stakeholders, from the CFO and Finance Department to the Executive Leadership Team down to the Line Managers. Improvement of processes outside of one's control and authority presents its own set of problems.

How to Improve Management Accounting and Reporting Quality

The assessments conducted above should give you an indication if and where your Budget Planning processes may be broken.

Use the classic Plan-Do-Check/Study-Act cycle described in TIQM P4 "Improve Information Process Quality," in Chapter 7. You may also use Six Sigma TIQM and apply the DMAIC (Define-Measure-Analyze-Improve-Control) format, which implements the same TIQM processes but in the DMAIC format. See the TIQM Six Sigma DMAIC mapping in Chapter 7, "The Step-by-Step Guide to *Improving Information Process Quality*," in Table 7-7, TIQM Processes and Steps Mapped to Six Sigma Phases and Steps.

NOTE Always measure the costs of IQ defects in Budget Planning Information *before* you conduct a Process Improvement. This becomes a *baseline* for measuring the *effectiveness* of the Improvement. Once the process is Improved and In Control, measure the *reduction* in the Costs of Failure and Information Scrap and Rework, and in Manufacturing Scrap and Rework as a result of the improved process. This will establish the ongoing *Value* of Process Improvement. See TIQM P3, "Measure the Costs of Poor Quality Information," in Chapter 6, "The Step-by-Step Guide to *Measuring the Costs and Risks of Poor Quality Information*."

Define a Project for Management Accounting Process Improvement (TIQM P4.1)

This Process step creates a Process Improvement Initiative, following your organization's project management protocol. See TIQM P4.1 "Define Project for Information Quality Improvement" in Chapter 7.

Plan for a Management Accounting Process Improvement: Root Cause Analysis (TIQM P4.2.1)

The first step of "Plan" Process Improvement (TIQM P4.2.1) is to define the "Effect," that is the IQ issue requiring improvement, such as Budget Codes are *ambiguous* and amounts are posted in *wrong* Code categories. This would indicate a need for an *improvement* of the Data Definition process. See how to conduct a Root-Cause Analysis session in Chapter 7, Step TIQM P4.2.1.

Another problem is knowingly posting amounts in different Codes because of lack of funds in the appropriate Code.

NOTE Posting expenses in *wrong* Accounts skews the *financial reality* of the Enterprise. This prevents the Enterprise from understanding exactly where its money is spent, or where its income comes from. This effectively prevents the Analysis of Financial Results, possibly hiding real Risks to the Enterprise.

For External Financial Reporting Root Causes, see Figure 12-3.

NOTE You must ensure that you isolate the Root Cause or Causes of the Information Effect. You may have to use observation or conduct a Design-of-Experiment (DOE) to isolate the Root Cause.

If you do not find the real Root Cause, your defined improvements will be sub-optimized at best, and fail at worst.

Plan for a Financial Management Information Process Improvement: Define Improvements to Eliminate the Root Causes

Process Improvement Considerations are shown in Table 12-5.

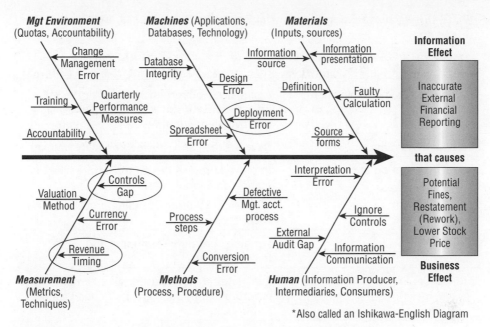

Figure 12-3: Inaccurate External Financial Reporting Causes and Effects

Table 12-5: Defective Budget Income/Expense Posting Root Causes and Improvement Considerations

INACCURATE INCOME/EXPENSE POSTING ROOT CAUSE	PROCESS IMPROVEMENT CONSIDERATIONS
Inadequate training	Train new Employees and provide refresher training.
Missing data at time of entry	Redefine process or create special processing routines for data capture at point of capture.
Human error	Implement Double-Entry Accounting Systems.
Process complexity or lack of clarity	Simplify process. Use bar Codes for improved accuracy in Inventory transaction processing.
Poor setup of new products	Improved new product introduction process with checklists
Lack of accuracy metrics or management oversight	Measure accuracy and cost of poor quality. Define specific goals for management and data entry personnel.
Internal or external fraud	Special fraud detection and Analysis processes

Table 12-6: Inaccurate External Financial Reporting Root Causes and Improvement Considerations

INACCURATE EXTERNAL FINANCIAL REPORTING CAUSES	PROCESS IMPROVEMENT CONSIDERATIONS
Improper Software Deployment	Adequate Requirements Analysis of Information and Process, testing, and validation by independent Auditors
Inadequate training	Develop, test, and provide adequate training
Lack of Information at time of posting	Improved process design to capture all information on a timely basis
	Improved exception-handling process to discover causes
Internal Controls failure	Periodic Control Assessments and Improvements
Spreadsheet Errors	Eliminate spreadsheets for all external reporting information chains or add Quality Controls.
Consolidation Errors	Reconciliation Controls and Full Information Traceability

"Do" Implement Budget Planning Process Improvements in a Controlled Way to Study Effectiveness

Changes in the Budget Planning and Budget Operations require planning to fit into the budget cycle. See TIQM Step P4.3 in Chapter 7.

1. Select a representative set of Managers to *pilot* the "improved" process.

2. Orient and train the pilot Team in the new procedures and objectives.

3. Implement all error-proofing techniques identified. Some error proofing techniques may require independent implementation and testing.

4. Allow the pilot Team to exercise the new procedures for the first two quarters as their learning period, in which the procedures should have become a habit.

Check and Study Impact of the Process Improvements on the Budget Planning Information Process and its Results

Review TIQM Step P4.4 in Chapter 7 for implementing the improvement(s) in a controlled way.

1. During the third quarter, "Check and Study" the results of Actual to Budget on a category by category basis. Review the Actual to Budget against the actual income and expense transactions. By the end of the second quarter, the pilot group of managers will have had the improved process and it will either become part of their behavior or they will have resorted to their old habits.

2. If old habits prevail, you must conduct a new Root Cause Analysis to identify why the improved process failed. Then re-implement or re-plan the improvements based on the identified cause.

3. In this process step, you *study* the *effectiveness* of the Improvements on the Clarity and Accuracy of Budget Planning Information. Ensure that you do not introduce negative side effects that create new IQ problems.

4. Study the impact to see if the Budget Planning Information meets the needs of your internal Knowledge Workers and external Stakeholders.

Act to Standardize the Budget Planning Process Improvements

See TIQM Step P4.5 in Chapter 7. Once you have an *effective* Improvement for posting income and expenses to the correct Budget Codes, get the process under control with actions to standardize the Improvements and "hold the gains" (keep Improvements "in control") and roll the process out to all Business Areas on an appropriate schedule.

Best Practices in Management Accounting and Reporting Quality

Best practices from the Information Quality perspective for Budget and Accounting information include:

- Create and maintain Rigorous Financial Information **Policies** and **Procedures** that are clear and executable.

- Active and ongoing **Governance that includes the** *Executive Leadership Team* to set strategy, standards and goals, including federation or collaboration with other Governance bodies such Information Architecture Board and Risk Governance

- Well-designed **Processes** with clear **Roles** and **Accountabilities**

- **Financial Forecasts** present a conservative estimate of the organization's expected financial position, results of operations, and changes in cash flow. Forecasts are based on assumptions regarding conditions actually expected to exist and the course of action anticipated.[10]

- **Financial Projections** present the organization's expected financial position, results of operations, and changes in cash flow. These should be based on conservative estimates about conditions expected to exist and the course of action anticipated to occur, given hypothetical assumptions.[11]

- **Architectural** quality through Enterprise-Strength Information Models, including: Customer and or Account Master, Vendor Master, (or as part of a "Party Master"), Material Master, Securities Master, and others with flexible hierarchies or networks to document the Real-World relationships of Entities in the real world of your Enterprise

▪ Develop "Enterprise-Strength" Information Models and Databases that support all internal Business Areas and that support all internal requirements for Management Accounting as well as all external Regulatory Rules for external Financial Reporting.

NOTE Financial and Party Information Models require both stability to meet all needs and the flexibility to support the required Organizational Structure, Relationship, and Process changes.

Effective Measurement System to drive *proactive* Preventive Improvements and Corrective actions via seamlessly integrated and automated (or semi-automated) controls such as:

▪ Content and Format Checks

▪ Duplicate Detection

▪ Cross Reference Checks

▪ Balancing Checks

▪ Reconciliation Checks

▪ Timeliness Checks

▪ Statistical Trending Checks

Applying IQ to Risk Management

Risk Management is a critical process within the Strategic and Tactical Leadership of the Enterprise, required to *mitigate catastrophic* Enterprise failure.

Risk Management Information Quality Issues

Common IQ issues and their costs in Risk Management process failure include those shown in Table 12-7.

Table 12-7: Information Quality Issues and Costs in Risk Management Information

IQ ISSUES	COSTS OF POOR INFORMATION QUALITY
Missing Information required by regulations	Fines and Regulator actions
Poor name matching	Fines, creation of duplicate Customers or financial transactions

IQ ISSUES	COSTS OF POOR INFORMATION QUALITY
Poor management of Privacy Preference Information and processes	Fines, Loss of Customers and Reputation Risk
Missing/inaccurate Credit History Information	Increased loan losses
Incorrect Risk Rating	Paying too much for an investment or loss because of a realized Risk failure event
Poor Counterparty Information	Inability to measure the full Risk exposure of a Counterparty or Trading Partner
Internal fraud event	Loss of money and threat to the Enterprise
External fraud event	External Reputational Loss, with Potential Lost Business with High Costs of Damage Control, especially when sensitive information is accessed and stolen
Lack of *due diligence* in Critical Information in M&A transactions	Overpayment or complete loss in the M&A transaction

How to Measure the Quality of the Risk Management Process

Risk Management will always be an imprecise estimate because of the many variables in analyzing Risk. The real measure of the Accuracy will be in the ultimate Value of the Outcome of a Decision or Investment as compared to the cost and potential consequences.

Risks will always be a part of any Enterprise that seeks to increase its business and its Value Proposition for its Customers.

How to Measure the Quality of the Risk Management Information Definition

Follow the baseline assessment steps in Chapter 4 "The Step-by-Step Guide to Assessing Information Product Specifications and Information Architecture Quality" (TIQM P1).

Identify Information Definition Quality Measures

If you have not identified and standardized the basic Information Definition Quality Characteristics by now, review steps TIQM P1.1.1 through steps TIQM P1.1.5 in Chapter 4 and seek to establish a standard set. These Quality Characteristics should be the same for the Assessment of all discrete Information Types.

One group of Risk Management Attributes are the Risk Codes that are assigned to various investments, strategies, or major decisions. The second group defines the Variables or Attributes used to determine which Risk Code to assign to an investment, strategy or decision.

Identify Risk Management Information Attributes for Definition Quality Assessment

Follow TIQM P1.2 in Chapter 4 to develop a Pareto Diagram based upon importance of Risk Management Attributes and the costs and impacts of poor quality. Identify the Critical-to-Quality Attributes and create an Information Group as the first set of Attributes to measure, followed by the B-priority or near-CTQ Information as the second Tier information to measure. See TIQM Process P3.3 in Chapter 6 for how to estimate the impacts of poor quality, and how to measure the actual direct and opportunity costs of poor quality to confirm the relative priority.

Risk Management information includes, but is not limited to, the following:

- **Risk Code:** A classification of the potential of an investment, strategy, or decision to fail

- **Risk Definition:** A statement describing the Risk

- **Risk Code Factor:** A Variable that influences the Risk of an investment, strategy, or decision

- **Risk Probability of Occurrence:** Likelihood of a Risk event happening

- **Geographic or Political Risk Factors:** Political or Geographic events that can disrupt business, such as the 2008 Russian invasion of Georgia

- **Product Risk Factors:** Characteristics of Products that can cause injury or death, such as hazardous materials with no proper handling instructions, or food subject to bacteria or disease

- **Customer Type Risk Factors:** The Customer's ability or willingness to pay. The Customer may be politically exposed or involved in prior fraud or other crimes.

- **Labor Action Risk Factors:** Labor actions, such as the Longshoremen's strike on the West Coast in 2002 that tied up Supply Chain shipping until a temporary injunction stopped the action

Identify Risk Management Information Stakeholders

Follow TIQM P1.3 in Chapter 4 to identify representatives from each of the Risk Management Information Stakeholder business areas. See Stakeholders listed in the Internal and External Stakeholder lists in Tables 12-1 and 12-2.

The representatives will participate in the Information Stakeholder feedback sessions in a subsequent Data Definition Assessment, step TIQM P1.6 in Chapter 4.

Assess the Risk Information Model and Database Design Quality

Assess the Technical Quality of your internal Risk Information Model following TIQM P1.5 in Chapter 4 for the basic process step description with tips.

Is the Risk Information Model intuitive to the real world? Is the model flexible enough to support all of the Factors that contribute to Risk in the real world as it affects your Enterprise? See Process P1.5 in Chapter 4. Quality Characteristics include:

- The Risk Information Model and Database Design are *Stable* enough to accommodate new Applications and Knowledge Workers with only additive changes, with no structural changes.

- The Risk Information Model and Database Design are *Flexible* enough to support Process Reengineering of the Risk Analysis with minimal structural change.

- The Risk Information Model and Database Design are *Reused* by *all* Risk Information Stakeholders.

- The Risk Models, which are models of Risk scenarios, have clear definition of the type of Risk, the conditions and probability of the Risk occurring, and the seriousness of the impact of occurrence, and are clear and as precise as necessary to meet Risk requirements.

Assess Stakeholder "Satisfaction" with Data Definition of Risk Management Information

Follow steps TIQM P1.6.1–P1.6.6 in Chapter 4. Step activities include:

Step 1. Identify 10 to 25 A-Priority (CTQ) Attributes about Risk Management Information that are the most important to decision making (P1.6.1).

NOTE Risk Management Information Stakeholders must be able to easily understand the meaning of Risk Codes and Risk Variables. If definitions are confusing, incorrect Risk conclusions may be drawn.

TIP Focus on Risk Codes and the Variables that contribute to Risk in all Risk scenarios pertinent to your Enterprise.

TIP Ensure that your Risk Model allows for tracking actual Risk Events of all Types of Risk you are exposed to.

TIP When evaluating investing in or acquiring other Organizations, assess Critical Information, such as Customer, Complaint, Financial, and Product Experience Information with due diligence.

TIP Be sure to develop your Risk Codes for *historical* Analysis. This is critical for the ability to evaluate Risk over time with changing circumstances.

Step 2. Compile the Data Names, including Abbreviations if any, Definitions, Valid Value Sets, Business Rule Specifications on the Information Product Specifications Quality/Value Assessment form in Step P1.6.2 in Chapter 4. Customize this for your organization if necessary.

TIP Conduct this assessment with representative Stakeholders of Risk Information. See Tables 12-1 and 12-2 in this Chapter for potential Stakeholder Groups.

NOTE Without a consensus understanding of Risk Codes and Variables, people may misinterpret the real Risks of a decision and make a wrong decision.

> **GLOBAL BANK LOST OVER $600 MILLION BECAUSE OF DISPARATELY DEFINED RISK CODES ACROSS BUSINESS UNITS**
>
> Investing in a company based upon a Risk Code value that indicated a sound investment proved fatal when the company failed, costing the bank its $600 million investment, which was non-recoverable.

Measuring Accuracy of Risk Management Information

The second assessment measures Accuracy and other IQ Characteristics of selected Risk Management information. Follow the general steps described in TIQM P2 in Chapter 5 "The Step-by-Step-Guide-to *Assessing Information Quality*." Here are tips for Risk Management Information Quality measurement.

TIP Identify all places where Risk Codes are defined. Ensure that they are defined properly and have *consensus* Definition when consensus is required.

Identify a Set of Risk Management Information for Measuring Quality

You will probably select the same 10 to 15 A-priority, CTQ Risk Management attributes for which you measured "information product specifications" quality. Follow TIQM P2.1 in Chapter 5 if needed.

Plan IQ Objectives, Measures and Tests

Follow TIQM P2.2 in Chapter 5 to identify Assessment Objectives, IQ Characteristics, and develop Assessment tests. Again, Risk Analysis is an estimating process based on heuristics of analyzing the Variables that cause something to be a risky endeavor. Knowledge Workers develop their own heuristics based on their experiences with the Variables and Correlation to Risk of failure. Gather this knowledge in ways that it can be reused electronically for Risk Analysis.

Measure the completeness of the Variables that correlate to Risk of an Investment, Strategy, or Decision.

Measure the correlation of those Variables and the Failure or Success of the Investment, Strategy, or Decision.

> **NOTE** The information here will not be clear-cut values. Accuracy is an appropriate IQ characteristic, but Precision of Accuracy can be quite variable. The degree of *Uncertainty* needs to be established to *interpret* the Assessment results.

Identify the Information Value Circle

Follow TIQM P2.3 in Chapter 5 to understand process capability. You must understand the processes that make up the Information Value Circle that creates the Risk information and the downstream processes that require it. Document this Value Circle using a Value Circle format,[12] or other Process and Information Work Flow models. Identify the various Information Stakeholders.

> **NOTE** This Value Circle should be the Enterprise Risk Management Life Cycle.

Determine the Information Store or Process to Assess

Follow TIQM P2.4 to identify the process to be assessed. The Risk Management Life Cycle is the process being assessed.

> **TIP** Conduct experiments to isolate and analyze impacts of the variables independently. Then measure combinations to determine relative strength of Risk in the decision.

Identify Accuracy Verification Sources

See TIQM Step P2.5 in Chapter 5 "The Step-by-Step Guide to *Assessing Information Quality*." The Assessment of the Accuracy of the Risk predictions is to compare them to actual outcomes of various Risk Variables, Risk Codes and Risk Incidents.

Extract a Statistically Valid Sample of Data

Follow Step TIQM P2.6 "Extract Statistically Valid Sample" in Chapter 5. The sample consists of actual decisions based on Risk Codes and the correctness of the decision to follow the behavior as established in the Risk Code Classification.

Measure Risk Management Information Quality in the Selected IQ Characteristics

Follow TIQM P2.7 in Chapter 5 to measure the Accuracy and Precision of the selected Risk decisions by comparing the actual income and expected behavior, as indicated by the Risk Variables.

Measure completeness. Identify Risk Variables that may not have been identified earlier.

Interpret and Report Risk Management Information Quality

Follow Process Step TIQM P2.8, "Interpret and Report Information Quality" in Chapter 5 and communicate assessment results to all key Information Stakeholders.

If there are significant and costly problems as a result, initiate an Information Process Improvement Initiative [TIQM P4], described in the next section.

How to Improve Risk Management Process Quality

Given the knowledge gained in the IQ Assessment, establish an IQ Improvement initiative to address the improvement of the process of assigning Risk and the accuracy of the variables as Factors contributing to Risk.

How to Improve Risk Management Process Quality

The assessments conducted above should give you an indication if and where your Risk Management processes may be broken.

Use the classic Plan-Do-Check/Study-Act cycle described in TIQM P4 "Improve Information Process Quality," in Chapter 7. You may also use Six Sigma the TIQM Six Sigma DMAIC (Define-Measure-Analyze-Improve-Control) format, which implements the same TIQM processes but in DMAIC format. See the TIQM Six Sigma DMAIC mapping in Chapter 7 TIQM, Table 7-7, "TIQM Processes and Steps Mapped to Six Sigma Phases and Steps."

> **NOTE** Measure and document the costs and consequences of IQ Defects in Risk Management Information *before* you conduct a Process Improvement. This includes losses incurred when the Risk was deemed acceptable or good. This also includes lost opportunity by rejection and the actual value that could have been realized with an affirmative decision. Once the process is improved and in control, measure the reduction in the Costs of Failure from Risk Incidents and Information Scrap and Rework, and in manufacturing or service Scrap and Rework because of the improved process. This will establish the ongoing Value of Process Improvement. See TIQM P3, "Measure the Costs of Poor Quality Information," in Chapter 6. This especially includes the opportunity costs and losses.

Define a Project for Risk Management Process Improvement

This Process step creates a Process Improvement Initiative, following your organization's project management protocol. See TIQM P4.1 "Define Project for Information Quality Improvement" in Chapter 7.

Plan a Risk Management Process Improvement: Root Cause Analysis (TIQM P4.2.1)

The first step of the "Plan" Process Improvement (TIQM P4.2.1) is to define the "Effect," that is the IQ issue requiring improvement, such as Risk Codes are assigned incorrectly to a given Investment, Strategy, or Decision. See how to conduct a Root Cause Analysis session in Chapter 7, Step TIQM P4.2.1.

Plan a Risk Management Process Improvement: Defining Improvements to Eliminate the Root Causes

Process Improvement Considerations are seen in Table 12-8. Follow TIQM 4.2B in Chapter 7 for defining Process Improvements.

Table 12-8: Defective Risk Information Root Causes and Improvement Considerations

INACCURATE RISK RATING ROOT CAUSE	PROCESS IMPROVEMENT CONSIDERATIONS
Missing Risk Factors	Periodic updates of Risk Models. Create independent "Challenger" Risk Models and pick the best Model.
Use of Old Risk Factors	Defined routines for Risk Factor updates and special updates during times of unusual change such as the Credit crisis in 2008
Incorrect weightings assigned to each Risk Factor	Advanced statistical Analysis and tools
Definition issues	Create a clear taxonomy of Risk Codes with specific Business Rules and Training materials.
Management is Risk-averse	Establish a Risk Analysis mindset in the Executive Leadership Team.

NOTE Be sure that you have identified improvements that *mitigate* the real Root Cause or Causes. Failure to do this will sub-optimize your defined improvement or cause it to fail.

"Do" Implement Risk Management Process Improvements in a Controlled Way to Study Their Effectiveness (TIQM Step P4.3)

Regulators and Auditors of Banks look for adequate Risk assessments to prioritize improvement activities. This is often an annual Risk Assessment.

Check and Study Impact of the Process Improvements on the Risk Management Information Process and Its Results (TIQM Step P4.4)

Failure Mode and Effects Analysis (FMEA) is a tool or method that considers the impact of a Risk, the likelihood of occurrence for each Risk and the ability to detect the Risk. The result is a Risk Priority Number for each Risk. The higher the Risk Priority Number, the higher the need to prevent or remediate it. You can see a sample template of an FMEA form in Figure 12-4.

Mortgage Application	FAILURE MODE AND EFFECTS ANALYSIS (FMEA)					
Project Leader Information Steward	**Project Name** Simplistic Example	**Project Number**	**Date**	**Project Type** Improvement	**Project Coach** Information Governance Manager	

Process Step / Function Requirements	Potential Failure Mode	Potential Effect(s) of Failure	Severity	Potential / Cause(s) / Mechanism(s) of Failure	Occurrence	Current Process Controls Inspection Prevention Detection	Detection	RPN	What is the Recommended Action(s) to mitigate the risk and target resolution date(s)?	Who is Responsible for Action(s)?	Action Results — Actions Taken	Sev	Occ	Det	RPN
	Identify potential failures that could occur for each step of the process. Note: There may be several potential failures in each step.	Identify the potential effect each failure will have. Note: There may be multiple effects for each failure mode.		Identify the potential root cause for each failure mode. Each failure mode may have multiple causes.											
Acquire Information	Incorrect data on Credit Application	Customer has too much debt. May not be able to pay.	5	Poor record keeping by customer	3	Prevention via Credit score check	4	60	Check balance with 2 or more Credit Agencies.	Credit Risk Team	Implemented Q3	5	1	2	10
Enter Information in Application System.	Data entry error on risk factor	Incorrect lending decision	5	Human error	2	Inspection	3	30	Automatic comparison of data to other source(s)	Credit Risk Team	Tested Q1 Implemented Q2	5	2	1	10
Move Information from Application System to Loan Processing System.	Data lost or corrupted	Missing or incorrect data	5	Computer job abends and is then restarted.	1	Detection via checksums	1	5	None, current controls are sufficient.						

Severity Key:
5= Certain Loss
4= High Probability of Loss
3= Noticeable Effect
2= Minor Effect
1= No effect

Occurrence Key: Likelihood of occurring
5= Very High: Failure is Almost Inevitable
4= High: Repeated Failures
3= Moderate: Occasional Failures
2= Low: Relatively Few Failures
1= Remote: Failure is Unlikely

Detection: Ability to Detect
5= Little to no chance of detection
4= Very low chance of detection
3= Moderate chance of detection
2= High chance of detection
1= Almost certain detection

Risk Priority Score
A detailed failure action plan should be created when RPN >30.

Figure 12-4: FMEA Form for Mortgage Application Risk

Failure mode and effects Analysis, also called FMEA is a tool or method that considers the severity of a Risk, the likelihood of occurrence for each Risk and the ability to detect the Risk. Each of these Factors (severity, occurrence, and detection) is rated on a scale of one to five and then they are multiplied together. The result is a Risk Priority Number from 1 to 125 for each Risk. The higher the number, the higher the need to remediate it. Typically, Risks over 30 require an action plan.

Severity Key: Loss Severity

> 5 = Certain Loss
>
> 4 = High Probability of Loss
>
> 3 = Noticeable Effect
>
> 2 = Minor Effect
>
> 1 = No Effect

Occurrence Key: Likelihood of Occurring

> 5 = Very High: Failure Almost Inevitable
>
> 4 = High: Repeated Failures
>
> 3 = Moderate: Occasional Failures
>
> 2 = Low: Relatively Few Failures
>
> 1 = Remote: Failure Unlikely

Detection Key: Ability to Detect

> 5 = Little to No Chance to Detect
>
> 4 = Very Low Chance to Detect
>
> 3 = Moderate Chance to Detect
>
> 2 = High Chance to Detect
>
> 1 = Almost Certain Detection

In a work Team of Subject Matter Experts, develop independent estimates of Risk and then normalize them. You may achieve a consensus or you may end up with a range of Risk values.

Act to Standardize the Risk Management Process Improvements (TIQM Step P4.5).

Ensure that the Process is In Control and roll it out to all Risk Managers.

Best Practices for Risk Management Information

- Creation of a *centralized* Risk Management Organization that drives a consistent approach to Risk measurements, calculation of reserves, initiation of strategic, and tactical Risk reductions and mitigation plans

- Enterprise Risk data warehouses and the use of Enterprise Risk Management tools are enabling organizations to analyze, understand, and act on a more complete view of the Risks.

- An Enterprise Risk Information Quality Specialist in the IQ Team that identifies key Risk IQ Issues and implements Root Cause Preventive Actions and Improvements

- The development and use of a "Challenger" Risk Model. The approach is to have a second, usually independent, Team create a statistical model to make the same Risk Analysis or Model. The best Model wins or a combined Model emerges that integrates the best features from each Model.[12]

Applying Quality to Audit and Compliance Information Processes

Major Information Quality issues in the Audit and Compliance Information affects internal Stakeholders, but especially external Stakeholders, such as Customers, Regulators, Communities, and Investors. The Audit and Compliance processes ensure internal and external Stakeholders that the Enterprise is healthy and a good Steward for its Stakeholders.

Audit and Compliance Information Quality Issues

Common IQ issues and their costs in Audit and Compliance failure include:

Table 12-9: IQ Issues and Costs in Audit and Compliance Information

IQ ISSUES	COSTS OF POOR INFORMATION QUALITY
Missing, legally required Information	Fines and the need to remediate defects, both of which can cost millions of dollars
Out-of-date information	Reputational cost of wrong actions, such as charging a wrong price
Conflicting Definitions across organizational units	Misinterpretation, leading to wrong actions, missing a required regulatory deliverable, or errors in the deliverable; fines and remediation
Inadequate Controls such as Separation of Duties	Internal fraud losses
Inadequate Information Access Controls, allowing inappropriate information access	Theft, fraud, data loss or corruption, lawsuits, and reputation damage

IQ ISSUES	COSTS OF POOR INFORMATION QUALITY
Inadequate Controls such as Monitors and Management Oversight	Trading losses, process failures, lawsuits, and reputational damages
Material inaccuracies in Financial Reporting	Stock price collapses, shareholder lawsuits, possible jail time, and reputational damages
Inaccuracies or missing Compliance Information	Fines, Information Scrap and Rework, and Sanctions in some cases
Poor Quality in Third-Party provided Information	Inability to provide feedback and corrective actions to Third-Party Information Providers
Broken Compliance Information Processes fail to provide accurate and timely Compliance Information.	Fines for failure in timely reporting

Quality in Audit and Compliance Information Processes

While internal Management Accounting needs to be Accurate to ensure that an organization is achieving its Mission, External Financial Reporting Information is critical for external Compliance with applicable Regulatory Requirements. Organizations subject to Sarbanes-Oxley require the CEO and CFO to sign the periodic Financial Reports to verify that they are accurate in that they correctly reflect the *true* financial health of the Enterprise.

The Impact of Basel II in the Financial Sector

Basel, Switzerland is where bankers from around the world meet to make recommendations for regulations and to set industry standards for capital reserves for banks. The Basel Committee on Banking Supervision was founded in 1974 and meets four times a year with members from bank supervisory agencies from the G-10 countries. The basic concept is that banks hold capital reserve appropriate to the Risk in its portfolio. The higher the Risk, the higher the capital reserves need to be. The more accurately a bank can predict and manage its Risk, the better it can mange its capital reserves. The Basel II accord was passed in 2004 and has been implemented in phases.

Basel II has directly impacted Information Quality programs positively at banks by making the *Accuracy* of the Risk Modeling process drive the amount of capital reserves. Risk Models can be complex statistical calculations, using dozens of Data Elements. The Timeliness and Accuracy of these Elements is *vital* to the calculations and, therefore, critical Data Elements to Information Quality Management.

Impact of Sarbanes-Oxley and Management Accountability for Information Quality

The Sarbanes-Oxley Act, often called Sarbox or simply Sox, has been a catalyst for improved Information Quality and Processes in public companies.

Senator Paul Sarbanes and Representative Michael Oxley drafted the Act to improve the *Accuracy and Reliability* of corporate reporting. The act was a response to the infamous issues with companies like Enron and WorldCom that covered up or misrepresented transactions, resulting in huge Investor, Employee, and Retiree losses.

The Act includes sections on new CEO and CFO Responsibilities and Accountability for Financial Information Quality (Section 302), prohibited Auditor activities (Section 201), Disclosure Rules (section 409), Criminal Penalties for Fraud (Section 807), and Criminal Penalties for Document Alteration (Section 802).

While some argue that Sox has increased the cost of corporate compliance, others argue that these Requirements can be leveraged into Increased Shareholder Value.

Impact of the USA PATRIOT Act on National Security

Customer Information, which is part of "Know Your Customer Information" is a *regulatory requirement* within the USA PATRIOT Act and exists in similar legislation in many countries. While this isn't Financial Information in the form of pounds, yen, or dollars and cents, it is *essential* Information for conducting business and running operations in most organizations. Various laws require it in the Financial Services Industry. It is used in business operations like billing, statement mailing, regulatory compliance, and cross-selling. Customer information includes Attributes such as:

- Customer Name
- Customer Address(es)
- Person Date of birth or
- Organization Date of Inception
- Party Tax ID Number
- Identification such as Passport or Drivers License Number
- Household or Organizational Relationships

Customer Organizational Relationships are another key part of Customer Information. Companies and individuals have many-to-many relationships that link the "whole" Extended Party together in a process called "house-holding." Multiple processes require this to aggregate and quantify the *total* Credit Risk exposure for the whole relationship. The linkage data itself is a common source of Definition Quality and Data Maintenance issues.

More information about the USA PATRIOT Act, the Financial Crimes Enforcement Network, and regulatory fines can be found at www.FINCEN.gov.

The Information Quality Act (OMB Section 515) and Federal Agency Accountability for Information Quality

The official title of this federal law is, Guidelines for Ensuring and Maximizing the Quality, Objectivity, Utility, and Integrity of Information Disseminated by Federal Agencies. The Information Quality Act is generally mislabeled "The Data Quality Act." However, the term "Information Quality" appears 15 times in the original document, while the term "Data Quality" appears only once. Enacted in 2001, it binds federal agencies that provide "influential" Information to the public or industry to ensure the quality of the information disseminated. It further requires agencies to provide an Information Consumer "Complaint" mechanism that identifies questionable Information that may need correction. The agencies must provide annual reports as to the *number and nature* of Information "Complaints" and *how they were handled and mitigated*.

OMB Section 515 denotes four substantive terms regarding information disseminated by Federal Agencies: Quality, Utility, Objectivity, and Integrity, with "quality" defined as an encompassing term.

Key Terms in the Information Quality Act

Quality: "an encompassing term comprising utility, objectivity, and integrity. the guidelines may refer to these four statutory terms, collectively, as 'quality.'"

Utility: "the usefulness of the information to its intended users [sic.] Information Consumers, including the public. In assessing the usefulness of information that the agency disseminates to the public, the agency needs to consider the uses of the information not only from the perspective of the agency but also from the perspective of the public. As a result, when reproducibility and transparency of information are relevant for assessing the information's usefulness from the public's perspective, the agency must take care to ensure that reproducibility and transparency have been addressed in its review of the information."

Objectivity: consists of two distinct characteristics: presentation and substance:

- *Objectivity includes whether disseminated information is being presented in an accurate, clear, complete, and unbiased manner. This involves whether the information is presented within a proper context. Sometimes, in disseminating certain types of information to the public, other information must also be disseminated in order to ensure an accurate, clear, complete, and unbiased presentation. Also, the agency needs to identify the sources of the disseminated information (to the extent possible, consistent with confidentiality protections) and, in a scientific or statistical context, the supporting information and models, so that the public can assess for itself whether there may be some reason to question the objectivity of the sources. Where appropriate, supporting information should have full, accurate, transparent documentation, and error sources affecting information quality should be identified and disclosed to users*

- *Objectivity also involves a focus on ensuring accurate, reliable, and unbiased information. In a scientific or statistical context, the original or supporting information shall be generated, and the analytical results shall be developed, with statistical and research methods.*

If results have been subject to formal, independent, external peer review, the information can be considered of acceptable objectivity.

In situations involving influential scientific or statistical information, the results must be capable of being substantially reproduced, if the original or supporting information are independently analyzed using the same models. Reproducibility does not mean that the original or supporting information have to be capable of being replicated through new experiments, samples or tests.

Making the information and models publicly available will assist in determining whether analytical results are capable of being substantially reproduced. However, these guidelines do not alter the otherwise applicable standards and procedures for determining when and how information is disclosed. Thus, the objectivity standard does not override other compelling interests, such as privacy, trade secret, and other confidentiality protections.

> **Integrity:** *security of information — protection of the information from unauthorized access or revision, to ensure that the information is not compromised through corruption or falsification*

> **Information:** *any communication or representation of knowledge such as facts or information, in any medium or form, including textual, numerical, graphic, cartographic, narrative, or audiovisual forms. This definition includes information that an agency disseminates from a web page, but does not include the provision of hyperlinks to information that others disseminate. This definition does not include opinions, where the agency's presentation makes it clear that what is being offered is someone's opinion rather than fact or the agency's views.*

> *Government information: information created, collected, processed, disseminated, or disposed of by or for the Federal Government.*
>
> *Information dissemination product: any book, paper, map, machine-readable material, audiovisual production, or other documentary material, regardless of physical form or characteristic, an agency disseminates to the public. This definition includes any electronic document, CD-ROM, or web page.*
>
> *Dissemination: agency-initiated or sponsored distribution of information to the public and does not include distribution limited to government employees or agency contractors or grantees; intra- or inter-agency use or sharing of government information; and responses to requests for agency records under the Freedom of Information Act, the Privacy Act, the Federal Advisory Committee Act or other similar law.*
>
> *Influential: when used in the phrase "influential scientific or statistical information" means the agency expects that information in the form of analytical results will likely have an important effect on the development of domestic or international government or private sector policies or will likely have important consequences for specific technologies, substances, products or firms.*
>
> *Capable of being substantially reproduced: independent reanalysis of the original or supporting information using the same methods would generate similar analytical results, subject to an acceptable degree of imprecision.*

This federal law is an excellent example for private sector companies as well as not-for-profits and all levels of government. It should be applied to Information Brokers who sell information.

The one limitation of The Information Quality Act is that it does not necessarily mean that High-Quality Information is produced by *improved, error-proofed, and controlled processes*. The accomplishment of quality could be "ensured" by exhaustive inspection processes prior to dissemination. This means of ensuring Quality Information is a reactive, Scrap and Rework activity.

NOTE Do not rely on last-minute Quality Assurance for "ensuring Quality of *critical* Information."

NOTE The best way to ensure Information Quality is to Design Quality into the Processes that Create, Maintain, Deliver, and Present Information, without having to perform the double work of inspection prior to dissemination.

Best Practices in Audit and Compliance Information Quality

The measurement of Quality of Audit and Compliance will be conducted externally by the applicable Regulatory Authority. However, you must conduct your own internal audit and assessment to ensure that you are in compliance and all reporting is done per regulatory procedure and compliance rules.

The Audit and Compliance process is an Assessment process in and of itself. It seeks to ensure that the Information audited is Correct, Complete, and meets Compliance Requirements. Develop a Pareto Diagram based upon the importance of the Audit and Compliance Attributes and the Costs and Impacts of Poor Quality. Identify the A-priority or CTQ Attributes and create an Information Group as the first set of Attributes to measure, followed by the B-priority or near-CTQ Information as the second tier Information to measure. See TIQM Process P3 in Chapter 6 for how to measure the actual Direct and Opportunity Costs and Risks of Poor Quality to confirm their relative priority.

Audit and Compliance Information includes, but is not limited to, the following Attributes required for Conformance Audit and Conformance Assessment:

- Source Attributes required to conduct an audit of the "Books"
- Attributes required for reporting on the audit:
    - GAAP or other National or Standard Accounting and Audit Principles
    - Circumstances in which Accounting Principles have not been consistently followed for the Audited Accounting Period
    - Reasonability of Informative Disclosures in the Financial Statements
    - Either, a Statement of an Opinion regarding the Financial Statements as a Whole, or a Statement that an Overall Opinion cannot be expressed along with reasons. The four types of opinions are:
        1. Unqualified (represents fairly, in all material aspects, the financial position);
        2. Qualified (represents fairly, in all material aspects, *except for* noted aspects);
        3. Adverse opinion (statements do *not* represent fairly the financial position); and
        4. Disclaimer of opinion (no opinion is expressed one way or another)[13]
- All Attributes required *for determining conformance* to Regulatory Policy

Best Practices in Audit and Compliance Information Process Quality

The improvement of Audit and Compliance processes requires cooperation among the Stakeholders, from the CFO and Audit Unit to the Executive Leadership Team down to the line managers and staff. Improvement of processes outside of one's control and authority presents its own set of problems.

How to Improve Audit and Compliance Process Quality

Use the classic Plan-Do-Check/Study-Act cycle described in TIQM P4 "Improve Information Process Quality," in Chapter 7. You may also use Six Sigma TIQM Six Sigma DMAIC (Define-Measure-Analyze-Improve-Control). See the TIQM Six Sigma DMAIC mapping in Chapter 7 TIQM, Table 7-7, "TIQM Processes and Steps Mapped to Six Sigma Phases and Steps."

NOTE The Risks of Audit or Compliance failure are regulatory actions, reputational loss, and lost business and Customers. Measure the Costs and Risks of IQ defects in Audit and Compliance information *before* a Process Improvement. This becomes a baseline for measuring the effectiveness of the Improvement. Once the process is improved and put in control, measure the reduction in the Costs of Failure and Information Scrap and Rework, and in Manufacturing Scrap and Rework, because of the improved process. This will establish the ongoing value of Process Improvement See TIQM P3, "Measure the Costs of Poor Quality Information," in Chapter 6.

Root Causes and Process Improvement considerations are shown in Table 12-10.

Table 12-10: Inaccurate Audit and Compliance Information Process Improvement Considerations

INACCURATE AUDIT AND COMPLIANCE ROOT CAUSE	PROCESS IMPROVEMENT CONSIDERATIONS
Poorly defined Audit and Compliance Assurance and Reporting Processes and Procedures	Update all processes and procedures and keep them current as changes occur. Document date and version numbers along with changes to the process or procedure.
Lack of Controls	Add the controls. Consider automatic or semiautomatic controls where possible.
Duplicate entries	Add check/control edits to detect and prevent duplicate entries.
Post the wrong amount	Consider range checks, trend checks, and reconciliation steps.
No Separation of duties	Separate Duties in Financial Processes.
Lack of Traceability of financial transactions	Establish Chain-of-Control Custody of Financial Transactions and modifications.
Internal/external Fraud	Implement Fraud Detection routines.

Best Practices in Audit and Compliance Information Quality

- Appoint a full-time person to maintain Documentation, Policies, and Procedures to each Audit or Compliance Regulatory body.
- Well-designed Audit and Compliance Processes
- Maintain the *currency* of Compliance Regulations and Compliance Reporting processes and Requirements.
- *Separation of duties* between performing work and auditing work
- Use Double-Entry Accounting System or other Controls to prevent keying errors.
- Use GAAP or other National or Standard Accounting and Audit principles.
- Set clear Policies with *effective* Procedures.
- Provide *regular* Training on Compliance and Signs of Non-Compliance.
- In-line and automated Audit checks on *key* Information
- Reward Self-Identification of issues.
- Internal Auditors should be skilled in:
  - Evaluating the *strength* of Internal Controls
  - Testing Compliance with the organization's Policies and Procedures
  - Measuring the Effectiveness of the Organization's performance
  - Developing suggestions for improving operational effectiveness and efficiency
  - Ascertaining whether or not assets are sufficiently safeguarded

Summary

The most interesting thing about IQ Applied to Financial Management is that our financial resources are not physical resources, like people and facilities. Banks do not manage "money," as in physical currency and coinage. Rather, they manage the Information *about* the money.

Success in organizations is how well they *manage* and *invest* money in the things that help them accomplish their Mission and *delight* their Customers.

Critical Financial processes in the Financial and Risk Management Value Circle "Budget-to-Profit" include:

- **Planning and Budgeting:** Required for ensuring the *effective use* of Financial Resources

- **Risk Management:** Required *to mitigate against failure* based on lack of knowledge of Critical Factors

- **Management (Internal) and External Financial Reporting:** Required for *effective decision making* about strategy and financial resource investment by the Enterprise *and external reporting* to the markets and investors.

- **Audit and Regulatory Compliance:** Required to ensure that your Financial Management processes *are working well*.

This chapter has described how to measure and improve Financial Management processes to improve effectiveness and ensure sound stewardship of Financial Information for the effective management of all other resources for the sake of Customers, Employees, Investors, and Communities in which the organization resides.

CHAPTER 13

Information Quality Applied to Internet and e-Business Information: *"e-Surfer-to-Satisfied-e-Customer"*

"Word of mouse is much faster than word of mouth."
"In e-Business, the Information is the Business."

Larry P. English

Introduction to Information Quality in the Internet and e-Business

Internet and e-Business Information Quality poses real challenges for the organization because Gemba is in cyberspace. The interaction of the organization with Customers and Suppliers is not physical but electronic. This chapter describes fundamental Information Quality (IQ) Principles and Techniques applied to Internet and e-Business Information Quality. It describes IQ problems unique to Web information and its presentation along with e-Business processes created and collected through the Internet. This chapter describes a Customer-centric e-Business Value Circle for e-Customer Care and business effectiveness.

In cyberspace, the Information *is* the Business, making Information Quality a *strategic* requirement for successful e-Business.

Two Categories of Internet and e-Business Information Requiring Quality

There are three categories of information in the Internet environment to which Quality Principles must be applied:

- Web-based Documents and Web Content
- Information collected or created in e-Commerce and e-Business Value Circles, including Information from Third-Party Business Partners. For a discussion of IQ principles applied to Third-Party Information, see Chapter 15, "Information Quality Applied to Information Management and Information Systems Engineering." See section "Best Practices for Purchased or Third-Party Information Quality."
- Web 2.0 Information for networking and collaboration

We will describe how to apply IQ to these two areas later in this chapter.

Internet and e-Business Information Stakeholders

The Internet has transformed how work is performed today. The end-Consumers and Business Partner Employees have become the new Information Producers, replacing Employees as order takers, eliminating an "intermediation point," but introducing new challenges for Information Quality Management and Control.

Internal Stakeholders

Internal Information Stakeholders include those listed in Table 13-1.

Table 13-1: Internal Information Stakeholders and Their Information Interests

INTERNAL INFORMATION STAKEHOLDERS	INFORMATION INTERESTS
Web site Designers	Categories of Information required on the site; Web design styles
Web Content Providers	e-Customer Information needs in Web content; Quality of Content and Presentation
Supply Chain Managers	Logistics Information for the Web channel
Quality Management Personnel	Quality Requirements to ensure that Quality is Designed in and achieved in the various processes of Development, Production, and Delivery
Service Product Developers	Market, demand, and Customer requirements to create new services, such as Financial, Insurance, or Investment "products" available online

INTERNAL INFORMATION STAKEHOLDERS	INFORMATION INTERESTS
Product Managers	Accountable for Product Descriptions and Pricing on Web site.
Marketing Staff	Content and Presentation Quality of Marketing material and Product or Service Descriptions; Clickstream analysis of e-Customer behavior.
Accounts Receivable Staff	Accountable for determining and providing Payment options to e-Customers.
Accounts Payables Staff	Electronic Invoices received and payments made.
Customer Care	Handling Complaints and mitigating problems.
Business Analysts	Analyze Product Sales and Customer patterns.
Sales Forecast Analysts	Analyze Sales data for trends and Supply Management.
Executive Management and Directors	Provide Strategic Direction for the organization.

External Stakeholders

Information Stakeholders outside the Enterprise include those in Table 13-2.

Table 13-2: External Information Stakeholders and Their Information Interests

EXTERNAL INFORMATION STAKEHOLDERS	INFORMATION INTERESTS
Web Visitors	View product/service information, Interact with the Business.
e-Customers	View Product/Service; Create Order; View/Update Customer Information.
Business Trading Partners	Various information exchanged between Trading Partners.
Buyers	Product Specification Information compared to Product Quality Requirements.
Warehouse Managers	Create Order to Replenish Stock.
Suppliers	Catalogs to and Purchases, Shipments from.
Supply Clerks	Order fulfillment, Shipment Information.
e-Business Partners	Creating Orders or Receipts, Invoices, or Payments.
Shareholders	Business and Financial Performance Information.

The Web Content Value Circle: "e-Concept-to-Educated-e-Customer"

The Web Content Value Circle follows the same Value Circle as the Document Value Circle described in Chapter 14, "Information Quality Applied to Document & Knowledge Management: *'Words-to-Wisdom' and 'Ideas-to-Innovation',*" Figure 14-2, "Document Management Value Circle "Words-to-Wisdom.""

The Internet and e-Business Information Value Circle: *"e-Surfer-to-Satisfied-e-Customer"*

The Value Circle "e-Surfer-to-Satisfied-e-Customer" is about making it easy for Customers to conduct business with you on *their* time table without the need of intermediation.

This creates new demands on the Quality of Information provided to and received from e-Visitors and e-Customers. A generic Value Circle describes the relative sequence of critical activities (see Figure 13-1).

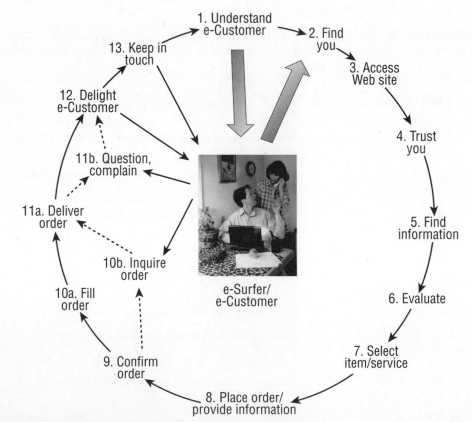

Figure 13-1: e-Surfer-to-Satisfied-e-Customer Value Circle

"e-Surfer-to-Satisfied-e-Customer" Value Circle Activities

Every Value Circle begins and ends with a Customer, from understanding their needs to providing products and services — and information — that meet or exceed their expectations and with active listening to their feedback, if you want to continue to do business with them. Information Quality is even more important for communicating with and conducting business in Cyberspace.

1. Understand e-Customer Information Needs

Before you develop Products or Services, your organization must understand the marketplace and the Customer Product and Service needs and expectations. In the same way, before you create or enhance your Web site, you must understand your marketplace, the prospective Customers, and their *Information* needs. If your Web site is "Informational," what do e-Surfers need to "know" in order to engage you? If your Web site is "Business Transactional," you must know *how* your Customers will want to conduct business with you, whether they are end-Consumers or Business Partners who ultimately serve your end-Consumers.

The Web site Design and Content and Information-gathering services must be well thought out and consistent so that your e-Customers will put their trust in you and conduct business with you.

Only after you have discovered your e-Customers likes and dislikes, identify and study your competitors, both in traditional and e-Business offerings. Otherwise, you may bias your thinking and fail to identify true breakout products and services. Analyze and highlight your differentiators. Study and understand your competitors' differentiators. Narrow the gap.

Realize that your e-Customers are becoming increasingly savvy and will react unfavorably to overhyped or biased messaging.

An e-Customer-focused approach to planning and delivering valuable online Information and Services uses Quality Function Deployment, a set of techniques that involves Customers in the design of products and services. David Siegel describes such an approach in his book, *Futurize Your Enterprise: Business Strategy in the Age of the E-Customer*, in which he describes the six "Customer-led" meetings required to develop and deliver the "Customer-Led Web Site."[1] They include:

- Meeting 1: Commitment
- Meeting 2: Customer Segmentation
- Meeting 3: Active Listening
- Meeting 4: Measuring Success
- Meeting 5: Customer Modeling
- Meeting 6: The Plan

The focus of the six meetings are as follows:

Meeting 1: Commitment

- "Forget" your current vision — the rules of Customer "engagement" and expectations have changed.

- "Forget" your competitors' Web sites — you must concentrate on delighting your e-Customers.

- Appoint an e-Business executive who reports to the Chief Operating Officer.

- Appoint a Chief Information Quality Officer who can help you ensure that you are not wasting money or alienating e-Customers through Poor Quality Information, both that you provide and that you receive from your e-Customers or e-Business Partners.

- Deal with resistance to change. You must change the paradigm to be successful in the emerging "realized" Information Age.

Meeting 2: Customer Segmentation

- Customer groups — not "user" groups! — will lead the new economic revolution.

- Start at the top of the loyalty pyramid.

- Identify your key e-Customer Segments.

- Target an *outrageous* level of e-Customer Satisfaction.

Meeting 3: Active Listening

- Question: "How are online Customers going to change our company?"

- Address: "What is our next Business Value Proposition?"

- Conduct Customer surveys and hold Focus Group meetings with existing or prospective e-Customers.

  - Identify a range of ideas with open, non-judgmental brainstorming.

  - Identify the most forward-thinking Customers willing to work with you and listen to their Visions and Dreams, but also to their Complaints.

  - Develop open-ended questionnaires to enable e-Visitors to provide open "Voice-of-the-Customer" Expectations and concerns.

  - Conduct one-on-one conversations

  - Create a Customer Advisory Board to guide you in the design of your e-Business environment.

Meeting 4: Measuring Success

- Identify the right measures; you must measure Customer Satisfaction, not just "on-time, within-budget," or "time-to-market" Characteristics.

- Measure Near-term Business Results that matter, such as Customer Lifetime Value (profit) and Complaints, not just the financials.

- Measure Long-term Business Results for e-Customer Satisfaction and delight along with Employee or Associate Satisfaction and Morale. Registered and delighted e-Customers and Employees are the true currency.

Meeting 5: Customer Modeling

- Develop a profile of a "typical" representative of each e-Customer group.

- Develop an entire part of your business around that e-Customer.

- Design around the beginner, intermediate and expert e-Customer.

- Develop the e-Business features for each need/action requirement.

Meeting 6: The Plan

- Plan the Web site from a Customer-led approach that focuses on the e-Customer experience versus a content-led approach, where each department wants to monopolize the home page.

- Develop the home page to direct target groups to their own neighborhood pages.

- Design the home page for both newcomers, with a few vital statistics, and for regular e-Customers.

- Design the Web site to "exceed" your e-Customers' expectations.

Now you can implement your plan with the confidence that, when your e-Customers find you, they will have a more than satisfactory experience.

2. e-Customer Finds Your Web Site

Web site design must make it easy for e-Customers to find you and the specific products or services of value to them. Here are some guidelines for optimizing search engine placement of your Web pages, from ICGLink.[2]

Search Engine Placement

Search engines visit your Web site using a "spider" to crawl over the pages in a site that they "see" and report back to the search engine about how many pages there are and what keywords are being used on each page.

Each search engine has its own set of algorithms that analyzes a number of factors to determine how to list pages in keyword searches. Long equations evaluate each keyword they find on each page of your site and compute a "weight" value for that keyword on each page. Search engines will list Web pages in sequence, according to each site's "keyword" weight compared with other sites that have the same keyword, with the highest weighted page listed first.

Keys to Keywords and Keyword Phrase Placement

- Find the keyword phrases e-Visitors use through a "Keyword Popularity Tool" that shows how many searches were made per month using specified keyword phrases.

- Select 30 or more keyword phrases you plan to emphasize on your site with the number of searches done for each one.

- If you are creating a new Web site, register a domain name that reflects what your site is about. Your company's name is not always the best choice. If you make Cookware you may want to have your domain be BestCookware.com rather than JaneSmith.com. This helps inspire people who have not heard of Jane Smith the Cookware maker to go to your site.

- Use your keyword list to *name* the pages in your site. There should not be a keyword phrase that doesn't have a page URL associated with it. If you are using a multiple-word phrase, use a hyphen rather than an underscore, for example, Nonstick-Frying-Pans.html, as underscores get lost in the underlined URL.

- Emphasize *only* two to three keyword phrases per page with the exception of the home page, which should describe the site as a whole. This spreads out keywords and phrases over many pages and creates additional ways that e-Visitors can enter your site through search engines. The more pages your site has, the more credibility the search engines will give it.

- Keyword phrases on a page should not exceed 6–12 words in 64 characters including spaces. The title of your home page should reflect what your Web site is about as a whole. The title of main pages should reflect the services or products, such as Cookware, on that page. Each internal page linked from there should reflect the specific details of the products offered on that page, such as "Nonstick Frying Pans."

- Use appropriate page titles with e-Customer-friendly headers that contain your keywords.

- Use critical keywords in the first text on a page.

- A page will receive a higher value for a keyword if the keyword appears in each paragraph on the page.

- Use description meta-tags with no more than 200 characters, including spaces, with 12–24 words and no more than three commas, because some search engines use meta-tags for calculating keyword density.

- Use keyword meta-tag to show the search engine the main keywords important to that page. Even though this tag is not weighted, it helps keyword density, and some smaller search engines will not accept a site without it. Keep keyword meta-tags to less than 1,000 characters, including spaces with no more than 48 words.

- Do *not* use the same keyword more than three times. Always use a *comma and a space* to separate keyword phrases. Keywords listed here *must* also appear on the page.

- Always create HTML heading tags for your keywords. Every page needs a main heading (H1) tag and secondary (H2) heading tags if possible. These reinforce the title meta-tag and give the page more credibility for search engines. You must have an H1 tag to have H2 tags.

- Image alt tags (words that pop up when you place your mouse over the picture) add value to the keyword density on a page. The image alt tag should have 5 to 8 words, using the keyword phrases for that page.

- Design pages to have between 250 to 500 words of clear, correct, and relevant content on each page. Search engines look for unique and original content that will interest the e-Visitor. Do not duplicate the content found on your other pages or other Web site pages, except where you have an abstract on the linking page and on the content page.

- Search engines need content readable in Hypertext Markup Language (HTML). Search engines cannot see text in a picture or a Flash movie. If an image has text in it, use an appropriate alt tag that can be read by the search engine.

- Web site navigation is also important for the search engine spiders. "Dropdown menus" for navigation are normally created in JavaScript or Flash. This type of navigation is attractive and can make e-Visitors more interested in a Web site, but Google is the only search engine that can read JavaScript. An easy way around Flash navigation is to have straight HTML links at the bottom of your pages. This allows spiders from all search engines to navigate through your site without restrictions

- Use "Anchor Text Links" using your keywords on each page so that search engines can find their way to the rest of your site. Search engines give these more weight. Use the keyword list to name links. For example: "Nonstick Frying Pans" would point to the page for "nonstick frying pans"

- Avoid using frames because some search engine spiders find them difficult to navigate and are not able to report the page content back to the search engine.

- Design your HTML code to maximize spider analysis. Minimize the nesting of tables and extensive use JavaScript or other content that moves your keywords far down in the page's HTML code. Search engines read from left to right and top to bottom, by reading the HTML code rather than the page directly. Columns are read in order from left to right, with content on the right considered less important than that on the left.

- Avoid using the "?" symbol in URLs that you want search engines to index. Some search engines test these pages by making up URLs at random to see if a database will generate a page. If not, the search engine may penalize the site.

- Create a site map linked from your home page to help spiders find all your content easily. Large Web sites should list only the main pages. The spiders can easily find the rest of the internal pages from there.

- Use a "robots.txt" file, so search engines know what to do when they arrive at your site.

Web Site Databases

Web site content can be entered into the HTML code of the pages, or the code can include calls to a database where the content is stored, using a non-technical content management system.

- Use Web site databases for volatile data such as product descriptions and prices to create dynamic pages. This causes search engines to reaccess the data from the URL as opposed to the cache, allowing your Clickstream analysis to have a more complete picture of e-Visitors' tracks. The e-Visitor sees no difference, but from a search engine's standpoint, not all databases are created equal.

- A basic database will allow you to add content to your pages.

- More sophisticated systems allow you to change the page title, description tag, keyword tag, alt tags, navigation links, and even Web page addresses. The more capabilities you have, the more they will help you influence your search engine listing.

Web Site Age

Your Web site's age is measured from the time it is submitted to a particular search engine. Search engines consider the age of a site important for reasons of credibility. Some search engines lower the value of a new site compared to an older one. It can take 6–8 months before your results improve, and it may take several more months to finally get well-listed.

Inbound Links

- Use various marketing channels to bring e-Consumers from your market to your site. Seek to get other credible Web sites to add a link from their Web site to your site. Not only does this drive more traffic to your site, but search engines will list you higher because of the number and quality of incoming links from other sites.

- Ask other Webmasters with sites that have a theme similar to yours for a link in exchange for a link back. Always ask for anchor text links like "Nonstick Frying Pans."

- Make sure the link from their site is relevant and that it has some Page Rank value (is not buried so deep that no one will ever find your link)

- Make sure that the link "feels" good and that it has no nasty surprises such as redirect, or unexpected pop-ups.

Pay per Clicks

This option is good if you don't often change the content of each page, or if you have so many different products that optimization would be too expensive. You buy your way to the top by bidding against your competitors for the top listing. The price can range from $.05 per click to well over $1.00 per click, depending on the field your company is in. There are about 640 Pay-per-Click Services out there to choose from, and the number is growing, so assistance from an expert is probably helpful in this area. A downside is that savvy e-Visitors may know about and avoid Pay-per-Click links. And pranksters or competitors may abuse them with massive access to drive up a sponsor's costs.

3. e-Customer Accesses Your Web Site

Web site availability is critical to the global community and your e-Customers, who shop in various time zones. Use techniques such as:

- Ensuring that backing up of your Web site and Information is performed on an appropriate schedule, according to your Customers' dependence on your site

- Publishing any times that the site is *not* available for scheduled site maintenance or other downtime, if any, when known

- Providing Web site redundancy and automatic fail-over where possible and practical, to mitigate inevitable technology failure

4. e-Customer Trusts Your Organization

With myriads of unscrupulous and unreliable Web sites, along with a growing incidence of identity theft, reputable e-Businesses must establish credibility and trustworthiness in their Web sites and e-Business operations.[3] There are benefits, but also "buyer beware" aspects in Web publishing. The benefits are that "people can easily make their works public [on a timely basis] as Web material can be published almost instantaneously. However, the steps that contribute to the accuracy of traditional media are frequently condensed or even eliminated on the Web."[4] The ease of making information available on Wikipedia has resulted in a situation where misinformation can go undetected for months.[5]

Establish your credibility by adopting a Customer-focused Code of Ethics and Warranty that include rigorous editorial and Quality Principles for Web Information publishing. Remember that you are no longer a few miles from your competitors — you are only a few mouse clicks away! A Customer-focused Code of Ethics and Warranty include the following elements.

Integrity, Credibility, and Legality

This establishes professional credibility and authority, by committing to comply with an industry or professional body's Code of Ethics that the e-Customer can verify. As one example, TRUSTe is an independent, non-profit privacy initiative dedicated to building Knowledge Workers' trust and confidence on the Internet and accelerating growth of the Internet industry. Sponsors a third-party oversight "seal" program that alleviates Knowledge Workers' concerns about online privacy, while meeting the specific business needs of each of their licensed Web sites. The TRUSTe program is backed by a multi-faceted assurance process that establishes Web site credibility, thereby making Knowledge Workers more comfortable when making online purchases or providing personal information. "Industry certifications, such as the VIPPS certification that is provided by the National Association of Boards of Pharmacy (NABP), are available for pharmacies. Certification requires that pharmacies must comply with NABP criteria, including quality assurance, patient privacy rights, state licensing and inspection, security of prescription orders, and provision of meaning consultation between patients and pharmacists."[6]

Security

"The highest level of security must be provided to Confidential and Proprietary or Identity Information exchanged to assure no accidental disclosure of or unauthorized access to personal data or confidential or sensitive business data. Data must be classified as to its security requirements, including regulatory and privacy, and implemented with the proper level of security control, such as firewalls, secure servers, effective log-in ID and password techniques, and encryption."[7]

Privacy and Confidentiality

"Consumers are increasingly frustrated with what they perceive as 'intrusive' invasion of their privacy. The UK and EU Data Protection Acts and the U.S.

Gramm–Leach–Bliley Act require organizations to take a more Customer-focused stance on privacy. These laws confirm Customer 'rights' as to what data may be collected about them and how it may be used. Conforming to the letter of the law is only the *entry point* for privacy. A quality organization understands its individual Customer's privacy expectations and honors them. Reputable organizations develop Customer-centric privacy policies and have third-party certification of their privacy statements through organizations such as TRUSTe (1997) or BBBOnline (1996)."[8] Only true Customer-focused e-tailers would list themselves on BizRate.com. Operated by Shopzilla, a leading comparison shopping service founded in 1996 and now owned by E. W. Scripps Company, the company compiles Customer satisfaction data in seven categories, including ease of finding information, timeliness of delivery, Customer support, and the product's meeting expectations. Serving e-Customers in the U.S., UK, France, and Germany, they rate e-tailers on 12 Quality Characteristics. They rank e-tailers based on thousands of e-Customer evaluations, providing a "Customer-Certified" designation for those who attain satisfactory or higher evaluations on all 12 quality characteristics, and providing a "Best-of-the-Best" designation for those with consistently "outstanding" ratings.[9] Figure 13-2 illustrates BizRate's summary rating of Quill Corporation.[10]

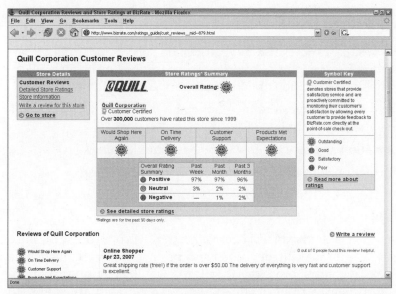

Figure 13-2: BizRate's Customer Satisfaction Rating for Quill Corporation

Information Quality Warranty

Credible Web sites will *not* just post a *disclaimer* disavowing responsibility for the completeness, accuracy, or currency of the information they post. Rather, they will *claim* what they *are* doing to ensure High-Quality Information. See the upcoming section "Applying Quality to Web-Based Documents and Web Content Value Circles." Only after they communicate what they are doing to provide High-Quality Information will they describe any disclaimer for legal purposes. Figure 13-3 illustrates an actual disclaimer on a major Information Technology Information Provider's Web site. There is no statement as to what, if any, Quality Management Controls are applied. Describing what the organization is doing to *ensure Quality* Information increases Customers' trust in their Information. U.S. federal law requires federal agencies to ensure and maximize the Quality, Objectivity, Utility, and Integrity of the *Influential* Information (including statistical information) they disseminate. "Agencies must issue their own implementing guidelines that include 'administrative mechanisms allowing affected persons to seek and obtain correction of Information maintained and disseminated by the agency' that does not comply with the OMB guidelines."[11] The National Science Foundation Web site illustrates its "warranty" and procedures for how to communicate an information complaint and how the complaint will be handled.[12] Information Consumers can identify suspected poor quality information and describe how the Information Consumer uses the information, how they are "hurt" by the information in error, and reasons for correcting the suspected error. This law may be a forerunner of laws requiring *warranties for Information Quality* and Customer recourse in the private sector if Consumers' well-being is put at risk."[13]

Customer Satisfaction

- "Credible e-Businesses post Customer satisfaction policies and product/service warranties. It is even more important when conducting business without prior physical evaluation of goods and services. See Table 13-1."[14]
- Remember that your investors may have lent you money, but it is the Customers who pay the bills.
- Treat Information as a product just as real as manufactured goods.
- Verify Information with independent corroborative sources.
- Use peer reviews of critical articles or Information you want treated as authoritative.

Information Brokers *must warrant the Information* they sell or provide because their Customers use it for making decisions and performing work. Defective Information causes Customers' processes to fail. You would not buy an automobile if it had the equivalent warranty. Why should you buy Information without a warranty? If Customers do not demand a warranty, there is no motivation for the broker to design Quality into their processes.

At the opposite end of the spectrum is the Customer-focused warranty of Carfax, which guarantees that its Information is Correct or it will compensate you if a car you purchased as a result of their Information is not free and clear. See Figure 13-4.

Disclaimer

1. **Disclaimer of Warranties.**
   COMPANY does not make any warranties, express or implied, including, without limitation, those of merchantability and fitness for a particular purpose, with respect to the Products. Although COMPANY takes reasonable steps to screen Products for infection by viruses, worms, Trojan horses or other code manifesting contaminating or destructive properties before making the Products available, COMPANY cannot guarantee that any Product will be free of infection.

2. **Accuracy of Information.**
   The information contained in the Products has been obtained from sources believed to be reliable. COMPANY disclaims all warranties as to the accuracy, completeness or adequacy of such information. The reader assumes sole responsibility for the selection of the Products to achieve its intended results. The opinions expressed in the Products are subject to change without notice.

3. **Limitation of Liability.**
   In no event will COMPANY be liable for:

   3.1 damages of any kind, including without limitation, direct, incidental or consequential damages (including, but not limited to, damages for lost profits, business interruption and loss of programs or information) arising out of the use of or inability to use COMPANY's Web site or the Products, or any information provided on the Web site, or in the Products.

   3.2 any claim attributable to errors, omissions or other inaccuracies in the Product or interpretations thereof.

Figure 13-3: Actual Information Quality Disclaimer with a Poor Quality Focus (with the Term "COMPANY" Replacing the Actual Organization's Name)

Figure 13-4: Carfax Warranty for the Quality of Its Title Certification

5. Customer Finds Information about Your Products and Services

Your e-Visitors need to be able to *easily and quickly* find the Information they want or to conduct business the way they need to.

- Ensure site navigation is intuitive for your audience.
- Provide examples and help mechanisms as informal training for novices.
- Ensure headings and labels are clear and intuitive.
- Ensure access to clear definitions of any technical terminology.
- Provide Information in a tiered approach from high-level and general information to detailed and specific information.
- Provide FAQs for novices or newcomers to answer common questions they may have.

6. Customer Evaluates Your Products, Services, and Information

If your organization is in a competitive market, you will want to ensure that your products or services are presented in the best way, without bias or overpromising.

Here is where newcomers will be looking for signs that indicate you are reputable and can be trusted. You must earn their trust, first with your stated Code of Ethics, Privacy Policy, and Security features. You must retain their trust through the behavior with which you treat them.

- Clearly describe the products or services and features.
- If you have pictures or images, ensure that they have a resolution that enables the e-Customer to have an accurate visualization of the product.
- Second-hand or used items should have any damage or flaws identified.
- Warranties for products and services should be accompanied by Warranties for the Information provided.
- Do not overwhelm e-Visitors with unnecessary common features. Instead, point out the distinguishing or differentiating features or make it easy to differentiate your products and services — with *realistic and accurate claims*.

7. Customer Selects Items, Services, and Information

e-Customers will now become their own clerks in a self-service environment. It must be easy for them to transact their business, whether conducting electronic banking, ordering a book, buying a DVD player, or downloading music — legally. It must all be able to be done easily and securely.

- Keep the business processes simple.
- Ensure that there are no "surprises" in the selection process, such as asking for more personal information just prior to completing the business transactions.
- Offer something of value that e-Visitors do not find elsewhere.

8. Customer Places Order and Provides Information

At this point, the e-Visitor has retrieved information as a Knowledge Worker and now becomes an Information Producer, creating information about themselves and the information required to conduct business transactions.

- Make the procedures easy to use.
- Error-proof the procedures for e-Customers to provide information accurately.

See also the "Preventive Actions for Keying Errors by e-Customers" section later in this chapter.

9. Organization Confirms Order and Provides Shipment Information

Communication requires confirmation that the sender's message has been satisfactorily received and understood. e-Business and e-Commerce require confirmation that business transactions have: (1) been received, and (2) once all transaction verification and validation procedures have been done, that the transaction has been conducted properly.

- Remember that e-Customers do not differentiate between your using third parties for shipment or for e-Customer interactions and your doing these activities yourself. Any interaction and process execution will be seen as having been done by your organization with you as the accountable entity.
- Design confirmation and other email communications to minimize the chances that spam filters will stop or delete your messages.
- Keep confirmation messages clear, simple, and Customer-focused. Do not use this as a marketing opportunity. e-Customers have enough problems with unscrupulous spammers.
- If errors or problems are found in the e-Customer's transaction, provide clear instructions for remedying this.
- Include estimated delivery data time and window to manage expectations.

10a. Organization Fills Order or Executes the Transaction

Whether your organization fills e-Customer Orders or it uses third parties for products or product delivery, the e-Customer will consider the source and distribution parties as part of your organization. This may be the first or only personal human contact the e-Customer has.

- Ensure that you have reputable, reliable Business Partners. Your organization will be judged by the behavior of your partners. To the e-Customer, they are merely an extension of you.

- Ensure that Third Parties share your Quality Philosophy and agree with your Warranties.

- Put in place processes to acquire e-Customer Feedback of all steps in the process.

10b. Customer Inquires about the Order or Transaction

e-Customer queries will generally be by email, but they may also wish to speak to a "live" person, depending on the nature of the query.

- Provide prompt access to a person, if the e-Customer requests it, through multiple means if possible: phone, Web form, email, and live chat.

- Be proactive. By alerting e-Customers to out-of-stock items or delays proactively, you can avoid frustrated e-Customer calls, possibly turning a negative situation into a positive "moment of truth."

If your organization uses an offshore third party as its call center, see Chapter 15, "Information Quality Applied to Information Management and Information Systems Engineering" in the section on "Best Practices for Third-Party Information Quality" for further tips and techniques.

11a. Organization or Partner Delivers Order or Provides Service

The Customer will have an expectation for delivery based upon the original commitment. In a world of ever-increasing "Just-In-Time" expectation, delays will create frustration. Tips for dealing with this include:

- Ensure that delivery of goods, services, or information is prompt and within an acceptable time window. Always communicate if there is a delay or problem with the order.

- Provide for contingencies for when conditions prevent delivery or a service provision that includes something of value for any inconvenience.

- Hold the delivery Business Partner *accountable* for having adequate capacity and delivery capability with remedies for failure to deliver to e-Customer Satisfaction.

- Make it easy for e-Customers to give you their comments and feedback — both positive and negative.

11b. Customer Questions or Complains about Products, Shipment, or Services

The bottom line is that the e-Customers will provide the final Quality Rating of the organization's performance, in Product Quality, and Information Utility. Tips:

- Proactively seek, analyze, and understand e-Customer Feedback.

- If the Feedback is less than satisfactory, analyze the Causes of various categories of complaints (such as a Service, Specific Product(s), Delivery, and Information) and *Improve* the Process to prevent recurrence.

- Formalize a Complaint-Handling procedure with logs and recorded remedies implemented in the general script to mitigate unrealistic expectations.

- Automate Feedback where possible and provide personal Customer-focused remediation quickly, on the e-Customer's timetable.

12. Satisfy e-Customer

In e-Business, the burden for e-Customer Satisfaction is more difficult than in face-to-face encounters. You do not have the communication feedback seen in body language or in speech inflexion. Because e-Customers cannot hand inspect the product, they and sales personnel cannot weed out Defective products at the point of sale. Tips for dealing with this include:

- Ensure that all pictorial and textual Information represents the Item or Service without bias or overhype.

- Ensure that you have immediate person-to-person contact through a variety of methods when the e-Customer needs it.

- Be patient with e-Consumers, who are also communicating without seeing body language communication clues.

- Accept Accountability for errors, or slip-ups, even if the source is a third party. Remember, Customers do not care what the cause is. They just want you to deliver what they were expecting.

- Make it easy for e-Customers to tell you their Complaints.

- Resolve Complaints on the spot, when e-Customers do complain. Some Customer-focused organizations empower Customer-facing staff with the authority to resolve complaints on the spot with a significant monetary value without management's approval. Train and empower staff. This minimizes Customers' feeling that "they must *NOT* think I'm important."

13. Organization Keeps in Touch with Customer

The challenge for any provider is to identify the optimum rate of contact with its Customers. Tips include:

- Identify distinct market segments.

- Determine behavioral characteristics and communication preferences. Focus groups or surveys are useful here.

- Understand the Cost of Poor Quality Products, Service, and Information and its impact on Customer dissatisfaction. Then invest in a sound Quality Management approach to Prevent and Eliminate the Causes of Process Failure and e-Customer Dissatisfaction.

- Capture and Honor the e-Customer's Privacy Preferences.

- Find ways to make the e-Customer successful with the Products, Services and Information you provide them. This will help Customers increase their quality of life.

And this brings us back to the starting point in the Value Circle, where we now understand our Customers better.

1. Organization Understands Customer [Better]

As your e-Customers conduct business with you, you can evaluate their satisfaction and behavior much better. Use:

Clickstream analysis to evaluate the effectiveness of your Web site design and Information Quality from the perspective of meeting their Information needs. Do e-Surfers drop out with items in their shopping cart? If so, why? Did they feel they could not trust you (security or the kind of information you requested)? Clickstream analysis looks at pages and links that e-Visitors traverse in their journey through your Web site. Things to look for include:

- ☑ Where did your e-Visitors come from? Link from a third-party Web site, link from a banner, or via an external search engine (what key words were used?)

- ☑ e-Visitor IP address

☑ Browser type used

☑ URL of the first and subsequent pages, images, or scripts accessed

☑ URL of interior pages that may be linked via a bookmark

☑ Page sequences

☑ Page dropped off

☑ Was the drop off after starting a purchase or service request?

☑ Length of time on a page (see limitations below)

☑ Site map pages selected (shows specific interests)

☑ Site search engine keywords used

☑ Search engine "found pages" accessed

☑ Glossary words or help features used (may show ease-of-use issues)

Clickstream analysis does have some limitations. "Noise" can distort the Clickstream data. Limitations include:

- Search engines capture the site time of access, not the e-Visitor time of access. This limits the ability to see the local time of the e-Visitor.

- e-Customers may not accept cookies that provide clickstream data. To overcome this, have a strong Customer-focused privacy and security policy and honor it. Mention that you require cookies and explain why from a Customer care focus. This can prevent some Customers from rejecting cookies.

- If e-Customers are interrupted while on a page view, it skews time of stay.

- Search engines may use a cache to refresh previously accessed pages, skewing the page traversal data. To overcome this, use techniques that force the reaccessing of the page from your site.

Seek feedback on the nature of the Information by using Customer feedback forms. Keep them simple and easy to complete. Is the Information in Product or Service description, Assembly instructions, Owner's Manual the *right* Information presented in the *right* format? Is it accurate, complete, and timely?

Seek feedback on the ease of use of the Web site, including any written instructions. Was the process cumbersome? Were the instructions not clear? Was it hard to go through the various pages to conclude the transaction?

Use your analysis of e-Visitor and e-Customer behavior to discover ways to make your e-Customers successful. Especially:

- Proactively notify e-Customers of glitches in their transactions.

- Help e-Customers avoid mistakes by doing the following:

- Create FAQs (Frequently Asked Questions).

- Develop customized instructions for unusual situations. One manufacturer provided customized installation instructions for its car radio with CD players customized for the specific makes and models of vehicles.

- Provide e-Customer-friendly reminders or renewal notices.

- Create early warnings for e-Customers, such as reminders for prescriptions that are routine, for those who might be forgetful.

- Whenever you contact the e-Customer, always try to include information that adds value from their perspective.

Information Quality in Internet and e-Business Value Circles

No longer optional, organizations must conduct business in some way or ways through the Internet. At a minimum, the Internet and the new Web 2.0 environments are places for prospective Customers to find you and to become active Customers. Some businesses conduct their business solely through the Internet, such as Amazon.com and e*Trade. Failure to address Information Quality issues can produce "garbage in, garbage out at the speed of the Internet." Information Quality is one of the most important ingredients of a successful Web site whether the site is informational or operational e-Business.

On the Internet, Customers who have a "complaint" are just a few *clicks* away from your Competitors as opposed to several blocks or miles. If they cannot find something easily or perceive missing, out-of-date, inaccurate, or biased information on the Web, they only have to click to access the competition.

General Internet Information Quality Issues

The Internet has created an incredible new channel through which legitimate organizations can conduct business. At the same time, it has created a huge opportunity for unscrupulous scam artists and for access by members of the general population who may lack the knowledge or rigorous discipline to research facts or the ability to create information that is valuable content. Anyone can create a Web site and place any kind of information on it with little concern for its accuracy.

So the challenge is for legitimate organizations to differentiate themselves, as shown by the items in the following list:

- The ease of posting information on the Web, coupled with the emphasis on accelerated cycle times to publish on the Web, has had the impact of *decreasing* the Quality of the content.[15] On the positive side, in e-Publishing, it is easier to fix electronic document errors than in hard print.

- Poor Quality Information in Cyberspace can go unnoticed — except by the e-Visitors — for much longer periods of time than in a store, where staff can recognize and correct obvious errors.

- Internet Information sources can be unreliable, with pages being modified without documentation, or moved or removed without notice.

- Misinformation, complaints, and rumors spread globally, quickly and easily over the Internet, increasing risks and damage caused by poor quality. "Word-of-*Mouse*" is much faster than "word-of-*Mouth*!"

On the Internet, *Gemba* (the "real place" where information is collected, manipulated, or presented) is a virtual place, unlike the shop floor or at a sales counter where people can see when problems occur.[16] On the Internet, organizations expose both their information and business processes to their Customers and Business Partners. Without regular monitoring and keeping Information current, poor Quality Information and defective processes can go unnoticed for long periods, creating high costs of *process failure* and Information Scrap and Rework, along with significant indirect costs of Missed Opportunity and Lost Customer Lifetime Value.

Applying Quality to Internet and e-Business Value Circles

There are three categories of Information in the Internet environment to measure:

- Web-based Documents and Web Content
- Information collected or created in e-Commerce and e-Business Value Circles, including third-party Information Producers
- Collaborative Information and Web 2.0 Information Quality

Applying Quality to Web-Based Documents and Web Content Value Circle

Here are some common issues in Web content.

Web-Based Documents and Web Content IQ Issues and Costs

Misleading, inaccurate, or out-of-date Information provided to Web e-Visitors can cause harm to the Enterprise or drive Customers away without even being noticed by the e-Business. The pertinent Value Circle "Words-to-Wisdom" is found in Figure 14-2: "Document Management Value Circle 'Words-to-Wisdom'" in Chapter 14, "Information Quality Applied to Document & Knowledge Management: *'Words-to-Wisdom'* and *'Ideas-to-Innovation.'*

Information Issues include the following.

Issue: Out-of-Date Information Content

Web and other types of Documents and Information subject to becoming out-of-date, if not kept current, ends up with inaccurate Information at the time the Information is no longer current, such as when dates of "future events" become "historical" dates. Sometimes history is required, but it can be confusing for those who may try to attend a seminar that is no longer available.

Costs of Out-of-Date Information Content

Costs include:

- e-Customers making errors or wrong decisions
- Loss of credibility by e-Customers
- Lost opportunity, sales, or engagement of e-Customers

Issue: Lack of Visibility of Information Problems

Lack of visibility of Information errors, such as wrong product prices, in the Gemba of Cyberspace can go unnoticed, for no person is physically observing the virtual interactions. Excessive prices will alienate or cause e-Customers not to buy. However, underpriced items will cost the organization revenue, and alienate Customers if the organization fails to honor the prices or seeks additional money from the purchasing Customers.

Costs of Lack of Visibility of Information Problems

Costs include:

- Lost business if products are overpriced in error
- Lost revenue if products are underpriced in error and legal liability and reputation problems with cost-recovery initiatives attempted
- Lost profit in returns of products for which Information does not match product reality

Issue: Unclear, Misleading, or Biased Web Information

Incorrect, Unclear, or Misleading Information can drive e-Customers away if they have no means of clarifying the Information. Over and beyond the critical Discrete Information such as Product Codes and Prices, the Descriptive Information and instructions for conducting business can be confusing to the novice e-Customers.

Costs of Unclear, Misleading, or Biased Information

Costs include:

- Confusion of e-Customers, who may make a wrong decision or selection. If Information does not match the Customer's perception of a product or service, they may request their money back, costing you for the handling of the return or compensation to them.

- Inaccurate or Unclear Descriptive Information may make the organization look silly and unprofessional, leading to loss of reputation and Customer Lifetime Value.

- As e-Visitors become more experienced and savvy, biased or overhyped claims may cost you the trust of prospective e-Customers.

- Product or service description that is biased in a way that creates high expectations can be greeted with an unsatisfactory e-Customer evaluation (does not meet expectations, based on the overhyped promises). Brick-and-mortar store Customers can actually see, touch, and experience the physical products in the store. Graphic and other representations must be accurate to prevent unrealistic expectations in e-Customers.

- Unclear Instructions or Directions can frustrate your e-Visitors, causing them to drop out and go elsewhere, which they can easily do.

Tips for Measuring Web-Based Documents and Web Content IQ

Measuring the Quality of Web-based documents and Web content requires two kinds of assessments:

- Measure the Quality of Business Information Definition (TIQM P1) in Chapter 4, "The Step-by-Step Guide to *Assessing Information Product Specifications and Information Architecture Quality*."

- Measure Accuracy and Other Information Quality Characteristics (TIQM P2) in Chapter 5, "The Step-by-Step Guide to *Assessing Information Quality*."

Measuring the Quality of Business Information Definition: Correctness, Completeness, and Clarity

In a P1 Assessment of Information Product Specification and Information Architecture Quality, you are looking for instances where casual e-Visitors may be inclined to misinterpret Information or find the Information to be presented in a way that is not Customer-friendly, or that may cause them to provide you with defective Information.

Follow the baseline assessment steps in Chapter 4 (TIQM P1). Here are some tips for this assessment applied to Internet documents and Web content.

Identify Information Definition Quality Measures (TIQM P1.1)

The critical Quality Characteristics here are Correctness, Completeness, and Clarity of communication. Key measures include:

- Intuitive business term names and correct, complete, and clear definition
- Clarity in written text definitions and specifications
- Intuitive navigation through the site for both novices and experienced e-Customers
- Help mechanisms that are intuitive and truly helpful
- Relevance of descriptive Information to e-Customer needs
- Complex information that is presented in a way that illuminates, such as from (1) a general concept or abstract to (2) a more specific description to (3) the most detailed information.

Identify a Set of Information to Assess Definition Quality (TIQM P1.2)

First, consider the Web site and e-Business processes as a single entity. You should evaluate this environment as a single "Information Environment," as it represents your organization as a whole, even if it represents only one channel of your Enterprise.

Second, identify any technical terms that are used in the Web pages and Documents and in business transactions that may not be generally understood.

Assess Information Definition Technical Quality (TIQM P1.4)

For definitions of terms or data elements presented or requested in your Web site, measure them for conformance to Enterprise Information Standards and Formats, and Name and Definition Clarity and Correctness.

Assess Web Site Structure, Database, and Navigation Mechanism Design Quality (TIQM P1.5)

This assesses the integrity of the Web site structure, Web Database Design and navigation system design. Quality Characteristics include:

- Clarity in Web site navigation term names and definitions
- Structure and organization of Web site navigation that is intuitive and easy to use for both novices and experts
- Clarity in Web site map with intuitive groups of information by e-Customer segments
- Site search engine capable of finding complex combinations of terms and phrases, with a single search finding information in both HTML documents and Database Files, such as ColdFusion

The Web site structure has the Characteristics of Stability, Flexibility, Reuse:

- Web site Stability means that the Web site is easily usable by multiple e-Customer segments, with only additive modification.

- Web site Flexibility means that the Web site can be reengineered to add new e-Business processes, or to enhance and improve the processes with minimal change to the Web site.

- Web site Reuse means that the Web site Databases are reused without having to create redundant data stores for business information.

- Databases that house personal e-Customer information or sensitive Enterprise Information are on secure servers with encryption.

Assess e-Customer Satisfaction with Data Definition (TIQM P1.6)

The most important measure is that of the e-Customer's satisfaction with their experience in the Web site and e-Business processes. Step activities include:

1. Develop a customized questionnaire for e-Customers to rate their Web and e-Business experience.

2. Identify a set of e-Customers from whom to solicit feedback. Use statistical sampling to be sure that you do not have a bias in the e-Visitors selected. This should be conducted with those who were most recent, known e-Visitors to your Web site.

   This may be conducted independently of the normal e-Customer feedback, or it may be part of your regular e-Customer process.

   As a usability test for this assessment, recruit Employees who may use your Web site but who were *not* part of the development of the Web site. Those who developed the site will bring a bias to the evaluation. This will help you receive feedback on your assessment form. Use this to refine your questions and format as necessary.

3. Assemble and email your Customer feedback form to your sample of e-Customers. You may wish to offer incentives for your e-Customers to complete your form and return it in a timely manner. Sample questions and topics for e-Customer Feedback (regarding site information) include:

   How did you hear about us? (for first time e-Visitors)

   Did you find the Information you needed?

   Was the Information easy to find and use?

   Was the Information useful and current?

   Was the Information accurate and complete?

Sample questions for conducting business include:

Was the procedure easy to follow?

Were product assembly or operating instructions easy to follow?

Did we give you confidence that we can serve you reliably?

What improvements would help us serve you better?

For e-Business:

Did the product/service meet your expectations based upon its description, image and expectation?

4. Collate and analyze the results of your surveys. Establish a Process Improvement initiative (see TIQM P4 "Improve Information Process Quality" in Chapter 7) where required.

Figure 13-5 is an example of an effective and simple Web site evaluation form for Applied Materials.

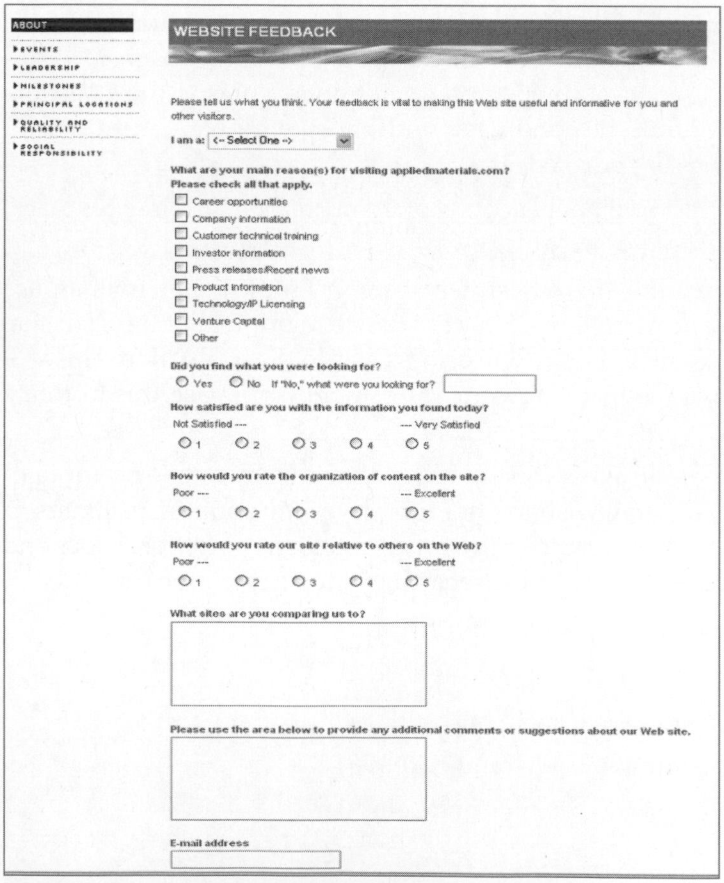

ABOUT
EVENTS
LEADERSHIP
MILESTONES
PRINCIPAL LOCATIONS
QUALITY AND RELIABILITY
SOCIAL RESPONSIBILITY

WEBSITE FEEDBACK

Please tell us what you think. Your feedback is vital to making this Web site useful and informative for you and other visitors.

I am a: <-- Select One -->

What are your main reason(s) for visiting appliedmaterials.com?
Please check all that apply.

- ☐ Career opportunities
- ☐ Company information
- ☐ Customer technical training
- ☐ Investor information
- ☐ Press releases/Recent news
- ☐ Product information
- ☐ Technology/IP Licensing
- ☐ Venture Capital
- ☐ Other

Did you find what you were looking for?
○ Yes ○ No If "No," what were you looking for?

How satisfied are you with the information you found today?
Not Satisfied --- --- Very Satisfied
○ 1 ○ 2 ○ 3 ○ 4 ○ 5

How would you rate the organization of content on the site?
Poor --- --- Excellent
○ 1 ○ 2 ○ 3 ○ 4 ○ 5

How would you rate our site relative to others on the Web?
Poor --- --- Excellent
○ 1 ○ 2 ○ 3 ○ 4 ○ 5

What sites are you comparing us to?

Please use the area below to provide any additional comments or suggestions about our Web site.

E-mail address

Figure 13-5: Web Visitor Evaluation and Comment Form

The form is simple, requiring only a couple of minutes to complete, yet it covers the key issues for Information Quality.

Measuring Accuracy and Other Information Quality Characteristics (TIQM P2)

The second assessment is an assessment of the accuracy of selected information found on your Web site. Follow the general steps described in Chapter 5 "The Step-by-Step Guide to *Assessing Information Quality*." Here are tips for measuring Web documents and Web content quality.

Identifying a Set of Information for Measuring Quality (TIQM P2.1)

Using a statistical means of random selection, select a set of 5 to 15 important facts presented on your Web site to measure for accuracy. These may be facts asserted in a document or in the text of a Web page, including such things as citations of quotations, product prices, service descriptions, addresses, or the spelling of a person's name available to your e-Customers.

Plan IQ Objectives, Measures, and Tests (TIQM P2.2)

Identify the Information Stakeholders to learn their IQ expectations. There are two major objectives for assessment:

1. Degree of Accuracy of the actual Information on the Web site
2. Degree of Accuracy of the process capability that provide Information to the Web site e-Visitor

Determine the IQ Characteristics to measure, such as Accuracy, Validity, Timeliness of availability, for example, based on their importance to e-Customers.

Identify the Information Value Circle (TIQM P2.3)

In order to understand process capability, you must understand the processes that make up the information Value Circle that creates the Information and propagates it to the Web site. Document this Value Circle using a Value Circle format as described in Chapter 5, Section "Step P2.3: Identify Information Value Circle," or use Information Value/Cost Chain[17] or Information or Work Flow Diagrams.

Determine Information Store or Process to Assess (TIQM P2.4)

The Web site as a whole will be the scope of the state of Quality of Information.

For the Process Capability Assessment, you will select the process that produces critical or influential content posted to the Web site. There will be many source processes for different types of information. Select one of the most critical Web content processes.

Identifying Accuracy Verification Sources (TIQM P2.5)

See Chapter 5 "The Step-by-Step Guide to *Assessing Information Quality*," Step P2.5 for how to identify the correct sources to verify Accuracy. This is the most critical Inherent Quality Characteristic for any Information.

Extract a Statistically Valid Sample of Data (TIQM P2.6)

A minimum number of occurrences to select from a statistical perspective is 30. You may want to select 100 occurrences of a fact type to measure Process Capability. The facts must be selected randomly to ensure an unbiased selection. See Chapter 5 "The Step-by-Step Guide to *Accessing Information Quality*," Step P2.6: "Extract Statistically Valid Sample of Data" for how to determine the sample size for your desired Confidence Level.

Measuring Information Quality in the Selected IQ Characteristics (TIQM P2.7)

To measure Accuracy of the selected Facts, compare the data value of the Fact to the Characteristics of the Real-World Objects or Events that the Facts represent. For Accuracy of a Product Price, compare the Web Product Price to the controlled Price provided by the Product Manager. Measure the "shipping" weight, by taking samples of the product, as packaged, and weigh them to determine an average Shipping Weight.

If there is wide variation in the actual Product Packaged Weights, then there is variation in the Packing process. Go find out the Root Cause and improve the process.

Interpreting and Reporting Information Quality (TIQM P2.8)

Report the data in the form of number or percent of *defects measured*. Use a statistical Quality Control Chart of the process measured over time. See Chapter 5, "The Step-by-Step Guide to *Assessing Information Quality*," Process Step P2.8 "Interpret and Report Information Quality."

Communicate assessment reports to Knowledge Workers who require the information so that they know about any issues with Information Quality. Communicate the assessments to Information Production Managers and Process Improvement Facilitators to address improvements as necessary. Maintain Control Charts to ensure processes stay "In Control."

Tips for Improving Web-Based Document and Web Content Process Quality

The information an organization provides to the public or its stakeholders is often neglected as "documentation" or a "necessary evil."

Remember that in e-Business the Information is the Business.

And this may represent the first "Moment of Truth" as Jan Carlzon would say. A Moment of Truth is an opportunity when a Customer, in this case an e-Customer, has to form an impression about an organization.[18] Will it be a positive or negative experience? Remember that you never get a second chance to make a first impression.

There will be slight variations in the improvement initiatives based on the specific nature of the data. Data such as product prices will follow the standard product pricing processes, and you should seek to understand the Root Causes of Inaccurate pricing.

However, documents and textual information provided on Web sites must follow classic publishing, Fact-Checking, Editorial, and Presentation Quality Guidelines.

Define a Project for Web Content Process Improvement (TIQM P4.1)

Identify a critical process requiring improvement. There are several possibilities:

- Web site Design
- Various Document and Content Development processes; these should be standardized.
- Processes that deliver Database data to Content pages, such as ColdFusion, PHP (Hypertext Preprocessor), SQL Queries, for example

Follow your organization's normal project planning procedures to establish a Process Improvement Initiative. Identify the process Owner, who is accountable for the process and for Implementing Improvements, Identify the Information Production staff, including Information Producers, Transcriptionists, or Translators. These will participate in the Root Cause Analysis and Process Improvement definition activities.

The facilitator for the Process Improvement Initiative should be the Process Owner. Develop the project plan for conducting the Process Improvement activities of the Plan-Do-Check/Study-Act cycle.

Plan for a Web Content Process Improvement (TIQM P4.2)

The first part of planning is to Analyze and Isolate the Root Cause or causes of the problem you are seeking to solve, such as "out-of-date content." See TIQM P5.2.1 "Analyze Root Causes of the IQ Problem" in Chapter 7. Analysis of the Root Causes requires understanding the needs and expectations of the e-Customers and facilitating the identification of precipitating causes to drill down to the Root Causes. Root Causes can include the following.

Causes of Out-of-Date Information Content

- Lack of attention to the Information Subject

- Lack of Management Accountability for Web Content produced in their area
- Lack of a Change Control Procedure for Outdated Information or a reminder date for updating or deleting obsolete Information
- Lack of Content Producer's understanding of e-Customer Needs
- Lack of Content Producer's understanding of Content domain
- Lack of Writing Skill, Concept Design, or Presentation Skill
- Time or Deadline issues with getting content out

Use the Ishikawa-English Cause-and-Effect Diagrams to define the IQ Effect (problem) and to collect, analyze, and identify the applicable Root Cause or causes.

The second part of planning is to define Process Improvements that eliminate the cause of defects described in the IQ effect. See TIQM 4.2.2 "Define Process Improvements to Prevent Recurrence of the Defects" in Chapter 7, The Step-by-Step Guide to *Improving Information Process Quality.*

Preventive Actions for Out-of-Date Information Content

Preventive actions include:

- Hold Managers of content producers *accountable* for the Quality and Currency of Web content. Once managers have accountability written into their job descriptions and are held accountable for Information Quality, and once training and resources are provided to Information Producers, then you may hold Content Producers accountable for their Information content.

- Understand the "shelf life" of the Information and create a schedule for when the Information "expires." If there is a known time of expiration, create calendar events to trigger a review to update or archive. At this time:

  - Update Information to keep it current, such as a new price for a current product following a scheduled, or event-driven protocol, such as interest-rate changes.

  - Replace content with correct, current information, such as when a new-and-improved product replaces a previous product.

  - Archive or delete information with no replacement, such as a discontinued product.

- If there is no arbitrary timeframe controlling when data goes out-of-date, such as when a product is retired, there must be a trigger created when the product retirement date is reached to communicate to the content steward that it is necessary to update or remove the information. Monitor information subject to IQ decay (going out-of-date) and verify the Information against its Accuracy source at an appropriate time interval.

Causes of Lack of Visibility of Information Problems

There is no real cause of the problem here. The lack of visibility is caused by the fact that e-Business takes place in the invisible reality of cyberspace. There is so much information online that it is difficult to control, and each e-Business entity must do its part.

Preventive Action for Lack of Visibility of Information Problems

Preventive actions include:

- Make the problems visible by creating internal Real-Time Monitors that can detect runaway or out-of-control transactions. Create thresholds of reasonable transaction limits, updated for sale or promotion events, to allow you to identify abnormal transaction patterns, both high and low. Then analyze the data associated with any runaway transactions to identify if an Information Quality issue is the cause, taking corrective action as necessary.

- Test Web links on a regular basis to ensure that they link correctly and remain relevant.

- Implement a process to ensure the correctness of content *before* uploading the information to the Web.

- Create incentives for your e-Customers to call to your attention problems in your Web information rather than calling them to the attention of other people. For example, if a product sales price is "too good to be true," encourage people to tell you by offering the first one or two Customers who identify it to buy the item at its "advertised" price and give them a gift certificate equivalent to its correct price that they can spend on anything else. This is an incentive for them to tell you rather than their email lists of family and friends! This will save you relationship problems and profits by learning and correcting the problem early.

Causes of Unclear, Misleading or Biased Information

Causes include:

- Failure to recognize and treat descriptive information as a critical component of communication — and as an integral part of the product or service — is a predominant cause of poorly written information. After all the business is about "selling" its products, not "writing" about them, isn't it? Wrong! The assumption that if we write it in English, anyone should be able to understand it is a misconception that can lead to significant business loss.

- Misleading promises about a product or service that cannot be substantiated or that are not attainable by the e-Customer

Preventive Actions for Unclear, Misleading, or Biased Information

Preventive actions include:

- To identify if there may be a problem, conduct a Clickstream analysis to identify patterns that may indicate confusion or the dropping out of prospective e-Customers.

- Analyze your writing and ensure that it has a reading difficulty index of three grade levels below that of the intended readership.

- Create definitions of technical or complex terms with hyperlinks.

- Create focus groups of prospective e-Customers to react to sample descriptive information or instructions for conducting business. Listen carefully to their experiences, feelings, and frustrations. Then adjust how you word descriptions and instructions.

- Develop, test, and provide graphics to illustrate products. Note that the graphics must be of sufficient resolution to accurately represent the products themselves.

- Develop, test, and provide "Helpful Hints" to guide people through the transaction process.

- Allow e-Customers to have direct telephone access to real people who are truly knowledgeable to answer their questions.

- Use online live chat, where practical, for real-time dialog between e-Customer and the Customer Support Team.

"Do" Implement Web Content Process Improvements (Step P4.3)

In the "Do" step, you may take one section of content in the Web site and improve the processes related to that content. The selected process may be from a single Business Area or may address one critical Information Group from different Business Areas. Note: because it may be gathering or delivering content, you want to isolate the improvements to a controlled area separate from the status quo processes. In this way, you can subsequently test the effectiveness of the "improved" process compared with the status quo processes and your original process assessment.

Check/Study Impact of Web Content Process Improvements (Step P4.4)

This step analyzes the e-Customer behavior of those accessing this portion of the Web site. Clickstream analysis of activity of this section can be compared to the activity prior to the improvement.

For checking and studying "biased information," solicit e-Customer feedback from those visiting this part of the Web site or accessing the information from the improved process.

Analyze the nature of the e-Customer behavior. Is it a positive change? Are e-Customers more satisfied?

If not, conduct a Root Cause Analysis as to why the improvement was not satisfactory and either reimplement or replan depending on the cause of failure.

If the problem is out-of-date information, you should test the process results, after or on a timeframe that will allow you to see whether currency requirements are met. For calendar events, this may be three to six months or, for airline-ticket pricing, it might be three to six hours.

Act to Standardize Web Content Process Improvements (Step P4.5)

Once your have an effective improvement, put the process in control with actions to make the improvements "permanent" and roll them out to the other areas of the Web site.

Put in place monitors to measure the Quality with an appropriate frequency to ensure that the processes stay in control.

Be sure that all procedures are enhanced and clear, with checklists as necessary, and that training has occurred and is demonstrated to be effective with the content producers.

Document the knowledge you've gained from each IQ Process Improvement Initiative:

- Lessons Learned from the Root Cause Analysis
- Critical Success Factors learned from the Process Improvement "Do" implementation
- Lessons Learned from the final "Act" to put the process in control

TIP Measure the Cost of Poor Information Quality before you make improvements, following Steps TIQM P3.3–6, *and* afterwards follow Step TIQM P3.7 in Chapter 6 to document your Return-on-Investment. This helps you confirm the value of your IQ function and sustain critical management support.

Applying Information Quality Principles to Information Collected or Created in e-Commerce and e-Business Value Circles

Information collected from e-Visitors and e-Customers, including third-party Business Partners is a new challenge brought about by the Internet.

Issues with Information Collected or Created in e-Commerce and e-Business Value Circles

With e-Business, e-Customers have replaced trained Employees as the new Information Producers. Data created by Customers or Business Partners in e-Business is "outside" enterprise control and introduces new sources of Information Quality issues that must be addressed. Problems include:

- Keying errors by e-Customers. Lacking keying skills, e-Customers may make common transposition and other keying errors in providing information.

  Staff no longer control the capture of information. e-Customers are the new *Information Producers* in e-Business. Organizations cannot "train" e-Customers in the same way they train point-of-sales staff. Complex transactions produce higher error rates.

- Unclear labels and instructions can cause e-Customers to enter the wrong data.

- Privacy and security of e-Customer-provided information such as personal data, credit card numbers, and other identifying data add additional complexity to the processes of gathering and maintaining e-Customer information.

- The anonymity of the Web increases the potential for misinformation, maliciously provided information, and fraud.

Issue: Keying Errors by e-Customers

Transactions created by e-Customers and e-Business suppliers are subject to the level of experience in keying data and also to the lack of training in the process of performing business. This creates a "learning curve" for new e-Customers and will also result in a demand for ease of use in the Information-Gathering Processes.

Costs of Keying Errors by e-Customers

The costs of errors will be the same per error regardless of whether the error came from an e-Customer creating an order or a Call Center Rep taking an order from a call-in Customer.

Tips for Measuring Information Collected or Created in e-Commerce and e-Business Value Circles

There are three types of Information collected from e-Business Value Circles: Customer Demographic data, Transactional data related to the business transactions being conducted, and e-Visitor Feedback. The assessment tests will vary according to the *type* of Information.

Identify a Set of Information for Measuring Quality (TIQM P2.1)

There are slight differences in how you measure each of the types of Information, Customer demographic data, transactional data, and e-Customer feedback data.

Select the specific data elements that are most critical, where errors or omissions are the most costly in terms of process failure and Information Scrap and Rework.

Plan IQ Objectives, Measures, and Tests (TIQM P2.2)

There are two major objectives for assessment:

1. To establish the degree of accuracy of the data in the entire database
2. To establish the degree of effectiveness of the process that produces the data

Measuring the current process capability requires selecting data from the recent transactions and interactions to measure the variance of accuracy over time.

Generally, you will select a sample of records randomly from all the transactions, and new Customer records created in the last month. Capturing these every month allows you to see whether the process is "in control," that is, it is producing consistently accurate data that meets the needs of the respective Information Consumer groups for that Information.

Identify Information Value/Cost Chain or Circle (TIQM P2.3)

These processes will be the Web processes themselves, in which the e-Customer is providing the Information, both about themselves and about the Business Transaction being performed, such as making a flight reservation, ordering a product, paying a bill, transferring funds, and e-Customer Feedback.

Determine File or Process to Assess (TIQM P2.4)

To measure process capability, you must extract data from the *originating* database file on a timely basis before any updates or corrective maintenance can be applied to it.

Identify Accuracy Verification Sources (TIQM P2.5)

The participating e-Customer will be the authoritative source for Customer Information. They will also be the authoritative source for their "intentions" in the business transactions. It is possible, however, that a person intended to order one item but hit the icon or button for a different item, *inadvertently selecting* a different item from what they intended.

Extract a Statistically Valid Sample of Data (TIQM P2.6)

Select 100 to 300 records or more randomly from the current process to measure its capability. The selected facts must be selected randomly to ensure an unbiased measurement. See Chapter 5 "The Step-by-Step Guide to *Assessing Information Quality*," Step P2.6: "Extract Statistically Valid Sample of Data" for how to determine the size of a sample for your confidence level.

Measure Information Quality (TIQM P2.7)

Confirm the Accuracy of the selected facts by comparing the facts to the characteristics of the Real-World Objects the Facts represent. With e-Customer-created data, the Customer will be the authoritative source. Contact them via email, phone, or mail to confirm the accuracy of the data they created or provided.

See the "Measure" steps in Chapter 5, TIQM Process Step P2.7 for guidelines and controls for Accuracy and other IQ Characteristic measurements.

Interpret and Report Information Quality (TIQM P2.8)

Report the data in the form of number or percent of defects measured. Use a Statistical Quality Control Chart of the process measured over time. See Chapter 5, Process Step P2.8 "Interpret and Report Information Quality."

Report the two Information Groups (Customer Profile data and Business Transaction data), using Statistical Quality Control Charts over time, as illustrated in Chapter 5.

Tips for Improving Information Collected or Created in e-Commerce and e-Business Value Circles

Significant problems are encountered in data entered by e-Visitors and e-Customers. Some are unique to the e-Business environment itself. The following provides some tips and techniques for Improving e-Business Processes to Error-Proof them.

Define a Project for e-Business Created Information Process Improvement

Follow Step TIQM P4.1 as outlined in Chapter 7, "The Step-by-Step Guide to *Improving Information Process Quality*." The IQ Improvement project team should include typical e-Customers as either active participants or in the form of focus groups, survey questionnaire responders, or interviewees to gather the real Information Producers' experiences. These may be typical end-Consumers of your products or Employees of your Business Partners in e-Business transactions.

Develop a Plan for e-Business Created Information Process Improvement (TIQM P4.2)

The Plan step first analyzes and isolates the Root Cause(s) of keying or intentional errors or poor Web presentation that induces errors.

Causes of Keying Errors by e-Customers

Errors by e-Customers have many causes. Precipitating Causes include:

- Lack of typing skill
- Failure to follow the instructions
- Selecting the wrong options or failure to understand them

Root Causes include:

- Poor design of e-Customer-facing screens and data to account for lack of training and lack of keying skills
- Deliberate "falsification" of data because of privacy or security concerns, or general lack of trust of the organization

The next step of Planning is to identify Improvements that Error-Proof the process and prevent recurrence of the negative Information Effects encountered in collecting e-Business Information.

Preventive Actions for Keying Errors by e-Customers

e-Visitors will bring varying keying skills to their web input. The burden is on the organization to understand the kinds of problems that e-Customers have and how to Error-Proof the e-Business transaction input process. Use such Error-Proofing Techniques as:

- Allow e-Customers to click items and boxes where appropriate instead of entering known data.
- Require double entry of critical data, such as account numbers, tax ID numbers, driver's license numbers, or credit card numbers, and self-created Customer name and password data.
- Use Check Digits for Customer IDs to prevent keying errors from selecting an incorrect person.
- Verify in real time or near-real-time data that can be validated, such as addresses, product IDs.
- Allow e-Customers to keep their Information *current*.
- Use Edit and Validation Capabilities in technologies such as JavaScript and Ajax to instantly check entered data against valid values and to conduct business rule tests for validity.

NOTE Remember that Validity (Conformance to Business Rules) does not ensure "Accuracy." To ensure Accuracy, you must put in place verification correctness of the Information with the source or source provider who is able to verify the Accuracy.

Issue: Unclear Labels and Instructions That Cause Errors

In our earlier discussion of unclear, misleading labels, the issue at hand was the organization's reputation and the e-Customer's loss of confidence in it. Here, we discuss the issue of poor quality labeling and instruction wording as it causes errors in the Information captured through e-Business transactions.

It is much more than cost reduction that causes organizations to move to e-Business. The more significant rationale is that many e-Customers choose to conduct business electronically for their own convenience.

Because your organization cannot "train" its Customers, it must make it easy and Error-Proof for its e-Customers to transact business and provide and maintain Vital Information. In fact, if done properly, Customer data maintenance can be a significant cost reduction, too.

Costs of Unclear Labels and Instructions That Cause Errors

The costs of errors created by e-Customers is the same per instance as when an Employee creates the error. Experience shows that e-Customers make more errors than do trained staff when there is *ambiguity* in the meaning of data and unclear instructions.

However, e-Customers know their own Information and will enter it correctly, except when unintentional typos occur or if they fear that you will use their information inappropriately. Examples of costs of e-Customer-induced errors caused by unclear labels and instructions:

- Process failure in the processes storing and/or using the data
- e-Customer frustration in failing to get the products or services or in failing to get them promptly
- Alienated Customers and lost business

Causes of Unclear Labels and Instructions That Cause Errors

One must analyze Root Causes to understand which is most likely, for the preventive actions will vary by cause.

Precipitating Causes include:

- Labeling or instruction writing by technicians who do not understand the e-Customers and the way they think
- Labeling or instruction writing that uses internal jargon instead of Consumer language
- Failure to Proofread Instructions

Root Causes include:

- Failing to understand and treat information *as a strategic business resource* and a *product of business processes*

- Performance measures of speed as opposed to *Quality* (which *reduces* the cost of Process Failure and Information Scrap and Rework)
- Failure to understand the e-Customers and their real needs

Preventive Actions for Unclear Labels and Instructions That Cause Errors

Preventive actions include:

- Treat Information as a *strategic resource* of the Enterprise. Acknowledge that information is *the* resource required to manage every other resource of the organization whether internal (Human Resources or Financial Resources) or external (Customer Resource or Business Partner Resources).

- Treat information in the same way that you treat a product. To produce a product with high quality, you must understand the Customer Requirements, and Design Quality Into the Process that produces the product and check your work. The same is true for the "Information Product." Data names, definitions, valid value sets or ranges, and specific defined business rules make up the "Information Product Specification Data" for Information.

- Treat information in the same way that you treat Financial Resources and Human Resources. General ledger account codes should be standardized across the enterprise with a clear precise definition of each revenue or expense category. Job descriptions should be standardized for clarity of the position's description, skill requirements, and job accountabilities. The same must be true for the definition of facts or Information.

- Understand the "Requirements" of your e-Customers. What Information do they need? What products or services do they need? Then, design your Products and Services and the Information to meet or exceed those e-Customer needs.

- Analyze the performance measures that create negative side effects that increase the "Cost-of-Ownership." Speed or "productivity" measures invariably create the opposite effect. They drive up the operational costs by *decreasing* quality in product and information that, in turn, *increases* the Costs of Process Failure and Scrap and Rework

Implement Defined e-Business-Created Information Process Improvements in a Controlled Environment (TIQM P4.3)

Of course, you will implement e-Business Process Improvements in your test environment first to ensure the software is operating properly on your test data.

However, you must also implement the Improvements in an environment where real e-Customers conduct real business, so you can study the e-Customer experience. Internal staff who simulate e-Customer behaviors can only approximate the experience of a typical Consumer. Improvements must Error-Proof the transactions for Customers who have a wide range of technological experience and knowledge. Improvements must be easy and Mistake-Proof. Enhancements to software tools like Java Script and Ajax make this easier to implement certain Validity tests.

Check and Study the Impact of e-Business-Created Information Process Improvements (TIQM P4.4)

Unlike checking and studying the impact of an improvement, when internal Information Producers will have (probably) gone through training on the Improved Process procedure and have written procedures or scripts to follow, your "e-Customer-turned-Information Producers" have to live with their existing knowledge and experience.

> **TIP** Make it easy for e-Customer Information Producers. Keep reading difficulty three grades less than the typical e-Customer education. Ensure all terms are defined with easy access to definitions. Provide helpful hints for unusual procedures.

With internal Information Producers, you must conduct final checks of implemented improvements after a "burn-in" time when the training is over and Information Producers will have either incorporated any improvements into their habits or not. Checking too early after the implemented improvements can produce biased results because the Information Producers will be focused on learning the new procedures and will be "trying" to perform them properly. The key is to Check and Study, once the learning curve attention span is over and the new behavior is routine.

But with e-Business improvements, you must check immediately after implementing the process improvement, to verify the experiences of first-time e-Customers. Your e-Customer feedback mechanisms should ask questions about how long they have been a Customer and how frequently they use the e-Business, in order to study errors by experience segment.

Act to Standardize the e-Business-Created Information Process Improvements (TIQM P4.5)

The key to Acting to Standardize and putting the process in control for consistent quality involves continued Electronic Monitoring to identify errors early so that they can be corrected with minimal expense before the defects cause process failure.

Applying Information Quality Principles to Web 2.0 Information

Information provided through new Internet technologies address collaboration and the combining of Information from multiple sources to increase value to Knowledge Workers.

Quality Principles for Web 2.0 Creation and Maintenance

The Internet information environments are continually evolving both in business use and in social use. While there is ongoing debate about the definition of "Web 2.0," the term refers to the newer technologies that enable non-traditional Web use in collaboration, communication and social networking.

Examples of Web 2.0 applications, technologies or content include:

- **Blog**: short for weblog, a running journal, diary or commentary of personal interest or topical discussion, often allowing comments or questions to be posted by readers

- **Podcast**: (1) technology that enables audio broadcasts to be made from a Web site; (2) an audio broadcast made from a Web site

- **Wiki**: (1) computer software that allows Knowledge Workers to collaboratively update and edit Web content and link other content; (2) Web sites, Web pages or online content that can be updated collaboratively by many individuals

- **Social networking** (YouTube, MySpace, Facebook): a Web site or online resource that allows individuals to share personal information, photos, videos, and other information informally. LinkedIn is a business networking site.

- **Mashup**: a Web site or application that combines content from multiple sources and *offers* it as an integrated whole

IQ Applied to Blog Information

Using Blogs in business communications requires using guidelines for verifying the accuracy of information exchanged. IQ Principles include:

- All parties should abide by the Journalistic Code of Behavior that includes verification of facts by independent, reliable sources.

- All parties should stay on topic of discussion thread or threads.

IQ Applied to Podcast Information

This is classic sharing of Information to an audio audience. The IQ Principles include:

- Ensure the content is relevant and value-adding to the audience.
- Ensure the content is accurate.

IQ Applied to Wiki Information

Wiki provides for collaborative work and development. Key IQ principles applied to collaborative Information development, such as the Wikipedia is to follow the Document Management Value Circle, "Words-to-Wisdom" described in Chapter 14, "Information Quality Applied to Document & Knowledge Management: *'Words-to-Wisdom'* and *'Ideas-to-Innovation.'"* IQ Principles include:

- Establish clear policies and procedures for the collaborative work.
- Establish a governance mechanism for achieving consensus in final results or of enhancements as you go.
- Ensure accuracy of factual Information provided by contributors by verifying the facts by independent, reliable sources.

IQ Applied to Social Networking Information

In Business, the counterpart to FaceBook or YouTube is LinkSys. The general purpose is to increase business connections with other persons or organizations where collaboration or partnerships can be developed for mutual value.
    IQ Principles include:

- Ensure you abide by privacy considerations
- Investigate backgrounds of potential link references to ensure integrity of the party consistent with your reputation
- Warrant the Quality of Information shared among networking parties

IQ Applied to Mashup Information

Mashups combine information that adds value beyond the value of each information product used separately, such as combining Google Earth with census or demographic data.
    IQ Principles include:

- Ensure you do not violate Copyright or Trademark laws.
- Ensure the combinations of Information are relevant to each other. For example, if the Google Earth image encompasses a geographic area, but the census demographic information does not fall exactly within the visual boundaries of the geographic area, you have created two errors — the demographics do not match the geographic area, and the area does not match the demographics.

Summary

In e-Business the Information *is* the Business.

The Internet and e-Business environments require a special focus on Information Quality, as all interactions are conducted in the electronic exchange of cyberspace. People no longer have to physically interact face-to-face. Information Quality problems can go unseen by Enterprise personnel, unless they regularly surf their own Web site.

On the Internet, Customers who have a "complaint" are just a few *clicks* away from your competitors as opposed to having to drive several blocks or miles. If they cannot find something easily or perceive missing, out-of-date, Inaccurate, or Biased Information on the Web, they only have to click to go to the competition.

By taking a strong e-Customer focus and concentrating on making certain that your Information Quality is high, your site can be the one that unhappy Web surfers gravitate to instead of *from.*

Exploiting new Web 2.0 technologies require new rules to provide new avenues for communicating your messages to a wider Prospective Customer audience. Be sure to understand the limitations of the new mechanisms, and how to exploit them with Quality of Information created or exchanged. Error-proof your processes of creating, updating and presenting the Information for value to the Knowledge Workers and end-Consumers.

CHAPTER 14

Information Quality Applied to Document & Knowledge Management: *"Words-to-Wisdom" and "Ideas-to-Innovation"*

"Avoid the Nice to Know — write the Need to Know"
John M. Smart

Introduction to Information Quality Applied to Document and Knowledge Management

This chapter applies Information Quality principles to complex Information Types, such as in Documents, Annual Reports, Catalogs, Policy and Procedure Manuals, Financial Statements, Meeting Notices, and in visual representation of quantitative information, such as statistical analysis of trends. While these are often called "unstructured" information by systems personnel, procedure manuals and annual reports are very "structured" documents. A more appropriate term for documents and information representations are "Complex" Information Types. More than 90 percent of technical information is contained in Complex Information Types, as opposed to data held in classic Databases and electronic Files.

Key terms:

Data: The representation of Facts in language, numbers, or symbols

Information: The meaning of Data in the form of a clear, precise Definition and Presentation understandable to a Knowledge Worker

Knowledge: An understanding of the Significance of Information

Wisdom: Correct, optimized Actions or Decisions based on one's Knowledge

Information Producer: One who *creates or captures* Data at its source

Knowledge Worker: One who *applies* Information in the *performance* of his or her work

The majority of an Enterprise's Information resides in complex information types, such as documents, policy and procedure manuals, product catalogs, in PDFs and HTML on Web sites, and in formal and informal communications, such as hard mail and email. Information also exists in phone conversation recordings, such as Call Center orders, oral stock trades or bank transactions, or Customer complaints.

To that extent, Quality Principles and Processes must be applied to these "Complex" Information Types, because Poor Quality Information in Documents and other Complex Information types will cause internal and external failure of business processes or of Customer expectations.

Global Communications 400 to 2010

Figure 14-1 shows the Codex Sinaiticus, courtesy of the British Library. It is the earliest copy of the Christian New Testament hand-written in Greek and published in the middle of the fourth century. Ironically, Greek, the universal language of the world in the first century AD, cannot be read by 99.9 percent of today's world population.

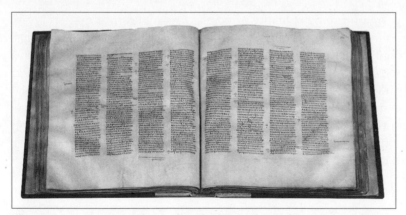

Figure 14-1: Picture of the Codex Sinaiticus, the Earliest Copy of the Christian New Testament[1]

Even as emoticons are in vogue in the teenage population, Controlled English is emerging as the new Lingua Franca for business communication, where "failure to communicate" is not an option.

While email is replacing postal mail, it is not as formal as traditional business communications. Employees often take less time to plan and develop emails, introducing errors and ambiguous wording. A survey of 560 email recipients concluded these facts:[2]

- 53 percent say they do not understand what action is expected of them
- 49 percent say the emails they receive are not understood
- 15 percent say that they do not know how the email is relevant to them

Categories of Information in the Documentation and Knowledge Management

There are several modes in which Document, Textual, or Visual Information is presented to Knowledge Workers internally and externally that must be presented in a *clear, concise, and correct* way:

- **Technical, Procedural, and Textual Documentation:** Information-bearing electronic and paper Documents, such as Owner's Manuals, Technical Procedures, or Customer Catalog Product Descriptions; or Assembly Instructions, Equipment Operating Procedures, for example
- **Data Capture Forms Design:** The design of Information Collection Mechanisms on Paper, in electronic Surveys, or on Computer Screens
- **Quantitative Information Presentation and Signage:** Numeric, Scientific, or Quantitative data presented Graphically or Visually
- **Shared Knowledge and Lessons Learned:** Experience and Knowledge *gained and documented* in work and problem solving for sharing

Document and Knowledge Stakeholders

Almost everyone is a Stakeholder of Documents of one type or another: Forms, Surveys, Graphics, Maps, Signage, and other Information-gathering and Presentation mechanisms.

Internal Information Stakeholders

Information Stakeholders within the organization include many specific and generic roles for various documents, textual, and visual information. See Table 14-1.

Table 14-1: Internal Document and Knowledge Stakeholders and their Information Interests

INTERNAL INFORMATION STAKEHOLDERS	INFORMATION AND KNOWLEDGE INTERESTS
Engineers and Designers	Engineering specifications, with emphasis on CAD (Computer-aided Design)
Manufacturing Personnel	Engineering Specifications to transfer actions to manufacturing processes
Customer Relationship Personnel	Customer Complaint descriptions and guidance
Quality Management Personnel	Customer Complaint descriptions and documentation
Service/Product Developers	Service or Product descriptions in Customers' or Suppliers' communications
Catalogers	Product Information that they create for sharing with Customer Trading Partners so partners can evaluate and select the right materials for their products
Contract Officers	Contract and product or Statement-of-Work information to develop formal relationships with Trading Partners for buying or selling raw materials, products, or services
Procurement Staff	Supply Information, contract terms, and supply pricing to order goods or supplies from Suppliers
Sales Representatives or Agents	Promotional, Product, and Pricing information to develop relationships with Customer Buyers to understand their requirements in order to sell goods and services that Customers require
Marketers	Product Feature and Differentiator Information to advertise and promote products and assess emerging Customer Requirements, along with sales and Customer Feedback Information to evaluate marketing campaigns
Policy and Procedure Writers	Guidelines for clear writing and error-proofed procedure writing
Executives	Policies and Procedures
Managers and Staff	Work procedures; concise and actionable emails, and office-layout signage

External Information Stakeholders

External Information Stakeholders include organizational Customers, Business Partners, and end-Consumers of your products or services. Their information interests in document, textual, and visual information are listed in Table 14-2.

Table 14-2: External Document, Textual, and Visual Information Stakeholders and their Information Interests

EXTERNAL INFORMATION STAKEHOLDERS	INFORMATION AND KNOWLEDGE INTERESTS
Consumers	Information about Products and Services, including Requirements conformance, Assembly and Operating Instructions, Warranty, Service and Disposal Information
Purchasing Personnel	Technical and Descriptive Information about the Products or Services under procurement
Trade Partners	Product Description, including features and differentiators, quality and price information to purchase products or materials that meet their end-Consumers' needs
Supplier Sales Representatives or Agents	Supply Materials and Quality requirements to produce products for the readers organization Customers to meet their expectations
Supplier Product Catalogers	Product Specification Information of their Products compared to our Customers' Requirements to assure our products meet Customer expectations
Logistics Partners	Bills of lading and way-bills, location and directions
Regulatory Authority Compliance Personnel	Industry applicable regulation requirements, compliance procedures, inspection results, and conformance information
Communities in which the Enterprise Resides	Economic and environmental impact information to ascertain the organization's social and environmental stewardship
Shareholders	Financial and Annual Reports with business and financial performance information to make, buy, or sell decisions
Regulatory Agencies	Reports about Financial Information, procedures for documenting conformance, and regulatory compliance

The Document Management Value Circle: "Words-to-Wisdom"

The "Words-to-Wisdom" Value Circle is a closed-loop process that ensures that document and textual information meets the respective Knowledge Workers' needs for their work or why they, as Customers, buy your Products and Services.

The generic Value Circle in Figure 14-2 describes the cycle of activities to produce and maintain quality documentation, signage, and graphical Information.

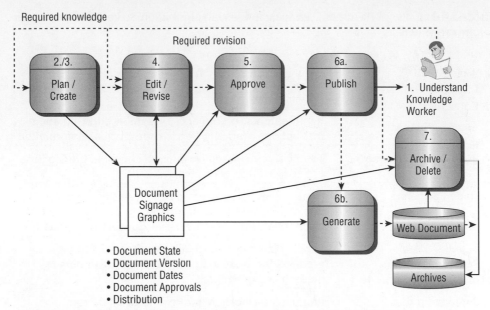

Figure 14-2: Document Management Value Circle "Words-to-Wisdom"

"Words-to-Wisdom" Value Circle Activities

Every Value Circle begins and ends with Customers, from understanding their needs to providing Products and Services — and Information — that meets or exceeds their Expectations. It also includes active listening to their feedback to develop and maintain long-term relationships with Customers.

1. Understand Internal or External Knowledge Worker Needs

Before you ever develop Products or Services, your organization must understand the marketplace and the Customer Product and Service needs and Expectations. Beyond the products and services, you must understand what Information your Customers need to know to exploit the products and services, such as Consumer-friendly Instruction Manuals and accurate Marketing Literature with Consumer-centric Warranties. Internal Knowledge Workers need to have access to information, shared learning, and experience that enables them to innovate and *continually improve* the Processes, Products, and Services for the benefit of the end-Consumers.

2. Plan the Information Presentation Based on Knowledge Worker Requirements

For any Information Content Product or Service, you need to understand your Customers, internal or external, and discover what they need to know to be successful in their job or in Customers' use of your Products or Services, or to ensure that Investors' monies are applied wisely.

3. Create the Information Presentation to Meet Requirements

Use techniques such as:

- Simplified Technical English (STE) for aerospace or Controlled English (CE) to write clear, correct, and concise language that will communicate to your Customers

- Information Chunking to organize Information into meaningful groups around a key topic or thought.

- Clear writing guidelines ensure that procedures and communications are *error-proofed* and that can be *translated into other languages without error* if translation is required.

4. Edit and Revise Information Presentation

For Policy and Procedure Manuals and other critical writing, such as Annual Reports, you will have one or more edit and review readings with key personnel required to approve the *critical* Documents.

Normally revisions will be required before the final documents are approved.

5. Gain Approval from All Required Approvers

Use the technique of *Nemawashi*, a Japanese term that literally means "going around the roots to prepare a tree or plant for transplanting. This tool is used to evaluate all alternative solutions before a final decision is made, or" to gain consensus approval of important documents.

Once final approval is made by all necessary reviewers, the document is ready to publish when required.

> **NOTE** Do not make the approval process so rigorous as to bog down the document development process.

6a. Publish to Your Intended Audience

This may be put on the Web site, or in the policy and procedure manual, or sent to Stockholders in the form of an annual report.

> **NOTE** For Owner's Manuals or Assembly Instructions make sure you have error-proofed the instructions to prevent Customer errors and frustration.

6b. Generate to Web Site

For Internet content, the document can be generated to an HTML, PDF, or other format document on the Web site.

> **NOTE** Use animation in ways that enhance the e-Visitor's experience.

> **NOTE** Use video for multimedia communications in ways that enhance the e-Visitor's experience. Video is becoming a common Web information source, as are blogs, podcasts, and other Web 2.0 collaboration and information disseminating mechanisms.

7. Archive or Delete When No Longer Required

The archival process is important for enterprise-critical documents, like company history, annual reports, and other information required by regulatory entities or by corporate management for historical retention.

Delete those documents if and when they lose value or become a liability to the enterprise.

1. Understand Knowledge Worker Requirements [Better]

Again we come full circle in understanding our Information Consumers better and increasing their value, whether internal Knowledge Workers or external Customers.

As you get feedback from your document Customers, you will be better able to improve quality to increase Customer Lifetime Value.

The Knowledge Management Value Circle: "Ideas-to-Innovation"

Virtually everyone in the enterprise requires information to perform his or her job. For certain operational processes, such as order placement and payment application, the procedures are straightforward for capturing, maintaining, and applying the information in Knowledge Workers' normal activities. The Value Proposition of information is not just knowing its meaning. The real Value Proposition is translating that information into *knowledge*, based on one's experiences and heuristics based on Lessons Learned. Knowledge means knowing the significance or importance that leads an empowered Knowledge Worker to take the *Right Action* or make the *Right decision*.

Sometimes the most valuable use of acquired information is not in the normal, day-to-day activities, but the insights it provides to understand trends or patterns in Customer behavior, product performance, risk assessment leading to product and service innovation, or identification of potential fraud.

The "Ideas-to-Innovation" Value Circle is illustrated in Figure 14-3.

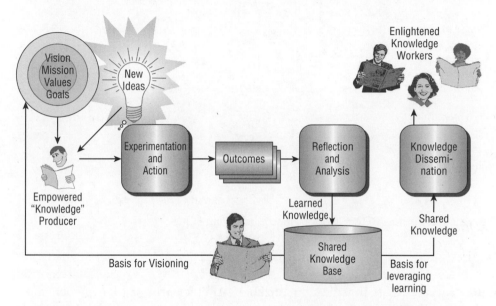

Adapted from R. Shaw and D. Perkins as cited in James Martin *Cybercorp*, p 267-8

Figure 14-3: The "Ideas-to-Innovation" Value Circle

Here, Knowledge Workers are empowered to explore new ideas and try unproven theories to find the next-generation products and services without fear of reprisal if they should take a misstep. Knowledge in shared knowledge bases encourages open collaboration, which can confirm experience or identify weaknesses in alternatives.

Figure 14-4 illustrates the typical barriers and lack of empowerment to explore new ideas.

Without freeing staff to explore new ideas, and, often, punishing them for "mistakes," the enterprise suffers, as key Employees who feel threatened will fall into patterns of survival, working to protect their own jobs due to fear in the workplace.

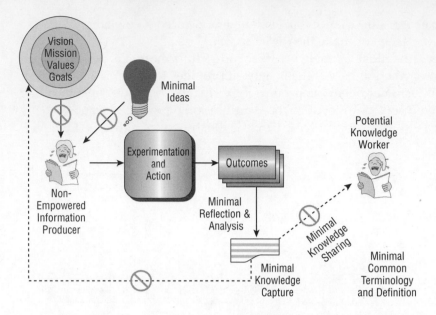

Adapted from R. Shaw and D. Perkins as
cited in James Martin *Cybercorp*, p 267-8

Figure 14-4: Barriers to the "Ideas-to-Innovation" Value Circle

Barriers to Organizational Learning

Our observations are that most organizations inhibit learning. Management must
remember that *all ideas* come from the Human resources. Management must
cultivate and empower this most important resource of the enterprise. Not all
Employees have the creative and innovative skill sets to create masterful new
products or services, but we must employ them and equip them with breakout
training to identify those who will innovate the enterprise's future.

Insufficient Motivation for Innovation

This comes when we do *not encourage, reward, provide training for, and stimulate*
staff. Often, management by the "numbers" (quotas) causes exceptional staff
to withdraw, caught up in preserving their own jobs, not realizing they may be
contributing to the self-fulfilling prophecy of enterprise failure because no one
is creating the products for the future.

Insufficient Capacity to Act

We create good innovative ideas, but do not have the equipment, resources, or
capacity to bring the innovative ideas into fruition of products and services or
in implementation within our organization.

Insufficient Capacity to Reflect

The Quality Improvement Cycle of "Standardize-Do-Check/Study-Act" causes us to focus on studying the results of new ideas, their implementation, and their effects or potential effects in the market or for changes within our organizations.

In my early career, I worked for a retailer whose philosophy was "Hire entry level and promote from within." This philosophy can work well when people are *empowered, trained, and rewarded* for their work.

Many job roles require repetitive work, but even Knowledge Workers in these roles can innovate and improve their own processes, if empowered.

Insufficient Recording of Lessons Learned

Lack of documentation of Lessons Learned from our experiences will surely cause us to stop reflecting on our work, and possibly stop innovating.

We observe that many organizations do not capture vital information that is not mandatory from an operational standpoint, especially that information some deem damaging to the company. We must analyze the "bad news" of Customer complaints, regulatory actions, and subtle warnings from those closest to the Customers to identify enterprise-threatening problems that must be addressed for the well-being of the enterprise.

Insufficient Capacity to Disseminate Learning

In our observations, many managers do not encourage sharing of knowledge. Rather they become Information *hoarders*, with the worst-case scenario that they use this Knowledge *for their own career advantage or personal gain*, not for the welfare of the Enterprise, its Customers, Shareholders, and other Stakeholders.

If we do innovate, we must study the results of the innovation and have the capacity to move it to production. We must share our ideas and innovations to allow others to identify gaps and think further outside the box, for true break-out thinking and innovation.

In the last section of this chapter we will come back to revisit this topic.

Now we look at applying quality principles to Technical, Procedure, and Documentation writing.

Applying Quality to Technical, Procedure, and Documentation Writing

Modern Technical, Procedure, and Documentation delivery plans must refocus on Web-based techniques. In the days of the British Empire, exporters proudly packed printed technical manuals into used tea chests. The British invented the three-ring binder for loose-leaf page delivery, an inefficient distribution technique today.

Today, if the maintenance manuals for the new Boeing 787 were printed the sheer volume of pages would render it virtually impossible to use. The airlines receive updated documentation modules every hour.

Why are Toyota vehicles rarely stolen? The reason is that vehicle maintenance records are transmitted by satellite to dealers and registered by Vehicle Identification Number (VIN). Car thieves who know that VINs are hidden on the chassis and encoded in the diagnostic tools go elsewhere. Toyota knows that accurate maintenance records help dealers provide better Customer Service. These industries rely on chunks of mission-critical information on time, at the right time.

Globalized firms like IBM and Microsoft publish technical information in 80 languages, mostly to the Web and in portable document format (.pdf). The European Economic Union mandates 23 languages for Instruction Manuals. The International Atomic Energy Agency's most expensive budget item is translating official Documents into the seven required languages. This requirement for multilingual documentation adds to the complexity of Quality Control in writing in a regulated industry.

FINANCIAL TIMES EXPOSES ERROR IN GOOGLE TRANSLATE

Google's Translate product incorrectly translated the humble "cheeseburger" as a "Cheeseburgury" in Polish.

Civilized society works because there are codes of conduct, formal and informal rules and laws that guide a society's behavior. In business we see this in the form of Policies and Procedures and defined Process Instructions.

Customers see this in the form of Assembly Instructions for products, Owner's Manuals with instructions on how to maintain products to increase usefulness and longevity, and in Warranty coverage and requirements.

The Correctness, Clarity, and Accuracy of Technical, Procedure, and Documentation writing contributes to effective work and personal success.

This section is dedicated to the development of processes that create and maintain Quality of Technical, Procedure, and Documentation writing that leads to error-proofed *communication*, locally and globally.

Technical, Procedure, and Documentation Writing IQ Issues and Costs

See examples of issues and costs in *poor quality* Procedure Writing in Table 14-3.

Table 14-3: IQ Issues and Costs in Technical, Procedure, and Documentation Writing

IQ ISSUES	COSTS OF POOR INFORMATION QUALITY
Passive voice in procedures	Can cause actors to perform work out of sequence, causing process failure.
Customers or Knowledge Workers making errors or wrong decisions from unclear Information or Instructions	Loss of credibility by Customers and Knowledge Workers
Out-of-date Procedures	Produces a wrong result due to superseded Procedure or Instruction. With it comes failure to comply to regulatory guidelines with fines and penalties.
Failure to comply with Regulatory Guidelines	High costs of fines and penalties, loss of Customer confidence
Lack of conciseness; excessive wordiness	Obscures understanding and distracts or confuses the reader, impeding efficient and effective work.
Acronyms and Ambiguous Terms	Causes wrong actions or decisions with costs of failure and recovery.
Terms or phrases that do *not* translate into required languages	Costs more to translate and error-proof translations and recovery from communication failure.
Disconnect between text and illustrations	Causes frustration and not knowing whether the illustration or text are correct.

Quality Applied to Technical, Procedure, and Documentation Writing

To *control ambiguity*, Airbus invented a global standard Language called ASD Simplified Technical English (STE). This Controlled English (CE) vocabulary uses a 985-word Technical Vocabulary, plus Aircraft Nomenclature for Global Aircraft standards. The use of STE is mandatory for all Airbus and many other aircraft. When you consider that an Airbus A400M has a Maximum Take-Off Weight (MTOW) of 100 tonnes, failure is not an option.

Notably, organizations like Lloyds of London, will *not underwrite insurance unless* manufacturers agree to procedures to mitigate risks of accidents. The use of STE ensures consistency of Terminology, Phraseology, and Visual Presentation. This book is designed by a publishing company that publishes books in many shapes, sizes, and styles. Publishers of aerospace documentation must use *rigid templates* for design, mostly dictated by EuroControl, FAA, NATO, military, and other Standards Bodies. Aircraft manuals are factual and easy to read and understand.

Elegance and prettiness are neither relevant nor required. Clear and correct understanding *is* relevant and required.

THE HUMAN FACTOR IN AIRBORNE MEDICAL EVACUATION

The highest form of civilian risk is the use of helicopters for medical evacuations. The pilots have no room for error in the cockpit. These units operate 24/7/365 (all-time availability) in good and bad weather, flying to highways and hospitals. Fatigue is the leading Causal Factor for human error. When a dispatch call comes into the center, pilots scramble into action. Many of these operations occur between the hours of 2:00 and 5:00 am. The pilots, mostly young, must learn and memorize checklists for all types of procedures, weather, aircraft readiness, and above all, good communications with the ground crews. The equipment that fills the cockpit of a modern helicopter is far superior to that of a simple automobile. The pilots must read and understand how to operate and manage those resources. The use of Simplified Technical English (STE) is the only method to control risks. Many accidents still occur when pilots fly into fog or hit electrical wires. Some helicopters now have wire-cutters to address this risk.

Issue: Out-of-Date Information in Documents

Document facts and procedures may be subject to obsolescence or "information decay" if not kept current. Modified aircraft components *must be documented when installed* on the plane. Without documentation, subsequent aircraft maintenance may cause component failure if incompatible parts are installed.

Facts and procedures may be out-of-date when retailers change product prices or substitute products, and airlines change their flight numbers and departure and arrival times. Sometimes history is required, but it can be confusing for those who may try to attend a seminar that is no longer available.

Of course, certain documents, such as Annual Reports, present a picture of the Enterprise at a single point in time, from which the future performance of the enterprise can be compared. However, for current cultural and business norms in an unfamiliar country a company is seeking to expand into, the Information must be current.

Issue: Incorrect, Unclear, Ambiguous, or Misleading Procedure, Direction, or Graphic Representation

Incorrect, unclear, or misleading Information can cause Knowledge Workers or the end-Customers *into taking a wrong action or making a wrong decision.*

Costs of Incorrect, Unclear, or Misleading Information

- Confusion in Customers who may make a *wrong* product selection. If Information does not match the Customers' perception of a product or service, they may request their money back, costing you the handling of the return and/or compensation to the Customer.

- *Inaccurate or unclear descriptive Information* may make the organization look unprofessional, leading to loss of reputation and Customer Lifetime Value.

- Product or service description that is biased in a way that creates high expectations can be greeted with an *unsatisfactory* Customer Experience (does not meet expectations, based on the over-promises). Graphic and other representations must be accurate to prevent unrealistic expectations in Customers.

- *Wrong* Instructions waste time and cause expensive technical problems.

Issue: Incorrect, Unclear, or Misleading Assembly Instructions

The illustration in Figure 14-5 shows the original English written in engineering-ese. The right side shows the same Information rewritten in ASD-STE100 Simplified Technical English for the new NATO Helicopters.

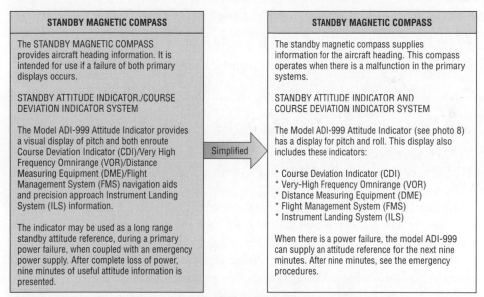

Figure 14-5: Example of Poor Technical Documentation in "Engineering-ese" on the Left, Compared to Improved, Simplified Technical English on the Right

Note that the STE version uses a bulleted list, a component of Information Mapping that makes Information more easily understandable. A key advantage of STE is that organizations like NATO can quickly understand technical

English. NATO has coined a term, "interoperability," which means combined forces can service the others' equipment.

The following list describes writing characteristics that cause miscommunication. This list is followed by a list of error-proofing techniques used in Simplified Technical English.

Characteristics of Poorly Written Communications:

- Weak phrases like "is intended for use" adds *no* Information.
- Text *is dense and not easy to read* in an emergency.
- The use of the *slash or "either or"* is not legal and causes exposure to liability claims.
- Long sentences *reduce readability*. The US Navy requires no more than 17 words or less per sentence. Controlled English *recommends 21 words or less per sentence*.
- The authors of Figure 14-5 ignored what happens after the nine minutes are up.
- The lack of white space intimidates readers who use English as second language.

Characteristics of Simplified Technical English and Controlled English:

- Text authored for global readers in 191 countries
- English grammar and syntax is simplified for use in an emergency.
- A simplified term like "loss of power" is a synonym for the more ambiguous "power failure."
- The STE text is 30 percent smaller and translates into significant cost savings.

While Simplified Technical English (STE) is designed specifically for aerospace, two versions are derived from the aerospace base. The first derivation is called Controlled English (CE).

The number of verbs is expanded and some of the restrictive rules are removed. However, the same objective remains: how to write clear, concise English sentences. The use of Controlled English has a big following in multinational companies like Siemens, Alcatel-Lucent, Citibank, Symantec, and IBM. The control allows the use of Six Sigma quality metrics on documentation.

A Controlled English vocabulary uses approximately 1,200 words out of the more than one million words in the English language as of June 2009. This reaches 95 percent of Knowledge Workers in 180 countries. This method of language control *removes ambiguity, increases readability*, and *enhances the usability of complex* technical documentation. The CE vocabularies are designed for mission-critical procedures and instructions. Examples include procedures to maintain a nuclear power plant, oil rig, or medical device.

A typical CE Vocabulary has a "basic" 1,200-word Vocabulary, with required *product* Terminology added. One can describe most product and service instructions with from 5,000 to 8,500 words out of the English language of more than 1,000,000 terms, which grows each day.

Controlled English uses a simplified English grammar and set of style rules that make English texts very easy to read and understand. The CE texts are easier to translate into other languages by hand or computer. Companies will achieve an immediate 30 percent cost savings in translation costs. See Figure 14-6 for a sample of words in the CE vocabulary.

HANG-s,-hung *[Vb]* To fasten from above with no support from below.
hard,-er,-est *[Adj]* Difficult to cut, not easy to go into or through.
HAVE-has,-had *[Vb]* To possess as a part or quality.
head *[N]* The top of something.
HEAR-s-d *[Vb]* To know by sound in the ear.
heat *[N]* Energy measured as temperature rises.
heav(y),-ier,-iest *[Adj]* Indicates a large mass, weight or force.
height *[N]* The vertical measurement of an object.
HELP-s,-ed *[Vb]* To give assistance.
here *[Adv]* In, at, or to this position.
high,-er,-est *[Adj]* Indicates larger than normal amount.
HIT-s,-hit *[Vb]* To touch suddenly and with force. (Do not use as a noun.)
HOLD-s,-held *[Vb]* 1. To continue to have in the hand or grip. 2. To continue to have in a specified location, position or condition.

INCREASE-s,-d *[Vb]* To make greater in value.
increment *[N]* One of a sequence of regular operations done one after the other, to increase or decrease an adjustable quantity.
independently *[Adv]* Not controlled by other events or things.
indication *[N]* Something that is shown.
INFLATE-s,-d *[Vb]* To pressurize a flexible container with gas.
initial,-ly *[Adj/Adv]* Occurring at the beginning; first. At the start.
injur(y),-ies *[N]* Damage to a person.
inner *[Adj]* Nearer to the center of an object.
input *[N]* The data, power or energy put into equipment or a system.
inspection *[N]* The procedure to check something to its standard or specification.
INSTALL-s,-ed *[Vb]* To attach an item to a second item; to connect an item in a system.
installation *[N]* The procedure which installs an item.

Figure 14-6: Sample Dictionary Page of Words in Controlled English

How to Implement Controlled English

1. Identify the area of written communication.

2. Use a tool like the SMART Text Miner or IBM Miner to identify product terminology for the dictionaries.

3. Use a grammar checker tool like the MAXit Checker to enforce the grammar rules. These tools check the texts for compliance to the vocabulary, which is a key measure of Quality.

4. Teach Technical Writers how to write procedures in clear English.

NOTE **A grammar checker tool interactively reads the text and makes suggestions. This critique uses 9,500 rules found in the *Chicago Manual of Style* or IBM's Style Guide. The rules function with a program that uses *artificial intelligence* to show the errors, corrections, and suggestions.**

A Real-World Application of Controlled English

An automated teller machine (ATM) looks simple to the Consumer, an indication of good design. However, the maintenance of ATMs is complex. First, there are all the banking software links to accounts. Now, add the cameras and security systems, and finally, the actual cash dispensers, which look like the device in Figure 14-7.

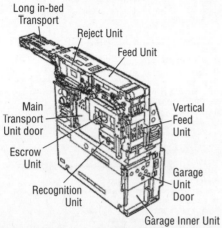

Figure 14-7: An ATM Unit with Poor Labels for Repair and Servicing

The engineering terminology for an ATM unit is exotic and ambiguous. For example, most readers find the phrase "Escrow Unit" vague. The engineers who designed the units were automobile enthusiasts and for fun, called the access door a "Garage Unit Door." To add more confusion, the engineers named the part that seizes stolen credit cards and rejects bad currency bills as the "Reject Unit." An average ATM unit has 96,000 pages of maintenance information. These pages can be required by law to be translated into more than 10 languages. By predefinition of product and technical terms along with the use of the Text Miner lets Controlled English improve textual Information Quality in the majority of Technical and Procedure Writing applications.

A typical ATM has a Controlled English vocabulary of 6,500 terms. Engineering terms are accepted after validation. A simple test validates the part name against the NATO databases. In this example, the term "Escrow Unit" is misleading. A better name is "Currency Holder."

Text Mining Software

The Smart Text Miner or other text miner tools quickly extract key terminology from Customer texts in seconds. From the extracted terms, a linguist makes the final choice. The *Approved* Terms are stored in an Approved Word Dictionary. The *unapproved* Terms are stored in a *reverse dictionary* that points the Knowledge Worker to a *correct replacement term*. Dictionaries can be built by hand, but text mining is fast, precise, and efficient.

Controlled English for a Medical Device

Figure 14-8 is a poor example of maintenance procedure writing. The right side shows the Controlled English procedure for the service technician.

In this example, we have the pump of a heart-lung machine. What Figure 14-8 shows are the original and improved CE instructions to test a pump in a medical device. Pump failure can cause injury or death and legal liability. This outcome demands Six Sigma Quality Procedures. The cost of Quality Procedure writing is pennies per word; the cost of a medical error is millions of dollars.

Figure 14-8 illustrates a poorly written procedure for maintaining a medical device (left) and an improved procedure (right).

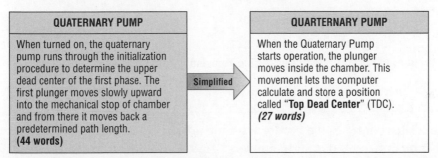

QUATERNARY PUMP

When turned on, the quaternary pump runs through the initialization procedure to determine the upper dead center of the first phase. The first plunger moves slowly upward into the mechanical stop of chamber and from there it moves back a predetermined path length.
(44 words)

Simplified →

QUARTERNARY PUMP

When the Quaternary Pump starts operation, the plunger moves inside the chamber. This movement lets the computer calculate and store a position called "**Top Dead Center**" (TDC).
(27 words)

Figure 14-8: Poor Documentation Writing on the Left with Improved Documentation Using Controlled English on the Right

Explanation of errors in the original writing include:

- **"turned on":** Confused meaning. "When the switch is set to the ON position."

- **"runs through":** Phrasal verbs, never translate.

- **"zation":** All of these suffixes confuse readers who fully understand English.

- **"determine"** is a human verb, machines cannot "think," they calculate

- **"upper dead center":** Wrong terminology. Every automobile engine has a timing mark, "TOP DEAD CENTER". The writer used an invalid term.
- **"upwards":** A fancy term that means to the top.
- *"mechanical stop"* of chamber is wrong terminology.
- **"moves back"** is another phrasal verb that means "returns."
- **"pre":** Bad prefix.

The original text is 44 words. To translate into 80 languages at 25 cents per word is (44 words) times ($.25) = ($11) times (80 countries) = $880 for the paragraph. The rewritten text is 27 words, with a savings of $340. IBM Corporation has determined it can save millions of dollars with Controlled English.

Another example of poor wording is seen in Figure 14-9.

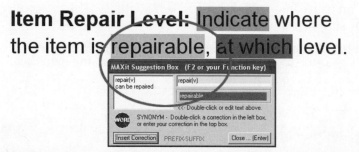

Figure 14-9: Item Repair Level with Impossible Translation and Confusion

Problems identified:

- The writer confuses the reader with the adjective "repairable" that will never be understood in 180 countries. Controlled English renders "repairable" as *"you can repair."* The introduction of the pronoun *"you"* provides immediate understanding of who does what to whom.
- The "at which" prepositional phrase is difficult in languages like Russian, Arabic, and Mandarin Chinese.

The computer gives the clues to simplify, and the writer recasts the thoughts. For example:

- **"Indicate where the item is repairable."** Improved wording: *"Show the location where you can repair the item."*
- **"at which level."** Improved wording: *"Show the level of repair."*

Now we have two ideas in two sentences.

At the time of the printing of this book, computers can not yet recast the sentence as fast as a human writer.

Olde English Is Our Legacy

Most English words are actually French. Example, the French "fôret" is the English "forest." That transition took 400 years. A legacy of the French heritage is the reflexive pronoun. The use of "itself" and "themselves" is very French and is vanishing fast.

Another problem is the use of a number in both words and digits. This legacy comes from 1864 when the typewriter emerged. Typists (also vanishing) wanted to make sure there were no errors so the numbers were repeated. Fast forward to computerized publishing systems that use items called "callouts." Numbers in circles indicate the part names.

English evolves daily. The noun "text" is now made into a verb. This process accelerates with the introduction of digital devices with larger keyboards. For English, the QUERTY keyboard survives, but the Apple iPhone has a digital keyboard that works with touch and word prediction algorithms.

Most Japanese Executives never use computer keyboards because the writing of Kanji is complex. The modern English evolving is easy to write and enter into a computer. How many of us hand-write business letters today? Not many, I imagine.

There is no way, except through a *grammar checker tool* to control grammar, syntax, and style.

STOP, STOP Your Sentence Runneth Over

A few years ago, the former General Motors provided a Corvette Service Manual that contained a paragraph with several sentences that averaged 150 words each. A well-intentioned writer at GM explained that they wanted to give the dealers as much information as possible on each page. The writer actually rendered the Information useless. Keep sentences no longer than 24 words. Best practice is to divide long sentences into short 17–21-word sentences. The "New GM" will now deliver electronic documentation to Dealers without any paper.

Read the first sentence in Figure 14-10 to see if you understand its meaning.

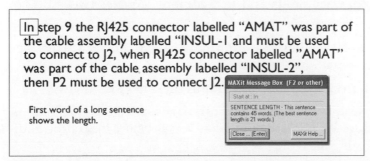

Figure 14-10: The Smart MAXit Calculates the Sentence Length for Guidance

You must read each sentence four times to get the idea.

One more example of Controlled English is in the procedures for mixing lime into the process of cement mixing. Note the improvement in readability in Figure 14-11.

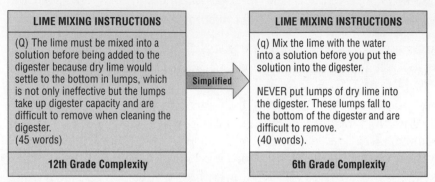

Figure 14-11: Poor Lime Mixing Instructions on the Left, with Controlled English on the Right

Explanations of problems in this procedure:

- Original sentence for the entire instruction is too long at 45 words. Improved is 40 words, separated into two distinct instructions.

- Passive voice "lime must be mixed." Better "Mix the lime with water…."

- "Because dry lime would settle…." This is a reason. State actions to take clearly. Better is: "NEVER put lumps of dry lime into the digester."

- Original sentence has a reading grade level of 12th grade. The improved instruction has a 6th grade reading level in the American Educational System.

Tips for Measuring Technical, Textual Information Quality

Measuring quality of documents and text content requires two kinds of assessments:

- Measure the Quality of Business Information Definition (TIQM P1; see Chapter 4).

  - Look for Clarity, Simplicity, and Intuitiveness of terms used

  - Ensure the Reading Difficulty Level of data, Business Term Definitions, and Procedure Writing are *three* grade-levels below that of the audience performing the work

- Measure Accuracy and Other Information Quality Characteristics (TIQM P2; see Chapter 5) in the facts within the procedure or text.

- Select a random sample of work performers from different levels of experience, age, gender, education level, and other variable characteristics.

- Observe typical Work Performers following the procedures being assessed, observe their behavior, and document the end results of their work. Compare the work of each for zero-defect results.

Assess Customer Satisfaction with Definition of Business Terms and Attributes in Technical, Textual Information in the Procedures or Operating Instructions (TIQM P1.6)

The most important measure is that of Information Stakeholders' Satisfaction with the Data Names, Defined Meaning, set of Valid Values, and Specification of the Business Rules describing the Validity Requirements for the Data and Calculation Formulae that create Derived Data values. Step activities include:

1. Take the introductory instructions and each procedure step as unique assessment items.

2. Have each sampled participant define the Critical-to-Quality Terms in the introduction, and describe *how* they would perform each procedure step.

3. Compare this with the procedure as intended with its expected outcomes.

This applies to the following and other procedural writing:

- Policy and Procedure development
- Owner's Manual development
- Manufacturing Equipment Operating Procedure development
- Product Assembly Instructions development

Identify Accuracy Verification Sources (TIQM P2.5)

See Chapter 5 "The Step-by-Step Guide to *Assessing Information Quality*," Step P2.5 for how to identify the correct sources to *verify the* Accuracy of the Information. See Table 14-4.

Table 14-4: Accuracy Verification Sources and Methods

Fact Checking	Identify credible sources to confirm or dispute Third-Party Information provided.
Calculated Data	Confirm the Calculation Formula and recalculate the figures independently.
Quotations	Identify *original source* and confirm the Quotation or Reference, or confirm with multiple corroborative citations.

(continued)

Table 14-4 *(continued)*

Assembly Instructions	*Follow the Assembly Instructions* to assemble the product, to find incorrect, ambiguous, or missing instructions.
Form Instruction Procedures	Follow the *form instruction procedures* for clarity and correct form completion results. Involve typical Customers of the form to be created.

Interpret and Report Information Quality of Technical, Textual Information (TIQM P2.8)

Report the data in the form of number or percent of defects measured. Use a statistical Quality Control Chart of the process measured over time. See Chapter 5, "The Step-by-Step Guide to *Assessing Information Quality*," Process Step P2.8, "Interpret and Report Information Quality."

Communicate assessment reports to Knowledge Workers who require the information so that they know about any issues with the quality of information. Communicate the assessments to Information Producer Managers to address improvements as necessary.

Best Practices: Error-Proofing Written, Technical Communication to Prevent Miscommunication

Procedural Instructions direct how work is performed and how formal actions must be performed. Errors and mistakes, including ambiguity, wordiness, and missing or incomplete Information or Instructions will cause work failures.

The Quest for the Perfect Manual ...

A *quality* Procedure or Technical Manual has no more than a 2 percent error rate, Measured by an index quantified by readability, usability, and translatability. Technical Manuals written in Controlled English can easily achieve Six Sigma Quality.

Common Errors in Documentation

The following list shows 23 common errors in technical documentation that lower the quality of the writing:

- Spelling errors caused by the failure to use a spell checker or context errors
- Automatic selection of first spell checker option
- Unclear or ambiguous writing with confused wording and jargon

- Long sentences that are more than 24 words
- Failure to ensure that the reading level is three grade-levels below the reader audience reading level
- Key information is missed, confused, or omitted
- *"Failure to Warn" — missing or wrong* Safety Warnings
- Wrong or non-existent page number references
- Readability levels above the U.S. 8th grade level
- Incorrect labels or setting references for instrumentation
- *Nice to know* content instead of *"need to know"*
- *Wrong or multiple* Names for parts or nomenclature
- Texts *written by engineers in technical language* as opposed to lay language
- Measurements are *vague, missed, or wrong* in the texts
- Use of gerunds ("-ing" words) *that cause ambiguity* in English
- Wrong metric *conversions* or omitted dual dimensions
- Obsolete telephone numbers, URLs, and product names
- Wrong or missing illustrations, graphics, and call-outs
- Multiple *meanings* for the same abbreviation
- Creation of *acronyms* that do not follow International Standards
- Tools and materials that are not available in reader locations
- Failure to ensure *technical* Accuracy
- *Failure to provide* translations for key markets and business advantage

Best Practices: Technical and Procedure Writing Guidelines

- Develop and use a standardized procedure-writing process. The procedures should be standardized and organized for consistency where people are performing more than one procedure. Procedures include a unique identifier or number, a clear business objective or purpose, and required administrative information in the header or footer on each page.
- Use *visual, graphic* procedures where possible.
- Where procedures must be translated to multiple languages, use words, phrases, and styles that are *NOT* ambiguous.

- Write steps as *imperative* sentences with *positive* commands.
- Use correct grammar.
- Use standard punctuation.
- Use Simplified Technical English for Technical Procedures and Complex Documentation, and Controlled English for textual Information and Documentation.
- Set reading difficulty three grade levels below the level of the Reader.
- Procedures must NOT be workarounds. Workarounds indicate a broken process. Workarounds in formal processes indicate that Employees are performing Information Scrap and Rework *by design*, without realizing it!
- Avoid *ambiguous* words or phrases.
- Avoid Acronyms and Abbreviations (without a legend).
- Use checklists for complex procedures to ensure no missed Steps or Information.
- Make Procedures *easily accessible* for performers.
- Specify ranges versus error bands: "31 – 47 (Normal = 39)," not "39 $\pm$ 8." This forces someone to make a mental calculation that can easily be miscalculated.
- If the step requires a calculation, provide calculation formula or calculation steps.
- Use formal logic rules (IF, WHEN, THEN, AND, OR, NOT) for conditional statements:

    "IF the Customer does not want to provide a birth date,
        THEN leave the field blank
        AND select Reason Code of "Refused"
- Use "NOT" for a negative condition or prohibition:

    "IF the amount of coverage is NOT sufficient . . ." versus "IF the amount of coverage is insufficient … ."[3]

Applying Quality to Data Capture Form Design

Two types of forms are described here:

- Forms that are filled out by hand
- Forms captured online, as found on Web sites or in electronic kiosks

Form Design Quality Issues and Costs

Typical problems and costs include the following:

Issue: Failure to Consider Information Producer or Knowledge Workers' Needs in Form Design

Forms not designed to be natural and intuitive for the work at hand will induce *errors in data collection or misinterpretation* of Information by Knowledge Workers.

Issue: Failure to Understand the Purpose of the Information Gathered

Is the data asked for relevant and critical for the purposes required?

Are the security and privacy issues considered and addressed?

Will the gathered Information *add value* to the overall Business Mission and Customers' Purposes?

Costs of Poor Ergonomics in Form Design

Costs include:

- Customers or Information Producers enter the wrong data or enter it in the wrong place
- Customers *become frustrated with long, laborious forms* that they are not sure provides Value to themselves for the Information they provide
- Lost sales opportunity and Customer Goodwill

Issue: Data Capture Fields Placed Far from the Data Labels

Incorrect *placement of data fields* induces errors by putting information for a field in the wrong field box.

Issues and costs include the following:

- *Missing or ambiguous labels* for necessary data fields. People have to *guess* at what is asked for.
- Lack of lookup for definitions of data fields. Novice Information Producers require this to prevent errors of interpretation.

Costs of Incorrect, Unclear, or Misleading Information

Costs include:

- Confusion in Customers who may make a wrong product selection. If information does not match the Customers' perception of a product or service, they may request their money back, costing you the handling of the return and or compensation to the Customer.

Tips for Measuring Information Form Design Quality

Measuring Quality of Form Design requires two kinds of assessments:

- Measuring the Quality of Business Information Definition (TIQM P1; see Chapter 4)
- Measuring Accuracy and Other Information Quality Characteristics (TIQM P2; see Chapter 5) of the facts within the procedure or text

How to Measure the Quality of Definition of Business Terms and Facts in Data Capture Form Design (TIQM P1)

Conduct a TIQM P1 Assessment of Information Definition Quality. You are looking for instances where casual readers may be induced to misinterpret information, or find the information to be presented in a non-Customer-friendly way that alienates them.

Follow the baseline assessment steps in Chapter 4 "The Step-by-Step Guide to *Assessing Information Product Specifications and Information Architecture Quality*" (TIQM P1). Also see TIQM P1 in my first book.[4] Here are some tips for this assessment applied to documents and text information.

Identify Information Definition Quality Measures (TIQM P1.1)

The CTQ Quality Characteristics here are Correctness, Completeness, and Clarity of communication in Form Labels and in Instructions. Key measures include:

- Intuitive Business Term Names and Correct, Complete, and Clear Definitions
- Clarity in written Definitions and Specifications
- *Intuitive navigation through* the form for both novices and experienced Customers
- Available *help mechanisms* or *explanatory notes* that are easy to use, intuitive, and helpful

- Relevance of Descriptive Information to Customer needs
- Complex information is presented in a way *that illuminates,* such as with a (1) general concept or abstract, to (2) more specific description, to (3) the most detailed information, and (4) examples and templates

Identify Form Design Attributes to Assess Definition Quality (TIQM P1.2)

Develop a Pareto Diagram based upon Knowledge Worker–defined *importance* of Facts, Quotations, References, and Calculations and on the costs and impacts of Poor Quality Information in such documents.

Identify a Set of Information Consumers of the Form Design Information (TIQM P1.3)

To assess Definition Clarity and Correctness, you should identify representatives from each of the different Stakeholder areas that require the information to perform their work. Also include representatives of those who create the information, as they must have a clear understanding of the "Information Product Specification Data," so they know how to capture and maintain it correctly.

The representatives you select here will participate in the Information Stakeholder feedback sessions in a subsequent Definition Assessment step (TIQM P1.6). The Stakeholders of each document type will be different audiences, from investors reading your annual reports, to Consumers owning and operating Products seeking to understand how to use the Products, to Employees needing to follow Procedures to perform their work correctly.

Assess Information Definition Technical Quality in Form Design (TIQM P1.4)

For definitions of Terms or Data Elements requested in your form, measure them for conformance to Enterprise Information Standards, Formats, and Name and Definition Clarity and Correctness.

Assess Information Model and Database Design Quality Supporting Form Design (TIQM P1.5)

This assesses the integrity of the Information Model and Database Design to house the knowledge collected. Quality characteristics include:

- Are all required attributes found in the Information Model and Database Design?
- Are all Attributes defined Correctly, Completely, and Clearly to the Information Stakeholders?
- Are all Business Terms that may be used in Attribute and Data Element definitions in the database available on a timely basis, and are they correct and complete for the purpose of each and every document requiring them?

Assess Stakeholder Satisfaction with Data Definition of Terms and Attributes in Form Design (TIQM P1.6)

The most important measure is that of the Information Stakeholders' Satisfaction with the Data Names, Defined Meaning, set of Valid Values, and Specification of the Business Rules describing the Validity Requirements for the data and Calculation Formulae that create Derived Data values. Step activities include:

1. Develop a customized questionnaire for Customers to rate their experience in completing the form. See the template example in Figures 4-8, 4-9, and 4-10 in Chapter 4.

2. Identify representative Information Stakeholders for assessing the Quality of the Information Product Specifications (IPS).

3. Schedule an Assessment meeting (in a conference room or in an electronic meeting).

4. Describe your expectations and rules for evaluating the Data Names, Definitions, Valid Value sets, and Code Meanings as required, and Business Rule Specification descriptions.

5. Conduct the assessment with participants submitting their assessments of the various IPS Quality Characteristics.

6. Develop a Pareto Diagram, illustrating the Stakeholders' responses.

7. Post or circulate the responses along with the Information Resource Quality Specialist's identification of next steps.

Measuring Accuracy and Other Information Quality Characteristics in Forms Design (TIQM P2)

The second assessment is an assessment of the Accuracy of selected Facts contained in the Data Capture Form. Follow the general steps, "Measuring Accuracy and Other Information Quality Characteristics" described in Chapter 5, "Step-By-Step Guide to *Assessing Information Quality*." Here are tips for documents and text content quality measurement.

Identify a Set of Attributes for Measuring Quality That the Form Captures (TIQM P2.1)

The key for this assessment is to ensure the Information Producers provide the correct and complete information in the right data fields for the use you need to make of their provided information.

NOTE   Ensure that the Information Producers have a positive and satisfying experience in filling the Information in for you. The more cumbersome the form, the more likely there will be gaps in the Information they provide or there may be unintentionally wrong information that you will have to deal with later.

Plan IQ Objectives, Measures, and Tests (TIQM P2.2)

See Chapter 5, "The Step-by-Step Guide to *Assessing Information Quality*," for identifying critical quality characteristics for your Data Capture Form. Major quality characteristics for assessment of facts in a document include:

- Degree of Accuracy of Facts provided
- Degree of Accuracy capability of the *processes* that capture or create facts
- Completeness of Facts
- Consistency of Facts in Documents to an authoritative, reliable Source
- Accurate Calculation and Presentation of Quantitative information
- Timeliness of Information
- Ease of Usability of Owner's Manual and Assembly Instructions

Ensure measurement of the IQ Characteristics to measure, such as Accuracy, Validity, Timeliness of Availability, and Presentation Utility, based on importance to Customers.

Identify the Information Value Circle (TIQM P2.3)

In order to understand process capability, you must understand the processes that make up the Information Value Circle that creates Documents and other types of Textual Information. Document this Value Circle using a Value Circle format, Value/Cost Chain[5] or use data flow or work flow diagrams.

Determine the Information Process to Assess (TIQM P2.4)

The process to assess is that process which captures the data in the Data Capture Form. All critical Facts captured in the Data Capture Form are in scope of Accuracy assessment.

Identifying Accuracy Verification Sources (TIQM P2.5)

See Chapter 5, "The Step-by-Step Guide to *Assessing Information Quality*," Step P2.5 for how to identify the correct sources to verify the Accuracy of the Information. If data is captured from people, then the accuracy source will be the person for whom the data represents or the event observed. See Table 14-5.

Table 14-5: Accuracy Verification Sources and Methods

INFORMATION TO ASSESS	ACCURACY ASSESSMENT TECHNIQUE
Data about the Customer	Verify Customer Information with the Customer unless it is sensitive information that they may not want you to know.

(continued)

Table 14-5 *(continued)*

INFORMATION TO ASSESS	ACCURACY ASSESSMENT TECHNIQUE
Data about purchases	Verify sales receipts or orders.
Data about instructions to fill out the form	Intuitiveness and ease of use of form.
Form instruction procedures	Assess if People are able to follow the form instruction procedures for clarity and correctness by assessing the form completion results. Involve typical Customers of the form. Observe people in filling out the forms and review their information for correctness to the intended answer or response.

Extract Statistically Valid Sample of Completed Forms (TIQM P2.6)

For documents that are widely published and read, you must verify *all* substantive and materially important Facts and Information. See Chapter 5, "The Step-by-Step Guide to *Assessing Information Quality*," Step P2.6, "Extract Statistically Valid Sample of Data" for how to determine the size of a sample for your Confidence Level.

> **NOTE** Do not make this too complex. The form-completion process is what is being measured. Sample the forms based on the importance of the Information captured in them. Forms must be selected by statistical sampling to prevent bias.

> **NOTE** Follow the guidelines in TIQM Process P2.6 in Chapter 5 to determine the proper sample size for the forms sampled. Sample size is dependent on standard variation, the confidence you want, and the confidence interval or Bound.

Measure Information Quality in the Selected IQ Characteristics of the Information and Process (TIQM P2.7)

To measure Accuracy of the selected facts, compare the Data Value for the fact to the Characteristic of the Real-World Object the Facts represent where you can. Confirm third-party–provided Facts with *independent and authoritative* sources. Follow the guidelines in Table 14-5 for conducting Accuracy and Usability tests.

Interpreting and Reporting Information Quality of Information Assessed (TIQM P2.8)

Report the data in the form of number or percent of defects measured. Use a Statistical Quality Control Chart of the process measured over time. See Chapter 3, "Implementing and Sustaining an Effective Information Quality Environment," Process Step P2.8 "Interpret and Report Information Quality."

Communicate Assessment Reports to Knowledge Workers who require the Information so that they know about any issues with the Quality. Communicate the assessments to Information Producer managers to address Improvements as necessary.

Form Design Quality Issues and Costs

Common issues in design of forms completed by hand include:

- Failure to design the form from a Human perspective
- Failure to *allow enough room* for the answers in data capture fields
- Failure to use the *best-suited mechanism for capturing data*, such as check boxes, free-form text, or drop-down window, for example, to decrease Information Producer effort,
- Asking for Information *not relevant* to your needs or the Customer's needs
- Failure to provide adequate *assurances* that you will protect the privacy, confidentiality and security of their personal information
- Asking for the same Information *multiple times* when it is *not* necessary

Best Practices in Form Design for Forms to Be Filled in by Hand

Forms not designed to be natural and intuitive for the work at hand will induce *errors* in data collection or *misinterpretation* of Information by Knowledge Workers. Forms must have appropriate instructions as to how to complete them properly. Forms should ask for only the information that is relevant and pertinent for the entity requiring the form, such as a health care provider, insurance agent, bank officer, telephone servicer, frequent flier, guest, or shopper, for example.

The first form I would like to illustrate is the infamous Palm Beach "Butterfly Ballot" that literally changed the course of history, in Figure 14-12.

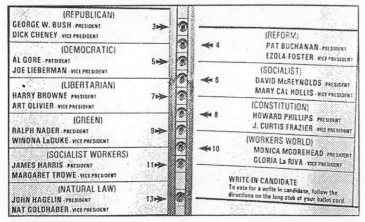

Figure 14-12: The Infamous Palm Beach Butterfly Ballot in the 2000 Presidential Election

This ballot design literally changed the course of history by throwing the 2000 presidential election into turmoil. The confusion was evident only on the morning of Election Day, November 8, 2000, when people came out of the voting booths concerned that they may have voted for the wrong candidate. Many not only were confused by the punch-card ballot, but actually invalidated their ballot by attempting to correct their vote to a different choice.

The errors in this ballot design guaranteed wrong choices, invalidated choices, and confusion throughout the recount process. Poor design features include:

- The use of the butterfly design was used for the first time in this county because of the number of candidates, so it was confusing to those who had always voted on "straight-line ballots" before.

- The design of the butterfly in essence asks the voter to conduct a zig-zag way of reading the ballot, not at all like the left to right thinking.

- The information in the choices are distant from the voting action box, where the stylus was to be used to punch the "chad" out of the ballot for their candidate of choice.

- The inner choices from Pat Buchanan on down have overlapping punch choices. Each information box (Candidate) is touching three chad-selection options. Based on the angle in which the voters would be observing the ballot, the angle exacerbated the location of the relevant selection.

- The names of the candidates are outside justified, not close to the vote choice option.

If the ballot requires the zig-zag butterfly design, the form should look more like that in Figure 14-13.

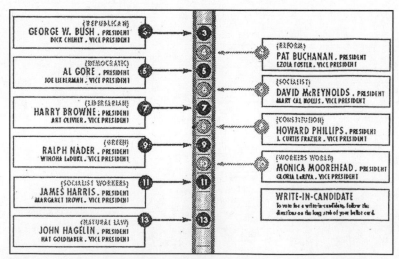

Figure 14-13: Butterfly Ballot with Error-Proofing Techniques

While the butterfly design is not optimum, error-proofing techniques here include:

- Separation of each Information Box from others

- Affinity of the Information Box to the Action punch, including lines with different shading separating the different choices

- Text is inside justified instead of outside justified, closer to the action punch selection.

The optimum design for this ballot is a straight-line ticket as illustrated in Figure 14-14.

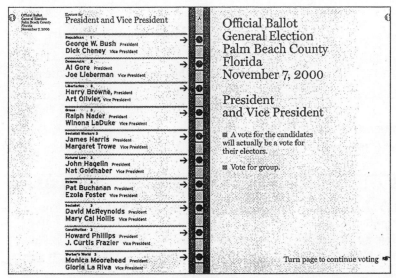

Figure 14-14: A Straight-Line Ballot without the Overlapping Possible Choices

However, there is another problem in the design of this ballot. The wording of the voting procedure is most ambiguous:

- The procedure reminds people that "A vote for the candidates will actually be a vote for their Electors." This is the heritage of the U.S. Electoral College mechanism for electing the U.S. President.

- The actual — and only — instruction for voting reads, "Vote for group." This actually misled many voters, not just in straight-line ballots and butterfly ballots, but in optical scan ballots as well. The statistics of "over-voting," the voting for more than one candidate in Florida, are shown in Table 14-6. The over-vote combinations in Florida alone illustrate the extent of the *ambiguity of the instructions for voting*.

Table 14-6: Over-Vote Combinations in the Florida 2000 Presidential Election

COMBINATION	BALLOTS	COMBINATION	BALLOTS
Gore + Buchanan	10,234	Bush + Hagelin	2,442
Gore + Browne	9,321	Bush + Phillips	2,047
Bush + Gore	8,956	Gore + Harris	1,782
Bush + Buchanan	4,957	Bush + Moorhead	1,771
Gore + Moorehead	3,989	Bush + Browne	1,711
Gore + McReynolds	3,976	Bush + Nader	1,529
Gore + Phillips	3,868	Gore + write-in-vote	1,292
Gore + Nader	3,405	All 10 candidates	957
Gore + Hagelin	3,015	Gore + Nader + Hagelin + McReynolds + Moorehead	911
All candidates, except Bush	3,007	Bush + write-in-vote	790

The total number of the top 20 over-vote combinations resulted in 69,960 ballot disqualifications (disenfranchised voters) in the state of Florida alone.

BROKEN ELECTIONS PROCESSES DISENFRANCHISE MILLIONS OF VOTERS

Four to six million U.S. voters lost their Presidential votes because of over-voting (voting for two or more candidates) or under-voting (not recording a vote, failed chad penetration, or too light pencil marks) or other process failures. This number of disenfranchised Voters was more than all voters who voted in Florida that year!

Shifting gears to a less significant, but common form design problem, Figure 14-15 shows a London hotel room service menu selection.

Problems with this design include:

- Too few Time selection options. A thirty-minute window will cause last in time group service to be cold.

- Check (tick) boxes in Continental Breakfast selection are mis-positioned; the affinity is with the second selection box. I wonder how many people got Muesli when they wanted "All Bran"?

- There are no clear instructions on restrictions, if any, for the traditional English Breakfast.

An example of a poorly designed medical history form is demonstrated in Figure 14-16.

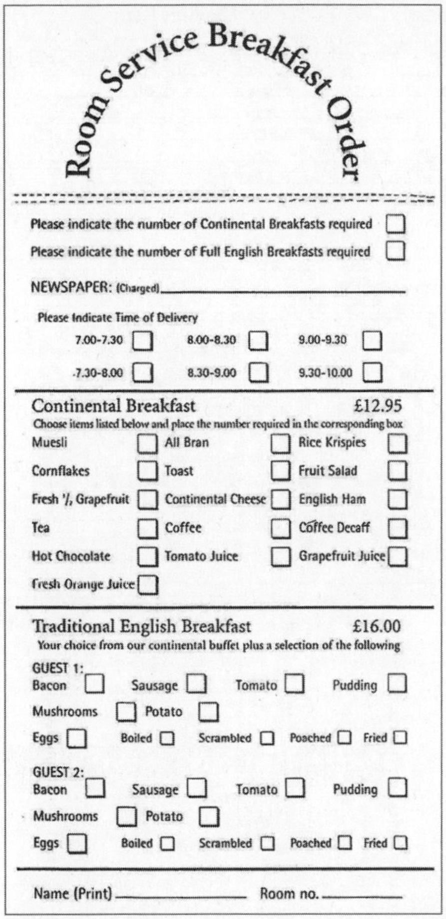

Room Service Breakfast Order

Please indicate the number of Continental Breakfasts required ☐

Please indicate the number of Full English Breakfasts required ☐

NEWSPAPER: (Charged) ____________

Please Indicate Time of Delivery

7.00-7.30 ☐ 8.00-8.30 ☐ 9.00-9.30 ☐

7.30-8.00 ☐ 8.30-9.00 ☐ 9.30-10.00 ☐

Continental Breakfast £12.95

Choose items listed below and place the number required in the corresponding box

Muesli	☐	All Bran	☐	Rice Krispies	☐
Cornflakes	☐	Toast	☐	Fruit Salad	☐
Fresh ½ Grapefruit	☐	Continental Cheese	☐	English Ham	☐
Tea	☐	Coffee	☐	Coffee Decaff	☐
Hot Chocolate	☐	Tomato Juice	☐	Grapefruit Juice	☐
Fresh Orange Juice	☐				

Traditional English Breakfast £16.00

Your choice from our continental buffet plus a selection of the following

GUEST 1:

Bacon ☐ Sausage ☐ Tomato ☐ Pudding ☐

Mushrooms ☐ Potato ☐

Eggs ☐ Boiled ☐ Scrambled ☐ Poached ☐ Fried ☐

GUEST 2:

Bacon ☐ Sausage ☐ Tomato ☐ Pudding ☐

Mushrooms ☐ Potato ☐

Eggs ☐ Boiled ☐ Scrambled ☐ Poached ☐ Fried ☐

Name (Print) ____________ Room no. ____________

Figure 14-15: Room Service Menu Form That Leads to Wrong Items Served

The Medical History Form in the following Figure 14-16 has serious defects.

- The form is too dense with not enough space for written text details.
- The section to capture your medical conditions and history have the check or tick boxes too far away from the pertinent column. They are actually closer to the adjacent column of conditions, except for the last column.
- To complete this section of the form, you have to keep looking back at the column to see which is "Yes" and which is "No."
- The instruction for completing this section is ambiguous, "Please check yes or no." Patients could literally check or tick either choice box without verifying that they did or did not have that condition. There was no instruction that said check "Yes" for the conditions you now have or have had in the past.

Patient Number _____ A.B.C. **HEALTH HISTORY & REGISTRATION**

Patient's Name _____ Sex: M F Birthdate _____ Age ____ Today's Date _____

Home Address _____ City _____ State ____ Zip ____

Previous Address (if less than 3 Years) _____ City _____ State ____ Zip ____

Please Circle One: Single, Married, Separated, Widowed   Occupation _____   Home Phone Number _____

Your Employer _____ How Long Employed? ____ Your Soc. Sec. # _____ Work Phone _____

Are you a full time student? ☐ Yes ☐ No If Patient is a minor we need: Mother's Birthdate _____ Father's Birthdate _____

Person Responsible For Account _____ Driver's License Number _____

Name of Spouse (Parent if Minor) _____ E-mail address _____

Spouse's (Parent's) Employer _____ Spouse's Soc. Sec. # _____ Work Phone _____

Referred to us by _____ EMERGENCY INFORMATION

Name, Address & Telephone of _____

Reason for this visit _____ a Relative Not living with you.

DENTAL INSURANCE INFORMATION (Primary Carrier)   If you have a double digit Insurance coverage complete this for the second coverage.

Insured's Name _____ DOB ____ SS# ____   Insured's Name _____ DOB ____ SS# ____

Insured's Employer _____   Insured's Employer _____

Insurance Co. _____   Insurance Co. _____

Insurance Co. Address _____   Insurance Co. Address _____

Phone No. _____   Phone No. _____

Group # _____ Local # _____   Group # _____ Local # _____

It is important that I know about your Medical and Dental History. These facts have a direct bearing on your Dental Health. This information is strictly confidential and will not be released to anyone. Thank you for taking the time to completely fill out this questionnaire.

•MEDICAL HISTORY•	YES	NO	If yes, explain:
Do you have any CURRENT HEALTH PROBLEMS?	☐	☐	
Are you under a PHYSICIAN'S CARE now?	☐	☐	
Are you currently taking any medication?	☐	☐	

Please check yes or no

	YES	NO		YES	NO		YES	NO
AIDS	☐	☐	Excessive Bleeding	☐	☐	Pacemaker	☐	☐
Allergies	☐	☐	Fainting	☐	☐	Phen Fen (if taken for > 1 month)	☐	☐
Anemia	☐	☐	Glaucoma	☐	☐	Pregnant-currently	☐	☐
Angina Pectoris	☐	☐	Hay Fever	☐	☐	Psychiatric Treatment	☐	☐
Arthritis	☐	☐	Heart Disease/Attack	☐	☐	Radiation Treatment	☐	☐
Artificial Heart Valve	☐	☐	Heart Murmur	☐	☐	Respiratory Problems	☐	☐
Artificial Joints	☐	☐	Heart Surgery	☐	☐	Rheumatism	☐	☐
Asthma	☐	☐	Hepatitis A	☐	☐	Scarlet Fever	☐	☐
Blood Disease	☐	☐	Hepatitis B	☐	☐	Sinus Problems	☐	☐
Bruise Easily	☐	☐	High Blood Pressure	☐	☐	Stomach Problems	☐	☐
Cancer	☐	☐	HIV Positive	☐	☐	Stroke	☐	☐
Chemotherapy	☐	☐	Jaundice	☐	☐	Thyroid Disease	☐	☐
Congenital Heart Lesions	☐	☐	Jaw Joint Pain	☐	☐	Tuberculosis	☐	☐
Diabetes	☐	☐	Kidney Disease	☐	☐	Ulcers	☐	☐
Dizziness	☐	☐	Liver Disease	☐	☐	Venereal Disease	☐	☐
Drug Addiction	☐	☐	Low Blood Pressure	☐	☐	Other	☐	☐
Emphysema	☐	☐	Mitro Valve Prolapse	☐	☐			
Epilepsy	☐	☐	Nervous Disorders	☐	☐			

Are you allergic or have you reacted adversely to any of the following medications?

	Yes	No		Yes	No		Yes	No
Aspirin	☐	☐	Percodan	☐	☐	Erythromycin	☐	☐
Darvon	☐	☐	Local Anesthetic	☐	☐	Valium	☐	☐
Nitrous Oxide	☐	☐	Codeine	☐	☐	Penicillin	☐	☐
						Other _____		

FAMILY PHYSICIAN: _____ PHONE _____

NO. _____

Is there any other Medical or Dental information that you feel I should know about? _____

CONSENT:

The undersigned hereby authorizes Doctor to take X-rays, study models, photographs, or any other diagnostic aids deemed appropriate by Doctor to make a thorough diagnosis of the patient's dental needs. I also authorize Doctor to perform any and all forms of treatment, medication and therapy, that may be indicated. I also understand the use of anesthetic agents embodies a certain risk. I understand that responsibility for payment for Dental Services provided in this office for myself or my dependents is mine, due and payable at the time services are rendered unless financial arrangements have been made. I further understand that a finance, rebilling, collection charge or attorney fee will be added to any overdue balance. I also assign all insurance benefits to the Doctor.

PATIENT Signature (Parent of Child) _____ Date: _____ DENTIST Signature _____

Pap-R Products WOR 002 142929 Rev. 3/16/00

Figure 14-16: Poor Medical Record Form Design

Now, let's compare this form with another, a form from my current dentist, shown in Figure 14-17.

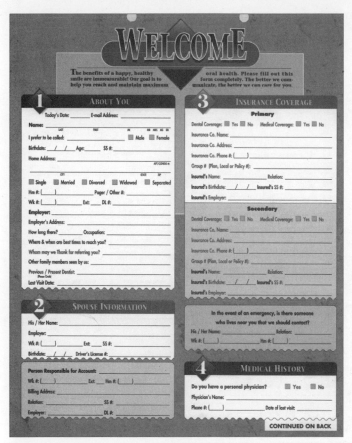

Figure 14-17: Improved Form Using Information Chunking, Color Coding, and Affinity to Check or Tick Boxes

This second form is well-designed. It begins with the greeting:

- The greeting at the top of the form shows a strong sense of Customer Care. "Welcome, the benefits of a happy, healthy smile are immeasurable! Our goal is to help you reach and maintain maximum oral health."

- The form is Information Chunked into sections of cohesive Information, (1) about You, (2) about Your Spouse, and (3) about your Insurance Coverage, for example.

- The Medical History (4) is radically different from the first form in that the instructions are clear. See Figure 14-18.

- This form has the correct instruction for medical history: "Have you ever had any of the following diseases or medical problems?"

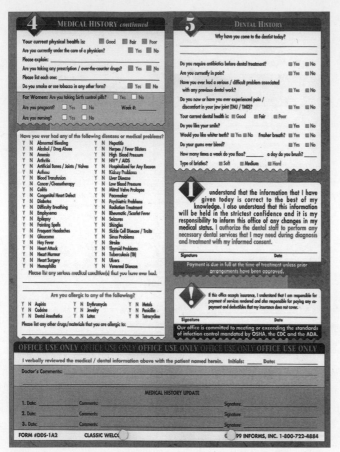

Figure 14-18: Much Improved Medical History Capture of Form 2

- There are no column headings, but the choice answers to circle, "Y" (yes) or "N" (no), for each disease or medical problem. This of course implies the understanding of the codes "Y" and "N." Note that these should be equated with their meanings.

- The placement of the choices is immediate to the left of the disease or problem to avoid confusion.

Both of these dental forms were purchased from forms makers. I have not identified the first form as it has significant problems, but the second form is available from INFORMS, Form #DDS-1A2 Classic Welcome (INFORMS, Inc., Telephone 1-800-722-4884).

Manual Form Design Checklist

Follow this checklist for a well-structured form.[6]

Get feedback from Knowledge Workers across the Enterprise who need the Information collected by the form:

- ☑ What decisions depend on the Information in this form?

- ☑ How much does it cost you when one of these decisions goes wrong because of misinformation?

- ☑ What facts do these decisions hinge on?

- ☑ What other facts are unnecessary?

- ☑ If problems strike, what facts do you need to make a quick recovery?

- ☑ In what areas do you need some extra space for exceptions, special cases, or special needs stories?

- ☑ Can you streamline the form, and avoid confusion from bad handwriting, by turning a form with questions into a checklist?

Now select a focus group of Customers or Information Producers who will be filling out the form. Ask:

- ☑ Which of these facts come easily to mind and can be written down without difficulty or error?

- ☑ What order do they naturally arrange these facts in? (How does this correspond to the order in which your staff wants to read the facts off the form?)

- ☑ Which facts fit into the same amount of space every time? Which vary significantly?

- ☑ Which responses seem hard to recall or look up? (Does your staff really need these? Can your staff stand the potential errors in this area?)

- ☑ Where would these people need extra space for comments? And what would they like you to leave off?

Group items so they make sense to the people who have to complete the form. The more iterations of proofing the form, the more improved the form will be, easier to fill out, more helpful to the readers, and faster to process. Conduct usability tests of each form version to text form completion from the Information Producers and form reading from Knowledge Workers. This helps you improve the form quickly with Customer and Knowledge Worker suggested improvements.

☑ Do your instructions point to the right slots, or do they hover vaguely in between several boxes?

☑ Can you read the labels without a magnifying glass?

☑ Have you kept your captions and labels consistent throughout?

☑ Have you eliminated lines, rules, and boxes wherever possible? Small boxes make for cramped handwriting; many boxes guarantee confusion.

☑ Have you put unimportant information, such as the form's number and your company logo, down at the bottom on the left?

☑ Have you put borders around or highlighted key boxes?

☑ Have you put boxes for totals and results down at the bottom, on the right, where most people expect them?

☑ Do you have wide left margins for forms that will end up in ring binders?

You can make forms easier to complete:

☑ Use check boxes where possible, to keep people from scribbling. Ask for "x's" or for shading the selection boxes, but not check marks, too. An "x" centers on the box; a check can sprawl over several boxes, leaving your staff unsure which box was meant.

☑ If the form gets filled out by staff while they're standing, make all boxes bigger.

The best form is none at all. The second best is the one you don't have to write anything on, just enter a few marks. The worst is an income tax form. That is one we would all rather not look at. Keep it in mind as a model of what to avoid.

Electronic Form Design Quality Issues and Costs

Common issues in design of forms completed electronically include:

- Failure to design the form for Human Factors
- Failure to allow enough space for the answers to text data fields
- Failure to use an easy mechanism for capturing data, such as check boxes, radio buttons for choice, and free-form text, for example
- Asking for information not relevant to your needs or the Customer's needs
- Asking for information that is not known or impossible to provide
- Failure to communicate assurances that you will protect the privacy, confidentiality, and security of personal information

- Asking for the same information multiple times when it is *not* necessary
- Layout that causes Customers or Knowledge Workers to enter data incorrectly or in the wrong data field
- Layout that causes confusion and loss of credibility of Customers
- Lost opportunity, sales, or engagement of Customers
- Unclear, cumbersome, confusing, or otherwise difficult to understand procedures will drive Customers away.

Poor Practices in Forms Design for Information Gathering

Jessica Enders provides her top five ways to make sure that Customers don't complete your Data Capture Forms.[7] Use these in good health and be sure to overstaff your Call Center. You will need extra help.

1. **Ask for information the person doesn't have at their finger tips.** If I have to leave my seat to complete your form, chances are that I won't return. If you do need to ask for obscure or arcane information from your person, prep them before they begin filling out your form. Tell them exactly what they are going to need before they ever type a single character into your form. If I'm at work and the info you require is at home, you ain't going to capture any data from me right then.

2. **Ask for a lot of information, but don't tell me why you need it.** The more extraneous the better. Extra points if the information you ask for makes me nervous about my privacy or security. Ask for a social security number when trying to sign up for your e-mail newsletter. See how well that works in scaring away your persons.

3. **Force me to input data according to how your system wants to see it.** Use a lot of "masks" for your data input, but don't show them to me until after I screw it up and put in the information wrong. Extra points for a phone number mask like: Phone numbers must be entered in the following format, +1 (###) ###-####. Not only is it hard to read, but it is nearly impossible to guess.

4. **Provide cryptic error messages that tell me to correct my mistake, but then give no information about what I did wrong.** Everyone makes mistakes now and then. Use this to your advantage to scare away your Customers.

5. **Divide your form into many segments without any indication of where I am in the process.** By forcing me to guess how much more information I have to enter, the chances that I will bail out go up with each step.

NOTE The overall lesson here is that if you can annoy me and make me feel stupid, inadequate, or nervous, you will definitely push me away.

Best Practices in Form Design for Electronic Forms to Be Filled in Online

Forms not designed to be natural and intuitive for the work at hand will induce errors in data collection from Information Producers or misinterpretation of Information by Knowledge Workers.

"Input elements should be organized in logical groups so that your brain can process the form layout in chunks of related fields."[8]

Information capture forms in Web applications require special attention to form design, layout and edit and validation for data input. Not all Web applications use forms consistently or with quality designed in. Variations in the alignment of input fields, their respective labels, edit and validation, calls to action, and their surrounding visual elements can support or impair different aspects of e-Customer and Knowledge Worker behavior. Thanks to Luke Wroblewski for his contribution to the Web Form Design as follows.[9]

Form Layout Considerations

When the time to complete a form needs to be minimized and the data being collected is mostly familiar to Information Producers (for instance, entering a name, address, and payment information in a check-out process), a vertical alignment of labels and input fields is likely to work best. Grouping each label and input field by vertical proximity and the consistent alignment of both input fields and labels reduces eye movement and processing time. Information Producers only need to move in one direction: down. See Figure 14-19 Data Input Form Design Layouts with vertical alignment.

Use *bold fonts* for input field *labels* to increase their *visual weight* and bring them to the foreground of the layout. Non-bold labels can compete with input fields for an Information Producer's attention as they have almost equal visual weight.

Left-justify data collected by a form if it is unfamiliar or does not fall into easy-to-process groups such as the parts of an address. This makes scanning the Information easier. Information Producers can just scan the left column of labels up and down without interruption by input fields. However, the distance between the labels and input fields is often increased by long labels, increasing entry completion time or causing data to be put in a wrong field. Avoid requiring Producers to have to "jump" from column to column to find the right input field for a label. See Figure 14-20 for Left-Justified, Horizontal Labels.

An alternative layout in Figure 14-21 right-aligns the input field Labels so the association between input field and Label is clear. However, the resulting left rag of the labels reduces the effectiveness of a quick scan to see what Information the form requires. In the Western world, we read from left to right, so our eyes prefer a hard edge along the left side.

The alternative layout in Figure 14-19 creates affinity between the Label and the data input Field.

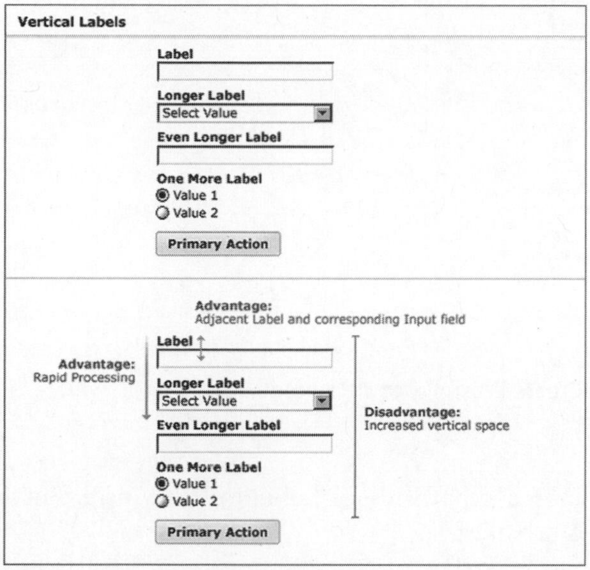

Vertical Labels

Label

Longer Label
Select Value

Even Longer Label

One More Label
◉ Value 1
◯ Value 2

Primary Action

Advantage:
Adjacent Label and corresponding Input field

Advantage:
Rapid Processing

Label

Longer Label
Select Value

Even Longer Label

One More Label
◉ Value 1
◯ Value 2

Primary Action

Disadvantage:
Increased vertical space

Figure 14-19: Web Form Layout Design with Alignment of Labels and Input Data Fields

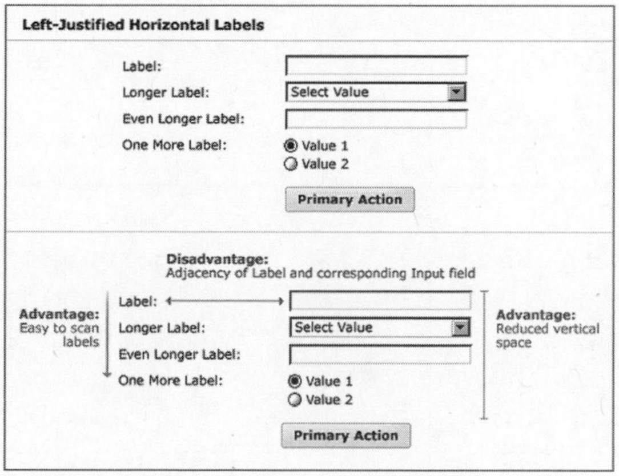

Left-Justified Horizontal Labels

Label:

Longer Label: Select Value

Even Longer Label:

One More Label: ◉ Value 1
                   ◯ Value 2

Primary Action

Disadvantage:
Adjacency of Label and corresponding Input field

Advantage:
Easy to scan labels

Label:

Longer Label: Select Value

Even Longer Label:

One More Label: ◉ Value 1
                   ◯ Value 2

Advantage:
Reduced vertical space

Primary Action

Figure 14-20: Web Form Layout Design with Poor Proximity of Labels to Input Data Field That Can Cause Errors

While Figure 14-20 solves the problem of proximity and affinity between Label and data input Field, it increases *noise* of the different elements in the layout. This can be irritating for large input screens, but it increases effectiveness of localizing the data Labels while retaining affinity to the data input Field or radio buttons.

Figure 14-21 shows Right-Aligned Labels with proximity to the Data Input Field.

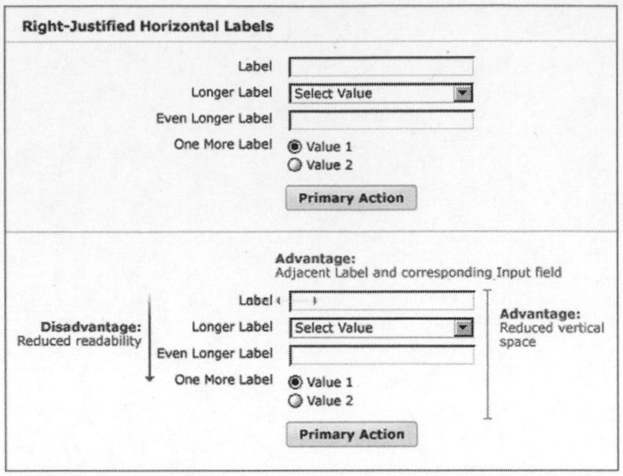

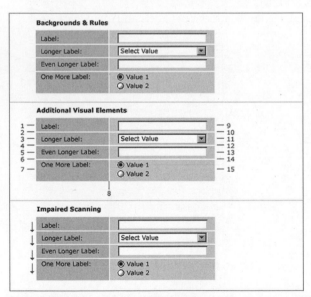

Figure 14-21: Right-Aligned Labels Create Proximity to Data Input Field, but Decrease Ease of Label Scanning

Finally, Figure 14-22 shows increased affinity of Label to Data Input Field through the use of Boxes and color Shading.

Figure 14-22: Increasing Affinity of Label to Data Input Field by Using Boxing and Color Shading

Primary and Secondary Actions

Primary action associated with a form (most commonly "submit" or "save") needs to carry a stronger visual weight as in the example in Figure 14-23 of bright color, bold font, and background color than the other form elements and should vertically align with the input fields. This illuminates a path for Information Producers and guides them to completion of the form.

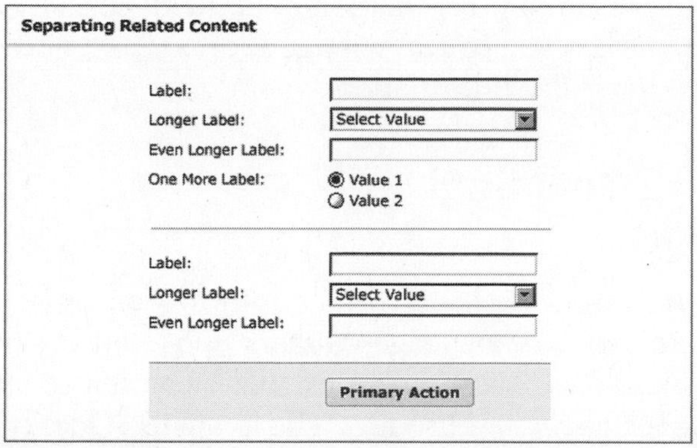

Figure 14-23: Separating Related Content in Data Capture Forms Design.

Reduce the visual weight of the secondary actions when a form has multiple actions such as "Continue" and "Go Back." This minimizes the risk for potential errors and further directs Information Producers to form completion. See Figure 14-24.

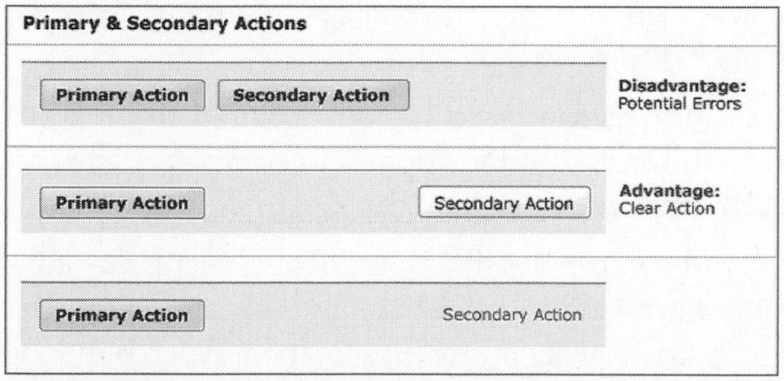

Figure 14-24: Separating Primary and Secondary Actions to Prevent Errors

In the top design in Figure 14-24, the proximity of the primary to secondary action does not have proper priority (on the primary action) causing potential for performing a primary action too early or too late. Use visual color, weight, and size to separate action choices where the sequence must be followed without variation.

Applying Quality to Information Presentation and Signage

Data must be turned into "Information" (the Finished Product) to present to the Knowledge Worker or the Customer who requires it. This means that we must *plan* the presentation based upon the circumstances and requirements of the Knowledge Workers and Customers.

Best Practices in Quantitative Information Presentation

Information must be presented in a way that *illuminates* the "truth" (Accurate presentation) in the data. Bias in presenting Information not only distorts the Information, but it will cause *credibility loss* in Knowledge Workers and end-Customers who see through *misrepresented* Information.

Quality Characteristics in Quantitative Information Presentation

Data residing in a Database is the *raw material* from which Information is produced and presented to end-Customers or Knowledge Workers who require it to perform their work or make required decisions. The Information as presented to the Knowledge Workers represents the *finished* Product. The following Quality Characteristics are required for presentation of Information to Knowledge Workers to minimize misunderstanding that results in wrong actions or decisions.

- **Accessibility:** Being able to *get* the Information
- **Availability:** Information is accessible *when* it is needed.
- **Presentation Media Appropriateness:** Being presented in the *right technology medium*, such as online, hardcopy report, email, audio, or video
- **Relevancy:** Information is appropriate for the task at hand, that is, Information required to *perform a process* or *make a decision*.
- **Presentation Standardization:** Formatted data is presented *consistently in a standardized way* across different media, such as in computer screens, generated reports, or manually prepared reports.
  - **Structured Values:** Structured Attributes like Dates, Time, Telephone numbers, Tax ID Numbers, Product Codes, and Currency Amounts should be presented in a consistent, standard way in any presentation. When numbers and identifiers are chunked, such as standard phone number formats (for example, [1] (615) 837-1211, they are easier to remember and use.
  - **Structured Documents:** Repeating reports should have a standard format with a style sheet that presents the information in a format that is consistent, easy to read, and easy to understand.

Documents should use readability-enhancing *Techniques* such as:

- Information Chunking to group Information around *cohesive topics*
- Use of simple, *unambiguous* words, such as in Controlled English
- Short sentences (17–21 words) with active verbs
- Bulleted items for lists
- A readability index of three grade levels below the reading audience

NOTE Methods such as "Information Mapping" significantly improve readability of textual information and documents. See www.infomap.com.

- **Presentation Clarity:** Information is presented in a way that communicates the truth of the information. Clear Labels, Footnotes, other Explanatory Notes, References, or Links to Definitions and/or Documentation that clearly communicate the meaning and any anomalies in the Information enhance Presentation *Clarity*.

  - Changes in Data Definition or in Business Rule Specification can cause comparing Information across time boundaries to be *inaccurate*.

  - If *different* Calculations are used for different periodic data, such as Unemployment or the Consumer Price Index, document the specific Calculations, illustrating how the data would compare over time if it were normalized to the new formula.

  - Ensure that all *calculated* Attributes are meaningful and relevant to the task at hand. See Figure 5-5 and its discussion in Chapter 5 for an example of a hypothetical "profit" calculated as the amount of interest ("profit") the bank would make if all loans went to maturity. This is an unreal and impossible number to achieve.

NOTE Never *calculate or present* Information that is never realizable.

- **Signage Clarity:** Signs and other information-bearing mechanisms like traffic signals should be standardized and made universal across the broadest audience possible.

Traffic signal lights are now standardized globally with red (stop), yellow (caution), and green (go) meanings. Furthermore, traffic signal lights have standard placements with red on top and green at the bottom for people with color-blindness, so that meaning is consistently associated with the position. This message "redundancy" reduces error.

- **Presentation Objectivity:** Information is presented *without bias*, enabling the Knowledge Worker to understand the meaning and significance *without misinterpretation*.

Numeric or quantitative data often requires graphical presentation for visual clarity. Objectivity means that the graphical or visual presentation of the information does not distort the truth represented in the data.

- **Presentation Utility:** Information is presented in a way that is intuitive and appropriate for the task at hand. The Presentation of Information will vary by the individual uses for which it is required. Some uses require *Concise* Presentation, while others require *a complete, detailed* Presentation, and yet others require *graphics, color-coding, or other highlighting* techniques.

Guidelines for Information Presentation Quality of Graphical Information

Edward Tufte provides guidelines for presenting Quantitative Information visually or graphically that clearly presents the Information without bias.

Guides for Visual Display Quality[10]

- Choose a proper Format and Design.
- Use Words, Numbers, and Drawings together.
- Reflect a Balance, a Proportion, a Sense of Relevant Scale.
- Display an Accessible complexity of Detail.
- Present a Narrative Quality or a story to tell about the data.
- Draw in a *professional* manner, with the technical details of production work done *with care*.
- Avoid *content-free decoration, including chartjunk*, that is, graphical designs or artistic decoration that is "non-data ink" and which does not communicate the message in the data.

Guides for Knowledge-Worker Friendly Graphics

Table 14-7 compares friendly and unfriendly characteristics of graphics.

Table 14-7: Friendly Versus Unfriendly Graphics Presentation[11]

KNOWLEDGE-WORKER FRIENDLY	KNOWLEDGE-WORKER UNFRIENDLY
Words are spelled out, mysterious and elaborate encoding avoided.	Abbreviations abound, requiring the viewer to sort through text to decode.
Words run from left to right, the usual direction for reading occidental languages.	Words run vertically, particularly along the Y-axis; words run in several different directions.
Little messages help explain data.	Graphic is cryptic, requires repeated references to scattered text.
Elaborately encoded shadings, cross-hatching, and colors are avoided; instead, labels are placed on the graphic itself; no legend is required.	Obscure codings require going back and forth between legend and graphic.
Graphic attracts viewer, provokes curiosity.	Graphic repels the viewer, lots of "chartjunk".

KNOWLEDGE-WORKER FRIENDLY	KNOWLEDGE-WORKER UNFRIENDLY
Colors are chosen so that the color-deficient and color-blind (5 to 10 percent of viewers) can make sense of the graphic (blue can be distinguished from other colors by most color-deficient people).	Design is insensitive to color-deficient viewers; red and green are used for essential contrasts.
Type is clear, precise, modest; lettering may be done by hand.	Type is clotted, overbearing.
Type is upper-and-lower case, with serifs.	Type is all capitals, sans serif.

Principles of Graphical Excellence

The following are characteristics of effective Graphics:[12]

- Well-designed presentation of relevant data — a matter of *substance*, of *statistics*, and of *design*
- Consists of complex ideas communicated with *clarity*, *precision*, and *efficiency*
- That which gives to the viewer the greatest number of ideas in the shortest time with the least ink in the smallest space
- Nearly always multivariate
- Requires telling *the truth* about the data

Principles of Graphical Integrity

The following are characteristics of Graphics Integrity:[13]

- The representation of numbers, as physically measured on the surface of the graphic itself, should be *directly proportional* to the numerical Quantities represented.
- Clear, detailed, and thorough Labeling should be used to defeat graphical *distortion and ambiguity*. Write out *explanations of the data on the graphic* itself. Label important Events in the data.
- Show *data* variation, **not** *design* variation.
- In time-series displays of money, *deflated and standardized units* of monetary measurement are nearly always better than nominal units.

- The number of Information-carrying Dimensions (Variables) depicted should *not* exceed the number of dimensions in the data.
- Graphics *must not quote data out of context.*

Graphical and visual information must be presented accurately without bias. See Figure 14-25.

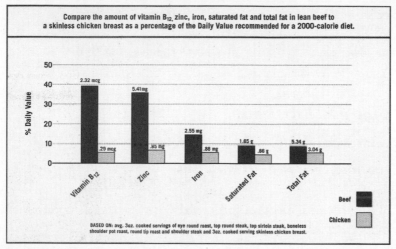

Figure 14-25: Presentation of Benefits of Beef over Chicken; This Graphic Is Biased because of What Is Missing, Not What Is Present

Presenting only *select* categories biases the Presentation in that it may omit categories that show nutritional features that favor chicken over the beef.

Poor Quality Information Presentation Can Lead to Disaster

The NASA Space Shuttle program's disastrous experience with the Columbia Shuttle is an example of how *not* to present Scientific Analysis Information for decision making. See Figure 14-26.

This slide comes from a presentation in which NASA evaluated the threat of the (2a) SOFI (Spray On Foam Insulation) chunk that broke off the fuel tank. The foam chunk impacted the Shuttle Columbia's left wing. The numbers within parentheses on the slide in Figure 14-26 are my insertions to refer to specific lines of information. I analyze critical quality problems in the written communication of this problem.

(1) The title of the slide provides the "Executive Summary," *biasing* the presentation, with the phrase "*Test Data Indicates Conservatism for Tile Penetration.*" This "conclusion" is stated *before* the evidence is presented and discussed.

---

(1)Review of Test Data Indicates Conservatism for Tile Penetration

- **(2)The existing (2a)SOFI on tile test data used to create Crater was reviewed along with STS-87 Southwest Research data**
  - **(3)Crater overpredicted penetration of tile coating significantly**
    - ♦ **(4)Initial penetration to described by normal velocity**
      - • (5)Varies with volume/mass of projectile (e.g., 200ft/sec for 3cu. In)
    - ♦ **(6)Significant energy is required for the softer SOFI particle to penetrate to relatively hard tile coating**
      - • (7)Test results do show that (7a) it is possible at sufficient mass and velocity
    - ♦ **(8)Conversely, once tile is penetrated SOFI can cause significant damage**
      - • (9)Minor variations in total energy (above penetration level) can cause significant tile damage
  - **(10)Flight condition is significantly outside of test database**
    - ♦ **(11)Volume of ramp is 1920 cu in vs 3 cu in for test**

Figure 14-26: Critical Slide in NASA's Foam Debris Impact on the Shuttle Columbia's Left Wing[14]

Here we describe the Information Presentation problems that led to confusion and a wrong decision.

(1) The term "conservatism" should mean we are highly confident that this problem is minor and will not cause shuttle failure on re-entry. However, no data is presented to support this conclusion. But the fact that this issue had to be addressed in crisis mode, after 112 shuttle flight missions, strains credibility.

(2) The Very-Big-Bullet phrase is not clear. The "Crater" is the name of a computer Model used to estimate damage to tiles protecting flat surfaces of the wing.

(3) "Crater 'overpredicted' penetration of tile coating significantly" is too generalized to have authority in decision-making. The meaning of "overpredicted" is not clear. It is not defined in *Webster's Third International Dictionary*, 3rd Ed, 2002.

(4) "Initial penetration to [sic. is] described by normal velocity." The grammar is flawed and its meaning is not clear.

(5) It seems that the test database used an estimated volume/mass (200ft/ sec for a three-cubic-inch chunk of foam), which is much smaller than the actual chunk (1920 cubic inches) that hit Columbia's left wing's leading edge.

(6) This line seems to support a conservative conclusion, but without concrete evidence.

(7) This line now indicates that based on sufficient mass and velocity that there could be tile damage.

(7a) The ambiguous reference "it" refers to *"damage to the left wing"* that could have occurred.

(7–9) These bullet lines indicate the possibility of damage to the shuttle's left wing.

(8) This third-level bullet now reveals that the test database had an incredibly poor (low) estimate of a typical size of SOFI that could break free from the fuel cylinder.

(9) This line is the "mea culpa" with the actual estimated size of foam debris at 1920 cubic inches, as compared to the three cubic inches in the test database.

(10–11) The actual size of the "ramp" (poor choice of words for "foam debris"). The actual volume of foam is 640 times larger than the amount used in the test database. This line tells us the two models were irrelevant to the actual scenario. Further to the point, the foam did not hit the underside of the wing — it hit the more delicate RCC (Reinforced-Carbon-Carbon) that was to protect the wing's *leading* edge. Throughout this presentation, the focus appeared to be on only the heat-shield tiles on the underside of the wing, a tragic omission of possibility.

Other issues in this presentation include:

- There are four typographic orphans that waste space: (1) Penetration; (3) significantly; (5) 3cu. In; (7) and velocity.

- There is a lack of standards in information presentation. The unit of measure "cubic inches" is presented in three different ways: 3cu. in; 1920cu in; and 3 cu in.

The sad tragedy of the episode was that the disaster could have been avoided. If NASA would have requested photographs from a military satellite or allowed the Astronauts to take a space walk to view the wing, they could have discovered the problem early, with time to solve the problem, attempt a repair, or hook up with the Space Station.

The result of the decision made in this critical situation was disastrous. *Yet, if this presentation had used quality principles to describe the facts and question the lack of data*, the tragedy might have been avoided.

Applying Quality to Shared Knowledge and Lessons Learned

Knowledge is derived from information. Information is derived from Data. *Data* is captured by Information Producers or Data Capture and Measurement

Devices and ultimately delivered to Knowledge Workers in the form of usable *information*. *Knowledge* is developed over time through personal experiences and the analysis of Lessons Learned and the heuristics we derive from them. With more experience, Knowledge Workers fine-tune their intuition and realize Critical Success Factors in performing their work or observing Phenomena in the Real World.

Blessed is the Enterprise that empowers its Knowledge Workers to experiment and share Knowledge *across* organizational boundaries *for the good of all* Stakeholders, internal or external.

Applying Information Quality to Signage

There are two types of Signage to consider, Warning Signs and Directional Signs. The creation of signs requires understanding the types; "Warning" versus "Directing" are the starting point.

Warning signs must clearly identify the threat and raise awareness of persons to avoid the threat, such as a fire alarm in a building, first alerting the threat, and secondly, providing direction to evacuate the building in the safest way.

Signage not designed to be natural and intuitive for the work at hand will cause wrong behavior that in the worst instance can cause injury or death.

Poor Information Quality and *ambiguity* in Signage causes people to get misdirected, miss appointments, or be late and decrease productivity.

Issues and Costs of Poor Quality Signage cause misdirection, misread warnings or other errors in behavior from misinterpretation. Issues include:

Issue: Signs Are Placed with a Wrong Orientation

Incorrect placement of Directional signs may cause one to go in a wrong direction.

Incorrect placement of Warning signs may cause one to take a wrong action that results in injury or death.

Issues include:

- Ambiguous signs cause wrong actions, with some violations breaking the law.

- Traffic warning signs placed too close or too far away can cause people to miss an exit or have an accident.

Costs of Incorrect, Unclear, or Misleading Signage

Costs include: Misleading Directional signs may cause one to go *in a wrong direction* or make a wrong action.

Misleading Warning signs may cause one to *take a wrong action that results in injury or death.*

Always use Universal Symbols when available. Figure 14-27 shows a sign from China that uses Universal Symbols with no written language.

Figure 14-27: Always Use Universal Symbols When Available

The upper middle symbol means "do not pick the flowers."

Best Practices in Signage

Best practices in Signage include the following examples, including *traffic signal improvements* in the city of Detroit, shown in Figure 14-28.

Figure 14-28: Detroit Has Replaced Its Traffic Signals with Larger LED Lights and Increased Backplanes

Detroit *increased the size* of the lights for *greater* visibility, using LED lights that are *more* efficient and *less subject to total failure.* It also increased the size of the backplanes to reduce glare and interference with background light and clutter. The results in accidents caused by running red lights has decreased 4 percent for drivers 25–64, but accidents have decreased 35 percent for drivers 65 and older.

In the center of Athens, office and apartment number ranges are on the corners of each intersection to direct visitors or shoppers, illustrated in Figure 14-29.

Figure 14-29: Street Number Sign Quality

The street sign depicted in Figure 14-29 provides an excellent way to let travelers know which direction to go based upon house numbers. This shows with an arrow the house numbers on this side of the street in this block. How much time is wasted when Americans come to a street corner and have no idea which direction is the up street numbers versus down? I estimate we make errors in unfamiliar neighborhoods about 50 percent of the time, wasting time and gasoline (petrol).

Guidelines for Clear, Intuitive Signage

Guidelines for Warning Signs include:

- Understand the purpose of the sign.
- Understand the Stakeholders of the signage.
- Ensure signage is designed for the Stakeholders in mind.
- Warning signs should be accompanied with audio messages and or, visual directions, such as lighting in airplanes that direct passengers to the nearest exit.

- Place the Warning signs in the most visible location for the nature of the risk or threat.

- Keep signage up-to-date if any components of the sign need to be changed, such as change of escape routes or actions, along with "change effective date."

Guidelines for Directional Signs include:

- Understand the purpose of the sign.

- Provide the proper orientation of the sign relative to the building or area.

- Follow the correct directional positioning, (North, South, East, and West).

- Ensure that all relative lines on the sign are proportional with the actual size of the building or area represented.

- Use "You are here" pointers to the point of observation of the area or building.

- Place location numbers or names for offices, retail departments or area places.

- Keep signage up-to-date if any components of the sign need to be changed, such as change of office numbers, along with "change effective date."

Summary

The art of writing *a clear, concise, and simple procedure* is a craft that *few* have mastered, but more must understand. The requirements are part common sense, but, the insurance costs will drive Six Sigma Quality in technical and procedure documentation.

The Presentation of Information to Knowledge Workers represents the final "Manufacturing" Process of Information by *assembling* the Information in a form and way that communicates the information *clearly* to the Customer. Information Presentation *cannot improve* the Quality of the data "Content." Information Presentation cannot improve the *"definition" or "meaning"* of data. It can, however, bring the truth in the data to light.

Information Presentation must "Tell the Truth" and *represent the data accurately*, without bias, and put Information in a context that is clear and understandable to the Knowledge Worker. Information Presentation must also call attention to any *seeming anomalies* in the data, such as degree of missing and inaccurate data, so that Knowledge Workers can apply their knowledge to take the right action or make the right decision.

Warning and Directional Signs are critical for Safety and Efficiency in getting people from where they are to where they need to get to in a building or in a physical area. Effective signage increases security, safety and efficiency of movement.

CHAPTER 15

Information Quality Applied to Information Management and Information Systems Engineering: *I-Need-to-Know-So-I-Can-Do to I-Can-Do-Because-I-Know*

"In the software industry, system development has largely been the result of work by very talented individuals. This approach has resulted in a style of business that relies too much on individuals, turning software development into a kind of craft dominated by a small group of craftsman. I do not feel that this approach is most appropriate for producing truly creative products."[1]

Shirou Fujita, NTT DATA CORPORATION, the first Information Services company to be awarded the Deming Prize

Introduction to Information Quality Applied to Information Management and Information Systems Engineering

Virtually everyone in the industrialized world and many in the developing world are directly affected by information technology today. People get money from ATMs, swipe their credit or debit cards to pay for groceries, gifts, and restaurant meals. They book airline tickets and search the Web for all sorts of things. They share information among friends and business associates via the collaborative Internet technologies available today.

Unfortunately, many of the experiences that laypeople have with Information Technology are negative — unless they happen to be technology savvy as many software developers are. These negative experiences do not involve identity theft or information fraud schemes. They arise from day-to-day failures and defects in Information System interactions. It is time for the information technology sector to become more *human-centric* in its Information System designs.

This chapter describes how to design Quality Information Models that can be translated into effective, Enterprise-Strength Databases that can house *knowledge* required by *all* Information Stakeholders to meet their needs in the accomplishment of the Enterprise Mission.

This chapter also describes how to specify Requirements and design Quality into the Screen Designs and Reports, with proper Quality Controls for Information Content and Presentation Quality.

Information Systems Stakeholders

There are many Information Systems Stakeholders throughout the enterprise, as well as many different Stakeholders outside the enterprise. Failure to provide High-Quality *Information* through the Value Circle will cause business activities such as product development, marketing campaigns, order fulfillment, financial management, and Customer Care processes to fail, sometimes with catastrophic results.

Internal Information Systems Information Stakeholders

Virtually everyone in the enterprise is dependent on the Information Systems and Databases that support work and house the collective knowledge of the enterprise. Table 15-1 shows an example of what information typical Stakeholders within an enterprise might need.

Table 15-1: Internal Information Stakeholders and Their Information Interests

INTERNAL INFORMATION STAKEHOLDERS	INFORMATION INTERESTS
Executives	Executive Support Systems that provide scientific measurement of Key Performance Indicators of various factors that show the health of the enterprise
Engineers	Customer Requirements Information to design products or components to meet Customer Quality expectations. In turn, they use this to create Product Design Specifications, generally in CAD/CAM (Computer-Aided Design/Computer-Aided Manufacturing) systems.
Manufacturing Personnel	Engineering Specifications in order to translate Product Quality Requirements into Process Quality Specifications to produce or assemble components or material into other Components or finished Products that meet Customer Quality Requirements

INTERNAL INFORMATION STAKEHOLDERS	INFORMATION INTERESTS
Quality Management Personnel	Quality Requirements to ensure that Quality is designed in and achieved in the various processes of development, production, and delivery, through measurement of various Quality Characteristics
Service Product Developers	Market, Demand, and Customer Requirements to create support services, such as financial, insurance, or investment "products"
Contract Officers	Systems support for Contract Management, including name and address information to develop formal relationships with trading partners
Sales Representatives or Agents	Automated Systems for Customer and Sales Information, such as name, address, and privacy and contact preference information to develop and maintain relationships with Customers
Marketers	Access to Customer and Prospect Information, including name, address, and profile preference and contact preference information for customized Marketing Campaigns
Accounts Receivable Staff	Information required for Customer Billing, Payment processing, and Risk Analysis
In Criminal Justice, Law Enforcement and Healthcare	Physical Identity Information, such as Fingerprints, DNA, scars, marks, and tattoos, to ensure that they have the right person of interest
Every Employee Who Is a Touch Point for Customers	Customer Insight Information. Each touch point with a Customer is a "Moment of Truth"[2] point in which the Customer has an interaction with an organization that makes an impression, positive or negative, about the organization. They also require application systems and access to information required to accomplish their work.
Systems Analysts and Designers	Develop Functional and Technical Requirements for Application systems
Information Architects and Modelers	Develop Enterprise-Wide Information Requirements to accomplish the Aim of the Enterprise
Programmers	Develop the code or logic in Information Systems
Database Designers and Administrators	Design, implement, and maintain the physical Databases that house the enterprise's data to support *all* Information Stakeholders
Information Producers	Those who capture information of any type required for the Enterprise

External Information Systems Stakeholders

Table 15-2 illustrates some of the external Stakeholders and their typical information needs.

Table 15-2: External Information Systems Stakeholders and Their Information Interests

EXTERNAL INFORMATION STAKEHOLDERS	INFORMATION INTERESTS
End-Consumers	Access to Customer-Care and help-desk Services about Products and Services, catalogs, or other promotional material with clear descriptions; whether buying directly from you or your agent, distributor, or retail outlet, they care that you understand their Requirements for the Products or Services and that you protect the Confidential Information they provide you.
Internet Shoppers and e-Surfers	Access to Surfer-friendly Web sites through which to conduct their business or personal needs, whether banking, shopping, selling on one of the auction sites, or making travel reservations
Trade Partner Buyers and Distributors, Retailers, or Agents	A source of end-Consumer Feedback, they need sound Supply-Chain communications for Forecast and Demand Information and product availability.
Supplier Sales Representatives or Agents	End-Consumer Product Requirement and preference information and Customer feedback, Complaint, and Warranty Information
Regulatory Authority Compliance Personnel	Regulation Compliance and Conformance, such as "Truth in Advertising," "Truth-in-Lending," and "Sarbanes-Oxley," Information to ensure that Customers and other Stakeholders are being treated properly
Information Brokers Who May Add Value to Information	Personal and Organizational Information to enhance organizational Information for sale or to add Attributes to enable organizations to better understand their Customers
Software Systems Suppliers	Develop, provide, and maintain purchased applications or systems support software.
Systems and Information Management Consultants	Provide services in Design and Development of Application Systems or in the development of Information Models and architecture.

The Information and Information Systems Engineering Value Circle: *"I-Need-to-Know-So-I-Can-Do* to *I-Can-Do-Because-I-Know"*

Knowledge Workers of the Enterprise, who *require* Information to perform their work and to accomplish the Enterprise Mission, are the center of the Information and Information Systems Engineering Value Circle. They perform the Value Work of the Enterprise to delight their Customers, both internal Knowledge Workers and external Customers, and end-Consumers of the enterprise's products and services.

Figure 15-1 illustrates the steps in the Information and Systems Engineering Value Circle in which Information Requirements become delivered Information.

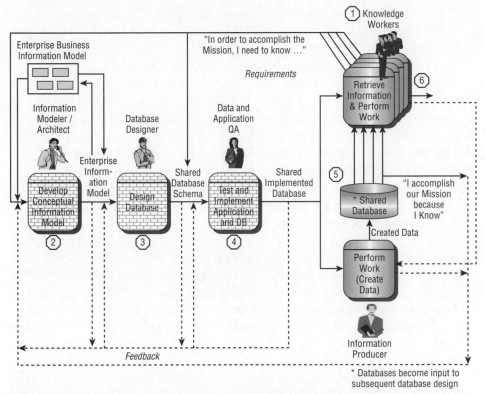

Figure 15-1: The Information Management and Information Systems Engineering Value Circle: *"I-Need-to-Know-So-I-Can-Do* to *I-Can-Do-Because-I-Know"*

1. **Knowledge Workers identify and define Requirements:** This is necessary to perform their work effectively. They receive Information from various Internal and External Sources required to perform their work. Knowledge

Workers request Information Systems that enable them to perform their work effectively and Databases that house the data they need to perform their work and make decisions effectively.

2. **Information Modelers or Architects facilitate the development of "Enterprise-Strength" Information Models:** Such Models capture Information Requirements by Business Resource, such as Party (Customer, Supplier, Employee, etc.), Product, Financials, Facilities, and Equipment, for example. They will involve Subject Matter Experts (SMEs) across the Enterprise who have a stake in the Business Resource being modeled. This Model documents and defines the fundamental Objects and Events, and the Attributes about those Objects and Events that the Enterprise needs to know about to perform its work and accomplish its Mission.

    Functional Requirements will be defined for the Application System to be designed, and Information Requirements will be defined for the Database Design to meet all dependent Knowledge Worker Requirements.

3. **Database Designers Develop "Enterprise-Strength" Database Designs:** "Enterprise-Strength" Databases ensure that *all facts* are able to be captured and stored for all Knowledge Worker Information Requirements with *integrity and fidelity* to the Information Model. Database designers must design integrity into the physical design to ensure the Stability and Flexibility to prevent unnecessary database reengineering due to faulty design.

NOTE Database Designers must first design integrity into the physical Database Design. Often, designers seek to provide performance (speed of Database transactions) by compromising the design integrity represented in the Information Model. Avoid this temptation, for it will come back to haunt you through inflexibility of the Database Design.

4. **Application Developers develop *prototypes* of the Human-Machine Interface and Application Logic:** These are given to Information Stakeholders to try out for conformance to requirements, and the Application Developers then refine the Interface Designs and Work Flows as required.

    Information Architects will ensure that the Information Model and Database Designs are "Enterprise-Strength" by reviewing additional Information Views required by Information Stakeholders. See TIQM Process P1.5 "Assess Information Architecture Quality" in Chapter 4, "The Step-by-Step Guide to *Assessing Information Product Specifications and Information Architecture Quality.*"

5. **Information Systems personnel will implement and test the application and Database and Application Design:** They do this in a controlled test environment that simulates the real-world working conditions.

The Business Information Stakeholders will review the Application and Database and ensure that they meet their Requirements. Information Architects will further ensure that the Subject Information Model and Database Design contain all information required by *all other* Stakeholders outside the application domain. This means that the Information captured meets all downstream Knowledge Workers' Requirements.

6. **Implement the Application and Database in Production and Perform Work:** Now the Knowledge Workers are performing their Value Work to delight their Customers and accomplish the Enterprise's Mission. Knowledge Workers will share their feedback and Lessons Learned in the implementation process.

7. **Enhance and improve the Application as required:** Improve the application to continually improve Ergonomics, Functionality, and Information Quality.

Value-Centric Information and Systems Engineering

In Japan, companies have Information and Systems Engineers. The United States tends to have Systems Analysts and Systems "Developers." Is there a difference in Quality in Information Systems effectiveness? The survey described in the sidebar "Obsolete Software Costs U.S. Companies Tens of Billions" illustrates significant problems in the Information Systems departments in U.S. businesses.

OBSOLETE SOFTWARE COSTS U.S. COMPANIES TENS OF BILLIONS

A survey of U.S. business and IT Executives conducted by the Business Performance Management (BPM) Forum found that more than 40 percent of the respondents estimate that unwanted applications drain more than 10 percent of their IT budgets, while 10 percent estimate the real cost to be more than 20 percent. Fully 70 percent say that their companies have redundant, deficient, or obsolete applications on the network, and the problem is even more serious in companies with revenues over $500 million.[3]

What would happen to these companies if *10 to 20 percent of their products were unwanted and unpurchased* by their Customers? It would spell disaster!!!

The following describes the Value Circle processes with their general activities and quality methods, and the IQ issues that can cause process failure. Figure 15-2 reviews this Value Circle to reflect the way that systems professionals look at their work.

Figure 15-2 identifies where to align TIQM process steps to the Information and Systems Engineering planning processes.

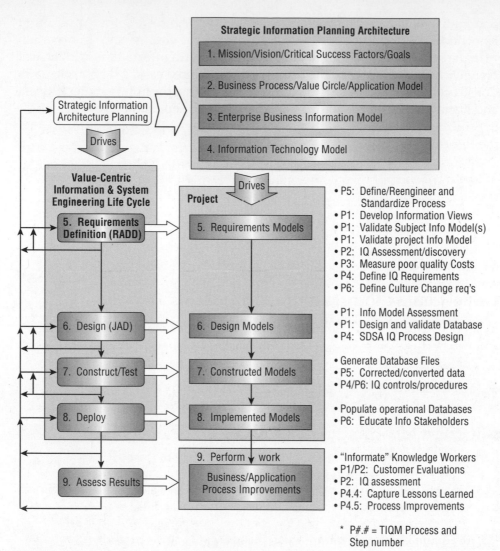

Figure 15-2: Strategic Information Planning Architecture and Value-Centric Information and Systems Engineering Processes and Steps

Strategic Information Planning

In the same way that the Executive Leadership Team conducts Strategic Business Planning, so must it also conduct Strategic Information Planning to identify what Information is critical for accomplishing the Mission of the Enterprise.

Strategic Information Planning is missing from the Information Systems Development Life Cycle. Especially insidious are methods such as "Extreme Programming" or RAD (Rapid Application Development). They focus mainly on one criteria — (Application) Time-to-Market. Little or no emphasis is placed on Quality with insufficient emphasis placed on Information Producer and Knowledge Worker Requirements.

In the same way you would not build a 100-story skyscraper or nuclear power plant without a *rigorous* Blueprint, Engineering Requirement Specifications, and Construction Specifications, you should not develop a complex Information System and Database Design without *rigorous* Information, Function, and Technology Specification Requirements along with Information Quality Requirements for the Information produced.

We further know now that without Quality Requirements being specified on the front end of the Systems Requirements and Engineering, the resulting application systems will be *sub-optimized at best*, and fail at worst.

Strategic Information Planning is required to ensure that the Enterprise has all of the major components required to develop high-Quality Information Systems and Database Designs. Strategic Information Planning must take place as an Executive Leadership Team initiative, as this is required to see the full set of interdependencies among the various Business Areas, and for them to carry out their work as an ensemble. The problem is that most organizations operate as islands of autonomy, creating conflict and chaos across *interdependent* Business Areas.

The Enterprise must be managed as a single system, according to Peter Drucker[4] and W. Edwards Deming[5] just as a Symphony Orchestra operates as a single ensemble according to any Symphony Conductor.

There are four architectural components in the Strategic Information Plan:

1. Understand the Mission, Vision, Critical Success Factors, and Strategic Goals.

2. Identify the core Business Processes or Value Circles, along with their interdependencies. These will subsequently be translated into Information Systems Models or Blueprints with *interdependencies*.

NOTE When developing Information Systems Requirements and Models, you must identify the Information *dependencies* on other Business Areas outside of the Business Area in which the processes are automated. Business Areas that are the natural creation point for Information about a given Business Resource must capture all data needed by downstream Business Areas.

3. Develop the Enterprise Business Information Model. This identifies all fundamental "Business Resources," called Information Subjects, within Information Management, that the Enterprise must manage effectively. These include Customer, Supplier, Business Partner Information, usually represented in a Party Information Model. Other resources include Products, Financials, Facilities and Equipment, Locations and Addresses, and Relationships among these resources, such as Customer Purchase or

Order, Order Shipment, Customer Account, and Account transactions. Orders and Shipments represent the relationship between Customer and Product resources.

4. Develop an Information Technology Model that documents the Information Technology Components that house the Databases, execute the Information Systems' processes, and maintain the computer network. The Enterprise Architecture Planning method by the late Steve Spewak and The Open Group Architecture Framework (TOGAF) are good methods for Strategic Information Planning.

Strategic Information Planning is a critically vital process for the Enterprise. Unfortunately, it is one of the most neglected processes.

1. Identify and Understand the Mission of the Enterprise

Because the Enterprise is a *single System*, we must understand the *ensemble*, or *synergy*, of the various parts of the Enterprise, so that we manage it effectively to accomplish the *Enterprise* Mission.

Before you Design a Database or Develop an Application System, you must understand your Enterprise Mission, the Vision, and core Business Processes or Value Circles required for your Enterprise to function effectively to accomplish its Mission.

All Employees, from top management to Knowledge Workers and Information Producers must subscribe to the Mission of the Enterprise and be driven by that Mission and Vision.

Process Activities

These steps are required before you can begin planning for Information Systems and Databases required to support the enterprise.

1. Understand the Mission and the purpose of the Enterprise. Ensure that all who are developing the Strategic Plan have a common understanding.

2. Understand the Vision of the Enterprise.

3. Define the Critical Success Factors required to succeed at *attaining* the Mission and Vision.

4. Define the Strategic Goals required for success and how to measure them.

Customer-centric organizations think first of the prospective Customer audience and seek to understand their Customers' needs in the products and services they offer. Mass marketing is out — Customer Care is in. Mass communication is out — personalized communication is in.

NOTE Organizations are only as successful as their ability to delight their Customers, externally *and* internally.

Common Information Quality Issues

- Business goals, Targets, Quotas, and Bonuses that *sub-optimize* cross-organizational Value Circles and create *harmful* competition across Business Areas instead of cooperation

  Application inventory is an *unplanned* collection of unintegrated systems.

- Purchased application software packages are *not* evaluated against Enterprise Information Requirements.

- Databases are developed for *performance* of Functional activities and **not** for housing of *Enterprise Information.*

- Information Systems Screens are designed by technical people for technical people, without much consideration for the ergonomics and look and feel for lay persons, so screens and work flow are **not** intuitive to the Information Producers or Knowledge Workers.

- Systems fail to capture **all** Attributes (Facts) that can be valuable for Knowledge Workers, only those in the *functional scope* of Requirements.

- Applications tend to lack the implementation of rigorous Business Rules that can test Validity and conformance to Valid Values and other Business Rules.

- Applications tend to be designed for response time performance and not for Quality Information.

You must design Quality into Information Systems and Databases if the organization *values* its Customers and is interested in their Lifetime *Value*. In order to design Quality into the processes and Information Systems that produce products, acquire Customers and manage your Financial and other resources and transactions, you must have organized Applications and Databases that **interoperate effectively.**

An effective Strategic Information Plan addresses the problems of short-term application *"solutions."*

2. Develop Business Process (Value Circle) Models

Functions are the alignment of activities that perform work to manage an *Enterprise Resource*, such as Financial Management, Operations, or Marketing and Sales, for example. Business Processes, (Value Circles), however, are the connection of activities that produce Products or Information required for interdependent activities requiring the output of one process to another. This process defines the core Business Processes or Value Circles required to accomplish the Enterprise Mission and to meet **all** Requirements of all Information Stakeholders.

NOTE Business Processes require true "Breakthrough" thinking to reengineer. Most organizations are in trouble because of the Status Quo Processes and Management Systems. Simply tweaking the current processes and application systems will yield minimal positive results.

TIP Ask the Process Team questions that lead to Breakthrough thinking.

Process Activities

Each major process or Value Circle should have an Executive Process Owner. Each Owner will ensure that the process is standardized and designed with Quality to meet all Stakeholders' Quality Requirements for the Products or Information produced by the process.

The objective is to ensure that the process is designed with controls to produce consistent results. Process activities include:

1. Identify a process (Value Circle) and its objective and expected outcomes.

2. Determine its correlation and alignment with the Mission.

3. Identify and define each process step with controls.

4. Identify the quality Requirements for each process step with Quality Controls.

5. Document the IQ Requirements for each Information Production step and the Information Presentation Quality Requirements for each Information Presentation Process step.

6. Document each actor (by role) for each process step. See the sample Value Circle for order fulfillment in Chapter 5, Figure 5-14.

7. Describe the Accountability for each role, whether it produces a *tangible* product or an *intangible* Information product.

8. Describe the Quality Controls implemented for each process step.

Common Information Quality Issues

- Uncontrolled processes
- *Poor or little* documentation of existing processes
- Failure to develop *breakout-level* alternative process designs
- Lack of SMEs who know the current processes and problems
- Poor Human-Factor Interface Design in the application
- Functional *bias* in Database Design

- Lack of *validation* of data at source of creation in human and automated processes

- Hidden Information Factories housing important Information because Knowledge Workers had to create their own Databases to keep their Information accurate and complete

- Purchased Software Packages that provide *minimal support* for the Information Requirements of Knowledge Workers

3. Develop Enterprise High-Level and Detailed Business Information Models

Before automating processes, the Enterprise must have a clear understanding of the process, its expected outputs, and its required inputs, as well as how the process or Value Circle interoperates with the other processes or Value Circles.

This detailed Business Information Model is a *business-friendly* Model that lists and describes the *critical* Objects and Events, and the Facts about those Objects and Events, that the Enterprise must know in order to accomplish its Mission and delight its Customers. Each Model represents a critical Business Resource, such as Party (consisting of Persons and Organizations in roles, such as Customer, Employee, Supplier, Business Partner), Product and Service, Materials, Financial Resources, Locations, and Equipment, each of which will make up a fundamental Subject Database that can be shared across operational processes in the Enterprise. Each Subject Database will have its mirror Operational Data Store with historical date and time-stamped records for Strategic and Tactical Data Analysis.

Process Activities

The Customer and Business Requirements and Analysis phase seeks to identify the features, functions, quality Requirements, expectations, and Customers' needs for the application system, Information Model, and Database Design.

The key Quality technique for this phase is Quality Function Deployment (QFD), used to discover Information Producers' and Knowledge Workers' Requirements for system design and Information Quality. QFD is also useful for capturing end-Customer Information Quality Requirements. Finally, QFD calls for the **involvement** of Information Producers and Knowledge Workers in the design of the Information System's Screens, Work Flow Specification, and Report of the Information Presentation Design. Key steps in the process are:

1. Identify Knowledge Worker and end-Customer needs and expectations.

2. Translate the Voice of the Customer (VOC) into measurable Information Requirements.

3. Ensure all process steps in the Value Circle(s) have Information Consumer Requirements specified.

4. Capture Information Requirements on Information View Charts. See the P1.5.I1.F1 Subject Information View Form in the Appendix on this book's Web site at www.wiley.com/go/IQApplied.

5. Specify *Functional* and *Information* Quality Characteristics and Specifications and *Process* Quality Characteristics and Specifications for the Information Production (Capture or Create, Maintain or Update, and Present) activities.

Process Quality Methods

- **Quality Function Deployment (QFD)**[6]: A method for involving Customers (here, Knowledge Workers and Information Producers) in the Quality Specifications for the Information Systems being developed. See the detailed description of QFD in Chapter 10, "Information Quality Applied to Product Development: '*Product-Idea-to-Product-Retire*,'" in the section "How to Measure and Improve Customer Requirement Information and Customer Requirement Information Process Quality."

- **Voice of the Customer (VOC):** Part of QFD that captures Customers' Requirements and Expectations in their *actual words*.

- **Voice of the Business (VOB):** Part of QFD that captures the organization's Requirements to develop the Product *effectively and with quality*. If there are inconsistencies between the VOB and VOC, the VOC must control. For example, "process an order quickly" VOB must be subservient to "capture my order accurately" VOC requirement.

- **SIPOC (Supplier-Input-Process-Output-Customer) Chart:** This captures the Customers' Information Requirements along with Expectations and Needs from Information Producers throughout the Value Circle. This enables you to discover downstream Knowledge Workers and their Information Requirements from the Information captured in the processes.

- **CRUD Matrix:** CRUD stands for "Create, Retrieve, Update, Delete" for the actions applied to Information in a Database from an Application Program. This technique is very helpful in identifying interdependencies of applications on the data they create or require.

Common Information Quality Issues

Issues here involve the correct design of QFD sessions, in which Information Producers and Knowledge Workers *participate actively* in the requirements definition and design phases of application systems. Issues include:

- Bias in the Requirements and Information-gathering process fails to identify real Information and IQ Requirements for all Information Stakeholders.

- Bias in the Stakeholder participation in Information-Modeling sessions stems from a small group of business Areas that create a *functionally-biased* Information Model.

- Misidentification of required Functions and Functional Requirements important to the Information Producers, along with poor Quality Characteristics and weightings for the Information *required by downstream* Knowledge Workers that causes the process to fail with defects in work outcomes

- Missed discovery of previously unstated Information Requirements leaves gaps in the Information Model and Database Design that will require subsequent reengineering.

- Failure to verify that the Systems Requirements (for Function and Information Quality) are consistent with the VOC requirements that leads to Information System "Customer" dissatisfaction.

TIP Use QFD to understand the Information Consumer Requirements for Information and Information Quality.

NOTE For applications that are Customer-facing, such as Web interactions, you must ensure that you understand the end-Customer's Information and Information Quality Requirements and that Human Factors Designs are intuitive to e-Surfers and non-technical e-Customers.

The Business Information Model represented in Figure 15-3 illustrates the core Business Resources, called Information Subjects in Information Management. They list the *fundamental* Types of Objects and Events that need to be known by the Enterprise. The Business Information Models will vary by industry type and nature of work. Each Industry Information Model will be very similar across different organizations within that Industry.

This High-Level Information Model is appropriate for Executives and Managers if it presents the *fundamental* Business Resources that they need to manage. Executives must also see Key Performance Indicators (KPIs) in the Information Model that they need in order to ensure Enterprise effectiveness.

These High-Level Models will be decomposed into more atomic-level Entity Types with *attribution* of all Characteristics that the Enterprise needs to know about critical Objects and Events of interest. This provides the framework of Business Resource Information Models to be developed into Enterprise-Strength Databases.

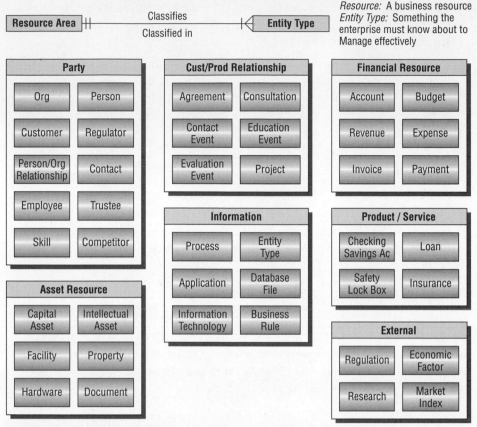

Figure 15-3: Example of High-Level Enterprise Business Information Model for a Financial Institution by Business Resources and Fundamental Object and Event Types

NOTE Always ensure that KPI Attributes show up in the High-Level Business Information Model. Executives want to know that the Model reflects what they need to know to manage the Enterprise *effectively*. These will exist as a summarized attribute in an Entity Type, such "Product Monthly Sales Amount," "Customer Lifetime Value," or "Monthly Product Warranty Costs."

4. Develop the Information Technology Model

This model lists and describes the Information Technology from hardware to software to networks, application systems, and database designs in the Information Systems operations.

Process Activities

In process 4, you identify the Information Technologies you require to support your Enterprise through its Information Technologies and Systems. Information technologies include:

1. **Hardware:** CPUs, disk storage, database servers, networks, routers, terminals and workstations, desktops and laptops, email servers

2. **Software:** Operating systems, database management systems (DBMS), systems support systems (security; firewalls; data storage management; backup and recovery; extract, transform, load S/W), application systems (Enterprise Resource Planning (ERP), Customer Relationship Management (CRM), problem-specific applications (Oil & Gas Exploration, Asset Management, Accounts Receivable, Accounts Payable), internally developed applications, interface applications

3. **Facilities requirements:** Air conditioning, fire suppression, backup/failover facilities and equipment

4. **Application and Systems Inventory**

5. **Detailed Business Information Models and planned Enterprise-Strength Databases**

6. **Information Models and Database File Inventory**

7. **Planned Information Systems Model**

Common Information Quality Issues

- Failure to transform Information Quality Requirements into Information Product Specifications to ensure that the Quality of the Information produced meets all Knowledge Workers' Requirements and Expectations

- Failure to ensure that the Information can be produced at the expected cost within the expected timeframe with the expected Quality

- Failure to minimize *redundant* technologies such as reporting tools that perform essentially the same type of work to standardize on a "best-fit" technology rather than a "best-of-breed" technology that may require high costs of redundancy in training, maintenance and database design

- Failure to *identify and evaluate* purchased software packages against Enterprise Information Requirements. Functionality is a *commodity*; Knowledge is a *competitive differentiator*.

This Enterprise Information and Systems Architecture provides the framework for actually identifying, developing, implementing, and operating the applications and databases that will support the Enterprise Processes with the aim of accomplishing the Enterprise Mission.

Strategic Information Planning is a *major* Business Management Tool. It is too broad of a topic to be treated thoroughly here. Resources that address this topic include:

- *Enterprise Architecture Planning*[7]
- *The Open Group Architecture Framework*[8]

Information Management and Information Systems Engineering

The Strategic Information Plan will guide you in selecting the Information Models to develop and Information Systems to engineer to accomplish the functional requirements effectively.

Activities include the following:

- Design, Engineer, and implement Enterprise-Strength Databases and Information Systems that automate work and "informate"[9] Knowledge Workers.

- Design and engineer the System Architecture to create Value-Centric System Components that share data from Enterprise-Strength Databases with no unnecessary redundancy and focus on Retrieval applications for Information delivery, the Value Proposition for Knowledge Workers.

Now, for each of the major Value Circles of the Enterprise, you must identify the Information Requirements as an Enterprise-Strength set of Information within each required Business Resource. These must *not* be developed as *departmental or functional* data stores.

NOTE Departmental or functionally *biased* database designs are the cause of broken Value Circles across the Enterprise and result in data redundancy, often with disparately defined data.

1. Information Requirements, Information Modeling, and Database Engineering

This process creates the detailed Enterprise-Strength Information Models that will enable Database Engineers to design Enterprise-Strength Databases. Design principles call for developing exact detailed Information Product Specifications for all Object and Event types and all Facts about the Objects and Events within a given Business Resource (Information Subject Area).

Generally, Information Models are developed in the *context* of an Information System that is developed to perform critical processes of the enterprise. This does *not* mean that the Information Model and Database are developed to support *only* the application being engineered. The Information Model for each Business

Resource must represent all Object Types and all Attributes about those Objects and Events required for all Knowledge Workers to be able to perform their work effectively and accomplish the Enterprise Mission effectively.

It is fine to define *functional* requirements by application, **but it is not acceptable to define Information Requirements by application.** The reason is that the Model will be biased toward the Business Area or Functional activities. Knowledge Workers in downstream Business Areas will be forced to collect many of the facts (Attributes) they need to know, but were excluded from the functional database design, because they were not needed by the sponsoring Business Process Owner. If Information Producers in the sponsoring Business Area are already at a touch point to capture the Information required downstream, they should capture the additional Attributes. See Figure 15-4 for the obsolete Model used to define Information Requirements.

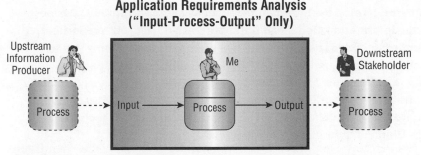

Figure 15-4: Defining Information Requirements by Business Area Only Causes Facts Required by Downstream Knowledge Workers to Be Overlooked.

This Input-Process-Output Model worked only during the pre-database management system era. In today's Internet and mature Database Management Systems environment, this Model has caused the building of excessive redundant databases as *departmental* databases that can only support *departmental* requirements and defeat the use of standardized data names and definitions. The old IPO (Input-Process-Output) Model must be replaced by an Enterprise-Strength Model that will create a standardized, Enterprise-Strength Database that will provide a standardized Chart-of-Facts of Information in the same way that there is a standardized Enterprise Chart of Accounts for Financial Management.

Figure 15-5 illustrates the Enterprise-Strength approach to Information Requirements and Value-Centric Information and Systems Engineering for Enterprise-Strength Databases that support all Knowledge Workers.

The Value-Centric Value Circle Information Analysis, looks across the entire Value Circle of activities to identify all Information Stakeholders for the Information being captured by the business area that is the natural Creation point for Information of a specific type, such as Customer, Product, financials, or Facilities.

**Value-Centric Value Circle Information Analysis
(Supplier-Input-Process-Output-Customer*)**

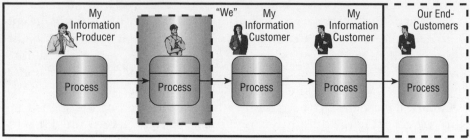

Figure 15-5: The Value-Centric Approach to Information Requirements Seeks to Understand All Information Requirements across the Value Circle So As to Capture All Facts Known to the Information Producers at the Point of Capture. (*SIPOC)

NOTE Do *not* develop the Information Model as an *Application-* or *Business-area* specific Information Model and Database Design. This will support only a narrow set of Knowledge Workers and will ultimately fail, causing you to have to build additional, redundant, cost-adding databases to support other functional areas. We must *break down barriers between staff areas* (Deming's Point 8 of Transformation). This means we must develop Information Models that will yield *shared* databases that are *Enterprise-Strength* in supporting Knowledge Workers' Information Requirements.

The Customer and Business Requirements and Analysis phase seeks to identify the features, functions, Quality Requirements, Expectations, and Customers' Needs for the Information they need to perform their work effectively.

See "Best Practices in Information Management" later in this chapter.

Process Activities

1. Develop a *detailed* business Information Model for *each* Business Resource in the scope of the business process or Value Circle in which an Information System is to be developed.

2. Identify the Information System to be developed.

3. Document the Information Value Circle of the process or processes to be automated.

4. Identify all Stakeholders (Information Producers and Knowledge Workers) across all different business areas that depend on the Information.

5. Select representative Subject Matter Experts (SMEs) from each Business Area or Function affected.

6. Have each Knowledge Worker develop two or three Information Views representing their Information Requirements for each Business Resource Area.

7. Bring all the participating Stakeholders together in a group Information Modeling workshop. This enables all Stakeholders to see and hear each other's Information Requirements and needs for Information about the subject or resource being modeled.

8. Conduct the Information Modeling workshop.

9. Compare the Information Model with the gathered Information Views and additional Information Views to confirm the completeness of the Model.

10. Define the Object Types and Attributes as you discover them.

11. Confirm the Definitions with a Consensus-oriented process.

12. Refine the Information Model as overlooked Requirements are discovered. Usually this will add to the Model but not "modify" it.

Process Quality Methods

- **Quality Function Deployment (QFD):** This involves Information Producers and Knowledge Workers in the design of Information systems that support their work.

- **SIPOC (Supplier-Input-Process-Output-Customer):** This approach analyzes downstream Knowledge Worker requirements for upstream creation applications.

- **Breakthrough Thinking:** This seeks to identify counterintuitive solutions to problems, including Information System designs.

- **Standardize-Do-Study-Act (SDSA) Cycle:** This uses *poka yoke* to error-proof Information Systems designs, human-machine interfaces, and Information Systems screen and report designs.

- **Lean Design:** Techniques to eliminate waste in systems design, such as redundant databases requiring Interface or ETL programs that transform and move data from one place to another. Also eliminates unnecessary redundancy of Information Technologies, such as multiple query or reporting tools.

Common Information Quality Issues

- Incomplete or Inaccurate Definition of Information

- Functional *bias* that will distort the data definition to a functional *orientation*, not an inherent definition of the Characteristics of Entity Types

- Developing an Information Model that does *not* capture all Entity Types and Attributes of the Real-World Objects and Events that the Enterprise needs to know about, so all data can be collected once in a way that allows it to be shared for all uses

2. Process Requirements Definition, Information Systems Design, Prototyping, and Engineering

This process specifies the Functional and Process Requirements for various processes that require Information about a given Business Resource, such as Customer (Party), product or financials to support all Knowledge Workers' Requirements across the Enterprise. Design principles call for developing exact detailed Information Product Specifications and Quality Requirements for all Object Types and Facts (Attributes) required not just for the process and application at hand, but for *all* downstream processes that depend on Information produced by this system to operate properly.

Requirements include the Information System Objectives, Functional Requirements, and Process design around the Information System, along with the IQ Requirements to support the system and all downstream Information Consumers.

Process Activities

1. Develop an exact, detailed purpose and objective of the process and how they relate to the Enterprise Mission.

2. Translate the Functional Requirements and Human Factors into Screen or Report prototypes.

3. Select a set of Business Stakeholders (Information Producers and Knowledge Workers) as part of the Information Systems Engineering Team to provide input, hands-on prototyping of the system designed to ensure business-friendly Application Design and Navigation. This ensures that the Presentation Quality of Information-gathering and Information Presentation screens and reports meet Information Producers' and Knowledge Workers' Expectations.

4. Develop a prototype that *satisfies* the Functional and Quality Requirements (design parameters) of the Information Stakeholders.

5. Build prototypes of the Information System with the Information Stakeholders.

6. Conduct process testing, adjustment, and validation with prospective scenarios of input and conditions with the Information Producers.

7. Install required hardware, system support software, and equipment.

8. Validate Process, Product, and Information output Quality.

9. Identify any ongoing IQ issues.

10. If any IQ issues, conduct Root Cause Analysis and define Process Improvements to mitigate IQ issues.

11. Prototype and Verify the Human Factor Design meets Information Producers' and Knowledge Workers' Requirements. See Figure 15-6 and 15-7 for interface screens with poor Human Factors Design.

12. Ensure compatibility for all downstream processes that require the Information produced by this Information System.

13. Provide training for all Information Producers and Information Consumers.

Figures 15-6 and 15-7 illustrate poor Human Factor Design.

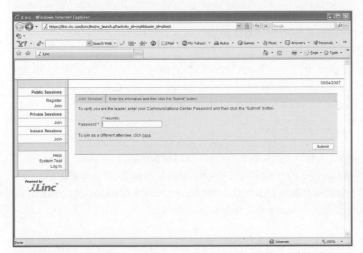

Figure 15-6: "Session Join" Screen Is Poorly Designed and Causes Frustration in Joining. See Join Results in Figure 15-7.

Note that in Figure 15-6, the first instruction line is looking for the password for the *leader*. Note how far away the Submit button is.

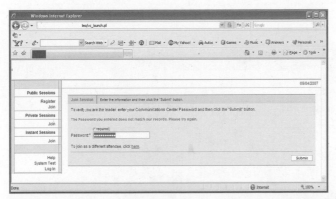

Figure 15-7: Filled-In Password Screen Was Rejected after Submission Because I Was a "different attendee" (See Figure 15-6) Required to Go to a Different Screen by Clicking the Link, "here."

Note in Figure 15-7 that my password was rejected. After about four tries, I noticed the first line reads "To verify you are the leader, enter your

Communications Center Password and then click the 'Submit' button." I was not the leader, but rather a "different attendee," and I should have clicked on the *barely visible* "click <u>here</u>" link to join the session.

You may argue that I should have been more observant — but this screen has confused many session attendees. It is poorly designed.

The message "The Password you entered does not match our records. Please try again." This further confuses the issue in that the password for session attendees will never be accepted, because none of the attendees, except the leader, has a matching password.

The most important point to note is that, while there is only one leader for the section, there might be 3 or 5 or 50 attendees to the session. The best design is, therefore, one that makes the screen easy to use for the attendees who may not be familiar with the technology.

NOTE By virtue of using QFD to involve the actual Information Producers and Knowledge Workers in the Process and Application Design, there should be minimal training required. Also, there should be minimal resistance, as the Workers have "designed" the Human-Machine Interfaces.

See Figure 15-8 for an example of poor data presentation on a screen.

Figure 15-8 presents the column heading "Onhand," which should read "On-Hand Qty." Note that the values in that column have a decimal point and four trailing zeroes. Is it ever possible that you maintain inventory counts to a precision of one-ten-thousandth of a unit? On-Hand Quantity will always be an integer. A quantity value cannot be fractional, and the width of the column is much larger than the potential quantities possible and wastes valuable real estate on the screen.

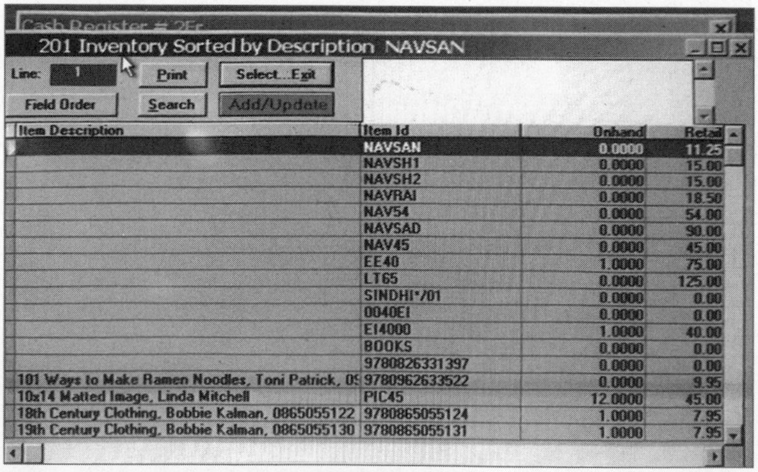

Figure 15-8: Poor Inventory Screen Design in a Retail Cash Register Application

Figure 15-9 is an example of a hotel's TV greeting for its guests.

Figure 15-9: Smart Hotel — Dumb Message!

Even though the hotel in Figure 15-9 was a state-of-the-art smart hotel, it still had IQ issues. Our TV greeted my wife, Diane and me as, "Welcome Linda Johnson." The message displayed a British flag to indicate the expected language spoken is English, not that the occupant is British, which was one of many languages in which guests could see messages. This is a quality feature for non-English speaking guests.

However, this *very* Customer-facing process was broken.

Process Quality Methods

- **Quality Function Deployment:** Gathers the Voice of the Customer Requirements

- **SIPOC (Supplier-Input-Process-Output-Customer) charts:** Identify Requirements of each Information Producer's process that creates Information required by others.

- **Standardize-Do-Check/Study-Act Cycle:** The process to define and ensure quality in a new process

- *Poka Yoke*: Error-Proofing techniques for Information Quality

- **Prototyping screen and report designs and work flow:** The application of Human Factors Design in Information System–Human interactions

- **Quality Control:** The application of techniques to ensure that the process *performs* to Requirements

Common Information Quality Issues

- Incomplete or *inaccurate* Definition of Functional and Quality Requirements (design parameters)

- *Inaccurate or imprecise* Information or System Requirements as compared to required Critical-To-Quality (CTQ) Requirement Specifications

Costs of Poor Quality Software before Implementation into Production Include:[10]

- Building defects into the system
- Finding the defects
- Correcting the defects
- Testing to determine that the defect causes are removed

Costs of Poor Quality Software after Implementation into Production Include:

- Specifying and coding the defect into the system
- Detecting the problems within the application system
- Reporting the problem to Information Services and/or the Process Owner/ Manager of the process
- Correcting the problems caused by the defects
- Operating the system until the defect is corrected
- Correcting the defect
- Testing to determine that the defect no longer exists
- Integrating the corrected program(s) into production
- Regaining Customer Trust and Goodwill (Customer Satisfaction)

Software Defect Categories:[11]

- **Requirements are Improperly Interpreted.** The Information Systems personnel *misinterpret* what the Knowledge Worker wants but correctly implement what the Systems Personnel believe is wanted.

- **Knowledge Workers Specify the Wrong Requirements**. The Specifications given to Information Systems are not correct or only partial.

- **Requirements are Not Correctly Recorded.** Information Systems personnel *fail to record* the Specifications properly.

- **Design Specifications are Not Correct**. The Information System Design does not achieve the System Requirements, but the Design as specified may be correctly implemented.

- **Program Specifications are Not Correct.** The Design Specifications are not correctly interpreted, making the program Specifications *inaccurate*, but the program can be properly coded to achieve the correct program specifications.

- **There is a Program Coding Error.** The program is not coded according to the Program Specifications.

- **There is a Program Structural or Instruction Error.** The programming capabilities are *improperly utilized*, resulting in Defects attributable to the *misuse* of a program instruction or the method in which the instruction is used.

- **There is a data Entry or Capture Error.** The System and or Program Information is *not* correctly entered into the Database.

- **There is a testing Error.** The test either detects an error *where there is no* error or *fails to detect* an existing Error in the application system.

- **There is an error Correction Mistake.** In the *process of correcting an error*, a Defect *is introduced* into the corrected condition.

- **The corrected Condition Causes Other Defects.** In the process of correcting a defect, the *correction process itself causes* additional Defects to be created by the Information System.

- **Screen or Report Designs are Unintuitive or Misleading.** Screen designs *are not easily usable, causing wrong* actions or decisions.

3. Information System Deployment

This step deploys the Information System into "production" mode to allow execution of the automated processes. At this point, the process should be in control, after final Systems and Stress Testing.

Process Activities for Information Systems Deployment

1. Implement the Information System in production mode.

2. Monitor the system production though the entire Value Circle to ensure that it is working properly with **no negative side effects**. If side effects are observed or if Information Quality problems appear, immediately stop the process and rectify the causes.

3. Ensure the process is In Control:

   - Implement Information Quality monitoring for CTQ Data Elements.
   - Ensure that Information Producers are capturing data accurately.
   - Ensure that any real-time equipment *is, and stays, calibrated* properly.
   - Ensure that equipment *calibration procedures are documented properly* and that there is adequate training.
   - Apply Continuous Process Improvement as necessary.

4. Gather downstream Knowledge Worker feedback.

5. Conduct Information System Process Testing, adjustment, and validation.

6. Install and Calibrate Manufacturing or Information Create applications and equipment *to meet* Nominal Values for Product or Information Quality Characteristics.

7. Conduct and adjust final Information System Process Design.

8. Provide ongoing Information System Process Training to staff.

Process Quality Methods

- **Standardize-Do-Check/Study-Act:** To define processes *with quality*

- **Information Quality monitoring:** To ensure *process control*

- **Business Rule Validation invoked from a Rules Engine or IQ Software:** To ensure *validity* of data at the source of capture or Information production

Common Information Quality Issues

- *Incomplete, inaccurate or unclear* Process Definitions and Work Procedures or Instructions

- *Incomplete, inaccurate, or imprecise* Business Rule Specifications

- *Inaccurate, incomplete, or unclear* Calculation Instructions

4. Information Systems Operation

This process represents the full-scale Information Systems and service operations.

Quality Management in this process ensures the Information delivered conforms to the Requirements and Expectations of the Knowledge Workers and end-Consumers. If your products and services do not meet your end-Customers' Expectations, Management will be faced with the following choice: Reinvent your Enterprise — or fail!

Process Activities

1. Perform *regular* measurement of Critical to Quality (CTQ) Characteristics of Requirements and Specifications based upon CTQ Information.

2. Use Statistical Process Control (SPC) charts to measure the CTQ Characteristics.

3. Ensure Conformance with all Information Quality Requirements to meet *Nominal Values*.

Process Quality Methods

- **Statistical Process Control charts**
- **Troubleshooting and Diagnosis**
- **Assessment of CTQ IQ Characteristics**
- **Pareto Diagrams of nonconformance**
- **Plan-Do-Check/Study-Act** applied to nonconformance discoveries
- **Root Cause Analysis** to identify the Root Causes of defects to eliminate
- **Poka yoke:** Techniques to Error-Proof Processes against defect cause

Common Information Quality Issues

- Lack of *intuitive and clear* Information Systems procedures
- Lack of *intuitiveness and ease of use* of Systems Screens and Navigation
- Unclear and or Biased Information *gathering Forms or Reports*
- *Inaccurate Measurement* of Information Process Quality

5. Information Consumer Feedback

This is a vital process. It is the process where the end-Consumers share their experiences with you about your Information and Service and Product Quality. The Customer-focused Organization will have *designed* Quality into their Products and Services, so the Customer feedback should *not* produce negative surprises, except in the most unusual circumstances. The Customers will always have the final say. If they walk away from your Products or Services, they will take with them their pocketbooks and will share their complaints with others.

Process Activities

1. Get *frequent* and *regular* feedback from your Customers as to their satisfaction with your products and services, as well as your Information.
2. *Act* on what you learn from your Customers to improve.

Process Quality Methods

- **Quality in after-system implementation service**
- **Customer Satisfaction Evaluation and Action**

Common Information Quality Issues

- Bias in Customer Satisfaction form questions; see Chapter 14, "Information Quality Applied to Document and Knowledge Management"

- Incomplete Customer Satisfaction Surveys
- Inaccurate interpretation of Customer Satisfaction Surveys
- Inaccurate or incomplete Warranty Claim data
- Inaccurate process and product measurement data in CTQ Requirements

6. Information Systems Enhancement, Redesign, and Retirement

As the Information System is deployed, it will succeed or fail subject to the Stakeholders' evaluation. As we have seen with the onslaught of new Information Technologies, it is difficult to keep up with the so-called state-of-the-art. However, technology is becoming more and more of a commodity. The key to success is how you apply the technology — not that you have it!!!

End-Customer experience will determine Enterprise success or failure. My file of "Business Success-to-Failure" is growing by the week. If Products and Services do not meet Customer needs consistently, management will be faced with the following choice: Reinvent your Enterprise or fail.

Information Systems Process Enhancement/Improvement Activities

There are three scenarios here:

1. Information System or Database needs minor improvements that keep the system effective. This requires a small project version of the Value Circle, beginning with process 2, "Customer and Business Requirements Analysis." Modifications to original requirements must be verified and implemented with Quality.

2. Information System or Database needs *major* redesign to meet market changes. This requires a major project reengineering, beginning with Process 2. Generally, this results in a new System or Database being reengineered to replace the now-deficient Application.

3. The Information System or Database is no longer Value-Added (not needed) in the marketplace and will be retired. Such is the evolution of computing technology that has seen semiconductors replace magnetic core RAM, which replaced transistors, which replaced vacuum tubes, which replaced mechanical relays, all in the space of 60 years.

Process Quality Methods

- Service Quality
- Customer Care

Common Information Quality Issues

- Inaccurate or incomplete Requirements data related to a decision to enhance, redesign, or retire an Information System or Database

- Inaccurate, incomplete, or irrelevant Information captured by an Information System that prevents the accomplishment of the Enterprise Mission

Information Quality Problems in Information Management and Information Systems Engineering

Having Quality problems in Systems Development, Information Modeling, and Database Designs is like incorrectly calibrating manufacturing equipment. It will introduce defects into the Information Production and Presentation processes.

The Fundamental Paradigm for Value-Centric Information Management and Information Systems Engineering

Information Systems Development is not an art. It is — or should be — an Engineering discipline.

Information Systems are *not* the products of the Information Systems Department!!!

The following manufacturing metaphor should apply to Information Systems Engineering:

- Manufacturing Equipment is used to produce the Products of the Enterprise. Each product feature or component has specific Quality Characteristic Requirements, such as precise diameter and weight. When Customers require product changes, the equipment is retooled

- Application Systems are used to produce the *Information Products* of the Enterprise. Each Information Attribute (Data Element) has specific Quality Characteristic Requirements, such as Accuracy, Validity, and Completeness. When Knowledge Workers require changes to their work processes, the application is retooled

  Application Systems are not an end in themselves. They are only the *tools* (machinery) that facilitate business processes' efforts to capture, maintain, and deliver the Information *required* to accomplish the Enterprise Mission.

  Enabled work, shared Knowledge, and empowered Knowledge Workers *are* the true *products* of Value-Centric Information and Systems Engineering.

Consequences of Poor Quality in Information and Systems Engineering

Following are examples of problems in Information Systems and Information process quality.

J SAINSBURY PLC WRITES OFF US$ 526 MILLION INVESTMENT IN FAILED AUTOMATED SUPPLY-CHAIN MANAGEMENT SYSTEM

The giant British food retailer J Sainsbury PLC had to write off its US$526 million investment in an automated Supply-Chain Management System. It seems that merchandise was stuck in the company's depots and warehouses and was not getting through to many of its stores. Sainsbury was forced to hire about 3,000 additional clerks to stock its shelves manually.[12]

COMPUTER SOFTWARE FAILURE CRASHES F-22 ON-BOARD COMPUTERS

The new U.S. stealth fighter, the F-22 Raptor, was deployed for the first time to Asia on February 11, 2007. Twelve Raptors flying from Hawaii to Japan were forced to turn back when a software glitch crashed all of the F-22s' on-board computers as they crossed the International Date Line. Every fighter completely lost all navigation and communications. They reportedly had to turn around and follow their tankers back to Hawaii by visual contact. Had they not been with their tankers, or the weather had been bad, this would have been serious.[13]

CALIFORNIA'S EFFORTS TO REDUCE PAY THWARTED BY SOFTWARE

As the state of California was trying to slash its budget and reduce the pay of thousands of individuals, the controller, John Chiang, found that the state's payroll system was so antiquated it would take months to make the changes to Workers' checks. "In 2003, my office tried to see if we could reconfigure our system to do such a task," Mr. Chiang told a State Senate committee on Monday. "And after 12 months, we stopped without a feasible solution"!!![14]

Best Practices in Information and Systems Engineering

Now, how do we get out of this mess? Here we describe best practices for Engineering Information Systems and Information Management.

Information Systems Requirements Definition

The key to any Product Quality is the Quality of the Requirements, whether Consumer Products or Information Systems. Systems must be designed for humans with error-proofing to prevent errors and omissions.

Use Quality Function Deployment techniques to identify and define Information Producer and Knowledge Worker requirements for both Information and the Functional capabilities of the proposed system.

Quality Function Deployment (QFD) is an effective tool for gathering Customer Requirements and Expectations for Information Systems as well as for consumer goods. Yoji Akao introduced QFD in Japan in 1966 to proactively involve the Customer in the design of products. This led to the maturing of Quality Management by moving from Quality Control of Requirements as understood by production to assuring that there was Quality Control of Requirements that were critical to *Customers*.

Here we illustrate how QFD effectively involves Information Stakeholders in Information Systems Requirements and Design and in Information Requirements gathering and enterprise Information Model development for Enterprise-Strength Databases.

QFD is a set of specific methods for ensuring Quality throughout each process of the Information and Systems Engineering Life Cycle. From concept and Knowledge Worker Requirements, through design, development, deployment and system enhancement or reengineering, QFD involves capturing the Voice of the Customer (VOC) to:

- Identify and understand their Functional Requirements for the application.

- Identify and understand the Information Requirements from all Information Consumer areas in order to perform their process(es) effectively.

- Translate the VOC into Quality Specifications for the Information Quality and Systems Functionality.

- Translate the Information Quality Requirements into Information Quality Error-Proofing techniques.

- Ensure Quality at each application System's Information Creation or Updating process step to provide Quality aimed at satisfying the Information Consumers, internally and externally.[15]

In the context of Information Systems Engineering, QFD involves Information Producers and Knowledge Workers in the development of the Requirements, Functions, Features, and Capabilities of the Information Systems they will use. QFD gathers the VOC as *verbatim* statements of Knowledge Worker needs,

Requirements, and Expectations and translates this into Requirements and Specifications that can be designed into the Information System. A critical part of the QFD process is to identify the *relative* importance of each Customer Requirement to identify the *vital few* or Critical-to-Quality (CTQ) Requirements from the more peripheral requirements.

Next, you identify Voice of the Business (VOB) to determine the Enterprise Requirements and the Enterprise's capability to produce the product or deliver the service with the *required* Quality. In essence, the VOB addresses Requirements and constraints in the development of the product. In Information Systems Development, this may identify Software or Hardware constraints such as Database Management System (DBMS) technology or purchased software required to implement the automated processes.

Information System Design for Quality

Here you translate the VOC and VOB Requirements into Design Specifications for the Information System Design.

Best Practices for Information System Design and Operation

Ellen Isaacs and Alan Walendowski have developed excellent guidelines for Human Factor Design in Information Systems in their book, *Designing from Both Sides of the Screen*.[16] "Human Factor Guidelines for Information Systems Engineering," on the "IQ Applied" book Web site at: www.wiley.com/go/IQApplied encapsulates their guidelines for Human Factors Design in the following categories:

- **Respect Physical Effort**
- **Respect Mental Effort**
- **Be Helpful**
- **Requirements Gathering**
- **Human Factor Structure**
- **Human Factor Layout**
- **Architecture**
- **Project Management**
- **Designer-Engineer Collaboration**
- **Development and Usage Studies**

Best Practices for Information Creation and Maintenance

These are the processes that "acquire" the raw material of data that will be assembled into useful Information for the Knowledge Workers to perform their knowledge work.

- **Ensure that the data *Capture* process is placed at the most natural point by the person who can capture the Information at the point of Knowledge.** The person at the natural point of contact with people or events about which we need Information, is the best point of Knowledge acquisition.

- **Design *Intuitive* Information Create/Update Screens and Forms.** Information collection devices must be designed in a way that is natural to data creation or collection, in the most logical sequence of data capture.

- **Capture data *electronically and automate capture* where possible.** If data can be captured from electronically readable forms such as bar codes or Radio Frequency IDs (RFIDs), it decreases data capture errors. Errors can still be introduced by the processes that create the bar codes or RFIDs, however.

- **Have the Information Producer enter data electronically if data must be captured on paper at the point of origin.** The Information Producer will have the best knowledge of what is written down, resulting in fewer transcription errors.

- **Use the Carpenter's Rule of Thumb (*Measure Twice, Cut Once*).** This *ensures* the Accuracy and Completeness of captured data before you commit, store it, or release it to others.

- **Capture *all* data required for *all* Downstream Processes.** The most serious flaw is to capture *only* the data required by the Business Area that captures the data. If the downstream Knowledge Workers need several other Attributes not required by the capturing Business Area, downstream Knowledge Workers will have to hunt and chase to get the additional Information, spending five to ten times as much or more than it would have cost for the original Information Producer to capture all required data while at the point of Knowledge.

- ***Train* Information Producers and *Required* Intermediaries.** Ensure that Information Producers *know* all their Information "Customers," the uses Information is required for, and the Costs and Impacts of Poor Quality.

- **Capture data *as soon as* it is known at the *origination* point, and capture it *once* in a way that can be shared by all who need it.** If data is captured in an Enterprise-Strength Database accessible by all, it increases the Value of the Information significantly. By *eliminating* the need to have *multiple Databases* that house the same Information, you eliminate the costs of having to move and transform the data, and you eliminate the potential for introducing errors as it is moved.

- Calibrate Automated Data Capture (Measurement) Devices and ensure Accuracy and Precision of measurement with minimal noise or bias.

- Implement edits at the source process that can be invoked by the source Create Application Program to validate reasonability and business rule conformance at the source of data capture.

- **"Error-proof" Handwritten data by allocating enough space, with blocks for individual letters.** All handwriting should be upper-case block letters, unless text is required to be case-sensitive as is the case with people's names or strong passwords. For Best Practices in Manual and Electronic Forms, see Chapter 14, "Information Quality Applied to Document and Knowledge Management," sections "Best Practies in Form Design for Forms to be Filled in by Hand," and "Best Practices in Form Design for Electronic Forms to be Filled in Online."

- **Capture the Pronunciation of Customer Names.** Do this if oral communication will take place, such as through a Call Center or Customer representative.

- **Don't assume you know correct spelling — *confirm* it.** Unique spellings of people's names are becoming more popular.

- *Repeat* **Vital Information given orally.** Repeat the information back in a way that is different from how it was given to you. If you get a phone number, such as "555-123-4466," you might repeat it back as "five-fifty-five, one, twenty-three, forty-four-sixty-six." This causes the person to think about the number, instead of giving you a rote, "'yes, that's right" answer.

- **Capture and maintain *historical* and *nonvolatile* identity data to minimize the potential for duplication.** For persons, such attributes include mother's maiden name, the last four digits of the Social Security number or other nonvolatile identifiers. Capture former addresses also, to use in duplication tests. If you acquire mailing lists from others, there will often be significant numbers of records with old addresses and maiden names or names changed to legal names required for security purposes.

- **Capture and maintain *historical* and *permanent* data.** If you have out-of-date addresses or other personal Information, having it may prevent you from creating a duplicate record because of the differences in the out-of-date information from the current information.

- Capture *all* data, including full names, not just abbreviations of names.

- **Minimize data entry keystrokes.** Use check boxes or automatic propagation from known data, such as postal codes from address and city and state data or postage amounts from weight and postal destination. If you use automatic propagation of data, you must Error-Proof it to ensure it is a *correct* value for the field propagated to.

- *Verify* the accuracy of automatically captured data often.

- Do not assume that *default* spell check options are correct — verify they are correct in context.

- **In spreadsheets, protect cells containing calculations.** This prevents inadvertent overwriting and losing the formula.

- **Ensure that Controls are implemented for OCR-scanned data.** Small fonts can be more difficult for the scanner to decipher. Enlarge original documents that have light print or small fonts to increase the scanner's accuracy.

Best Practices in Information Management

Information Management is a Business Management Function. While the function generally resides in the Information Systems area, it should be managed as a *Business* rather than a *Technical* activity.

Applying Information Quality Principles to "Shared" Information

One of the most significant problems in Information Design is developing "functionally biased" Databases. It is tragic to read books on Information Design that state that the purpose of an Information Model or Database Design is to identify and house data required by an *application*!!!

Nothing could be further from the truth. The purpose of an Information Model and Database Design is to identify *all* Information Requirements needed by the Enterprise and to house the collective Knowledge of the *Enterprise* in shared, Enterprise-Strength Subject Databases for all Knowledge Workers who need that Information to perform their value work and help accomplish the Mission of the Enterprise.

Functionally *biased* Databases are defective outputs of a defective Information Management process. This will cause Information Quality Problems because defective or *poorly or functionally defined* Data Definition ("Information Product Specifications") causes Information Content Quality problems, in the same way that defects in Manufacturing Product Specifications cause *defects* in the Products produced.

Issue: Disparate, Redundant Information and Databases

Two types of problems occur here. The first is having *redundant* Databases in which the Record-of-Origin (ROO) Database supplies a downstream *redundant* Database through an interface or ETL program. Problems with this approach are:

- This introduces an "Information Float" delay in data moved to the redundant Database. If "Timeliness" of Information is important to the downstream Database Stakeholders, they may miss opportunities because of the transmission delay.

- If this is not a controlled (replicated) database, Knowledge Workers downstream may make updates to the data, making the two Databases *no longer* Equivalent and not knowing which one is correct, if either.

If the two databases have different architectures (for example, because one is an internally designed Database and the other is a software package data structure), the domain value sets are probably different and may have different meanings of the Attributes. Problems in this scenario include:

- Out-of-sync values from the ROO Database to the downstream *redundant* data store. This requires Knowledge Workers to learn multiple sets of values and their meanings.

- Invariably, externally developed data stores will **not** contain **all** Attributes required by the Enterprise, and Knowledge Workers will have to access data from multiple places, or migrate data to a third (new redundant) Database, increasing the complexity and potential for errors in data values and interpretation.

Costs of Disparate, Redundant Information Required in Web-Accessible and Internal Databases

Costs include:

- Costs of developing and maintaining redundant databases when a single Record-of-Reference, Enterprise-Strength Database could be shared across the Value Circle. This is true for such databases as pricing databases or product/service descriptive Information. Of course, security is an issue and must be provided to protect critical Information.

- Non-value-adding Costs of developing the *interface module or ETL routine* to propagate the data from the ROO to the downstream redundant data store

- Out-of-sync Information because of time delays in moving data can cause errors as a result of *non-current* Information in the downstream data store.

- *Disparate* Definition or Valid Value sets in the *redundant* Database creates *different* meanings in the different Databases, causing internal and external communication problems.

Tips for Measuring Data "Shared" by Internal Processes and Internet Processes

The pertinent measure in redundant data stores is "Equivalence" and "Concurrence" of the data in multiple data stores. Equivalence means that the data values in the two Databases represent the same Real-World Attribute *correctly*. If you have "F" for female gender in one database and "2" for female gender in the second database, these two values are Equivalent. They represent a person who is a woman. Concurrence means that the data is Equivalent in the two Databases at all times. This requires *distributed* Database *replication*.

Equivalence means that you have the same, semantically equivalent data values in the two Databases, such as product price for an item or a Customer name and address.

Concurrence is the degree of delay, if any, between when the same facts are knowable to Knowledge Workers using one data store and using the other data store(s). This is a measure of "Information Float," or the lag time for data to be propagated to a downstream data file.

See Chapter 5, "The Step-by-Step Guide to *Assessing Information Quality*," for guidelines for measuring and improving Information Quality.

Tips for Improving Data "Shared" by Multiple Business Areas

Because electronic Information that is stored in a single Database is *Non-Consumable*, it can be accessed and retrieved by anyone with read access authority. The Principle of Information Value is that all Knowledge Workers should have access to required Information from Enterprise-Strength Databases.

If redundant Databases exist, is there a real "business reason," such as security and/or privacy; an insurmountable technical reason (such as the incompatibility of required hardware platform or operating systems that cannot physically be integrated); or is it just *standard practice* to create **redundant** Databases for each application? Application specific Databases should not be allowed if the Enterprise is engineering its own Information Systems and Databases.

Defining a Project for Redundant Data Process Improvement (TIQM P4.1)

The Project Team will need a mix of Information Systems specialists, and Business Managers and Professionals with a stake in the Information across the Enterprise. This problem involves Systems processes that move data as well as Business Processes that are functionally oriented.

Developing a Plan for Redundant Data Process Improvement (TIQM P4.2)

Plan an Improvement by analyzing Root Causes of *redundant* Databases (TIQM P4.2.1). Root Causes of redundant data include the treatment of Information as an *application or departmental resource* by Systems and/or Business personnel.

Causes of Disparate, Redundant Databases, and Information

Causes include:

- The *precipitating* cause is the application development methodology that treats Information as an *application resource* and not an Enterprise Resource.

- Having *different technology platforms* may drive separate physical databases, but it should not require different data names or definitions for common facts required across different business areas.

- Treatment of Information as a *technical and application system resource*

- Treatment of Information as a Departmental or Business Area, and **Proprietary**, Resource

- *Lack of a process* to develop Enterprise-Strength Information Models and Database Designs

- *Lack of training* in how to develop Enterprise-Strength Information Models and Database Designs

- *Deadline date and budget constraints* prevent developing Information Models and Database Designs from an *Enterprise* perspective.

- Failure to implement proper transformation or data movement across redundant databases

- The **ultimate** Root Cause, however, is that Business Management, from the top down, generally manages the organization by Functional area, not as a single Enterprise entity or a single "System." As a result, the *larger* the organization, the less a given Business Segment knows about how it fits into the larger business Value Circles of the Enterprise. This causes Business Areas *to create their own databases* with their *functional definitions* of data, and *with their own performance measures* for their work.

The second part of Planning for Process Improvement is to define Improvements that will eliminate or minimize redundancy, or the discrepancy between redundant Databases (TIQM P4.2.2). Design single Databases for each fundamental Business Resource (Subject Area), unless there are **real** Business Reasons, such as security requires total separation of Information in Web-accessible Databases to prevent the most capable hackers from getting into critical internal Information Systems and Databases.

If, however, data is **not** Equivalent across required redundant Databases, the *causes and improvements* will be in the technical processes that move and transform the data between the databases.

If the data has *different* Definitions and Values, requiring transformation, the Root Cause is, once again, having a *Departmental* view of "my Information," irrespective of that fact that Knowledge Workers in other Business Areas need that Information as well. The corrective maintenance process (TIQM P5) is to standardize Data Names, Definitions and Value sets, and Business Rules across *redundant* data stores. This requires participation from all Information Stakeholders.

But the preventive maintenance (TIQM P4.2.2) in Chapter 7, "The Step-by-Step Guide to *Improving Information Process Quality*," is to improve the process of Information Requirement Specification and Data Definition to ensure that Information is *standardized* across the Enterprise for all Information Stakeholders. Data should be named and defined with representatives of all Stakeholder areas, with Customer-facing data having Standard Names and Definitions understandable by the Customers.

Preventive Actions for Disparate, Redundant Databases

- Recognize and begin to manage Information as an *Enterprise Resource* — not a *departmental or business area* Resource.

- Develop Information Standards and Guidelines for *naming and defining* Entity Types and Attributes with Enterprise-Consensus Names, Definitions, Valid Value Sets, and Business Rule Specification guidelines. Confirm that the Names and Definitions are Enterprise-centric by involving Stakeholders who require the data to confirm the appropriateness of Data Names and Definitions.

- Involve *representative* Knowledge Workers and Information Producers in the Information Modeling and Data Definition processes.

- Encourage Business Areas to use Enterprise-Strength Record-of-Reference Databases by making them easy to access and manipulate.

- Define Improvements to eliminate or minimize data Redundancy in the Information Systems and Information-Engineering processes.

- Provide *training* in how to develop Enterprise-Strength Information Models and Database Designs.

- Improve Information Modeling and Data Definition processes to provide clear Definition of data and Business Rule Specifications.

- Identify and use Enterprise-Strength "Record-of-Reference" Databases as shared Databases for *all* operational processes (where possible).

- Tune DBMS *performance controls and physical file management controls*, indexes, and buffer capabilities to maximize performance, including parallel processes where required, to increase shared DBMS performance. These are technical Database Management tools.

- Tune the Application Design to increase performance before compromising the physical Database Design away from the conceptual Information Model.

- Ensure that the definition of data is *Accurate* and Complete and that Business Rule Specifications are correct and complete *across the Enterprise*.

Do Implement Redundant Data Process Improvements (TIQM P4.3)

Once the defined Improvements are implemented in the process for Information Modeling and Data Definition, the Information Modeling and Data Definition Process Improvements should be tested with a controlled project requiring Information to be defined. Representatives of every Business Area requiring the Information to be defined should have *representative* participation in the Identification, Naming, and Definition of the Information of common interest.

Conducting this new data definition process in a controlled way enables you to check to see that it works properly. Study what you learned to minimize risk of implementing a potentially ill-defined modeling process before it is in control.

Check/Study Impact of Redundant Data Process Improvements (TIQM P4.4)

Check and study the results of the new definition process by conducting an Information Stakeholder Assessment (see TIQM P1.6 in Chapter 4) in which Information Stakeholders, who were *not part of the definition process*, review the Data Names, Definitions, and Valid Values for Correctness, Completeness, and Clarity. Study the results of the improved process.

- What did we learn?
- What Critical Success Factors made it successful? Or,
- What factors caused it to *not* be successful? If this is the case, you must conduct a Root Cause Analysis to see if you:
  - Did not implement the Improvement properly
  - Did not define the *right* Improvement
  - Did not correctly understand the Root Cause
  - Solved the root problem, but introduced a Negative Side-Effect

If the result of the controlled improvement failed, you must resolve the causes of the failure and eliminate them to achieve a satisfactorily improved process. You must replan or re-implement the improvements until you eliminate the failed process definition.

Act to Standardize Redundant Data Process Improvements (Step P4.5)

Once the improvement has been certified as successful and effective, *Act* to formalize the improved process, get it in control, and maintain ongoing TIQM P1.4, 5, and 6 assessments to ensure consistent Data Definition Quality is achieved in every development project.

The end result of this will be the creation of Information Models that support *all* Knowledge Requirements for *all* Knowledge Workers across *all* Business Areas implemented in shareable Enterprise-Strength Databases. By *eliminating redundant databases*, you eliminate the cost of developing, maintaining, and operating them and the interface programs that move data from one proprietary database to another without adding any Value — only cost of operation — from your sub-optimized value/*cost* circles.

Best Practices for Evaluating Application Software Packages

Commercial Application Software Packages are often misused, and misevaluated during the selection process. The most serious mistake is to not understand both Functional *and* **Information** Requirements necessary to evaluate the software capabilities. The second most serious mistake is to not understand the Costs-of-Ownership of an Application Software Package being considered. Remember that the Software is designed without understanding *your* specific Functional and Knowledge Requirements. They are developed to make a profit while meeting what the Vendor *perceives to be your* Functional Requirements. Very few, if any, Commercial Application Software Developers consider Information required by downstream processes and Knowledge Workers that are not relevant to the Application Functional Area.

Following is a list of best practices for evaluating application software you want to purchase:

- Define your *functional and technical* Requirements (operating systems, other internal applications the software must interface with, and hardware limitations, for example).

- Evaluate the *Warranty* offered for the software. Is it Customer-friendly? Would you buy an automobile with the same "warranty"? Be sure that you make your purchase decision for the best interests of your enterprise. There are alternatives, external and internal.

- Define a detailed, Enterprise-Strength Information Model for each Business Resource (Information Subject Area). This is required to determine what Information gaps exist between the application's data structure and your Information Requirements.

  - Map the Data Elements in the application software to the Attributes in your Enterprise Information Model, so you know where you have a match, and where the package's data structure has Data Elements that are missing from your Information Model.

  - Evaluate whether the software has *Customer-definable* fields for additionally required Attributes.

  - Evaluate whether the application software allows you to implement or invoke additional validity tests for Customer-defined fields.

- Study the data dictionary very carefully to evaluate whether it has *high quality* in the Information Product Specification data, such as whether Naming Standards are followed, and Definitions are Correct, Clear, and Complete.

  - Conduct a TIQM P1 Assessment of the Information Product Specification data. Conduct Steps TIQM P1.4 and TIQM P1.6, involving Knowledge Workers who require the Information created by the application software and Information Producers who will be creating the Information in the application software. What are the ergonomics designed into the Information Capture Screens?

  - What are the standard reports and queries that are available from the Application? Are they easily understandable? Do they provide the kinds of statistics or reporting required for your Knowledge Work?

  - Do not accept *poor quality* in Data Definition. Require the software provider to rectify any deficiencies in Data Definition, Valid Value sets, and Business Rule Specifications.

- Identify data you require in your Information Model that does not exist in the Software Package Data Structure. These are gaps that should be filled in the software data structure, at no additional charge, or handled with an internal application.

- Calculate the total Costs-of-Ownership of the software package:

  - Costs to develop and operate the Interface Programs required to move data from the Software Package data store to your Record-of-Reference (ROR) or from your ROR Database to the Software Package data structure

  - Costs to make required modifications to the Application Software Package. Be careful in modifying software package code. The modifications will be rendered null and void with each release update. Rather, create your own Enterprise-Strength Information Model and ROR Database Design for your Enterprise View of the Information Subject.

  - Costs of maintenance and Warranty of the Software Package. No Customer should have to pay for the costs to fix bugs and defects in a purchased software design or code.

  - Costs of Technical Service Support. The System should be easy to use and train for.

  - Calculate the costs of in-house development against your own Enterprise-Strength Information Models translated to Enterprise-Strength Databases, Subject by Subject.

> **NOTE** The key to successful purchased Software Evaluation is the data — not
> the functionality. How well the package data structure meets your *Enterprise*
> Knowledge and Information and Quality Requirements is the key differentiator
> among options. If a Software Provider will not let you review their physical data
> model and data definitions, do *NOT* buy their software. You, as the Customer,
> must *See* what you are getting.

Best Practices for Purchased or Third-Party Information Quality

There are two types of *external* sources that data comes from. The first are
Information Brokers, who *sell* information. The second are Business Partners,
who voluntarily provide you with Information, such as their catalog of products,
or their delivery schedules for shipping.

Best Practices in Purchased Information

Information provided by Information Brokers are captured for specific purposes,
such as Name and Address or Email lists for prospecting, Census information for
demographics by census area, or Pharmaceutical sales information. Some information brokers conduct research as special studies for clients. These can include
studying your Customer Satisfaction and that of your competitors' Customers.

Information Broker–Provided Information

When you *buy* Information from Information Brokers, you should evaluate
them in the same way that you evaluate any major purchase, such as a home
or an automobile. You expect a Warranty on a new car. You will probably buy
a Homeowner's Warranty to cover major defects in your house. Because you
will use the Information to make *significant* decisions, you will want to ensure
that your Broker *Warrants* the Information. Here are important considerations
for Information Quality:

- Develop Contracts with Warranties and set expectations for Accuracy,
  Completeness, Non-duplication, Timeliness, and other required Quality
  Characteristics with *Remedies* for non-compliance.

AERA ENERGY REQUIRES WARRANTY FROM INFORMATION BROKERS

When C. Lwanga Yonke, Information Quality Process Manager, and his Team
at Aera Energy LLC began requiring the company's Information Brokers to
provide a warranty for the quality of the Information the Brokers sold to Aera
Energy, the number of errors rapidly decreased by 50 percent.

See CARFAX's warranty for branded titles in Figure 15-10.

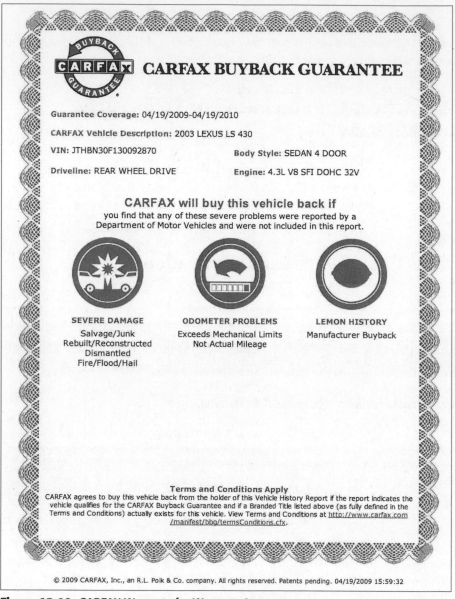

Figure 15-10: CARFAX Warranty for Warranty Accuracy

- Conduct Quality Assessment upon receipt of the information:
    - Assess Data Definition Quality as a one-time event prior to contract so you know the meaning of the data you have purchased.
    - Assess Quality of the purchased Information in comparison to the real-world objects, events or other sources, especially for name and address information or information such as the Consumer Price Index or prime rate that affects decisions.
    - Send defective Information back to the Broker and request a remedy.
- Provide Quality training to all Stakeholders as to the meaning and potential use of the Information.
- Provide Feedback (Pareto Diagrams, Control Charts), especially if the Information comes on a regular basis.
- Conduct Process Improvement Initiatives as needed with the Broker.
- Allow your Information Broker's Information Producers to attend your Information Quality training.
- Give Brokers your Information Quality Requirements to use as Product Specifications.

AERA ENERGY ALLOWS ITS INFORMATION BROKERS TO ATTEND ITS IQ TRAINING

Aera Energy empowers its Information Brokers by allowing them to attend its Information Quality training. This has increased the Quality of Information that external Information Suppliers produce and provide to Aera Energy.

FEDERAL AGENCIES THAT DISSEMINATE INFLUENTIAL INFORMATION MUST ENSURE (WARRANT) ITS QUALITY, OBJECTIVITY, INTEGRITY, AND UTILITY

Federal agencies are required by law (OMB Section 515) to provide Quality of influential Information to the public or the private sector. They must provide a mechanism for Information Consumers who see potential IQ issues to file a "Complaint." The agencies must report annually on the number and nature of Complaints and how they resolved the problems. See the section "The Information Quality Act" (OMB Section 515) and Federal Agency Accountability for Information Quality" in Chapter 12, "Information Quality Applied to Financial and Risk Management: *Budget-to-Profit*.'"

Business Partner-Provided Information

These Business Partners provide or exchange Information with you for mutual benefit in a working partnership, such as the Customer-Supplier relationship.

- Rather than develop a warranty for information from your partner, develop *Information Stewardship Agreements* (ISAs) for Information produced by one party and provided to the other.

- Assess the Quality of Information according to the various IQ Characteristics, especially Accuracy, Validity, and Completeness.

- Provide immediate feedback if there are problems.

- Allow your partner's Information Producers to attend your IQ training as a win-win proposition.

- In exchange for the High Quality Information they provide to you (at no charge), provide *value* in return to your Partner. Not only is it economically feasible, it is also Value-Adding when each party benefits.

Best Practices in Quality of Outsourced or Third-Party Information Systems Engineering

If you outsource the development of Information Systems, you must remain in control of the design of the Information Models that represent your real Knowledge Requirements and your Database Designs. These components represent your shared Knowledge — what you must know in order to accomplish your Mission and delight your Customers. In health care, we can transplant hearts, kidneys, lungs, and faces. But we cannot transplant "brains." Information is your means of *competitive differentiation*. What you know that your competition doesn't can set you apart and give your Enterprise Competitive Advantage.

If you *outsource* your Information Design, you will have lost control of your Information and Knowledge Assets that provide you with the means of Competitive Differentiation.

Best Practices for Information Management in Outsourced Information Systems Engineering

- Define a detailed, Enterprise-Strength Information Model for each Business Resource (Information Subject Area) that will be required for use by the outsourced Information System. This is required in order to keep your Information in sync across the Enterprise. The Information System should operate against the Enterprise-Strength (Operational) Databases to prevent redundancy.

- Define your Requirements for the specification of CTQ IQ Characteristics, including Accuracy, Completeness, Timeliness, and other Requirements. Define these as Warranties in your Contract for the development.

- Establish an effective Quality Assessment Process to ensure that Quality Requirements for the Application and Quality of Information are met.

Best Practices in Information Management Quality

- Ensure the Quality of your Information Standards and Guidelines. Poor Information Standards create problems when they are replicated.
  - Involve Representative Information Stakeholders from across the Enterprise in the development of Information Standards and Guidelines.
  - Create Standards with clear examples of Data Naming, Data Definition, Valid Value Specification and Definition, Data Value Formatting, and Business Rule Specification.

- Name and Label data Clearly and Consistently across the Information Value Circles.
  - Involve Business Stakeholders in facilitated Information Model development.

- Ensure *consensus* on Information Definitions among *all* Knowledge Workers and Information Producers requiring or creating them.

- Define all Code Values and ensure consistency across the Information Value Circles.

- Appoint Business Information Stewards for Critical Information to ensure *consensus* on Definitions across all Stakeholders and to ensure updates so Data Definitions are documented with effective end dates.

- Ensure Information Architecture *Stability* and *Flexibility* and that it supports *all* Information Views.

- Define Primary Key Identifiers with no embedded Meaning and no volatility.

- Design the Primary Key as numeric with Check Digits for Entities with a high volume of transaction data (Customer IDs and Credit Card Numbers).

- Control redundant data through common definition; ensure that the replication schedule meets all needs.

- Include Audit and Verification Attributes, so you know the Information Quality actions and currency of those actions.

Best Practices for Error-Proofing Information Capture

The following are best practices in Information Capture and Maintenance:

- Allow a value of "Unknown" for Attributes whose value may not be known to the Information Producer at create time.

- Define Attributes for personal Information that do not change over time, for example, mother's maiden name and last four digits of a Social Security or Social Insurance number. This is important for duplicate matching.

- Capture and retain historical data, such as name change or address change to help identify potential duplicates.

- Ensure appropriate contact with persons or entities whose characteristics can change over time, especially if there are frequent changes, such as product price changes.

- Develop comprehensive duplicate-matching algorithms, including soft matches for phonetic spellings, and partial matching to identity attributes (last four digits of the Social Security number), for example.

- Develop Reasonability Tests but include capability that allows the Information Producer to capture data that is Accurate but outside of reasonable (valid) values.

- Ensure Editing and Validation routines test for Reasonability.

- In capturing data orally, *repeat* data values in a way that causes the Provider to have to stop and reconsider the provided value.

- Implement Business Rules in the data, Tables, and callable Modules, not in the application code.

- Require Double Entry for Zero-Defect Data.

- Implement Double Checks for high-risk Business Rules.

- Record Oral Transactions for Quality Control.

Best Practices in Software and Systems Engineering Quality

Best practices in Software and Systems Engineering include the following:

- Reengineer processes before automating them.

- Do *not* design *unnecessary Interfaces* or Intermediation.

- Involve Knowledge Workers throughout development, including in Human Factors Design and active prototyping.

- Reuse data — do *not* create *redundant* data structures.

- Eliminate *redundant* data entry. Create a single "Create" application program for data of a given type, such as Customer, Product or Order. Create modules for subtypes as necessary, such as Personal Customer or Organizational Customer.

- Automate data capture where feasible — do *not* require people to capture data if machines can capture it accurately.

- Place data capture at the point of Knowledge Acquisition.

- Allow a value of "Unknown" or "missing" for attributes whose value may not be known to the information Producer at creation time.

- Use Standard data Names and Labels across the Enterprise — not by department or Business Area.

- Make Forms and Screens simple, intuitive, and unambiguous — actively prototype (QFD*).

- Check Information capture activites for span of attention.

- Place text and check boxes unambiguously close together to prevent wrong selection.

- Allow for explanations of anomalies in data.

- Use value selection as opposed to free-form entry where possible.

- Avoid long pick lists — break codes into multi-level codes.

- Minimize data entry keystrokes.

- Use multi-sensory techniques (dynamic color, highlighting, audio), but be considerate of color-blindness.

- Incorporate comprehensive duplicate-matching logic for Customer or Party creation.

- Provide automated help with data definition using in-line Help mechanisms to access the Data Dictionary.

Applying Information Quality Principles to "Shared" Information

Often, applications are designed in a "vacuum" outside of normal Business Process Design, and without consideration for how the processes *interact* and how the Information is shared across the Enterprise. The result is redundant, functionally biased and *poor quality* databases.

BEST PRACTICE: BELGACOM IMPLEMENTS QUALITY GATES FOR SYSTEMS DEVELOPMENT CONTROL

Filip van Hallewijn explains that the business problem is that products, interfaces, tables, and applications are often developed and launched into production without involving the Information Quality Management (IQM) Team, resulting in the IQM Team detecting issues too late, with retroactive data correction instead of proactive design of quality into the process. Without involvement of the IQM Team in the whole design, development, testing, and launching process, the IQM Team has difficulty implementing Quality Controls in the processes and applications.

The IQM Team implemented a Quality Template in the Requirements, Solution and Estimates Form (RSE) in its Systems Development Methodology, so people completing this form should validate, verify, and confirm with signature that they conform with the "Quality Goals and Requirements" established for Information Systems development. With this the IQM Team is able to advise management in advance of potential problems if certain KPIs are not taken into account during the process.

Benefits include the ability to anticipate likely issues with processes, applications, or the database.

During the RSE process (Fusion: ready for scoping, designing, developing, testing, etc.), the responsible parties are obligated to sign which quality gate (KPI, control) has been reviewed along with a sound business reason!

The IQM Team keeps track of each RSE launched as it passes through the process phase. The IQM Team expects this to become part of the information governance process soon.

Best Practices: Information Presentation Quality

- Ensure that you understand the Knowledge Workers' Requirements: "What do you mean by … .?"

- Design for the Information Consumer(s).

- Ensure Quality across multiple types of media (printed and online, for example).

- Ensure the Clarity and Objectivity of presented Information.

- Use the "Who, What, Why, Where, When, How" checklist to ensure that all pertinent information is gathered.

- Use intuitive, standard, "correct" data Names, Labels, and Terms.

- Ensure that recurring Document types have standardized style sheets and guidelines for consistency of reporting.

- Apply Information-Mapping techniques to *"chunk"* Information into meaningful groups.

"UNSTRUCTURED" DATA *IS* STRUCTURED

Documents that are routine and standard are NOT unstructured data! The term "unstructured" is biased to the database view of the world, which deals with attributes, not information layout and design. Product catalogs, annual reports, and financial statements are all "structured."

- Use an Intuitive Idea Presentation Sequence.
- Ensure that the Reading Difficulty is three grade levels below the reader's education level.
- Ensure that Data Definition is available and standardized for the Enterprise among representatives of all Information Stakeholders.
- Provide help and access to Data and Glossary definitions.
- Make it easy for Customers to provide Feedback.
- Present Information in a way that is Complete and Objective.
- Use a Presentation Format that is Intuitive for the Context and audience.
- Make it minimalist and concise, with drill down as needed.
- Use a consistent order sequence of data and linkage.
- Use graphic representations that are accurate to the text or quantitative data presented.
- Include Abstracts or Executive Summaries for reports, articles, and presentations.
- Use meaningful Names, Titles, Keywords, or Meta-tags.
- Add Legends, Footnotes, or Links to explain "apparent" Anomalies; otherwise, someone may challenge the conclusion.
- Identify Data Sources to ensure that the Information is corroborated.
- For sampled or scientific data, list population size, sample size, and confidence level, and describe sampling techniques.
- Test your Information Presentation with Information Consumers.

Summary

Information Systems Engineering is to the Information Age what Machinery was to the Industrial Age. Machinery is the means to automate the Production of Products. Information Systems are the means to automate Work, capture data, and produce Information Products.

Information Management has become a core competency in the Management of the intangible Information Resources (or Assets), replacing Financial Management as the second most important resource.

As Stephen Covey says, the Information Systems and Databases represent the "Production Capability" of an organization.

The development of Information Systems and Enterprise-Strength Databases are critical to Operations, Management, and Leadership of the Enterprise, if it is to accomplish its Aim.

Information Systems and Databases must be designed and engineered with high Quality to meet internal Information Producers' and Knowledge Workers' needs. They are also required to make work more efficient and to make Knowledge Workers more effective in accomplishing the Mission of the Enterprise.

Quality is vital in the development of these capabilities.

The Journey Is the Key to Success

Except for my experiences with my wife, Diane, and my two children, Ashley and Chancellor, the most exhilarating experiences I have had have been those working with Knowledge Workers who really care about increasing their effectiveness and value to their organizations by improving their Information Processes.

You do not accomplish a mature IQ culture in one fell swoop. It takes time. After all, you did not get the broken Information Processes overnight. They evolved over time purely as the result of the status quo of designing processes without considering the causes of defective information.

If you have read the major parts of this book, you understand the problem, the causes, and the way out of the problems by analyzing and isolating Root Causes of defects and by proactive Information Process Improvement and Error-Proofing to prevent recurrence of the defects.

As you go, you will establish the Culture of Continuous Process Improvement involving everyone and every business area in assessment and Process Improvement activities. This will be part of your journey in moving people and the organization to new, higher levels of IQ capability.

Figure 16-1 illustrates the ultimate journey as you mature your Enterprise on the path to Continuous Process Improvement of your core, critical processes.

Success Is in the Journey

Each step you make in the journey takes you a step higher in the maturing of your IQ practices.

Chapter 3 describes the steps you must take to accomplish a truly effective and sustainable IQ culture and environment. As you implement more and more Process Improvements, you deliver more *Value* to your organization and your Customers, both internally and externally.

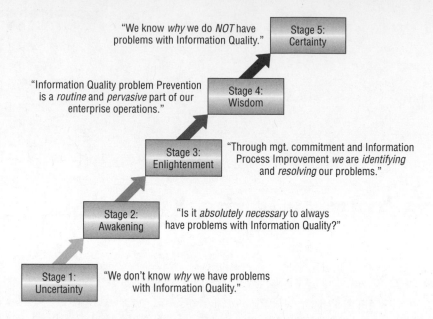

Adapted from P. B. Crosby's Quality Management Maturity Grid
See L. English, *Improving Data Warehouse & Business Information Quality*, pp. 427-437.

Figure 16-1: Maturing Your Enterprise through the Five Stages of Information Quality Maturity

Please let me hear from you about your best practices and results as you apply the TIQM principles, process, and practices in your organization.

Do not hesitate to let me know if you need assistance in implementing your Information Quality environment. It is not an easy task to overcome what may be years of the status quo of performing work fast (Costs of Acquisition) as opposed to performing work with quality (Total Costs of Ownership).

Figure 16-2 illustrates the recipe for attaining success in transforming your organization's culture.

1. Take action. Any action is better than nothing. Conduct a Customer satisfaction survey. Go measure the Costs of Poor Quality Information. Bring people together to discuss their IQ problems.

2. Create a symbol that can rally the troops around TIQM as a business management tool.

3. Identify new role models, not the reactive problem solvers who jump in to save the day by corrective maintenance of problems without understanding Root Causes. Rather, seek out *people who are ready to start the new journey* of proactive Information Process Improvements to prevent defects.

4. Do not worry about structure and organization concerns early on. Everyone ultimately has a role in IQ, and everyone must assume accountability for it.

Figure 16-2: Kevan Scholes' Recipe for Success in Culture Transformation

5. Develop your "systems," that is the processes of assessing IQ, measuring the Costs of Poor Quality Information, and Improving Processes using Plan-Do-Check/Study-Act or Define-Measure-Analyze-Improve-Control to Improve the Processes and put them in control to meet all Knowledge Workers' Requirements.

6. Challenge the *rewards and incentives* that promote poor behavior, which is a major cause of defective information.

7 Develop new routines that become habits for Continuous Process Improvement.

8. Now, you are sharing new *Success Stories* of your Process Improvements and recovered profits, no longer just the anecdotes of poor quality and their costs.

1. This leads you back to take more Action and increase your circle of influence and grow the new Culture of Information Quality.

When you think things are not going well, do not fret. Rather:

1. Seek out like-minded colleagues who believe in the TIQM vision. There is comfort and strength in numbers.

2. Look for the highest level of Management that is feeling the pain. Go meet with them to find out their problems.

3. Take action to help them solve their IQ problems and help them accomplish their goals in the Enterprise Mission. It is very likely that they will in turn become your *champions*, helping you to get to the next highest level.

4. Let them introduce you to the next level of Management to increase your *circle of influence*.

5. Do not hesitate to bring skilled counsel in, should you have problems you cannot seem to overcome. Everyone needs outside help from time to time. It is *not* a character flaw to ask for help. It is a problem, however, to not take advantage of help when you need it.

Conclusion

There is no conclusion to the High IQ Journey. It is a continuous journey of Information Process Improvement that continually increases business effectiveness.

Stay tuned with us at Information Impact International, and through this book's Web site at www.wiley.com/go/IQApplied. Let us hear of your best practices and success stories. We will publish these as we continue to develop the IQ Body of Knowledge.

Together we will bring in the emerging *Realized* Information Age.

Endnotes

Chapter 1

1. Joseph M. Juran, *Juran on Quality by Design: The New Steps for Planning Quality into Goods and Services*, New York: Free Press, 1992, as cited in Hélio Gomes, *Quality Quotes*, Milwaukee, WI: Quality Press, 1996, p. 37.

2. Elizabeth Weise, Gannett News Service, "Study reveals medical errors claim 98,000 annually in U.S.," *The Tennessean*, May 18, 2005.

3. Christopher Drew, "Navy Says Sub Hit Mountain That Was Not on Its Charts," *New York Times*, January 11, 2005.

4. "Fatal Aerobatics," USA Today, March 5, 1999.

5. BBC News, "Typing error left rapist at large," published March 23, 2005 at: `http://news/bbc.co.uk/go/pr/fr/-/1/hi/england/kent/4375611.stm`. No longer available at this URL.

6. Darrell Giles, "Health's big blunder: Dialysis equipment sent to the wrong place," *The Mail* (Australia), February 27, 2005.

7. "Euro coins ordered reminted," *The Tennessean*, July 7, 1998.

8. Nancy A. Youssef, "U.S. forces mistakenly bomb house," *The Tennessean*, January 9, 2005.

9. The Associated Press "'Friendly Fire' Video: 'I'm going to be sick.'" *The Tennessean*, February 7, 2007.

10. Alan Levin, "FAA changes weight rules for aircraft," *USA Today*, May 13, 2003.

11. John Hechinger and Robert Tomsch, "Colleges review Applications after SAT Errors," *Wall Street Journal*, March 9, 2006.

12. BBC NEWS: "Many labels on food 'misleading.'" Accessed August 27, 2009 at: `http://news.bbc.co.uk/go/pr/fr/-/1/hi/health/4311087.stm`. Published: 03/03/2005.

13. BBC News: "28% of motor licences inaccurate." Accessed May 8, 2009 at: `http://news.bbc.co.uk/2/hi/uk_news/england/devon/3636453.stm`.

14. Bush Bernard, "Firm seeks tires from recall," The Tennessean, 7/22/2006.

15. Robin Lloyd, "Metric mishap caused loss of NASA orbiter." CNN website, November 30, 1999. Accessed August 21, 2009 at: `http://www.cnn.com/TECH/space/9909/30/mars.metric.02/`.

16. James S. Liebman, Jeffery Fagan, Valerie West, "A Broken System: Error Rates in Capital Cases 1973-1995," Columbia Law School, July 3, 2000, `http://www.law.columbia.edu/news`. No longer at this location.

17. Larry P. English, "Information Quality Mandate for Election Reform," originally published in *DM Review*, beginning October 2001, available in PDF format from `www.infoimpact.com`. (Select Tools and Resources, then Other Resources, then click on Article: Information Quality Mandate for Election Reform.) Accessed August 21, 2009.

18. Alison Cassady, "Mistakes Do Happen: A Look at Errors in Consumer Credit Reports." National Association of State PIRGs, June, 2004.

19. Peter Drucker, *The New Realities: In Government and Politics/In Economics and Business/In Society and World View*, New York: Harper & Row, 1989, p. 207ff.

20. Genichi Taguchi, S. Chowdhury, and Y. Wu, *Taguchi's Quality Engineering Handbook*, Hoboken, NJ: John Wiley & Sons, 2005, p. 171.

Chapter 2

1. Masaaki Imai, *Gemba Kaizen: A Commonsense, Low-Cost Approach to Management*, New York: McGraw-Hill, 1997, p. xvii.

2. W. Edwards Deming, *Out of the Crisis*, Cambridge, MA: Massachusetts Institute of Technology Center for Advanced Engineering Study, 1986, p. 3.

3. Ibid., p. 18.

4. W. Edwards Deming, *The New Economics*, 2nd ed., Cambridge, MA: Massachusetts Institute of Technology Center for Advanced Engineering Study, 1994, p. 95.

5. P. B. Gove, ed., *Webster's Third New International Dictionary*, unabridged, Springfield, Mass: Merriam-Webster, 2002 p. 755.

6. Peter Drucker, *The New Realities: In Government and Politics/In Economics and Business/In Society and World View*, New York: Harper & Row, 1989, p. 207.

7. Ibid., p. 207.

8. Larry P. English, *Improving Data Warehouse and Business Information Quality, (IDW&BIQ)*, Hoboken, NJ: John Wiley & Sons, 1999, pp. 337–399.

9. Larry P. English, "Data Quality: Meeting Customer Needs," *DM Review*, November 1996, p. 46.

10. Armand Feigenbaum, *Total Quality Control*, 3rd ed., rev., New York: McGraw-Hill, 1991, p. 7.

11. Peter F. Drucker, *Management: Tasks, Responsibilities, Practices*, New York: Harper & Row, 1973–1974, p. 61.

12. English, *IDW&BIQ*, p. 27.

13. Masaaki Imai, *Kaizen: The Key to Japan's Competitive Success*, New York: McGraw-Hill, 1986, p. 43.

14. Philip Crosby, *Quality Is Free*, New York: Penguin Group, 1979, p. 1.

15. Ibid., p. 15.

16. Joseph M. Juran, *Juran on Planning for Quality*, New York: The Free Press, 1988, p. 1.

17. Samuel Boyle, "Quality, Speed, Customer Involvement & the New Look of Organizations," seminar, Excel, 1992, p. 17.

18. Siegel and Shim, *Accounting Handbook*, 3rd ed., Hauppauge: Barron's Educational Series, Inc., 2000, p. 88.

19. L. P. Carr, "Applying Cost of Quality to a Service Business," *Sloan Management Review*, 1992, pp. 72-77 cited by Rust et al, *Return On Quality*, Chicago: Irwin Professional Publishing, 1994, p. 92.

20. Larry P. English, *IDW&BIQ*, p. 12.

21. Ibid.

22. Larry. P. English, "IQ 301: Measuring the Costs of Poor Quality Information," seminar, Brentwood, Tennessee: Information Impact International, 2006, p. 101.

23. Deming, *Out of the Crisis*, p. 26.

24. Mary Walton, *The Deming Management Method*, New York: Perigee Books, 1987, p. 57.

25. Juran, *Juran on Planning for Quality*, p. 14.

26. Ibid., p. 10.

27. Crosby, *Quality Is Free*, p. 151.

28. Imai, *Kaizen*, p. 52.

29. Feigenbaum, *Total Quality Control*, p. 4.

30. Charles A. Sengstock, Jr., *Quality in the Communications Process*, Schaumburg, IL: Motorola University Press, 1997, p. 11.

31. Baldrige. *2007 Criteria for Performance Excellence*, Gaithersburg, MD: Baldrige National Quality Program, 2007, p. 21.

32. Peter F. Drucker, *The Effective Executive*, New York: Harper & Row, 1966, p. 3.

33. Peter F. Drucker, *Management Challenges for the 21st Century*, New York: Harper Business, 1999, p. 135, cited by Stephen R. Covey, *The 8th Habit: From Effectiveness to Greatness*, New York: Free Press, 2004, p. 15.

34. Juran, *Juran on Planning for Quality*, p. 59.

35. Imai, *Gemba Kaizen*, p. 44.

36. Kaoru Ishikawa, *Guide to Quality Control*, Tokyo: Asian Productivity Organization, 1982, p. 1.

37. Imai, *Kaizen*, p. 48.

38. Philip B. Crosby, *Quality Without Tears*, New York: McGraw-Hill, 1984, p. 66.

39. Imai, *Gemba Kaizen*, p. 13.

40. Ibid., p. 7.

41. Deming, *Out of the Crisis*, p. 49.

42. Crosby, *Quality Is Free*, p. 149.

43. Juran, *Juran on Planning for Quality*, p. 248.

44. David Hall Partnership Ltd., *Quality in Practice:BS 5750 and Kaizen Training Notes*, London: BBC Training Videos, 1993, p. 47.

45. J. M. Juran, "The Quality Improvement Process," *Juran's Quality Handbook*, 5th ed., Joseph M. Juran and A. B. Godfrey, eds., New York: McGraw-Hill, 1999, p. 5.67.

46. Deming, *Out of the Crisis*, p. 401.

47. Imai, *Kaizen*, p. 13.

48. Imai, *Gemba Kaizen*, p. 3.

49. Ibid., p. 18.

50. Drucker, *Management*, p. 45.

51. John Naisbitt and P. Aburdene, *Re-inventing the Corporation: Transforming Your Job and Your Company for the New Information Society*, New York: Warner Books, 1985, p. 5.

52. English, *IDW&BIQ*, p. 407.

53. Ibid., See how to conduct an Information Quality Management Maturity Assessment, p. 427–437.

54. Publilius Syrus, *Quotations Book*, Accessed on August 21, 2009 from: `http://www.quotationsbook.com/authors/7102/Publilius_Syrus`.

55. Adapted from L. English, "The Essentials of Information Quality Management," *DM Review*, September, 2002.

Chapter 3

1. Einstein, as cited in Stephen R. Covey, *The 8th Habit: From Effectiveness to Greatness*, New York: Free Press, 2004, p. 19.

2. Larry P. English, *Improving Data Warehouse and Business Information Quality: Methods for Reducing Costs and Increasing Profits*, (IDW&BIQ), Hoboken, NJ: John Wiley & Sons, 1999, Chapter 11, "The 14 Points of Information Quality," pp. 337–399.

3. W. Edwards Deming, *Out of the Crisis*, Cambridge, MA: Massachusetts Institute of Technology Center for Advanced Engineering Study, 1986, p. 24.

4. Mary Walton, *The Deming Management Method (DMM)*, New York: Putnam Publishing, 1986, p. 57.

5. English, *IDW&BIQ*, p. 341.

6. Deming, *Out of the Crisis*, p. 58.

7. Walton, *DMM*, p. 59.

8. L. English, *IDW&BIQ*, p. 343.

9. Deming, *Out of the Crisis*, p. 29.

10. Ibid., p. 49.

11. Walton, *DMM*, p. 66.

12. Mark Brown, D. E. Hitchcock, and M. L. Willard, *Why TQM Fails and What To Do About It*, Chicago: Irwin Professional Publishing, 1994, pp. 2f.

13. Ibid., p. 5.

14. D. A. Benton, *How to Think Like a CEO: The 22 Vital Traits You Need to Be the Person at the Top*, New York: Warner Books, 1999, p. 453f.

15. Brown, *Why TQM Fails*, p. 18.

16. Adapted from Brown, *Why TQM Fails*, pp. 7–8.

17. Ben Margulio, *Human Error Prevention* Seminar, Cold Spring, NY: 2003, p. 16.

18. Lori L. Silverman and Linda Ernst, "SEDUCE: An Effective Approach to Experiential Learning," *The 1999 Annual: Volume 1, Training*, San Francisco: Jossey-Bass/Pfeiffer, 1999.

19. Adapted from English, *IDW&BIQ*, p. 366–367.

20. Brown, *Why TQM Fails*, pp. 69–134.

21. W. Edwards Deming, *The New Economics: For Industry, Government, Education*, 2nd ed., Cambridge, MA: The MIT Press, 2000, orig. ed. 1994, p. 121.

22. Brown, *Why TQM Fails*, p. 137. 23.

23. Jan Carlzon, *Moments of Truth*, New York: Harper& Row, 1987, p. 1.

24. *Quality, Speed, Customer Involvement and the New Look of Organizations, Boulder: Career Track, 1992.*

25. Brown, *Why TQM Fails*, p. 143–145.

26. Macy, Izumi, Bliese, and Norton. "Organizational Change and Work Innovation: A Meta-Analysis of 131 North American Field Studies 1961–1991," *Research in Organizational Change and Development*, Vol. 7, Woodman and Passmore, eds. Greenwich, CT: JAI Press, 1993, as cited in Brown, *Why TQM Fails*, p. 144.

27. See Lawler, *High Involvement Management*, as cited in Brown, *Why TQM Fails*, p. 145.

28. Eight Ss™ is a trademark of R. T. Pascale, in *Managing on the Edge: How the Smartest Companies Use Conflict to Stay Ahead*, New York: Simon & Schuster, 1990, as cited in Brown, *Why TQM Fails*, pp. 183–191.

29. John P. Kotter, *Leading Change*, Boston: Harvard Business School Press, 1996, p. 4.

30. Ibid., p. 6.

31. Beckhard and Harris, 1987 as discussed in Dannemiller, K. D. and R. W. Jacobs, "Changing the Way Organizations Change: A Revolution of Common Sense," *The Journal of Applied Behavioral Science*, December, 1992.

32. Kathi Dannemiller, *Real-Time Strategic Change*, Ann Arbor: Tyson Associates, Inc., 1994.

33. Kotter, *Leading Change*, p. 21.

34. Ibid., p. 66.

35. Nemawashi, Accessed July 8, 2009 at: `http://captain.grog.googlepages.com/nemawashi`

36. *"Nemawashi*: Toyota's way to good decisions," *The Vertical Slice*. Accessed May 10, 2009 at: `http://www.bestbrains.dk/Blog/2008/01/27/Nemawashi ToyotasWayToGoodDecisions.aspx`. No longer at this location.

37. Jeffrey Liker, *The Toyota Way*, New York: McGraw-Hill, 2004, p. 34.

38. Peter Block, *Stewardship: Choosing Service over Self-Interest*, San Francisco: Berett-Koehler, 1993, p. xx.

39. English, *IDW&BIQ*, p. 402.

40. English, Ibid.

41. Adapted from English, Ibid., p. 407.

Chapter 4

1. American Heritage Dictionary.

2. Oxford Dictionary.

3. Webster's Dictionary.

4. Oxford Dictionary.

5. American Heritage Dictionary.

6. American Heritage Dictionary.

7. Larry English, *Improving Data Warehouse and Business Information Quality*, *(IDW&BIQ)*, Hoboken, NJ: Wiley & Sons, 1999, p. 91.

8. Ibid., pp. 87–118.

Chapter 5

1. Kaoru Ishikawa, *Guide to Quality Control*, Tokyo: Asian Productivity Organization, 1982, p. 5, as cited in Larry English, *Improving Data Warehouse and Business Information Quality*, Hoboken, NJ: Wiley & Sons, 1999, p. 184.

2. Kevin Rechin, "A Full Minute of Warning for Airline Pilots," Allied Signal Aerospace, *USA TODAY*, Oct 16, 1996.

3. Deanna Oxender Burgess, "Exaggerating the Positive," *The New York Times*, September 15, 2002.

4. Edward Tufte, *The Visual Display of Quantitative Information*, 2nd ed. (Visual Display), Cheshire, CT: Graphics Press, 2001, p. 57.

5. Associated Press, "Missing Pyramid Found by Egyptian Archaeologists," FoxNews Website, June 5, 2008. Accessed May 29, 2009 at: `http://www.foxnews.com/story/0,2933,363472,00.html`. Story no longer at this location.

6. Larry English, *Improving Data Warehouse and Business Information Quality*, Hoboken, NJ: John Wiley & Sons, p. 175.

7. Michael Brassard and D. Ritter, *The Memory Jogger II*, Goal/QPC, 1994, p. 39.

8. Ibid., p. 45.

Chapter 6

1. Frank M. Gryna, "Quality Costs," in *Quality Control Handbook*, 4th ed., New York: McGraw-Hill, as cited in Rust, R., Anthony Zahorik, and Timothy Keiningham, *Return on Quality*, 1988, p. 94.

2. Frank M. Gryna, "Quality and Costs," as cited in, Joseph M. Juran and A. Blanton Godfrey, *Juran's Quality Handbook*, 5th ed., New York: McGraw-Hill, 1998, p. 8.22.

Chapter 7

1. Source unknown.

Chapter 8

1. Joseph M. Juran, *Juran on Quality by Design: The New Steps for Planning Quality into Goods and Services*, New York: Free Press, 1992, as cited in Hélio Gomes, *Quality Quotes*, Milwaukee, WI: Quality Press, 1996, p. 37.

Chapter 9

1. Jan Carlzon, *Moments of Truth: New Strategies for Today's Customer-Driven Economy*, New York: Harper & Row, 1987, p. 3.

2. Craig Whitlock and S. Smiley, "Non-European Ph.D.'s find use of 'Dr.' verboten," *The Tennessean*, March 14, 2008.

3. Thomas Frank, "TSA says airlines could face $35,000 fines over mistaken terrorist IDs," *USA Today*, July 31, 2008.

4. Laurie Kulikowski **"E*Trade Hit With $1 Million Fine,"** The Street.com, January 2, 2009. Accessed on August 21, 2009 at: `http://www.thestreet.com/story/10455801/1/etrade-hit-with-1-million-fine.html?puc=_tscrss`.

5. Claude Johnson, **"Duplicates: Seeing DOUBLE,"** Jems from Johnson, August 26, 2005. Accessed 2/4/2009 at: `http://www.smartreply.com/work_case_jem03.html`. Story no longer at this location.

6. Graham Rhind, *Practical International Data Management*, Aldershot, UK: Gower, 2001.

7. Rhind, *Global Sourcebook for Address Data Management*, Amsterdam: GRC Database Information, 2009.

8. John Yunker, "Beyond Borders, Web Globalization Strategies", Indianapolis, IN: New Riders, 2003, p. 82.

9. A number of resources will help you keep your data up-to-date, accurate, and a truer representation of the entities it represents. These include:

   - "The Global Sourcebook for Address Data Management" by Graham Rhind, updated twice annually, Accessed on February 4, 2009 at: `http://www.grcdi.nl/book2.htm`.

   - "Guide to Worldwide Postal-code and Address Formats" by Merry Law, Accessed on August 21, 2009 at: `http://www.worldvu.com/`.

   - Updated links to postal code, post office and address information quality management pages. Accessed on August 21, 2009 at: `http://www.grcdi.nl/links.htm`.

10. "Serbia," U.S. Department of State. Accessed August 21, 2009 at: `http://www.state.gov/r/pa/ei/bgn/5388.htm`.

11. Samuel Boyle, "Quality, Speed, Customer Involvement & the New Look of Organizations," seminar, Boulder, Co: CareerTrack, 1992, p. 8., (study conducted by e-Satisfy/ TARP), as cited in English, *IDW&BIQ*, p. 234.

Chapter 10

1. We will use the inclusive definition of product to also include service, except where we need to differentiate between product and service.

2. Stephen Covey, *The Seven Habits of Highly Effective People*, New York: Simon & Schuster, 1989, p. 54.

3. W. Edwards Deming, *Out of the Crisis*, Cambridge, MA: MIT Center for Advanced Engineering Study, 1986, p. 26.

4. Armand Feigenbaum, *Total Quality Control.* 3rd ed., rev., New York: McGraw-Hill, 1991, p. 99.

5. Kai Yang and Basem El-Haik, *Design for Six Sigma: A Roadmap for Product Development*, New York: McGraw-Hill, p. 5. The phase names have been adapted.

6. Ibid., p. 309.

7. P. O'Grady. and J. Oh, "A Review of Approaches to Design for Assembly," *Concurrent Engineering,* 1991, Vol. 1, pp. 5–11.

8. P. Sacket and A. Holbrook, "DFA as a Primary Process Decreases Design Deficiencies," *Assembly Automation*, 1988, Vol. 12, No. 2, pp. 15–16.

9. G. Q. Huang, ed., *Design for X: Concurrent Engineering Imperatives*, London: Chapman & Hall, 1996.

10. Ibid.

11. S. Arimoto et al., "Development of Machining Productivity Evaluation Method (MEM)," *Annals of CIRP*, 1993, Vol. 42, No. 1, pp. 119–122.

12. G. Boothroyd et al., *Product Design for Assembly Handbook,* WakefieldRI: Boothroyd-Dewhurst Inc., 1994.

13. Huang, op. cit., 1996.

14. Foo et al. "Design for Material Logistics," *AT&T Technical Journal*, 1990, Vol. 69, No. 3, pp. 61–67.

15. Huang, *op cit.*, 1996.

16. W. Beitz, "Design for Ease of Recycling (Guidelines VDI-2243)," *ICED Proceedings 90*, 1990, Dubrovnik, Heurista, Zurich, Switzerland.

17. D. Navichandra, "Design for Environmentality," *Proceedings of ASME Conference on Design Theory and Methodology*, 1991, New York.

18. S. Gardner and D. F. Sheldon, "Maintainability as an Issue for Design," *Journal of Engineering Design*, 1995, Vol. 6, No. 2, pp. 75–89.

19. D. F. Sheldon et al., "Designing for Whole-life Costs at the Concept Stage," *Proceedings of ICED*, 1990, Heurista, Zurich, Switzerland.

20. J. Gershenson and K. Ishii, "Life Cycle Serviceability Design," *Proceedings of ASME Conference on Design and Theory and Methodology*, 1991, Miami, FL.

21. H. Mughal and R. Osborne, "Design for Profit," *World Class Design to Manufacture*, 1995, Vol. 2, No. 5, pp. 160–226.

22. G. Zaccai, "The New DFM: Design for Marketability," *World Class Manufacture to Design*, 1994, Vol. 1, No. 6, pp. 5–11.

23. J. Wang. and T. Ruxton, "Design for Safety of Make-to-Order Products," *National Design Engineering Conference of ASME*, 1993, Vol. 93-DE-1, American Society of Mechanical Engineers, New York.

24. F. Tayyari, "Design for Human Factors," in *Concurrent Engineering*, H.R. Parsaei and W.G. Sullivan, eds., London: Chapman & Hall, 1993, pp. 297–325.

25. Herbert Friedman, "The Hubble Space Telescope: Ten Times Better." Originally from: `http//www.cosmos-club.org`. No longer at this location.

26. Sally Stephens, "The New and Improved *Hubble Space Telescope*," *The Universe in the Classroom*, Winter, 1994. Accessed August 21, 2009 at: `http://www.astrosociety.org/education/publications/tnl/26/26.html`.

27. Jay Bucher, "Calibration — The Good, the Bad And the Ugly," *Quality Progress*, November 2007, p. 53.

28. Rivian Bell, "Smith Corona announces asset purchase agreement with Carolina Wholesale," Cortland, NY, May 23, 2000. Accessed Aug 1, 2007 at: `http://www.smithcorona.com/About_Smith_Corona/Press_Releases/Corporate_News/purchase.cfm`. No longer available at this location.

29. Kim L. Hubbard, "Smith Corona Changes Focus and Bounces Back," CNY Business Journal, Dec 10, 1999. Accessed at: `http://findarticles.com/p/articles/mi_qa3718/is_199912/ai_n8878337`.

30. Carter Doughtery and Leslie Wayne, "FedEx Rescinds Order for Airbus A380s," *New York Times*, Nov 8, 2006. Accessed August 21, 2009 at: `http://www.nytimes.com/2006/11/08/business/worldbusiness/08airbus.html?ex=1320642000&en=8f716890dfe44356&ei=5088&partner=rssnyt&emc=rss`.

31. Marilyn Adams, "Giant plane gives Airbus giant headaches," *USA Today*, July 17, 2007, p. 1B.

32. David Kiley, "Deposition: Tiremaker knew about problems before recall," *USA Today*, August 15, 2001.

33. Akao Yoji, ed., *Quality Function Deployment: Integrating Customer Requirements into Product Design*, Portland, OR: Productivity Press, 1988, p. 3.

34. Lou Cohen, *Quality Function Deployment: How to Make QFD Work for You*, Reading, MA: Addison-Wesley, 1995, p. 256.

35. Ibid.

36. Ibid., p. 257.

37. Ibid., p. 260.

38. John Terninko, *Step-by-Step QFD: Customer-Driven Product Design*, 2nd ed., Boca Raton, FL: St. Lucie Press, 1997, p. 103.

39. See also Larry P. English, *Improving Data Warehouse and Business Information Quality*, Hoboken, NJ: John Wiley & Sons, 1999, Chapter 5, "Assessing Data Definition and Information Architecture Quality," pp. 83–136.

40. *Ibid.*, p. 162.

41. Yang and El-Haik, p. 442.

42. Yang and El-Haik, p. 442.

43. Yang and El-Haik, p. 442.

44. Yang and El-Haik, p. 443. Source improve mean performance

45. Yang and El-Haik, p. 443. Source improve by reducing variation

Chapter 11

1. Gomez, Helio, *Quality Quotes*, Milwaukee: ASQ Quality Press, 1996, p. 2

2. Editorial, "Mortgage default rate first domino to fall?," *Portland Press Herald and Maine Sunday Telegram*, August 23, 2007. Accessed August 21, 2009 at: http://pressherald.mainetoday.com/story.php?id=129152&ac=PHedi.

3. Ibid.

4. Larry Margasak, "High-security labs mishandle a rogues' gallery of germs," *USA Today*, Oct. 3, 2007, p. 6D.

5. Ibid.

6. B2B = Business-to-Business, B2C = Business-to-Consumer, G2G = Government-to-Government, and G2C = Government-to-Constituent.

7. See also Larry P. English, *Improving Data Warehouse and Business Information Quality*, Hoboken, NJ: John Wiley & Sons, 1999, Chapter 5, "Assessing Data Definition and Information Architecture Quality," pp. 83–136.

8. Masaaki Imai, *Gemba Kaizen: A Commonsense, Low-Cost Approach to Management*, New York: McGraw-Hill, 1997, pp. 146–147.

9. Ibid.

10. See also Larry P. English, *Improving Data Warehouse and Business Information Quality*, Hoboken, NJ: John Wiley & Sons, 1999, Chapter 5, "Assessing Data Definition and Information Architecture Quality," pp. 83–136.

11. Donna Rosato, "Airlines may be doctoring arrival time data," *USA Today*, April 3, 1998.

12. GS1, *GDSN Package Measurement Rules: GS1 Standards Document*, Issue 1.7, 12-Sep-2007. Accessed Jan. 19, 2008 at: http://www.gs1.org/docs/gsmp/gdsn/GDSN_Package_Measurement_Rules.pdf. No longer at this location.

13. See also, *GSDN Standard Package Measurement Tolerances: Best Practice Guidelines*. Accessed Jan. 19, 2008 at: http://www.gs1.org/docs/gsmp/gdsn/GDSN_Standard_Package_Measurement_Tolerances_Best_Practice_i1.pdf. No longer at this location.

Chapter 12

1. Basel II Accord Section 644.

2. Jack King, *Operational Risk Measurement and Modeling*, Hoboken, NJ: John Wiley & Sons, Ltd., 2001, p.7.

3. dictionary.com. Accessed November 26, 2008 at: `www.dictionary.com`.

4. Data Governance and Data Quality Insider. Accessed August 21, 2009 at: `http://data-governance.blogspot.com/2008/03/mergers-and-acquisitions -datas.html`.

5. Ed Mierzwinski and Jen Mueller ,"One In Four Credit Reports Contains Errors Serious Enough To Wreak Havoc For Consumers," U.S. PIRG Consumer Program. June 17, 2004. Accessed 7/29/2009 at `http://uspirg .org/uspirgnewsroom.asp?id2=13650`.

6. ACFE's *2006 Report to the Nation on Occupational Fraud and Abuse*. Accessed on August 21, 2009 at: `http://www.acfe.com/resources/publications .asp?copy=rttn`.

7. Reuters, "Two Units of E*Trade Financial Fined $1 Million," *New York Times*, Jan 2, 2009, accessed January 6, 2009 at: `http://www.nytimes .com/2009/01/03/business/03bizbriefs-TWOUNITSOFET_BRF.html`. No longer at this location.

8. See also Larry P. English, *Improving Data Warehouse and Business Information Quality*, Hoboken, NJ: John Wiley & Sons, 1999), Chapter 5, "Assessing Data Definition and Information Architecture Quality," pp. 83–136.

9. Ibid.

10. Joel G. Siegel, *Barron's Accounting Handbook*, Hauppauge, NY: Barron's Educational Series, 2000, p. 840.

11. Ibid.

12. English, *IBW&BIQ*, p. 162.

13. Reference: `http://www.occ.treas.gov/ftp/bulletin/2000-16.txt`. Accessed August 21, 2009.

14. Siegel, *Accounting Handbook*, p. 829–830.

Chapter 13

1. The following has been adapted from: David Siegel, *Futurize Your Enterprise*, Hoboken, NJ: John Wiley, 1999, pp. 81–100.

2. Jack Massari, "Search Engine Knowledgebase," ICGLink. Retrieved August 21, 2009 from: www.icglink.net/.

3. Larry P. English, "Information Quality in Internet and E-business Environments," *The Internet Encyclopedia*, Vol 2, Hossein Bidgoli, ed., Hoboken, NJ: John Wiley & Sons, 2004, p. 166.

4. Janet E. Alexander and M.A. Tate, *Web Wisdom: How to Evaluate and Create Information Quality on the Web*, Mahwah, NJ: Lawrence Erlbaum, 1999, p. 12.

5. Ralph Loos, "Wary of Wikipedia: Global search engine's accuracy questioned," *The Tennessean*, February 18, 2007, p. 21A.

6. National Association of Boards of Pharmacy (NABP), *VIPPS*, retrieved August 21, 2009 from: http://www.nabp.net/vipps/intro.asp, as cited in English, "IQ in Internet and E-business," p. 167–168.

7. Ibid., p. 168.

8. Ibid.

9. BizRate.com Merchant Ratings FAQs. Accessed on August 21, 2009 at: http://www.bizrate.com/content/ratings_guide.html#3.

10. Quill Summary rating for the current 90 days. Accessed on December 1, 2007 at: http://www.bizrate.com/ratings_guide/cust_reviews__mid–879.html.

11. OMB, "Guidelines for ensuring and maximizing the quality, objectivity, utility, and integrity of information disseminated by federal agencies," *Federal Register, 66*, p. 189. September 28, 2001, with supplements January 3, 2002. Retrieved August 21, 2009 from http://www.whitehouse.gov/omb/inforeg_agency_info_quality_links/.

12. English, "IQ in Internet and E-business," p. 168.

13. Ibid.

14. P. J. Calvert, "Web-based misinformation in the context of higher education," *Asian Libraries*, *8*(3), 1999, pp. 83–91. Retrieved January 2, 2003, from: http://www.emeraldinsight.com/pdfs/17308cb2.pdf. No longer at this location.

15. English, "IQ in Internet and E-business," p. 165.

16. See also Larry P. English, *Improving Data Warehouse and Business Information Quality*, Hoboken, NJ: John Wiley & Sons, 1999, Chapter 5, "Assessing Data Definition and Information Architecture Quality," pp. 83–136.

17. English, *IBW&BIQ*, p. 162.

18. Jan Carlzon, *Moments of Truth: New Strategies for Today's Customer-Driven Economy*, New York: Harper & Row, 1987, p. 3.

Chapter 14

1. Picture of Codex Sinaiticus, courtesy of the British Library.

2. "E-mail Communications," Information Mapping. Accessed August 21, 2009 at: `http://www.infomap.com/index.cfm/Learning/Learning FocusAreas/E-mail_Communications`.

3. Adapted from: D. Wieringa, *Procedure Writing: Principles and Practices*. Columbus, OH: *Battelle Press*, 1998, p. 130.

4. See also Larry P. English, *Improving Data Warehouse and Business Information Quality*, Hoboken, NJ: John Wiley & Sons, 1999, Chapter 5, "Assessing Data Definition and Information Architecture Quality," pp. 83–136.

5. English, *IDW&BIQ*, p. 162.

6. Jonathan Price, *Put That in Writing*, New York: Viking, 1984, p. 126–128.

7. Jessica Enders, "5 Ways To Make Sure That Users Abandon Your Forms," Accessed August 21, 2009 at: `http://www.egmstrategy.com/ice/direct_link.cfm?bid=FBCF08E7-DEE8-F2D5-48AEF8A07371777B`.

8. Information Mapping, Inc., Home page last accessed August 21, 2009 at: `http://www.infomap.com/index.cfm/`.

9. Luke Wroblewski, "Web Application Form Design," Luke Interface Design. Accessed July 23, 2009 at: `http://www.lukew.com/resources/articles/web_forms.html`.

10. Tufte, *The Visual Display*, p. 177.

11. Ibid., p. 183.

12. Ibid., p. 51.

13. Ibid., p. 77.

14. Rendering and commentary of a critical slide from Boeing engineers' presentation to NASA for evaluating the likelihood of a safe reentry for the Shuttle Columbia, from Edward Tufte, *Beautiful Evidence*, Cheshire, CT: Graphics Press, 2006, pp. 164–165.

Chapter 15

1. Shirou Fujita, *A Strategy for Corporate Innovation*, Tokyo: Asian Productivity Organization, 1997, p. x.

2. Jan Carlzon, *Moments of Truth*, New York: Harper & Row, 1987.

3. "Obsolete Software Costs U.S. Companies Billions of Dollars in Unnecessary IT Spending," Survey Finds," BNET, 12/2004. Accessed on August 21, 2009 at: `http://findarticles.com/p/articles/mi_pwwi/is_200412/ai_n8562166`. Contributed by Don Carlson.

4. See Peter Drucker, *The New Realities*, New York: Harper & Row, 1989, p. 207.

5. See W. Edwards Deming, *The New Economics*, 2nd ed., Cambridge: MIT Press, 2000, p. 96.

6. Shigeru Mizuno and Yoji Akao, *QFD: The Customer-Driven Approach to Quality Planning and Deployment*, Tokyo: Asian Productivity Organization, 1994.

7. Steve Spewak, *Enterprise Architecture Planning: Developing a Blueprint for Data, Applications and Technology*, 2nd ed., Wellesley, MA: QED Information Sciences, 1997.

8. TOGAF, "The Open Group Architecture Framework," Accessed June 15, 2009 at `http://www.opengroup.org/togaf/`.

9. Shoshana Zuboff, *In the Age of the Smart Machine*, New York: Basic Books, 1988, p.10. Coined by Zuboff, the term is applied to the highest benefit of technology in which the important information about events in the enterprise can be used to "informate" Knowledge Workers.

10. William E. Perry, *Effective Methods for Software Testing*, 2nd ed., Hoboken, NJ: John Wiley & Sons, 2000, p. 162.

11. Ibid., pp. 162–163.

12. Robert N. Charette, "Why Software Fails," IEEE Spectrum online, August 21, 2009. Accessed June 15, 2009 at: `http://www.spectrum.ieee.org/search?media=articles&q=Why+Software+Fails&x=36&y=11`

13. K. Dawson, "Software Bug Halts F-22 Flight," *The Sun*, February 25, 2007. Accessed August 21, 2009 at: `http://it.slashdot.org/article.pl?sid=07/02/25/2038217`.

14. Jesse McKinley, "In California, Retro-Tech Complicates Budget Woes," *The New York Times*, August 5, 2008. Accessed August 21, 2009 at: `http://www.nytimes.com/2008/08/06/us/06computer.html?_r=1&scp=1&sq=California+Payroll+old+systems&st=nyt` (courtesy of Don Carlson).

15. Yoji, Akao, ed., *Quality Function Deployment: Integrating Customer Requirements into Product Design*, Portland, OR: Productivity Press, 1988, p. 3.

16. Ellen Isaacs and Alan Walendowski, *Designing From Both Sides of the Screen*, Indianapolis: New Riders Publishing, 2002, pp. 298–311.

Index